周雖舊邦其

命維新 詩經

'Chou is an old people,
but its charge is new'

The Book of Songs, trans. A. Waley
(New York, Grove Press, 1960)

A History of the Chinese Communist Party 1921-1949

A History of the Chinese Communist Party 1921-1949

JACQUES GUILLERMAZ

Translated by Anne Destenay

RANDOM HOUSE

New York

Published in the United States
by Random House, Inc., New York.
Originally published in France
as *Histoire du parti communiste chinois 1921-1949*
by Payot, Paris.
English translation first published in Great Britain
by Methuen & Co. Ltd., London.

ISBN: 0-394-46479-6
Library of Congress Catalog Card Number: 72-2736

Manufactured in the United States of America

First American Edition.

9 8 7 6 5 4 3 2

Contents

Maps

Plates

Acknowledgements

The publishers wish to thank The Associated Press Ltd, London, for their permission to reproduce Plates 18, 20, 21, 22, 23, 24, 25, 26, 27, 28, 29, 30, 31, 32, 33, 34, 35, 36, 37, 38, 39, 40, 41 and 42, and the Hsin Hua News Agency for their permission to reproduce Plates 6, 12, 13, 14 and 19. Other plates were supplied by the Centre de Documentation sur L'Extrême-Orient, Paris.

Foreword

Events sometimes urge the historian to speed up his work. However incomplete this work may be, it is needed to help analyse and understand what is happening today and tomorrow. This is true for the China of our time, and particularly for the Communist Party, which is the life of the country, transforming it and attempting to put it in command of part of the world, perhaps of the world as a whole.

At a time when access is rarely given to the archives of Peking or T'aipei, or is granted only after strict calculation, when access to the Moscow archives is denied in spite of strong polemics, when the greatest protagonists and their companions still observe strict silence regarding the main secrets of their former collaborations and quarrels, it may well appear that to attempt to write a history of the Chinese Communist Party is both rash and premature.

This same history has been unfolding itself before our eyes for the last fifty years, however. The actors and their writings, the facts and their sequence, are well known, as is the national and international context that provides the key to them. We now know the major causes and stages of the evolution which has taken but one generation to bring the Chinese communists to power. Yet we remain in ignorance of some of the immediate or fortuitous causes which hastened or slowed down this evolution, and of the special role played by certain men at critical moments.

All things considered, we are well enough informed to be able to pick out the essential facts from a view of the whole which has become indispensable. Perhaps the time is ripe as far as history itself is concerned. The official versions from each side of the Straits of Taiwan have already begun to modify or blur established facts, as the authoritarian aspect of both Chinese regimes forces independent witnesses into submission or silence.

Considering this last point, it is perhaps fitting that a synthesis be attempted by a Western observer who has had the rare good fortune to be able to contemplate at length the changing face of contemporary China – that of the last warlords, of the Kuomintang, and of the Communist Party – to breathe the atmosphere of this troubled era and to meet its chief personalities. Although near enough to love and admire China, his foreign origins provide the distance necessary to escape involvement in the terrible passions that have been wearing out the country for the last half century.

This work sets out to sum up what is known today of the history of the Chinese Communist Party, giving a comprehensive outline and a synthesis of available knowledge; it is above all intended to be a balanced account in which equal importance is given to the events themselves, to their interpretation and to relevant documents. It is to be hoped that it will provide the background for more detailed reading and study and contribute to the understanding of the problems of China today.

A second volume based largely on information brought to light by the Cultural Revolution will trace the history of the Party since it took over in 1949. The last volume will deal with events that the author himself witnessed, or in which he took part between 1937 and 1967; it will include portraits of some of the chief personalities of the Kuomintang and communist regimes and descriptions of some of the outstanding events in recent Chinese history, and it will dwell on the prodigious political and social evolution of contemporary China.

Notes on the Text

1 Except in well-known places and personal names, the Wade-Giles transcription has been used rather than the new Chinese system, 'P'in Yin Tzu Mu', as the latter is not yet well known in Europe, and is not used in Chinese publications for foreigners.
2 The bibliography of Chinese and Western works consulted appears at the end of this volume. Works of major importance for the understanding of certain events are mentioned in the notes to the relevant chapters.
3 Apart from one or two exceptions, the passages quoted have been translated into English from the author's own translation, or are taken from various translations published separately or in larger volumes by the Foreign Languages Press in Peking. Passages from the *Selected Works* of Mao Tse-tung have been taken from the English translation, volumes I to IV, published by the Foreign Languages Press, Peking, 1960-1965.

Introduction

Less than ten years passed between the collapse of the three thousand year old Chinese empire and the emergence of the modern Communist Party. In fact, however, nearly a century of concealed decadence and changes, which were becoming increasingly apparent, had been paving the way for the revolutions of our time that eventually gave birth to it.

The Emperor Ch'ien Lung was the last great sovereign the monarchy produced. By the end of his long reign, which lasted from 1736 until his mysterious abdication sixty years later in 1796, China's frontiers were roughly as they are today. The Mongols and the Tibetans had at last been subdued. Korea, Burma and Vietnam were still under imperial protection. An almost unprecedented era of peace more than doubled the population, which increased during his reign from 140 to over 300 million. The classical arts, particularly those of painting and porcelain, flourished brilliantly for the last time. Traditional wisdom and philosophical and literary works were gathered into vast encyclopedias. In the eyes of Europe, China was still the most civilized and perhaps the most ably governed country in the world; the extraordinary reception that the court of Peking gave to Lord Macartney's embassy in 1793, treating it as a mission of tributaries, aroused stupefaction rather than indignation and China lost none of her prestige.

Six sovereigns, all either mediocre or too young, followed Ch'ien Lung, but even if they had shown as much intelligence, firmness and energy as their ancestor, the rough impact of the West would nonetheless have caused China to embark on an era of revolution in the fullest sense of the word.

The year 1840 can rightly be said to mark China's entry into the modern world. The myth of the Chinese Colossus crumbled in a few months in the face of a few English warships. The greatest empire in the world had to stoop to the humiliation of the Unequal Treaties, so that it became, as Sun Yat-sen so strikingly puts it, 'the colony and slave of all nations'. Chinese civilization as a whole and the people themselves fell into discredit, becoming the victims of a disfavour which had been unknown during the previous century.

From 1850 to 1864, the dynasty and indeed the empire itself were shaken to the very roots by the T'ai p'ing Rebellion, the first Chinese revolution to be inspired, at least partially, by the West, and which was acclaimed by the Chinese communists as the origin of all the others, including their own.

Wars against Western or Westernized powers continued. The Anglo-French expedition of 1860 was followed by the Sino-French war of 1885, and the Sino-Japanese war of 1894-5. All these wars, and particularly the last, drew China into a reluctant imitation of Europe. This imitation was at first intended to be limited to technical achievements, but it was soon found that the production and use of the materials themselves inevitably involved evolution in ideas, customs and systems. Reformers and conservative elements came into open conflict, a conflict that began on a bad footing for the former with their defeat in 1898 in spite of the support of the Emperor Kuang Hsü. The Boxer Rebellion of 1900 and the wounding spectacle of a war between Russia and Japan in 1904-5 for the control of Chinese Manchuria, completed the ruin of the dynasty, together with the old institutions and traditional doctrines. The imperial house fell in 1911 with scarcely any resistance. General Yüan Shih-k'ai, the first President of the Republic, maintained the political and administrative unity of the vast body of China as best he could until his death in 1916. After him, China entered the era of military cliques. This was not yet over in 1921, when the history of the party that governs the country today begins.[1]

[1] The communists consider that the 'feudal' society in existence before 1840 becomes by degrees 'semi-feudal' and 'semi-colonial', and that the struggle of nationalism against feudalism upheld by imperialism represents the chief contradiction of that time. This theory is hard to accept, as are the terms in which it is expressed.

Part 1

The Origins and Birth of the Chinese Communist Party

During those crowded months and years of endeavour,
All of us students together and all of us young,
Our bearing was proud, our bodies strong,
Our ideals true to a scholar spirit;
Just and upright, fearless and frank,
We pointed the finger at our land,
We praised and condemned through our writings,
And those in high positions we counted no more than dust.

Mao Tse-tung

1 The Situation in China in 1921

The political situation

When the congress inaugurating the Chinese Communist Party opened on 1 July 1921, China was in a state of complete political anarchy, although her modern economic sector was gradually developing and the lives, ideas and customs of certain social categories were beginning to change. On the political plane, the state of anarchy was to last until 1928, or indeed until 1949, when the present regime took over, for the unity of the country was constantly challenged by the provincial clans, the communists, and finally by the Japanese and their collaborators. In spite of the fragmentation, only one Chinese government was in existence: its chief task was to continue dealings with abroad, particularly with the privileged powers. It consisted of a President of the Republic, a cabinet, which was formed or dismissed according to the whim of the faction occupying the capital, Peking, and a corrupt parliament which was little better than a mockery and scarcely ever summoned. The administration of the provinces was carried out in the government's name and, although some of the appropriate fictions were maintained, the provincial authorities themselves were in the hands of the local military powers.

Yüan Shih-k'ai, the first President of the Republic, died on 6 June 1916, after trying to re-establish the empire in his own name. He was succeeded by Li Yüan-hung, a former army officer, a person of slight importance who became involved in the Revolution of 1911 against his will. Li Yüan-hung was forced to retire in 1917, when General Chang Hsün, a picturesque individual whom the president had summoned to Peking, failed in a brief attempt to restore the Manchu monarchy.

The next new president was an old, inoffensive scholar, Hsü Shih-ch'ang, a former member of the Han Lin Academy (the 'Forest of Brushes') and the foster-brother of the late president Yüan Shih-k'ai. Hsü Shih-ch'ang was still in office in 1921, but was replaced by General Ts'ao K'un the following year.

Towards the middle of 1921, the power was held by three rival cliques who shared the provinces among themselves. The Fengtien clique, which took its name from the region surrounding Mukden, was based in Manchuria. Its leader, Chang Tso-lin, was a former 'red beard', an ex-bandit who went over to Japan during the Russo-Japanese war of 1904-5. His son, Marshal Chang Hsüeh-liang, who was later to succeed him, was 23; he was later to take part in the Sian Incident. The stubborn resentment of his victim, Generalissimo Chiang Kai-shek, has kept Chang Hsüeh-liang in Taiwan until this day.

The Chihli (present Hopei) clique was centred at Paotingfu, the provincial capital. It had direct control over Hopei, Honan and Shantung, and indirect control over Hupei and Hunan. Its leaders were Ts'ao K'un, Feng Kuo-chang and later the famous Marshal Wu P'ei-fu, one of the last scholar-generals of old China.

The third clique, the Anfu, was called after the street in Peking where its members first met. Pro-Japanese in its allegiance, it had control of the government until 1920, then lost its power in the north, while retaining its influence in the lower Yangtze valley. Its leader, Marshal Tuan Ch'i-jui, was to become a sort of President of the Republic from 1924 to 1926, under the title of 'Chief of Executive Power'.

Finally, the outlying provinces – Yunnan, Kwangsi, Szechuan, Sikang, Sinkiang, Shansi and Ninghsia – were all in fact independent, acknowledgement of this being more or less open, depending on their position and the circumstances. The best known of their governors were Yen Hsi-shan in Shansi, Liu Hsiang in Szechuan, Liu Wen-hui in Sikang, and the Moslem generals, Ma Pu-fang in Chinghai and Ma Hung-k'uei in Ninghsia.

On 25 April 1921, only a few weeks before the modest and clandestine opening of the First Congress of the Chinese Communist Party, three of the great warlords of the moment – Ts'ao K'un, Chang Tso-lin and Wang Chan-yüan – held a conference in Peking. They rearranged the cliques' spheres of influence and strongly expressed their opposition to the imminent formation of a national government in Kwangtung, which was to rival the Peking government. Both items on the agenda were characteristic of the habits and the political conventions of the times.

On 7 April 200 deputies, members of the old parliament elected in 1913 just after the fall of the empire, had in fact met in Canton to decide on the constitution of a legal government whose president was to be the great Chinese revolutionary, Sun Yat-sen, then 65 years old.

Sun Yat-sen had already presided over a military government in the province of Kwangtung from September 1917 until May 1918, when he was deposed by the Kwangsi provincial clique. His second government was destined to be no more fortunate than the first, as it was to disappear in June 1922, and a third Sun Yat-sen government was formed, in Canton once more, in 1923.

The general situation in 1921 as summarized above was little different from that of 1926 during the Northern Expedition, when the Kuomintang and its communist allies set out from Canton, a longstanding seedbed of revolution, to begin their task of reuniting the nation. The military cliques were almost the same, as were the men themselves. Meanwhile, great changes had taken place in the organization and the means at the disposal of the revolutionary troops of the Kuomintang and the Communist Party. They now represented an almost irresistible force, meeting with rapid success, in spite of initial financial and military inferiority, and in spite of the dissensions, which began with the death of Sun Yat-sen on 12 March 1925 and increased until the final break in the spring and summer of 1927.

Although the fall of the empire resulted in a complete renewal of the upper administrative structures, it scarcely affected the administration of rural areas, which by tradition were largely autonomous. The former regime was content with a simple framework: a few thousand civil servants: governors-general, provincial governors, prefects and district magistrates with locally recruited assistants. State intervention stopped at the level of the district (hsien), which included from 200 to 500 villages, or between 200,000 and 300,000 inhabitants. The towns and villages governed themselves by an authority which they exercised under unwritten law. Common sense and habit played a far more important role than coercion or law.

The duties falling to the heads of the villages were generally fulfilled by unpaid 'gentry' chosen by the influential families from among themselves. The heads of villages and the gentry who helped them were responsible for taxes (particularly the tax paid in grain), for collecting recruits for the army or the militia, and for the maintenance of order and morality in general; they directed the life of the community, ignoring the individual and taking the family into consideration as the recognized base of the social pyramid. Intermediate groups sometimes grew up between the family and the village. In this way, the old system of 'pao' (groups of ten families) and 'chia' (groups of ten 'pao'), inherited from the Sung, was brought into force once more in 1932. In fact, the Chinese village, with its large families and clans (tsu) embracing families of different social standing, all bearing the same name and revering the same ancestor, its associations for mutual help in times of natural calamity or against bandits, its religious associations, even secret societies, was an astonishingly well balanced social structure, which was often almost incomprehensible to the outsider, especially when its unusual customs were also taken into consideration.

Nothing had changed perceptibly by 1921 and, in spite of a few efforts from 1930 onwards, the central Kuomintang government did not manage to modify this situation, which had ensured the survival of the civilization and the empire itself over the centuries. Until 1949 China was to remain a completely decentralized country, where provincial regionalism, the village and the family formed a screen that quickly dulled the impact of any move the government made. The countryside was outside the main current of national and international life, and was only dimly aware of it.

One factor was, however, to have far-reaching consequences in the peasant's world: the disappearance of the social and moral example set by the scholar. Wherever he was, in the remote chief city of a district or the village where he lived in retirement, and whatever his personal qualities or failings may have been, the scholar embodied an ideal of knowledge and helped preserve the old order based on clearly defined human relationships, summed up by the Five Cardinal Relationships: sovereign and subject, father and son, elder and younger brother, husband and wife, friend and friend.

Many scholars of the old order still existed in 1921, but socially they had already been replaced by the landlords, merchants and modern civil servants who did not represent the same traditional moral values or stability. The consequent weakening of conservatism in the country districts made matters easier for those who had dealings with the peasants; they were mainly the Communist Party.

The economic situation

The economic situation in China in 1921 was as deplorable as the political one. China is above all an incredibly poor country, possessing the classic features of an underdeveloped country to a rare degree, particularly that of an inadequate food supply. Sun Yat-sen's phrase, 'in our country there only are the poor and the even poorer', was truer than ever.

The chief cause underlying this situation was the over-rapid population growth in the eighteenth and early nineteenth centuries. The demographic increase at that time was extraordinary. From the beginning of the Christian era until the birth of the last dynasty (1644), the population had remained below 100 million inhabitants. By 1741 it was 143·4 million, and by 1841, a hundred years later, it had risen to 413 million. A partial census in 1928 produced an estimate of 462,873,793 inhabitants, a precise though possibly inexact figure.

Although the population tripled in the space of one century, the area of cultivable land scarcely increased by a seventh between 1724 (6,837,000 'ch'ing')[1] and 1833 (7,375,000 'ch'ing'). Towards 1921, however, this figure had risen to about 13,900,000 'ch'ing', or 92 million hectares.

The national income naturally remained small; the economists' estimates vary between 12,000 and 25,000 million Chinese dollars.[2] The standard of living was extremely low. No figures exist for the year 1921, but according to an enquiry made by the Academia Sinica twelve years later, the average personal income was twelve U.S. dollars per annum; the value of the dollar has since fallen by 50 per cent. Accumulation of capital and investment both remained low, whereas political and military troubles, administrative waste and a total lack of technicians of any sort prevented the carrying out of plans for development on a national scale. China was, and remained, essentially a country of farmers and artisans; until the Sino-Japanese war of 1937, over three-quarters of the consumer goods were produced by town or country dwelling artisans.

Although nearly 80 per cent of the population was employed in agriculture, no progress was made in this sphere and, owing to lack of implements, fertilizers and money, the traditional fragmented and intensive system persisted. The yield, particularly of wheat, the staple diet of the northern provinces, was mediocre. Natural calamities, frequent in a country governed by the vagaries of the monsoon, produced famines, which the incompetent authorities were unable to remedy.

However, thanks to the natural vitality of the Chinese, and with the help of loans from outside, the example set by the foreign concessions led to the development of a small modern economic sector, which grew up alongside the traditional crafts. At first it was concerned with transport (railways and coastal and river traffic), arsenals and mines; later light

[1] The 'ch'ing' contains 100 'mou' and is equal to 6·6 hectares.

[2] At the rate of four Chinese dollars for one U.S. dollar, as it was valued in 1933.

industry and particularly the textile and food industries were included as well. Heavy industry, which needs more capital and technical ability and is slow to produce results, developed little.

These new undertakings were naturally almost all concentrated in the large coastal towns such as Shanghai, Tientsin and Tsingtao, where foreigners were more active, providing some measure of security. The nature of these towns and their level of development will be examined later on, in connection with the industrial bourgeoisie and proletariat created by the modern sector of industry and the part these were to play in the political life of the country (see Chapter 3). Meanwhile, the following general statistics reveal the low rate of production in mining and industry and the inadequate agricultural output, particularly when considered alongside the enormous figures given for the population.

Coal	19,876,375 tons
Iron ore	1,311,697 tons
Steel (modern steelworks)[1]	4,851 tons
Antimony (regulus)	8,900 tons
Tin	11,500 tons
Petroleum	85,000 tons
Cotton mills	1,422,000 spindles
Mixed cereals[2]	150,000,000 tons

The social situation

The chief characteristic of Chinese society in 1921 was the rapid transformation affecting its upper classes, as a result of the casting off of the former educational system and the disappearance of the old imperial administration. The mandarin, unique in his ability to combine the duties of scholar, magistrate, even military commander at the head of regular or militia troops, and chosen by examinations that had remained identical for centuries from one end of the empire to the other, was gradually disappearing.

New, completely different categories of men were appearing to take

[1] A large proportion of the iron ore was exported to Japan. The modern ironworks produced little more than 250,000 tons of pig iron per year. Production of indigenous iron amounted to about 150,000 tons per year.

[2] This is a rough estimate including eleven cereals, or other foodstuffs grouped with them, for an average year. Rice represents about 50 million tons, wheat about 25 million; the rest includes millet, kaoliang, barley, oats, beans, soya beans, sweet potatoes, etc. For details on the Chinese economic situation, see the relevant *China Year Book*. See also Yuan-li Wu's book, *An Economic Survey of Communist China* (New York, 1956), which has an excellent bibliography.

his place. The modern intellectual, a teacher or student with revolutionary sympathies (or at least ready to reject the old culture), was still influenced by some of the scholars' traditions: pride in his class, and an inclination to criticize the authorities in power. He usually sobered down rapidly on entering the administration or business. The local military chief was in fact the one who had the means of enforcing authority in a country where the old administrative system was crumbling. He tended to replace the civil servant and the politician, who then became his assistants, while he looked for military help from a higher level and eliminated all possible rivals. Some of these military chiefs were not without nationalist and revolutionary aspirations, but they were prisoners of a system from which they could escape only if the revolution came to them. The businessman, engaged either in industry or commerce, came from the landowning or the civil servant class; his interests either allied him with foreign capitalists or else brought him into competition with them. These three social categories corresponded to a new Chinese middle class. The military feudalistic regime and the nationalist (Kuomintang) and communist (Kungch'antang) regimes all filled their administrative posts from among its members.

The outstanding feature of the Chinese society of 1921 was the existence of an enormous peasant class, which was docile, patient, hard-working, usually illiterate, and incapable of change in its habits and mentality. Its members were even worse off than in preceding centuries, owing to demographic pressure and financial chaos, which raised the price of land. Although few large estates existed, the distribution of land was unequal; this was later to form the basis for the communists' somewhat oversimplified classification: landlords, rich peasants, middle peasants and poor peasants.

Among the many statistics published on this subject, it is interesting to compare the following figures referring to later years, one set given by a communist author, the other by a supporter of the government:[1]

	Percentage of households		*Percentage of land owned*	
Landlords	4	3	50	26
Rich peasants	6	7	15	27
Middle peasants	20	22	20	25
Poor peasants	70	68	15	22

[1] The figures in the left-hand columns were published by Ch'en Han-seng in 1950, those on the right were given by Wu Wen-hui for the year 1934. They are quoted by Yuan-li Wu, *An Economic Survey of Communist China.*

In both cases, 10 per cent of the rural population (landlords and rich peasants) hold over 50 per cent of the land, about 70 per cent of the population (poor peasants) being obliged to rent land at a rate that is rarely, if ever, lower than half the harvest. This particular situation was to give considerable help to the Communist Party when it was forced to rely on the countryside, having lost all solid support in the towns. Mao Tse-tung himself included poor peasants and middle peasants, who rented part of the lands they worked, in a semi-proletariat.[1]

Even though the proportion of land to population was so ill balanced that it brought the size of the average farm to 1 hectare, the basic problem of Chinese agriculture was in fact one of lack of modernization rather than of equal distribution of land.

Whereas weight of numbers, ignorance and difficulties of communication rendered the peasantry immune to change, and the proletariat was too small and lacking in organization to be fully aware of its own existence, currents of all sorts began to penetrate the towns, particularly those on the coast. New political, intellectual and ethical ideas created tension between generations. All contemporary literature bears witness to it. The voluminous novels of Pa Chin were probably the best examples of this kind.[2]

However, it must be admitted that these currents had made no far-reaching changes in customs by 1921, even in the cities. The Chinese family was still all-powerful and claimed all individual loyalties. In the words of Lin Yü-t'ang, it was 'a walled castle outside which everything is legitimate loot'. The family, the clan, the guild, the village, or the secret society, were infinitely more important than the nation and the state, even as regards basic morality. The sacrifice of public interest to these private interests, as well as nepotism and corruption, was still the rule at all levels of society and the administration. The Chinese Communists put themselves at a considerable advantage by a violent attack on the family, which ceased to exist in the eyes of the Party. Within the movement, this won the undivided loyalty of their members to the hierarchy, while outside it earning a well-deserved reputation for honesty, incorruptibility and, consequently, efficiency, which gained the support of part of the younger generation who were attracted by change.

The international context

In the summer of 1921, China was still in an unfavourable and uncertain international context as far as her relations with Japan and with her former

[1] 'Analysis of the Classes in Chinese society', *Selected Works*, vol. I.

[2] Pearl Buck's trilogy, *The Good Earth*, *A House Divided* and *Sons*, gives a fairly accurate idea of the way in which the different generations evolved at this time.

Western allies were concerned. The Twenty-one Demands, presented by Japan on 18 January 1915 and accepted in part by Yüan Shih-k'ai on 9 May, had awakened a section of public opinion to international problems. China's entry into the war against Germany (14 August 1917) and the Allied victory seemed to justify hopes of a release from the Unequal Treaties and of the restitution of the German rights and interests in Shantung, which had been seized by the Japanese. The sensitivity and disappointment of the Chinese were clearly shown during the May 4th 1919 Movement, a movement the Chinese communists later affected to link up with the worldwide proletarian revolution (see Chapter 3).

When the Chinese Communist Party was born, in July 1921, the questions laid aside or deferred by the peace conference, particularly that of the German rights in Shantung, had not been resolved, but the Washington Conference which opened the same year provided at least a partial solution. This was expressed in two diplomatic documents of great importance, which were to direct Chinese foreign policy for ten years: the Nine-Power Treaty of 6 February 1922 and the Sino-Japanese Treaty of 4 February 1922.

The Nine-Power Treaty, signed by Belgium, China, France, Great Britain, Italy, Japan, the Netherlands, Portugal and the United States:

1. Reaffirmed China's sovereignty, independence and territorial and administrative integrity.
2. Stated that the powers agreed to give China the chance of having an 'efficient and stable' government.
3. Recalled the 'open door' principle, or the equal chance policy defined in 1899 by the American Secretary of State, John Hay.
4. Made provision for the autonomy of the Chinese customs and the end of extraterritoriality, but gave no details as to date or means.

China was thus protected from the territorial ambitions of the powers, particularly Japan, who dared not seize Manchuria for another ten years (the Mukden Incident, 18 September 1931), and tried to efface the memory of the Twenty-one Demands. On the other hand, China's situation was still undeniably semicolonial, owing to its inability to furnish a government capable of undertaking international responsibilities. 'But', wrote Sun Yat-sen, 'Whose colony is China after all? She is the colony of each country with which she had signed a treaty, every country which has signed a treaty with her is her master. So China is not a slave of one country but of all countries.'[1]

This position of inferiority offered distinct advantages for the growth

[1] Sun Yat-sen, *Selected Works* (Peking, 1957: in Chinese).

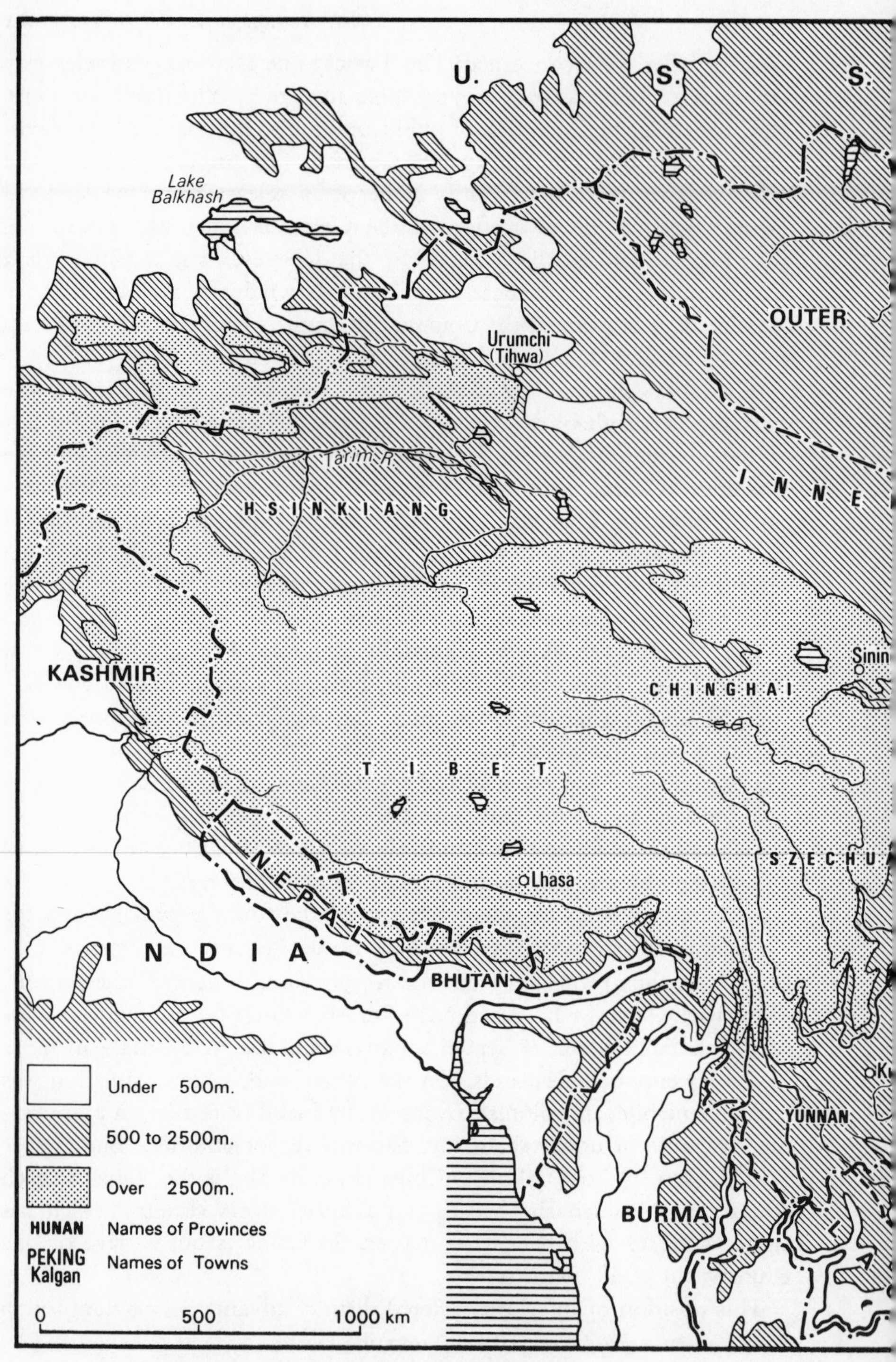

Map 1. Physical map of China and provinces

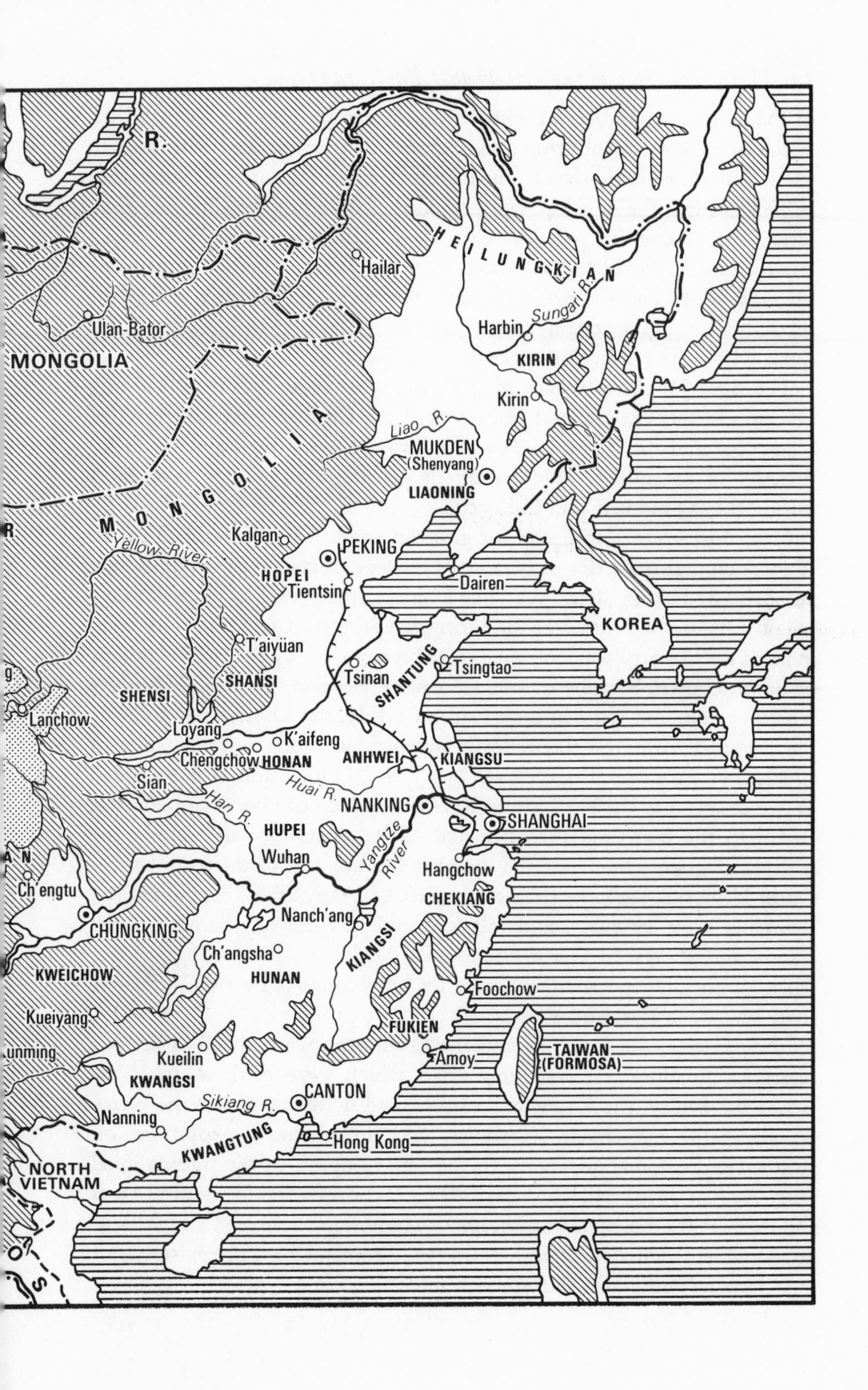

R.
MONGOLIA
Ulan-Bator
Hailar
HEILUNGKIAN
Harbin
Sungari R.
KIRIN
Kirin
Liao R.
MUKDEN
(Shenyang)
LIAONING
M O N G O L I A
Kalgan
PEKING
HOPEI
Tientsin
Dairen
KOREA
Yellow River
T'aiyüan
Tsinan
SHANTUNG
Tsingtao
SHENSI
SHANSI
Lanchow
Loyang
K'aifeng
Chengchow
HONAN
ANHWEI
KIANGSU
Sian
Huai R.
Han R.
NANKING
SHANGHAI
HUPEI
Wuhan
Yangtze River
Hangchow
Ch'engtu
CHEKIANG
CHUNGKING
Nanch'ang
KIANGSI
Ch'angsha
KWEICHOW
HUNAN
Foochow
Kueiyang
FUKIEN
Kueilin
Amoy
TAIWAN
(FORMOSA)
KWANGSI
Sikiang R.
CANTON
Nanning
Hong Kong
KWANGTUNG
NORTH
VIETNAM

of the nationalist and communist revolutionary movements. It furnished both causes with an enduring and irrefutable argument, and both were to use it with equal enthusiasm. The maintenance of the foreign concessions helped towards the development and concentration of the Chinese proletariat, sharpening its political awareness. The concessions and leased territories also facilitated contacts with the West, whether directly or through books and the press. Finally, they were to provide a refuge for revolutionary agitators on more than one occasion, and above all for those who were ready to respect their neutrality.

The Sino-Japanese Treaty of 4 February 1922 settled the Shantung question in theory. Japan at last restored the German leased territory of Kiaochow and the Tsingtao-Tsinan railway (Kiaotsi line) against an indemnity of 66 million gold francs; the retrocession was to take effect during the six months that followed.

China lost Outer Mongolia for good in 1921. Although linked to the Chinese emperors by ties of personal vassalage, it ceased to recognize the authority of Peking after 1911. The Chinese tried, with some success, to regain a foothold there in 1919, during the Siberian Civil War. Urga and most of the country was occupied in February 1921 by the 'white' troops of Baron Ungern-Sternberg, who joined the Hetman Semenof. When the red troops entered Urga in their turn on 5 July, the Chinese had to leave the country. Although theoretically independent once more, in spite of Chicherin's promise of evacuation (15 June), Outer Mongolia remained in fact attached to the Far Eastern Republic, which had been formed from Baikal to the Maritime Province with Chita as its capital. Neither the nationalist government nor the People's Republic of China were to win Outer Mongolia back. In spite of the fact that they are of the same race, share the same language and religion, and in spite of a similar social system and allegiance to the communist world, the two Mongolias are still as politically separate today as are the two Koreas or the two Vietnams, shared between East and West.

In July 1921, the U.S.S.R. and the Comintern went through serious internal difficulties: an economic crisis which gave birth to the New Economic Policy, the Kronstadt mutiny, and divisions within the European socialist movement. However, adopting Lenin's resolutions on national and colonial questions, the Second Congress of the International (July-August 1920) had, the year before, laid down the ideological basis and defined the practical conditions of communist action in China as in other non-emancipated foreign countries. From then on the existence of the Chinese Communist Party was assured.

Thus in 1921, when the Chinese Communist Party was born, China was beginning to enter the modern world, through her upper classes first of all. The old civilization was still present everywhere, however. This dualism is often reflected in the personality and conduct of the future leaders of the Party, who were educated or completed their education during this period of transition. Mao Tse-tung, who was born in 1893, was 18 when the empire fell and 28 when his Party was formed; his was a common case, though an illustrious one.

When tracing the adventurous course of these men's lives, it must never be forgotten that two or even three widely differing currents contribute to their intellectual and moral education: Confucianism, democratic and liberal ideas, and Marxism-Leninism. From this point of view at least, the Chinese communists of the new generation, who are nearer the international model, should be easier to understand than the original ones. This is not necessarily so, however, for the old civilization continues to leave its mark on both individual and national psychological processes.

2 The Introduction of Western Political Ideas 1894-1919 The Forerunners of Socialism

The technical revolution

Socialism, particularly the Marxist brand of socialism, made a late appearance in China and it could almost be said that this coincided with the formation of the Chinese Communist Party in 1921. At first sight it seems surprising that China should be half a century behind Europe in this respect and a quarter of a century behind Japan, where a socialist party had existed since 1901.[1] On examination, this was only to be expected considering how long it took for China to become receptive to Western ideas. In any case, new political concepts could only be introduced slowly, once the old culture, with its overwhelming originality, had lost ground or been uprooted. Conservative ideas in China, whether held by the people or by the scholar class, held out for a long time against Western intrusion each defeat they suffered being the result of a disastrous war against the foreigner: the Opium War (1840), war with France and England (1860), war with France (1885), war with Japan (1894), the Boxer Rebellion (1900), and the Russo-Japanese war for the control of Chinese Manchuria (1904-5).

At first Western material superiority alone was acknowledged. For some time technical advances in the military and naval fields were the only ones introduced, followed by some industrial developments with a direct bearing on national defence. Tseng Kuo-fan, the governor-general

[1] The first Japanese socialist party was founded by Katayama Sen, later vice-president of the 1904 Amsterdam Congress, but Hiromichi Ozaki had described socialism in 1881 in the review *Rokugo*, 'The Cause of Modern Socialism'.

who had defeated the T'ai p'ing, created the first arsenals in the Yangtze valley; Li Hung-chang and Chang Chih-t'ung built the first spinning mills and the first railways, launched a modern fleet, opened up mines and founded offices where Western techniques were studied, etc. These remarkable men and their imitators never seem to have contemplated introducing political or administrative reforms along Western lines. They doubtless knew how far they could go without condemning themselves, and above all they had boundless confidence in China's superiority in all but scientific fields; the social order, the moral foundations of the empire, and its customs, all left nothing to be desired when compared with those of the West: 'Chinese learning for the fundamental principles, Western learning for practical application'[1] became the slogan of the era.

Chinese revolutionaries have been unjust to these great innovators, and especially to Li Hung-chang. The communists in particular, instead of being grateful to them for founding Chinese industry and the proletariat, saw them only as the first representatives of a new class of 'compradors' in the service of 'feudalism' and 'imperialism', a class that was to wreck the traditional economy and at the same time paralyse its evolution towards modern capitalism. In fact these men were neither conservatives nor revolutionaries; they merely served progress in the light of their origins and their times. When seen from this angle, they were undeniably the last great men that the old empire produced.

The reformers of 1898

After the Sino-Japanese war and the deplorable Treaty of Shimonoseki, true thinkers tried to introduce new political ideas of Western origin, adapting them to traditional philosophy with varying degrees of sincerity: K'ang Yu-wei, T'an Ssu-t'ung and Liang Ch'i-Ch'ao, all three closely linked with the 1898 Reform Movement, are the most original and the most important of them. Although their writings and personalities were completely different, they all shared a feeling of courageous patriotism, a deep-rooted hostility to the old social order, and a tendency, which was sometimes vague, towards anarchism and a socialist Utopia. Finally, all three were both theorists and men of action, and enjoyed immense personal prestige.

K'ang Yu-wei and the 'Great Harmony'

K'ang Yu-wei (1858-1927) came of an old family of scholars from Kwangtung province. After receiving a classical education from teachers of a

[1] Translated by Ssu-yu Teng and J. K. Fairbank in *China's Response to the West* (New York, Atheneum, 1967), p. 164.

neo-Confucian tendency, he went to Peking where he joined the reformist movement just after the first defeats inflicted by the Japanese in the war. The titles of some of his writings show how preoccupied he was by national issues: *Notes on the French Revolution*, *Notes on the Division of Poland*, *The Meiji Revolution* and the *History of Peter the Great*. Even before 1894 he had tried to find support for his theories of reform in the works of Confucius himself; he gave a new interpretation, denouncing the passages in the Classics which were mere inventions: *Study of the Classics Forged during the Hsin Period*, *Confucius as a Reformer*. The *Ta T'ung Shu* or *The Book of the Great Harmony* is the most important of his works as far as the history of Chinese socialism is concerned.

Basing his theories on the *Spring and Autumn Annals*, and particularly on the *Li Yün* (*Evolution of Rituals*), one of the chapters of the *Li Chi* (*Record of Rituals*), K'ang Yu-wei traces an evolution in the history of humanity consisting of three stages: an age of disorder and individualism, an age of nationalism, and finally an age of universal peace. In this new age, described at length in the *Ta T'ung Shu,* the nations vanish, regional administrations are elected, private property and even the family are abolished; the family is seen as the source of all selfishness, and as an encouragement to an unhealthy instinct for private property.

K'ang Yu-wei ascribed all the sufferings of humanity to nine 'spheres' or 'barriers', which reveal his astonishingly destructive personality: barriers between nations, class barriers, barriers of race, sex, family, profession, individual disorders, species (human and animal) and poverty. He proposed thirteen solutions to remedy these evils, which, once applied, would bring about the era of Great Harmony.

The communists could not fail to condemn the theories of K'ang Yu-wei. They saw in them the reflection of an era of rising capitalism already at loggerheads with decadent feudalism. K'ang Yu-wei was classed as a member of the capitalist bourgeoisie; pressure from the foreigner and from traditional 'feudalism' led him to search for a new solution, and, in pursuing his own dreams, he laid bare his own weaknesses. They also pointed out, justifiably, that K'ang Yu-wei used material from many conflicting sources to form the ideology of his Utopia: Confucianism, Buddhism, Christianity, European socialism, etc. However, they admitted that his work expressed a reaction against the evils of capitalism and opposed the exploitation of the masses, while acknowledging the evolution of society to be inevitable. For this reason, they conceded that it contained elements of a romantic socialism. These elements were also recognized by Liang Ch'i-ch'ao, the disciple and expounder of K'ang Yu-wei, whose originality of thought he much admired: 'When he wrote this book thirty years ago, he relied on nothing and he plagiarized nothing [from others]; yet his ideas correspond in many ways to the internationalism and socialism of today, and in statement of high principles he even surpasses them.'[1]

K'ang Yu-wei was summoned by the Emperor Kuang Hsü to guide the abortive Hundred Days' Reform (1898). He was forced to flee to Japan where he remained loyal to the monarchy, founding the Society for the Protection of the Emperor, before gradually retiring from political action. On his return to China, he supported Yüan Shih-k'ai in his attempt to restore the empire in his own name. He died in Tsingtao, an old man who had completely reverted to a thoroughly orthodox conservatism.

T'an Ssu-t'ung and the 'Philosophy of Jen'[2]

T'an Ssu-t'ung (1865-98) was a disciple of K'ang Yu-wei, and another distant forerunner of socialism. Liang Ch'i-ch'ao called him 'a meteor in the intellectual world of the late Ch'ing period'; he was executed in 1898 at the age of 34 after the failure of the 1898 Reform Movement. He refused to flee the country, saying that no nation had been reformed without martyrs, a gesture that admirably illustrates his wholehearted generosity and idealism.

T'an Ssu-t'ung, though indisputably Confucianist, as the name alone of his work *The Philosophy of Jen* (*Jen Hsüeh*) shows, rose up in protest against all the obstacles hemming in the old society: the individual selfishness, the hypocrisy of the Five Cardinal Relationships, and the formalism, particularly in connection with culture. He attacked the Manchus with unusual violence, while at the same time rejecting nationalism, and preached universal love and the abolition of frontiers. The following short passage shows the extent of his determination in the cause of total emancipation:

> . . . to break out of the entangling net [created by] the pursuit of selfish interests and of official emoluments; to break out of the net of such vulgar teachings as those of the school of textual criticism and of stylistic formalism; to break out of the net of all [confining] theories and teachings throughout the globe; to break through the trammels imposed by rulers; to break out of the net of the 'basic human relationships'; and to break out of the net of 'heaven'.[3]

[1] Liang Ch'i-ch'ao, *Intellectual Trends in the Ch'ing Period,* tr. Immanuel C. Y. Hsü (Cambridge, Mass., Harvard University Press, 1959), p. 97.

[2] Jen, which can be translated more or less adequately by 'benevolence', with 'righteousness' (yi), formed the foundation of classical moral philosophy.

[3] Cf. Liang Ch'i-ch'ao, *Intellectual Trends in the Ch'ing Period,* p. 107.

It is interesting to note that T'an Ssu-t'ung was a Hunanese from the little town of Liuyang, and that he took an extremely active part in politics in Ch'angsha, the provincial capital, where he helped produce the first modern newspapers: the *Hunan Journal* (*Hsiang pao*), which was a daily paper, and the *Hunan Students' Journal* (*Hsiang-hsüeh pao*). He also had several anti-Manchu works, such as the *Record of the Ten Days in Yangchow*, reprinted and distributed secretly, and joined in discussions held by several reformist societies, one of which was the 'Nan-hsüeh hui'.

A generation later, his compatriot, Mao Tse-tung, was stirred by the memory of the young, romantic revolutionary, for he too became aware of political ideas and activities for the first time in Ch'angsha. Mao Tse-tung's official biographers, particularly Li Jui,[1] mention this, laying justifiable emphasis on the province's strong revolutionary tradition. Present-day communist writers show more understanding of T'an Ssu-t'ung than of K'ang Yu-wei, saying that in spite of his fidelity to Confucianism, he still inclined towards the bourgeois democratic revolution necessary to the advent of the socialist revolution.

Liang Ch'i-ch'ao, a lover of controversy

Liang Ch'i-ch'ao achieved importance through the stir created by his essays and newspaper articles widely circulated in Chinese political and intellectual circles at the beginning of the century. Until the failure of the 1898 Reform Movement, he was a disciple of K'ang Yu-wei, but he grew away from him and gradually abandoned Confucianism for Rousseau and Montesquieu. His political convictions were always uncertain and even frankly contradictory; he declared himself to be a supporter of constitutional monarchy and the Emperor Kuang Hsü, while opposing the Manchus. As Liang himself put it: 'The point of greatest contrast between Liang and K'ang is that the latter had too many fixed ideas and the former too few.'[2] However, he was undeniably a liberal, a democrat, in favour of scientific knowledge, against materialism, and an upholder of morality, simultaneously. Even if he cannot, strictly speaking, be described as a forerunner of socialism, he can at least be said to have prepared the way for it by giving wide, though somewhat haphazard circulation to Western political concepts, helped by a style that probably made him the first modern Chinese journalist.[3]

[1] Li Jui, *Comrade Mao's Early Revolutionary Activities* (Peking, 1957: in Chinese).
[2] Cf. Liang Ch'i-ch'ao, *Intellectual Trends in the Ch'ing Period*, p. 106.
[3] His most important articles are to be found in *The Collected Writings of the Yin Ping Room* (1902), which unfortunately does not exist in translation.

Liang Ch'i-ch'ao lived for a time in Japan, where he founded several newspapers (the *Ch'ing I-pao* and especially the *Hsin-min Ts'ung-pao*) which were in opposition to those of Sun Yat-sen. After 1911 he returned to China; he then held several ministerial posts, taught at Tsinghua University and directed the National Library in Peking, where he died in 1929.

The great translators: Yen Fu, Ma Chün-wu

Although the political thinkers were the most influential, it should not be forgotten that the translators, who were at the same time outstanding scholars, exercised indirect influence through the choice, the number and the style of their translations. The most distinguished of these was probably Yen Fu (1853-1921). A native of Fukien, he intended at first to enter the navy and spent some time in England before becoming Director of the Translations Office in 1902, and then Rector of Peking University and counsellor to Yüan Shih-k'ai after 1911. His liberal ideas lost their force as he grew older, and after the death of Yüan Shih-k'ai, like K'ang Yu-wei, he returned to the classical sources of Confucianism before dying in his native province. The titles of his translations speak for themselves:

> *Evolution and Ethics*, Thomas Huxley (1898); *The Wealth of Nations*, Adam Smith (1901); *A System of Logic*, John Stuart Mill (1902); *On Liberty*, John Stuart Mill (1903); *Study of Sociology*, Herbert Spencer; *L'Esprit des lois*, Montesquieu (1906); *History of Politics*, E. Jenks; *Logics*, W. S. Jevons.

Another translator who was instrumental in the spreading of Western ideas was Ma Chün-wu. He was the first to introduce Darwin with his translations of *The Descent of Man* and *On the Origin of Species*, and also made Rousseau known in China when he published the first Chinese edition of the *Contrat Social*.

The names of these first translations are to be found repeatedly in biographies of the Chinese communist leaders, and particularly in connection with Mao Tse-tung, whose only knowledge of Western political thought, until 1919 at least, was acquired through them.

The first Marxist texts

Marxist works were translated into Chinese for the first time in Japan, chiefly during the controversies that arose between the different groups of Chinese emigrants, some of whom were reformist and some revolutionary. The first text appears to have been *Modern Socialism* by Fukui

Junzo, published in 1889 and translated in 1903. In 1906 the *Min pao*, the newspaper run by Sun Yat-sen in Japan, published the Communist Manifesto, translated by Chu Chih-hsin, the most radical of Dr Sun's supporters. This date, however, is less important than would at first appear. Chinese papers from Japan only rarely reached the mainland, and when they did it was in secret. Their writers tended to gather Western political ideas and offer them to their readers all at once, as they came, with no rearrangement or selection. The concrete problems facing China and practical solutions to them held their attention more than did theoretical systems.

China opened up considerably to Western political trends after the 1911 Revolution. The slackening of police control, the intellectual ferment generated by contemporary events, and the prospect of a parliamentary regime provided a favourable climate in which ideas of all kinds could circulate freely.

Socialist ideas lagged behind, however, and a truly representative selection of Marxist works was not available in China until 1919. This will be mentioned again later on in connection with early writings by the founders of the Chinese Communist Party, particularly those of Ch'en Tu-hsiu and Li Ta-chao. As for translations, the Communist Manifesto was published in November 1919 in a student newspaper[1] and was put on sale in bookshops in 1920 (translated by Ch'eng Wang-tao); *The Class Struggle* by Kautsky and Kirkup's *History of Socialism* seem to have appeared in Chinese a little earlier on. Mao Tse-tung was to read all three before 1920 and admitted that they influenced him considerably.[2] Marx, Engels and Lenin were not systematically translated until 1923; the choice of Marxist works available in Chinese remained limited until 1930.[3]

Anarchism: the forerunner of Marxism

Revolutionary anarchism seems to have held more attraction for Chinese intellectuals than did socialism during the early years of the century. As several authors most aptly put it, it was at the same time 'the antithesis and the logical predecessor' of Marxism-Leninism in China.[4] In fact, the

[1] 'Salary, Work and Capital', also by Marx, was published in May-June 1919 in the *Morning Post,* the newspaper of the Progressive Party (Chin pu Tang).
[2] Edgar Snow, *Red Star Over China.*
[3] A list of the sixty reviews and works in English and Chinese available to the small Marxist study group at Peking University in 1922 is given in *Modern Historical Material* (*Chin-tai shih tzu-liao*), 1955, No. 2, p. 167.
[4] R. A. Scalapino and G. T. Yu, *The Chinese Anarchist Movement.*

Chinese anarchist movement, which developed chiefly among Chinese students in France, guided some revolutionaries towards Marxist writings and vocabulary, but supplied few cadres for the future Communist Party. The relative success of anarchism among Chinese intellectuals can be explained by its progress in Europe during the years before the First World War. Its noisy demonstrations, often causing bloodshed, could not fail to impress some students, and acts of terrorism were committed in China, too, sometimes in cooperation with the 'T'ung-meng hui' led by Sun Yat-sen, the first version of the Kuomintang.

In its rejection of society and glorification of individual liberty, as well as in its negative aspects, Western anarchism had much in common with old Taoist trends and for this reason was easy to grasp. The following passage by Sun Yat-sen is particularly eloquent in this respect:

> As far as anarchism is concerned, it is a doctrine which has been spoken of in China from the earliest dynasties. Are the theories of Huang and Lao[1] anything other than anarchism? The *Lieh Tze* says: 'In the kingdom of Hua Hsü, the people have no sovereign, there are no laws and they follow nature'. Is not that anarchism again?
>
> In China, we have been speaking of anarchism for several thousand years, but the younger generation have not examined it and go off, picking up what other countries cast away. They have no idea that the anarchism of which they speak today is something which we have been speaking of for thousands of years, which they took no notice of.[2]

The first anarchist nucleus appeared in Paris towards 1907. Its most important members were Li Shih-tseng, Wu Chih-hui, and later Chang Chi. They published a newspaper in Chinese entitled *The New Century*, with a subtitle in Esperanto (*La Tempo Novaj*).[3] *Mutual Aid: a Factor of Evolution* by Prince Kropotkin was translated by Li Shih-tseng and also by Chou Fo-hai. A small group of anarchists, led by Chang Chi, Dr Ch'u Min-i and Liu Shih-p'ei, was formed in Japan as well; their newspaper was the *T'ien-i pao* (*Celestial Justice*).

The 1911 Revolution brought these different groups back to their own country. The anarchists continued for a few more years, sometimes in the form of societies with startling names and rules, such as the Society for the Promotion of Virtue (Chin Teh hui), to which Wang Ching-wei

[1] Of Lao Tze and the Yellow Emperor (Huang ti), the mythical master of Taoism.

[2] Sun Yat-sen, *Selected Works* (Chinese edition), p. 581.

[3] An anarchist paper published by Jean Grave from 1895 to 1914 had the same title.

belonged, or the Society of Cocks Crowing in the Dark,[1] whose name comes from a passage of the Classics; the *Min-sheng* (*The Voice of the People*) was the best known of their papers.

In the main, the Chinese anarchists became dispersed in 1915-16. The chief figures among them filled senior administrative posts in the Kuomintang and held them until the end. This is true of Chang Chi who ended his days in 1947 as Director of the National Institute of History, Dr Ch'u Min-i who was shot as a collaborator, Li Shih-tseng who for a long time was in charge of Sino-French cultural relations and Chairman of the National Peking University, and is now in Taiwan, and finally Wu Chih-hui. Chou Fo-hai was the only one to join the Communist Party, and he left it fairly rapidly. Several anarchists attached to small socialist groups formed in 1919-20 were eliminated from them as early as 1921.

Anarchism lasted a little longer, particularly in literature, largely thanks to the novelist Pa Chin who translated several of Kropotkin's works: *The Conquest of Bread, Memoirs of a Revolutionist,* and *Ethics, Origin and Development*. A few controversies arose between communists (Ch'en Tu-hsiu) and anarchists (Ou Sheng-pai), and a few anarchist leaflets appeared, but the movement quickly lost its vigour and influence once its founders had abandoned it.

Anarchism played no part in the great events leading up to the spreading of the revolution in 1926-7 and the political unification of China. Even though some of the present leaders were briefly affected by it, among them Mao Tse-tung who admits to it himself, the Communist Party's doctrinal strictness has eliminated all trace of it.

The socialism of Chiang K'ang-hu

Two groups laid claim to the title of socialist in the years before the First World War: an uncertain and ephemeral group led by Chiang K'ang-hu and that led by Sun Yat-sen himself. Both claims were doubtful, but the use of the word influenced the propagation of authentic Marxism.

Chiang K'ang-hu, who was born in Shangjao, Kiangsi, in 1883, made three stays in Japan between 1900 and 1907, teaching Japanese in Peking

[1] R. A. Scalapino and G. T. Yu, in *The Chinese Anarchist Movement*, give details of the extremely rigorous rules imposed on members of these associations. The Society of Cocks Crowing in the Dark forbade its adherents to smoke, drink alcohol, eat meat, marry, be civil servants or soldiers, belong to a political party, have a religion, use their surnames, etc. Several different classes of membership existed, as members could undertake to obey all or some of the rules.

in the intervals. He was without any doubt influenced by anarchism, and his first article, published under the name of Hsü An-ch'eng, was a violent attack on the family. According to one of his biographers,[1] he liked to contrast the concept of the Three Negations (San Wu Chu I) – that of the family, the nation and religion – with the Three People's Principles (San Min Chu I) of Sun Yat-sen. When he returned to China from Belgium in 1911, he organized an Association for the Study of Socialism followed by a 'Socialist Party' (Chung-kuo she-hui Tang) in Shanghai, and published a review called *The Star*, which soon became *The Socialist Review*. At this stage, Chiang K'ang-hu advocated the equal distribution of land and the nationalization of production. The rest of his programme lumped together the abolition of war and armies, the death penalty, prostitution, inheritance and direct taxation, and called for the introduction of free, compulsory education.

If certain historians are to be believed,[2] thirty deputies of the first Chinese National Assembly elected in 1912 were supporters of Chiang K'ang-hu. Once Yüan Shih-k'ai had dissolved the assembly, Chiang K'ang-hu continued his activities, which were by then somewhat disorganized. He came to accept both the dictator and the concept of nationalism, and asked that the island of Ch'ungming in the mouth of the Yangtze be put at his disposal to conduct an experiment in socialism. After teaching for a time in the United States, he spent two years in Europe. In 1921 he visited the Soviet Union, where he attended the Third Congress of the Communist International and possibly had interviews with Lenin and Trotsky, before spending some time in Europe once more. In 1924 he again tried to create a Chinese Social-Democrat Party in Peking (Chung-kuo she-hui min-chu Tang), but nothing came of it;[3] the various authoritarian regimes then sharing control of China were not favourable to liberalism. In 1939 Chiang K'ang-hu ruined his chances for the future by throwing in his lot with the Sino-Japanese collaborators.

It seems that Chiang K'ang-hu never offered a coherent picture of socialism to his compatriots, or organized a real party, or even had any true contact with the proletariat. His individual brand of socialism reflects both his humanitarian and anarchist tendencies, and his political ambitions. He left no disciples behind him. He was influential, however, and it was

[1] Professor Wu Hsiang-hsiang of Taiwan University in 'Chiang K'ang-hu and the Chinese Socialist Party', *Modern Chinese Historical Review* (in Chinese).

[2] Professor Yang Yu-chiung in *A History of Chinese Political Parties* (in Chinese).

[3] In 1925 this Party changed its name to the Neo-Socialist Democrat Party, based in Peking, with a branch in Shanghai.

probably he who first introduced a socialist vocabulary into China. Mao Tse-tung read some of his pamphlets as early as 1911.[1]

The socialism of Sun Yat-sen

Sun Yat-sen seems to have called himself a 'socialist' for the first time towards 1905, in Japan, where he had just founded the 'T'ung-meng hui'. The influence of the first Japanese socialist groups, combined with his early concern with humanitarianism, which inspired his third principle, 'min sheng' or 'people's livelihood', probably led him to use the term. The fact that he had adopted a definite position, and the nature of various controversies between his paper, the *Min pao*, and that of Liang Ch'i-ch'ao, the *Hsin-min Ts'ung-pao*, have led scholars to look for traces of socialism in the original thought of Sun and Liang. It is generally agreed today that, even though traces do exist, they correspond to sentimental leanings towards a state socialism or a reformist policy with a substantial social content, rather than to authentic Marxist ideas. The conclusion reached by some is that it is still true to say that Sun and Liang, by linking socialism with nationalism and democracy, particularly in the Three People's Principles, helped to make it respectable, and made it easier to introduce it into China.[2]

This would appear to be as much as can be said for it. Later declarations and commentaries by Sun Yat-sen were to show that his nebulous socialism betrayed a romantic temperament and a lack of discipline in his thought.[3] His tendency towards syncretism in political and social fields could not fail to borrow from Marxism, just as it borrowed from many other doctrines. But since his whole work represents an effort to reconcile the Confucian tradition, nationalism and modern society he could hardly accept Marxist philosophy with its exclusive political consequences. Although they praise him for his role in the revolution and his efforts towards closer contact with the Soviet Union, and celebrate the anniversary of his birth, modern Chinese communists have never considered him as anything but a bourgeois revolutionary. Lin Po-ch'ü, who is now dead, expressed this clearly during the Eighth Congress of the Chinese Communist Party:

> He [Sun Yat-sen] proposed to overthrow the Manchus and establish a bourgeois republic. This programme earned the people's support,

[1] Cf. Edgar Snow, *Red Star Over China*. The best known works of Chiang K'ang-hu are: *The Flood, History of Chinese Civilization, A Study of Chinese Science*.

[2] R. A. Scalapino and H. Z. Schiffrin, 'Early Socialist Currents in the Chinese Revolutionary Movement', *Journal of Asian Studies*, May 1959.

[3] See the *Three People's Principles*, the description of the 'people's livelihood' principle.

because they detested the Manchu domination. The parliamentary system was then considered as the way to salvation, and thus the 1911 Revolution broke out.[1]

This is yet another proof of the general ignorance of Marxism in China before the May 4th 1919 Movement, which will shortly be discussed. At least it can be said that a way had at last been cleared through the thicket of classical philosophy, and Western political philosophy had become well enough known, if not always well expounded and understood, for Marxism to make an appearance.

The prestige of the parliamentary democracy

The Chinese first awoke to the military and technical superiority of the West through their contact with the great democratic states: France, England, the United States of America. Once they realized that they could not ensure the same advantage for themselves merely by adopting the technical advances of their adversaries, they naturally turned their attention to the political institutions. Reformers and revolutionaries were divided into two camps: those who supported a constitutional monarchy (K'ang Yu-wei and Liang Ch'i-ch'ao) and those who supported a parliamentary republic after the French model, or a presidential republic based on the American system. They were unanimous in their rejection of the 1908 constitution, an artificial constitution conceded by the court and copied from the Japanese model. On the other hand, both sides gave an enthusiastic welcome to the provisional constitution of 1912, which established a parliamentary regime similar to those of France and England, but which proved completely unsuitable. This infatuation for a system that the great Western nations had already put to the test helped to leave Marxism to one side, as Lin Po-ch'ü admitted.

China's main difficulty at the end of the nineteenth century and the beginning of the twentieth was to bring about the political and economic emancipation of the bourgeoisie from the Manchus and the warlords who succeeded them. When they embarked on a bourgeois democratic revolution, the Chinese were conforming to a historical process for which they had plenty of models. The proletariat was still small, concentrated in a few places, and largely in the employment of foreign firms, so that its emancipation could not take on the urgency or the proportions of a nationwide problem, or even attract much attention. Numerically weak

[1] Speech entitled 'Lessons in the History of the Chinese Revolution' (22 September 1956).

and ignorant as it was, the proletariat was incapable of organizing itself, producing its own leaders, or taking on its own political education and developing trade union activities, which were in their infancy.

As for the intellectuals, the awakening of their interest in the masses was delayed by traditional Chinese prejudices against those who live by their physical strength alone. Finally, and above all, owing to the presence of foreigners and to the Unequal Treaties, they were chiefly engrossed by national rather than social problems. Before the October Revolution and the Second Congress of the Communist International, Marxism appeared to be a movement leading to social rather than national emancipation. Its pretensions to internationalism, as far as many Chinese intellectuals were concerned, came into direct collision with feelings of isolation and mistrust which were hundreds of years old. After half a century of war and pressure from outside, a close association, even on a purely ideological plane, with well-organized and powerful foreign political movements, was bound to be regarded with reserve. Internationalism, as understood by the West at least, had little meaning or attraction for a country that had long lived in isolation, drawing on its own resources to create its civilization.

Lastly, the Chinese were repaid for their lack of interest in Marxism before 1919 by the Marxists themselves. For them, China had the reputation of being a conservative country; it was a country little known and universally misunderstood, apparently less likely than any other to be destined for socialism, which was usually born of an industrial society. It seemed improbable that China would produce a new force capable of contributing to the victory of the revolution in Europe, which alone was important in their eyes. The conjunction of many new factors – the nationalist crisis of 1919, the example of the Russian Revolution, the development of the modern proletariat following the Great War – was required before Marxist ideas finally gained a permanent foothold in the Chinese world.

3 The Prelude to Marxism

The May 4th 1919 Movement

1919 was a vital year in the political and cultural history of China, but the importance of the May 4th Movement, its main event, only became apparent some time later. The expression applies to several currents, which arose in about 1916 to combine and develop into a huge wave of nationalism during the years that followed. Marxism was one of the elements present; the wave of feeling then subsided, only to reappear in 1925. In the narrowest sense of the term, the May 4th Movement was a spontaneous student movement, which quickly spread to the bourgeoisie and to some artisans and workers in the big towns. At first it was directed against the Allied Powers and the Treaty of Versailles, but it soon turned against the feeble, corrupt regime then in power. Although it made no immediate change in the political situation of the country, it played a large part in arousing public opinion against the politico-military cliques. The Kuomintang, who shared in it to a very limited degree, was to profit by it more than anyone else.

Japan declared war on Germany on 23 August 1914. On 7 November of the same year the Japanese seized the German settlements in the Chinese province of Shantung (the leased territory of Kiaochow and the naval bases of Tsingtao protecting it). They then extended their occupation to the whole of the Kiaotsi railway line (Tsingtao to Tsinan) built by the Germans in 1898, and to the mining concessions lying alongside the line. A few months later, once Japan had been rendered free by events in Europe to do as it pleased, the Japanese presented China with the

Twenty-one Demands, which, if applied, would have transformed China into a mere Japanese protectorate.

China, however, had also entered the war against Germany on 14 August 1917. As this entitled them to a seat at the peace conference, the Chinese tried to have a series of items added to the agenda, which, if decided in their favour, would have restored full sovereignty to their country: the renunciation by the Powers of their policy of spheres of influence, the withdrawal of foreign garrisons, the abolition of foreign consular jurisdiction and foreign post offices, the return of the concessions and leased territories, and the freeing of the customs tariffs.

As the peace conference decided that these questions were beyond its scope and therefore could not be discussed, the Chinese tried to bring up the question of the withdrawal of the Twenty-one Demands made by Japan in 1915. They were still unsuccessful, but their request to discuss the retrocession by Japan of German possessions in Shantung could not be denied. In spite of President Wilson's ardent support, China obtained no satisfaction. The French and the English, who were bound by various promises made to Japan during difficult moments of the war, fearing that Tokyo would boycott the future League of Nations, refused to commit themselves. Tsingtao, the leased territory of Kiaochow and the Kiaotsi railway remained in the hands of the Japanese; their fate was to be decided by a later conference (Articles 156, 157 and 158 of the projected peace treaty).

When these decisions were made known in Peking, a strong protest movement arose among the students there. Three or four thousand of them demonstrated in front of T'ien An Men (the Gate of Heavenly Peace); among their slogans were: 'Fight for Equal Rights!', 'Down with the Traitors', 'We Refuse to Sign the Peace Treaty!', 'Withdraw the Twenty-one Demands!', 'Die for Tsingtao!' and 'Boycott Japanese goods!'

Although the movement was at first directed against foreigners, it soon turned against the government itself. Public indignation rose to its highest pitch when it was learned that the Japanese delegates at the conference had quoted Yüan Shih-k'ai's acceptance of the Twenty-one Demands in 1915, and also a secret agreement in which his successor, Tuan Ch'i-jui, had consented 'with satisfaction', in the words of a diplomatic note, to the transfer of the German rights to Japan, in return for a loan of 20 million yen. The mention of this arrangement incited the students to make a direct attack on the Chinese responsible for negotiating loans from the Japanese: Ts'ao Ju-lin, Minister of Communications and Vice-Minister of Foreign Affairs at the time of the Twenty-one Demands, Chang Tsung-hsiang, Minister to Japan, and Lu Tsung-yu, director of the Finance Bureau. Ts'ao Ju-lin's house was burned down, Chang Tsung-hsiang was beaten by the crowd, and Lu Tsung-yü managed to escape. Thirty-two students were arrested. The university went on strike.

This movement against politicians who were either in league with foreigners or simply incapable, continued for a month and spread to other universities, among them Shanghai, Nanking, Tientsin and Paoting. In all these towns the students swept a section of the shopkeepers, workers and artisans along with them. This was relatively easy in places like Shanghai where Japanese firms employed large numbers of workers. Nationalism took on a commercial form as well: Japanese goods were boycotted, and the sale of Chinese goods was encouraged, measures that sometimes injured individual shopkeepers, but helped Chinese engaged in industry.[1] Even so, the numbers of strikers, workers and artisans remained low – 20,000 at the beginning of the movement and 70,000 at the end. Between 3 and 11 June more students were arrested on a still larger scale (1,000 were put under arrest in Peking on 3 and 4 June), bringing the different forms of demonstration to their height. The agitation gradually died down, but the main objects had been secured, for the Chinese government refused to sign the Treaty of Versailles on 28 June 1919 – the war with Germany was ended by a special declaration in September of the same year – and the three pro-Japanese ministers were forced to resign.

Over the last twenty years or so, considerable work has been done on the May 4th Movement, both in China and abroad, in the way of research, studies and interpretation.[2] The Chinese communists consider it as the turning point in contemporary Chinese history and the start of a new era for culture and ideology. They maintain that, before 4 May 1919, the Chinese revolutionary movements of the nineteenth and twentieth centuries belonged to the old category of bourgeois democratic movements. Several classes took part in them, but from the T'ai p'ing Rebellion to 1911 all the movements were halted by 'imperialism' and 'feudalism' because they lacked real targets; furthermore, 'imperialism' and 'feudalism' were not yet clearly defined and opposition to them was too intermittent.

But, as the communists point out, the May 4th Movement was different. For a start the international context was no longer the same. The Powers had revealed their rivalries, their selfishness and also their weaknesses;

[1] The Japanese share in Chinese foreign trade was 39·45 per cent in 1919.

[2] The most recent and fullest work on the subject in a Western language is the book by Chow Ts'e-tsung, *The May Fourth Movement*.

some had collapsed during the war, while others had suffered loss of influence and of material and financial means. 'National liberation' appeared to be a possibility at last.

In the eyes of the Chinese communists, the example of the Russian Revolution had also been a decisive factor and Mao Tse-tung affirmed this against all contrary evidence: 'The May 4th Movement came into being at the call of the world revolution, of the Russian Revolution and of Lenin. It was part of the world proletarian revolution of the time.'[1]

With the same disdain for history, the Chinese communists, Mao Tse-tung among them, also claim that communist intellectuals, none of whom then existed as such, played an essential role in the movement. In the same way they present the May 4th Movement as a sort of prelude to a pseudo June 3rd Movement, essentially proletarian and even more authentically revolutionary than the first one:

> In the beginning the May 4th Movement was the revolutionary movement of a united front of three sections of people – communist intellectuals, revolutionary petty-bourgeois intellectuals and bourgeois intellectuals (the last forming the right wing of the movement). Its shortcoming was that it was confined to the intellectuals and that the workers and peasants did not join in. But as soon as it developed into the June 3rd Movement, not only the intellectuals but the mass of the proletariat, the petty bourgeoisie and the bourgeoisie joined in, and it became a nationwide revolutionary movement.[2]

Lastly, the communists would have everyone believe that the proletariat and 'its party' inspired and led the Chinese revolutionary movements after 4 May:

> After the May 4th Movement, the political leader of China's bourgeois-democratic revolution was no longer the bourgeoisie but the proletariat, although the national bourgeoisie continued to take part in the revolution. The Chinese proletariat rapidly became an awakened and independent political force as a result of its maturing and of the influence of the Russian Revolution.[3]

In fact, the Chinese proletariat in 1919, if it did exist, was completely lacking in organization and was to remain so for several more years. The workers belonging to a few large firms joined in the anti-Japanese agita-

[1] Mao Tse-tung, 'On New Democracy', *Selected Works*, vol. II, pp. 373, 374.
[2] Ibid.
[3] Ibid., p. 348.

tion in a spirit of patriotism, and were guided by the students (and not the contrary). Although the Chinese proletariat took an active part in the revolution between 1925 and 1927, its role was to become insignificant after the liquidation of the trade unions in Shanghai (12 April 1927) and the failure of the Canton Commune (December 1927). The leading part in the 'bourgeois revolution' was to be taken by the bourgeoisie represented by the Kuomintang. This was made easier for them by the fact that until the first few years of the Sino-Japanese war, the Communist Party, driven back into a few mountainous districts in Central and North China, and all but eliminated in the rest of the country, had virtually no direct contact with the population.

The role of the Chinese Communist Party in the May 4th Movement could only amount to nothing, because it did not exist, and because not one single avowed communist existed in the whole of China, Mao Tse-tung being no exception. No ideological interpretation of the motives of the patriots of 4 May, and no attempt to see in them a pointer to the future of the Chinese Communist Party can prevail in the face of this evidence.

In spite of this, the spirit and consequences of the May 4th Movement make it without any doubt an authentic revolutionary movement. Essentially nationalistic in its origins, it led many intellectuals to ponder once more the political and social situation of their country and it prepared the way for the appearance of Marxism. Movements directed against foreigners were by no means without precedent in China; the Boxer Rebellion is a striking example. They were, however, always more or less identified with an element of political and cultural conservatism. The May 4th Movement, which was hostile to the West and to Japan, was different in that it also opposed a morally indefensible political regime, incapable of representing the country's interest either at home or abroad.

The students were naturally the first to react. Their education enabled them to evaluate better than anyone else the full extent of the injustice and humiliation inflicted by the decisions taken at Versailles. They were also fully conscious of the fact that they enjoyed the prestige, greater in China than elsewhere, inspired by learning. They stirred up other classes, but often almost by accident. Their contact with the shopkeepers arose from a desire to control the boycott on Japanese goods, rather than to swell the movement. They became interested in the workers less for what they were than because they were employed by numerous Japanese firms, but this interest was in itself an important innovation. Little by little the climate of hostility to 'imperialism' and 'feudalism' spread to the whole nation; both expressions became part of the vocabulary of all Chinese revolutionaries, including the communists. This climate was naturally an important element in the evolution of the Communist Party, although the Party's development was slow: in 1921 it had fifty-seven members, all intellectuals, two years after the May 4th Movement, and not until 1925 did its numbers exceed a thousand.

The Communist Party also stood to gain from the final triumph of the vernacular speech (pai-hua) over the classical written style (wen-yen). Ch'en Tu-hsiu, who later became its founder, had been one of the chief advocates of this reform since 1915; it was to facilitate the spread of new cultural and political ideas among the public at large through the press and printed publications. Later on, the communists claimed the monopoly of this anti-Confucianist cultural revolution, 'overthrowing Confucius and Sons', as they said, in the words of the famous writer Lu Hsün. Although they sometimes had reluctantly to acknowledge the part played by great non-communist intellectuals like Hu Shih, they were quick to accuse them of renouncing the traditional culture solely in order to impose that of the 'imperialists'.

The May 4th Movement appears to have been a nationalist student movement, which succeeded in sweeping various urban elements along with it. It was no mass phenomenon, but represented rather a reaction among intellectuals; its importance and its meaning should be sought in the realm of ideas and culture.

The salvoes of the October Revolution

While the May 4th Movement was developing, the Russian Revolution, which was to have an enormous influence on the course of Chinese history, was beginning to arouse the attention of members of Peking University, even though little was known about it at that time. The events themselves could not be thoroughly known or properly understood, for they were obscured by the confusion of civil war, by the screen of the Siberian 'white' armies, and by a widespread lack of understanding of socialism in general, and of Bolshevism in particular. However, Russia was so close to Chinese history that she could not fail to awaken a special interest, and the Russian Revolution, since it was a national event, revealed Marxism to China. This is how Mao Tse-tung's famous comment should be understood: 'The salvoes of the October Revolution brought us Marxism-Leninism.'[1]

[1] Mao Tse-tung, 'On the People's Democratic Dictatorship', *Selected Works*, vol. IV.

All at once the Chinese became aware that a theory of revolutionary socialism existed, and that it had been adopted as a system of government by a neighbouring country which, moreover, had many characteristics in common with China, as far as size, backwardness in the technical field, a vast rural population, feudal elements, and even ethnic diversity were concerned.

The first evidence of Chinese interest in the Russian Revolution, taken in its international context, is to be found in three articles by Li Ta-chao, one of the future founders of the Chinese Communist Party, published in 1918 in various magazines; their titles alone are revealing: 'The French Revolution' (the *Yen Chih Review*, published on 1 July 1918), 'The Victory of Bolshevism' and 'The Victory of the Masses' (15 October 1918). The last two articles appeared in the review *Youth*, which will be mentioned again from time to time later on. Although the ideas and terms are somewhat confused, some statements foreshadow the ideological evolution of their author. A new age had been born with the Russian Revolution: 'The French Revolution of 1789 heralded the revolutions of the nineteenth century in every country. The Russian Revolution heralds the worldwide revolution of the twentieth century.' ('The Victory of the Masses')

Internationalism must be spread throughout the world, beginning with the peace conference: 'At this conference, the majority ought, I think, to be formed of supporters of justice who want to break down frontiers between states. . . .' ('The Victory of the Masses')

The world should no longer belong to capitalists and militarists, but to the workers, and China, a beggar nation, must prepare herself for this evolution, so that she may occupy an honourable position among the peoples: 'When the world has become a huge factory, and work and food are to be had for all, will there be room for a lazy people like ours? We must be one of the world's peoples, a people of workers! Gentlemen, hurry to work!' ('The Victory of the Masses')

The new age, to be born amid suffering, was inevitable; humanity could only accept it and comply with it.

Li Ta-chao's articles met with no response; not until May 1919 did a special number of *Youth* publish a fairly complete account of Marxism-Leninism, and although its appearance coincided with the May 4th Movement, this was purely a matter of luck.

It took the leaders of the new Russia only two years to create a situation in both diplomatic and ideological fields in which Marxism could be propagated in China. On 4 July 1918, Georgi Chicherin, People's Commissar for Foreign Affairs, in his address to the Fifth Congress of Soviets, declared that Russia was prepared to renounce her special privileges and to give the Chinese Eastern Railway back to China, in return for compensation.[1] Little attention was paid to this first declaration, but a year later it was renewed, on 25 July 1919, by Karakhan, and with it came a proposal to establish diplomatic relations. The Soviet declaration, contrasting as it did with the attitude to China recently adopted by the Allied Powers at Versailles, gained sympathy for Moscow which had hitherto been reserved for Paris, London or Washington. However, the Russians were in no hurry to exploit this advantage in the revolutionary field. At that moment, they were interested in traditional targets rather than in a group of powerless intellectuals and a proletariat in its infancy. Their aim was to make sure of the former frontiers of the empire against the Japanese, who were still at Vladivostok and in the Maritime Province. They also intended to open normal relations once more with the Peking government, however reactionary it might be, and to help it to resist Western influence.

Several diplomatic missions were exchanged: a Chinese mission led by General Chang Shih-ling in October 1920, and Russian missions led by A. K. Paikes in December 1921 and A. A. Joffe in 1922. Not until 31 May 1924 did the conversations between the two powers result in the signature of an 'Agreement on the methods to be used in solving general questions'. But from then on relations continued between Moscow and the various Chinese governments that succeeded each other after 1924, and were sometimes very close indeed; they often had a profound effect on the relations between the Comintern and the Chinese Communist Party, in which the latter usually came off worse.

From 1920 onwards, the Comintern took a direct interest in Chinese affairs, mainly as a result of the evolution of Lenin's personal attitude towards Western countries after 1917. Between 1900 and 1917 Lenin had written about ten short articles on China, the only country that lies within the scope of this book. The most interesting of them, 'Democracy and Populism in China', appeared on 15 July 1912.[2] In an effort to analyse the country's situation after the 1911 Revolution, Lenin acknowledged Sun Yat-sen to be a progressive in spite of a lack of precision in his doctrine. The bourgeois democratic revolution led by the Kuomintang seemed

[1] This railway consisted mainly of the Manchouli-Harbin-Suifenho line, which ran from west to east across Manchuria, and another running perpendicular to it, from Harbin to Ch'angch'un.

[2] See Allen S. Whiting, *Soviet Policies in China,* for an analysis of this document, and of an extract from the *Pravda* of 8 November 1912, concerning China.

to him to be worthy of interest inasmuch as it opposed Western 'oppression'. He acknowledged the important role the peasantry was to fulfil, though he had doubts as to its revolutionary value in the absence of a proletariat: 'Whether the peasants, who are not led by a proletarian party, will be able to retain their democratic positions *against* [in italics] the liberals, who are only waiting for an opportunity to shift to the right, will be seen in the near future.'[1]

He foresaw the eventual appearance of a proletariat which would instil new life into Sun Yat-sen's doctrine:

> Lastly, the Chinese proletariat will increase as the number of Shanghais increases. It will probably form some kind of Chinese Social-Democratic Labour party, which, while criticizing the petty-bourgeois Utopias and reactionary views of Sun Yat-sen, will certainly take care to single out, defend and develop the revolutionary-democratic core of his political and agrarian programme.[2]

The Great War showed how vulnerable were the Powers in their colonial empires, leading Lenin to look for revolutionary possibilities in that direction. These ideas were expressed in 'Imperialism, the Highest Stage of Capitalism', written in 1916, and now a classic. However, as A. Whiting says, 'Lenin called attention to the ferment in Asia but never gave it priority over European developments.'[3]

The adoption of the Theses on the National and the Colonial Questions by the Second Congress of the Communist International (19 July to 7 August 1920) finally allowed a clearly defined programme of action concerning underdeveloped countries to be drawn up. The circumstances of this congress, the incidents involving disagreement between various delegates, including the Indian, M. N. Roy, and Lenin himself, belong to the history of Marxism in general and fall outside the scope of this book. Its most important results should be borne in mind, however. When the Third International was founded at the First Congress of Communist Parties on 4 March 1919, the emphasis had been laid on the struggle of the proletariat to gain power. This position was due above all to the hopes born of the political and social situation in Europe just after the Great War. The Second Congress, held at Petrograd in July and August 1920, was still centred on Europe, but it was a calmer Europe, in which the

[1] V. I. Lenin, 'Regenerated China', *Collected Works*, vol. 18 (Moscow, Foreign Languages Publishing House, 1963), p. 401.

[2] V. I. Lenin, 'Democracy and Narodism in China', *Collected Works*, vol. 18, p. 163.

[3] Allen S. Whiting, *Soviet Policies in China*, p. 21.

German and the Hungarian revolutions had failed. The importance of national and colonial questions was shown by the adoption of Lenin's theses, certain points of which could not fail to find an application in China:

(*a*) Affirmation of a close union between Soviet Russia and all national and colonial liberation movements (Article 6).

(*b*) An invitation extended to all communist parties in the world to give active support to revolutionary liberation movements.

(*c*) The necessity of helping peasant movements against landowners and all feudal survivals: 'One must strive to give the peasant movements the most revolutionary character by organizing as far as possible the peasants and all the exploited into soviets. . . .'

This categorical expression of support for the peasants in contrast to former reservations made by the Marxists was to be quoted by Mao Tse-tung to justify his own proposals.

(*d*) The Communist International's duties: . . . The Communist International must enter into temporary alliance with bourgeois democracy in the colonial and backward countries, but should not merge with it, and should under all circumstances uphold the independence of the proletarian movement even if it is in its most embryonic form; . . . (Point 11/e)[1]

This passage was to govern in theory all future collaboration between the Kuomintang and the Chinese Communist Party.

The theses submitted by the Indian, M. N. Roy, were adopted by the congress alongside those of Lenin, in spite of the fact that they contained contradictions of the latter's ideas. They were of interest to China, not only because of their author, who was to be the Comintern's representative there during the 1927 crisis, but also because they raised the difficult question of 'leadership' of revolutionary movements in colonial and semi-colonial countries. Roy declared that in these countries revolution should follow a programme allowing bourgeois reforms and agrarian reforms to be included, but 'it does not in the least follow that the leadership of the revolution will have to be surrendered to the bourgeois democrats'. On the contrary, he added, proletarian parties must 'carry on vigorous and

[1] V. I. Lenin: 'Preliminary draft theses on the national and the colonial questions for the Second Congress of the Communist International', *Collected Works*, vol. 31 (Moscow, Progress Publishers, 1966), p. 150.

systematic propaganda for the idea of soviets, and must organize peasants' and workers' soviets as soon as possible'. This question was to be at the heart of the Comintern's policy for China.

The theses for the Second Congress more or less adapted Marxism to the needs of China, which was a typical example of a semicolonial country. The offer of official support from the Soviet Union and world communist parties at the very moment when the Western powers refused to comply with China's requests, and when the Peking government itself seemed to make light of national interest, certainly encouraged many intellectuals to turn their thoughts towards Marxism. The theses also enabled those definitely opposed to Marxism, and particularly the national bourgeoisie, to collaborate with the then nascent Chinese Communist Party. They amounted to a promise of moral and material support, both urgently needed by the nationalist movements. The Kuomintang-Communist 'united front' originated in the Second Congress; it lasted until the Northern Expedition and the summer of 1927, enabling Chinese revolutionary nationalism to get the better of the feudal elements and achieve some measure of unity in China once more.

Another conference that concerned China was held in 1920, which proved to be an important year: the Eastern Peoples' Congress, held at Baku from 1 to 8 September. As the choice of meeting place indicates, the congress was directly aimed at the Near Eastern nations (Turkey and Iran), but it was also addressed to all 'oppressed' peoples, and created a precedent in this. The Chinese sent a delegate of some importance, Chang T'ai-lei, the future founder of Communist Youth, as well as the future leader and victim of the Canton Commune in 1927.[1]

In 1920 the Siberian Soviet Communist Party also created a propaganda bureau at Irkutsk for the peoples of the Far East. In the following year it began publication of a propaganda bulletin, in Russian and English: *Narodny Dalnego Vostoka*, *The Peoples of the Far East*, run by B. Z. Shumiatsky.[2]

Lastly, 1920 saw the appearance of the first Soviet envoys or Comintern agents in China. The earliest arrivals were Yurin, who had an official mission as ambassador, Voitinsky, the Secretary-General of the Comintern Far Eastern Bureau, Maring (alias H. Sneevliet), an agent of the Communist International, and a few other, less well-known men. They were the first to make contact with the early Chinese Marxists; they regrouped

[1] Two Chinese delegates, one of whom, Lao Hsin-chao, made a speech of little importance, had attended the Second Congress of the Communist International.

[2] Cf. X. Eudin and R. C. North, *Soviet Russia and the East, 1920 to 1927*.

them, purged them, helped them to get organized, and united them into a real, disciplined and homogeneous party.

The awakening of the proletariat

Before going into the history of communist organizations and their founders, a third factor contributing to the development of Chinese Marxism should be noted: the growth and awakening of a small proletariat, which appeared towards the beginning of the century, based on the transport, mining, textile and rice-milling industries. Its numbers are hard to estimate accurately, as the definitions were elastic and statistics inadequate. P'eng Shu-chih, one of the assistants of the first secretary-general, reckoned that the Chinese proletariat amounted to between 1·6 and 1·8 million people, and included several tens of thousands of railway workers and seamen, several tens of thousands of miners, and 60,000 textile workers, who were the most advanced element; the rest were manual workers and labourers.[1] In 1927, Su Chao-cheng, then Minister of Labour in the Wuhan government, declared at the Pacific Workers' Conference that industrial workers amounted to 2,750,000 and artisans to 12,160,000, out of a population reckoned at 450 million inhabitants. Other communist writers gave a figure of 1 million for industrial workers in 1911, and 2 million just before the foundation of the Party. Ten million is the figure given for artisans.[2]

A fairly accurate set of statistics found in the work of an authorized Chinese author is quoted below, with the usual reservations:[3]

1913 approximately 650,000 workers

1919 approximately 2 million workers, distributed as follows:

Industrial workers	702,488
Workers employed by foreign firms	320,000
Miners	596,990
Railway workers	142,991
Seamen	150,000
Post Office workers	23,154
Electricity workers	10,741
Total	1,946,364

[1] Cf. the review *Youth*, December 1924: 'Who is Leading the Chinese Revolution?'

[2] Liao Chu-Hsiang, *History of the Communist Party: A Summary* (Peking, 1959).

[3] Hu Hua, *Essays on the History of the Chinese Revolution* (in Chinese). The author bases his account on statistics supplied by the Ministry of Commerce and Agriculture, which omit eleven provinces and a special zone, but these are probably outlying provinces barely affected by modern industry.

Statistics from the same source, for the year 1925, give an idea of the geographical distribution of this proletariat, which was particularly concentrated on the coast:

Shanghai	500,000 at least, 1 million at most
Wuhan	400,000
Tientsin	350,000
Hong Kong	250,000
Canton	100,000
The North-East	600,000

Artisans, who were more evenly distributed, amounted to 12 million.

If statistics referring to the number and size of firms are used, rather than uncertain and suspect figures representing individuals, the rate of progress is easier to follow:

Cotton industry	*Factories*	*Spindles*
1915	22	540,000
1922	62	1,590,000
1927	119	3,690,000

Sixty-three new silk factories were built in the region of Shanghai from 1912 to 1927, and capital investment increased fivefold between 1914 and 1919. As far as modern rice mills are concerned, 2 factories existed in 1900, 67 in 1916, and 107 in 1927. As regards modern factories as a whole, 673 factories employing over 30 workers existed in 1920, and 1347 factories with more than 30 workers existed in 1927. The fall in foreign imports, due to the Great War, furnishes a partial explanation for the development of national industries:

1914	213,014,752 customs dollars	at the rate of 0·661 U.S. dollars per customs dollar[1]
1915	35,624,555 customs dollars	
1919	16,188,270 customs dollars	

The proportion of foreign investment and factories under foreign management was still considerable. The figures vary according to the method of assessment used by different authors. That given for 1914 is roughly 1000 million U.S. dollars.[2] In some industries the reckoning is more accurate; in 1923, for instance, according to P'eng Shu-chih,

[1] Hu Hua, *Essays on the History of the Chinese Revolution.*

[2] 1610·3 million, according to Lavallée, Noirot and Dominique, *Economie de la Chine Socialiste* (Geneva, 1957).

foreigners owned over half the spindles in the cotton industry.[1] This is not confirmed, however, by other communist authors. Hu Hua states that 66·4 per cent of the spindles and 58·5 per cent of the looms belonged to Chinese firms in 1921.[2]

The communists assert that the Westerners ruined the traditional economy based on handicrafts and the peasantry, and then prevented national industry from developing freely, as it had in nineteenth-century Europe. They claim that but for the First World War, which forced the Europeans to relax their pressure, Chinese industrial capitalism would never have survived or advanced. In fact, China was in complete chaos at the beginning of the twentieth century, and no more capable of creating a modern national industry than was the backward China of the century before. The basic elements of the industrial power that is her pride today were received from foreign capitalism, in the form of financial, material and technical investments.

At the same time, foreign capitalism created in China the two social categories that are by tradition revolutionary:

(*a*) A 'national' bourgeoisie, which took over the leadership of the democratic revolution.
(*b*) A proletariat, 'twin brother of the bourgeoisie', in the words of Mao Tse-tung, which, according to Lenin, was destined to assume the leadership of the socialist revolution.

As its numbers swelled during the years after the Great War, the Chinese proletariat gradually developed a modern outlook. Workers in precapitalist China belonged to various types of organization resembling those formerly in existence in Europe. As in Europe, their aim was to defend each trade and its products, and to safeguard the interest of the producers (employers and associates) *vis-à-vis* the consumer through associations and by means of rules. Three kinds of associations existed: corporations, regional guilds and secret societies. The corporations (hang hui) were sometimes entrusted to the protection of a celestial spirit, who was generally Taoist; they were controlled by the employers, their members being divided into employers (yeh-chu), workers (ku-kung) and apprentices (hsüeh-t'u). Guilds (pang-k'ou, t'ung hsiang hui) grouped workers in the large towns, according to their province or place of origin. They usually sought the patronage of an influential citizen or civil servant

[1] 1,106,801 spindles altogether, 499,346 of which were Chinese, according to this author, whose statistics do not entirely agree with those mentioned above.
[2] Hu Hua, *Essays on the History of the Chinese Revolution.*

from the same region. Secret societies (mi-mi chieh-hui) grouped backward or doubtful elements, and were sometimes under the direction of professional criminals; some workers were forced to join, or did so to obtain protection.

These traditional organizations lasted for a long time, in the large coastal towns as well as in the interior of the country. Chinese workers were used to them, they offered plenty of human contact, and they were sometimes based on family ties. The more anonymous trade unions, usually led by men considered too young, when judged by traditional standards, had great difficulty in gaining acceptance until after the great strikes of 1925; the two systems then existed side by side for some time.[1]

Historically, the first trade union organization dates back to the years 1850-61, when a Porters' Association and a Packers' Association in Canton joined to form one union. The first strike is supposedly that of 20,000 Hong Kong coolies who returned to Canton during the 1858 war to avoid working for the French or the English. But even if this first strike against 'foreign imperialism' really did take place, it has little value except as an anecdote.

The communist authors claim that seventy-eight strikes took place between 1875 and 1913. They were, however, purely fortuitous movements, lacking coordination, but justified by appalling local conditions. The usual records reveal that several strikes of a more traditional nature took place after 1913:

1913: postmen's strike in Peking, strike at the Hanyang arsenal.
1914 (October): seamen's strike.
1915: strikes in the Anyang and P'inghsiang mines.
1916: printers' strike in Peking.
1917-18: small textile workers' strikes.

These demonstrations were short lived; the authorities, who saw no reason to admit the right to strike, suppressed them brutally, and they were also thwarted by a permanent labour surplus. They developed more freely in Hong Kong and in foreign firms, although working conditions were less hard there than in the Chinese-owned industries. Lastly, they had not as yet taken on a political aspect. A few workers were private members of the first organizations led by Sun Yat-sen (out of 105 of the first members of the Hsing-chung hui three were workers, and the T'ung-meng hui had a few more). Some miners from P'inghsiang, in Kiangsi, joined the

[1] Seventy-two guilds were still in existence in Canton in 1924. Guilds survived until 1949, in fact, and exist today in Chinese colonies abroad.

abortive revolt of 1906, and some Canton trade unions (especially the hairdressers' union) had shown anarchist tendencies, but it can safely be said that the only people to take political action were members of the bourgeoisie.

The May 4th Movement lent political colouring to strikes for the first time, and illustrated the progress made by the proletariat in organization. On 3 May 3000 workers in Tsinanfu, the capital of Shantung, staged a demonstration demanding that Tsingtao, the other large town in the province, be given back to China. On 15 May workers from Peking demonstrated at Chang Yi Gate, demanding the return of all territory in foreign hands to the nation. In Shanghai the strikes did not begin until early June; although they affected the textile and transport industries and the telephone, they only involved 60,000 or 70,000 workers out of half a million, which gave a total of 140,000 when the shopkeepers and their employees were counted in as well. The T'angshan mines in Hopei (3000 workers) and the railway works at Ch'anghsintien, near Peking, were also seriously affected, as the workers' organization was better there than elsewhere. As in the case of the students, both strikes and demonstrations fostered a feeling of solidarity and sometimes resulted in the creation of new, patriotic associations.

The May 4th Movement certainly helped to widen the scope of the workers' struggle. But it should not be forgotten that this struggle began its true development only under the impetus of nationalism: the May 4th Movement, the Hong Kong seamen's strike and the K'ailan mines strike in 1922, and particularly the strikes in 1925, all correspond exactly to anti-foreign movements. When this motive did not exist, the number of strikes and strikers fell, partly because of the authorities' intolerance: twenty-six strikes involved 91,400 strikers in 1919, nineteen strikes in 1920 involved only 46,000 strikers. A similar lull occurred in 1924. The workers' share in the May 4th Movement helped to make a certain number of intellectuals aware of the existence and importance of the proletariat and, later on, was to move some of them to turn to communism. The newly formed Chinese Communist Party was quick to found a Trade Union General Secretariat in Shanghai; its activities, nationalist and social in aspect, developed rapidly.[1]

In 1919, three factors – the Russian Revolution, the patriotic 4th May Movement, and the first signs of the awakening of the proletariat – all contributed to create a situation eminently suitable to a new wave of

[1] See Jean Chesneaux, *Le Mouvement Ouvrier chinois de 1919 à 1927*, for details on the development of the Chinese labour movement.

revolutionary activities. This movement, however, needed a solid organization behind it, in the shape of coherent revolutionary parties, with freedom for their activities to a certain extent. The Kuomintang had been in existence since 1895, but it was not strict enough regarding matters of doctrine or discipline within the party, and these defects were not corrected until 1924. As for the Communist Party, it was as yet unborn and, although its founders were soon to come forward, it was not to develop either in numbers or importance until 1925. Both these parties had the good fortune to be able to base their existence on a small area, the region surrounding Canton, and this made a considerable contribution towards their success.

4 The First Chinese Marxist-Leninists

Ch'en Tu-hsiu

Two university professors, Ch'en Tu-hsiu and Li Ta-chao, founded the Chinese Communist Party; their aims and methods of action were similar, though they were different in temperament, and later events were to carry them in opposite directions. The first, better known than the second, was the organizer of the first Marxist study groups, and became the first Secretary-General of the Party. He has the appearance of a man of transition, whose origins were firmly rooted in the old culture and society, though he came round to Western democratic and liberal ideas, and was finally seduced by Marxism after the May 4th Movement and the Russian Revolution. In 1927 he was forced to resign from his post as Secretary-General, and later on was expelled from the Party; he was briefly a Trotskyist, before becoming a nationalist once more, and may even have been a more or less sincere member of the Kuomintang before his death near Chungking on 24 May 1942.

Communist official historians treat him harshly and accuse him of never having been anything but a 'bourgeois democratic revolutionary', full of prejudice and contradictions. Only his mistakes have outlived him, and he is now scarcely mentioned by the historians, who credit Li Ta-chao, executed by Chang Tso-lin in 1927, with the leading role in the introduction of Marxism in China. It need hardly be added that it is not easy to find very much material on Ch'en Tu-hsiu, a deserter from the Communist Party whom the Kuomintang could accept only with the greatest possible reservations.

Ch'en Tu-hsiu (sometimes known as Ch'en Ch'ien-sheng or Ch'en Chung-tzu) was born in 1879 in Huaining, a town in Anhwei province, into the family of a military mandarin. Brought up by his grandfather and later by his brother in the spirit of the old culture and education, he became a bachelor (hsiu-ts'ai) in 1898 and began to study naval science. This may possibly have been inspired by nationalist feelings, for sea power was then the main expression of the superiority of the foreigners. He began a course at Hangchow, in Chekiang, at the Ch'iu Shih (Truth-seeking) School, but quickly gave it up. He then spent from 1900 to 1902 in Japan, where he attended the Tokyo Normal School and then Waseda University. It was there that he first began to take part in politics. He became a member of the Chinese Youth Society, founded by Feng Tzu-yu, one of the first associates of Sun Yat-sen. In 1902, when he returned to China, to Shanghai, he helped launch a new review, and worked on the *Anhwei Vernacular Magazine* in 1904.

After another brief trip to Japan in 1906, Ch'en Tu-hsiu went to France in 1907, and appears to have stayed there until 1910. Nothing is known about this long stay, although it had a lasting influence on him. France seemed to him, above all other countries, to be the home of culture and liberalism. One of the first articles which he wrote for *Youth*, entitled 'France and Contemporary Civilization', stresses his attachment and admiration for the country. The gist of his argument is that the world is indebted to France for three things: political equality stated in the declaration of the rights of man, the theory of evolution, discovered by Lamarck before Darwin, and the socialism of Baboeuf, Fourrier and Saint-Simon, which would prolong the political revolution and inspire greater justice in society. Whatever the outcome of the war (he was writing in 1916), France had already conquered all the peoples of the world by bringing them civilization, he concludes, quoting what Nietzsche had said after 1870.[1]

After his return to China in 1910, the future Secretary-General of the Communist Party does not seem to have played a particularly active part in the 1911 Revolution. He was, however, appointed Commissar of Education for Anhwei province almost immediately afterwards. When Yüan Shih-k'ai dissolved the first Chinese parliament and took up the reins of the administration, Ch'en Tu-hsiu abandoned his post and spent a further two years in Japan, from 1913 to 1915. From there, he returned to Shanghai once more. He settled in the French Concession, and in September 1915

[1] Later on, in 1920, Ch'en Tu-hsiu sent two of his sons, Ch'en Yen-nien and Ch'en Chiao-men, both communists like him, to France; they made only a short stay there.

he founded his famous review *Ch'ing Nien* there, adding the French title *Jeunesse* later on.[1] His public life begins, properly speaking, with the launching of the review.

In the first issue Ch'en Tu-hsiu made an immediate appeal to the force represented by Chinese youth. Youth, whose strength ensures the renewal of nature, has its parallel in society. Unlike Western societies, which undergo constant change, Chinese society is old and stagnant, and youth itself is corrupted by it: 'Out of ten young men, five are already old in physique, and out of ten young men, young both in age and physique, nine are old in their mentality.'

He proposed six principles to the new Chinese youth, developing each one in turn:

1 'Be independent, not servile' (example taken from Nietzsche).
2 'Be men of progress, not bound by routine' (reference is made to Bergson and *l'Evolution créatrice*).
3 'Be brave, not fearful' (condemnation of Tagore and praise of Christopher Columbus).
4 'Be internationalist, not isolationist' (at least half of a nation's future depends on other nations; examples taken from Chinese history).
5 'Be practical, not formalistic'.
6 'Be scientific, not imaginative' (an appeal to reason and science as opposed to religion, art and literature).

The theme of youth and the renewal of society was to reappear often. Ch'en Tu-hsiu's new magazine also appealed to 'Democracy and Science', both of which, like youth, generated new forces capable of emancipating the individual, destroying the old, conservative, passive society, and rebuilding China: 'If the Europe of today is ahead of other peoples, it is because scientific development is no less important there than the theory of the rights of man.'[2] Although it contained violent attacks on tradition, and spread modern Western ideas, *Youth* took no real part in the political struggle.

Two events were to add considerably to the popularity of Ch'en Tu-hsiu and consequently help to spread Marxism. The first was the success of the movement for cultural and literary revolution, one of whose main points was the rejection of the classical written style in favour of the written vernacular. Hu Shih, one of the great figures in education, who died in 1962, discussed the problem in the January 1917 number of *New Youth*.

[1] From September 1916 onwards the magazine was called *Hsin Ch'ing-nien* (*New Youth*).
[2] Ch'en Tu-hsiu, 'Appeal to Youth' (1915).

Ch'en Tu-hsiu wrote an extremely vigorous article in support, entitled 'Revolution in Chinese Literature', which appeared the following month. As was to be expected, the aim was to eliminate the artificial literature accessible to a limited number of people, and to create, as he put it, 'the popular literature of a living society'.

The question of the reform of the literature and the language provoked heated disputes, which created an enormous stir in intellectual and university circles. As for the more and more widespread use of the written vernacular, it was bound to enlarge the audience of the future Communist Party. Later on, workers' newspapers even made their appearance; they were known as 'mosquito papers', and used not more than a thousand simple characters, three or four thousand being needed normally.

The other important event was the formation of a team of modern, liberal teachers under the new Rector of Peking University, Ts'ai Yüan-p'ei. Ts'ai Yüan-p'ei, who at first had leaned towards anarchism, became Minister of Education after 1911 and played a considerable part in sending several thousand Chinese students to France. When he was in office, the University became, as he hoped it would, a meeting place for people with differing views, according to a criterion that he defined himself: 'Regardless of what schools of academic thought there may be, if their words are reasonable and there is a cause for maintaining them, and they have not yet reached the fate of being eliminated by nature, I would let them develop in complete freedom.'[1] Ch'en Tu-hsiu was appointed to a post at the Arts Faculty of Peking University in 1916, and naturally found himself growing involved in the political preoccupations of this new circle, where he came across many contributors to *New Youth*, particularly Li Ta-chao. He and Li Ta-chao founded the *Weekly Critic* together in December 1918; it was more openly political than was the *New Youth* of the same period.

In May 1919 *New Youth* published a special number on Marxism. The most interesting contribution was that of Li Ta-chao, entitled 'My Views on Marxism'. At the same time, on 11 June, Ch'en Tu-hsiu was imprisoned for distributing tracts; this active participation in the May 4th Movement was to boost his reputation. He was not freed until September, however, and *New Youth* ceased publication from May to November. This difficult period in his life seems to have made Ch'en Tu-hsiu even more radical in

[1] Letter from Ts'ai Yüan-p'ei to Professor Liu Shu (May 1919), quoted by T'ang Leang-li in *China in Revolt*. A more complete and slightly different version is to be found in Ssu-yu Teng and J. K. Fairbank, *China's Response to the West* (New York, Atheneum, 1967), Document 58.

his political opinions. As soon as he was out of prison, he organized a New Youth Society, and in honour of this he launched an unusually violent manifesto in the name of the magazine:

> We believe that militarism and the cult of force have already caused incalculable evil in the world and should be rejected.
>
> We believe that in each country, concepts inherited from the past, concerning politics, ethics and economics, contain many elements that are obstacles in the way of evolution and are unreasonable.
>
> If we want to make the old society progress, we cannot do otherwise than to shatter these 'sacred' and 'unchangeable' prejudices.
>
> On one hand, we should reject these old concepts and on the other we should combine the ideas of the sages of old with those of the sages of today, and with our own ideas, to create new concepts concerning politics, ethics and economics, to implant the spirit of the new age, to adapt us to the environment of the new society.
>
> Our ideal society of the new age will be honest, progressive, active, free, egalitarian, creative, beautiful, good, peace-loving, brotherly, hard-working and joyful and will give happiness to all.
>
> We hope that some phenomena will gradually fade away till they disappear, such as: hypocrisy, conservatism, negativism, constraint, social classes, tradition, ugliness, evil, war, the causes of disorder, laziness and boredom, happiness reserved for the few. . . .

The political programme, however, which was somewhat vague in expression, was liberal, without a trace of communism:

> Although we do not hold the superstitious belief that politics are all-powerful, we acknowledge their importance in public life. We believe that in a true democracy, political rights should be shared among everybody, and even though there may be limitations, work rather than possessions should be the criterion. . . . As for political parties, we acknowledge their function in politics, but we will never join any party that supports the interests of the minority or of one class, and does not work for the happiness of society as a whole. . . .

Some authors consider that this manifesto was influenced by the 'Déclaration d'indépendance de l'esprit', published in France and signed by many French and foreign intellectuals (Barbusse, Rolland, etc.); a Chinese version appears in the same number of *New Youth*.[1]

It is impossible to say exactly when or in what circumstances Ch'en Tu-

[1] Cf. Chow Ts'e-tsung, *The May Fourth Movement,* ch. VII.

hsiu became an avowed Marxist. He seems to have been liberal and democratic in his views at the end of 1919, but he was certainly neither of these in the summer of 1920. Meanwhile, he had to leave Peking and take refuge in the French Concession in Shanghai. There he came into contact with various small groups with socialist, anarchist, syndicalist and nationalist tendencies who had joined together in May 1920 to form a heterogeneous group, which some people see as an early version of the Chinese Communist Party. He also met Voitinsky in Shanghai, sent by the Comintern on a mission of information and organization among circles with Marxist sympathies. Then early in 1921 Ch'en Tu-hsiu was summoned to Canton by the nationalist General Ch'en Chiung-ming, who invited him to reorganize national education in the province of Kwangtung. In Canton, as in Shanghai and several large towns, a small Marxist group was formed. Representatives of these groups were soon to found the Chinese Communist Party. From the spring or summer of 1920 onwards, Ch'en Tu-hsiu's personal history becomes entangled with the history of the communist movement, and as such it will be continued later on.

Li Ta-chao

Li Ta-chao (Li Shou-ch'ang), born on 6 October 1888 in the Lot'ing district of east Hopei, was younger than Ch'en Tu-hsiu. He also came of more humble origins. He was brought up by his grandfather, entered the Peiyang College of Law and Political Science in Peking in 1907, and then spent two or three years at Waseda University in Japan, from 1913 to 1916. Like most Chinese students in Japan, he was a keen nationalist, and the Twenty-one Demands were to make him even more so. His first true political writings, 'Notes on a National Shame', 'National Bitterness', 'Advice to our Elders', 'Don't be Discouraged', etc., date from this period. He was also, naturally, hostile to Yüan Shih-k'ai, and even founded a patriotic society (Shen-chou hsüeh-hui). He returned to Shanghai, went on from there to Peking, and worked on the *Morning Post* (*Ch'en pao*) for a short time, before joining the team that published *New Youth*.

In February 1918 Ts'ai Yüan-p'ei appointed him Director of the Peking University Library and then, a few months later, Professor of History, both of which posts he held at the same time. In the same year, 1918, he became one of the principal collaborators of Ch'en Tu-hsiu, with whom he founded the *Weekly Critic*. He also helped with the beginnings of the literary magazine *Hsin ch'ao* (*New Tide*), founded on 18 November by a group of young writers interested in criticism, science, and the renewal of the language. Like Ch'en Tu-hsiu, Li Ta-chao placed his trust in the country's youth, whom he wanted to turn against tradition, and whose enthusiasm he tried to arouse. This confidence in youth, which later became identified with the best 'revolutionary optimism' of every good communist, appeared as early as 1916 in one of his most famous articles, with the symbolic title of 'Spring' (Ch'ing Ch'un), and was to reappear often.[1] It also found expression in his active part in the founding of the Young China Society. He abhorred the past and the 'dry skeleton' of Confucianism, and realized how many difficulties stood in the way of the application of Western political and moral ideas in his own country, impregnated as it still was with tradition. The contradictions of contemporary China, to be found in the constitutional texts themselves and symbolized by the survival of the Manchu court within the republican regime, were forcefully illustrated by a brief article written in May 1918: 'The New! The Old!'[2]

As has already been stated in the last chapter, Li Ta-chao was the first person in China fully to realize the importance of the Russian Revolution, and to introduce Marxism in a special issue of *New Youth* (May 1919).[3] From then on, as his communist biographers say, quite rightly, the 'abstract hope', the 'spring', the 'new', take on a concrete form for him: 'Bolshevism'. From then on he considered that the contradictions existing in Chinese society would be resolved under the leadership of the proletariat.[4] As with Ch'en Tu-hsiu, the May 4th Movement undoubtedly precipitated Li Ta-chao's conversion to Marxism. It also helped to divide intellectuals who were more or less avowed Marxists from liberals who were influenced by the pragmatism of Dewey, whose lecture tour in China in 1920 caused a great stir. Among the latter was the great writer Hu Shih, who is now portrayed as the chief ideological adversary of Li Ta-chao. One of his most serious faults was to have attributed China's ills to its backwardness in the scientific field, and to its own disorders, rather than to 'foreign imperialism'; he is also accused of being afraid to face reality. The 'Problems and Isms' controversy opened in July 1919, after a few preliminary skirmishes.[5] Hu Shih published 'More Study of Problems,

[1] Cf. above all 'Now', which appeared in April 1918.
[2] This article appeared on 15 May 1918 in *New Youth*.
[3] 'My Views on Marxism'.
[4] See 'Li Ta-chao opposes Bourgeois Reformism during the May 4th Movement' by Kao Ch'uan-pu and Chang Chi-chih in the magazine *Li-shih Yen-chiu* (*Historical Studies*), 1959, No. 6.
[5] Hu Shih, 'Pragmatism' (April 1919); Li-Ta chao, 'My Views on Marxism' (May 1919). Hu Shih died early in 1962.

Less Talk of Isms', which, as its title suggests, was practical in its approach. The next month, Li Ta-chao replied with 'One More Discussion of Problems and Isms'. He thought that the Russian Revolution supplied the model needed for the essential changes to be made in the realm of production. Finally the controversy was extended to foreign affairs. Li Ta-chao attacked 'colonialism' as being responsible for the First World War, denounced the 'open door' concept, etc. After the 'Problems and Isms' controversy, Hu Shih retired from politics for a short time. He returned in 1922, giving a witty justification for his decision: 'for if the slaves of Confucius and Chu Hsi are less numerous, those of Marx and Kropotkin are more so'.

Li Ta-chao's radical views became more apparent in his writings over the years 1919 and 1920. He made violent attacks on political institutions, ethics, and the family: 'All the evils of present Chinese society come from its family system'. But above all he defined the meaning of class struggle and emerged as the official introducer of Marxism, the role that history has since assigned to him. It should be noted that he was probably one of the first Chinese intellectuals to 'go to the people'. The May 4th Movement was in fact followed by a kind of movement in favour of manual work, or at least for the association of manual and intellectual work; mutual aid groups were founded. Li Ta-chao exhorted the students to draw nearer to the peasants, and to share their work, not only in order to understand them better, but also to learn from them.[1] These views, completely new to China, were at first restricted to theory alone, but after 1921 and the foundation of the Communist Party, Li Ta-chao revealed himself to be a man of action and an organizer who reached far beyond the scope of his usual university circles.

As in the case of Ch'en Tu-hsiu, it is not easy to judge when Li Ta-chao reached the point of no return and became a convinced and avowed Marxist. As B. I. Schwartz points out, his conversion was complete by December 1920 at least, as is proved by the article 'The Value of Historical Materialism in Modern Historical Science', which appeared in *New Youth*.[2] The verdict of communist authors is that, even after his conversion, Li Ta-chao, who spanned the transition from the 'bourgeois revolution' to the 'neo-democratic revolution', never managed to rid himself entirely of all traces of capitalism and liberalism. They do acknowledge his merit, however, in adopting the ideological weapon of Marxism to fight the old

[1] Youth and the Villages', February 1919.

[2] Cf. B. I. Schwartz, *Chinese Communism and the Rise of Mao*, and M. Meisner, *Li Ta-chao and the Origins of Chinese Marxism*.

society, and they praise his courage; Marshal Ch'en Yi, in a long poem composed in memory of the thirtieth anniversary of his death, wrote:

> You walked bravely in the forefront,
> Like the pine, you did not fear the cold of the years.[1]

The Marxist study societies and the first organized groups

By December 1920 a Society for the Study of Marxist Theory, probably founded by Li Ta-chao, had been in existence for nearly a year at Peking University. Its example was followed by other small groups, which sprang up here and there, sometimes in disguise, all trying to find their way through the labyrinth of revolutionary political theory and literature of a social trend. They were as yet largely ignorant and undecided. Chou Yang, who until his disgrace in 1966 was responsible for cultural affairs under the present regime, gives perhaps the best description of all in an article published in September 1957:[2]

> . . . we must look back along the road that intellectuals like ourselves have travelled. . . . We eagerly absorbed everything new from abroad, unable at the time to differentiate between anarchism and socialism, between individualism and collectivism. Nietzsche, Kropotkin and Karl Marx attracted us almost equally. It was not till later that we came to see that Marxism-Leninism was the only truth and the weapon for the liberation of mankind. . . . We believed in communism in the abstract, but our actions were often motivated by personal ambitions and the longing to prove ourselves heroes. We were not in close touch with the workers and peasants, and seldom even approached them. The democratic revolution was our immediate goal, the socialist revolution a distant ideal. . . . For a long time we were strongly influenced by individualism. . . . We revered Ibsen and cherished his famous dictum: 'The strongest man in the world is he who stands most alone'.

It was high time for the Comintern to come and deal with the organizing and purging of these little groups. This duly happened in June 1920, when the Secretary-General of the Far Eastern Bureau of the Comintern, Gregory Voitinsky (alias Zarkin), arrived in Peking accompanied by a militant Chinese communist educated in Russia, Yang Ming-chai. Few details are known about Voitinsky's work. Opinions also differ widely as to the com-

[1] *People's Daily*, 28 April 1957.
[2] Chou Yang, *A Great Debate on the Literary Front,* 16 September 1957 (English translation: Peking, Foreign Languages Press, 1958).

position and dates of foundation of the first socialist groups or the Socialist Youth Corps groups, which appeared in 1920. Some authors hold that a Communist Party existed as early as the spring of 1920, others claim that a meeting to prepare for the foundation of the Communist Party was held in September 1920. The best way to clarify the question a little is no doubt to give a brief account of each group in existence just before the First Congress of the Communist Party, with a short historical outline.

The Peking group seems to have grown out of the Society for the Study of Socialism founded in 1919 at Peking University. A Society for the Study of Marxist Theory appeared in March 1920, however, and may have been simply a development of the first group.[1] Once it had been re-organized and purged, just before the First Congress, the Peking group had about ten members, among whom were Li Ta-chao, Teng Chung-hsia, Chang Kuo-t'ao, Lo Chang-lung, Liu Jen-ching and Ho Meng-hsiung. Three of them were later executed, three more left the party, and one alone, Chang Kuo-t'ao, who took refuge in Hong Kong, is still alive today. The Peking group edited a weekly paper, *The Voice of Labour* (*Lao-tung yin*). In September 1920 a branch of the Socialist Youth Corps, whose main branch had formed a base in Shanghai in August 1920, was founded in Peking. The Shanghai group, which was probably founded in May 1920 by Ch'en Tu-hsiu, is said to have consisted of fifty to seventy members. Four of these were to become well known, but not one of them remained in the Party: Chou Fo-hai was shot in 1946 for collaboration with the Japanese, Tai Chi-t'ao went over to the Kuomintang, Shao Li-tzu left the Party for the Kuomintang but declared his allegiance once more to the Peking government in 1949, and Li Ta gave up political activities early to devote himself to teaching. The Shanghai group began publication of a magazine, *Labour Circles* (*Lao-tung chieh*), on 15 August 1920. After 7 November it became a monthly magazine and changed its name to *The Communist* (*K'ung-ch'an tang*). The Socialist Youth Corps created in August 1920 became the Communist Youth Corps at the Third Congress in 1923.

In Canton, where Ch'en Tu-hsiu still was in July 1921, a small group of about ten people was formed: Ch'en Kung-po, who was soon to turn traitor and later came to a miserable end, shot by the Chinese in 1946, after succeeding Wang Ching-wei as head of the pro-Japanese government in Nanking; T'an P'ing-shan, who also left the Party later on; P'eng P'ai, who was to take command of the Soviet districts of east Kwangtung;

[1] Several authors, among them Chow Ts'e-tsung, hold that this society did not really become active until the end of 1921; others state that the Society for the Study of Socialism goes back to 1918. They may be referring to different societies.

Lin Po-ch'ü, who remained faithful until his death in 1960; Tan Chih-t'ang, etc. The group published a periodical, *The Voice of Labour* (*Lao-tung sheng*). Four or five people had formed a group in Wuhan: Tung Pi-wu, now Vice-President of the Republic, Ch'en T'an-ch'iu, possibly Yün Tai-yin, even at this early date, Hsü Pei-tao and Ssu Yang. Wang Shu-mei and Teng En-ming were together in Tsinan (Shantung). In Ch'angsha, the capital of Hunan, were Mao Tse-tung and Ho Shu-heng. A Society for the Study of Marxism had been in existence there since September 1920, and a branch of the Socialist Youth Corps is reported to have been founded there in October of the same year. One or two people stood on their own: Shen Ting-i in Hangchow, Chekiang, and Kao Tsung-su in Shansi.

This list, and the fact that the groups were scattered geographically, should not create any illusion as to the numbers involved. The official sources state that those present at the First Congress represented a total of fifty-seven people. As for the members of the Socialist Youth Corps, they are generally reckoned at one or two hundred at the most within China itself. In February 1921 a small branch of the Socialist Youth Corps was founded in Paris, preparatory to the founding of a proper French branch of the Chinese Communist Party (see Chapter 5). The First Congress was to mould all these little groups of hesitant intellectuals, driven to search for a faith by feelings of nationalism and repulsion for traditional society and culture, into a true orthodox and disciplined party. But, apart from a few exceptions, the early Chinese communists were not to survive the first revolutionary upheavals. Most of them were to abandon communism, several were to be executed by their political adversaries, and Mao Tse-tung and Tung Pi-wu are virtually the only ones of the original fifty-seven to have triumphed along with their Party.

5 The Birth of the Party

The First Congress

The First Congress of the Chinese Communist Party is still shrouded in mists, which the official historians seem unwilling to disperse. The anniversary of 1 July is celebrated each year, but is never accompanied by any details to clarify this important event. This reticence is easily explained. At least six of the twelve who took part were to leave the Party, whereas a future apostate, Ch'en Tu-hsiu, was elected Secretary-General. As for Mao Tse-tung, who was 28 at the time, the unobtrusive part he played was unworthy of the great destiny awaiting him; legend has nothing to gain by following history too closely.[1]

The most reliable sources agree that the congress was held in the French Concession in Shanghai (in the Po Wen Girls' School, Szechuan Road),[2] from 1 to 5 July, which tallies with the date of 1 July given by the Party itself. Some authors, however, give 9 and 10 July. Ch'en Kung-po, one of those who took part, wrote in 1923 that the congress began on

[1] The *Communist International*, in an issue dating from January 1936 (Paris publishing office), attempted to write a biography of Mao Tse-tung and managed to gather together an incredible number of falsehoods and errors about the congress; it was attended by 'several dozen' (*sic*) workers, peasants, coolies, intellectuals; dialogue between Ch'en Tu-hsiu and Mao Tse-tung, in which the latter preached a lesson in proletarian morality, etc. In fact, Ch'en Tu-hsiu, then in Canton, could not attend the congress and was elected 'in absentia'.

[2] Now Hsin Yeh Lu, No. 78. A small museum has been opened there. A quotation from Mao Tse-tung's works has been put up: 'A Single Spark can Start a Prairie Fire', but the commemorative plaque does not mention the Party's founders. The first meetings seem to have been held at the house of Li Han-chün.

20 July, lasted two weeks, and was then ended in a pleasure boat on a well-known lake. Hsiao Yü, one of Mao Tse-tung's schoolfellows, states that the congress was interrupted for fear of police intervention and continued on Lake Chiahsing; this is confirmed by the official version.[1] Ch'en T'an-ch'iu, who was also present, says that the congress took place in the second half of July and lasted for four days.

The same uncertainty surrounds the first meetings, which may have been held successively in different places. The communists of that time may also have given several false addresses and dates as a measure of security. The Chinese habit of approximation, the use of the lunar calendar alongside our own, the lack of minutes and archives, the disappearance of three-quarters of the witnesses, the silence of those who are left, all help to produce inaccuracy and confusion. Many similar examples exist.

Twelve communists represented fifty-seven belonging to seven regional groups. Their names have been transmitted by historical accounts with some measure of certainty: Chang Kuo-t'ao, Ch'en Kung-po, Ch'en T'an ch'iu, Ch'en Wang-tao, Chou Fo-hai, Ho Shu-heng, Li Han-chün, Li Ta, Liu Jen-ching, Mao Tse-tung, Pao Hui-seng, Tung Pi-wu. Some people may possibly have replaced others at some meetings, or have attended as private individuals. This explains why the names of Teng En-ming and Wang Shu-mei, who were both to give their lives for the Party, are sometimes mentioned. Also present was a delegate from the International, a Dutchman called Maring, alias Sneevliet, a former agitator in the Dutch East Indies; he too was to abandon communism, though some time later, and to disappear during the Second World War.

Part of the discussions centred round points of doctrine, which seem fairly elementary today; they arose from the inadequate education of the first Chinese communists as well as from conditions in the country itself. Most of the members seem to have supported one of two extreme views. Some advocated 'legal Marxism', and held that the new ideology should be spread openly, through the press and through parliamentary rather than revolutionary action. The Party should be loosely organized and not overcentralized. Li Han-chün, who may have been supported by Li Ta and Ch'en Kung-po, is said to have represented this line. A radical and 'adventurist' tendency opposed it, refusing in advance to cooperate with

[1] A few hours away from Shanghai, on the line from Shanghai to Hangchow, the capital of Chekiang. A monument has been built on an island in the lake to commemorate the episode. Chou Fo-hai wrote of his memories of the occasion in the magazine *Ch'un-ch'iu*, Nos. 209 and 223 (Hong Kong, 1966).

the bourgeois nationalist and democratic parties, and intending to count on the support of the working class who were to be brought to power as soon as possible, though the likelihood of this seemed extremely slender. Liu Jen-ching and Pao Hui-seng defended this point of view. If this were in fact so, it is piquant to note that Liu Jen-ching was later to be accused of rightist deviationism and that he left the Party at the same time as Ch'en Tu-hsiu. If Ch'en Kung-po is to be believed,[1] the Party's attitude was one of isolation, if not frank hostility, with regard to all other parties, including that of Sun Yat-sen, who was considered responsible for the political chaos in the same way as the northern warlords. The principle of simultaneous adherence to several political organizations was thus brought up early and implicitly condemned. This is of interest in that the question of collaboration with the Kuomintang, advocated by the Comintern, was to be the subject of tough discussion at the following congresses and remained in the forefront of affairs in the history of the Communist Party until just before its rise to power. It was also natural that the question should arise, considering the powerful nationalistic current among all Chinese intellectuals, and the personal prestige surrounding the man later to be called 'Kuo Fu', the Father of the Nation, not to mention the fact that the Kuomintang was the only revolutionary party at that time.

As far as organization was concerned, the statutes and programme drawn up at the First Congress were to remain secret.[2] Officers were elected, and first of all the first Secretary-General, Ch'en Tu-hsiu. The leadership of the Party seems to have been put in the hands of a body consisting of three members, an embryo of the future Political Bureau: Ch'en Tu-hsiu, Chang Kuo-t'ao and Li Ta, assisted by three deputy members: Chou Fo-hai, Li Han-chün and Liu Jen-ching. The Organization Department of the Party probably fell to Chang Kuo-t'ao, and that of Propaganda to Li Ta.[3] Mao Tse-tung's position does not appear to have been particularly clear cut; at the end of the congress he went back to Hunan, the province whose delegate he was. Fifteen years were still to pass before he rose officially to the leading post in the Party; his rival to

[1] Ch'en Kung-po, *The Communist Movement in China.*

[2] Ch'en Kung-po gives an account of this, though it cannot be checked against other texts (cf. title mentioned above).

[3] Li Ta left the Party in 1927. In 1966 Red Guards accused him of repudiating communism, writing 'reactionary' articles and serving the Kuomintang. Chou Fo-hai states that he was elected Assistant Secretary-General, replacing Ch'en Tu-hsiu, who was absent. In his account, the term Committee Leader (Wei-yuan chang) is substituted for that of Secretary-General.

it in 1935 was Chang Kuo-t'ao, whose claim was clearly the more justifiable.

The Chinese Communist Party, as it was at the First Congress, appears weak, lacking all means of taking action, and above all absurdly small. 1 July 1921 is, however, the greatest date in its history. It marks the end of the period of confusion and hesitation. The Party had acquired leaders, a centralized organization and an embryonic status; the uncertain and undisciplined elements were to disappear of their own accord. Now, under the guidance of a clear-cut and independent ideology, with the political and material help of Soviet Russia and the Comintern, it was able to begin to concentrate on its true aim, on the masses and especially the urban proletariat. Progress in this field was rapid, at least as far as trade unions were concerned. Political progress, which came later, was slower, and did not really begin until 1925. The alliance with the Kuomintang was to help. The union of these two revolutionary parties, which lasted until 1927, was to restore, temporarily at least, the national unity that had been lost in 1911.

The Chinese Communist Party abroad

While the Chinese Communist Party was beginning to become organized in China, groups of Chinese communist workers and students were also being formed in Europe, chiefly in France, and in Japan. France was in a special position in this respect. The country's revolutionary tradition, toleration in the field of politics, and hospitality which was open to all had already encouraged the formation of small groups of Chinese nationalists and anarchists at the beginning of the century (see Chapter 2). The Great War was to produce a wave of interest in France, the first of the Allied nations, and also an unusual form of Chinese emigration.

For the first time, Chinese workers, who as a rule never went further than Asia and the Pacific when they left the country, went to Europe. Nearly 150,000 of them were to spend some time in France from 1917 onwards, as a result of the agreements signed by the French and Chinese governments. Several thousand of them stayed there for good. Although many of them were to have their first experience of trade union organization, learning new ideas from the life of the French workers, very few seem to have shown any interest in political ideas or activities, either in France or in China, once they returned. Most of them went back to their native province, Shantung, and resumed their old lives as coolies or peasants. None of them became well known in the history of Chinese communism, or even the Chinese trade union movement.

On the other hand, a student-worker movement launched in 1912 by the former anarchists, Li Shih-tseng, Wu Chih-hui, etc., took on a new lease of life in 1915 when the Society for Frugal Study by Means of Labour (Ch'in Kung-chien hsüeh-hui) was re-established in Paris. Chinese students in France, mostly from Hunan and Szechuan, numbered over 400 in 1919. In 1920, they probably amounted to 1600 or 1800, and the movement was active until 1923. This group, whose history is beyond the scope of this book, included Marxists who now hold some of the highest posts in the Party and the government.

Chinese communists in France[1] appear to have developed from a small mutual aid association formed within the student-worker group. The two leaders of the group, Ts'ai Ho-shen and Wang Jo-fei, who were already convinced socialists, introduced politics from the beginning. The former is said to have posted the Communist Manifesto in the association's premises, and the latter encouraged students to 'follow the soviet working class road'. Lively discussions took place, however, between representatives of the socialist and the anarchist tendencies. The date of the inaugural meeting is not known with certainty, but it probably took place in 1920. In 1921 the association changed its name and became the Student-Workers' Association (Kung-hsüeh shih-chieh hui), which later had about 400 members.

Those who founded the Chinese Socialist Youth Group (She-hui chu-i ch'ing-nien t'uan) in February 1921 were probably members of this group. Acting on instructions from the Chinese Communist Party, it changed its name in July 1922 to French Section of the Chinese Communist Party (Chung-kung lü Fa Chih-pu).[2] It grew fairly rapidly, for just before it disappeared, in 1923, it had nearly 500 members, which amounted to more than the Communist Party in China.[3] The Chinese communists in France published a paper, *Youth* (*Shao nien*), run by Ch'en Yen-nien (one of Ch'en Tu-hsiu's sons) and Chao Shih-yen; from 1924 onwards this was replaced by a magazine, *Ch'ih Kuang* (*Red Light*), which appeared every two months and was edited by Teng Hsiao-p'ing, later Secretary of the

[1] Cf. Ho Ch'ang-kung, *Memories of my Life as a Student-Worker* (in Chinese). Ho Ch'ang-kung, first of all Minister of Heavy Industry and later Vice-Minister of Geology, was one of the victims of the Cultural Revolution.

[2] The Section's address was a hotel in rue Godefroy, near the Place d'Italie. The Bibliothèque du Travail, 144 rue Pelleport, is said to have sent works of communist propaganda to China.

[3] Nym Wales, *The Chinese Labor Movement*.

Political Bureau. They also were in constant opposition to the nationalist groups led by Tseng Ch'i and Li Huang, and their paper, *The Awakening Lion Weekly*.

The list of members of the French section of the Chinese Communist Party later made impressive reading: Chou En-lai, Prime Minister, Marshal Ch'en Yi, Foreign Minister, Li Fu-ch'un, Plan Commissar, Teng Hsiao-p'ing, Secretary to the Central Committee, all four members of the Political Bureau, Li Wei-han (alias Lo Mai), who was for a short time in charge of the 'united front', Ts'ai Ch'ang (the wife of Li Fu-ch'un), who was Minister of Justice, Li Li-san, who once was Secretary-General of the Party, Wu Yü-chang, and Hsü T'e-li, Mao Tse-tung's former teacher. Marshal Nieh Jung-chen and Jao Shu-shih also came to France later on. Some others, who have since disappeared, held important posts in the Party as well: Wang Jo-fei, Yeh Ch'ing (alias of Jen Cho-hsüan), etc., not to mention distinguished militant members such as Ts'ai Ho-shen,[1] who died early. The French Section of the Chinese Communist Party was responsible to the European Branch of the Chinese Communist Party, led by Chou En-lai, then in Germany.

The other sections, in Belgium and Germany, were smaller than the French one. The Belgian section left no names behind it; Marshal Chu Teh, former Commander-in-Chief of the Chinese Red Army, Chang Shen-fu, now a professor at Tsinghua University, and Kao Yü-han, etc., all belonged to the German section.

In 1924, however, Chou En-lai returned to China. He was at first succeeded by Li Fu-ch'un and Fu Chung. Then the student-workers gradually left, without being replaced. A few communist and Kuomintang cadres were sent to the Sun Yat-sen University in Moscow. The French Section of the Chinese Communist Party dwindled and finally disappeared completely. Although they still hold many leading posts, the Chinese communist 'returned students' from France have never again created another group, even for the sake of renewing old friendships and memories. Many years have passed; they have almost forgotten the language, and if they ever mention France it is solely in connection with their youth.[2]

Few Chinese communists were educated in Japan. Chou Fo-hai is the

[1] A hundred and ten students who were living in the Fort Saint-Irénée at Lyons were expelled on 14 November 1921 and put on a ship at Marseilles. Ch'en Yi, later to be Foreign Minister, was among them.

[2] Among the most prominent leaders educated in France, Jao Shu-shih was eliminated in 1954; Teng Hsiao-p'ing and several others were removed from office during the Cultural Revolution.

best known of them, and he was to leave the Party early. Several factors contributed to this state of affairs, unprecedented in Chinese revolutionary history, and out of proportion with the large numbers of Chinese students in Japan – the severity of the ever-present Japanese police, the fact that the Japanese socialist groups were both ignorant and insignificant before the appearance in August 1921 of the Japanese Communist Party, led by Eizo Kondo, and the lack of contact between the Chinese students and the Japanese workers.

Thus the Chinese Communist Party was founded in the summer of 1921, and began its historic career. It was, however, so weak that it had to look to the Kuomintang, the nationalist revolutionary movement and its elder, for support, and to merge with it to a certain extent. This union, which at first brought success, before resulting in the momentary loss of the Party, was a tragic experiment, as passionately interesting today as it was fifty years ago.

Part 2

The Chinese Communist Party from its Foundation to its Break with the Kuomintang (1 July 1921-1 August 1927)

The whole course of the Chinese revolution, its character, its prospects, undoubtedly indicate that the Chinese communists ought to remain in the Kuomintang and intensify their work in it.

Stalin, Declaration at the Seventh Enlarged Plenum of the Executive Committee of the Communist International, 30 November 1926

6 The Foundations of the Collaboration between Nationalists and Communists The Second and Third Communist Party Congresses

The period from the founding of the Chinese Communist Party up to the break with the Kuomintang is known by communist historians as the First Revolutionary Civil War. The common enemy of nationalists and communists was naturally the Peking government, a term which included different groups of warlords who were both allies and rivals, and were roughly the same as those in existence in 1921.[1]

The Kuomintang, Dr Sun Yat-sen's Nationalist Party, organized and led the struggle, a fact which must be made clear straight away. This party alone, more or less, deserves the credit for having eliminated the most powerful warlords, or having stripped them of their power. We should not be misled in this by the final victory of the Communist Party in China and the distorted picture given by some modern historians, who either claim that both parties were on the same footing, or describe the youthful Communist Party as taking the more active part in the nationalist reconquest.

At the same time it is true that communist organization and discipline provided the Kuomintang with a badly needed example. It is also true that Soviet military help, although amounting to very little, enabled it to survive in the Canton region before achieving its first successes against

[1] See Chapter 1. The expressions 'militarists', 'northerners', 'cliques', 'warlords', 'tuchün', etc., are all of them vague; Kuomintang and communist terminologies are the same in this respect. It should be remembered, however, that the Peking government representing them was recognised as the legal government for the whole of China by all the Powers, including the Soviet Union.

the northerners; these early successes were soon to develop into full-scale victories. Lastly, it cannot be denied that the communists converted a whole section of the Kuomintang to radical views, and remains of it still exist in Peking today, known as the Kuomintang Revolutionary Committee.[1] Its large membership, power and prestige made the Kuomintang in its third phase (when it launched the reorganization of 1924 and the Northern Expedition) the main, if not the sole incarnation of the revolution. The communists of that period were themselves forced to acknowledge this. Although it was above all a nationalist party, the Kuomintang also represented a class: the bourgeoisie, which was the only one fully aware of revolutionary ideas and anxious to maintain control of the revolution in both social and political fields.

The communists, who were active though few in number, also claimed to represent a new class, the proletariat, and intended to make use of the nationalist feelings, the reputation and the organization of the Kuomintang to make themselves known and to further the development of their own party. They maintained their own partisan organization, as they were required to do by the theses of the Second Congress of the Comintern, in order to keep themselves separate from their allies, and to be able to fight against them when the time was ripe.

The vital importance of the relations between the Nationalist Party and the communists (whether Chinese or Russian) from 1924 to 1927 was not restricted to Chinese history alone. The repercussions they produced in Moscow provided material for the bitter controversy which developed in Russia in 1927 between the Stalinist majority and the Trotskyist opposition.[2] The Comintern's experience in China is still valuable today in so far as it can be taken as a precedent; it has even acquired further meaning, now that underdeveloped countries on the way to total emancipation are more numerous than they were. There, as in the China of 1927, which was a perfect example of an underdeveloped country, international communism is faced with several choices as regards allies, methods and themes of propaganda. This fact was clearly perceived and expressed by Bukharin as early as the Fifteenth Congress of the Communist Party of the Soviet Union (10 December 1927):

> The experience of the Chinese revolution is of enormous importance to us, and not only from the point of view of the further successful development of the revolutionary struggle in China. The Chinese

[1] The Cultural Revolution has caused them to disappear almost completely.

[2] For further details see Pierre Broué, *La Question chinoise dans l'International communiste (1926-1927)*.

> revolution has confronted us with the colonial problem in its most concrete form. . . . The experience of the Chinese revolution has brought us into actual touch with a diversity of problems of colonial revolutions in general.[1]

The Russians and the Chinese of today cannot draw the same conclusions from the experience of their elders during the period from 1923 to 1927. Although the Russian leaders of that time have disappeared, many of the present Chinese leaders were among the protagonists and victims of the dramatic events of 1927.

In 1923 the Kuomintang-Kungch'antang collaboration seemed natural at least, if not strictly necessary. In the eyes of patriotic Chinese at that time, the two great evils of post-war China were 'feudalism' and foreign ascendancy. It was only natural that all true revolutionaries should join forces to defeat them. Rivalry for power could only develop once a joint victory appeared a distinct possibility.

The communist view of the collaboration

The communists were scarcely in a position to act alone. Their party still consisted of a few dozen intellectuals with no practical experience of politics. The proletariat, whom it claimed to represent, had hardly heard of it, and the mass of the peasants were highly conservative, if not backward, and, what is more, hard to approach. A strictly Marxist programme was meaningless in this context and could only shock established ideas and customs. On the other hand, a programme of national emancipation, as the May 4th Movement had already shown, could rally widely differing sections of the population to their cause, including – proof of this was shortly to be forthcoming – large military groups from the North. From a doctrinal point of view, the resolutions laid down by the Second Congress of the Comintern had made special provision for alliances between communist parties and bourgeois revolutionary movements; the Kuomintang had been included among the latter by Lenin as early as 1912. The same theme had been taken up once more at the Third Congress of the International (June-July 1921) at which the Chinese delegate Chang T'ai-lei had advocated a temporary and watchful alliance with the Chinese bourgeoisie, in opposition to the radical views expressed by the Indian, M. N. Roy. A new and more direct expression of the resolutions established by the Second Congress was to come a few months later at the Eastern Peoples' Congress, which held a preliminary conference at

[1] Quoted by X. Eudin and R. C. North, *Soviet Russia and the East, 1920 to 1927*, p. 391.

Irkutsk (November 1921), followed by official sessions in Moscow and Petrograd (21-27 January 1922).

The Eastern Peoples' Congress was in a sense a reply to the announcement that the Washington Conference was to take place, and it was a continuation of the Congress of Baku held in September 1920 (see Chapter 3). But whereas this last appealed mainly to Near and Middle Eastern nations, the new congress included chiefly Japanese, Chinese and Koreans.[1] The Chinese delegation consisted of at least thirty-seven full members and five advisory members. Fourteen communists, eleven members of socialist youth movements and fourteen people with no party allegiance made up the delegation of full members. The most important roles seem to have been played by Chang T'ai-lei, representing the communists, and a man named Tao, who represented the Kuomintang. Other well-known people were present: Chang Kuo-t'ao, and also Chiang K'ang-hu, the founder of the 1911 Chinese Socialist Party (see Chapter 2).

The Soviet delegates, above all Zinoviev and Safarov, took the opportunity afforded by the congress of stressing once more the solidarity of all revolutionary movements fighting for national emancipation, at the same time offering Russian help to bourgeois revolutionaries. In a special reference to China, Safarov, in his reply to the Kuomintang delegate, acknowledged that it was a truly revolutionary and democratic party, and declared:

> We are convinced that this Party has done great revolutionary work which was absolutely necessary in China, and we hope to fight side by side with this Party in the future. . . . We say: In colonial and semi-colonial countries the first phase of the revolutionary movement must inevitably be a national-democratic movement.

The delegates from the Soviet Union made no secret of the ultimate aims of communism, or of their intention of becoming the sole leaders of the proletariat:

> The proletarian and semi-proletarian masses of China and Korea have a greater task to fulfil than that of national emancipation. They are confronted with the task of *complete* liberation of their countries.
>
> But on the other hand, the proletarian and semi-proletarian elements must organize independently in their class unions. The unions which are now being formed as guild and craft organizations directly connected

[1] Sometimes called the Congress of the Toilers of the East, or the Far Eastern Revolutionary Organizations' Congress.

with the Homindan [Kuomintang] cannot be recognized by us as class unions. They do not understand the class principle, they are not the organs of the class struggle of the proletariat for its emancipation. Therefore, in dealing with you, followers of the Homindan, as with our allies, friends and comrades, we at the same time tell you openly and frankly: we are supporting and will continue to support your struggle in so far as it is a matter of nationalistic and democratic uprising for national emancipation. But at the same time we shall independently carry on our communist work of organizing the proletarian and semi-proletarian masses of China.

This is the cause of the proletarian masses themselves, and must be done by the Chinese workers, the Chinese proletariat. In this sphere the Chinese labour movement must develop quite independently of the radically minded bourgeois and democratic organizations and parties....

On the other hand, however, we definitely demand from these bourgeois democratic, these radical-democratic elements, that they make no attempt to dominate over the young labour movements of China and Korea and that they make no attempt to divert it from its true path and substitute its ideals by radical-democratic ideals painted in Soviet colours. We will more easily come to an understanding if we tell each other what we really are.[1]

The Eastern Peoples' Congress thus gave a clear definition of the nature and limitations of a collaboration between the Kuomintang and the Communist Party; future conflicts were foreshadowed in the text. The agrarian question in particular had already brought the Kuomintang delegates into open opposition to those from the Soviet Union. The Kuomintang policy was to postpone reform until after the reunification of China under a nationalist government, whereas the Russian delegates were in favour of launching a far-reaching reform immediately, beginning at the lowest level. A passage from Safarov's declaration paves the way for some of Mao Tse-tung's most vigorous writings on the subject: 'Without a correct attitude on the land question, the great masses cannot be drawn into the struggle on our side. It is not enough to work out a good programme, it is not enough to advocate this programme in a small circle of so-called well-educated society, it is necessary to make it the burning demand of the toiling masses. . . .'

Once the communists had admitted the collaboration with the

[1] Safarov's declaration of 27 January 1922. Cf. Eudin and North, *Soviet Russia and the East*, pp. 227-9.

Kuomintang as correct in principle and necessary in the circumstances, the practical aspects had to be considered, particularly the form these were to take: Should the revolutionary activities of the two parties converge, or be coordinated? Should they act in close alliance with each other, and, if so, what form should this take, and at what level should it be made?

As the Communist Party was anxious to maintain its own organization, two types of solution were possible, known by Chinese authors as 'open door' and 'closed door'. The first proposed that the Communist Party should become a sort of homogeneous and autonomous element within the framework of the Kuomintang, and the second that the Communist Party should remain entirely outside the Kuomintang, while linking its activities with those of the other party. As will be seen later on, a variant of the first solution was adopted in the end; the communists became individual members of the Kuomintang, while still members of their own party. This solution was agreed upon with great difficulty.

The communists gave expression to their efforts towards collaboration with the Kuomintang in two documents dating from the summer of 1922. The earlier of the two, a Chinese Communist Party manifesto dealing with the contemporary situation, states the problem somewhat cynically, but goes no further:

> The Chinese Communist Party, as the vanguard of the proletariat, struggles for working-class liberation and for the proletarian revolution. Until such time as the Chinese proletariat is able to seize power in its own hands, considering the present political and economic conditions of China's development and all the historical processes now going on in China, the proletariat's urgent task is to act jointly with the democratic party to establish a united front of democratic revolution to struggle for the overthrow of the military and for the organization of a real democratic government.[1]

In spite of these advances, the same document still contains a violent attack on the Kuomintang, which, although doubtless a revolutionary party, still 'possesses only a relative amount of democratic and revolutionary spirit' and 'must renounce once and for all every policy of vacillation, compromise and endless zigzags'.

The manifesto of the Second Congress (July 1922) is a little more explicit: 'At present, in the interest of the workers and poor peasants, the Chinese Communist Party must bring the workers to help the democratic

[1] Conrad Brandt, Benjamin Schwartz and John K. Fairbank, *A Documentary History of Chinese Communism*, p. 62.

revolutionary movement and get the workers, the poor peasants and the petty bourgeoisie to set up a democratic united front.'

A list of the seven chief aims of the party follows. These include:

(*a*) As far as the nation is concerned, the constitution of a federal republic, including Mongolia, Tibet and Turkestan, and, of course, the elimination of 'foreign imperialism'.

(*b*) As far as internal politics are concerned, the fundamental right to vote, hold assemblies, and enjoy free expression.

(*c*) As far as social conditions are concerned, modern legislation on labour (the eight-hour day was part of this), educational reform, tax reform.

The same document lays particular emphasis on maintaining the independence of the proletariat *vis-à-vis* the bourgeoisie.

Although the Second Congress raised the question of collaboration between the Chinese Communist Party and the Kuomintang in July 1922, it was not until the following month that Maring suggested to the Central Committee that the Party should be contained within the Kuomintang, probably as the result of a suggestion or stipulation coming from Sun Yat-sen himself. Maring's proposal, which was that each member of the Chinese Communist Party should at the same time become a member of the Kuomintang appears to have aroused violent reactions, which were to be renewed and expressed more clearly at the Third Party Congress, held in Canton in June 1923. The opposition assumed two forms, which used different arguments but arrived at the same conclusion.

The 'leftist' opposition, led by Chang Kuo-T'ao, was based on doctrinal reasoning. The Chinese Communist Party was by definition the party representing one class, the proletariat, and could not therefore represent other classes without creating confusion of all sorts, first and foremost in the minds of its members and those who sympathized with it. Such confusion could only weaken the Party's cohesion and determination, and lead to serious practical mistakes. The leftist opposition also pointed out that the leaders of the Kuomintang were not to be trusted, and that in fact, the Kuomintang of 1922-3 did not inspire much confidence, for it bore too close a resemblance to the party it had been during the first years of the Republic. Its lack of doctrinal rigour, its heterogeneous composition and the frequent hesitations and compromises of its leader were all too obvious, and were damaging its revolutionary spirit.

The 'rightist' opponents, later to be described as 'rightist capitulationists', and particularly Ch'en Tu-hsiu, the Secretary-General, considered that it was logical, indeed preferable, to let the Kuomintang carry through its bourgeois democratic revolution, so that the communists could follow it up with the proletarian revolution. This position seemed orthodox to a certain extent, and took account of the fact that the Communist Party was still too weak to consider leading the Kuomintang from within. It was an attitude that reappears under different forms in the Party's history.

Maring's proposal was finally accepted, probably because Sun Yat-sen's intransigence left no other choice to the Comintern. The official communist history describes Mao Tse-tung and Ch'ü Ch'iu-pai as the two most determined supporters of the collaboration under the form proposed, and their 'correct' attitude is the object of particular emphasis as their adversaries have since become the two most famous deserters from the Party. Mao Tse-tung and Ch'ü Ch'iu-pai were both elected to the Central Committee for the first time during the Third Congress.

The manifesto of the Third Congress, although it gave no details as to the practical aspects of the collaboration, announced it and acknowledged the Kuomintang's role as leader: 'The Kuomintang must be the central force in the revolution, and assume the leadership of it. . . . We therefore hope that all the revolutionary elements in Chinese society will gather round the Kuomintang so that the national revolution may be achieved more quickly.'

Although it had stated its position and published an invitation to support the Kuomintang, this did not prevent the Party from making yet another vigorous denunciation of its ally's weaknesses:

> The Kuomintang must be the central force of the revolution and should assume its leadership. Unfortunately, the Kuomintang maintains two mistaken ideas:
>
> (1) It hopes that the foreign powers will help the Chinese national revolution. If it appeals to the enemy in this way, not only will it lose its role as leader, but also the people will be led to depend on foreign power, and will lose their self-confidence and their spirit of national independence.
>
> (2) It concentrates all its efforts on military action, neglecting propaganda among the masses. Consequently the Kuomintang will lose its political leadership; also a national revolutionary party that does not obtain the sympathy of the entire people will never be able to succeed by military action alone.

This is an excellent example of the reluctant, compelling support which communist parties of all countries give to their allies of the moment.

The nationalist view of the collaboration

It would perhaps be as well to give a brief summary of the numerous transformations the Kuomintang went through during the twenty-five years of its existence, before examining the collaboration question as it appeared to Sun Yat-sen and the nationalists. From its foundation in 1895 until 1905 the Kuomintang was known as the 'Hsing-chung hui' or 'Revive China Society'; from 1905 until 1912 it was the 'Chung-kuo t'ung-meng hui' or the 'United League', an anti-dynastic, republican, democratic and vaguely socialist organization, whose illegal and secret activities consisted in attempts to provoke uprisings, which either originated abroad or received foreign help. In 1912, just before the election of the first Chinese Parliament, the 'T'ung-meng hui' became a true political party, the 'Kuomintang' or 'Nationalist Party', and undertook to take part in legal parliamentary activities. When, after the dissolution of the parliament (1913) in which it had a majority, the Kuomintang was banned in China, it became the 'Chung-hua Komintang' or 'Chinese Revolutionary Party' in Japan in 1914. On 10 October 1919 Sun Yat-sen, who had returned to China after the death of Yüan Shih-k'ai in 1916, restored the former name of Kuomintang.

These different names followed the changing fortunes of Sun Yat-sen himself, but his personal vicissitudes did not end with the disappearance of his chief enemy. Although he created the first 'military government' in Canton in September 1917, he was driven out of the same town in August 1919. He returned in 1920 and was elected president of a new government there on 5 May 1921, only to be exiled once more, to Shanghai, from June 1922 to February 1923.

One of the main causes of his failure was the lack of unity in his party, which stood for widely differing currents of feeling in nationalism and sentiment. Although he excelled when engaged in revolutionary or even parliamentary opposition, Sun Yat-sen revealed himself incapable of drawing up a clear-cut programme for the rebuilding of his country. His socialistic tendencies, vague in content though radical in their vocabulary, worried many of his supporters. The political context and circumstances drove him to look for help from unreliable sources, whether in China itself where he approached military factions, or abroad where he approached powers who were over-anxious to assume political and economic control of the country (Japan, Great Britain). In this respect, things might have gone far indeed, for it is rumoured that the Kuomintang leader even approached the United States Embassy secretly in 1923, asking that

Washington should assume the leadership of an international military expedition (composed of troops from England, France, Germany, Italy and the United States) to rid China of the 'tuchün', keep Japanese ambition at bay, and set the country on its feet again, all of which was to be accomplished during the five years of occupation.[1] That the Kuomintang survived all these difficulties was due solely to the personal reputation of its leader, who became a symbol of truly disinterested and tenacious revolutionary nationalism in spite of his misjudgements and weaknesses.

In February 1923, when Sun Yat-sen returned to Canton for the last time, the Nationalist Party was as vulnerable as it ever had been. The 'military government' supporting it was in the hands of local generals who were more interested in using its own and its leader's popularity for their personal ends than in helping the Kuomintang. This time, however, Sun Yat-sen managed to remain in Canton, making the town and the surrounding province into a proper revolutionary base, which later became the starting point of the expedition to reconquer the country. Soviet technical and material help was a determining factor in this initial phase.

The beginning of the collaboration

Sun Yat-sen must have grown aware of the Russian revolutionary movement and the October Revolution at a very early date. Shortly after the Revolution he sent a message to Lenin, expressing his sympathy (1918). A little later, a correspondence began between Sun and Chicherin, opened by the latter who was then People's Commissar of Foreign Affairs.[2] Chicherin affected to treat Sun Yat-sen as the leader of a proletarian and peasant revolution, whereas Sun Yat-sen seems to have been more anxious to give his own life history, describe his country's situation, and warn the Russians against their neighbour, Chang Tso-lin, than to establish contact on an ideological plane. When Sun Yat-sen expressed a polite desire for further information on the characteristics of the Soviet regime, particularly in the fields of military organization and education, he saw Bolshevism primarily as a nationalist and antimonarchical movement of emancipation. It was for this reason, and also because it set an example to China, that Sun Yat-sen's sympathy was aroused.

When he replied to Chicherin, Sun Yat-sen had already personally encountered the first Comintern envoy to China, Voitinsky. This meeting

[1] Cf. H. Abend, *My Years in China* (London, J. Lane, Bodley Head, 1944).

[2] Cf. text of a letter from Chicherin to Sun Yat-sen (August 1918) and from Sun Yat-sen to Chicherin (28 August 1921), quoted in Eudin and North, *Soviet Russia and the East*.

took place in the autumn of 1920, in the French Concession in Shanghai, but it does not appear to have been followed up. On the other hand, in November 1921, when he was in Kueilin in Kwangsi preparing a first 'Northern Expedition', which was eventually called off, Sun Yat-sen received a visit from another agent of the International, the Dutchman Maring (real name Sneevliet). Sun Yat-sen thought that Russia and China shared identical problems, and was considerably struck by this, and also by the moderation of Lenin's economic policy. He describes his pleasant surprise in a letter to Liao Chung-k'ai, drawing a somewhat unexpected parallel between his own ideas on the economy and the N.E.P.[1] The presence of Kuomintang delegates at the Eastern Peoples' Congress held in Moscow and Petrograd the following year (see p. 70) was perhaps the most important outcome of his interview with Maring.

In the summer of 1922 Sun Yat-sen was driven out of Canton by the revolt led by Ch'en Chiung-ming, and received a visit in Shanghai from another Soviet envoy, Dallin; they seem to have had lengthy discussions. But the meeting between Sun Yat-sen and Adolph Abramovitch Joffe finally decided the matter of collaboration between the Chinese communists and the Kuomintang. Joffe, the former leader of the Soviet Delegation at Brest-Litowsk, and the former Soviet Ambassador in Berlin and a supporter of Trotsky, who was later to commit suicide on 16 November 1927 leaving a most moving political testament behind him, arrived in China in August 1922 to prepare the ground for the reopening of diplomatic relations between Peking and Moscow. When this attempt failed, he went to Japan via Shanghai, where he met Sun Yat-sen in December 1922, when the latter was about to return once more to Canton.

The conversation between Sun and Joffe culminated in the famous joint manifesto of 26 January 1923, which was intended to pave the way for collaboration between the two parties and to reassure sections of the Kuomintang:

> Dr Sun Yat-sen thinks that as none of the conditions needed for their successful application exist in China, neither the communist nor even the soviet system can be introduced there. Mr Joffe shares this belief and thinks that the most urgent and important problem in China is that of unification and national independence. With regard to this

[1] Cf. Chiang Kai-shek, *Soviet Russia in China: A Summing-up at Seventy*, p. 20; see also extracts from the text of the letter from Sun to Liao Chung-k'ai in C. Brandt, *Stalin's Failure in China (1924-1927)*.

great task, he has assured Dr Sun Yat-sen of the warmest sympathy of the Russian people for China and of the unfailing support of Russia.

Several paragraphs followed, dealing with the principle of the Soviet Union's renunciation of extraterritorial privileges, the maintenance of the *status quo* with regard to the Chinese Eastern Railway, and the presence of Soviet troops in Mongolia.

The meetings between Joffe and Sun Yat-sen were followed by more detailed conversations, at Atami in Japan, between Joffe and Liao Chung-k'ai, the future Minister of Finance of the Canton government. They probably dealt with two essential points: the form which cooperation between the two parties should take, and the nature and extent of the help to be furnished by the Comintern in military matters – and perhaps already in the organization of the Kuomintang itself.

The agreement between the Kuomintang and the Comintern, ratified by the Third Congress of the Chinese Communist Party in June 1923 after considerable opposition, was crowned in the autumn of the same year by Chiang Kai-shek's official visit to Moscow. The nationalist Chief of Staff, accompanied by a small delegation – Shen Ting-i, Wang Teng-yun and the communist Chang T'ai-lei – stayed in Russia from 2 September to 25 November. He studied the organization of the Red Army and the Soviet Communist Party, and met Trotsky and several well-known Russians. If his memoirs are to be believed, this visit quickly removed all illusions as to the sincerity of his hosts; he reported on this, so he says, to Sun Yat-sen, and above all to Liao Chung-k'ai in a letter written 14 March of the following year.[1] However, as far as external appearances were concerned, the Chiang Kai-shek of the 1920s was considered a radical general, and none would have doubted his pro-Russian sympathies.

On 6 October 1923 Borodin arrived in China, with a first group of Russian advisers (Joffe, who was ill, had meanwhile been replaced by Karakhan). His first task was to help with a complete reorganization of the Kuomintang. Borodin, whose real name was Michel Grusenberg, was Jewish, born in Lithuania in 1884; he emigrated to the United States in about 1906, and his varied international experience had made him a highly adaptable person who knew when ideology should give way to common sense. He seems to have had no difficulties in his dealings with Sun Yat-sen and with Chiang Kai-shek himself, at least until the launching of the Northern Expedition in 1926.[2]

1 Chiang Kai-shek, *Soviet Russia in China*, pp. 25 ff.

2 Mao Tse-tung, on the other hand, had extremely unpleasant memories of him (cf. Edgar Snow, *Red Star Over China*).

The reorganization of the Kuomintang began on 25 October 1923. It was led by a committee of nine, advised by Borodin and the communist Li Ta-chao, for whom an exception had been made to enable him to become a member of the Kuomintang. The communist T'an P'ing-shan, soon to be head of the Organization Department of the Kuomintang – a significant fact – also seems to have shared in the work of the committee. The new statutes of the Kuomintang were approved by the First Congress of the Party, held in Canton from 20 to 30 January 1924. In spite of opposition raised by some nationalist elements, to which Li Ta-chao replied with great skill, the congress also ratified the admission of members of the Chinese Communist Party and the Socialist Youth Corps to membership of the Kuomintang.

From then onwards the true period of collaboration between the Communist Party and the Kuomintang began. It was helped by similarities in the organization of the two parties, by the fact that groups of communists were present at all levels in the Kuomintang hierarchy – including the highest of all – and by the revolutionary spirit, which undeniably existed, and whose immediate aims were common to both parties. The new Kuomintang was a strong party with a sterner discipline than before, in spite of the fact that several different trends still existed. It was also an authoritarian party, placing itself on a higher plane than the people it was to lead step by step to true democracy.

The communist influence is clearly reflected in its structure. This is hardly surprising, as Borodin himself is said to have drawn up the party's constitution in English, which Liao Chung-k'ai then translated into Chinese. Broadly speaking, it consisted of:

(*a*) A National Party Congress, which was to meet every two years to elect members of a Central Committee and hear government reports.

(*b*) A Central Executive Committee, consisting of a chairman, twenty-four permanent members and seventeen deputy members. The Central Executive Committee was to meet every six months. Between meetings it was replaced by a Standing Committee with five to nine members, which constituted a real political bureau.

Further party organizations, divided into eight sections, came under the control of the Central Executive Committee: Organization, Propaganda, Youth, Labour Questions, Peasant Questions, Military Affairs, Questions concerning Women, Foreign Policy.

(*c*) Party Offices (Tangpu) existed at the provincial, district and local levels (with a minimum of five members), each organization holding a congress from time to time and electing a small executive committee.

(*d*) A Committee of Control (consisting of five members and five deputy members) supervised Party members at all levels.

The Chairman of the Central Executive Committee (Sun Yat-sen) had the title of 'Tsung li' (Party Leader), and his authority was considerable; he was elected for life.

The Three People's Principles of Sun Yat-sen, given a new interpretation at the First Congress, were naturally acknowledged to form the basic doctrine of the Party's ideology. This was to a certain degree complemented by the 'Three Great Policies': 1 Collaboration with Soviet Russia; 2 Collaboration with the Chinese Communist Party; 3 Support for the workers and peasants.

These Three Great Policies, which from then on were considered inseparable from the Three People's Principles, enabled the communists to find a justification for their collaboration with the Kuomintang; Mao Tse-tung gives a long explanation in 'On New Democracy'.[1]

Some of Sun Yat-sen's ideas became more clearly defined during this new stage, particularly his theory of three periods in the political evolution of China: the military period, the period of tutelage and the constitutional period.[2] However, he came no nearer to accepting Marxist philosophy than he had in the past. He remained essentially liberal in his aims, a nationalist still basically attached to the Chinese cultural tradition. The Kuomintang's collaboration with the Chinese communists and Soviet Russia was born not so much of choice as of the circumstances, at a time when the Western nations refused their help to the man who had unceasingly sought their support for a quarter of a century.

The Soviet advisers' influence was particularly strong and successful in two fields, which were both essential to the development of the new Kuomintang: propaganda and military affairs. Propaganda, which had up till then been left to the initiative of local representatives, was centralized, organized and disciplined, and controlled by an office of which Mao Tse-tung was once temporarily in charge.[3] The number of papers and magazines increased: *Reconstruction* (the official Party organ), *The Republic of Canton*, *The People of Shanghai*, etc. The propaganda machine of the

[1] Cf. Mao Tse-tung, 'On New Democracy', *Selected Works*, vol. II, p. 339.

[2] Cf. Sun Yat-sen, *Chien Kuo Ta Kang* (*Principle of the Reconstruction of the Nation*) (Peking, 12 April 1924: Chinese ed.), p. 569.

[3] In February 1926 he was also editor of a Kuomintang magazine, the *Political Weekly* (*Cheng-chih chou-pao*).

Kuomintang, based on a solid substructure of supporters, came into its own during the Northern Expedition. The 'Propaganda Corps' of the nationalist armies, armed with revolutionary and patriotic themes and slogans, played a large part in the collapse of the northern armies and administrative system.

In the military field Russian advice and material help enabled Sun Yat-sen's government to found its own army, thus avoiding pressure from local generals or the representatives of private commercial and financial interests. Chiang Kai-shek, inspired by his visit to Russia the previous year, created the Whampoa Military Academy[1] in May 1924; he himself took over the leadership of it, appointing the communist Chou En-lai Assistant Political Director. This military academy had another, even more important role as a school of revolution, which Sun Yat-sen called the 'Party's Army' (Tang Chün). It had many carefully chosen Russian advisers, under the orders of Galen, alias Blücher, whom Chiang Kai-shek described as 'an excellent strategist, a man of sound common sense, and a friend'.[2] Many Russian military advisers moved on from there into units of the army, and some died for the cause of the Chinese revolution.[3]

Eminent communist military leaders like Marshal Yeh Chien-ying, Marshal Lin Piao, Marshal Nieh Jung-chen, and a few other men who were equally outstanding but who disappeared early in the struggle – like Yün Tai-ying – were instructors or pupils at the Whampoa Military Academy, which can also rightly be called the first military school of the future Chinese Red Army. Russian material aid, which took some time to arrive, was modest: 26,000 rifles, 100 machine guns, 24 field guns, 15 aeroplanes and 116 vehicles are the figures given in official sources.[4] Armament was completed by buying directly from Europe or the United States. It was more important to provide equipment for a first nucleus of cadets and trustworthy troops than to gather large armies together. These troops, who were loyal and keen, though few in numbers, were to save the nationalist regime twice over: once in October 1924, during the Canton Merchants' Rising, and then again early in 1925, when General Ch'en Chiung-ming attacked the government.[5]

[1] Whampoa is the Cantonese for Huangp'u.

[2] Chiang Kai-shek, *Soviet Russia in China.*

[3] Dan N. Jacobs, 'Recent Russian Material on Soviet Advisers in China, 1923-1927', *The China Quarterly*, No. 41 (January-March 1970), deals with known Soviet works on the subject.

[4] Lai Hsin-hsia, Wei Hung-yin, *Historical Essays on the 1st Revolutionary Civil War* (Wuhan, 1952: in Chinese).

[5] André Malraux based his novel *Les Conquérants* on this episode.

While the Kuomintang was renewing its own organization and that of its propaganda machine and its army, it was also preparing the governmental and administrative institutions of the new regime set up once more in Canton. The government, organized on the basis of a committee with sixteen ministers, was called the Military Government until July 1925. Until his death Sun Yat-sen's title was that of Grand Marshal (Ta Yüan-shuai).

The Chinese communists quickly took over many important posts in the administrative and governmental framework, as well as in the Kuomintang itself, to which they helped give a special character and working style. Consequently, in January 1924 three communists were to be found among the twenty-four members of the Kuomintang Central Executive Committee: Li Ta-chao, T'an P'ing-shan and Yü Shu-te. The seventeen deputy members included six more: Mao Tse-tung, Ch'ü Ch'iu-pai, Chang Kuo-t'ao, Lin Tsu-han, Han Lin-fu and Yü Fang-chou. Other communists held high executive posts, such as T'an P'ing-shan, head of the Organization Department, or P'eng P'ai, head of the Workers' Section. A certain proportion of them disguised their loyalties as much as possible. The dangers of this communist infiltration into the governmental framework later gave rise to attacks from Kuomintang members who were opposed to the collaboration between the two parties.

When a left and a right wing could gradually be distinguished within the Kuomintang, the communists naturally worked in close alliance with those of leftist tendencies. They tried to attract the most radical and dynamic members to their own cause. In this they were often successful. But, above all, the Kuomintang enabled them to spread wherever nationalist agitation was gaining ground. The Chinese Communist Party began its rise to power thanks to the forcefulness of the nationalist ideal.

7 The Chinese Communist Party from the First Congress to the Northern Expedition The Fourth Congress

The May 30th 1925 Movement

The vitality of the new Kuomintang, which now had Russian advisers and military aid as well as the communist contribution at its disposal, the social and economic changes that were slowly but steadily taking place, and wholehearted participation in the international incidents of 1925, all helped to bring about a rapid increase in the strength of the Chinese revolutionary movement. The Communist Party directed most of its efforts towards the workers, taking over the leadership of the trade unions almost entirely. Progress was slow at first, but the Party then gained ground during the vast campaign of anti-foreign agitation and strikes known as the May 30th Movement. Its membership figures show how much it owed to these particular events:

1921 (First Congress): 57 members
1922 (Second Congress): 123 members
1923 (Third Congress): 342 members
1925 (Fourth Congress): 980 members (Youth Corps: 2635 members)
1925 (November): 10,000 members (Youth Corps: 9000 members)
1926 (July): 30,000 members
1927 (April): 57,963 members (Youth Corps: 35,000 members)

The Communist Party increased tenfold in the six months between April and November 1925, and its membership was tripled during the following year. On the eve of the break with the Kuomintang, its membership had risen to nearly 100,000 (including the Youth Corps), while it exercised indirect control over 2,800,000 workers belonging to trade unions, and 9,700,000 peasants – though the latter were only loosely organized.

To understand the Communist Party's activities and success in the different sections of Chinese society (intellectuals, proletariat and peasantry), it must be remembered that an atmosphere of feverish excitement reigned in 1925, above all during the May 30th Movement, which set the May 4th 1919 Movement in motion once more, enlarging it considerably. Numerous local strikes had occurred in 1922 and 1923, sharpening the awareness of a section of the proletariat in the large towns. In 1922 the Hong Kong seamen went on strike in January, and in September a strike occurred in the K'ailan mines. The first strike began on 13 January and at first only affected part of Hong Kong's merchant seamen; it gradually spread to include all of them (6500 men) and 100,000 workers and office staff also joined in, paralysing the port of Hong Kong. It lasted until early in March and caused a considerable stir throughout the country in so far as it attacked the prestige of Great Britain, a supreme example of an 'imperialist power'. On the other hand, the strike at the K'ailan mines in north-east Hupei, for which the communists rightly or wrongly claim the responsibility, failed after three days (23-6 September 1922). The strike on the Kinhan (Peking to Hankow) railway, which began on 4 February, ended in tragedy. The railwaymen and repair-shop workers decided to combine several local unions in a single general union based at Chengchow. They met with opposition from the authorities and the strike that grew out of this situation resulted in considerable bloodshed. Marshal Wu P'ei-fu and his subordinate, the governor of Hupei, dealt out brutal repression; four strikers were killed, over a hundred were injured, and the leaders were either imprisoned or dismissed. The trade union movement, faced with the suppression meted out by the Chinese warlords, who were far more intractable than the 'foreign imperialists' of Hong Kong or Shanghai, went into hibernation for two years. It became active again in 1925, under cover of agitation, which was of nationalist rather than socialist content.

On 15 May 1925 a Chinese worker, Ku Cheng-hung, was killed by a Japanese foreman as a result of a quarrel in a Japanese textile mill in the Shanghai international settlement. After two weeks' agitation, the students decided to stage a large demonstration there on 30 May. Several were arrested, while others tried to seize a police station in Nanking Road. A British officer, fearing he was losing control of the situation, gave the order to fire; twelve demonstrators were killed and several dozen more injured. This incident immediately set off further demonstrations and strikes, which spread to several other towns. On 23 June Chinese demonstrators in Canton, including cadets from the Whampoa Military Academy, seemed about to attack the little island of Shameen, containing the French and English Concessions. Several shots were fired on the Chinese side, the French and English replied, and about fifty of the assailants were killed. Other less serious incidents occurred in Hankow on 11 June.

The events of 30 May and 23 June resulted in violent anti-foreign opinion. The Peking government itself gave its sanction to the xenophobic demonstrations, the Russians fanned the flames and Karakhan offered his condolences. A group of Chinese invaded their legation in Paris and tried to force the minister to sign an 'anti-imperialist' proclamation. The British, who bore the brunt of the accusation, laid the responsibility at the door of Moscow and the Chinese communists. The Communist Party could not fail to gain by this clumsy handling of the situation, and by the fact that the wave of patriotism had originated in a workers' conflict, with one of their own supporters as the victim.[1]

Nationalist feelings were encouraged enormously by the May 30th Movement; it lasted for several months, affecting areas where industry was already advanced, and those where foreign interests were most obvious. In the China of 1925 the foreign textile mills employed more workers than the Chinese mills and two-thirds of the cotton industry was concentrated in Shanghai and Tsingtao. The presence of foreigners was therefore not a mere abstract propaganda theme; demonstrators everywhere drew up clearly formulated demands: the departure of foreign troops, the end of foreign jurisdiction, the return of the concessions to China. This explosion of patriotic feelings spread even to the regions under the control of the 'tuchün' and contributed towards the triumphal aspect of the Northern Expedition when it was launched the next year, with revolutionary nationalism as its motto.

Communist Party activities and means of action

Communist publications

During the first period of the Party's history, communist publications developed considerably. The official organ was a weekly paper, *Hsiang-tao* (*The Guide Weekly*) published from 15 September 1922 onwards, first of

[1] The Central Committee of the Communist Party met in Shanghai on 28 May and decided that the demonstration on 30 May should be directed against 'imperialism'. It met again on 30 May and decided to call for strikes in industry, commerce and the university.

all in Shanghai and later in Canton, with first eight and then sixteen pages. From June 1923 onwards the magazine *Hsin Ch'ing-nien*, formerly edited by Ch'en Tu-hsiu, was considered as the Party organ. *Ch'ien-feng* (*Advance Guard*) was published in Canton from June 1923 onwards. Local papers and those with a specialized appeal also increased rapidly in number: *Chung-kuo Ch'ing-nien* (*Chinese Youth*), the official organ of the Socialist Youth Corps, *Chung-kuo Kung-jen* (the *Chinese Worker*), the official trade union paper, *Kung-jen chou-k'an* (the *Workers' Weekly*), the railwaymen's paper. Over a dozen weekly or monthly publications existed in 1926 at the time of the Northern Expedition and, although they could not circulate freely outside the nationalist zone, they were to be found in large towns and industrial centres in the Yangtze valley and North China.[1]

Cadres

The Party constantly needed more cadres, who were carefully trained in different sorts of schools: schools for agitators, where the length of the course varied between two weeks and a month, and regional schools turning out militants; these latter institutions were usually disguised under various different names.[2] The Party soon sent people to be trained in Russia, at the Toilers of the East University founded in Tashkent in 1920, and later to the Sun Yat-sen University opened in Moscow in January 1926, under the leadership of Karl Radek.

The Party and the intellectuals

Party activities in intellectual and student circles do not seem to have caused any anxiety to the leaders, who themselves came from the same background. The Chinese university world was one of such acute political consciousness that the Party had little difficulty in finding sympathizers and supporters. The situation ought to have been the same in literary circles, where some communist leaders, such as Ch'en Tu-hsiu, enjoyed considerable personal prestige. However, although Ch'eng Fang-wu and Kuo Mo-jo showed Marxist leanings as early as 1924, no authentic revolutionary literature appeared until 1930, when the League of Leftist Writers was formed; even then it was anti-Kuomintang rather than truly pro-communist (see Chapter 18).

[1] Cf. *Essays on the History of the First Civil War* (Hupei People's Press: in Chinese).

[2] For details on the syllabus in Communist Party schools, cf. C. Martin Wilbur and Julie Lien-ying How, *Documents on Communism, Nationalism and Soviet Advisers in China, 1918-1927*, Document No. 9. A few deserters from the Party have also described their experiences in the schools (cf. especially Sze-Ma Lu, *18 Years of Combat* (*Tou-ch'eng shih-pa nien*): in Chinese).

The Party and the workers

From the First Congress onwards, the Chinese Communist Party made a special effort to win over the workers. In August 1921 a Chinese Labour Union Secretariat was founded in Shanghai, led by Chang Kuo-t'ao. The aim of this organization was to give political instruction to the workers, and to create and develop workers' publications, while at the same time fighting for their liberation. Another paper, the *Labour Weekly* (*Lao-tung chou-k'an*), began publication alongside the few workers' papers created under the influence of the Marxist groups in 1920 (see Chapter 4).

The First Chinese Trade Union Congress, held in Canton on 1 May 1922 and organized by the new Secretariat, was attended by 162 delegates representing 270,000 union members in twelve towns; about 100 unions of different persuasions participated (Kuomintang, anarchist and purely professional unions). The congress expressed its opposition to 'imperialism' and 'feudalism', called for the eight-hour day and introduced the principle of mutual help in time of strikes. Finally, it put forward a sort of workers' charter, which, though inapplicable in China and clearly never destined to become law, nonetheless helped to awaken the workers. This successful First Congress, and the success of the Hong Kong seamen's strike in 1922 encouraged the Secretariat to stir up further agitation among the workers, and to develop the union organizations that supported it.

The failure of the strikes at the K'ailan mines and on the Kinhan railway, as well as those at the Hanyang ironworks (Hupei) and the Anyüan mines (Kiangsi), slowed down communist progress among the proletariat for a time.[1] However, if communist writers are to be believed, the number of unions and their membership continued to increase, especially in Shanghai: 1922, 24 trade unions (40,000 members); 1923, 50 trade unions (84,000 members); 1925, 100 trade unions (180,000 members).

The Fourth Congress of the Chinese Communist Party, held in Shanghai on 11 and 12 January 1925 (see p. 90), paid particular attention to labour movements and to the revolutionary role of the proletariat, whose special duty was stressed once more:

> In semi-colonial China the working class must not enter the struggle in its own interest alone, it must also take part in the national revolution. What is more, it must take over the leadership of the national revolution. . . .

[1] The ruinous, usurper's role supposedly played by Liu Shao-ch'i in the Anyüan strike, of which Mao Tse-tung was said to be the true organizer, was one theme of the attacks made on Liu Shao-ch'i by Mao's supporters during the Cultural Revolution.

> The national revolution cannot win unless the most revolutionary class shares in it with all its might and leads it.

Finally, the Party acknowledged that momentary difficulties existed, and advised its unions to establish closer contact with those of the Kuomintang.

The Second Trade Union Congress held in Canton from 1 to 7 May 1925 showed further progress, however, as it was attended by 281 delegates from 166 unions, representing 540,000 members. The disappearance of the Secretariat created by Chang Kuo-t'ao in 1921 and the creation of the General Labour Union in its place, was also a sign of progress. The General Labour Union was run by a committee of twenty-five members, with the seaman Lin Wei-min as its chairman; regional and local committees were set up in the provinces and large towns. The Second Trade Union Congress laid particular stress on the political role to be played by the unions, in the spirit of the Fourth Party Congress resolutions.

The events of 1925 gave a new impulse to the trade union movement. At the Third Congress, held in Canton in May 1926, 502 delegates were present, representing 1,240,000 members: more than twice the number of the previous year. The Northern Expedition was about to be launched, and the theme of the congress was, naturally enough, the union of all revolutionary forces and classes. Su Chao-cheng, another seaman and a communist, was elected Chairman of the Union's executive committee. When the Communist Party broke with the Kuomintang, the Chinese trade unions included 2,800,000 members. The communists' influence was stronger than any other (Su Chao-cheng represented them at a national level, Chou En-lai in Shanghai, and Liu Shao-ch'i in Hankow). The proportions assumed by the trade union movement, which now had groups of armed men at its disposal, was the factor that made Chiang Kai-shek decide suddenly to break with the Communist Party on 12 April 1927.

The Communist Party and the peasants

At the beginning and until the Fourth Congress at least, the Chinese Communist Party's interest in the peasants was limited; this was in character with the general trends of its predecessors, as well as with the movement itself, which was essentially attached to the big cities. However, the first rural base was founded at a very early stage, without any particular efforts from the Party, in east Kwangtung in the East River region, round the two coastal districts of Haifeng and Lufeng. The population of this area was used to emigration, and its constant contact with Hong Kong and Canton made it more receptive to new ideas than people elsewhere (see Map 2, p. 89).

In 1921 P'eng P'ai, a local agitator who had been educated in Japan, where he had been won over to Marxism, took the initiative of organizing the peasants and publishing a small local paper. In 1922 the movement had already spread to twenty-eight villages; in 1923 a quarter of the population of Haifeng and part of that of the neighbouring districts belonged to his peasant unions, which tried to reduce land rent and

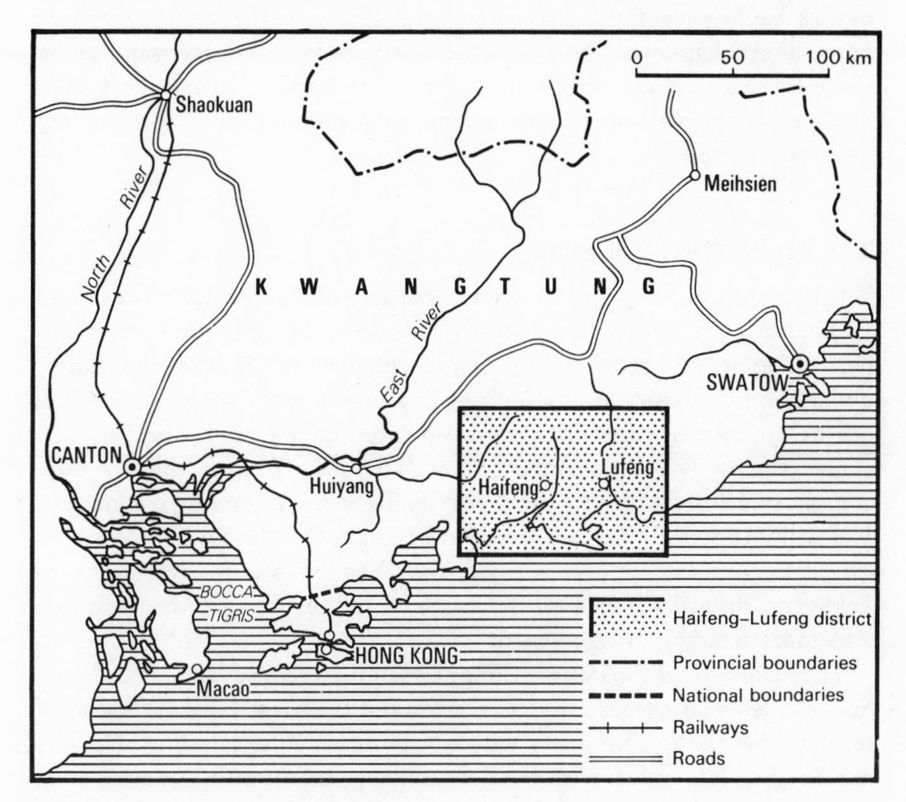

Map 2. The Haifeng-Lufeng region

abolish the *corvée* system. This movement, known as the 5 July 1923 Movement, failed temporarily, only to reappear in May 1925 and, above all, in May 1926; it then created peasant soviets in November 1927, which lasted until February 1928. P'eng P'ai, who was shot by the Kuomintang in 1929, was the forerunner of Mao Tse-tung in this respect, and his experiment is one of the most astounding and interesting episodes in the history of the Chinese revolution in the country districts.[1]

[1] Cf. 'The Eight Years' Struggle of the Hai-Lu-Feng Peasant Movement', in *Modern Historical Material,* No. 1 (Peking, 1955: in Chinese).

Communist activity among the peasants was carried out in the province of Kwangtung alone, under limited protection from the nationalist administration. At the First Congress of the Peasant Unions on 1 May 1925, official statistics give the figure of 200,000 affiliated members, belonging to twenty-two districts. 600,000 peasants belonging to sixty-six districts were represented at the Second Congress on 1 May 1926. These figures are low, even if they relate to the province of Kwangtung alone (36 million inhabitants). Not until the Northern Expedition began did the Communist Party, encouraged by a few of its leaders – particularly Mao Tse-tung – approach the peasants, and even then contacts were limited to certain places.

The Fourth Party Congress

The Fourth Congress of the Communist Party met in Shanghai on 11 and 12 January 1925. Twenty delegates attended, representing 980 Party members. A report was given on the general situation in China, as the leaders understood it. Struggles for power had begun once more among the northern generals, particularly between those belonging to the Fengtien clique (Chang Tso-lin) and the Chihli clique (Wu P'ei-fu); matters were complicated still further by the revolt led by Feng Yü-hsiang against Wu P'ei-fu, his superior. Feng occupied Peking on 23 October and a provisional executive government was formed. Sun Yat-sen was invited to go to Peking to discuss China's future. He accepted, expressing the wish that a national assembly be convened.

The manifesto of the Fourth Congress refers to these events. It endorses Sun Yat-sen's initiative, and draws up an outline for a social and political programme, though probably with no illusions. When dealing with the matter of collaboration with the Kuomintang, the Fourth Congress tried to keep to a middle path, while opposing the still present errors of the left and the right. The former consisted of basing all policy on the dictatorship of the proletariat and refusing all collaboration with the Kuomintang, and the latter – more widespread than the first – in working for the Kuomintang alone, leaving the Party's true aims to one side, at least in the immediate future. The error of today is an error of all time, as the Party put it, and in fact both these trends were to recur when the communists and the Kuomintang entered into collaboration once more during the Sino-Japanese war.

The Fourth Congress witnessed the first clear pronouncement by the Communist Party on the peasant question. It recognized the peasants' 'special' importance, and the 'need to encourage them as much as possible, and systematically, and to organize them everywhere, so that they enter the economic and political struggle step by step', otherwise, as the text of the resolution on the peasants puts it: 'Our hopes of seeing the Chinese revolution crowned with success, and of taking over the leadership of the national movement, will come to nothing.' As far as practical details were concerned, the above resolution attacked several abuses committed by landlords and advocated the creation of peasants' unions and a militia. However, it contained no clear-cut agrarian policy as yet, and even stated that reduction of land rent ought not to be left to the discretion of the unions.

The other resolutions passed by the Fourth Congress dealt with organizations. Finally, the Party's constitution was modified, allowing for a tightening of authority and enlargement at the lowest level, where three members were enough to form a cell, and five or more could organize a committee. The training of militants also received attention, and the duties of the various communist publications were redefined: *Hsiang-tao* (*The Guide Weekly*) was to deal with the main political interpretations, *Hsin Ch'ing-nien* (*Youth*) was to examine the concrete problems arising from the Chinese revolution, and *Chung-kuo Kung-jen* was to be adapted to the needs of the workers and peasants, and reflect their problems. The Fourth Congress was not a turning point in the history of the Party, but it did at least prepare the Party to fulfil its role when faced with the sudden development brought about by the great wave of nationalism of 1925.

8 The Collaboration between the Chinese Communist Party and the Kuomintang until the Eve of the Northern Expedition

The years of agreement

Generally speaking, good relations between the Chinese Communist Party and the Kuomintang lasted through 1924 and 1925 and until the *Chung Shan* Incident on 20 March 1926. From then on the situation worsened until the summer of 1927, when the final break came; even so, the process of deterioration was interrupted from time to time. The reasons for the original climate of understanding between the two parties were many.

The communists, thoroughly aware of their own weakness compared with the Kuomintang (a few hundred members, as opposed to two hundred thousand), were at first discreet and careful. The Nationalist Party had granted them many important posts, out of all proportion to their numbers, and they were anxious to avoid any shadow of suspicion as to their loyalty. They were also fully conscious of the precarious position of the government set up in Canton by Sun Yat-sen. Its very weakness compelled them to support it in order to secure a territorial base for the Chinese revolutionary movement as a whole, without which it could not develop in safety. In 1924 and 1925 it was constantly threatened by armed groups from within and without. In 1924 the government had to disarm the Canton merchants' militia, thus putting an end to a quarrel which had lasted for several months, during which the merchants, encouraged from Hong Kong and supported by the rebel General Ch'en Chiung-ming, almost triumphed. In February 1925 the nationalists again had to organize a large expedition against Ch'en Chiung-ming's forces, which were based on the East River area and preparing to attack the government. In two months Chiang Kai-shek occupied all the east of the province as far as Swatow and Ch'aochow. On 13 June 1925 troops from Kwangsi and Yunnan, led by Liu Chen-huan and Yang Hsi-min and amounting to almost 20,000 men, had to be disarmed as their loyalty could no longer be counted on.

In October and November 1925 another campaign was launched against Ch'en Chiung-ming, who had once more gained a foothold in Kwangtung. In fact, until these persistent rivals and uncertain allies had been eliminated, early in 1926, just before the start of the Northern Expedition, the nationalist government did not have full control over the whole of Kwangtung province.

The great 'anti-imperialist' and 'anti-feudalist' movements of 1925, and the strikes accompanying them, also brought the communists and the nationalists together momentarily; they shared the same hatred for the foreigners, it was in the interests of both to make skilful use of propaganda, and the united front seemed more important than ever. On each side, Sun Yat-sen and the Comintern managed to enforce collaboration on even the most reluctant elements of the Kuomintang and the Communist Party. Dr Sun's moral authority within his party was such that he could easily resist the attacks and insinuations of those who accused him of 'turning red' (chih hua). Borodin and the Comintern, for their part, acted with great circumspection and, on the whole, honesty. They exercised a moderating influence on the Chinese communists when necessary, and rejected some of their requests. When, for instance, the communists asked for arms for their supporters among the Kwangtung militia, they met with a refusal. In the same way, the Russian advisers restrained sections of the Kuomintang prepared to make war on Great Britain during the events of 1925.[1] Finally, for a long time they advised against the launching of the Northern Expedition, both because of the nationalists' lack of military equipment and men as compared with their adversaries, and also for fear of provoking a reaction from the Western powers; this prudence also served the cause of the Communist Party, which was not yet powerful enough to exercise any control over events.

There came a moment when the Northern Expedition, which had been planned for so long, seemed hardly necessary, for in the autumn of 1924

[1] In connection with this, see C. Martin Wilbur and Julie Lien-ying How, *Documents on Communism, Nationalism and Soviet Advisers in China*, Document No. 13, an interesting letter from Chiang Kai-shek to Galen.

the politico-military Chihli clique, led by Wu P'ei-fu and President Ts'ao K'un, who held Peking, was suddenly driven out of the capital by a rebellion instigated by one of its members, Feng Yü-hsiang, the 'Christian General'. This event promised to turn out differently from all similar ones preceding it, as General Feng, a picturesque giant of a man, who observed the utmost simplicity in his habits and dress, was also attracted by revolutionary and democratic ideas, and sympathized with the Soviet Union.[1] True to the traditions of Chinese warfare, Feng Yü-hsiang formed an alliance with Chang Tso-lin, although his instructions were to fight him. His former chief, Wu P'ei-fu, once ousted, was treated with supreme irony: he was appointed Agricultural Commissar of the distant north-western province of Chinghai. Ts'ao K'un was forced to relinquish office on 2 November.

On 24 November Marshal Tuan Ch'i-jui, former Prime Minister of the Anfu clique, accepted the title of Chief of Executive Power, and the new government proposed, with a doubtful degree of sincerity, to call a National Rehabilitation Conference in Peking, aimed ostensibly at demobilizing part of the armies and paving the way for the country's political reunification. These entirely new possibilities upset the plans of Sun Yat-sen, who had just announced, on 18 September 1924, that the Northern Expedition was about to be launched. The leader of the Kuomintang was invited to attend the conference; he accepted, leaving Canton on 13 November. After visiting Shanghai and Japan, he arrived in Tientsin, where he had to take to his bed; from there he was conveyed to Peking, where he died on 12 March 1925 of cancer of the liver.

His last act, apart from writing his political testament, was to address a message to the Soviet Central Executive Committee, written the day before his death, probably by Wang Ching-wei. As a document, it could have no political consequences. It deserves to be made known, however, because of its bearing on the history of the relationship between the two parties and because it is constantly quoted by the communists:

Dear comrades,

As I have an incurable illness, my thoughts turn towards you, towards the future of my party and my country. You are the leaders of

[1] General Feng was to remain an important figure on the Chinese political scene until his death in 1948. He was burned to death in the Black Sea on his return from a journey. He was the author of several interesting works on contemporary history (see Bibliography). Madame Feng (Li Te-ch'uan) is now in Peking and is Chairman of the Chinese Red Cross; before that she was for a long time Minister of Public Hygiene.

a free and great union of republics. This union is the true legacy left to all the oppressed peoples of the world by the immortal Lenin. Thanks to it, the unhappy peoples under imperialist rule will be guaranteed their freedom and will be emancipated from an international system founded on former slavery, conquest and selfishness.

I am leaving the Kuomintang as my bequest. I hope that the Kuomintang, while accomplishing its historic task of liberating China from imperialism, and of liberating other countries too, will be able to work in close cooperation with you. Fate is making me leave my work unfinished and entrust it to those who, while upholding the principles and teaching of the Kuomintang, will know how to organize our true comrades. For this reason I have given the Kuomintang the order to carry on the national revolutionary movement so that China may escape from the constraints of the semi-colonial condition forced upon her by imperialism. To this end, I have given the Kuomintang instructions to continue hand in hand with you. I am sure that your government will continue to help my country as in the past.

My dear comrades, as I leave you I hope with all my heart that the dawn will soon break, when the Soviet Union, her friends and her allies will welcome a strong, prosperous and independent China. In the great struggle for the emancipation of all the peoples of the world, our two countries will walk hand in hand to victory.

Your friend and brother,

Sun Yat-sen[1]

Sun Yat-sen's last wish was not to be realized; two years were enough to complete the break between the two revolutionary parties.

As far as the nation was concerned, all hopes of achieving the reunification of China by peaceful means quickly faded. A switching of allies followed; Wu P'ei-fu became reconciled with Chang Tso-lin again, while Feng Yü-hsiang withdrew, after dividing the zone under his control (the north-western provinces) between five of his subordinates. He then left for Russia, to examine the industrial development of the country – a variation of the accepted practice of taking a journey for the purpose of study indulged in by all Chinese politicians or generals wanting to retire temporarily from public life, or forced to do so. The situation became once more much as it had been in the previous autumn.

[1] Cf. Sun Yat-sen, *Selected Works* (Peking, 1957: in Chinese), p. 922. This text has now been engraved on a marble slab in the Pi Yün-Ssu Temple, where the body of Sun Yat-sen lay for several years before it was moved to Nanking.

The first storms

The disappearance of Sun Yat-sen was quickly followed by complications in the relations between the Communist Party and the Kuomintang, since the individuals and rival groups who inherited his authority held entirely different views on the subject. Two extremist currents and one representing a middle way existed within the Kuomintang. The highly conservative extreme rightist current was led by Hu Han-min, an old comrade of Sun Yat-sen and an excellent journalist. The leftist current was centred round Liao Chung-k'ai, another of Sun Yat-sen's former comrades.

The two leading figures of the Kuomintang after the death of Sun Yat-sen, however, were without any doubt Wang Ching-wei and Chiang Kai-shek; for twenty years they were rivals, though not always openly so, until Wang Ching-wei, in spite of his intellectual qualities and his career as a revolutionary fighter and terrorist, was driven to collaborate with the Japanese during the last war. At that time, it was generally understood that Wang Ching-wei was the true successor of Sun Yat-sen; he occupied all the important government and Party posts: he was Chairman of the Political Affairs Committee created by Sun Yat-sen on 11 July 1924, Chairman of the Military Council created on 6 July 1925 and, above all, President of the National Government, which on 1 July 1925 had replaced the former Military Government founded by Sun Yat-sen in 1922. Chiang Kai-shek, his opponent, had the support of the young army cadres whom he had trained or gathered about him at the Whampoa Military Academy, and he could also count on the loyalty of a large proportion of the army itself.[1] Both men were considered to have radical rather than conservative leanings, but their actions were governed above all by opportunism, and their temperaments and ambitions brought them constantly into conflict with each other; their behaviour towards the communists was no exception to this.

As early as the First Congress of the Kuomintang in January 1924 some of its members openly opposed the principle of collaboration with the Communist Party; the double political allegiance of communist members aroused still more violent opposition. The communists were reproached with intransigence in international affairs, which could well

[1] The biographies of Chiang Kai-shek and Wang Ching-wei, both central figures in the contemporary history of China, fall outside the scope of this book. Chinese sources can be consulted for information on the former (see Bibliography), and see also S. I. Hsiung, *The Life of Chiang Kai-shek* (London, Davies, 1948), and Hollington Tong, *Chiang Kai-shek* (T'aipei, 1953).

compromise the Canton government's relations with foreign powers from the outset, by adding another argument to normal hostility of the foreigners. Their social policy was naturally regarded with mistrust and considered liable to disturb the regime's economy. But the true basis of the anti-communist opposition was a strong nationalist feeling, which, by definition, could not ally itself with a movement whose obedience lay elsewhere. The nationalist argument gradually forced people of great personal merit, like Hu Han-min and especially Tai Chi-t'ao, both former members of the Shanghai socialist group, to become increasingly conservative. The latter, a journalist and lawyer by profession, was later to be one of the most important theorists of the Kuomintang; he was for a long time personal adviser to Sun Yat-sen and then to Chiang Kai-shek, before committing suicide in Canton in 1949, just before the continent was relinquished, a gesture true to the greatest traditions of the mandarins.[1]

The open hostility of a section of the Kuomintang towards the communists became apparent for the first time in a resolution passed by the Control Committee on 18 June. Proposed by Chang Chi, a former anarchist educated in France (see Chapter 3), it was based on several documents and articles from the communist press encouraging militants to work for their own cause, as well as that of the Kuomintang.[2] Chang Chi's resolution was laid on one side by Sun Yat-sen and the Central Executive Committee, which merely reaffirmed the duty of each member of the Kuomintang (including the communists) to comply with the Party's requests.

A serious incident occurred on 20 August 1925: Liao Chung-k'ai, then Finance Minister, was murdered. Liao was an ardent supporter of the alliance with the communists, who lost no time in laying the blame on their political adversaries. Hu Han-min was implicated in the affair through his brother Hu I-sheng, and had to leave Canton; strangely enough, he went to the Soviet Union, though possibly against his will.[3] The crime was never fully explained; it may have been a crime with no political motives, committed by a few individuals who were irritated by Liao Chung-k'ai's intransigence as Minister of Finance.

[1] The chief works of Tai Chi-t'ao, *The Philosophical Foundations of Sun Yat-senism* and *The National Revolution and the Kuomintang*, have not been translated.

[2] Chiefly publications of the Socialist Youth League (March 1924).

[3] Some foreign journalists claimed that he was seized in Shanghai and taken to Vladivostok.

The Western Hills Group

A few months later, the question of collaboration with the communists gave rise to a major crisis within the Kuomintang itself, almost splitting its ranks. On 23 November 1925 about ten important right wing members of the Kuomintang met in Peking to form a group. With an astute blending of romanticism and a sense of propaganda, they held their first meeting before the coffin of Sun Yat-sen, in the Temple of the Azure Clouds (Pi Yün Ssu) in the hills about 20 kilometres west of Peking. The group, soon to be known as the Western Hills Group, included Lin Sen, the future President of the Chinese Republic, Chang Chi, Chü Cheng, a lawyer who later became Chairman of the Judicial Yüan, Tsou Lu, Hsieh Ch'ih, etc. A resolution was quickly passed, demanding – among other things – the expulsion of the communists from the Kuomintang, and the departure of Borodin. When the resolution was rejected in Canton, the group set up a dissident faction in Shanghai and held what they claimed to be a session of the Central Executive Committee (29 March).

At roughly the same time another anti-communist group, led by Tai Chi-t'ao, was created in Canton. It proclaimed its opposition to the Shanghai group, which it considered reactionary and aimed at undermining the authority of Wang Ching-wei and Chiang Kai-shek, but it also demanded the communists' expulsion, in the name of the true thought of Sun Yat-sen. Its political position is summarized fairly accurately in the sentence attributed by Mao Tse-tung to one of Tai Chi-t'ao's partisans: 'Raise your left fist to knock down the imperialists and your right to knock down the communists.'[1] As the communists had created a Union of Military Youth, whose very name constituted a threat, Tai Chi-t'ao founded a Society for the Study of Sun Yat-senism, to thwart both the Union and young communists in general; Wang Po-ling, Ho Chung-han and Miao Wu were the best known of its members.

However, the Second Congress of the Kuomintang, over which Wang Ching-wei presided in Canton from 4 to 19 January 1926, revealed that the majority was in favour of cooperation with the communists. Out of a total of thirty-six members of the Central Executive Committee, seven communists[2] were elected by the 258 delegates present at the congress, and seven others – one of whom was Mao Tse-tung – were elected

[1] Mao Tse-tung, 'Analysis of the Classes in Chinese society', *Selected Works*, vol. I, p. 14.
[2] Lin Tsu-han, T'an P'ing-shan, Wu Yü-chang, Yang Pan-an, Yu Shu-te, Yun Tai-ying, P'eng Che-ming.

deputy members. Mao Tse-tung took over the Propaganda, although Wang Ching-wei was the titular head, T'an P'ing-shan remained in charge of Organization, and Lin Tsu-han took over Agriculture. The Kuomintang's different factions seemed to be in agreement once more.

The March 20th 1926 Incident

Less than three months later, another violent incident occurred, this time not within the Kuomintang itself, but between Chiang Kai-shek and the communists. It was known as the March 20th Incident, or the gunboat *Chung Shan* Incident; its consequences, particularly the resolution passed by the Kuomintang Central Executive Committee of 15 May, were to raise yet again the question of the conditions of the collaboration between the two parties. On the night of 18-19 March the gunboat *Chung Shan* (formerly the *Yung Feng*), commanded by a communist naval officer Li Chih-lung, who was also Assistant Director of the Naval Bureau, moored about 20 kilometres east of Canton opposite the Whampoa Military Academy, where Chiang Kai-shek was thought to be. The Generalissimo, who was in fact in Canton, called her back and had her commander arrested, in the belief (or pretended belief) that he had acted without orders, with the intention of seizing Chiang Kai-shek himself. During the night of 20 March at 3 a.m. Chiang Kai-shek had most of the communist cadres in the Academy, a total of twenty-five men, including Chou En-lai, either arrested or kept under close supervision, while the Soviet advisers were placed under house arrest. In Canton other arrests were made, the trade union headquarters were kept under a close watch and the strike pickets belonging to the Kwangtung–Hong Kong strike committees were disarmed.

No one was able to give a clear explanation of the affair. The nationalists claimed that the Communist Party, with the support of Kissenka, the temporary head of the Russian mission, had begun a campaign to discredit and threaten Chiang Kai-shek, whom they wanted to have eliminated, if not assassinated. The communists considered that the whole affair had been contrived by Chiang Kai-shek himself, helped by the Director of the Naval School, Ao Yang-ko, his sworn brother, who was also a member of the Society for the Study of Sun Yat-senism. Whatever the case may be, the March 20th Incident had far-reaching consequences. The first, which was unexpected, was that Wang Ching-wei retired. Irritated by the way in which Chiang Kai-shek had left him in ignorance of what was going on, the president of the national government temporarily abandoned his duties and, on a pretext of illness, left for France on 11 May. This decision left his rival a free hand for the first part of the Northern Expedition, and enabled him to bring a large section of the Kuomintang to accept right wing ideas and the principle of breaking with the communists.

The other consequence became apparent on 15 May when the Kuomintang Central Executive Committee held an extremely tense meeting, at which it was decided to limit the positions and the role of the communists in the Party and its institutions. Several special measures were adopted:

(*a*) The communists were asked to abide by the Three People's Principles.
(*b*) A complete list of the communists who were members of both parties was to be submitted to the Kuomintang.
(*c*) The communists were henceforth forbidden to take up leading posts in the Kuomintang or to hold more than a third of the administrative posts in the Party and the state.
(*d*) Members of the Communist Party were forbidden to form organized groups within the Kuomintang.
(*e*) Directives from the Comintern and the Communist Party were to be submitted for approval to a committee consisting of communists and members of the Kuomintang.
(*f*) Members of the Kuomintang were forbidden to join the Communist Party without first obtaining permission to leave their former party.[1]

The Communist reaction to the March 20th Incident and the events of 15 May was restrained, both in Moscow and in Canton. Borodin, on his return from Peking, proved to be 'conciliatory' and 'reasonable', in the words of Chiang Kai-shek himself. Moscow showed discretion. The revolutionary front continued. Chiang Kai-shek confirmed its existence once more, on a new basis; he was skilful enough to give way a little. The Society for the Study of Sun Yat-senism, whose extreme views might be an embarrassment to him, was dissolved, and a few communists were invited to take up their former posts once more. The Communist Party lost several important posts, however: Ch'en Kuo-fu replaced T'an P'ing-shan at the head of the Department of Organization of the Kuo-

[1] Chang Ch'i-yün, the nationalist historian, gives 5 July as the date on which most of the above measures were passed. They formed part of a resolution proposed by Chiang Kai-shek to the Central Executive Committee.

mintang, Mao Tse-tung was replaced by Ku Meng-yü in the Department of Propaganda, and Kan Nai-kuang took over the Department of Peasant Affairs from Lin Tsu-han.

It is hardly surprising that official historians today lay yet another charge against the memory of Ch'en Tu-hsiu, accusing him of 'capitulationism' once more. Although Ch'en Tu-hsiu did in fact write an article of conciliatory tone in the *Hsiang-tao* entitled 'The Canton Incident and the Unity of the Revolutionary Forces', his first reactions seem to have been violent, for he suggested to Moscow that the Communist Party members should withdraw from the Kuomintang and that the collaboration between the two parties should take the form of a mere alliance. His views were disapproved of and were even severely criticized by Bukharin.[1]

Later on, the Trotskyist opposition sharply reproached the Stalinist majority for the attitude of passivity and silence adopted by the Comintern in the March 20th affair.[2] It is, however, hard to believe, as official historians do today, that the Chinese communists could have won over the Kuomintang left wing and eliminated Chiang Kai-shek. In any case, the nationalist leader's success drew the majority of his party to his side, inclining the Kuomintang still further towards the bourgeois right wing; in short, it paved the way for the brutal show of force which was to take place during the following year in Shanghai, Wuhan and Canton.

The fact that the Northern Expedition was imminent probably explains why the collaboration between the two parties continued. The preparations for this great enterprise were under way. Power was handed over to the expedition's military leader, social problems were momentarily put on one side, the most redoubtable of the foreign powers were discreetly appeased, and negotiations were opened with the British on the subject of boycotting and the Hong Kong strike, both called off on 10 October 1926. On 1 July, the first anniversary of the formation of the nationalist government, Generalissimo Chiang Kai-shek sent a message to all his armies, announcing that the Northern Expedition had been launched. It was the beginning of a new and turbulent phase in the history of the Chinese revolution. This time its activities were to extend far beyond the limitations of the home base in Kwangtung and cover the whole of China.

[1] Cf. B. I. Schwartz, *Chinese Communism and the Rise of Mao.*

[2] See in particular Leon Trotsky, *Problems of the Chinese Revolution* (New York, 1932), pp. 221 and 347.

9 The Northern Expedition[1]

The armed forces involved

At the start of the Northern Expedition, the Kuomintang army was unquestionably loyal politically and its numbers, though inferior to those of its enemies, were large. The armies of its adversaries were modern as far as organization and arms were concerned, but they had inherited many of the failings of the old imperial armies.

Until the fall of the empire in 1911, the Chinese armed forces fell into two categories: the Manchu army, known as the Army of Eight Banners, which had degenerated to a certain extent since the eighteenth century, and the Chinese troops proper, known as the Army of the Green Standard. Pressure of circumstances had inspired a first attempt at modernization of the Chinese armed forces during the T'ai p'ing Rebellion. The inefficiency and lack of discipline of the imperial troops had led several senior civil servants to form provincial armies, based on the militia. The scholars in command of these peasant armies, which were carefully recruited and well treated, even gave them an education in morality and sometimes politics as well, based on the Confucian tradition. At the time, traditional values were used to fight the pseudo-Christian beliefs preached by the T'ai p'ing. The Huai Army created by Li Hung-chang, the Hunan Army created by Tseng Kuo-fan, and the Ch'u Army, all became great names, and some followed their former commanders when they moved to a new appointment. Thus the Peiyang Army, created by Yüan Shih-k'ai in 1902, the first army formed entirely along Western lines, was a descendant of the

1 See Map 3, p. 103.

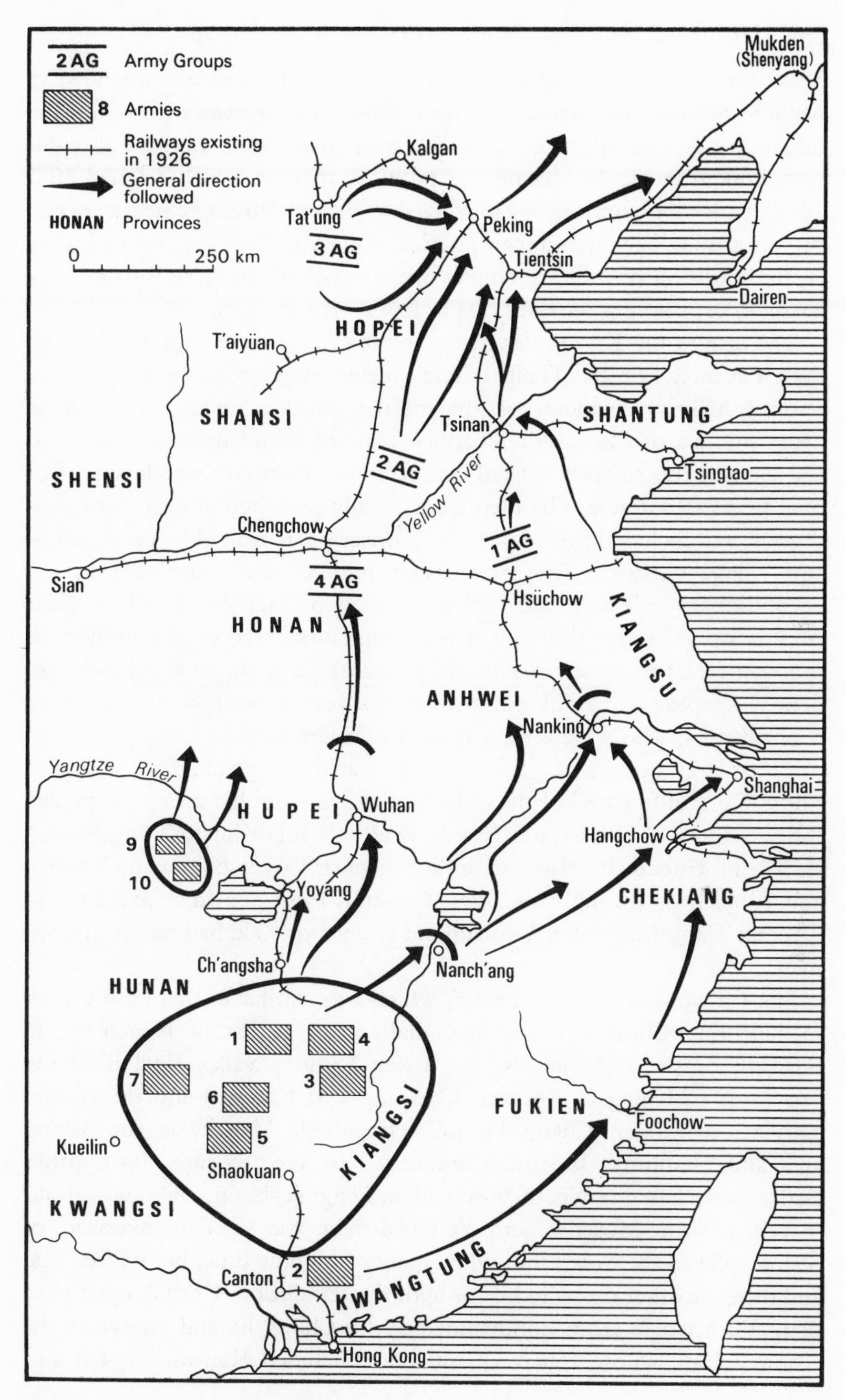
2 AG
Army Groups
8
Armies
Railways existing in 1926
General direction followed
HONAN
Provinces
0
250 km
Mukden (Shenyang)
Kalgan
Tat'ung
Peking
3 AG
Tientsin
Dairen
HOPEI
T'aiyüan
SHANSI
Tsinan
SHANTUNG
SHENSI
2 AG
Yellow River
Tsingtao
Chengchow
1 AG
Sian
4 AG
Hsüchow
HONAN
KIANGSU
ANHWEI
Nanking
Yangtze River
HUPEI
Wuhan
Shanghai
9
10
Hangchow
Yoyang
CHEKIANG
Ch'angsha
Nanch'ang
HUNAN
1
4
7
3
6
FUKIEN
KIANGSI
Foochow
5
Kueilin
Shaokuan
KWANGSI
2
Canton
KWANGTUNG
Hong Kong

Map 3. The Northern Expedition

Huai Army. The Land Army (Lu Chün) created in 1906 was intended to become the national army, but the military reform was affected by the temporary retirement of Yüan Shih-k'ai in 1908. After the 1911 Revolution, and in particular during the political anarchy which reigned after 1916, the local governors began to raise their own forces, which were real private armies, backing up their political influence. This was the beginning of the tradition of military cliques which marked the period from 1911 to 1928, or, it might almost be said, from 1911 to 1949.

The armies the Kuomintang was about to face were provincial rather than national armies. Their officers, often regular soldiers from the Paoting Military Academy or provincial military academies, but also as often soldiers of fortune or reformed bandits, could have no loyalty to the state, as this scarcely existed, and followed their commanders or their own personal interest. The men were usually recruited in very poor conditions, and included ruined peasants, conscripts recruited by press gangs, and village outcasts. They were poor fighters and went over to the revolutionary side with no difficulty when ordered to do so by their commanders. Lastly, although these troops numbered over 1 million altogether (ten times the revolutionary forces), each clique acted independently, keeping a careful watch over the rest as well as over its own subordinates, who were always ready to change sides.

Three large groups of warlords existed at the beginning of the operations. Wu P'ei-fu (head of the old Chihli clique) and his group controlled the provinces of Honan and Hupei, while his subordinate T'ang Sheng-chih held Hunan; he also had indirect control over Szechuan, Yunnan and Kweichow through his allies, General Yang Sen in Szechuan, and General T'ang Chi-yao in Yunnan and Kweichow. He had about 250,000 men.

Sun Ch'uan-fang and his group, which was similar to that of Wu P'ei-fu, held East China from the Shanghai region to that of Nanch'ang in Kiangsi, or, in other words, the lower Yangtze valley (including the provinces of Kiangsu, Anhwei, Chekiang and Kiangsi) and the coastal province of Fukien. Chang Tso-lin's clique held Manchuria, the Peking area and Shantung. Its forces amounted to 300,000 men. Two other leaders were based in North-West China: Feng Yü-hsiang, who was about to return from Moscow, and Yen Hsi-shan, the 'model governor' of Shansi, played their own individual games for some time, before first one and then the other threw in his lot with the revolution. Until August 1927 Feng Yü-hsiang's army, commanded by Lu Chung-lin and known as the Kuominchün, whose sphere of influence included Kansu, Suiyuan and

Chahar, held the Nank'ou Pass near the Great Wall, about 40 kilometres west of Peking, against Wu P'ei-fu and Chang Tso-lin.

The nationalist forces had grown rapidly. At the beginning of 1924 they did not exist, but by July 1925 they consisted of three small armies (40,000 men); by December of the same year these had become six armies (85,000 men). At the start of the Northern Expedition approximately 100,000 men were grouped in eight armies, including the Kwangsi and Hunan armies – the latter having come over to the revolutionary camp, led by its commander who had abandoned Wu P'ei-fu. Theoretically at least, each army consisted of three divisions of three regiments of 1620 men each, making a total of 14,580 officers and men to each army. The soldiers were carefully chosen and, thanks to the system of political commissars introduced by the Soviet advisers, they all were given a political training. Many students joined the army as fighters or as members of the propaganda machine. This homogeneous nucleus was quickly to be joined by sections from the northern armies rallying to the Kuomintang, and the nationalist army changed rapidly both in size and in character, while rivalries within the revolutionary ranks were also going to affect its zeal and purity. Lastly, the Russian advisers took a large part in staff work and their leader, General Vasili K. Blücher (alias Galen), was to make a great contribution to important decisions.[1]

At the beginning of July the battle order and strategic deployment of the nationalist forces was roughly as follows:

First Army: Commander, Ho Ying-Ch'in (in fact it was Wang Po-ling), Hengyang area in south Hunan (the 2nd Division was the only one in operation at first; the 1st and 3rd Divisions were guarding Kwangtung).

Second Army: Commander, T'an Yen-k'ai (in fact it was Lu Ti-p'ing). Political Commissar: Li Fu-ch'un, later Plan Commissar under the present regime. The Second Army was kept at Canton at first, and then sent to the Nanch'ang area (Kiangsi).

Third Army: Commander, Chu P'ei-teh (a former subordinate of Yüan Shih-k'ai). Its headquarters was at Ch'aling in east Hunan.

Fourth Army: Commander, Li Chi-shen (in fact the Fourth Army was commanded by Chang Fa-k'uei and, before him, by Ch'en Ming-shu). Many communists, among them Lin Piao and Su Yü, belonged to this army, and they were to rebel at Nanch'ang on 1 August 1927. The Fourth Army was at first in east Hunan (headquarters at Yuhsien).

[1] Blücher was to become commander of the Far Eastern Red Army, before he disappeared in 1938 during the great Russian Communist Party purges.

Fifth Army: Commander, Li Fu-lin, who was later to overcome the Canton Commune. The Fifth Army was stationed in south-west Hunan.

Sixth Army: Commander, Ch'eng Ch'ien, a native of Hunan who joined the present Peking government after having been a candidate for the Vice-Presidency of the central Nanking government in 1948. It was stationed in south Hunan. Lin Tsu-han (alias Lin Po-ch'ü), a leading communist, now dead, was Political Commissar.

Seventh Army: Commander, Li Tsung-jen. This army was composed of Kwangsi provincial troops, nominally included in the nationalist army; it operated in west Hunan, and had its headquarters at Yung-feng.

Eighth Army: Commander, T'ang Sheng-chih. This was an army of Hunanese which joined the revolutionary forces on the spot.

Although several units had communist commanding officers, like the Independent Regiment of Yeh T'ing, no distinct, entirely communist element existed in the nationalist army.

On 27 July the Generalissimo went to his headquarters at Shaokuan in north Kwangtung. By this time, the campaign had been under way for two weeks. During the first series of operations the revolutionary armies took the central provinces of Hunan, Hupei and Kiangsi; this step was completed before the end of 1926. A second series of operations began in the Nanch'ang area; by the next spring the armies had reached the lower Yangtze, in the region of Shanghai and Nanking. Then the front became stationary for a year, roughly along the line of the Yangtze, while a serious political crisis arose, which lasted until the end of 1927, and until the alliance between the Kuomintang and the Communist Party came to an end.

As early as 12 July 1926 T'ang Sheng-chih and the Eighth Army, with the support of the Fourth and Seventh Armies, entered Ch'angsha. From there the revolutionary armies advanced northwards towards Yoyang and P'ingchiang and a violent battle took place on about 25 August at T'ing Szu-ch'iao and Ho Sheng-ch'iao, on the road to the three towns which made up Wuhan (Hankow, Wuch'ang and Hanyang). Wu P'ei-fu, who was engaged in a vast campaign against Feng Yü-hsiang's troops, driving them out of Nank'ou as far as Chahar and Suiyuan, had left Hupei inadequately protected, and his personal intervention came too late to save the situation. Hanyang and Hankow were taken on 7 September, but the walled city of Wuch'ang put up a courageous resistance and did not fall to the assailants until 7 October after several violent attacks.[1] Meanwhile Chiang Kai-shek was trying to win Sun Ch'uan-fang over to the revolutionary cause, but the latter decided once and for all to turn against it. The nationalist armies managed to take Nanch'ang for the first time on 20 September, only to lose the town again almost immediately, winning it back again on 8 November. Canton now controlled the entire province of Kiangsi.

Further south, two divisions of the First Army, sent from Kwangtung under the command of Ho Ying-ch'in, occupied Foochow and Fukien, which were defended by a subordinate of Sun Ch'uan-fang. To the west of this vast area of operations, two armies, which had only recently been formed from local troops – the Ninth and Tenth Armies – controlled the boundaries of Hunan, Hupei and Kweichow. The nationalist army's numbers rose rapidly; five months after the campaign began, they totalled 264,000 men.[2] On 16 September Feng Yü-hsiang, just back from Russia, once more declared his allegiance to the revolutionary cause, and his return helped restrain the movements of Wu P'ei-fu and Chang Tso-lin. Early in 1927 operations began in Chekiang, whose capital, Hangchow, was occupied on 17 February, and in south Anhwei, whose appointed defender joined the revolutionaries without fighting at all. Finally, Shanghai was occupied on 22 March; the trade unions under communist leadership there rose up in arms for the third time when the advance of the nationalist armies was announced. Nanking was occupied two days later. Hofei, in north Anhwei, was taken on 18 March. Less than a year after the beginning of the Northern Expedition, the revolutionary troops held the Yangtze valley, and about ten provinces in South and Central China were under their control. The advance did not begin again until the following year. The nationalists reached Tsinan in Shantung on 3 May and Peking was taken without a fight on 4 May 1928 by troops from Shansi.

When Chang Hsüeh-liang, the son and successor of General Chang Tso-lin, whose train was blown up on 4 June 1928 (he died a few days later), rallied to the nationalist government on 29 December 1928, political unity of China was achieved once more, at least as far as appearances were concerned. Meanwhile, as has already been mentioned, a serious crisis had arisen, threatening the existence of the Kuomintang and provoking the Chinese Communist Party to resort to armed opposition for the first time, a phase which was to last for ten years, from 1927 to 1937.

[1] For a description of the atmosphere of the operations in Hupei and round Wuhan, see Kuo Mo-jo, *Revolutionary Spring* (in Chinese).

[2] S. I. Hsiung, *The Life of Chiang Kai-shek* (London, Davies, 1948).

The reasons behind the nationalist victories

The rapid success of the revolutionary armies was due first and foremost to the deep-seated lack of unity among their enemies. The northerners never managed to agree on a single line of action. On the contrary, each tried to turn his ally's momentary difficulties to his own advantage, at the risk of humouring the enemy. All through the years of complicated and baffling struggles, full of comic and dramatic situations, reversals and treasons, the golden rule followed by the 'tuchün' had been 'today's friend is tomorrow's enemy, and vice versa'. It remained valid in the face of danger, which in fact was only a mortal danger for those actually engaged in fighting. Spectacular changes of allegiance took place in favour of the revolutionary cause, the same thing happening when the Communist Party finally triumphed in 1949. The traditional Chinese concept of ideal warfare, in which diplomacy made battles useless, weighed heavily for a long time on the history of this century.

The revolutionaries made great use of military diplomacy both at the beginning and throughout the campaign. First of all, the Kwangsi armies (commanded by General Li Tsung-jen and General Pai Ch'ung-hsi) had to be won over to the Kuomintang, the defection of General T'ang Sheng-chih's Hunan army had to be achieved, a conspiracy was begun with some of the Szechuan military cliques to counterbalance the Yunnan troops preparing to invade Kwangsi, Sun Ch'uan-fang had to be restrained, an alliance was concluded with Feng Yü-hsiang, and lastly different groups had to be played off against each other wherever possible. With barely 50,000 men at their disposal, the nationalists took Central China, particularly Wuhan and Hupei, while Wu P'ei-fu was busy holding at bay Feng Yü-hsiang's 'bolshevik' troops threatening Peking. Sun Ch'uan-fang could easily have stood in the way of the nationalist advance northwards by advancing into Kwangsi himself, but he did not intervene and instead he negotiated with Chiang Kai-shek. When Sun Ch'uan-fang eventually decided to take action, the situation was different. The taking of Wuhan set free several nationalist armies and its impact on morale was such that it helped bring about the defection of several of Sun's subordinates, among them the governors of Chekiang and Anhwei and the Commander of the Fleet.

A similar situation arose several months later, when Chang Tsung-ch'ang, the governor of Shantung, intervened too late to save Shanghai and Nanking. Lastly, the governor of Shansi, Yen Hsi-shan, a long-standing enemy of Feng Yü-hsiang and an ally of the Kuomintang, took

Peking in 1928 in the name of the revolution. It is easy to imagine the degree of determination and eagerness to fight shown by the less conspicuous military leaders when one considers these well-known events. A few hard battles took place, but they were short and limited to small areas, and the advantage gained was lost through intrigue.

From 1927 onwards disagreements also plagued the nationalists, halting the Northern Expedition for nearly a year, and bringing the whole enterprise temporarily to the verge of disaster. All the nationalist generals were, however, kept in the same camp by their loyalty to the same patriotic and revolutionary ideals. None went over to the northerners, although they were ready to fight among themselves. The nationalist ideal, composed of legitimate aspirations – the desire to restore political unity, efface the 'national shame of the Unequal Treaties', and modernize the country – was a powerful influence among the merchant and industrial bourgeoisie and the young intellectuals. The personal prestige of Sun Yat-sen was identified with it and his death lent a quality of sanctity to the whole undertaking. The Kuomintang's enemies had nothing similar with which to answer these ideals; their sole support was founded on regionalism, the ignorant loyalty of their troops, or, from time to time, personal qualities shown by one or other of their leaders. The Kuomintang, helped by advice from the Soviet Union, also created a political propaganda organization particularly well suited to the times and the country itself. The Party's ramifications, whether working secretly or in the open, reached as far as the territories controlled by the 'tuchün', providing the means for a long-range psychological offensive.

Thanks to the corps of political commissars, which went down as far as company level, the nationalist army was an immense publicity machine on the move. The communists held many posts in this branch, some of them important. Whenever a locality was occupied, a meeting was held, posters were put up and the masses organized into taking part in various rallies. Later on, 'propaganda trains' with modern equipment – printing presses, a photographic unit, mobile exhibitions, etc. – travelled up and down the railway north and south of Wuhan. A volunteer corps was formed in Peking, consisting of 3500 students who tried to join the nationalist army and its political departments. It goes without saying that nationalist propaganda was aimed directly at the enemy's army, where it met with great success, particularly among the officers; the men in the ranks were generally passive and indifferent.

In their counter-propaganda, the northerners tried to pass the Kuomintang off as a Bolshevik party acting under Borodin's orders; they denounced its opposition to established Chinese traditions, in an effort to stir all conservative elements into reaction against it. But their time was past and once they lost military power they had no support left.

The nationalist troops were in many ways inferior to the northern troops, most of whom were experienced professional soldiers using better arms. But the nationalists were volunteers with a political education, kept under strict discipline and led by young officers from Whampoa, many of whom gave up their lives; they proved to be excellent operational units. Many of these qualities were lost when they were abruptly amalgamated with troops who until very recently had been enemies. The quarrels of the nationalist leaders were soon to make them lose sight of national aims. Up to the end of the Sino-Japanese war, two sorts of armies existed – those directly controlled by the central Nanking government, and the provincial armies, usually known as 'route armies'. The new order reigning in the Kuomintang did not extend to military any more than to political unity.

The Hankow and Nanking incidents

Given the prevailing climate of xenophobia, it was perhaps inevitable that the Northern Expedition should result in incidents involving foreigners. At the time, and sometimes even now, the most serious of them were attributed to the communists, who wanted to create difficulties between Chiang Kai-shek and the foreign powers, and to stress the fact that the Northern Expedition was both revolutionary and anti-Western. The earliest incident occurred on 3 January 1927. An anti-British demonstration was staged by the Hankow trade unions on the edge of the British Concession.[1] Anxious to avoid a repetition of incidents like those of 30 May 1925, the British left the responsibility for maintaining order to the Chinese themselves, and gave up their concession in the town of Kiukiang. Both concessions were officially given back to the Chinese by the agreements signed by Eugène Ch'en and O'Malley on 19 February and 2 March 1927. This affair, which had given rise to several minor incidents, ended in a great success in the diplomatic field, due to the realism and foresight of the British, always quick to sense the winners, and also to the efforts of the masses and the trade unions, which were led by the communists. In this last respect, it helped to strengthen the radical influence at Wuhan, causing

[1] Anti-British feeling was exacerbated by the Wanhsien incidents (August-September 1926) during which the Szechuanese troops and population had killed several Englishmen (the H.M.S. *Cockchafer* Incident); as a reprisal, British gunboats opened fire on the town and killed about a hundred of its inhabitants.

widespread anxiety among the foreign colonies, particularly those in Shanghai; reinforcements from both the army and the navy were sent there by the foreign powers.[1]

The Nanking incidents were more serious and involved several nations. On 24 March nationalist troops belonging to the Sixth Army, led by General Ch'eng Ch'ien, entered Nanking, which had been evacuated by the northerners. During the morning foreign establishments were attacked and looted – the British, American and Japanese consulates, Roman Catholic missions, and various commercial firms. About a dozen foreigners were killed; the rest, gathered as best they could near the town wall, were saved only by a barrage of fire from foreign gunboats. Chiang Kai-shek arrived soon afterwards to reduce the tension and reassure the foreigners. He took exemplary action against the 3rd Division of the Sixth Army, held to be responsible for the outburst; this unit was almost entirely disarmed, and thirty or forty men were executed. The Sixth Army returned to the Hankow area, where it was soon to throw in its lot with the Wuhan government.

Later on, however, the communist Political Commissar of the Sixth Army, Lin Tsu-han, was accused of having taken the initiative in the anti-foreign incidents. This seems surprising to say the least, for although the communists certainly nourished no special sympathy for the Westerners and their interests, intervention by the foreign powers might well compromise the success of their own revolutionary task, as well as that of the Kuomintang. Whatever the truth may be, the Nanking Incident certainly helped make Chiang Kai-shek and the Kuomintang right wing still more anti-communist. To avoid a confrontation near foreign concessions, it now seemed more important than ever to establish firm control over all the different forces at work in Shanghai – especially the trade unions and their armed pickets, known for their communist loyalties. This object in particular, combined with other, more far-reaching aims, was to result in a preliminary break with the Communist Party, depriving it of almost all possibility of action in half the territory recently won over for the revolution.

[1] The visit of Doriot, Mann and Browder – all notorious members of the international communist movement – to Canton and Wuhan, where they gave violent speeches and incited foreign troops (particularly the Indo-Chinese) to rebel, was a source of grave anxiety to foreign residents in China.

10 The April 12th 1927 Coup and the Expulsion of the Communists from the Kuomintang Right Wing and from the Nanking Government

Kuomintang: right wing versus left wing

Relations between the Kuomintang and the Chinese Communist Party were difficult after the March 20th 1926 Incident and the resolution adopted by the Kuomintang Central Executive Committee on 15 May of the same year, but they were maintained as far as possible for a year longer. After that, a double break took place; the first occurred on 12 April 1927 with the right wing faction of the Kuomintang represented by Chiang Kai-shek, who was shortly to set up a government in Nanking, and a further break occurred later in the same year, on 15 July, with the Kuomintang left wing, led by Wang Ching-wei who had returned from Europe, and was at the head of the Canton government, now transferred to Wuhan. This is one of the most obscure and complicated periods in the history of the Chinese revolution: intrigues between individuals and factions within the Kuomintang itself, bargaining between the governments and the provinces and with foreign powers, a working relationship between the Comintern and the Chinese Communist Party, the repercussions of the Stalin-Trotsky quarrel on Chinese affairs, all combine to shroud events in mystery which history is slow in dispelling.

Complications and difficulties appeared first within the Kuomintang. Chiang Kai-shek was given considerable power just before the Northern Expedition. His title of Commander-in-Chief gave him the control of all the nationalist armies, while his other posts – Chairman of the Government Political Council and of the Kuomintang Central Committee's Standing Committee, and head of the Department of Organization – gave him the control of the governmental and Party structures. In these various capacities Chiang Kai-shek was still subject to the Central Executive Committee of the Kuomintang. Many of the thirty-six members of this committee, elected by the Second Congress in January 1926, were his personal enemies. They included the seven communist members already mentioned (see Chapter 7) and radicals whose temperament or beliefs made them naturally hostile to the concentration of power in the hands of one man, or who were guided by their own personal ambition. They reappear throughout Chinese contemporary history; on the whole they behave as pure individualists, quick to criticize their own party in the name of liberalism, but remaining silent or acquiescent when faced with the worst authoritarian excesses on the part of the Communist Party. Among the best-known of them were Madame Sun Yat-sen, widow of the great Chinese revolutionary, sister of Madame Chiang Kai-shek and now Vice-President of the People's Republic of China; Madame Liao Chung-k'ai, widow of Sun Yat-sen's Minister of Finance who was assassinated in 1925; Sun Fo, Sun Yat-sen's son, who was so volatile and unpredictable that his political enemies called him Sun Wu-k'ung, after the monkey pilgrim in the famous novel *Hsi Yu Chi*;[1] Sung Tzu-wen (T. V. Soong), Sun Yat-sen's brother-in-law, much influenced by the United States; Eugène Ch'en, a Chinese lawyer from Trinidad of wholly English education; George Hsü (Hsü Ch'ien), another lawyer, formerly Minister of Justice and a Protestant bishop, whose violent character had become a legend; Ku Meng-yü, a professor; Ch'en Kung-po, a former communist; and Teng Yen-ta, one of Chiang Kai-shek's most trusted men, who had turned radical. In these circumstances, disagreements were virtually inevitable and owing to the rapid success of the revolution and the fierce competition between the two revolutionary parties, both going through a period of lightning development, the confrontation came earlier than might have been expected.

Future difficulties were foreshadowed by the meeting of the Central Executive Committee of the Kuomintang, held in Canton from 15 to 28 October 1926, and also attended by the Party's Provincial Bureau. The transfer of the capital to Wuhan was discussed, but above all – possibly at the instigation of the communists and particularly of Wu Yü-chang – resolutions opposing personal power were carried, while some members called for the return of Wang Ching-wei, who was still in France. The policy of collaboration between the Kuomintang and the Communist Party, already reaffirmed by the Second Congress, was approved once more.

[1] *Record of a Journey to the West* or *Monkey*.

The communists and their friends seem to some extent to have regained the influence which they had lost a few months earlier on 20 March and 15 May. Another disturbing event occurred on 13 December 1926, when a special committee was formed at Wuhan (Wuch'ang) made up of members of the government and of the Kuomintang Central Executive Committee. Sun Fo, T. V. Soong, Hsü Ch'ien and Eugène Ch'en were on the committee, whose function was to direct the affairs of the state and the Kuomintang until the official transfer of the capital from Canton to Wuhan. Hsü Ch'ien was chairman and Borodin was adviser; the committee soon came into conflict with the Commander-in-Chief and, if the latter is to be believed, began a secret campaign to discredit him.

A primary source of difficulty was the question of the general direction to be taken by military operations, now that Chiang Kai-shek had abandoned his advance northwards and decided first of all to rid himself of Sun Ch'uan-fang who held the lower Yangtze valley and would have been a dangerous threat to his communication lines. Another disagreement arose over the choice of capital, for the Generalissimo wanted Nanch'ang, where his headquarters were, made a provisional capital. The special committee, basing their case on valid geographical reasons, wanted Wuhan to remain the seat of government; the communists, who for their part counted on the support of the large local proletariat, were bound to agree. Chiang Kai-shek went to Wuhan (Hankow) and stayed there from 11 to 18 January 1927, trying to win the committee over to his point of view, but in vain. Lastly, several financial and administrative questions gave rise to conflicts between the government and the Commander-in-Chief, as is inevitable in such circumstances.

A *de facto* territorial division gradually developed from 1927 onwards: Hunan, Hupei and later Kiangsi obeyed instructions from Wuhan, whereas Fukien, Chekiang, Anhwei, Kiangsu and Kwangtung obeyed the Generalissimo. Differences in the social and political climate of the two zones became more and more apparent. The Generalissimo suppressed disorder, and did his best to avoid difficulties with the foreigners, whereas the Wuhan government pursued or allowed a radical policy, tolerating excesses committed by the masses, and giving the communists a free hand with their propaganda and their workers' and peasants' organizations. Although the social disturbances had died down, and the Hankow and Kiukiang incidents with the British had ended happily, the more moderate sections of the population and the bourgeoisie were uneasy, particularly as trade union power was developing rapidly. The Hankow union, where the former President of the Republic, Liu Shao-ch'i, played an important part, had 300,000 members two months after the occupation of the town. Union membership in Hunan increased rapidly from 50,000 to 150,000.

At the same time the peasant associations were also growing in numbers and in confidence. The communist historian Hua Kang states that in November 1926, 1,071,137 peasants in Hunan belonged to an organization, and that this figure had increased to almost 2 million by January 1927. Another historian (Ho Kan-chih) mentions the existence of peasant associations in fifty 'hsien' (districts) in November 1926, with a total membership of 1,367,000. The Wuhan government did not have the peasant movements fully under control, and some excesses were committed. A situation of anarchy developed in some areas and the legal decision, taken in Canton, to lower the land rent by 25 per cent, was often flagrantly ignored. In some places the administration ceased to function altogether and the peasant associations represented the sole organized power. It is hard to assess the real power and extent of these agrarian movements. Later on the communists accused their Secretary-General, Ch'en Tu-hsiu, of failing to encourage their existence, of ignoring those that had grown up, and even of thwarting them by complying with the 'reactionary' measures of the Wuhan government; this in itself implies that they were limited in their scope.

Mao Tse-tung and the peasants

Mao Tse-tung now began to make a name for himself through his interest in the peasantry as a revolutionary force.[1] He was one of the few communist leaders to come of a peasant family and, for a time (1925-6), he was in charge of the National Peasant Movement Institute, created in July 1924 by the Kuomintang in Canton,[2] before taking over the responsibility for questions relating to the peasants within the Communist Party and becoming the Secretary-General of the National Peasant Association at Wuhan.[3] All this led him to make a close study of reactions in the rural areas to the Northern Expedition. His views are to be found in the pamphlet entitled *Report on an Investigation of the Peasant Movement in Hunan*. This document is the result of work carried out from 4 January to 5 February 1927 in five 'hsien' in Hunan province: Hsiangt'an, Hsianghsiang, Hengshan, Liling and Ch'angsha. It was written in March and published shortly afterwards.

[1] See Chapter 20 for an account of Mao Tse-tung's early years.

[2] A museum has been opened on the site of this Institute, where from March 1926 Mao Tse-tung taught the sixth class, consisting of 327 pupils.

[3] Ho Kan-chih, *A History of the Modern Chinese Revolution* (Peking, 1959).

The *Investigation* seems to prove that at the beginning of 1927 the peasant movement had not yet become widely generalized throughout Hunan, although the province had been conquered six months before, but that it had great possibilities.

> In a very short time, in China's central, southern and northern provinces, several hundred million peasants will rise like a mighty storm, like a hurricane, a force so swift and violent that no power, however great, will be able to hold it back. . . . There are three alternatives. To march at their head and lead them? To trail behind them, gesticulating and criticizing? Or to stand in their way and oppose them? Every Chinese is free to choose, but events will force you to make the choice quickly.[1]

Events were to show that these vigorous words had only a local and momentary significance, but they faced the Communist Party squarely with the question of the use of the peasantry as the main revolutionary force, and Mao Tse-tung was in fact to save his party twice over, thanks to the peasant force once it was militarized. At this particular moment, Mao Tse-tung not only asked the question, but gave a categorical reply, first of all excusing and approving excesses committed by the peasants in the name of the revolution:

> A revolution is not a dinner party, or writing an essay, or painting a picture, or doing embroidery; it cannot be so refined, so leisurely and gentle, so temperate, kind, courteous, restrained and magnanimous. A revolution is an insurrection, an act of violence by which one class overthrows another. A rural revolution is a revolution by which the peasantry overthrows the power of the feudal landlord class.[2]

Mao Tse-tung justifies the excesses the first results obtained, listing 'fourteen great achievements' ranging from the elimination of the political and economic tyranny of the landowners and gentry (tu-hao and lieh-shen) to the changing of habits and customs and the practice of a system of mutual help. Lastly, though under no illusions, he urged the government and Chiang Kai-shek to give their approval to the 'revolutionary' action undertaken by the Hunan peasants. The rightist leaders already seemed to him to be afraid of the revolution, although constantly talking about it; he was reminded of the pointed fable of the legendary figure, Sheh Kung, who loved dragons so much that he had them carved all over his weapons, his possessions and his house, but fled, terrified, when a real celestial dragon came out of curiosity to look round it: 'To talk about "arousing the masses" day in

[1] *Selected Works*, vol. I, p. 23. [2] Ibid, p. 28.

and day out and then to be scared to death when the masses do rise – what difference is there between this and Lord Sheh's love of dragons?'[1]

The crucial period of the crisis which arose between the government, which had been based in Wuhan since 1 January, and the Generalissimo, whose headquarters were to be Nanch'ang for a few weeks more, could be said to have begun on 10 March 1927. On that day, Chiang Kai-shek made a violent speech against the Wuhan section of the Kuomintang, and Hsü Ch'ien in particular. He also made his position clear with regard to the communists, whom he humoured and threatened simultaneously:

> I have never intended not to cooperate with the communists. In fact, I can claim to have brought them into the Kuomintang. . . . The communists have now reached the zenith of their power and arrogance; if their activities are not checked, they will bring disaster upon the Kuomintang. . . .
>
> I must say again that I am not opposed to the communists, I appreciate their support and sympathy, but I advise them not to take advantage of their influence in the Party to oppress the moderate elements of the Kuomintang. If a break were to come about, the revolution would inevitably be weakened.

The Wuhan government was quick to reply, for the Third Session of the Second Central Executive Committee, held at Hankow from 10 to 17 March, provided the opportunity. During this session the Kuomintang left wing and its communist allies passed several resolutions showing their mistrust of the Commander-in-Chief, depriving him of almost all his special powers and undermining his personal status in the Party. Chiang Kai-shek was dismissed from the post of Chairman of the Political Council, the highest government organization. A bureau with seven members was created to replace the post of Chairman; it included Wang Ching-wei, Sun Fo, Hsü Ch'ien, Ku Meng-yü, T. V. Soong, T'an Yen-k'ai and T'an P'ing-shan, who was a communist at that time. Chiang Kai-shek did not belong to it. A military council was also created once more, to replace the former one abolished just before the outset of the Northern Expedition. It supervised all action taken by the Commander-in-Chief; at least six of its members had to belong to the Central Executive Committee, and the rest (at least three and at most seven) could be generals. From now on Chiang Kai-shek was to be kept firmly in hand by this committee, of which he was simply a member, while Wang Ching-wei supplanted him – theoretically – in all the important posts in the Kuomintang, including

[1] Ibid., p. 56.

that of Organization, on which his authority was founded. His humiliation was completed by a circular issued to Kuomintang members during the session of the Central Executive Committee, voicing with the utmost insolence the Committee's mistrust of the Generalissimo:

> Since the beginning of the Northern Expedition, all military, political and Party matters have been concentrated in the hands of one man. This means that the Party has been unable to carry out the administration, which has been conducted solely by military organizations. A system like this has many faults. Not only does it protect useless and corrupt elements in the Party, but it also attracts bureaucrats, merchants and other opportunists to the Party. Dictatorship and military autocracy are the result. . . .

The communists were rewarded for their policy. They won the chairmanship of the Political Council, to be held by T'an P'ing-shan,[1] and two ministerial posts: T'an P'ing-shan was appointed Minister of Agriculture, and Su Chao-cheng Minister of Labour. Several other measures reinforced the cooperation between the Kuomintang and the Communist Party in the administration as well as in the realm of revolutionary activity; the anti-communist measures passed on 15 May 1926 were virtually annulled.

Chiang Kai-shek was not one to remain unmoved by the loss of power and the consequent threat to his own personal future. Nor was the Kuomintang right wing going to accept without protest the increasingly radical trend followed by the Wuhan faction. Yet relations were not openly broken off until a few weeks after an attempt to form an agreement with Wang Ching-wei, who arrived in Shanghai from Europe on 1 April 1927. The city had been occupied by nationalist armies a few days before, and Chiang Kai-shek and Wang Ching-wei had several talks there between 1 and 6 April.

The conversations between the two nationalist leaders seem to have centred round two main themes – a bringing together of the two different groups within the Party, and the policy to adopt as far as the communists were concerned. They seem to have achieved a result, temporarily at least, on the first point. Chiang Kai-shek gave implicit acknowledgement to the authority of the Wuhan government, though he had never openly refused to acknowledge it, in a telegram circulated on 3 April. Wang Ching-wei,

[1] When expelled from the Communist Party in 1927, T'an P'ing-shan founded the Third Party, and then went over to the Kuomintang, which he left in 1947 to join Li Chi-shen and the Revolutionary Kuomintang. In 1949 he was a delegate at the Peking Consultative Assembly and is now a member of the Attorney General's Office, though he has not been re-admitted to the Communist Party.

for his part, seems to have agreed at one point to allow the session of the Central Executive Committee planned for 15 April to be held at Nanking, and to have considered the possibility of withdrawing the decisions taken a month earlier regarding Chiang Kai-shek. As far as the communists were concerned, if the historian T'ang Liang-li (one of Wang Ching-wei's most loyal supporters) is to be believed, the latter refused to agree to a change in policy unless the approval of the Central Executive Committee or a National Congress of the Party was obtained beforehand. This may well have been his attitude, for he had been abroad for over a year and had not yet re-established contact with the government organizations and those of the Wuhan party. As his position was reinforced by a majority in the Central Executive Committee, after the 10 March session, he clearly had nothing to gain by committing himself to any premature concessions to the Generalissimo's policy.

However – and this is important – on 4 April Wang Ching-wei and Ch'en Tu-hsiu, who was also in Shanghai, signed a declaration stating once more the principle of cooperation between the two parties, and silencing rumours of a communist *coup* or an anti-communist purge:

> We hereby declare that the Communist Party frankly and honestly recognizes and acknowledges that the Nationalist Party and the Three People's Principles laid down by our late leader, President Sun Yat-sen, are the central spirits of the Chinese Nationalist Movement. Only those who are opposed to the progress of the movement and who seek to bring about the downfall of the Kuomintang and the elimination of the Three Principles will think of the split. . . .
>
> According to the constitution of the International Communist Party, the membership qualification is confined to the non-possessing classes. This principle already has been adopted and enforced in the Union of Soviet Socialist Republics. The question now arises as to whether the situation which exists in one country, with its economic, social and political conditions, will be suitable in another and whether the same principles enforced in one country should and can be applied to another. Unlike other people, the Chinese are an oppressed race, and, therefore, in China a union is needed not only of the non-possessing classes but of all oppressed people in the revolutionary fight and in the struggle against the counter-revolutionaries. . . .
>
> Some people allege that the Communist Party is about to organize a labour government for the purpose of destroying the nationalist army and to attack the foreign settlement and the French Concession

> of Shanghai in order to bring about international complications. Others allege that the Kuomintang military leaders will soon disarm the uniformed pickets and drive the communist members from the Party. . . .
>
> The highest committee of the Kuomintang has formerly notified the world that the Kuomintang will not, at any cost, destroy the labour unions or drive the communist members from the Party, as the latter are friendly disposed towards them. . . . On the other hand, the communists love order and peace just as does any other party or person, and they have strongly supported the policy of the Nationalist government with regard to the rendition of the foreign concessions and they still are strongly of the opinion that these should be taken back by peaceful negotiations rather than by force. . . .
>
> The General Labour Union of Shanghai have also defined their aims and made a definite statement to the effect that they will make no attempt to attack the settlement or the French Concession. They go further by saying that they welcome the cooperation of other classes, apart from the labourers, in the administration of local affairs. In face of these facts, therefore, there is no ground for the counter-revolutionaries and imperialists to spread rumours.[1]

Although this declaration may be considered to have helped Chiang Kai-shek by lessening the mistrust of the pro-communist trade unions he was going to disarm and dissolve, it also convinced him that Wang Ching-wei would never consent to a break with the Chinese communists and Moscow. He had to act quickly.

Although the reverse might be expected, communist historians were to deal severely with Wang Ching-wei, accusing him of entering into a secret agreement with Chiang Kai-shek to prepare for the liquidation, then imminent, which took place on 12 April. No proof of such double-dealing exists. On the contrary, during the weeks that followed, Wang Ching-wei and the communists demonstrated side by side against Chiang Kai-shek and the Kuomintang right wing. The excesses and clumsiness of the Chinese communists and the Comintern combined were needed to make Wang Ching-wei also decide to undertake a purge, which in any case proved to be much less drastic than that of his rival.

The power of the Shanghai trade unions

At dawn on 12 April 1927 General Chiang Kai-shek had the pro-communist trade unions in Shanghai disarmed; this act of violence was to complete

[1] Cf. *The North-China Herald*, 9 April 1927.

his breaking off of relations both with the Communist Party and with the Wuhan government and Wang Ching-wei.

Since the creation of the first trade union secretariat in Shanghai by Chang Kuo-t'ao in 1921, the labour movement had been steadily developing and improving its organization; furthermore, Shanghai contained over half the Chinese industrial proletariat. During the Northern Expedition the trade union movement, which had distributed arms secretly to several hundreds of its supporters, was considered strong enough by its leaders to try on three different occasions to stage a rising and take the town. The first attempt, on 23 October 1926, coincided with the revolt of one of Sun Ch'uan-fang's subordinates. On 16 October General Hsia Chao, the governor of Chekiang, announced that he was going to take up the revolutionary cause and marched on Shanghai, where he was to be supported by a movement led jointly by Kuomintang elements under Niu Yung-chien (3600 men, 500 of whom were armed) and communist elements (2000 men, 130 of whom were armed). But when he got to within about 30 kilometres of the town, Hsia Chao was defeated, arrested and put to death. In spite of this, the rising began in several parts of Shanghai on the afternoon of 23 October, but it failed completely, being inadequately prepared and badly carried out. The next day the trade unions had to withdraw their order to strike, and give up the fight. About a dozen communists were killed in attacks on police stations and about a hundred were arrested. The second attempt, led by Li Li-san, Chao Shih-yen, Lo I-nung, Ch'ü Ch'iu-pai and other trade union leaders, was a more serious one. It began on 19 February 1927, when revolutionary armies from Nanch'ang occupied Hangchow, the capital of Chekiang. On the first day, 150,000 workers stopped work in reply to an appeal from a strike committee. They were followed by artisans, office workers and tradespeople. The number of strikers rose to 275,000 on the second day and 350,000 on the third, according to the communists, though the local foreign press gave the figure as 120,000. On 22 February an attempt was made to turn the movement into an insurrection and a temporary revolutionary committee was formed. For several hours the rebels gained control of certain areas in the Nanshih and Chapei districts. Two rebel gunboats gave them support, briefly shelling the Shanghai arsenal. But the local commander, General Li Pao-chang, reacted vigorously, beheading and shooting several rebels in the street to serve as an example. The uprising had to be abandoned and the order to strike withdrawn. The trade unions, now accused by official historians of failure to win over the soldiers, and above all of failure to mobilize the population, had 40 of their number killed and 300 taken prisoner.

The third attempt, which took place a month later, on 21 March, was to be successful. Nationalist troops, commanded by Pai Ch'ung-hsi, reached Lunghua in the western suburbs of Shanghai. They halted there while Chiang Kai-shek, in his anxiety to avoid any incidents near the

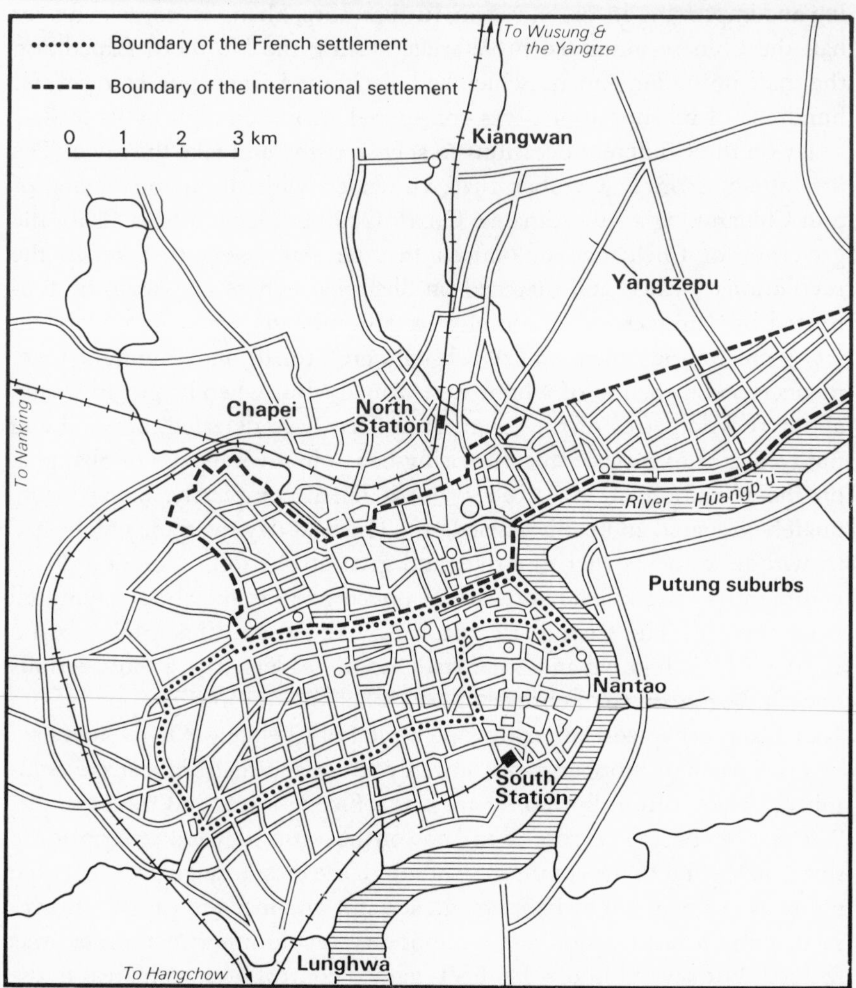

Map 4. The city of Shanghai

foreign concessions, carried out patient negotiations to obtain the withdrawal or the support of the northern troops commanded by General Pi Shu-cheng. The Shanghai trade unions, led by Chou En-lai, Lo I-nung and Chao Shih-yen, unwilling to wait for the end of the negotiations, staged a strike, which began with the railwaymen and eventually included

800,000 people. Several street battles occurred on 21 and 22 March, in which the rebel losses were 200 killed and 1000 wounded. The northerners, their communications with Nanking threatened by Pai Ch'ung-shi, withdrew, and by 22 March Shanghai was virtually in nationalist hands.

The communists tried to take advantage of their trade union victory straight away, for the military and political power of the unions had been strengthened. On 29 March they formed a temporary town council with nineteen members, though they were careful to offer the chair and several seats to non-communists, who refused them. The communists tried to appear moderate, avoiding anti-foreign incidents, and doing their best, as the manifesto signed by Wang Ching-wei and Ch'en Tu-hsiu on 5 April proves, to prolong a collaboration from which they stood to gain, but all in vain. As Commander-in-Chief, Chiang Kai-shek could not tolerate the presence of any other power in Shanghai, particularly when that power was armed and claimed to have the support of a large section of the population. He had once more had occasion to judge the extent of the young Communist Party's power; the clash was now inevitable and imminent. The action taken by Chiang Kai-shek and the Kuomintang right wing against the communists was not restricted to Shanghai alone, and was carried out after extensive political preparations.

The communists claim that the nationalist Commander-in-Chief had begun careful preparations for the break between the Kuomintang right wing and the Communist Party some time before, in his headquarters at Nanch'ang. This being so, they have tried to collect every possible proof of premeditation on the Generalissimo's part. The legitimate reassurances he gave to the foreign powers worried about their own subjects and their interests are interpreted as shameful compromises with 'imperialism', damaging the cause of the Chinese revolution. Chiang Kai-shek's relations with the Shanghai industrial and merchant bourgeoisie, who had to be persuaded to help finance the Northern Expedition, are said to have had the sole aim of fixing the price of the blood shed by the workers who fell on 12 April.[1] Lastly, the fact – whether true or false – that Chiang Kai-shek belonged to secret societies in Shanghai (the Green and the Red), which did in fact provide information and help in his undertaking, was also denounced with the utmost violence.

[1] Chiang Kai-shek is said to have received 15 million yuan in this way before the formation of the Nanking government, and 30 million immediately afterwards.

April 12th 1927

On 2 April, at Chiang Kai-shek's instigation, several members of the Kuomintang Control Committee, one of them Wu Chih-hui, called together those of their colleagues present in Shanghai (eight out of a total of twenty) to discuss the purging of the party. Theoretically, the purge was to affect landlords and gentry who opposed the revolution, and the many opportunists which the Northern Expedition had attracted, but it was directed above all against the communists; Wu Chih-hui's report to the meeting made no secret of this:

> ... Borodin uses particularly loathsome methods to provoke and divide. Outwardly, he is very friendly, but this façade is the one which their training gives to both Russian and Chinese communists. They are extremely affable in their social dealings and their speech. When speaking of their relations [with us], they profess solidarity, but in action they are evil and harsh. Deceit is the first verse of their gospel.

On 5 April it was decided to carry out a purge and a special committee was formed by Teng Tse-ju and Chang Hsi-ming. On 10 April a decree was passed giving effect to various new rules: the suspension of applications for membership of the Party, the renewal of membership subject to the result of an enquiry lasting three months, and a requirement that each Party member should give a report on his political activities to his home branch every two weeks.

The decree of 10 April furnished the Generalissimo and the Kuomintang with a legal cover for their anti-communist activities in all the provinces under their control. As far as Shanghai was concerned, the disarming of the workers' militia had been prepared by a series of special measures. On 6 April all armed groups, whoever they might be, were placed under the control of the military authority, under pain of being considered rebels and treated as such. On 8 April a Shanghai Provisional Administrative Committee was formed, to eliminate the temporary town council created by the communists. Then on 11 April the Commander-in-Chief gave a secret order to disarm the pro-communist trade union pickets, in all 2700 men. The operation began at 1 a.m. the next morning and was carried out with the help of non-communist trade union members, members of secret societies, and possibly of individuals from the town's underworld. All dressed in blue trousers and wearing a white arm-band, they attacked the picket guards. When the communist unionists refused to surrender their arms, General Chou Feng-ch'i's troops, newly won over to the revolution, intervened to maintain order. Scattered fighting continued throughout the day on 12 April, resulting in 120 killed and 180 wounded among the communist unionists; their headquarters at Chapei was occupied and turned over to the new trade unions. The general strike called the next day was obeyed by about 100,000 workers only, and was a failure. A demonstration, which took place in front of the headquarters of the 2nd Division of the Twenty-Sixth Army, Paoshan Road, ended in gunfire which killed or wounded about 100 people, while ten more were killed in the southern town.

The trade unions called off the strike on 14 April and the purge went on until the following day. The official communist figures for the April 12th Incident stand at 300 dead and 5000 missing. Among them were many leading communists and men of promise: Ch'en Yen-nien, former Party Secretary for Kwangtung and one of Ch'en Tu-hsiu's sons; Wang Shu-hua, Chairman of the Trade Union Federation; and Chao Shih-yen, former Party Secretary in France and Li Ta-chao's collaborator. Chou En-lai, who was one of the leaders at that time, succeeding in escaping.

Although the liquidation of communist cadres and trade unionists was coming to an end in Shanghai, it still continued in the provinces, where in places it had begun before 12 April. The leader of the unions in Kanchow in Kiangsi (Ch'en Tsan-hsien) had been assassinated on 11 March, while the union office at Kiukiang on the Yangtze had been closed on 17 March, and that at Hangchow in Chekiang on 29 March. On 3 April a movement to help the Generalissimo and the Kuomintang had been launched more or less everywhere; its slogan was 'Uphold the Party, protect China' (Yung Tang Hu Chiang). In Canton the toll of the purge was particularly heavy; 2100 suspects, most of them communists, were arrested. The headquarters of the trade unions and the strike committee were closed, and the Soviet advisers placed under a careful watch. In five of the provinces now under nationalist control, the communists were either arrested or went underground.

Searching of the Soviet Embassy: death of Li Ta-chao

The 12 April affair occurred during another anti-communist incident, which caused a great stir internationally because of the light it threw on Comintern activities in China. It was also important in the history of the Communist Party, as it ended in the execution of Li Ta-chao, one of the Party's first leaders. On 6 April at 11.15 in the morning, the Peking

Chinese police, acting on orders from Marshal Chang Tso-lin and with permission from the Diplomatic Quarter authorities, searched part of the Soviet Embassy – the club, residential quarters and, as a result of an incident, the Military Attaché's office. The police returned from their expedition bringing with them Li Ta-chao and thirty-five Chinese communists who had taken refuge in the Soviet Embassy after Feng Yü-hsiang's departure from Peking, and were continuing their clandestine activities under cover from the Embassy. They were tried before a special commission a few weeks later. Li Ta-chao and nineteen other communists including one woman were condemned to death and strangled on the afternoon of 28 April. This tragic event removed one of the two founders of the Communist Party, who had also played a leading part in bringing about the collaboration with the Kuomintang. He died when the collaboration was coming to an end and it is not unlikely that he would have shared the blame which was shortly to fall on Ch'en Tu-hsiu and his group. His death saved him from discredit and dissent, making him into the first great martyr in the Chinese communist cause.

The search on 6 April led to the discovery of many important documents, some of which were published in the papers at the time; those dealing with the collusion between Feng Yü-hsiang and the Russians and the encouragement given by Moscow to the anti-foreign agitation aroused special interest.[1] The Soviet Military Attaché's instructions, received after the Seventh Plenary Session of the Comintern Executive Committee, and made known a few weeks after the looting and massacres at Nanking, greatly shocked public opinion:

> It is necessary to organize anti-European riots on the territory held by Chang Tso-lin's troops. . . .
>
> To bring on interference by the foreigners [burned] do not hesitate to use any measures, including even robbing and beatings. . . .
>
> In directing this movement against Europeans it is extremely important to preserve the existing antagonism between the individual foreign powers. It is particularly important to isolate Japan as a country that might land large military forces in China very swiftly. For this purpose, during any demonstrations it is necessary to be careful to see that none of the victims are Japanese residents. However, in conducting agitation against foreigners, to set Japan apart might create an unfavourable

[1] These documents have been collected and translated by C. Martin Wilbur and Julie Lien-ying How, and entitled *Documents on Communism, Nationalism and Soviet Advisers in China, 1918-1927.*

> impression. Therefore it is necessary to conduct agitation against foreigners in the form of an anti-British movement.[1]

The anti-communist reaction was intensified throughout the country. Feng Yü-hsiang in the North-West and Wang Ching-wei in Hankow were the only ones to continue their collaboration with the Soviet advisers and the Chinese Communist Party. A few months were enough to wreck the collaboration and force Chinese communists everywhere into a position at once precarious and clandestine.

[1] See Wilbur and How, *Documents,* p. 16. Some experts doubt the authenticity of this particular document, parts of which have been burned.

11 The Wuhan Government versus the Nanking Government The Expulsion of the Communists from the Kuomintang Left Wing

The April 12th Incident naturally kindled great indignation in Wuhan. Chiang Kai-shek was almost immediately dismissed from all his posts and expelled from the Kuomintang (17 April), while all the troops under his command were placed, theoretically at least, under direct orders from a military committee. Indignation rose still higher when he set up a formal government at Nanking, with the support of the right wing faction of the Kuomintang – Hu Han-min, Wu Chih-hui, Ts'ai Yüan-p'ei, Li Yü-ying, etc. On 25 April an immense protest meeting, presided over by Wang Ching-wei and attended by 300,000 people, was held in Wuhan. An expedition against Nanking was proposed and China's political position seemed worse than ever, resembling the chaos that had reigned immediately after the 1911 Revolution.

The Chinese communists rejoiced loudly at the firm stand taken against Chiang Kai-shek by Wang Ching-wei and the Wuhan government. They published a long declaration on 20 April on the subject, with an urgent appeal for agrarian reform, illustrated by a curious comparison between the Northern Expedition and Napoleon's attempt to establish European unity:

> . . . As 50 per cent of the Chinese population are peasants, democratic revolutionary power can only be established through an agrarian revolution. The French peasants gave Napoleon their support for twenty years because of the agrarian reforms achieved by the Great Revolution. . . .

> The French peasants helped Napoleon to conquer feudal Europe. The Chinese peasants will uphold the Nationalist Government and the Nationalist Army in the liberation of China from imperialism and militarism.[1]

The Wuhan government, however, now reduced geographically to the three provinces of Hupei, Hunan and Kiangsi, isolated from the outside world and surrounded by enemies, was shortly to experience grave difficulties because of its communist allies.

The peasant question

Peasant associations began to multiply in the country districts, as Mao Tse-tung had foreseen they would. The peasants went beyond their rights and increasingly replaced the administration. The landlords sometimes had to take refuge in the towns, and sometimes managed to create defensive organizations, based on local associations, secret societies, or occasionally on the local sections of the Kuomintang. An atmosphere not unlike that of civil war was developing in some places. News of the April 12th Incident encouraged anti-communist reaction and even caused the army to intervene to maintain order. The most violent reaction, at Ch'angsha on 21 May, is known as the Ma Jih (Horse Day) Incident. Hsü K'e-hsiang, commanding the 33rd Regiment of the Thirty-fifth Army, began a harsh repression of the communists and groups of trade unionists and peasants who seemed to threaten the town from within and without. This particularly violent incident is said to have resulted in over 100 deaths. Liu Shao-ch'i, T'eng Tai-yüan, Hsü T'e-li and Hsia Yi escaped with the utmost difficulty.[2] The Hunan peasant militia did not take part; they were dissuaded from doing so by Li Wei-han and T'an P'ing-shan, Minister of Agriculture, who was rapidly dispatched from Moscow.

The policy of the Communist Party leaders was apparently to curb the peasants' excesses as far as possible and practise moderation. This moderation was to appear fairly clearly during the Fifth Party Congress, which met in Hankow on 27 April. The agrarian question was examined once more and land redistribution treated as both a national and a revolutionary necessity. The programme was limited in its scope, however:

> The estates of the large landlords and counter-revolutionaries must be confiscated. Rented land must be confiscated and given to the

[1] From an article in *La Politique de Pékin*, No. 21, 14th year, 22 May 1927.

[2] Cf. an article by Yin Tung-hsu on this subject in the *Chung-yang jih-pao*, 21 May 1963.

peasants to work. Small holdings will not be confiscated. The lands of those serving in the revolutionary army will not be confiscated either. . . .

Publicly owned land and lands belonging to family or religious temples, schools, foreign churches and agricultural undertakings were also to be confiscated and handed over to the peasants. When submitted to the Agricultural Department of the Central Executive Committee, this proposal was considered impracticable for the time being, and the Chinese Communist Party did not publish it.[1] The Kuomintang and the communists do not seem to have been able to come to an agreement as to the definition of large landlords; the Kuomintang suggested a minimum figure of 500 'mou', or 33 hectares, and the communists proposed 100 'mou' (6.6 hectares), which was still much higher than the figure for an average farm (1 hectare). Finally, the Wuhan government and its communist allies were content to fix a maximum land rent, amounting to 40 per cent of the harvest. The agrarian question remained a constant source of localized conflicts and caused much anxiety to both the Wuhan government and the communists. Ch'en Tu-hsiu was shortly to be severely reproached with not having turned it to advantage in order to take over the leadership of a second revolution.

At the very moment when the Ch'angsha Incident threatened to damage relations between the Chinese Communist Party and the Wuhan government beyond repair, the government was forced to distribute weapons to the pro-communist trade unions of the capital to deal with a military rebellion. On 17 May General Hsia Tou-yin, the commander of the 14th Independent Division, who had just declared his loyalty to the revolution and had the support of the Fifteenth Army (General Liu Tso-lung) and of the Twentieth Szechuanese Army (in spite of orders to fight the latter), rebelled and proclaimed his loyalty to the Nanking government. As most of the Wuhan troops were in Honan fighting Wu P'ei-fu, Hsia Tou-yin managed to reach the outskirts of Wuch'ang and cut the Ch'angsha railway line. The triple city of Wuhan had a narrow escape, being saved by mobilizing part of the population, and by a rapid transfer of troops carried out by General Yeh T'ing, one of the few nationalist army officers who favoured the communists. The contrasting

[1] The above extract is translated from Hu Hua, *Essays on the History of the Chinese Revolution* (Peking, 1959). A summary, with comments, of the Fifth Congress resolution on the agrarian question is to be found in Brandt, Schwartz and Fairbank, *A Documentary History of Chinese Communism,* where the sources used are in this case Japanese.

situations at Wuhan and Ch'angsha provide yet another example of the complexity of the situation during that period. The Wuhan government was forced to maintain an uncertain and dangerous equilibrium. To use military force against the peasant associations and the trade unions was to adopt the same policy as the rival government in Nanking, losing the backing of its more radical supporters and of the troops more or less under communist control. To fail to act was to let its authority wane, allowing its allies to rise and take over the leadership of the government. If the collaboration were to continue, strict order had to be maintained within the Party and the communists' loyalty had to be complete. Internal order was constantly threatened by local initiatives arising from conflicting currents of opinion. The communists' loyalty was severely tested both by instructions from Moscow and by pressure from the lowest strata of the population in the country districts.

Before examining the Comintern's policy during this first phase of the Chinese revolution, the contents of two documents dating from before 12 April 1927 should be mentioned: Stalin's declaration to the Seventh Enlarged Plenum of the Comintern Executive Committee (30 November 1926) and the theses with reference to the Chinese question which were adopted at the Plenum (22 November-16 December 1926).[1] These documents are perfectly clear on two essential points, stressing them heavily. First and foremost the Chinese Communist Party must continue its collaboration with the Kuomintang left wing and the Wuhan government. Stalin made a particularly vigorous declaration on this subject:

> It is said that the Chinese communists ought to secede from the Kuomintang. This is pure folly, comrades. It would be the greatest mistake for the Chinese communists to leave the Kuomintang. The whole course of the Chinese revolution, its character, its prospects, undoubtedly indicate that the Chinese communists ought to remain in the Kuomintang and intensify their work in it.[2]

The theses of the Seventh Plenum are equally insistent, quoting some of Stalin's remarks verbatim:

> The supreme necessity of influencing the peasantry also determines the relation of the Communist Party to the Kuomintang and the relation of the Canton government. The apparatus of the National Revolutionary Government provides a very effective way to reach the peasantry.

[1] See X. Eudin and R. C. North, *Soviet Russia and the East*, pp. 350 ff.

[2] J. Stalin, 'The Prospects of the Revolution in China', speech delivered in the Chinese Commission of the Enlarged E.C.C.I. on 30 November 1926.

The Communist Party must use this way. The whole course of the Chinese revolution, its character, its prospects, undoubtedly indicate that the Chinese communists ought to remain in the Kuomintang and intensify their work in it.[1]

Although the Comintern stressed the need for collaboration between the two Chinese revolutionary parties, it also laid equal stress on the necessity for the communists to seize the real power in the rural districts through the peasant associations:

> At the present moment, we must not raise the question of soviets, but of the formation of peasant committees; I mean committees, elected by the peasants, which are capable of formulating the fundamental demands of the peasantry and of taking all the necessary measures for realizing these demands by revolutionary methods. . . . In my opinion, it is high time to do away with the indifference and 'neutrality' towards the peasantry which is noticeable in the activity of certain elements of the Kuomintang. . . . What prospects open up in this respect and up to what limits an advance can and should be made – that depends on the course of the revolution. I think that it should finally be carried as far as the nationalization of the land. In any case we cannot dispense with the slogan of the nationalization of the land.[2]

The theses were still more detailed, listing the measures which the Chinese Communist Party and the Kuomintang ought to apply immediately to gain the support of the peasants. These initially moderate measures – lowering of land rent, confiscation of land corporately owned or owned by large landlords and gentry hostile to the revolution, and the creation of peasant militia – were to be 'imposed' on the Kuomintang, enabling the Communist Party to gain control over the rural masses:

> It is the task of the Communist Party to see that the Canton government enforces these measures as a transition to a more developed stage of agrarian revolution. This very important task will be carried on through the organization of peasant committees under communist leadership. In process of the development of the revolution the peasants' committees will assume the authority and power needed for the enforcement of the above demands and intensify the struggle by putting forward more radical demands. . . .[3]

[1] Seventh Enlarged Plenum of the E.C.C.I. *Inprecor*, November-December 1926.
[2] J. Stalin, 'The Prospects of the Revolution in China'.
[3] Seventh Enlarged Plenum of the E.C.C.I. *Inprecor*, November-December 1926.

The Comintern's basic position was changed little by the 12 April 1927 Incident and the 'betrayal' by the Kuomintang right wing. It was stated once more, with added emphasis, by the Eighth Session of the Comintern Central Executive Committee (8-30 May 1927), which seemed even to encourage initiatives taken by the peasants: 'The most important thing at the present time is to secure the "plebeian" revolutionary solution of the agrarian problem from below by the tens and hundreds of millions of the peasants themselves. And in this, the Communist Party must take the lead of the movement.'[1]

Cooperation with the Kuomintang left wing was to remain whole-hearted, in order to avoid 'the Kuomintang banner being captured by the Right Wing'.[2]

Faced with these two urgent duties – maintaining the political front with the Kuomintang and the Wuhan government at all costs, and at the same time enlarging the scope of the peasant revolution, taking over the leadership of it, at the risk of damaging the front – Ch'en Tu-hsiu and the Communist Party could neither find a middle way nor resign themselves to making a choice. Their irresolution finally checked the impetus of the peasant movement, while exciting the suspicion and hostility of a large proportion of the Kuomintang left wing, and eventually of Wang Ching-wei himself. The bourgeoisie rose in self-defence; as upholders of the theory of class struggle, the communists ought to have been better equipped than most to foresee this possibility.

The Fifth Congress

The Fifth Congress of the Chinese Communist Party, already mentioned once in connection with the agrarian question, reflected the state of bewilderment besetting its leaders at that time. The Congress opened on 27 April 1927, attended by eighty delegates theoretically representing 57,967 members, a figure which became meaningless after the break with Nanking. The Indian M. N. Roy was the delegate of the Third International. To varying degrees, all the Party leaders and their external advisers – M. N. Roy and Borodin – were in favour of temporizing. Ch'en Tu-hsiu's point of view, that the revolution should be allowed to spread under the leadership of the Kuomintang before being advanced to a further stage, was generally accepted in Wuhan and in Moscow,

[1] 'Resolution on the Chinese Question', Eighth Plenum of the E.C.C.I., May 1927. *Inprecor,* No. 35.
[2] Ibid.

where Trotsky alone uttered a violent and prophetic denunciation.[1] It may be that false hopes of an alliance between Wuhan and Feng Yü-hsiang against Nanking and Chiang Kai-shek helped make it more acceptable. Under these conditions the need for close cooperation with the Kuomintang left wing and participation with the Wuhan government without merging with either, had to be stated once more. True to the Comintern's directives – those of the Seventh and Eighth Plenary Sessions, though the latter had not as yet taken place – the Chinese Communist Party placed the need for alliance above that of revolution, especially agrarian revolution.

The official history relates how a small group including Mao Tse-tung, Liu Shao-ch'i, Jen Pi-shih, Ch'ü Ch'iu-pai and a few other delegates opposed Ch'en Tu-hsiu's 'rightist' line, but was rapidly silenced. Mao Tse-tung, who was ill and had lost his right to vote, retired from the Congress, which elected a Central Committee with twenty-nine full members and eleven substitutes, and returned Ch'en Tu-hsiu as Secretary-General once more. It is hardly surprising that Chinese communists today consider the Fifth Congress as the least interesting, if not the most unfortunate of all. Whether true or imaginary, it must be pointed out that Mao Tse-tung's attitude at the Fifth Congress was entirely consistent with the conclusions of his *Report on an Investigation of the Peasant Movement in Hunan*. It is by no means certain that the brutal measures he advocated had any chance of success. They probably involved the risk of endangering the revolutionary movement as a whole and leading Central China into a state of political chaos, which could have brought the return of the northerners with it. But they were the only course of action that could enable the communists to acquire the leadership of the revolutionary movement. When the communists wanted to carry out this plan a few months later it no longer had any hope of success, as the failure of the Autumn Harvest Uprising was to prove.

After the Ch'angsha Incident on 21 May the peasant movement deteriorated rapidly. Regular troops and the landowners' militia, backed up by proper organization and arms, dealt mercilessly with any trouble in the country districts. In the army itself, several military leaders like Ho Chien in Hunan (Thirty-fifth Army) or Chu P'ei-teh in Kiangsi (Third Army) ostentatiously expelled the communists from their units. More and more communist leaders were arrested.[2] By the middle of June

[1] Leon Trotsky, *Problems of the Chinese Revolution* (New York, 1932).

[2] Large figures are given by some communist authors: 4700 peasants massacred in Hupei, 20,000 in Hunan, after the 21 May Incident.

cooperation was non-existent except in the province of Hupei. Tension mounted, until matters were precipitated by a clumsy move on the part of the delegate from the International.

The final break

The Eighth Plenum's resolution on the Chinese question was handed over to the Communist Party in the form of instructions on 1 June. They were more concrete and detailed than the resolution itself, and although they confirmed the veto on creating soviets and the need for an agrarian policy based on concessions to members of the army and smallholders, on the other hand they prescribed the following measures, which seemed to prepare for a communist take-over of the government:

> Liquidation of untrustworthy nationalist generals; they should be brought before a tribunal presided over by a leading figure of the Kuomintang.
>
> Creation of an army consisting of 20,000 Communist Party members and 50,000 workers and peasants for the two provinces of Hunan and Hupei.
>
> Introduction of new members of peasant and working-class origins into the Kuomintang Central Executive Committee.[1]

The Comintern delegate in Wuhan, M. N. Roy, acting independently of Borodin, went so far as to hand over the text of this telegram to Wang Ching-wei himself. As he later said, somewhat naively, the head of the Wuhan government had to be prevented from drawing closer to Nanking by showing him that Moscow was ready to uphold him if he adopted a truly revolutionary policy.[2]

Wang Ching-wei, now convinced that the Communist Party intended to acquire the military power needed to control his government, found himself forced into an agreement with Nanking, as was only to be expected. What is more, this happened at an awkward moment. On the northern front, Wuhan troops commanded by General T'ang Sheng-chih had advanced along the Kinhan railway as far as the important railway junction of Chengchow (1 June), but had been sorely tried by the battle of Chumatien against Chang Hsüeh-liang. At the same time, Nanking armies had occupied Hsüchow (16 May) and were apparently prepared to

[1] The contents of these instructions are to be found in a declaration made by Stalin on 1 August 1927 (cf. Eudin and North, *Soviet Russia and the East*, Document No. 109), and in Ch'en Tu-hsiu, 'Letter to all Party Comrades', 10 December 1929.

[2] Cf. M. N. Roy, *My Experience in China* (Calcutta, Renaissance Publishers, 1945).

conquer North China as quickly as possible. If the situation arose, they were in a position to threaten Wang Ching-wei's own troops, part of which sympathized with Chiang Kai-shek and the Kuomintang right wing policy.

A new and important element then came to the fore in the general military situation in the person of Feng Yü-hsiang, who had taken advantage of the retreat of the northerners to advance from Shensi to north Honan. He had moved his headquarters to K'aifeng on the Lunghai railway between Chengchow and Hsüchow, taking up a position which made him seem like a sort of arbitrator between Wuhan and Nanking, though *a priori* his sympathies lay with Wuhan and the Russians, who had given him considerable military help, as well as hospitality in the Soviet Union from January to September 1926. On 10 June Feng Yü-hsiang invited Wang Ching-wei and several members of the Wuhan government to come to Chengchow to meet him, while negotiating simultaneously with Chiang Kai-shek. It may be supposed that he made a pressing offer of mediation and suggested that the communists should be expelled from Wuhan as a preliminary step towards drawing closer to Nanking. Meanwhile he obtained the right to occupy north Honan. Several days later, the 'Christian General', accompanied by several members of the Wuhan government, went to Hsüchow, where he met Chiang Kai-shek and members of the Nanking government: Wu Chih-hui, Hu Han-min and Ts'ai Yüan-p'ei. Immediately after these meetings he sent a telegram to Wang Ching-wei on 21 June in which he publicly stated his opposition to the Russians and the communists and urged Wuhan to go over to Nanking:

> . . . Borodin has already resigned and should go back to his own country without delay. Members of the Hankow Central Executive Committee wanting to visit foreign countries should be given permission to do so, while the others may join the Nanking nationalist government if they wish. . . .
>
> I must say once more emphatically that the time has come to unite the nationalist factions in the fight against our common enemies. My hope is that you will accept the above solution and carry it out immediately.[1]

This summons compelled Wang Ching-wei to act without delay. Although he remained faithful to his principle of hostility towards

[1] In his book, *Chiang Kai-shek as I know Him* (in Chinese), Feng Yü-Hsiang, who had changed considerably in the meantime, scarcely mentions this episode.

Nanking, even pretending to prepare a military expedition against Chiang Kai-shek, he also declared his opposition to the communists. They in their turn, in order to obey the Comintern's orders, tried to maintain the alliance which had forced them into countless concessions. On 30 June the Central Committee of the Party drew up a declaration in eleven points, whose terms reflected the conciliatory spirit behind it:

> The Kuomintang, being an alliance of workers, peasants and small capitalists against imperialism, ought naturally to assume the leadership of the national revolution.
>
> The communists belonging to the Kuomintang hold governmental posts (whether at a central or a local level) only as members of the Kuomintang; during meetings between the two parties decisions are negotiated for which responsibilities are shared; they [the meetings] do not stand for a combined political power (the communists who share in the work of the government at the moment may apply for leave of absence to lessen present political difficulties).
>
> Mass organizations – workers, peasants and others – must submit to the leadership and control of the Kuomintang authorities; the requests of the people's, workers', peasants', etc., movements must conform with resolutions passed by the Kuomintang Congress or by its Central Executive Committee, as well as with government laws and decrees. Members of the Kuomintang must also protect the liberty of organization and the interests of the masses of workers and peasants according to the resolutions passed by the Party and the government laws and decrees.
>
> The shop assistants' unions must be organized by the Party in agreement with the provincial trade union federation delegates. Material requests made by the shop assistants should not exceed the owners' possibilities, and the trade unions must not encroach on the owners' rights in matters of employment and management; still less must they humiliate owners, for instance by arresting, fining or putting tall paper hats on them. . . .
>
> The trade unions and pickets cannot apply legal or administrative sanctions, make arrests, pass judgements, or patrol the streets without the permission of the Party or the government.
>
> Young pioneer groups are strictly forbidden to carry out police activities, such as arresting people or interfering with passers by.
>
> According to the principles of the Kuomintang, the workers and

peasants must be armed, but all armed groups of workers and peasants must be trained and supervised by the government.[1]

No denials and no amount of going back on what had been said and done could save the collaboration now, for the experiment had proved a failure, and, as far as the Kuomintang was concerned, it was no longer based on trust. On 15 July the Kuomintang Political Affairs Committee decided to put an end to it. The communists had to leave the Kuomintang; a few days later they had to leave the army as well. Borodin left for his own country on 27 July, the communist leaders began to scatter and go into hiding, and the trade union headquarters were occupied by the army. The Communist Party leaders appeared to be at a complete loss as to what to do next. They alone had to shoulder the responsibility for a failure in which the Comintern had a considerable share; they were soon to find themselves entirely replaced by others.

The reunification of the Kuomintang

The expulsion of the communists was a first step towards a *rapprochement* with Nanking, but six more months were to pass before the Kuomintang and the national government were unified once again. On 13 August Chiang Kai-shek retired momentarily from political life and went first to his native town, Fenghua, and then to Japan. The official explanation was that an obstacle to agreement between the two capitals had to be removed. In fact the Generalissimo probably responded to pressure from some of those directly beneath him who were worried by the presence of a double military threat, from the North and from Wuhan. Sun Ch'uan-fang had taken advantage of the discord among the nationalists to take back Hsüchow and all the territory north of the Yangtze, and advance as far as P'uk'ow, opposite Nanking (17 August); some units of his troops had even crossed the river to the east of the town. Sun Ch'uan-fang was driven back, with some difficulty, at the end of August, but once the danger was past the regime went through a phase of serious military anarchy. Revolutionary generals inspired by personal or provincial interests quarrelled among themselves like the northern warlords; the national revolution and political reunification seemed further away than ever. The chaos was such that Chiang Kai-shek was called back from

[1] The above extracts have been translated from Hu Hua, *Essays on the History of the Chinese Revolution* (Peking, 1959). According to a witness, quoted by the Hsin Hua Agency on 10 November 1968, Liu Shao-ch'i ordered the workers' pickets to surrender their arms on 28 June: 3000 rifles for 5000 men.

Japan in November, to take up his duties and his military command officially once more on 1 January 1928.[1]

The Nanking government was reorganized again in February on the principle of the five 'Yüan', before the Northern Expedition was continued once more. The Wuhan government had meanwhile more or less disintegrated. A Conference for Unity held in Shanghai from September onwards, and the creation of a special central executive committee enabled the members of the Kuomintang left wing to come over to Nanking, one after another. T'ang Sheng-chih fled to Japan, having lost control of the army. Wang Ching-wei left for Europe once more at the end of 1927 after trying, with the help of Chang Fa-k'uei, to re-form a nationalist government in Canton. A few inflexible supporters of the left wing went into voluntary exile. Madame Sun Yat-sen went to Moscow, in loyalty to the principle of collaboration with the communists. Teng Yen-ta, the former liegeman of Chiang Kai-shek, also went to Russia, coming back in 1931 to be shot by his former leader; Eugène Ch'en disappeared from the political scene. Chiang Kai-shek was to retain power for the next twenty years.

Reasons for the communist failure

The first phase in the history of the Chinese Communist Party ended in a series of bad setbacks – the failure in Shanghai, and the failure in Wuhan, soon to be completed by the abortive Nanch'ang Military Uprising (1 August) and the crushing of the Canton Commune (12 December). The Party was rebuilt once again in its rural bases in Central China; ten years later it experienced a similar collapse and did not gain strength again until the Sino-Japanese war. Once the *a posteriori* doctrinal explanations or the concessions made to the infallibility of the Comintern are laid to one side, the deep-seated reasons for the Communist Party's defeat in 1927 are fairly obvious.

First of all, it is perfectly clear that nationalist and anti-foreign feelings outweighed all else among the Chinese intellectuals who initiated and then fostered the revolution. Even in the case of those who chose communism, true social feelings awoke late and remained in the background. China had first of all to be reunified politically, freed from the politico-military cliques and emancipated from her humiliating semi-colonial state by the abolition of the Unequal Treaties. The Kuomintang

[1] He married Soong Mei-ling, Madame Sun Yat-sen's sister, on 1 December 1927; this is worth mentioning because of the political consequences that were to follow.

embodied these nationalist aspirations better than the Communist Party, since the latter looked for inspiration and orders from abroad. In spite of weaknesses in its doctrine and organization, the Kuomintang had a twenty-five year start on the Communist Party. The overthrowing of the empire in 1911, the tenacious personality of Sun Yat-sen and the number of its martyrs combined to give it credit and prestige which the October Revolution obviously could not equal. The great majority of Chinese intellectuals were drawn first of all to the Kuomintang rather than the Communist Party.

The rising influence of the industrial and merchant class could not fail to give the Chinese revolution the colouring of a bourgeois democratic revolution. Ch'en Tu-hsiu understood this when he proposed to support it without the Communist Party taking its share of the direct responsibility. The communists stood to find themselves in a difficult position in the inevitable confrontation which would result if the revolution met with rapid success. Perhaps this is the main reason why Borodin and the Soviet advisers considered the Northern Expedition premature in the light of the communists' influence and numbers.

The proletariat's weakness and lack of experience and the passive mass of conservative and backward peasants also contributed to the communists' failure. In Canton, Shanghai and Hankow, in which almost all the modern proletariat was concentrated, the Party had made an excellent start and formed groups of enthusiastic and loyal supporters, as was shown by the refusal of the Shanghai strike pickets to surrender their arms, and by the Canton Commune. This proletariat was, however, lost among the countless mass of artisans and coolies, who were still tied by traditional ideas and habits and were concerned above all with the problem of survival. Risings happened only in places where the peasants had been indoctrinated and organized. This was true for the East River districts in Kwangtung and for some districts in Hunan and Kiangsi. The peasants remained inactive in the white zones and those occupied by northern generals; in regions conquered by the nationalists the stir was short lived.

The Chinese Communist Party had neither the time nor the cadres necessary to organize the revolution properly in the country districts. The proletariat in the large towns was easy to approach and the Party's principles and tradition tended in this direction; the same was not true for the peasantry. The structure of Chinese rural society made it above all strongly dependent on the bourgeoisie. Land remained the safest value of all in an underdeveloped country in the grip of political anarchy. The owners of small or middle-sized (rarely large) estates were civil servants, officers, merchants or overseas Chinese, all of whom were extremely sensitive to any disturbances in the agricultural situation. Communist agitators or organizers found they did not have a free hand to act as they liked; the nationalist government was quick to react to any excesses, as was the left wing itself. The disagreement opposing the Communist Party leaders of that moment to the Comintern was largely based on the question of possibilities of Communist Party action among the peasants.

At a more general level the question arises as to whether the mistakes of the Comintern and the Secretary-General of the Chinese Communist Party can be included among the causes of the communists' failure. The Comintern gave a clear definition to the general mission of Eastern communist parties among the resolutions of the Fourth Congress of the International held in November 1922: 'To struggle for the most radical solutions of the problems of bourgeois-democratic revolution . . . to organize the workers and peasants to struggle for their special class interests.'[1]

The importance of the peasant question was fully appreciated in Moscow. In spite of a tenacious legend, Mao Tse-tung was not in fact the first to discover the revolutionary potential of the peasantry. A year before he wrote his *Report on an Investigation of the Peasant Movement in Hunan*, the Sixth Enlarged Plenary Session of the International had pointed out:

> The fundamental problem of the Chinese national liberation movement is the peasant problem. The victory of the movement's revolutionary democratic tendencies depends on how many of the 400 million Chinese peasants are drawn, together with the Chinese workers and under their leadership, into decisive revolutionary struggle. . . .[2]

The same could be said for military questions:

> The Chinese Communist Party and the Kuomintang should give most decisive support to this work of organizing military forces; they should also work hard at revolutionizing both the army's internal relations (its formations, the selection and re-education of cadres, the serious organization of political work) and its mutual relations with the population in bivouac areas.[3]

Although these general views may have been correct, the Chinese situation made them extremely difficult to put into practice. A rightist policy, such

[1] X. Eudin and R. C. North, *Soviet Russia and the East*, p. 235.
[2] Ibid., p. 349. [3] Ibid., p. 348.

as Ch'en Tu-hsiu had advocated at first, was conceivable, but would have led nowhere under the regime of tutelage excluding all other possibilities, which the Kuomintang was to impose on China in obedience to the wish of Sun Yat-sen. A leftist policy such as that suggested by Chang Kuo-t'ao, allowing the communists full independence, would probably have caused their party to be banned by law well before 1926, or if not, they would have been eliminated as soon as they dared undertake any far-reaching action among the peasants or in the army. The proletariat alone could not carry them to power.

The one alternative was a policy of agreement with the Kuomintang, enabling the communist numbers to increase. Later on it might prove possible to take over the leadership of the Kuomintang and the revolution from the inside, attacking the Kuomintang right wing and mollifying the left. This 'popular front', which emerged before its time, was the only solution allowing the communists to take power, if luck were on their side. The communists' calculation failed. The nationalist bourgeoisie betrayed them before themselves being betrayed. The Comintern had foreseen this risk but it had to be taken.

The 12 April *coup* did not change this policy; it may even have strengthened it as far as the disappearance of the capitalist bourgeoisie from the coalition was considered to raise the revolution to a higher plane:

> The alliance between the bourgeoisie, petty bourgeoisie, the peasantry and the proletariat has collapsed and is beginning to be transformed into a bloc between the proletariat, the peasantry and petty bourgeoisie, in which the proletariat is assuming an increasingly leading role.[1]

Moscow was careful to maintain relations with Wuhan, while withholding permission for the Chinese communists to create their own state power, in the form of soviets. The popular front continued, either because the Comintern was caught out at its own game when it overestimated the revolutionary character of the Wuhan government, or, which is more likely, because it had no illusions as to the real weakness of the Chinese communists, particularly after the rapid liquidation of zones under Nanking's control. The radical measures proposed at the Eighth Plenary Session of the Comintern Central Executive Committee called for the prior approval of the Wuhan government; this is why the Comintern's representative M. N. Roy states that he communicated them to Wang

[1] 'Resolution on the Chinese Question', Eighth Plenum of the E.C.C.I., May 1927. *Inprecor*, No. 35.

Ching-wei. The only possible solution was to gamble on the revolutionary disposition of Wang Ching-wei and the Kuomintang left wing.

After this, the official histories could safely reproach Ch'en Tu-hsiu with 'sabotage' of Moscow's instructions, with 'capitulationism' and 'rightist opportunism'. They would have done better to reproach him for his uncomplaining loyalty, but the infallibility of the Comintern would have been insufficiently emphasized. Mistakes in policy and application existed as in every human enterprise, but they could not change the result which can be amply explained by essentially Chinese factors. As well as those already mentioned, one of the most important was the military factor.

In 1927 China was still in the hands of military cliques. In this respect the generals owing allegiance to the Kuomintang differed little from their northern equivalents. Chiang Kai-shek, T'ang Sheng-chih and Feng Yü-hsiang were military rather than revolutionary leaders and this is even truer of all those who were won over during the Northern Expedition. They all understood the interest and strength of the nationalist current, but none of them ever forgot that power still belongs to the man who has a strong army behind him, and they all worked to maintain their own. The Communist Party had no army, either because the Kuomintang would not allow it, or because it wanted first of all to base itself on the proletariat. It did little or no ideological work in the nationalist army, in spite of the fact that communist cadres existed there; Trotsky was to reproach them vigorously for this:

> A characterization of the Party attitude towards the army was given by comrade Chou En-lai in his report. He said to Party members; 'Go into this national revolutionary army, strengthen it, raise its fighting ability, but do not carry on any independent work there.' Up to recently there were no nuclei in the army. Our comrades, who were political advisers, occupied themselves exclusively with military and political work for the Kuomintang.[1]

Mao Tse-tung said much the same when writing of the Party's military history: 'It [the Party] did not then understand the supreme importance of armed struggle in China, or seriously prepare for war and organize armed forces, or apply itself to the study of military strategy and tactics.'[2]

Nor did the Chinese Communist Party manage to create an army from the workers' and peasants' militia, and when the idea took shape it was too late. In desperation it tried to organize a rising of part of the nationalist

[1] Leon Trotsky, *Problems of the Chinese Revolution* (New York, 1932), pp. 421 ff.

[2] Mao Tse-tung, 'Problems of War and Strategy', *Selected Works*, vol. II, p. 222.

troops at Nanch'ang, failed miserably and once more paid the price for its indifference to military matters. All things considered, this indifference was perhaps the major cause of the Party's misfortunes. Once this was understood, the Party looked for its main support to the army, creating it from the elements that escaped from Nanch'ang and Wuhan. The People's Liberation Army, born on 1 August 1927, was to ensure its triumph in the end, in justification of the saying of Mao Tse-tung: 'War is the highest form of class struggle.'

Part 3

The Kiangsi Period (August 1927-October 1934) and the Long March (October 1934-October 1935)

Forced to flee to Liangshan.

Shui-Hu-Chuan

The countryside, and the countryside alone, can provide the broad areas in which the revolutionaries can manoeuvre freely.

Lin Piao, 'Long Live the Victory of the People's War!'

12 The Change in Leadership and the Failure of the Nanch'ang and Autumn Harvest Uprisings, and of the Canton Commune

The first war between the national government, soon to be reunited in Nanking, and the communists marks the beginning of an extremely complicated chapter in modern Chinese history.[1] The civil war can be said to begin on 1 August 1927 with the Nanch'ang Military Uprising; theoretically it lasted until the agreement concluded by the Communist Party and the Kuomintang on 22 September 1937 when the Sino-Japanese war was a few weeks old. In fact it ended at least a year earlier, shortly before the Sian Incident on 12 December 1936. The military engagements between the nationalists and the communists during this period were concentrated in three main theatres of operations:

Central China (chiefly the provinces of Kiangsi and Hunan) from August 1927 to October 1934.
The western and north-western provinces, during the Long March (October 1934 to October 1935).
Northern Shensi (the Yenan area) in 1936 and early in 1937.

In the first theatre of operations the communists' military attitude went through two main phases. During the first, offensive phase, the communists endeavoured to stir up rebellion in vast areas and take

[1] In modern communist terminology the Northern Expedition constitutes the First Revolutionary Civil War, the period covering Kiangsi and the Long March is the Second Revolutionary Civil War, and the renewal of the war against the nationalist government (1946-50) is the Third Revolutionary Civil War.

several large towns, resulting in the Nanch'ang Military Uprising, the Autumn Harvest Uprising, the Canton Commune and sudden attacks on Ch'angsha and Hankow. A defensive phase followed after the summer of 1930. It was designed to keep the rural bases in Central China in the Party's hands, and it lasted until these bases were evacuated at the beginning of the Long March (October 1934).

The Kiangsi period was one of far-reaching changes in the political field. The Party's leadership was renewed several times, and several secretaries-general held office in succession, while Mao Tse-tung built up real administrative and military power for himself. Inevitably the Party shed its urban and proletarian characteristics, becoming a rural, military party. When it was finally driven out of Central China, reduced to several tens of thousands of cadres and fighters, the Party had at least acquired invaluable practical experience over the preceding seven years; this was to enable it to re-establish itself once more and develop with great rapidity over vast areas of nationalist territory during the Sino-Japanese war from 1937 to 1945.

The change-over in leadership: Ch'ü Ch'iu-pai

On 7 August 1927 the Central Committee of the Chinese Communist Party met at Kiukiang, a little port on the Yangtze not far from where Lake P'oyang joins the river, to hold an extraordinary meeting called by Besso Lominadze, the Comintern's new representative in China and successor of M. N. Roy.[1] Circumstances prevented the Committee from attending in full force, but the meeting was attended by twelve members, three deputy members, five members of the Central Committee of the Communist Youth Corps and two members of the local branch. Ch'en Tu-hsiu, the Party's Secretary-General, either unable to come or unwanted, was not present. The Committee's first decision was to replace him by another, deposing him and his supporters from the Central Committee, and accusing them of 'rightist capitulationism'. A Provisional Political Bureau was created to take over until the Sixth Congress (which was held a year later in Moscow), consisting of seven full members and five deputy members; it was to take over the functions of the Central Committee. In view of the circumstances, the Party was reorganized and its activities became clandestine. New cells were not to exceed five or seven members; local standing committees, consisting of a few people only, took over all

[1] Lominadze was helped by Heinz Neuman, alias Neuberg, the future author of *L'Insurrection armée*.

the Party's affairs, the Party itself was further centralized, and discipline was tightened. By means of a 'resolution' and a 'circular letter' to 'all party members', the new Political Bureau interpreted and condemned the mistakes and betrayals of the former Central Committee, and drew up a new policy based on the latest instructions from the Comintern.[1]

The agrarian revolution was still the central question of the bourgeois democratic revolution, and remained the only way of bringing the peasant masses into the fight. It was to have its roots in the masses themselves; the Communist Party was to take the leadership in military affairs:

> At the present time, therefore, the preparation by the Party of systematic, planned peasant insurrections, organized on as wide a scale as possible, is one of the main tasks of the Party. We should take advantage of the harvesting period this year to intensify the class struggle in the villages. The slogan of these peasant insurrections should be the transfer of political power in the villages into the hands of the peasant associations. The land of large and middle landlords should be confiscated and distributed to poor peasants. Small landlords should be forced to lower their rents (this is based on the strategy of neutralizing the small capitalists and small landlords whose power is much larger than their numbers would indicate). If our programme of agrarian revolution is carried out within a fixed period, we may proceed to the universal slogan of 'land to the tillers', carry out the nationalization of land, and proceed to the redistribution of land.

The practical meaning of this passage became fully apparent a few weeks later.

The decision taken on 7 August with reference to the workers' movement had little more than a theoretical value, owing to the weakening of the Party's position in the towns; they dealt chiefly with ways of fighting non-communist trade unions. On the other hand, it is interesting to note that the communists had not yet lost all hope of reconciliation and collaboration with the Kuomintang. It was understood, however, that if this object was to be achieved, the other party would have to be 'revolutionized' by the introduction of large numbers of workers and peasants into its framework. For this reason, the Nanch'ang Military Uprising was carried out in the name of the Kuomintang, under its flag.

[1] A Chinese text of the 'Letter to All Party Members' is to be found in Ch'en Ch'eng, *Reactionary Documents of the Red Bandits,* vol. II, collected in T'aipei. The original text of the 'Resolution' is not available. The following quotation is from Brandt, Schwartz and Fairbank, *A Documentary History of Chinese Communism*, based on a Japanese text.

The elimination of Ch'en Tu-hsiu brought Ch'ü Ch'iu-pai, a young revolutionary trained in Russia, to power, and with him a team of radicals: Li Wei-han (alias Lo Mai), Liu Shao-ch'i, Chou En-lai and, lastly, a true member of the proletariat, Hsiang Chung-fa, who lacked both personality and education. Chang Kuo-t'ao and Chang T'ai-lei, both old militant Party members who had often opposed Ch'en Tu-hsiu, seem to have been included in the Political Bureau as well. Ch'ü Ch'iu-pai, born in 1899 in Ch'angchow in Kiangsu into a poor schoolteacher's family, was just 28. He was a former student of Russian language and literature, a journalist who had translated Gorki, and he arrived in Russia in 1920 with no political views; he received his Marxist education in the Soviet Union, not in China. On his return to his own country in 1923, he became professor of sociology at Shanghai University and a contributor to *New Youth*. His age and political origins presented Moscow with some measure of security, which had been lacking in the person of Ch'en Tu-hsiu, a difficult man who had already reached maturity and was deeply imbued with the Chinese cultural tradition; Ch'en Tu-hsiu was accused of leading the Party alone, using patriarchal, if not completely authoritarian methods, and of having treated the Comintern's latest instructions too lightly.[1]

The Nanch'ang Military Uprising (1 August 1927)[2]

A few days before the meeting on 7 August at Kiukiang, the communists had attempted a military *putsch* several hundred kilometres away, at Nanch'ang, the capital of Kiangsi province. This date has symbolically become the date of the birth of the People's Liberation Army; it marks the beginning of a military phase in the Party's history, which was to last for over twenty years and have a far-reaching effect on both its spirit and its structure. The whole regime still bears its imprint today. As the expulsion of the communists from the Wuhan government and the Kuomintang left wing turned the latter into a 'counter-revolutionary' force, the only solution was to win back power within it by a military *coup*. The Central Committee of Lominadze seem to have decided this during the days that followed the break of 15 July. With this in view, Chou En-lai, Li Li-san and T'an P'ing-shan either took over or were ordered to take

[1] For a recent biography of Ch'ü Ch'iu-pai, see Tsi-an Hsia, *The Gate of Darkness*.
[2] For a more detailed account of this, see our article entitled 'Nanch'ang Uprising' in *The China Quarterly*, July-September 1962, and 'The Ashes of Defeat' by C. Martin Wilbur in the same publication, April-June 1964.

over the military and political preparations for the operation. A Front Committee, with Chou En-lai as its secretary, was formed at Nanch'ang; at the same time Chang Kuo-t'ao was sent there on a mission, possibly with the ulterior motive of preventing the *putsch*, which had not been fully approved by the Comintern and seemed to him doomed to failure. He arrived there too late to change the course of events.[1]

The Communist Party had no troops of its own, but it is known that the Northern Expedition forces included several communist officers, some of whom held important commands. Such was the case in the Second Front Army (ex Fourth Army), commanded by General Chang Fa-k'uei and recently transferred from Hupei to the Nanch'ang-Kiukiang area of Kiangsi, with its headquarters to Kiukiang (see Map 5, p. 152). A few units of three armies belonging to the Second Front Army were in Nanch'ang itself or in the neighbourhood of the town: the Fourth Army (the 25th Division), the Eleventh Army (the 10th, 11th and 24th Divisions) and the Twentieth Army (the 1st, 2nd and 3rd Divisions). General Ho Lung, in command of the Twentieth Army, and General Yeh T'ing of the 24th Division were either members of the Communist Party or sympathized with it, as did some of their officers. The Party was also fortunate in that the head of the Nanch'ang Public Security Bureau was also a communist – General Chu Teh, soon to be Commander-in-Chief of the Chinese Red Army. The rebels could count on the support of about fifteen regiments in all, numbering between 20,000 and 30,000 men. Within the town itself, the numbers of their future enemies were smaller, for they consisted of less than three regiments – two independent regiments belonging to the Third Army, and a few small units from the Sixth and Ninth Armies.

The uprising was fixed for 1 August at 1 a.m.; all went according to plan. The non-communist troops were taken completely by surprise; most of them were disarmed, while others were driven back through the northern suburbs. No disorder or looting took place; the population understood little about what was going on and took scarcely any notice of it. Political consequences quickly followed the preliminary success; on the same day a Revolutionary Committee was created, consisting of twenty-five members, including outstanding nationalist and communist figures, all of whom proclaimed their loyalty to the Kuomintang. The most important leaders – Madame Sun Yat-sen, Madame Liao Chung-k'ai, Teng Yen-ta and Chang Fa-k'uei himself – were all missing and had

[1] Cf. the memories of Chang Kuo-t'ao, which appeared in the *Ming Pao* (Hong Kong 1968), particularly issues No. 25 and 26.

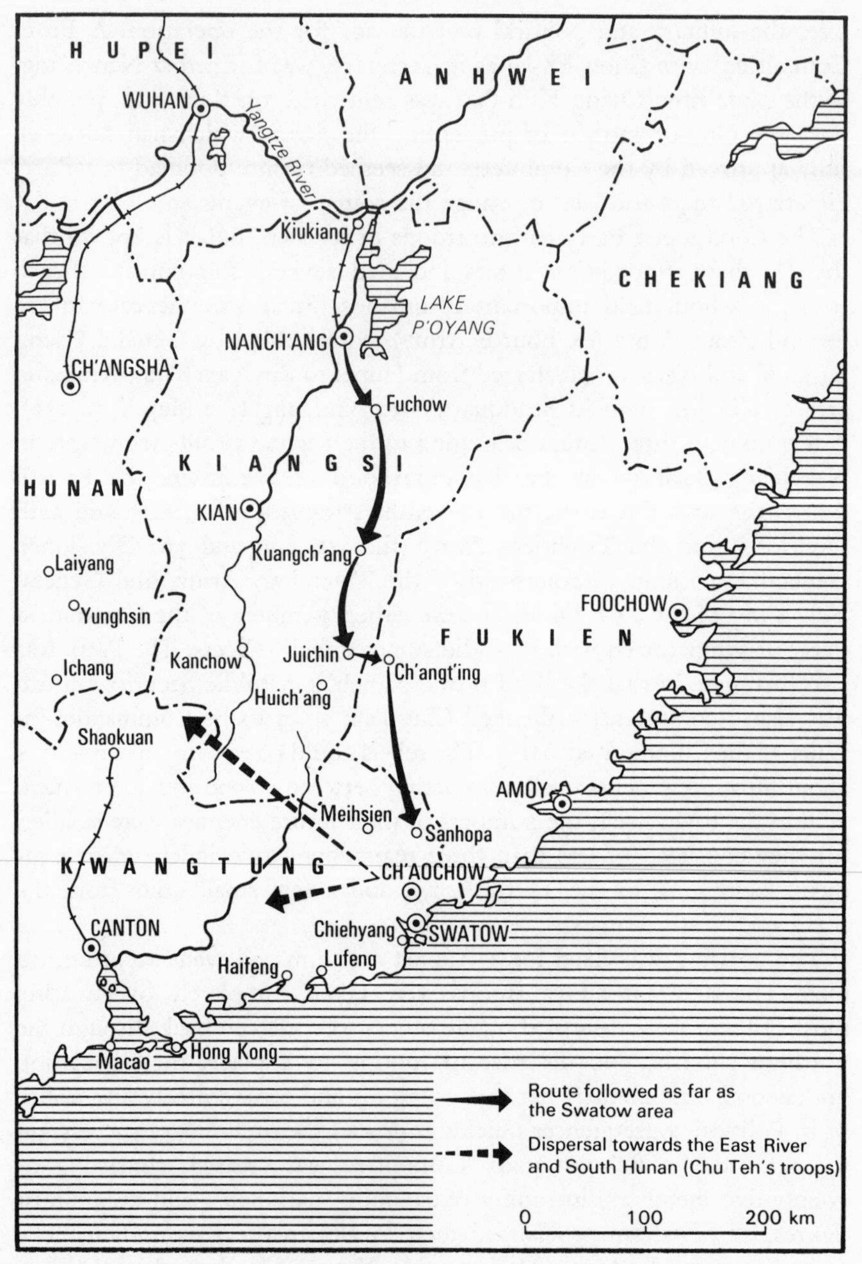

Map 5. The Nanch'ang Military Uprising and the retreat to Swatow

not even been consulted. The writer Kuo Mo-jo, a non-Party man who held an important post in the army Political Department, was also appointed to the committee. All the important posts went to the communists: T'an P'ing-shan was Chairman, Wu Yü-chang Secretary-General, Chang Kuo-t'ao took over the Workers' and Peasants' Department, Lin Tsu-han took over Finance, Li Li-san was appointed to the Political Affairs Department and Chou En-lai to the Military Affairs Department. Ho Lung, Yeh T'ing, Chu Teh, Yün Tai-ying and probably Jen Pi-shih and P'eng P'ai were also included on the committee. When Lin Piao, the present Minister of National Defence, Ch'en Yi, the present Foreign Minister, and Nieh Jung-chen, are added to the names already mentioned it may be said that a large percentage of the most important figures of the regime today were already together at Nanch'ang, though Mao Tse-tung was not with them.

The Revolutionary Committee issued a proclamation and covered the town with slogans – 'Down with Imperialism!', 'Down with the tuchün!', 'Agrarian Reform!', 'Confiscate Estates of over 100 mou!', 'Rights for the Workers and the Peasants!' The rebel troops were placed under the orders of a single headquarters; Ho Lung was in command, Yeh T'ing second in command, Liu Po-ch'eng was Chief of General Staff, and Kuo Mo-jo was appointed head of the Political Department, though he had not yet arrived and did not take up the post. The former battle order was only slightly changed – Twentieth Army (Ho Lung), Eleventh Army (Yeh T'ing), Ninth Army (Chu Teh). The name of Second Front Army was kept for the forces as a whole. The rank and file, who were convinced that preparations were under way for their return to Kwangtung, their native province, accepted the events and followed their leaders through force of habit.

Chang Fa-k'uei's reaction to the rebellion of half his units was extremely rapid, more so than his former tolerant attitude towards the communists might have suggested. He immediately marched on the town, with the support of part of the Third Army; the communists began to retreat on 3 August, and on 5 August they evacuated the town completely without a blow being struck. The rebel armies still under Ho Lung did not try to maintain their position in Kiangsi and Hunan within range of the Wuhan government, as might have been expected from a logical and political point of view. Nor did they turn for support to the hinterland, said to be in a state of great restlessness. They do not even appear to have considered looking for reinforcements in these two provinces when some of their number, such as Ts'ai T'ing-k'ai's 10th

Division, went back to the nationalist camp. The official version was that the Nanch'ang rebels decided to go back to Kwangtung to found a revolutionary base there for the Communist Party to use as the starting point for a second Northern Expedition, which would this time have the full support of a population won over by radical reforms. Their illusions were probably short lived. Kwangtung was firmly in the hands of rival Kuomintang generals, ready to be reunited immediately in the face of a communist threat; the Canton Commune was soon to bear this out.

In their retreat southwards, the communist leaders were perhaps complying with the wishes of their troops, who were not at home in Central China and lacked enthusiasm for the prospect of fighting Chiang Kai-shek's troops, who were nationalists like themselves. The rebels, aware of their weakness and (if Kuo Mo-jo is to be believed) in possession of a direct warning from Chang Fa-k'uei, did not try to approach Canton directly through the Kan valley (via Kian and Kanchow) and the North River valley. Anxious to avoid their enemies as far as possible, they chose a route through the mountains to the east, passing first through Fuchow, where they stopped for three days, and through Juichin (later to be the communist capital from 1931 to 1934), where they entered the town after a brief night engagement against two regiments from Ch'ien Ta-chün's army (18 August).

On 24 August the rebels met three or four regiments of the Nationalist Thirty-second Army (Ch'ien Ta-chün) at Huich'ang, where they lost 800 men in a battle lasting ten hours, which was particularly hard for the Eleventh Army commanded by Yeh T'ing. The communists then gave up their plan of advancing to Canton, and decided instead to return to Juichin and proceed from there to Ch'aochow and the port of Swatow, via Ch'angt'ing in western Fukien. They seem to have chosen Swatow partly because they wanted access to a port through which the Russians could send them the military aid they badly needed, and partly because they wanted the support of the soviet districts of Haifeng and Lufeng on the East River. Leaving Chu Teh with the 25th Division at San Ho Pa to cover their retreat, the majority of the communist troops moved on towards the coast. On 23 September the rebels took Ch'aochow without a fight; their vanguards reached Swatow the next day.

However, the Kwangtung nationalist generals Li Chi-shen, Ch'en Chi-t'ang and Li Fu-lin were quick to react and endeavoured to encircle the communists. Hard fighting took place on about 27 September in the region of Chiehyang and particularly at T'angk'eng, about 100 kilometres north-west of Swatow; the town itself was held by the 3rd Division of the Twentieth Army until 30 September. Finally, most of the red troops (1st, 2nd and 24th Divisions) were scattered in the Kueichi-Wushih area, west of Chiehyang. A few hundred fugitives with Yeh T'ing and the chief leaders of the uprising managed to reach the East River districts; others reached Hong Kong or Shanghai. Chu Teh's troops, among whom were Lin Piao and Ch'en Yi, left behind at San Ho Pa, were more fortunate. After the evacuation of Swatow, they managed to retreat to the Shangyu-Ch'ungyi area near Kanchow in south-west Kiangsi. Chu Teh, who had exhausted all his supplies, was lucky enough to find that the commander of the Sixteenth Nationalist Army, General Fan Shih-sheng, whose headquarters were at Shaokuan, north of Canton, was a former classmate from the Yunnan Military Academy. Chu Teh took the name of Wang K'ai, went over (or pretended to) to the nationalist cause, and settled at Lishih, north of Shaokuan; his unit (1200 men) became the 140th Regiment of the nationalist army, with Ch'en Yi as its Political Commissar.[1]

Chu Teh took no part in the Canton Commune. But early in the next year he left the Sixteenth Army and took his regiment to the Ichang area on the border of Hunan and Kwangtung. There, on 28 January 1928, he reorganized his troops to become the Fourth Red Army, with two regiments (28th and 29th) and a battalion (the Ichang Independent Battalion). For several months Chu Teh tried to maintain his hold in the area of Ichang, Leiyang, Pinghsien and Yunghsing, creating soviets and detachments of red guards, and driving back the small expeditions launched by the provincial troops or the nationalists. By April 1928 his situation had become so difficult that he decided to join Mao Tse-tung in the Ching Kang Shan, about 100 kilometres away.[2] The meeting of the two leaders and their little armies took place in the middle of April, in the village of Talung in the district of Yuhsien in Hunan. The moment has been commemorated in countless pictures by popular artists.[3]

The Nanch'ang Uprising had the merit of gathering able military cadres into one homogeneous group; had they been isolated or left to themselves, they might well have become lost to the Party during the worst

[1] Cf. Kung Ch'u, *I and the Red Army* (in Chinese). Kung Ch'u belonged to Chu Teh's group.

[2] According to some witnesses, it was Mao Tse-tung who wanted to go and join Chu Teh at first. Chu's troops – about 4800 fighters and cadres of various kinds – were at least as large as Mao's at the time.

[3] The meeting between Chu Teh's troops (29th Regiment) and those of Mao Tse-tung had taken place a few days before, in fact, in the village of Shuik'ou.

periods of Kuomintang suppression. The uprising had no hope of succeeding, of winning over the rest of the army or mobilizing the peasant masses, or even of attracting the more revolutionary factions of the Kuomintang. The communists represented a small minority in the army and were almost all to be found in the former Fourth Army, commanded by Chang Fa-k'uei. The peasant masses of Kiangsi were insufficiently organized and had too few trained men among them to be able to form a useful alliance for the rebels. Lastly, the movement came too late in some respects. Had it followed quickly on the liquidation of the communists in Shanghai and the creation of Chiang Kai-shek's government at Nanking, it might have been helped by the indignation this had aroused in certain quarters and might have gained firmer support from the Kuomintang left wing. After 15 July the Wuhan government declared its opposition to the collaboration; the rebels, by outlawing themselves, lost what little remaining outside support they still possessed and provided justification for all the severity shown them by their former allies.

The Autumn Harvest Uprising[1]

The Autumn Harvest Uprising was not destined to be any more successful than the Nanch'ang Uprising, but in the long run its results were just as fortunate for the communist movement. It was intended to be an attempt to put into effect the decisions taken at the meeting on 7 August, taking the form of an effort to mobilize the peasantry in places where the work of organization had begun, and to renew contact with some of the large towns and their proletariat. Ch'ü Ch'iu-pai directed the movement as a whole, but Mao Tse-tung, who was particularly well qualified by his social origins, his experience and his previous assignments to deal with the peasant question, was put in charge of the uprising in the areas best prepared for it, part of which at least had formed the subject of his *Investigation*, carried out the January before in the Hunan-Kiangsi border area, east of Ch'angsha. His activities were in fact limited to about six districts – P'ingchiang, Liuyang, Liling, P'inghsiang, Anyüan and Hsiangt'an – in the hills rising out of the great plain fed by the Hsiang valley and Lake Tungt'ing. Military and revolutionary traditions were strong in the 'rice bowl' of Hunan and the Northern Expedition, with its armies and propaganda machine, had passed through it the year before. Enthusiasm had been dampened, however, by the May 21st Incident and the liquidation of trade unions and peasant associations with communist leanings.

[1] See Map 6, p. 158.

Mao Tse-tung, although he was himself without military experience apart from six months spent in the 1911 revolutionary army, attempted to organize a proper army. With the help of Hsiang Ying he formed a small corps of 2000 men, divided into four modest regiments. The first of these consisted of the remains of a battalion of guards from the Fourth Army Group (in fact, the Second Front Army commanded by Chang Fa-k'uei) who had escaped from Wuhan. Workers from the Anyüan and P'inghsiang mines formed the second. The third was based on peasant militia, chiefly from the P'ingchiang and Liuyang areas. The fourth regiment, which came from the border between Hupei and Hunan, was made up of soldiers from the nationalist army who had come over during the May 21st Incident.

Operations began on 8 or 9 September round the districts of P'ingchiang, Liuyang and Liling; Liling appears to have been the only town occupied. Ch'angsha was never really threatened. The nationalist troops were quick to react; Mao Tse-tung's 2nd Regiment was surrounded in Liling, while the 4th Regiment changed sides once more and attacked the 1st Regiment. Disaster seemed imminent. Mao Tse-tung, abandoning his intentions of advancing on Ch'angsha and gaining control of the area, began to retreat southwards on 19 September, after a hard fight with the enemy at Luchi and the desertion of many of his men. When he reached the village of Sanwan in the Yunghsin district in Kiangsi, he organized the few remaining troops into one regiment of two battalions, and then pushed on until, in the last few weeks of 1927, he reached the Ching Kang Shan (Ridge of Wells), a mountainous, almost desert region shortly to become the first communist rural base in Central China.[1]

A few other more modest, badly coordinated efforts took place elsewhere: in southern Hupei, in the area round Hsienning, Chiayü, T'ungshan, T'ungch'eng and Ch'ungyang, where the rebels succeeded in cutting off the railway between Yochow (Yüehyang) and Hankow for a short time, and tried in vain to threaten Hankow itself; in north-eastern Hupei in the Tapieh mountains area (Mach'eng, Huangan); in south Hunan (near Kwangshan); and in south Kiangsi (round Wanan and Taiho). Attempts at rebellion also took place in Kiangsu in the Wushi area, and even in Hainan; in Shensi a local agitator, Liu Chih-tan, retreated to the north of the province not far from Yenan and prepared the ground, ten years before the event, for the settlement of the survivors of the Long March.

[1] On the Autumn Harvest Uprising, see the article by Roy Hofheinz Jr, 'Autumn Harvest Insurrection', in *The China Quarterly*, October-December 1967.

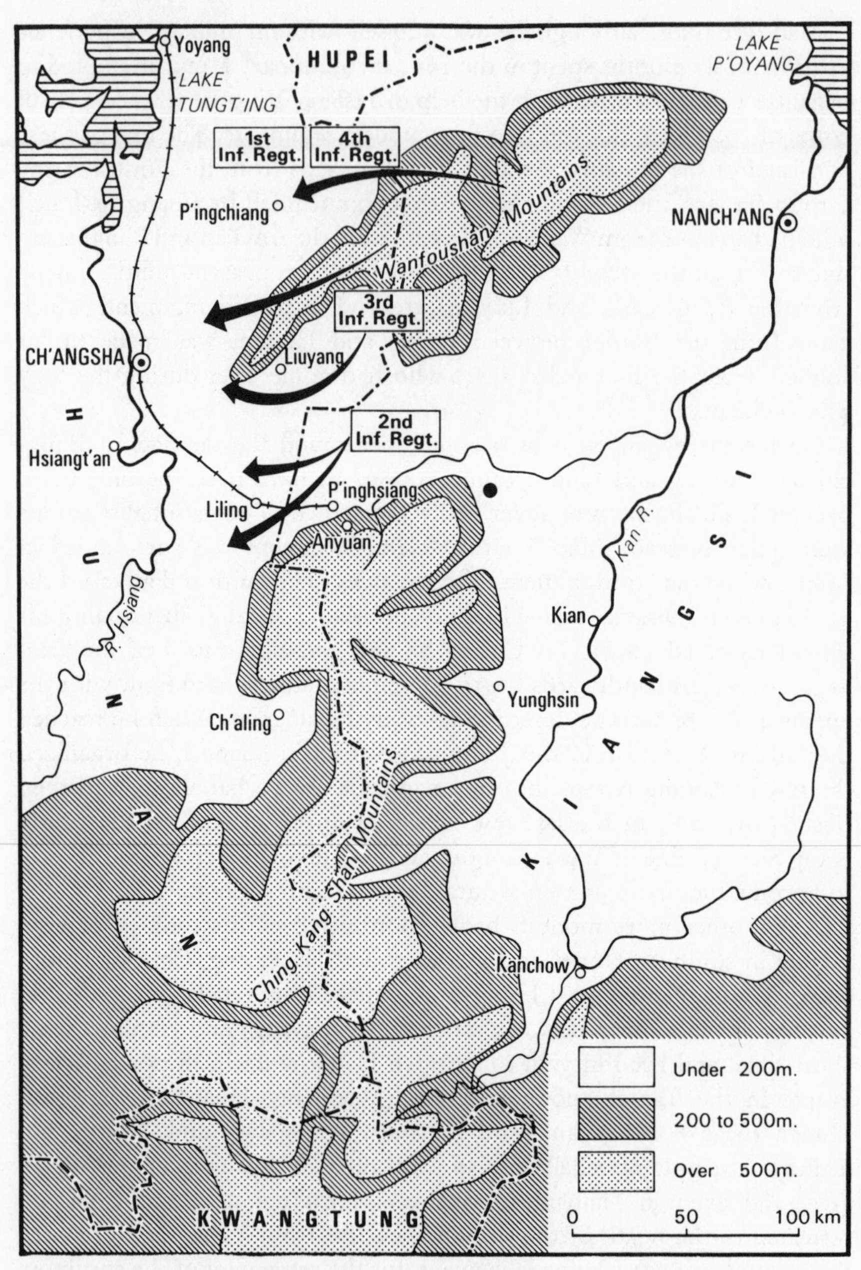

Map 6. The Autumn Harvest Uprising

The Autumn Harvest Uprising met with the same difficulties everywhere – a general apathy on the part of the peasant population, who lacked sufficient preparation, a shortage of cadres, lack of arms, and bad coordination of activities. It failed, as hundreds of peasant uprisings had failed in the past, while the Party lost energetic, valuable men who were to be sorely missed; its reputation in the country districts was undermined, just as the failures in Wuhan and Shanghai had undermined it in the towns.

The success of the uprising was slightly more durable in the East River region of Kwangtung, in the areas round Haifeng and Lufeng where P'eng P'ai had been at work for some time. The two chief towns in the area were taken for the first time in April 1927; a local red government was formed, but it did not last long (29 April to 9 May) and it was suppressed with as much cruelty as was the revolt itself. The September uprising produced no spectacular results, but paved the way for the October uprising, which ended in the occupation of the towns of Lufeng and Haifeng. The first congress of the soviets was held on 18 November 1927 at Haifeng. A soviet government was officially created in the Haifeng Lufeng region, controlled by a Chinese Communist Party Special Committee for the East River, with P'eng P'ai as Secretary-General. The first Chinese soviet regime was to last until the following February.[1]

The Party's new leaders did not realize how serious its failures were; instead, noting the quarrels dividing the nationalist camp since Chiang Kai-shek's departure for Japan, they thought the time had come to spark off revolutionary activities once more in the towns, as well as in the country districts. A 'leftist deviation' of 'petty bourgeois inspiration' developed, born – as was explained later on – of the feelings of indignation aroused by the anti-communist suppression in the white zones, and standing for a reaction against the spirit of abandon which was rife in Ch'en Tu-hsiu's leadership of the Party before 7 August 1927. This leftist policy found expression at the enlarged meeting of the Political Bureau, held on 8 November 1927. The Bureau adopted a proposal entitled 'The Current Chinese Situation and the Communist Party's Tasks', which was to be severely criticized at the Sixth Congress for its rashness and unwillingness to recognize the necessary stages of the revolution (see Chapter 14). For several months longer the Party went on sending out small expeditions with no hope of success; the apathy of the

[1] Cf. Shinkichi Eto, 'Hai-lu-feng: the First Chinese Soviet Government', *The China Quarterly*, October-December 1961 and January-February 1962.

masses limited their scope and, fortunately, the loss of life involved. They were sporadic and short lived, particularly in the Shanghai and Nanking areas. Events were to take a different turn in Canton, where the Party attempted to take over; it managed to gain control of the town from 11 to 13 December 1927.

The Canton Commune[1]

The communists planned to take action in Canton, traditionally the most revolutionary town in the country, as well as in the large towns of Central China, Ch'angsha and Hankow, designated by the decisions of 7 August as the final objectives of the Autumn Harvest Uprising. In September 1927, however, the situation had not matured enough to justify the use of force. The communist and workers' organizations had been intimidated by the March 20th 1926 Incident and the events of April 1927 had put them to a further test. When the Shanghai trade unions were liquidated on 12 April, this act was echoed almost immediately in Canton, where General Li Chi-shen disarmed the workers' pickets, and arrested and executed about 100 cadres and militants, according to communist sources. An attempt to launch a general strike on 25 April failed. The repression then became even harsher and the communists had to continue their activities in secret. The trade unions – particularly the powerful committee behind the Hong Kong strike from 1925 to autumn 1926 – had been reorganized and removed from red influence. The communists tried to maintain their hold among the militant members of the trade unions by using terrorism and encouraging as many strikes as possible. A series of incidents in October (14 and 23 October) gave rise to new, harsher measures. The Hong Kong strike committee's workers' canteens and dormitories were closed. It seemed likely that even the communists' secret activities would have to stop.

At one point the Party's leaders had considered the possibility of taking Canton from the outside, using the Nanch'ang Uprising as a cover. However, when Yeh T'ing, Ho Lung and Chu Teh were dispersed at Swatow, the remains of their troops were no longer in a position to threaten Canton. Several armies held the region firmly in hand: Li Chi-shen's army from Kwangsi, Li Fu-lin's Cantonese army (the Fifth Army), and the Fourth Army, commanded by Chang Fa-k'uei, which had returned to Kwang-tung from Kiangsi in the middle of October. This inauspicious situation, combined with the failure of the peasant operations

[1] See Map 7, p. 163.

during the Autumn Harvest Uprising, ought to have been enough, seemingly, to discourage the Party from operations against Canton. But this was not the case.

Several authors, among them Trotsky, consider that the Canton Uprising was launched from Moscow, to suit the Russians:

> Stalin's special emissaries had the task of preparing an insurrection in Canton timed for the Fifteenth Congress of the Communist Party of the Soviet Union, in order to cover up the physical extermination of the Russian opposition with the political triumph of the Stalinist tactic in China. On the declining wave, while the depression still prevailed among the urban masses, the Canton 'Soviet' uprising was hurriedly organized, heroic in the conduct of the workers, criminal in the adventurism of the leadership.[1]

Others claim that a sudden development in the local situation in November was enough to justify a daring intervention.[2] The nationalist generals in Kwangtung were at loggerheads among themselves, reflecting the climate in the Kuomintang itself. Li Chi-shen supported Chiang Kai-shek's faction; Chiang Kai-shek himself was still in exile in Japan, but was soon to come back. Chang Fa-k'uei, still loyal to the spirit of Wuhan and closer to Wang Ching-wei, was trying to create a new government for him in Canton. Li Fu-lin supported neither Wang Ching-wei nor Chang Fa-k'uei, but was displeased to see generals from Kwangsi settling in his native province.

Chang Fa-k'uei had his headquarters in Canton; he had driven Li Chi-shen out of the town on 17 November, and to protect it he deployed his forces round the outside of it, particularly on the North and West rivers. Only a few weaker groups remained within Canton itself: a training regiment of 3000 men, an artillery regiment, a militia regiment (Peace Preservation Corps), the troops belonging to the various services attached to Chang Fa-k'uei's headquarters, the headquarters of the 12th and 26th Divisions, and the depots of the Thirteenth Army, the 10th and 25th Divisions.

As at Nanch'ang, luck was on the communists' side, as the officer in command of the training regiment had just joined the Party or was in sympathy with it – Yeh Chien-ying, a future marshal and Chief of General Staff of the Red Army. Over 200 of his men were, like him, either Party members or secret supporters. The communist forces, however, were

[1] Leon Trotsky, *Problems of the Chinese Revolution* (New York, 1932).
[2] Cf. Hsiao Tso-liang, 'Chinese Communism and the Canton Soviet of 1927', *The China Quarterly*, 1967, No. 30.

still ludicrously weak compared with those of the enemy; they consisted of 2000 poorly armed red guards, whose ranks were swelled by workers, supplied with captured weapons, and above all by the training regiment. The rebels certainly did not number more than 10,000 men; the enemy numbered about 50,000. The only hope of success lay in a widespread movement of popular support, quickly backed up by the rural districts, which would bring with it the defection of part of the government troops.

On 7 December the Party's Provincial Committee called a secret meeting of eighty-five delegates from different trade unions, which approved the principle of an insurrection. The moment chosen was 13 December, but it was quickly changed to 11 December at 3.30 a.m. A committee of sixteen, presided over by Chang T'ai-lei, was put in charge of the preparations. Yeh T'ing, who could arrive only a few hours before the movement began, was given command of military operations. His assistant was Hsü Kuan-ying, a future communist general; he is also reported to have had help from a Russian and a German adviser. In the early hours of 11 December Chang T'ai-lei, Yeh T'ing and Yün Tai-ying went to the training regiment and roused it to rebellion. About fifteen officers and men who opposed them were killed on the spot, and others were taken prisoner. The general insurrection began as planned at 3.30 a.m.[1]

The training regiment consisted of nine companies, each of whom was given a special mission: the Goddess of Mercy Hill (Kuan Yin Shan) and the nearby ammunition factory (two companies), the Public Security main building and the nearby police headquarters (two companies), and the Sse Piao Barracks (two companies); the three remaining companies were put in charge of the artillery regiment, the Kowloon line railway station and the 300 police of the Sikuan district. The red guards were divided into seven detachments and assigned to various districts of the town. Their special task was to disarm the police and the Peace Preservation Corps forces attached to the Great Buddha Temple (Ta Fo Sse) and the T'ai p'ing Theatre. Two detachments supported the soldiers in their attack on the Public Security building. Almost everywhere, the enemy was taken by surprise; in a few hours the whole town was occupied, except for the Fourth Army headquarters and those of the 12th and 26th Divisions, which held out to the end. Chang Fa-k'uei had to leave the town, though he was shortly to lead some of his own and Li Fu-lin's troops against it, while Li Chi-shen sank his former differences and joined

[1] Some of the above details, especially the sharing out of the missions, are taken from *Historic Events of the Second Revolutionary War* (Peking, 1956: in Chinese).

forces with him. Large supplies of arms were captured in the depots or from the nationalist units: some witnesses give a total of 8000 weapons. They were used to arm volunteers and some of the 3000 liberated prisoners. A few hundred peasants from neighbouring villages were also reported to have joined the communists.

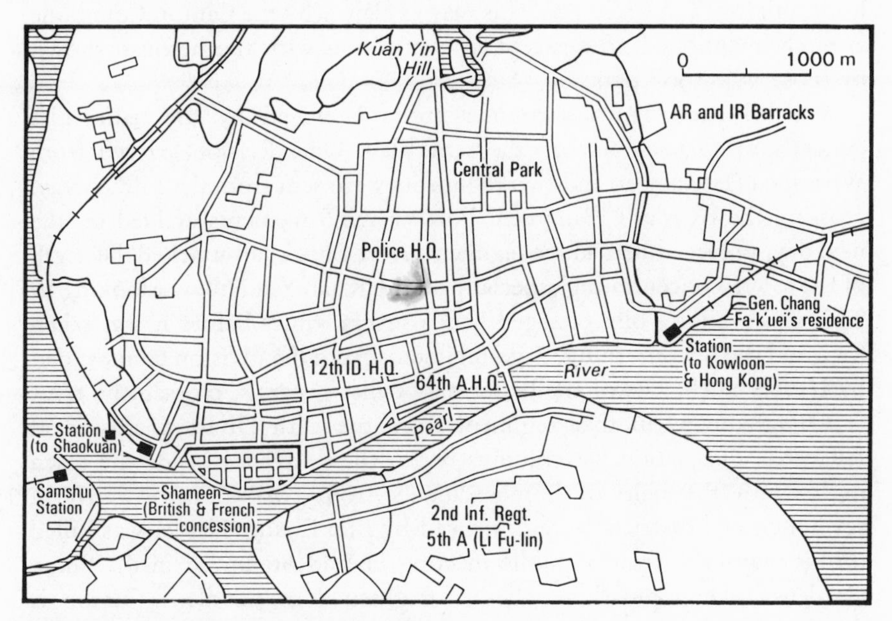

Map 7. The Canton Commune, Canton

On the morning of the same day (11 December) the rebels set up a local soviet government in the head offices of the Public Security, along with the military command. Its members were as follows: Su Chao-cheng (Chairman),[1] Yün Tai-ying (Secretary-General), Chou Wen-yung (Labour), P'eng P'ai (Agriculture), Ho Lai (Economy), Ch'en Yü (Justice), Yang Yin (Purges), Huan Ping (External Affairs), Yeh T'ing (Military Commander), Hsü Kuan-ying (Chief of General Staff) and Chang T'ai-lei (Party Representative).

The proclamation accompanying the Soviet's assumption of power naturally attacked imperialism and feudalism, and announced the most revolutionary measures concerning confiscations, nationalization, redistribution of wealth and cancelling of debts. It categorically rejected all relations with the Kuomintang and proclaimed all its factions illegal. Trotsky wrote a long commentary on these proposals, for, given the

[1] Su Chao-cheng could not get to Canton in time, and Chang T'ai-lei stood in for him.

circumstances, they inevitably set up a dictatorship of the proletariat, which he considered the only regime capable of carrying through the bourgeois democratic revolution.[1] In fact the radicalism of the Canton Commune went further than the 'leftist deviationism' with which the Sixth Party Congress and the Comintern were shortly to reproach the leadership of Ch'ü Ch'iu-pai. This may explain why the Canton Commune is rarely mentioned now except in connection with the heroism shown by those who took part.

A rapid and vigorous counter-stroke launched by the nationalist generals made itself felt on the same day. One division arrived from Whampoa (Huangp'u) and two regiments were sent from the Fifth Army, crossing the river at Chiangmen. Further reinforcements arrived on the next day, 12 December. Three regiments from Shaokuan attacked the north of the town, concentrating especially on the Kuan Yin Hill overlooking it. This observation point changed hands several times before it was taken for good the next morning. Two regiments from the division commanded by Hsüeh Yüeh, one of the better nationalist generals, crossed the river at Chinghaimen; another regiment from the 26th Division crossed at Huansha. The nationalist columns began their advance inside the town itself, with the help of bombardments from two Chinese warships; several central districts were destroyed by fire. Chang T'ai-lei was killed on his way back from a public meeting he had organized in the Sikua Gardens. The population, whether frightened or hostile – Canton is first and foremost a trading town – gave no help to the communists, who were attacked by groups from the newly organized trade unions, and also possibly by the local underworld.

The rebels could hope for no reinforcements, and their losses were heavy. Yeh T'ing gave the order to retreat, which was executed during the night. About 1000 men managed to escape eastwards through Tungshan and Lungyen Tung (the Dragon's Eye Cave). From there they went on to Huahsien and the soviet districts of Haifeng and Lufeng and the East River. A few small groups filtered through to the west via Hsi Mien Ch'ung and later organized the guerrilla operations on the Yü Kiang River in Kwangsi. A few pockets of resistance were still holding out on the morning of 13 December, particularly the Public Security building, which fell to the enemy at 2 p.m. that afternoon after a heroic struggle.

The movement was quelled with the utmost brutality, involving more loss of life than the insurrection itself. The exact number of victims will

[1] Cf. Trotsky, *Problems of the Chinese Revolution* (The Canton Insurrection).

never be known: some communist authors give it as 4000 or 5000, others as 8000, while a nationalist author gives 15,000. The communist cadres were hunted down mercilessly, and about ten Russian subjects were massacred when their consulate was attacked. Yeh T'ing, Hsü Kuan-ying and a few others (among them the future general, Hsü Hsiang-ch'ien, who was then in command of a company), managed to go into hiding and reach Hong Kong, before taking up their eventful careers once more. The crushing of the Canton Commune, coming as it did after the liquidations in Wuhan, Shanghai and other towns, completed the collapse of the Chinese proletariat as an effective revolutionary force. The Communist Party lost its last support in the towns. One way still lay open – to lead the peasants into action, working from the bases where it had taken refuge, and conducting a thorough, lasting mobilization of the entire population. In the circumstances it had no choice but to take this road; some time passed before the Party realized its worth, and it involved further 'leftist' mistakes, resulting in more changes in leadership.

13 Ching Kang Shan: the Sacred Mountain of the Revolution[1]

While the rearguard of the proletariat was being crushed in vain in the Canton streets, Mao Tse-tung, in his refuge in the Ching Kang mountains, was forming a small army from an ill-assorted bunch of men – survivors from the Autumn Harvest Uprising, peasants, former bandits and deserters from the nationalist armies. The barren massif of the Ching Kang mountains (Ridge of Wells), situated on the boundaries of Hunan and Kiangsi, is part of the great Lo Hsiao Shan range; it stretches over about 50 kilometres from north to south and from east to west, bordered by the districts of Ningkang to the north, Suich'uan to the east, Shangyu to the south and Linghsien to the west, while Kanchow, the largest town in south Kiangsi, is about 100 kilometres to the east. This tangled mass of scrub-covered or wooded hills, where irrigation is difficult in spite of abundant rainfall, was a poor, sparsely populated region. Its 2000 inhabitants lived in about ten hamlets, growing a little rice, sweet potatoes, beans, a little tea and some cotton. Providing supplies for an army, however small, was to prove extremely difficult.

On the other hand, the region had the characteristics of a natural stronghold: fairly high mountain peaks, between 1500 and 1700 metres, long valleys, narrow corridors and no roads. A handful of determined men could keep a much larger enemy force at bay for a long time. Groups of bandits had always retreated there and the authorities did not even bother to pursue them. It was an accepted fact under every dynasty that some mountainous regions were outside the law. In this particular case, the

[1] See Map 8, p. 168.

rebels were sure of added security, as the Ching Kang Shan lie on the borders of two provinces, each of which left the task of bringing them into submission to the other.

After reorganizing his troops, reduced to a few hundred men, at Sanwan, Mao Tse-tung arrived in the Ching Kang Shan at the end of October or the beginning of November 1927, joined by two small groups of peasants from the Ningkang region on the way. First of all he had to claim the territory from two bandit chiefs, two 'companions of the green forests', as the Chinese expression puts it. Wang Tso and Ai Wen-ts'ai, as they were called, at first agreed to be included, with their men (120 rifles), among Mao Tse-tung's troops, but these social outcasts eventually proved impossible to assimilate.[1] For reasons of security, and doubtless to facilitate supplies as well, two small but separate bases were formed – the first and larger of the two covered the central and southern parts of the massif in the Five Wells (Wu Ching) area, while the second, smaller base was to the north, in the Nine Dragon hills (Chiu Lung Shan) on the borders of the Yunghsin, Lienhua and Ch'aling districts.[2] The army set up its defences and installed its extremely rudimentary services in these two small areas of refuge. From there, the communists tried from time to time to spread their activities to the plain and the districts surrounding the mountains. Several districts – Ningkang, Yuhsien, Yunghsin, Ch'aling and Suich'uan – were occupied for varying lengths of time.

Mao Tse-tung's first task was to mould the heterogeneous group of his followers, to whom he had given the somewhat pretentious title of the First Division of the Workers' and Peasants' Army, into a disciplined force with political and military training, inspired by a true revolutionary ideal. Luckily for him, the arrival of Chu Teh with his Fourth Army in April 1928 was to increase his numbers three- or fourfold. The command and the units were reorganized once again. Chu Teh became Commander-in-Chief of the combined forces, now called the Fourth Red Army of the Chinese Workers' and Peasants' Army. Mao Tse-tung's title was Party Representative. In spite of difficulties in obtaining equipment and arms, the Fourth Army gradually developed and, at its largest, numbered between 8000 and 10,000 men (when Chu Teh joined Mao Tse-tung, it numbered little over half this total). It consisted of three regiments – the

[1] History relates that these two bandits remained loyal until the Ching Kang Shan were evacuated by the communists, when they returned to their former life. In February 1930, both were liquidated at Yunghsin by their former comrades in arms at the end of a 'friendly' banquet.

[2] See Mao Tse-tung, 'The Struggle in the Ching Kang Mountains' (25 November 1928), *Selected Works,* vol. I.

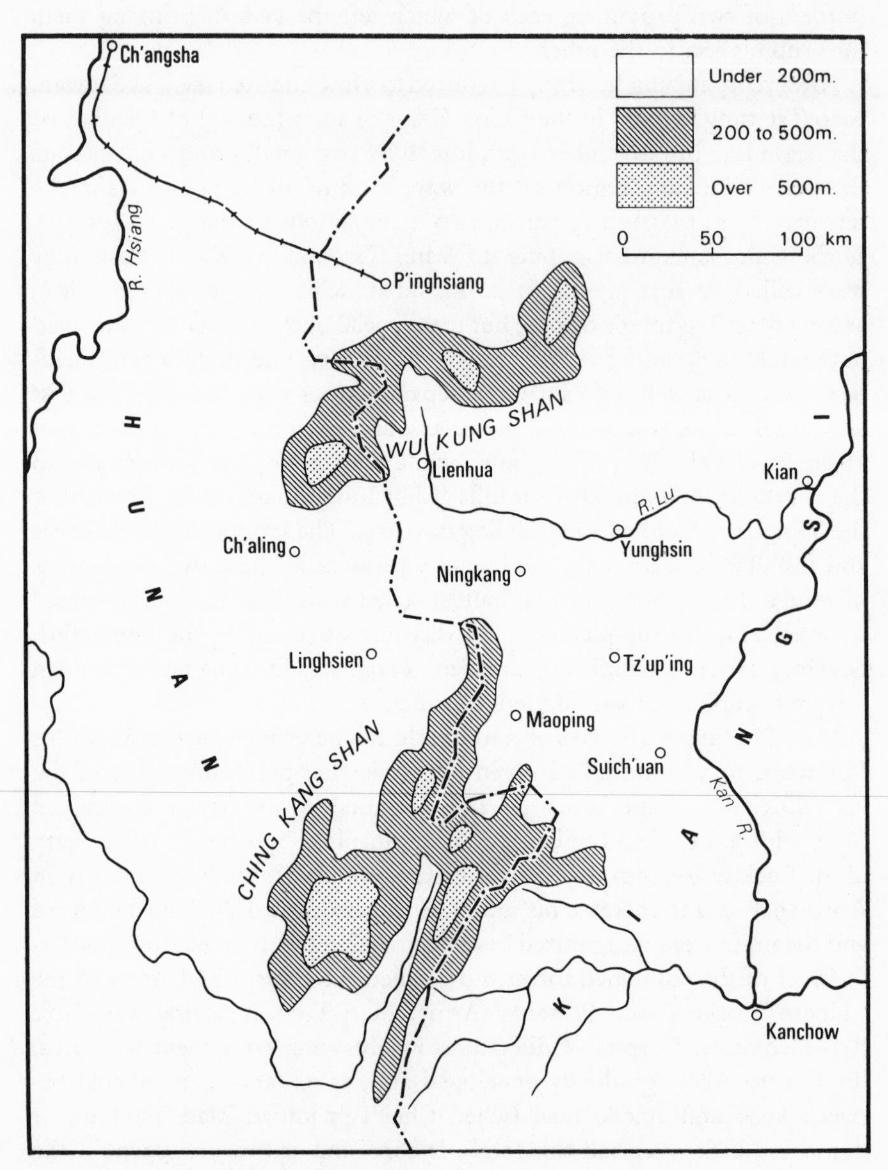

Map 8. The Ching Kang mountains

27th, 29th and 34th – the first two of which had been brought from Hunan by Chu Teh, while the third was the former 1st Division;[1] these were completed by a few service and training units.

Guerrilla units of red guards without uniforms were created alongside the regular army. To begin with, one 'unit' existed for each district (hsien) adjoining the Ching Kang Shan. At that stage the red guards were few in number and scantily armed (Mao Tse-tung, writing in November 1928, says they had 683 rifles), but they played an important part as auxiliary troops. They delayed the enemy and provided the regular army with information and supplies when it was working in their district. They were also responsible for ensuring collaboration between the army and the population. Red guards continued their civilian work and theoretically were under the command of the Party member for the 'hsien'; unlike the regular army, they fought in scattered groups. Alongside the red guards, organized at the 'hsien' level, 'rebel detachments' (Kung nung pao-tung) appeared at the level of the village; these were even less well armed. They were the forerunners of the militia which appeared much later; they helped maintain the new order, and kept the landlords' levies in check in places where the situation was not yet stable.

An army as heterogeneous and untrained as this one needed strict, simple discipline. Basic rules of tactics, taking into account its weakness and the kind of action it was to carry out among the population, had to be drawn up for its cadres. Rules of conduct and a doctrine of fighting emerged little by little, to be codified in the 'Resolution of the Fourth Army's Conference at Kut'ien' in December 1929 (see Chapter 15). It was already noticeable that all army activities, whether military operations or political work, were based on a close collaboration between the army and the population. It is safe to say that the agrarian reform and the cooperation between the army and the population were to be the two most important factors contributing to the success of the communist revolution.

No agrarian measures could be carried out until the revolutionary organizations and administration had been set up. A Front Committee was created to lead the struggle in the Ching Kang Shan.[2] It was responsible to the Hunan Provincial Committee and, through that, to the Central

[1] As a rule, the regiments had three battalions of four companies each, plus one special company, one machine gun company and one mortar company to each regiment. See Mao Tse-tung, 'The Struggle in the Ching Kang Mountains'. In April 1928 the 28th and 31st Regiments were known to be reasonably well armed, and the 32nd poorly armed.

[2] In November 1928 its members were Mao Tse-tung, Chu Teh, T'an Chen-lin, Sung Chiao-sheng and Mao Ke-wen. The last two were mere ciphers.

Committee, and its authority extended to all local Party organizations. A Party Special Committee (Secretary-General Mao Tse-tung) and a Party Military Committee (Secretary Ch'en Yi, and later Chu Teh) came under its orders. From February 1928 onwards, the Party set up its structure, and especially executive committees, in the districts wholly or partially under its control – Ningkang, Yunghsin, Ch'aling, Suich'uan, Lienhua and Linghsien. Party committees then set up governments of workers, peasants and soldiers, elected by local assemblies – in other words, local soviets. This was not easy; the establishment and functioning of the new administration was constantly hindered by such difficulties as finding qualified office-bearers, fear of a return of the Kuomintang, lack of understanding of the respective roles of assemblies and committees, and the special structure of Chinese rural society, with its countless ties. The local governments were supported by various para-revolutionary organizations appealing to the peasants, to young people, to women, etc.

For the first time, the outlying country districts were brought into contact with the political life in which everybody over the age of 16 had to take part. Artificial and directed from outside, it was an entirely new phenomenon. At the same time, wherever it went, the Party endeavoured to stamp out old, harmful habits like opium, gambling, bound feet, inequality of the sexes, etc. Schools (Lenin schools for children of 14 and under, and evening schools) and the army's Political Department played a large part in this field.

However, the revolution was to hinge on the agrarian reform. At the level of the villages in the Ching Kang Shan the reform was carried out to the letter. Confiscated lands were divided into three categories – good, middling and poor – and shared out as equally as possible, taking each family's labour force into consideration. The landlords who escaped physical liquidation were excluded from the sharing out of land, and rents were abolished. The one tax still in existence was theoretically meant not to exceed 15 per cent of the harvest (in fact it reached 20 per cent or more). This method was too radical and alienated the numerous middle peasants whose influence hindered the application of the reform itself. The Party was later to develop a more flexible approach.

The Hunan-Kiangsi red zone did not have the leisure to pursue its experiments far, as its development sparked off increasingly violent reactions on the part of the nationalists. A preliminary operation was carried out in June 1928 by two divisions from Kiangsi. Government troops took Yunghsin and made their way towards Ningkang, Hsinch'eng and Maop'ing. On 22 June they clashed with the 28th and 29th communist regiments, backed up by the Ningkang militia, in the area of the two Ridges of the Seven Steps (Lao Ch'i Chi Ling and Hsin Ch'i Chi Ling). Two columns, one consisting of three regiments commanded by Yang Ch'ih-sheng (9th Division), and the other consisting of four regiments commanded by Yang Ju-kan (27th Division), had to retreat after losing 1000 men who had either deserted or been taken prisoner. Hsinshui was occupied once more. An inscription there reads: 'With one third of its troops, the Red Army destroyed the two sheep from Kiangsi'.[1] West of the Ching Kang Shan, the communists had to evacuate Yuhsien in the face of government troops from Anjen in Hunan.

The nationalists launched another attack in July. This time, according to communist sources, they sent eighteen regiments from the Third, Eighth and Sixth Armies, commanded by Chin Han-ting. The Red Army retreated into its natural stronghold and abandoned the towns (Yunghsin, Ningkang, etc.) to the enemy, but harassed his communications. The government troops retreated after occupying the area for about twenty days. Nanking was to continue the Northern Expedition once more, and all its troops were needed elsewhere; the government lost interest in the red zones until the beginning of the winter, which was fortunate for Mao Tse-tung who had serious difficulties to deal with.

Difficulties arose first of all within the Party itself, from the economic hardships resulting from the nationalist blockade, from the importance assumed by military affairs compared with politics, and because the cadres needed by the Party were recruited too exclusively from among the petty bourgeoisie and the peasants. Mao Tse-tung explains this clearly in several passages on the situation in the Ching Kang Shan. He did not write at length on the subject until over a year after the evacuation of the area, in December 1929, when he produced: 'On Correcting Mistaken Ideas in the Party'. He himself gives a list of mistaken ideas, from which the following are taken:

> The purely military viewpoint . . . [these comrades] think that the task of the Red Army, like that of the White Army, is merely to fight. They do not understand that the Chinese Red Army is an armed body for carrying out the political tasks of the revolution. Other mistakes arise from this one: lack of interest in the masses, individualism, love of individual heroism, and the 'mentality of mercenaries'.
>
> 'Ultra-democracy' is a tendency to apply 'democratic centralism from the bottom to the top', while Party discipline obviously suffers.

[1] A pun on the word 'yang', which is a surname, and also means sheep.

'Failure of the minority to submit to the majority' and 'criticism made without regard to organizational discipline'.

'Absolute egalitarianism', pushed so far that it ruins discipline.

'Subjectivism' and 'individualism'.

Development of a 'vagabond outlook' which leads to the sacrifice of carefully created bases to a love of adventure and the search for material satisfaction.

These various 'mistakes' were no doubt widespread in the Party during the Ching Kang Shan period, as was proved by the 'energetic purge' which Mao Tse-tung admits took place in September 1928. The summer operations had exhausted the region economically, while the food situation in the army, which was scarcely ever paid, had grown still worse. Yuan Chung-ts'uan, in command of the 2nd Battalion of the 28th Regiment, rebelled and killed his colonel and part of his unit followed him in his revolt for a time.

Roughly at the same time, at the urgent request of the provincial Committee of the Party for Hunan which 'encouraged the 29th Regiment in their mistaken ideas', half the Red Army left the Ching Kang Shan for South Hunan.[1] Chu Teh led the 28th and 29th Regiments in the attack on Pinghsien (Ch'enchow), destroying part of the Sixteenth Nationalist Army commanded by his former protector, Fan Shih-sheng. The nationalists' counter-attack on Pinghsien caused the communists to suffer heavy losses in the Ichang region, and they led their troops from south Hunan back to the Ching Kang Shan. These defeats were partly compensated for in advance, as on 22 July a nationalist regiment (the 1st Regiment of the 5th Independent Division of the Hunan Army) stationed in the P'ingchiang area on the borders of Hunan and Hupei (the leader, P'eng Teh-huai, later became one of the best-known generals of the Red Army) went over to the communists. The rebel unit, backed up by local peasant groups, took the title of the Fifth Army. When forced to abandon P'ingchiang after 1 August, it retreated to the Hsiushui, T'ungku and Liuyang area and created the 'Hunan-Hupei-Kiangsi' borders guerrilla base. The Fifth Army then joined the Fourth Army in the Ching Kang Shan, under further pressure from nationalist troops, leaving only small groups behind.

Mao Tse-tung and Chu Teh were then asked by the Central Committee to move their troops eastwards into the Fukien-Kiangsi border area,

[1] Cf. Mao Tse-tung, 'The Struggle in the Ching Kang Mountains'. Kung Ch'u, Commander of the 29th Regiment, attributes the initiative of the movement to Mao Tse-tung and Chu Teh themselves.

leaving P'eng Teh-huai and the Fifth Army to defend the Ching Kang Shan. The transfer began in December; the three regiments of the Fourth Army moved 250 kilometres east of the Ching Kang Shan, fighting several engagements on the way, to settle in the area round Ningtu and Juichin (Kiangsi) and T'ingchow (Fukien), an area which was to be the great Chinese soviet base for five years.

The Fifth Army under P'eng Teh-huai, alone in the Ching Kang Shan, tried to gather together as many armed groups as possible to parry an expected attack from the nationalists, which came in January 1929. After a month of fighting, P'eng Teh-huai, at the end of his resources, also abandoned the Ching Kang Shan and joined the Fourth Army in south Kiangsi. The military history of the Ching Kang Shan does not end there, however, for in the following July the Fifth Army went back there once more, with four times as many men as before. In 1930 the communist attempts to take back Ch'angsha in Hunan and Kian in Kiangsi were launched from this dangerous stronghold with its shifting boundaries. In the autumn of 1934, when the Long March began, the sacred mountain of the Chinese revolution was at last abandoned. Fifteen years were to pass before the communists were able to return. In Western eyes, Juichin and Yenan have obscured the fame of the Ching Kang Shan, but Mao Tse-tung served his apprenticeship for power in their shadow, and they sheltered him while he created the first true Red Army. It is hardly surprising that he has dedicated one of his most beautiful poems to them:

> Below the hill were our flags and banners,
> To the hilltop sounded our bugles and drums.
> The foe surrounded us thousands strong,
> But we were steadfast and never moved.
>
> Our defence was strong as a wall already,
> Now did our wills unite like a fortress.
> From Huangyangchieh came the thunder of guns,
> And the enemy army had fled in the night!

14 The Sixth Congress of the Chinese Communist Party (July-September 1928)

Coming as it did after the great and tragic events of 1927, and faced with an entirely new political situation, the Sixth Congress of the Chinese Communist Party was an exceptionally important one. The revolutionary achievements of the last few years were reviewed, conclusions were drawn from the collaboration with the Kuomintang, and a new general line was drawn up; its lack of clarity caused the new leaders to make new leftist errors. The outcome of the special meeting held at Kiukiang on 7 August 1927 had been the failure of the Autumn Harvest Uprising and the Canton Commune; the Sixth Congress was to lead to the 'adventurism' of Li Li-san.

In February 1928 the Ninth Plenary Assembly of the Comintern Executive Committee had examined the Chinese situation, and purported to explain the causes of the year's failures and blame those responsible for the Canton disaster, particularly its own representatives, Neuman and Lominadze. It also outlined a future policy for China:

> The Party must prepare for the broad upsurge of a new revolutionary wave. That upsurge will confront the Party with the direct practical task of organization and leadership of the mass armed insurrection because only by means of an insurrection and the overthrow of the existing government can the tasks of the revolution be solved. But precisely for that purpose, and because of that, the centre of gravity of all Party activity at the given moment lies in the conquest of the millions of workers and peasants, their political enlightenment, and their organization around the Party. . . . The greatest danger of the present situation lies in the fact that the vanguard of the labour and

peasant movement as a result of a wrong appraisal of the present situation and the underestimation of the enemy forces may be torn away from the masses, run too far ahead, split up its forces and allow itself to be smashed into separate detachments. . . .

It is necessary to fight energetically against putschism among some sections of the working class, against unprepared and unorganized action both in the towns and the rural districts, against playing with insurrection. To play with insurrections, instead of organizing a mass uprising of the workers and peasants is a sure way of losing the revolution. Leading the spontaneous guerrilla actions of the peasants in the various provinces, the Party must have in view that these actions can be transformed into a victorious national uprising only on condition that they will be linked up with the new upsurge of the new revolutionary wave in the proletarian centres. . . .

In this connection it is necessary to fight against becoming carried away with guerrilla warfare in broken up and disconnected detachments which are doomed to failure.[1]

This text reflected the bad memories left by the Autumn Harvest Uprising and the Canton Commune, and showed little confidence in the military action which was confined to country districts, then mainly in the hands of Mao Tse-tung, who had just abandoned the Ching Kang Shan. It also stressed two ideas liable to misinterpretation – the preparation of a new revolutionary upsurge and the need to maintain contact with the towns. The Sixth Congress took them up and developed them, changing them slightly.

Exceptionally, the Sixth Congress of the Chinese Communist Party was held in Moscow, for security reasons, and also possibly to coincide with the Sixth Congress of the International (17 July-1 September).[2] The choice of the Russian capital stressed the fact that the Chinese Communist Party had become more dependent on the Russians since Ch'ü Ch'iu-pai and his team had replaced Ch'en Tu-hsiu and his group. Eighty-four delegates theoretically representing 40,000 members attended the congress, which was also attended by Bukharin and Mif. Among them were: Ch'ü Ch'iu-pai, Chang Kuo-t'ao, Chou En-lai, Li Li-san, Hsiang Chung-fa and Teng Chung-hsia, all of whom were later to have an important role to

[1] 'Resolution on the Chinese Question', Ninth Plenum of the E.C.C.I., 25 February 1928. *Inprecor*.

[2] The Sixth Congress of the Comintern also passed a resolution on the Chinese question, not mentioned here, as most of its suggestions appeared in the 'Political Resolution of the Sixth Congress of the Chinese Communist Party', summarized below.

play. Neither Mao Tse-tung nor any other member from the rural bases was present.[1]

Several important resolutions were passed by the congress, among them those on the political situation, the peasant movement, the agrarian question, the organization of soviets and a suggestion for the organization of the Party. The political resolution outlined the various phases of the world revolutionary movement, emphasizing the growing importance of the Chinese revolution in relation to this, and then defining the tasks lying before the movement. They naturally sprang from the bourgeois-democratic characteristics of the revolution in a country still a prey to 'imperialism' and 'semi-feudal oppression', and to exploitation by landlords. In other words, it called for the rejection of the 'imperialists' and their Chinese allies (warlords, compradors, landlords and Kuomintang bourgeoisie) and for the inauguration of an agrarian reform, beginning at the bottom and working upwards. Since the bourgeoisie had proved themselves traitors, the peasants and workers alone could be the instruments in these great undertakings. 'Ten Great Demands of the Chinese Revolution' were drawn up:

1 Overthrow imperialist rule.
2 Confiscate companies and banks controlled by foreign capital.
3 Unify China and acknowledge her people's right to self-determination.
4 Overthrow the government of the Kuomintang warlords.
5 Set up a representative government of workers, peasants and soldiers.
6 Enforce the eight-hour day, higher salaries, aid for the unemployed and social security benefits.
7 Confiscate all landlords' estates; give the land back to the peasants.
8 Improve the soldiers' livelihood, giving them land and work.
9 Abolish all levies and miscellaneous taxes, introduce a single, progressive tax.
10 Unite the proletariat of the world and the Soviet Union.

Official, highly arguable explanations were given for the failure of the united front. It was generally agreed that China was in a 'trough between two waves': 'The first revolutionary wave has now receded, owing to repeated failures; the new wave has not yet come, and the counter-revolutionary forces still surpass those of the workers and peasants.'[2]

In reality, the mistakes of the Party's Secretary-General were openly

[1] Chang Kuo-t'ao recalls this congress in his memoirs. See the *Ming Pao*, No. 29 (Hong Kong, 1968).

[2] Cf. Wang Chien-min, *A History of the Chinese Communist Party* (in Chinese), vol. II, p. 17.

held to be the cause of its failure: 'The chief cause of the failure of the revolution is the opportunist policy followed by the leadership of the Communist Party, vanguard of the proletariat.'[1]

The resolution gave other important causes as well – the power of the imperialists, which was considerable, the bourgeoisie's betrayal of the revolution, the numbers and strength of the reactionary armies, the vacillations of the petty-bourgeoisie, the backwardness of the peasant movement, as compared with the workers' movement, itself weak and scattered, and the fact that peasant agitation was too localized.

When dealing with the period following the change in Party leadership after a meeting at Kiukiang on 7 August 1927, the Sixth Congress acknowledged that a truly revolutionary road had been taken once more. Serious doctrinal errors and errors in application had, however, been committed. The underlying principle of the Nanch'ang Uprising, the Autumn Harvest Uprising and the Canton Commune was correct, but almost all these insurrections had been inadequately prepared among the masses themselves. No lesson had been learned from the failures. The value of the peasant movements in Hupei and Hunan had been overestimated. 'Adventurist' trends had persisted, while the patient organization of the masses had been neglected. The false concept of a 'permanent' revolution in constant progress had not been eliminated.

Future tasks were linked with the prospect of a new, inevitable revolutionary 'rising tide', and may be summarized by the following recommendations:

1 Unite the masses round the Party.
2 Make full use of all opportunities for agitation and class struggle.
3 Avoid 'military opportunism' and 'putschism'.
4 Become reconciled with the petty bourgeoisie, constantly fighting its exploitation.
5 Reinforce and 'proletarianize' the Party.
6 Expand the soviet regimes and develop the revolutionary military forces.
7 Vigorously oppose all Kuomintang groups and the Third Party of Teng Yen-ta and T'an P'ing-shan.[2]
8 Enter into contact with the communist parties of other countries.

[1] Ibid., p. 12.

[2] The Third Party was created by these two men. Teng Yen-ta, formerly one of Chiang Kai-shek's collaborators, and a member of the Kuomintang left wing, was executed in 1931. T'an P'ing-shan left the Communist Party in the autumn of 1927. He later gave his allegiance to the Peking People's Government.

The resolution of the agrarian question was to be more important in the immediate future of the movement. It assumed that the growing economic difficulties would intensify the struggle in the villages, although the struggle was uneven and carried out in a different way from one region to another. As many peasants as possible, both rich and poor, should be mobilized in a broad political front. Henceforward, the accepted principle was to neutralize the rich peasants, make allies of the middle peasants, and put the poor peasants in charge of the peasant associations. This was to remain at the centre of the Party's agrarian policy until the final victory. The system of land distribution was to be adapted to take account of local circumstances. In places where middle peasants were most numerous, it was not advisable to insist on systematic equalization. Peasant associations were to resemble vast battle organizations, some legal, some illegal, whose mission was to form the nucleus of future soviets. If the need arose, the Party was to take over without hesitation the traditional peasant secret societies (Red Spears, Long Knives, etc.) through action from the inside. If necessary, special peasant organizations were to be created.

Particular stress was laid on the peasants' struggles taking the form of guerrilla warfare. Two important results were expected of this – the practical application of the agrarian reform, and the gradual formation of a red revolutionary army of peasants and workers. It was essential that this guerrilla warfare be carried out within the framework of mass movements and backed up by a planned propaganda campaign. Excesses in the form of murders and systematic burning, both of which had occurred too often already, were to be avoided. Lastly, the Communist Party emphasized the need to link up the workers' and peasants' movements, and to make representatives of the proletariat responsible for the leadership.

Later on, Mao Tse-tung underlined several weaknesses apparent at the Sixth Congress, while acknowledging the importance of its work:

> On the other hand, the Sixth Congress also had its shortcomings and mistakes. It lacked correct estimates and policies concerning the dual character of the intermediate classes and the internal contradictions among the reactionary forces; it also lacked necessary understanding of the Party's need for an orderly tactical retreat after the defeat of the Great Revolution, of the importance of the rural base areas and of the protracted nature of the democratic revolution. Although these shortcomings and mistakes prevented the thorough eradication of the 'Left' ideas existing after the 7 August Meeting, and although they were made

> more extreme and were greatly magnified by the subsequent 'Left' ideas, nevertheless they cannot eclipse the correctness of the Congress in its main aspect.[1]

New Party statutes were also adopted at the Sixth Congress (fifteen chapters and fifty-three articles); they remained in use until the Seventh Congress, which revised them in April 1945. The Party leaders were also changed. Chü Ch'iu-pai, judged responsible for what was later called the 'first leftist opportunist deviation', lost his post as Secretary-General and was left behind in Moscow as the Chinese Communist Party's representative to the Comintern. Hsiang Chung-fa, a Hankow boatman of true proletarian stock, became the nominal Secretary-General. A returned student from France, Li Li-san, was the real head of the new Political Bureau, which appears to have had seven members at least: Chang Kuo-t'ao, Chou En-lai, Ch'ü Ch'iu-pai, Hsiang Chung-fa, Hu Wen-chiang, Li Li-san and Ts'ai Ho-shen.[2]

A few changes were made in the Central Committee, to which Mao Tse-tung was elected. This meant little in the light of the fact that he was already in charge of most of the revolution's organized military and rural forces. It marked the beginning of a return to grace, as in November 1927 the Central Committee had blamed him for his failures in Hunan; he lost both his seat as a deputy member of the Central Committee and his membership of the Provisional Political Bureau created on 7 August 1927 at the Conference of Kiukiang.

In the months that followed a serious disagreement was to arise between Mao Tse-tung, resettled in Kiangsi, and Li Li-san who acted as Secretary-General in Shanghai. It was aggravated by the fact that the two men, both Hunanese, had several things in common and had been at the same teachers' training college. Li Li-san, born in Liling in 1900, was seven years younger than Mao Tse-tung and unlike him had the advantage of having spent several years abroad, first in France (Lyons University) and then in Russia. He was a strong-willed, energetic man and, like Chang Kuo-t'ao, he was one of the two or three individuals capable of achieving the stature and destiny of Mao Tse-tung, had events been in his favour. Chou En-lai, in charge of military questions in the new Political Bureau, was a close friend of Li Li-san and without any doubt had a large share in the defeats of 1930, although his subtlety and flexibility enabled him

[1] 'Resolution on Certain Questions in the History of our Party', *Selected Works*, vol. III.
[2] According to R. C. North in *Kuomintang and Chinese Communist Elites*, Chang Kuo-t'ao gives the same list. Hu Wen-chiang was, however, replaced by Hsiang Ying.

to avoid the same disgrace. He was also able to realize sufficiently early that Mao Tse-tung, with the backing of the Party's administrative and, above all, military organization, was bound to get the better of a political organization suffering from the difficulties of operating in secret and virtually lacking in all popular support.

During the same year (1929) the troops who had left the Ching Kang Shan for Kiangsi had made great advances both in numbers and in quality. Mao Tse-tung was chiefly responsible for this. Here again, he managed to combine traditional experience of Chinese popular insurrections with a use of modern revolutionary tactics and of the geographical and human characteristics of his country, so that he appeared both an original thinker and an original military scientist on an international scale, capable of imparting inspiration directly to the rebel troops and, at the same time, to the troops sent to suppress them.

15 From the Ching Kang Shan to Kiangsi
The Development of Red Bases and Red Armies in Central China

The Kiangsi central base

Like the Ching Kang Shan bases, the Red Army's new main base was set among hills and relatively high mountains (500-1200 metres), in an area lying on the boundaries of several provinces: Kiangsi, Fukien and, to a lesser extent, Kwangtung. The jagged relief and shifting boundaries make it hard to define its area with exactitude. Roughly speaking, the base may be described as stretching eastwards from the Kan valley as far as the foothills of the Wu Yi Shan, or (to put it another way) a line from Ningtu to Juichin could be given as its north-south axis, and another from Kanchow to T'ingchow as its east-west axis. The area was nearly 200 kilometres long by 150 kilometres wide, covering about 30,000 square kilometres; its population was 5 or 6 million (see Map 9, p. 182). The climate was hot and wet, with plentiful summer rains and a fairly cold winter. Rice, tea and tung oil were the chief products grown on the red, not particularly fertile soil. Less wild and more hospitable than the Ching Kang Shan, the area had several market towns: Juichin, Ningtu, Chiangk'ou and T'ingchow, though on the whole it was a poor region where communications were difficult. These characteristics were to help the communists when the central government was able to set about dislodging them; five hard campaigns between 1931 and 1934 were needed to accomplish it. The Red Army from the Ching Kang Shan grew freely and quickly in its base in Kiangsi, considering its low numbers at the outset and the difficulties in obtaining supplies and equipment.

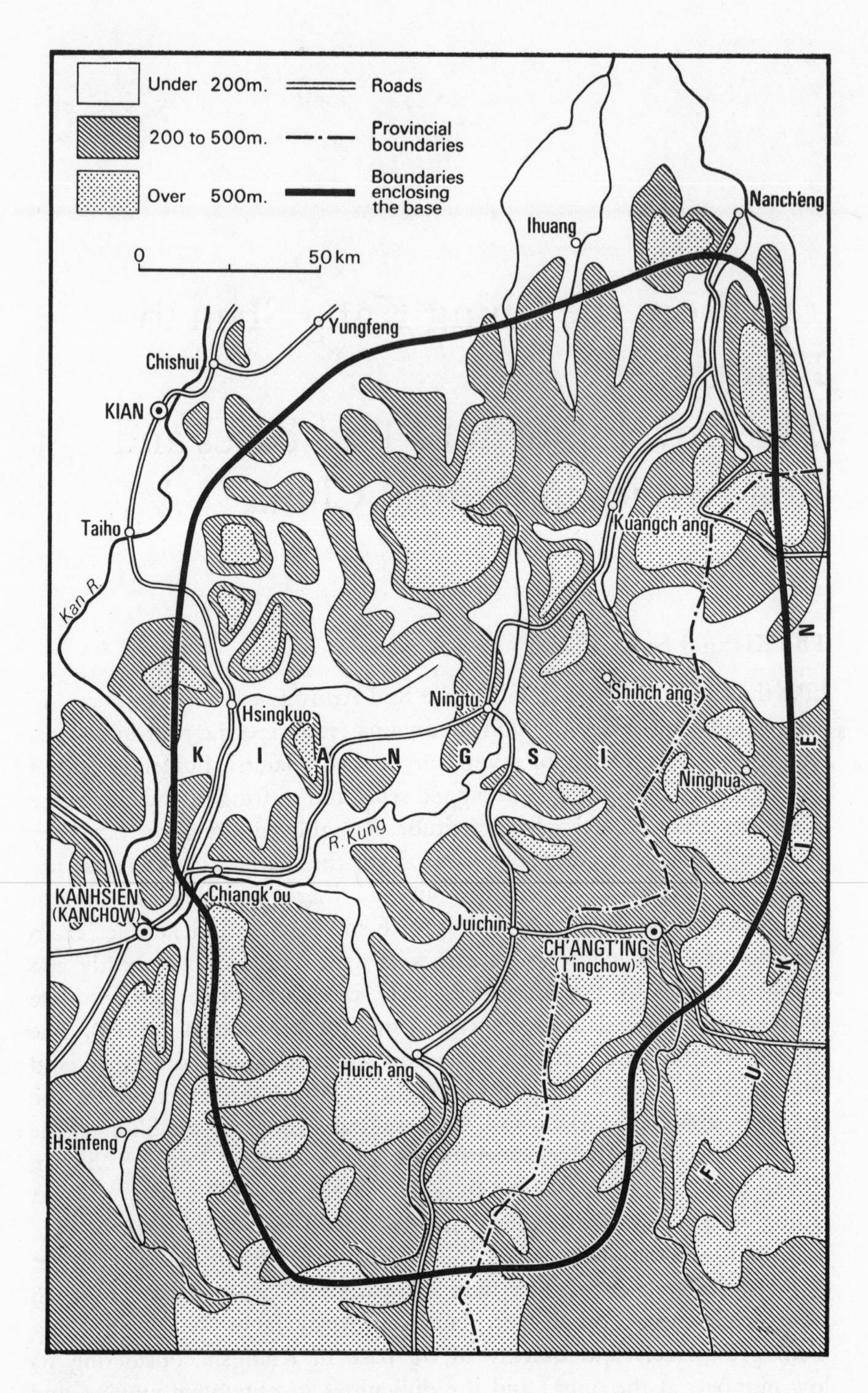

Map 9. The Kiangsi central base

The small bases in Central China

Following the example of the large Kiangsi base, small ones were to grow up or develop alongside it, generally situated in similar mountainous areas where several provincial boundaries converged. The communist historian, Hu Hua, reckons that by the summer of 1930 about fifteen bases existed covering one or several districts; the regular troops defending them numbered between 60,000 and 70,000 men, belonging to thirteen armies.

The political situation helped enormously towards the development of both the communist armed forces and the bases themselves. The Northern Expedition was coming to an end, but serious disagreements arose between the nationalist leaders, and soon degenerated into armed conflicts. In March 1929, a war took place between the Kwangsi generals, Li Tsung-jen and Pai Ch'ung-hsi, and Chiang Kai-shek. In May of the same year, Chiang Kai-shek made war on Feng Yü-hsiang. In 1930 another war broke out between Chiang Kai-shek and Feng Yü-hsiang who had the support of Yen Hsi-shan. The central government's first task was to bring the provincial generals into submission or eliminate them, to maintain the newly accomplished national unity, before attacking the communists who seemed but a minor danger now they had taken refuge in poor, outlying areas.

In the middle of 1930 the distribution of red bases (see Map 10, p. 184) and the battle order of the troops at their disposal was roughly as follows. The main Kiangsi-Fukien base centred on Juichin covered a more or less continuous stretch of land. A South Kiangsi government and a West Fukien government were created there in March 1930. Its troops had been reorganized. In June 1929 the former Fourth Army became the First Army Group, remaining under the command of Chu Teh. In May 1930 P'eng Teh-huai's Fifth Army became the Third Army Group. Then in August 1930 the First and Third Army Groups formed the First Red Front Army, with 30,000 men. Chu Teh naturally took over the command of it.[1] In May 1928 a communist agitator, Fang Chih-min, had created a rebel zone in the area round Iyang and Hengfeng in north-east Kiangsi, near the borders of Chekiang and Fukien. In 1930 he created a Tenth Army there. On the boundaries of Honan, Hupei and Anhwei the guerrillas from the Mach'eng and Huangan area who had taken part in the Autumn Harvest Uprising formed the Fourth Army Group under the

[1] The composition of the army groups naturally varied as time went on; the First Army Group generally included the Third, Fourth, Twelfth, Twentieth, Twenty-first and Twenty-second Armies, and the Third Army Group, commanded by P'eng Teh-huai, consisted of the Seventh, Eighth and Sixteenth Armies.

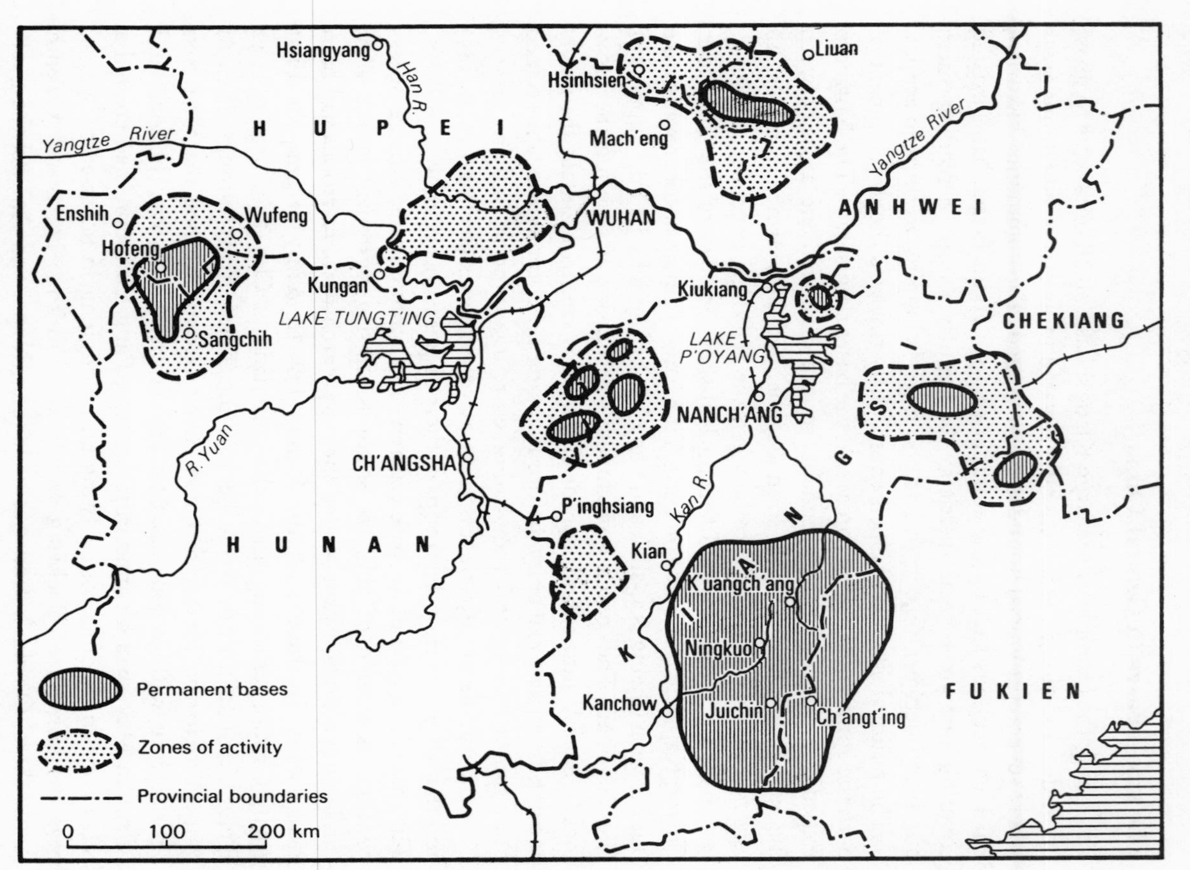

Map 10. The Central China bases

leadership of Chang Kuo-t'ao[1] and Hsü Hsiang-ch'ien.[2] This important base was to survive until 1933.

Ho Lung, one of the rebels who took part in the Nanch'ang Uprising, enlarged an existing red base, creating a Second Army, in the area round Sangchih, Enshih, Wufeng and Hofeng, at the other end of the province of Hupei, and in the west of the neighbouring province of Hunan. Not far from there a Sixth Army was formed, in the Kungan area, north of Lake Tungt'ing. At the end of 1930 these two armies became the Second Army Group. Another important but short-lived base with Chang Yün-i, Kung Ch'u and Teng Hsiao-p'ing was formed in the Paise and Lungchow area in south Kwangsi, on the rivers Tso Kiang and Yü Kiang. The Seventh and Eighth Armies created there were moved to Hunan in 1930 in preparation for the attack on Ch'angsha.[3]

The fact that red bases were scattered over about ten provinces should not give the impression that government rule was disintegrating, for this was far from the truth. The contemporary Chinese or Western press shows how little importance was attached to the communist question, from 1928 to 1931 at least. The Chinese communists, concerned above all with survival, tried not to draw any more attention to themselves than they could help. The discretion of the base leaders was not imitated by the new team that grew out of the Sixth Congress; its untimely, aggressive attitude almost caused the complete loss of the red zones and the army.

The development of the Red Army

Luckily for the communists, Mao Tse-tung and Chu Teh, as well as the leaders of the red zones dispersed throughout Central China, carried out a thorough organization and training of the Red Army, as well as giving it political instruction. Each zone underwent a separate military development, as local conditions and resources permitted. No real order or unity was established in the Army until the formation of the Chinese Soviet Government at the end of 1931. The following description applies to the period that began with this event, and does not claim to cover all the countless different situations.

[1] Chang Kuo-t'ao remained in Moscow, however, until 1931.

[2] The First and Fifteenth Armies. Hsü Hsiang-ch'ien gave an account of the origins of this base in the *People's Daily* of 29 July 1967. The Chengchow Museum (Honan) has devoted a room to it. See also MacColl, 'Oyüwan Soviet Area 1927-1932', *Journal of Asian Studies,* November 1967.

[3] A detailed history of the Kwangsi bases is given in Kung Ch'u's book, *I and the Red Army* (in Chinese). See also an article by Hu Wen-hua in the review *The Unity of the Minorities* (*Min-tsu t'uan-chi*), 7 July 1961.

As is often the case with movements of insurrection or resistance, the growth of the Red Army was punctuated by serious inner conflicts and disorders, leading to large-scale purges and executions. The Fut'ien Incident, which occurred in Kiangsi in 1930 and was severely repressed by Mao Tse-tung, and the incident at the Hupei-Honan-Anhwei base at the end of 1931, which resulted in several hundred victims (conveniently dismissed as 'counter-revolutionaries'), were far from being isolated cases (see Chapter 17).

Organization and recruitment[1]

The regular army was organized on a ternary system: three divisions (shih) in each army (chün), three regiments (t'uan) in each division, three battalions (ying) to a regiment, three companies (lien) to a battalion, three platoons (p'ai) to a company, three sections (pan) to a platoon. The basic unit consisted of twelve men, including the section leader and his assistant.

The following organization table of a typical infantry company is given as an example:[2] 1 company commander, 1 political commissar, 3 platoon leaders, 9 section leaders, 9 assistant section leaders, 90 riflemen, 1 section leader (light machine gun), 2 gun layers, 2 ammunition carriers, 1 headquarters platoon leader, 22 clerks, runners, medical orderlies, etc. (total: 141 combatants). Weapons: 6 pistols, 1 light machine gun, 11 rifles.

The battalion contained three companies, one service section of 20 men and a heavy machine gun company (four machine guns shared between two sections, plus a section of riflemen). As well as its three battalions, a regiment had a 'special unit' responsible for reconnaissance and intelligence, transport (porters), supplies and medical help. In addition to its services, a division included a mortar company, a company of engineers and an intelligence unit as part of its headquarters. Only at army level were there a little artillery and relatively large services, particularly a modern signals detachment. The numbers of these units amounted to about 500 men to a battalion, 1600-1700 to a regiment, 5200-5300 to a division, and 16,000 to an army. All these numbers should naturally be used with caution, particularly as far as the larger units are concerned, as here the titles represented intentions rather than reality.

[1] The following details and figures are taken from a communist document, *Historical Facts of the Second Revolutionary War Period* (Peking, 1956: in Chinese). Texts captured from the communists between 1929 and 1931 and published by the Kuomintang have also been used.

[2] Ch'en Ch'eng, *Reactionary Documents of the Red Bandits* (in Chinese), vol. VI.

Local troops took their place alongside the regular army. They were made up partly of red guards (chih wei-tuei) and partly of the 'young vanguard' (shao-nien feng-tuei). Theoretically, all citizens between 18 and 40, except former landowners, belonged to the red guards, apart from those between 18 and 23 who joined the 'young vanguard'. In fact, only the most able-bodied men were habitually used on military operations. They formed 'model units' always ready to march alongside the regular army. Their organization alone will be given here, which was as follows: a 'large subdistrict' (ta ch'ü) contained two to three companies; a 'small subdistrict' (hsiao ch'ü) contained one or two companies; one or two 'large subdistricts' made up a battalion of three to five companies; three to five battalions constituted a regiment. A division (three to five regiments) was created at the level of the district (hsien). The company (the basic unit) contained at least 120 fighting men.

With the existence of the model units, the red guards, the vanguard and women's groups, the whole population was almost entirely mobilized in times of crisis. Although the regular army's action on the battlefield was hampered by lack of weapons, it was nevertheless spared endless tasks concerning supplies, transport, medical services and the security of the rear. The support of the entire population created an atmosphere and state of mind eminently suited to the army's operations. A population that was already mobilized from the ideological and the practical point of view provided the army with trained volunteers ready to replace its losses almost instantaneously. When faced with an enemy superior both in numbers and equipment, though at fault as far as its methods of recruitment and its attitude towards gaining the population's support were concerned (unlike the communists, it did not need to rely on material support from the population), these advantages proved decisive for a long time, and explain the series of resounding victories won by the defenders of the red zones between 1931 and 1934.

Recruitment for the regular army was at first carried out as circumstances dictated, without any special rules; young men, mainly peasants, were called upon above all. The following statistics were given for April 1934, shortly before the end of the Kiangsi period.

Age:	%
Under 16	1
16 to 23	51
24 to 40	44
over 40	4

Social origins:	%
Peasants	68
Workers and artisans	30
Office workers	1
Miscellaneous	1
Place of origin:	
Red zones	77
White zones	12
Prisoners from the nationalist army	2
Deserters from the nationalist army	9

Twenty-eight per cent of the cadres and men were members of the Communist Party, and 16 per cent were members of Communist Youth.

Discipline

First and foremost, even before ideological questions are taken into account, a soldier must be disciplined; if rules are to be known and applied, they must be simple and easy to learn by heart. The 'three rules and eight points' answer these requirements. They are surprisingly elementary. Their content is explained by the fact that traditional Chinese society was selfish and the soldiers always badly behaved.

The Three Rules:

1 Obey orders in all your actions.
2 Do not take a single needle or piece of thread from the masses.
3 Turn in everything captured.

The Eight Points:

1 Speak politely.
2 Pay fairly for what you buy.
3 Return everything you borrow.
4 Pay for anything you damage.
5 Do not hit or swear at people.
6 Do not damage crops.
7 Do not take liberties with women.
8 Do not ill treat captives.[1]

The eight points should more accurately be called 'recommendations'.

[1] Mao Tse-tung, *Selected Works*, vol. IV, p. 155.

Military discipline quickly became one with political training. This political training awakened the soldiers' class consciousness, forging the disturbingly disparate collection that formed the first Red Army in the Ching Kang Shan into a unified whole. Here ideological concepts and practical necessity coincided. Mao Tse-tung's army was not simply an instrument of military power; its role as a revolutionary political organization was as important as that of an organized military force, if not more so: 'The Red Army fights not merely for the sake of fighting but in order to conduct propaganda work among the masses, organize them, arm them, and help them to establish revolutionary political power.'[1]

Over and over again, Mao Tse-tung denounced the 'purely military viewpoint' – *esprit de corps*, a tendency to individual heroism, the mentality of mercenaries, the vagabond outlook and 'putschism'.

It should be pointed out that the idea of a close link between the army and the masses was not a new one in China. The formation of local militia accorded with extremely ancient practices. The political and ideological T'ai p'ing movement based its military organization on Chou dynasty ritual and the Ming dynasty militia regulations. The concepts of the family and the army were so closely bound up together that the group of twenty-five families organized and commanded by a 'Liang Sse ma' was the political, social, military and religious cell on which military action, the agrarian reform, education, and control of public morality could all be based. On the other hand, the provincial armies formed from carefully recruited militia by the great viceroys (Li Hung-chang, Tseng Kuo-fan, etc.) to combat the T'ai p'ing were submitted to a neo-Confucian ideology aimed at counterbalancing the T'ai p'ing socio-Christian ideology. This last was particularly true of Hunan, Mao Tse-tung's native province. However, in the case of the Kiangsi red armies, ideological severity and all forms of discipline were ensured by the creation of a political organization far more powerful than that of the T'ai p'ing or the imperial militia.

The Red Army's political organization

Political organization existed at all levels of the Red Army: a Political Department for the 'large units' and political commissars for the smaller ones, down to company level. These were not only in charge of the political training and control of cadres and men, but of propaganda activities conducted among the civilian population as well. In newly liberated areas, the Political Department of the army or the division set up the new

[1] 'On Correcting Mistaken Ideas in the Party', *Selected Works*, vol. I, p. 106.

temporary administrative structures. This practice was to continue until 1949.

The means at the disposal of the Political Department naturally varied from one level to another. At the level of the Front Army at the head of the Army Groups the following services were to be found: general affairs, organization, local affairs, youth, propaganda. A political instructors' battalion (a school for cadres, in fact) and a company of guards also existed. At the level of the division, the Political Department contained about thirty people, twenty-one of whom belonged to the propaganda section. The political commissar of a regiment had only four or five

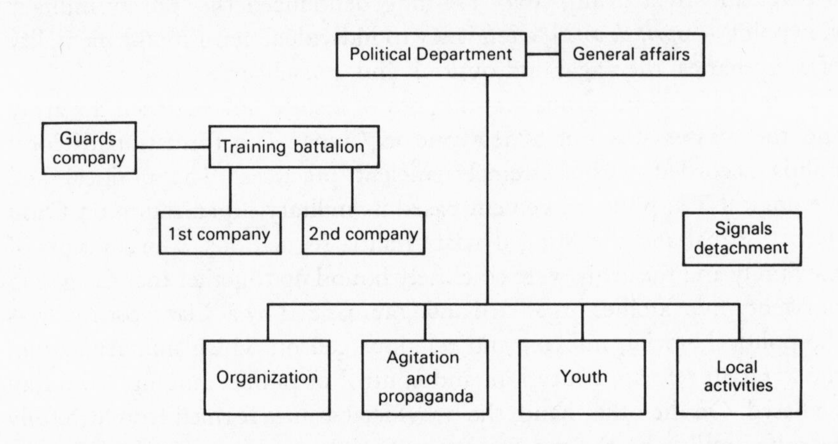

assistants, but as in the case of subordinate units, he naturally had the support of the Communist Party's own organization. Each unit's political activities were centred round the 'Lenin room', which existed in all established units. The political commissar's authority was considerable. He was virtually the link between his unit and the civilian population and its social or political organizations; he also took part in the commander's duties. He gave his approval to the latter's orders (except for operational orders) and was expected to be capable of commanding in the field. The same person rarely combined the duties of unit commander and political commissar. In spite of the strict organization and the watchfulness of its control apparatus, the Red Army's spirit and discipline left much to be desired at first. The Kut'ien Resolution affords proof of this (December 1929), as do the savage purges which were to affect some units.[1]

[1] Mao Tse-tung was responsible for this resolution, which was passed during the Ninth Conference of Army Representatives, and part of which appears in *Selected Works*, vol. I: 'On Correcting Mistaken Ideas in the Party'. It is considered to have shaped the fundamental military line followed since then.

The Red Army set itself apart from all the others above all by its behaviour towards the masses. It did not set out to be the Nation's Army, for this was an abstract notion difficult to grasp, but the People's Army, belonging to the population among whom it lived, claiming to liberate the masses from the foreigners and reactionary forces, while carrying out a reorganization of the population which was both superficial and far-reaching. Its powerful propaganda machine enabled it to overcome an extremely ancient pacifist and anti-militaristic current. At the same time the weak, scattered communist forces, with their lack of material means, had no choice but to win the support of the population. They were helped in this by the upheaval in peasant ownership of land which accompanied their own development; Mao Tse-tung was justified in his frequent use of the expression 'revolutionary agrarian war'.

Strategy and tactics

The withdrawal of rebel forces into mountainous regions or regions of little political or economic importance is a phenomenon of which countless examples exist both in Chinese and European history. One of the most famous of Chinese popular novels, the *Water Margin* (*Shui-Hu-Chuan*), listed by Mao Tse-tung as one of his favourite books, relates the adventures of 108 bandits or heroes sheltering in the Liangshan; under every dynasty, bands of men rebelled in the name of the people against the injustice and arbitrary decisions of the central power. Even so, Kiangsi is set up frequently as an unprecedented phenomenon:

> The long-term survival inside a country of one or more small areas under red political power completely encircled by a white regime is a phenomenon that has never occurred anywhere else in the world.[1]

This claim of an unprecedented phenomenon can only be allowed if the words 'white' and 'red' are underlined, with all the political conflicts they imply. The achievement of Mao Tse-tung and his party lay in their ability to give a new political meaning to an old situation. The agrarian reform and the identification, or at least close association, of the troops with the population gave a special character to the Kiangsi base which was to be cultivated in other parts of Central China before being transferred to North China in 1935, and above all after 1937. The support afforded by a population which was psychologically mobilized and thoroughly familiar with the surrounding area was to make Mao Tse-tung on several occasions

[1] 'Reasons for the Emergence and Survival of Red Political Power in China', *Selected Works*, vol. I, p. 64.

state his preference for a flexible 'strategic defensive' on interior lines.[1] The great successes of 1931 to 1933, like the military failures due to the Li Li-san line in 1930, and like the 1934 disaster, for which he declined to accept responsibility, were to prove him right.

Mao Tse-tung was also to realize that victory could not be won through guerrilla warfare alone. From the Kiangsi period onwards he endeavoured to change from this sort of warfare to a regular war in Chinese style, which, on his own admission, was no more than guerrilla warfare on a higher level.[2] Nothing in his tactics could justify Mao Tse-tung's claim to originality, for they tally with the normal evasive strategy adopted by light units of the type he was using: to scatter for the purposes of living and political work, to gather together to fight, to take the enemy by surprise as often as possible, to avoid all wastage in terms of men. Mao Tse-tung must have had immense faith in himself to be able to affirm that 'The tactics we have derived from the struggle of the past three years are indeed different from any other tactics, ancient or modern, Chinese or foreign.'[3]

The one new factor in these tactics – and it must be admitted that it was of the utmost importance – was the participation of the masses in the operations, whether direct, in the shape of model units of red guards, or indirect, in the shape of logistical help. In tactics, as in discipline, rules had to be simple; hence the choice of expressive formulae, whose meaning was concentrated in four characters and easy for all to understand: 'The enemy advances, we retreat', 'The enemy camps, we harass', 'The enemy tires, we attack', 'The enemy retreats, we pursue'. Other similar condensed sentences existed to deal with different situations in battle.

A glance at Mao Tse-tung's works is enough to gauge the extent of his interest in military questions, and his efforts to draw practical conclusions from each campaign and gather them into a coherent system. It should be added that he was the only person to write, while placing himself in such a high position; Chu Teh, his constant associate at that time at least, produced virtually no writings of any importance, and the same is true of his generals – P'eng Teh-huai, Lin Piao, Ho Lung – who nevertheless achieved remarkable results. Perhaps war was so closely tied up with and subordinated to politics and ideology that only the supreme head could draw up its doctrine.

[1] See particularly 'Problems of Strategy in China's Revolutionary War', *Selected Works*, vol. I, p. 179.

[2] Ibid. pp. 179 ff.

[3] 'A Single Spark can Start a Prairie Fire', *Selected Works*, vol. I, p. 124.

Mao Tse-tung's optimism

Direct contact with the problems of the country's general situation inspired Mao Tse-tung to begin to give a detailed account in his writings of his conception of the Chinese revolution. His idea, as expressed in two fundamental documents, 'Why is it that Red Political Power can Exist in China?' (5 October 1928) and 'A Single Spark can Start a Prairie Fire' (3 January 1930), is both optimistic and prudent. It also reveals the methods of action preferred by the man who was to guide the Chinese revolution. Mao Tse-tung's optimism was based on observable facts. The chronic disagreements between the Chinese warlords safeguarded to a large extent the survival of the red zones. At the same time the country's economic fragmentation enabled each region to carry on independently of the rest, while the national economy was unaffected by this secession. Lastly, the fact that a Red Army had been created ensured that the bases would last and develop in the future.

When considering methods, Mao Tse-tung held that 'adventurism' on the part of the army or the guerrilla forces was to be avoided. He spoke out vigorously against all who wanted first of all to enlarge the peasant revolt and spread political influence by guerrilla raids alone, conquering the masses and establishing political power afterwards. He considered it essential to organize power in the bases on solid foundations, further the agrarian revolution there, and develop the Red Army, destined to be the 'most powerful instrument of all in the coming great revolution'.

He also parried possible ideological criticisms of the peasants' military role: 'Therefore, it would be wrong to abandon the struggle in the cities, but in our opinion it would also be wrong for any of our Party members to fear the growth of peasant strength lest it should outstrip the workers' strength and harm the revolution'.[1]

Mao Tse-tung was already voicing disapproval in advance of the illusions and excesses of the 'Li Li-san line', which was to overestimate the 'subjective revolutionary forces', while underestimating those of the counter-revolution, and lead to 'putschism'. His judgement doubtless also reflects his anxiety to avoid any rash disturbance of the foundations of his own power, in the shape of his base in central Kiangsi and his armies. Events were to bear out his foresight and his anxiety.

[1] 'A Single Spark can Start a Prairie Fire', *Selected Works*, vol. I, p. 123.

16 The Li Li-san Line

Li Li-san[1]

Li Li-san's energy carried considerable weight in the decisions that launched the Communist Party on a wild project to reconquer the towns. Li Li-san's origins resembled those of Mao Tse-tung; like him, he was a native of Hunan province. Born in Liling in 1900, or as other sources state, in about 1896, he was younger than Mao; like him, he entered the Hunan Teachers' Training College. Mao Tse-tung has related the circumstances in which he got to know Li Li-san. After putting an advertisement in a local paper in an effort to form a group of young men who, like him, were interested in politics, he received, as he put it, three and a half replies: 'The "half" reply came from a non-committal youth named Li Li-san. Li listened to all I had to say, and then went away without making any definite proposals himself, and our friendship never developed.'[2]

Li Li-san went to France in 1919 as a worker-student and ended up by being expelled from Lyons University with others of his fellow-students. He was already a communist, and appears next to have gone to Moscow, where he stayed until 1923. Between 1923 and 1927 Li Li-san made a name for himself in the trade union movements in Canton and Shanghai; he was elected Vice-Chairman of the General Labour Federation (1926-7). As such, he went back to Moscow in March 1926 to attend the Fourth

[1] Alias Li Min-jan and Li Lung-chih, sometimes Li Cheng; a former collaborator of Voitinsky's.

[2] Edgar Snow, *Red Star over China*, p. 146 of the 1968 edition.

Congress of the Profintern. It is important to point out this interest in the workers and their world in so far as it helped to cut him off from his peasant origins and consequently from Mao Tse-tung's activities in the rural areas. Whereas Mao Tse-tung, who did not leave China until 1950, remained aware of his country's true situation, Li, a 'returned student' from France and Russia, was more ready to accept trends from abroad. For the same reason, and also because of his age and training, it was inevitable that his ideas should be different from those of Ch'en Tu-hsiu, a self-educated Marxist.

Although he was not among Ch'en's closest collaborators when he was Secretary-General, Li Li-san was a member of the Political Bureau elected by the Fifth Congress. When the Political Bureau was reshuffled at Kiukiang on 7 August 1927 he remained a member of it. He managed to remain in the Political Bureau during the Sixth Congress, taking over the leadership of it, in spite of a relatively unimportant post (Propaganda), thanks to the inadequacy of Hsiang Chung-fa. From September 1929 Li Li-san was the real, if not the only, head of the Chinese Communist Party.

The origins and the explanation of the military events of the summer of 1930, whose resounding failure was to provide the proof of Li Li-san's leftist deviation (the Party's second leftist deviation, according to the official Party history), are to be found in the resolutions passed by the Second Plenary Session of the Sixth Central Committee. This session, which was attended by only about half of the committee members, with the addition of seven other people, took place in June or July 1929 and lasted six days. The 9 July resolution is the result of its work.

The resolution analysed the world situation and that of China, concluding that the world situation was moving towards a period of even more severe crisis, for the progress of the Soviet Union and the revolutionary movement in various countries was provoking more and more hostile reactions from the capitalist powers. In the case of China in particular, it noted that competition between the imperialist nations – Japan, Great Britain and the United States – was becoming keener and that feudal classes were receiving more support from foreign interests and exploiting the people even more mercilessly; this exploitation was in return encouraging a revolutionary movement whose 'rising tide' seemed neither 'very remote' nor 'imminent'. The resolution of 9 July 1929 noted that the proletariat was awakening further in spite of the development of the Kuomintang trade unions and the relative success achieved by bourgeois reformism. It expressed consternation at its weakness and showed anxiety to begin bolder action among the workers in the towns once more.

The need to organize the workers and give them military training was clearly stated. The text of this long resolution is a document of enormous interest to anyone wishing to examine the internal situation in the Party during these difficult years. A little later the Comintern addressed a letter to the Chinese Communist Party, which appears to have urged the Party to undertake direct action on a vast scale as soon as possible.[1]

Li Li-san's intentions took shape from the spring of 1930 onwards. First of all, they were clearly set out in a letter from the Central Committee to the Fourth Army Front Committee – or, in other words to Mao Tse-tung (letter dated 3 April 1930).[2] The Central Committee showed alarm at the supposed intentions of Mao Tse-tung and Chu Teh, who appeared to want to spread their activities southwards, towards Kwangtung. It stated that the essential aim of the Red Army should be to take the big towns of the three provinces of Hunan, Hupei and Kiangsi, and particularly Wuhan; their success should then be developed on a national scale. Lastly, the Central Committee appeared to reproach the Red Army for its slow development and its tendency to scatter its material resources too widely. Until June 1930, however, no large-scale operations against the towns seem to have been imminent; a conference of delegates from soviet zones called by the Party and the General Labour Federation on 25 February, which met in May in Shanghai, was not to make much headway in preparations for a military insurrection.

The resolution of 11 June

The Central Committee's resolution passed on 11 June 1930, entitled 'The New Revolutionary Rising Tide and Preliminary Successes in one or more Provinces', is the key document in the Li Li-san affair. Referring to the atmosphere in the world as a whole, it restates the themes of the 1929 resolution, with greater emphasis: the importance of China for the Western powers and threats to the Soviet Union, an illustration of which was to be found in the United States of Europe suggested by Briand: 'Thus the chief danger of the moment is a war of aggression against the Soviet Union.'

The external and internal crises provoked a situation in which the opposition between the Chinese bourgeoisie and proletariat could quickly develop into a political struggle, or even an armed struggle.

[1] The letter, dated 26 October 1929, appeared in the *Red Flag* of 15 February 1930, No. 16. See B. Schwartz, *Chinese Communism and the Rise of Mao*, p. 134.

[2] See Hsiao Tso-liang, *Power Relations within the Chinese Communist Movement 1930-1934*, p. 14. Hsiao analyses this letter, the original of which he studied in Taiwan.

> Thus China is the weakest link in the chain of world imperialism; it is there that the volcano of world revolution is most likely to erupt. Consequently, thanks to the present aggravation of the world revolutionary crisis, the Chinese revolution may be the first to break out and spark off world revolution and decisive class war in the world.

The Chinese communist leaders of that time had big ideas about their mission or at least about their possibilities in the revolutionary field. They reproached the 'rightists' and 'opportunists' in the Party, particularly Ch'en Tu-hsiu, for their failure to give international importance to China, the 'largest colony of the world'.

The same document states that China's internal difficulties were so great that a 'new revolutionary rising tide' was beginning to flow. In the towns, the bourgeoisie was fighting a 'last-ditch battle': 'The greatest handicaps in our present task are the rightist ideas of doubt and pessimism with regard to the struggle of the workers.'

As the great revolutionary struggle was likely to happen in various different places, involving the activities of various groups (workers, peasants and soldiers), its technical preparation must be properly co-ordinated and organized. In practice, this took the form of 'action committees' belonging to different movements – the Party, trade unions and mass organizations – at the cost of harming security and normal missions. The role of the proletariat was still the most important:

> The great struggle of the proletariat is the decisive force as far as preliminary successes in one or several provinces are concerned. Without a wave of strikes staged by the working class, without armed insurrection in the key cities, there can be no success in one or several provinces. It is a wholly mistaken idea not to pay particular attention to urban work and to count on the villages to surround the towns.

The most important ideas in the resolution of 11 June 1930 relate to military matters. They are an implicit repudiation of the work of Mao Tse-tung and Chu Teh, in their obvious contemplation of a combined action at an early date, and they also reveal how cut off Li Li-san and the Shanghai leaders were from the realities of the military situation at that moment. Military strength was to be developed rapidly – the Red Army within the soviet zones, and the armed groups of workers within the cities. The plan of campaign was then to include a large increase in local risings aimed at conquering the towns and setting up soviet regimes. The concept of mere guerrilla warfare, reflecting a peasant mentality, was to be opposed. At the same time, the Red Army was to drop its tactics of harassing the enemy. It was to be encouraged to make resolute attacks on the enemy's chief forces, the large cities and the main communication channels. Military planning should be organized and coordinated to enable the war to be enlarged into a revolutionary war to liquidate the feudal class: 'The tactics of guerrilla warfare have become completely incompatible with this line and must undergo fundamental change.'[1]

The poverty of the Red Army at the time, its numerical weakness, its precarious situation far from all the important regions and even moderately well-populated areas, and the absence of all proper communist organizations within the cities – all these factors were unknown to or ignored by the Central Political Bureau and Li Li-san. Armed legions do not rise from the ground at the stamp of a foot, and bravery rarely replaces great battalions, as the communists were soon to learn from bitter experience.

The sight of the national government, torn apart by inner struggles and apparently about to founder, seemed to justify the optimism of the 11 June resolution. Chiang Kai-shek had had several rebellions to deal with in 1929. The most serious, led by the Kwangsi generals (and chiefly by Li Tsung-jen), ended in the occupation of Kueilin, Nanning and Wuchow by the central army troops (April-May 1929). Almost immediately after that, Feng Yü-hsiang, openly supported by Yen Hsi-shan who controlled Shansi and North China, staged a rebellion in the north-west. It took Chiang Kai-shek three months (October to December 1929) to win back Honan. A new and serious struggle then arose between Chiang Kai-shek and Wang Ching-wei, who was then backed by Chang Fa-k'uei and T'ang Sheng-chih, as he had been in 1927. Their troops were eventually beaten and disarmed in Kwangsi and West Honan (January 1930).

The year 1930 was to see even more serious conflicts. This time, Yen Hsi-shan, Feng Yü-hsiang, Li Tsung-jen and Chang Fa-k'uei joined forces and rose in opposition to Chiang Kai-shek and the central government. During the summer, operations took place first of all in Hunan and then in Honan and Shantung. Wang Ching-wei went to Peking and tried to seize power once more. Chang Hsüeh-liang, the 'Young Marshal' from Manchuria, intervened to save Nanking and Chiang Kai-shek by occupying Peking in the name of the central government; by the autumn of 1930 the situation was stable once more.

The Yangtze valley was almost emptied of regular troops while all this was happening in Central and North China. The fact that fighting was

[1] The preceding quotations are translated from Hsiao Tso-liang, *Power Relations within the Chinese Communist Movement 1930-1934*, vol. II, Chinese documents.

going on within the Kuomintang also suggested that the authority of both government and administration might be on the wane.

The communist offensive of the summer of 1930[1]

The communist plan of campaign for the summer of 1930 included three main objectives – the three large cities in the region, Ch'angsha, Wuhan and Nanch'ang. The first of these three, the only target to be reached, was entrusted to the Third Army Group under P'eng Teh-huai (Fifth and Eighth Armies). The attack on Nanch'ang was to be led by the First Army Group (Fourth, Third and Twelfth Armies), in other words the troops belonging to the Kiangsi zone in the strictest sense (commanded by Chu Teh and Mao Tse-tung). The Second Army Group, under Ho Lung (Second and Sixth Armies) who was in west Hupei-Hunan, was to be responsible for operations against Wuhan. The Fourth Army Group, under Hsü Hsiang-chien, was also to join in the attack on Wuhan, from its base in Anhwei-Honan-Hupei. Lastly, Fang Chih-min and the Tenth Army were to take Kiukiang on the Yangtze. Strikes, later to develop into uprisings, were planned for all the cities – Shanghai, Nanking, Canton, Tientsin and Tsingtao, and even the cities in Manchuria. Everywhere, action committees (Hsing tung wei-yuan-hui) containing delegates from the Party, Communist Youth and the trade unions were formed to undertake the organization of demonstrations, strikes and uprisings.

The main offensive spread over several provinces was to be a miserable failure. The one success – although short lived – was P'eng Teh-huai's attack on Ch'angsha; he took the town with comparative ease on 27 July, because hardly any troops were there to defend it. He maintained his position there for about ten days, during which he was treated with the utmost reserve, if not open hostility, by the population. Ho Chien, the governor of Hunan, drove him out without any difficulty, and while P'eng Teh-huai was retreating to the Liuyang area, taking with him 3000 people (men who had openly supported the communists, and specialized workers needed by the army), a savage purge destroyed the Party's secret organization in the Hunan capital for good.

The Ch'angsha failure played into the hands of Mao Tse-tung, who had enough military experience to foresee the inevitable results from the outset. He disobeyed his orders to attack Nanch'ang, and he and Chu Teh, with the First Army Group, headed for Liuyang, under the pretext of helping P'eng Teh-huai. United once more, the First and Third Army

[1] See Map. 11, p. 200.

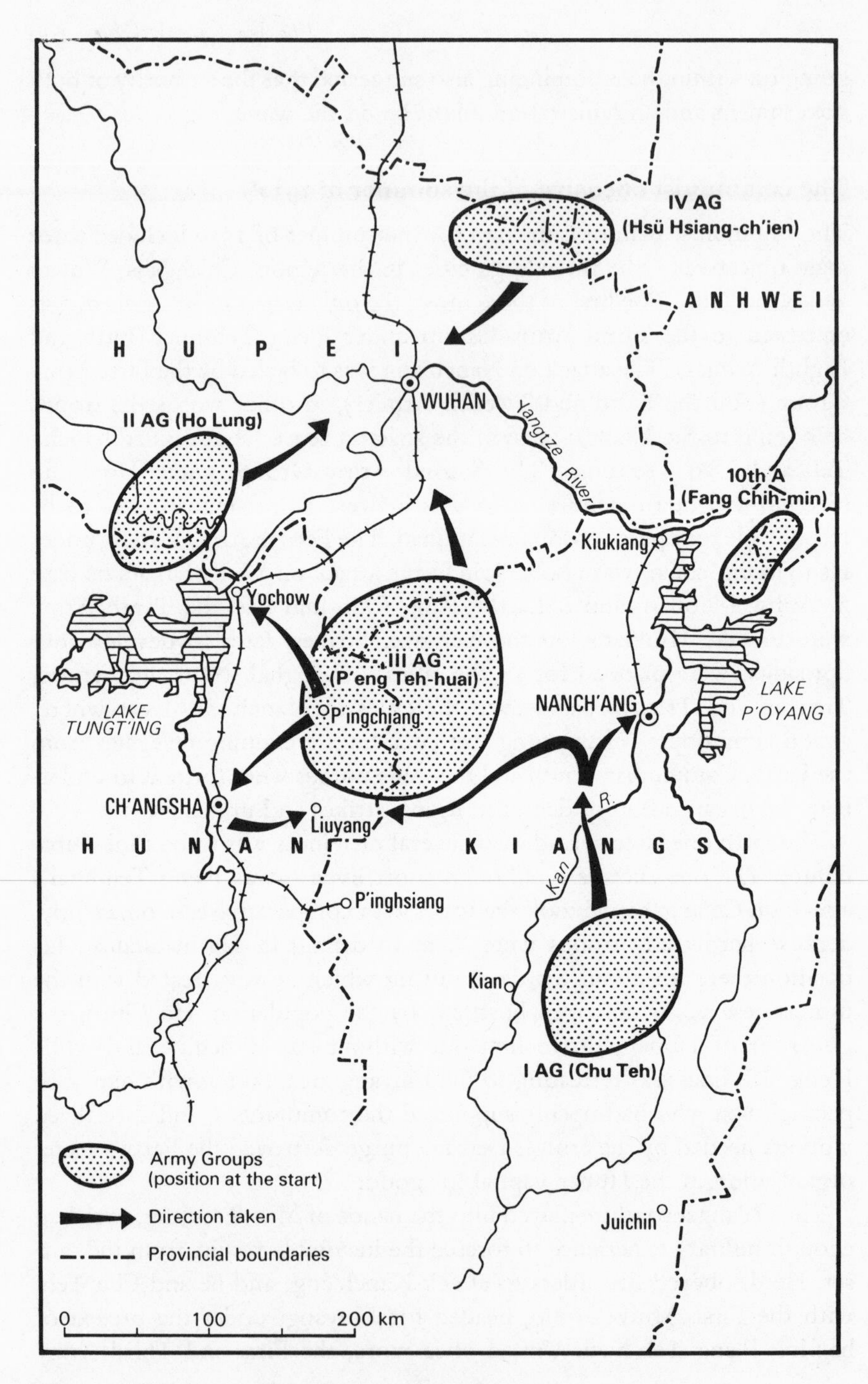

Map 11. The communist offensive of summer 1930

Groups became the First Front Army (Ti i fang-mien-chün), with Chu Teh in command and Mao Tse-tung as political leader; a 'Front Committee' was formed. In September of the same year, P'eng Teh-huai was pushed into making another attack on Ch'angsha. It was a half-hearted attempt, probably carried out in order to avoid openly disobeying the Central Committee's orders, and it was a failure. Four or five nationalist regiments were there to defend the town, and the enemy could no longer be taken by surprise; the communists had virtually none of the artillery needed for a proper assault. With the Central Committee's approval, Mao Tse-tung attacked and took Kian, in south Kiangsi. It was a weak and short-lived victory, though it enabled him to enlarge his base in the Kan valley, and slightly lessened the bad impression left by the semi-failure at Ch'angsha and the sham attack on Nanch'ang.

The communists met with no greater success at Wuhan, where they hardly got near the town. Nothing more than disturbances occurred in the other towns; the sole result was that the most deeply involved militant communists were forced into the open and put out of action. If the figures revealed since then are accurate, there were no more than 32,000 active communists for all the towns, 2000 of whom were in Shanghai, 1000 in Wuhan[1] and 500 in Tientsin; since these three cities each had several million inhabitants, their action could scarcely be expected to achieve much more than this.

As for the red armies, they represented between 70,000 and 80,000 men scattered over hundreds of thousands of square kilometres, among a population of between 100 and 200 million. Their experience of coordinated action was extremely limited, and their equipment did not allow them to attack places that were strongly defended. What is more, with the exception of the red zones, the rural population was totally unprepared to follow any revolutionary movement, even were it successful. A more blatant example of blind opportunism than the events of the summer of 1930 would be hard to find; Li Li-san was shortly to answer for this, before the Party itself.

The Third Plenum of the Sixth Central Committee

The Third Plenum of the Sixth Central Committee was held in September at Lushan, with Ch'ü Ch'iu-pai, the former Secretary-General, acting as

[1] Some authors give much lower figures: 200 members of the Chinese Communist Party and 150 red trade union members, if Isaacs is to be believed; his information is based on a letter from the Comintern to the Chinese Communist Party; cf. H. R. Isaacs, *The Tragedy of the Chinese Revolution.*

the Comintern delegate, in the chair. Chou En-lai, who had returned from Moscow at the same time as Ch'ü Ch'iu-pai, wrote the draft for the Committee's report, endeavouring with the utmost caution to reconcile the Comintern's view (letter dated 23 July 1930) and the Li Li-san line, at least as far as the principles to which it gave expression were concerned. As for the general situation, the Chinese Communist Party acknowledged that it had not yet fully realized how uneven the development of the revolution was from region to region. It also acknowledged that although a nationwide revolutionary situation was in course of preparation, it did not in fact exist when the July offensive was launched:

> Do the errors of the Central Committee arise from a difference of opinion with the Comintern? Certainly not. No difference in line exists. The present task of the Chinese Communist Party is to win over the broad masses, concentrate their revolutionary strength, organize revolutionary warfare, make active preparations for armed insurrection, reject the Kuomintang imperialist domination and set up a soviet regime. These aims do not differ in the slightest from the instructions of the Communist International and are in perfect agreement with them. It is only because of an overestimation of the evolution of the revolutionary situation and the speed of its development that the Central Committee has made tactical mistakes here and there.[1]

The Central Committee admitted that it had underestimated the role of the soviet zones. From now on, they should be extended and strengthened, with the help of a Central Soviet Government. At the same time, an effort should be made to mobilize the city workers; these two tasks were to be the chief work of the moment. The Red Army was to be developed, centralized and purged, in order to become the principal force of the civil war.

The Third Plenum's resolution shed a little light on the inner conflicts of a party whose organization was weak and whose lack of roots in the proletariat (2000 industrial workers out of a membership of 120,000, according to quoted figures) set it at a disadvantage. The rightism of Ho Meng-hsiung's faction was violently denounced, while Li Li-san's personal mistakes were skilfully laid at the door of the entire Central Committee.

[1] Cf. Ch'en Ch'eng, *Reactionary Documents of the Red Bandits* (in Chinese), vol. II, pp. 424 ff.

The Fourth Plenum of the Sixth Central Committee

The Central Committee's mild self-criticism did not satisfy Moscow. Four months later, in January 1931, the Committee held a fourth plenum, and this time Li Li-san's most determined enemies, Pavel Mif's young students from the Sun Yat-sen University, later known as the 'Twenty-eight Bolsheviks', were triumphant. The resolution of January 1931 began by recalling that in July 1930 the Comintern's instructions to the Communist Party had been correct:

> However, just at the critical moment when the revolutionary upsurge was beginning, the leadership of the Chinese Communist Party, which was dominated by the Li Li-san line, in spite of instructions from the Comintern, was following an adventurous policy of putschism contrary to the policy of the Communist International. Everyone now sees that the anti-Comintern line of Comrade Li Li-san caused considerable damage to the Party. It is impossible to enumerate all the serious and evil consequences resulting from the application of the adventurist and anti-Leninist line of Comrade Li Li-san.[1]

After such an introduction, a merciless indictment was to be expected. Li Li-san was in fact accused of having weakened the Party's action among the masses and within its structure. He was also reproached with having oppressed 'those who supported the Communist International line', making it possible 'for Trotskyists and Ch'en Tu-hsiu-ists on the one hand, and rightists within the Party on the other, to avail themselves of this opportunity to become more active'. This was clearly an exceptionally serious accusation. It was developed at length from an ideological angle:

> The mistakes of Comrade Li Li-san are not individual or accidental errors, they are based on many erroneous concepts forming a thoroughly anti-Leninist system. These erroneous concepts are by their nature a repetition of the theories of Trotsky. The Li Li-san line denies the uneven development of the revolution in the world, which amounts to a denial of the possibility of victory for the Chinese revolution and the consolidation of this victory. The Li Li-san line is in utter contradiction with the correct understanding of the nature and the phases of the Chinese revolution. It uses Trotsky's view which denies the bourgeois-democratic revolutionary phase, to replace Lenin's theory on the transformation of the revolution. This shows that he (Li Li-san) entirely misunderstands the tasks belonging to the present phase of the

[1] Ibid.

> Chinese revolution, and that he overlooks the unique characteristics of the Chinese political and economic development. . . . To sum up, the Li Li-san line is in complete contradiction with the Comintern line. However, its leftism is a cover up for opportunism and it shows opportunist passivism as regards the task of organizing the masses in a practical and revolutionary way.[1]

The last two sentences were obviously a reply to Chou En-lai, who had maintained that the Li Li-san line and the Comintern line were identical.

The practical leadership of the Party came in for equally violent and numerous criticisms: indifference to the peasant movements in the 'white zones', an over-tolerant attitude to the rich peasants in the 'red zones', negligence in the setting up of a central political regime by means of a 'Congress of Chinese Soviets'. As for the Red Army, it had been weakened by the 'premature' order to take the big cities and give up guerrilla activities. In a way that would be totally incomprehensible in any context other than that of the Communist Party, the Central Committee voiced violent criticism of its own past tolerance and blamed itself for limiting its criticisms of Li Li-san at the Third Plenum to his personal failings.

> The resolution of the Third Plenum proves that at that time, the leaders of the Party had not recognized all the errors of the policy of Li Li-san and had not realized that this policy was in complete contradiction with, and opposed in principle to the line of the Communist International.[2]

The Central Committee's relentless attacks on Li Li-san and even on Ch'ü Ch'iu-pai, who was held responsible for the moderate resolution passed in September, were accompanied, as was to be expected, by formal promises of obedience to the Comintern and its representatives, and of changes in the Political Bureau. Hsiang Chung-fa remained Secretary-General in name until his death (he was captured and shot by the Kuomintang in June 1931), but the power was in fact in the hands of the Comintern delegate Pavel Mif and his team: Wang Ming (alias Ch'en Shao-yü), Chang Wen-t'ien, Ch'in Pang-hsien (alias Po Ku), Wang Chien-hsiang, Ho Chih-shu, etc., names that will reappear in the next chapters.[3]

Li Li-san was to return to Moscow for several years. He made a brief

[1] Ibid. [2] Ibid.

[3] Wang Ming, born of a rich peasant family in Anhwei in 1906, member of the Communist Party from 1925 onwards and trained in Moscow, was considered the leading figure among Chinese communists with international leanings. He was a member of the Central Committee until the Ninth Congress (April 1969).

reappearance at Yenan during the Sino-Japanese war, and another in Manchuria in 1946, when Russian troops were in occupation. His special duties and close relationship with the Soviet Union made it seem likely at one point that he would have an important part to play once the Communist Party was triumphant. When the Eighth Party Congress was held in September 1956 Li Li-san made an extraordinary, almost abject statement, on the subject of his own errors as opposed to the infallibility of Mao Tse-tung, no doubt to appease the latter's watchful and tenacious animosity, which had probably been aggravated by the recent conspiracy of Kao Kang and Jao Shu-shih. Li Li-san explained his errors and relapses by his petty-bourgeois origins, and gave the following summary of events in 1930:

> In towns where the enemy's rule of 'white terror' was strongest, I did not take the trouble to work hard among the masses and build up revolutionary forces little by little. I did the opposite. Strikes and demonstrations were constantly fomented, and uprisings were repeatedly organized. In rural districts, instead of setting the peasant masses in movement to lead the revolutionary struggle for the land reform, instead of developing guerrilla warfare and building revolutionary bases little by little, the armed revolutionary forces, who were still young and few in number, were constantly ordered to assault the key cities. . . .[1]

From 1945 onwards Li Li-san became a member of the Central Committee once more; Vice-Chairman of the National Trade Union Federation (1958) and for a time Minister of Labour, he remained an important figure in the administration until the Cultural Revolution of 1966. However, his friendship with the Soviet Union, his Russian wife, and the difficulties in his dealings with Mao Tse-tung in the past, all singled him out for persecution by the red guards. Rumour has it that he committed suicide in 1967.[2]

[1] *People's Daily*, 24 September 1956.

[2] J. P. Harrison has written a study on the Li Li-san episode, 'The Li Li-san line and the C.C.P. in 1930', *The China Quarterly*, No. 14 and 15 (1963).

17 The Chinese Soviet Republic

When the offensives of the summer of 1930 had failed, and the likelihood of revolution on a national scale seemed more remote than ever, it was only natural that the military and rural bases in Central China should arouse renewed interest. Their development was a continuing proof of the vitality of the revolution and the Party, while the military and agrarian experiments under way had taken on great practical value. Their leaders, and chiefly Mao Tse-tung and Chu-Teh, without going as far as to be openly disobedient, had shown good sense when they hesitated to follow Li Li-san in his adventures. At the Third and Fourth Plenums of the Central Committee, the delegates from the rural bases had behaved with the utmost reserve, keeping their distance from Li Li-san, from the 'Twenty-Eight Bolsheviks' and from Ho Meng-hsiung and his rightist supporters. Perhaps they were already conscious of the fact that they represented the future of the revolution, and realized that it would be unwise to draw attention to themselves too early, or take part in struggles between different factions.

Since the retreat from the Ching Kang Shan, the rural bases, particularly the Kiangsi base, had progressed. According to accounts of official historians, their total extent covered part or all of nearly 300 'hsien' (districts) out of the existing 2000. The number is no doubt slightly exaggerated, but about 10,000 people probably lived more or less permanently under the Party's control with the local soviets acting as intermediaries; to set up a government was not an absurdity.[1] As this centralization inevitably worked in favour of the leaders on the spot, to the detriment of the Central Committee still in Shanghai, it helped reinforce national tendencies, at the expense of total subordination to the Comintern.

Until 1930 the soviets did not exist above the administrative level represented by the district (hsien); on 7 February 1930 the first provincial soviet appeared, that of Kiangsi, with its centre at Tungku. As 'red power' was scattered over about fifteen bases, it was decided to hold a meeting on 31 May 1930, in Shanghai, attended by regional delegates, to enable them to discuss their difficulties and pass a few resolutions concerning the political situation, agrarian measures (a provisional agrarian law), legislation concerning the workers, and even the defence of the Soviet Union. The assembly appointed a committee to organize a central soviet authority and convene a Soviet Congress. The First All-China Soviet Congress was fixed for 11 November 1930, but the date was changed to 7 February 1931; it was then postponed again, probably because of the lengthy settling of the Li Li-san affair, to 7 November 1931, when it met at Juichin, Kiangsi, on the anniversary of the Russian Revolution. The 610 delegates of the congress (from local soviets and also from trade unions, the Communist Party and the Red Army) ratified the constitution of the Chinese Soviet Republic, appointed members of a Central Government, and passed resolutions – the most important of which, as it had immediate practical effects, was the land law.

The provisional constitution of the Soviet Republic

The constitution of the Chinese Soviet Republic contains seventeen articles. The first gives its aim:

> To guarantee the democratic dictatorship of the workers and peasants in the Soviet districts, and to extend this to the whole of China.

This characteristic of a workers' and peasants' democratic dictatorship is stated once more in Article 2, which denied electoral rights and political freedom to militarists, bureaucrats, landlords, the gentry, monks, capitalists

[1] According to a declaration made by Chiang Kai-shek, the communists in Kiangsi controlled 70 'hsien', but the total probably refers to the Kiangsi-Hunan-Fukien border area. Cf. Hollington Tong, *Chiang Kai-shek* (T'aipei, 1953), p. 171. Mao Tse-tung gave the figure of 9 million inhabitants for all the bases in 1934 to Edgar Snow: Kiangsi, 3 million; Hupei-Honan-Anhwei, 2 million; Hunan-Kiangsi-Hupei, 1 million; Kiangsi-Hunan, 1 million; Hunan-Hupei, 1 million; Chekiang-Fukien, 1 million. Cf. Edgar Snow, *Red Star over China.*

and all those living by 'the exploitation of others'. Supreme power was to be exercised by an All-China Congress of Soviets of Workers', Peasants' and Soldiers' Deputies. Between sessions the power was entrusted to a Central Executive Committee with sixty-four members. The Central Committee in turn appointed a Council of People's Commissars, to 'conduct all governmental affairs, and promulgate decrees'. Everybody was entitled to vote and be elected from the age of 16. Elections were to take place at the place of work (factory or workshop) for the workers, the rest to vote wherever they lived. The text allows for a larger number of delegates from among the workers, 'since only the proletariat can lead the broad masses of workers and peasants to socialism'.

In practice, the elections were conducted so that one delegate represented fifteen proletarian electors, and the other categories were represented by one delegate to fifty electors. The new constitution proposed to pass labour legislation (Article 5) and a land law (Article 6), and to impose a single progressive tax (Article 7). Article 8, aimed against imperialism, abolished all foreign privileges in China and in particular refused to recognize the validity of the Unequal Treaties and foreign loans. Article 11 guaranteed the emancipation and protection of women. Article 13 proclaimed both religious freedom and the right to pursue anti-religious propaganda. Article 14 stated the right of the national minorities to total secession and the formation of an independent state for each one. The constitutions of 1949 and 1954 did not go as far in this direction. On the other hand, the policy of defence of the individual national cultures and languages was already outlined. The three last articles contain expressions of solidarity with the Soviet Union, the world proletariat and the oppressed nations.

In view of the difficulties at that time – the isolation of the red bases, the immense distances between them, the insecurity, and the lack of qualified cadres – the first Chinese communist constitution was inevitably rudimentary. In some ways it was harsher and more revolutionary than those that followed. The regime set out to be purely and simply a workers' and peasants' dictatorship; the bourgeoisie, whatever their category, did not enter into the picture at all. The bourgeoisie had just 'betrayed' the revolution and were not rehabilitated until the Sino-Japanese war.

On 27 November 1931 Mao Tse-tung was elected President of the new Chinese Soviet Republic. Two Vice-Presidents were also appointed: Hsiang Ying and Chang Kuo-t'ao, who was to return to his base – the Fourth Army Group base, on the Hupei-Honan-Anhwei borders. Chu Teh was nominated Chairman of the Military Committee, with Chou

En-lai as his assistant. Several men, now dead or fallen into disgrace, were among the commissars: Teng Tzu-hui (Finance), Wang Chia-hsiang (Foreign Affairs), Chan Ting-chen (Agriculture), Ch'ü Ch'iu-pai (Education), Hsiang Ying (Labour), Chang Kuo-t'ao (Justice), Teng Fa (Security), Ho Shu-heng (Control).

The formation of a soviet government could have but a limited effect on the development of the regime at the top, as it was still led by the Front Committee and the local Party structure where the same men as before continued in office. At the lowest level, however, the soviets had an important role in so far as they established the contact between the Party and the masses, so that the latter could be associated with the carrying out of the revolution. The Communist Party was still the soul of the regime, the soviets becoming its body, much like the People's Congresses which were created by the constitution of 1954. 'The local soviets', as Mao Tse-tung said, 'are the organizations which mobilize the masses directly and carry out practical duties.'

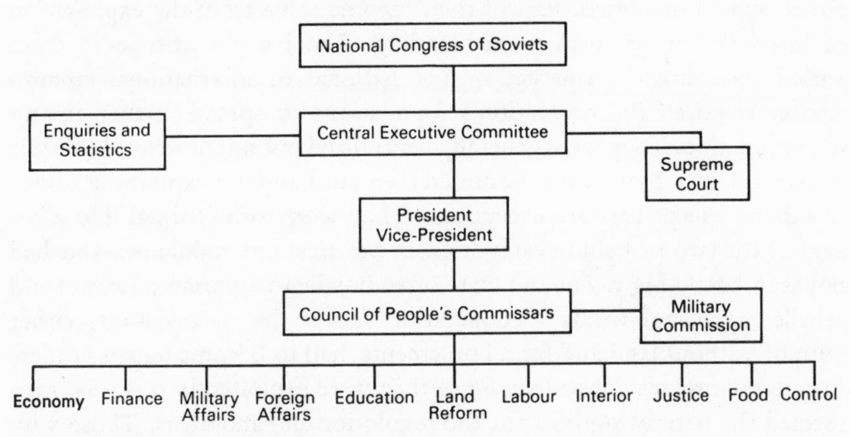

Organization of the Chinese Soviet Government (1931)

The Party had several times to pay attention to the views of the soviets, which forced it not to lose sight of certain local and human realities. In some cases, the Party and the soviets found themselves in opposition to each other.

The agrarian policy

The communists would have been unable to maintain their position in Central China, in view of their military weakness, if they had not had the support of the majority of the peasants; this support was mainly due to agrarian measures, which most of the peasants found satisfactory. It took several years to draw up a land policy coinciding with the Party's true interests, or in other words, one that won the masses over to its side without endangering the region's economy. Throughout this, Mao Tse-tung naturally played an important part. In October 1933 he defined the class distribution in the countryside once and for all; from the beginning, all communist land legislation has been based on this fundamental notion.[1] Leaving the artisans and workers – the latter were few in number – to one side, inhabitants of rural areas were divided into four main categories: landlords, rich peasants, middle peasants and poor peasants.

Landlords owned land without working it themselves, and therefore lived by 'exploiting the peasants': they exacted land rent, hired labour and lent money. 'Local tyrants' (tu-hao) and 'evil gentry' (lieh-shen) were included among them. They were natural enemies of the revolution and provoked economic and cultural stagnation; their assistants were to receive the same treatment. Rich peasants themselves worked land which they either owned or rented. Part of their income came from the exploitation of hired labour or from money-lending. The Party's attitude to them varied according to whether or not national or international circumstances required the revolution's foundations to spread further among the population. They were generally neutralized but not destroyed. Middle peasants, who either owned or rented their land, did not exploit the labour of others, except for rare exceptions. They were to be turned into allies against the two preceding categories. In practice, the middle peasants had hopes of becoming richer and were often hostile to agrarian measures and rebelled against all forms of cooperation. Lastly, the poor peasants, either with or without land and farm implements, had to become tenant farmers or hire themselves out to live. Since they were exploited in this way, they formed the natural support for the revolution in rural areas. Those who lived in the countryside were classed according to the way they worked rather than by the extent of their land; as a political principle, this was well adapted to local conditions, because of great differences in the quality of the land and in types of crops.

The Party's land policy, which was radical during the Ching Kang Shan period, and slightly less so at the beginning of the Kiangsi period, was to become a little more moderate later, taking on its final form after the First Soviet Congress. Initially, each base seems to have done as it pleased, guided more or less by the resolution passed by the Sixth Congress on the

[1] Mao Tse-tung, 'How to Differentiate the Classes in the Rural Areas', *Selected Works*, vol. I, p. 136.

land question. In the Ching Kang Shan the policy was based on a decree dating from December 1928, which was not widely applied owing to the sparse population and the precarious nature of the communist occupation. In 1930 the Revolutionary Military Committee, the true government at the time, published a law in four chapters and thirty articles. It was extremely strict, allowing for the confiscation of the land and houses of the rich peasants and landlords, leaving them with no means of livelihood. In May of the same year the delegates from the soviet zones met secretly in Shanghai and adopted a 'provisional law', which was less ruthless than the earlier one, in that it made some concessions to the rich peasants, though it forbade buying, selling and renting of land. In November 1931 the First Congress assembled at Juichin approved a final version of the land law, drawn up by a committee appointed in September of the previous year.

The land law of the Chinese Soviet Republic was appreciably more liberal than the earlier ones, which had estranged many middle peasants anxious to grow richer and who were particularly annoyed by the clause forbidding the sale of property. The preamble to its thirteen articles stated the motives behind it, describing the progress of the agrarian revolution and stressing the need for a uniform ruling.[1] Article 1 ordered the confiscation with compensation, 'whether they work them themselves or rent them out', of all lands belonging to feudal landlords, gentry, large landlords, bureaucrats and militarists; they were not to be entitled to receive land during the redistribution. The soviets would then distribute the land to poor, or even middle peasants, refugees and independent workers. Article 2 stated the right of every Red Army soldier to have a plot allotted to him, which the community would work in his absence. According to Article 3, the land of rich peasants could also be confiscated; in return they would be given poor quality land, on condition that they worked it themselves. Article 4 stated that land belonging to those who opposed the revolution would be confiscated, with the exception of soldiers 'who have been drawn into, and remain in the struggle against the soviets because of their ignorance'. Article 5, remarkable for its caution, revealed the difficulties encountered by the regime in the attitude of the poor peasants when the distribution was too strict:

> The First Congress considers that equal distribution of all the land is the most radical way of destroying all feudal relations of slavery

[1] The Chinese texts of the three land laws mentioned above are to be found in Ch'en Ch'eng, *Reactionary Documents of the Red Bandits*, vol. III.

connected with the land, and for putting an end to private ownership of land; even so, local soviets must not use force or appeal to authority. They must explain all the aspects involved to the peasants. Not until the mass of the peasants at the base – and above all the mass of middle peasants – desire it and give it their direct support, can this land reform be applied. When the majority of middle peasants so wish it, they may be allowed not to take part in this equal redistribution.

Article 6 recommended that similar care be taken when carrying out confiscation of public or temple lands, so as not to offend the religious feelings of the peasants. Article 7 provided for great flexibility in the application of the law, for each soviet was free to decide on the best way to redistribute land, basing its decision on local conditions and land productivity, on condition that the poor and middle peasants gained in comparison with the rest. The last articles (8 to 14) dealt with confiscated goods (buildings, farm implements, animals), the abolition of contracts and debts, and the use to be made of woods, lakes and pastures. They also set out in detail the role to be played by people's organizations, and especially by the poor peasants, in the application of the law. The advantages to be gained from the nationalization of land were explained, but renting, sale and purchase of land was not forbidden, except in the case of rich peasants and landlords who wanted to buy back their possessions (Article 12). The spreading of the law to regions not as yet under the control of soviets was dealt with. A new redistribution of land was to be carried out in districts not guided by the new law.

Although it was more moderate than the earlier laws, the law of November 1931 was later considered still too radical; this radicalism was blamed on the third 'leftist' deviation, led by Wang Ming, who was too quick to throw men who were recoverable back on the bourgeoisie and the Kuomintang. True enough, extremists had gone as far as to ask for the immediate creation of 'sovkhozes' and 'kolkhozes' during the First Soviet Congress. Mao Tse-tung, in charge of the economy of the red zones, was realistic enough to press for a moderate line not only in agrarian questions, but also in questions of artisans' production and trade. His aim was to strike a balance, so that the peasant was interested in the revolution in terms of what it had to offer, as well as what it allowed him to keep: 'Only since we have distributed land to the peasants and encouraged and rewarded production, has their labour blossomed forth and great success in production been achieved.'[1]

[1] Mao Tse-tung, 'Our Economic Policy', *Selected Works*, vol. I, p. 142.

The application of the communist land legislation gave rise to all sorts of difficulties which the texts do not record, and which the reticence shown by the Party may lead us to underestimate. It was not easy for the Chinese peasants to rid themselves of habits which had lasted for centuries. They greeted the social upheaval offered them with a suspicion which was far from unfounded, as red power everywhere was in a precarious position. Immediate advantages were balanced by the prospect of future uncertainty, and the population often took some time to swing over to the side of the communists. Rich peasants and former landlords retained their influence in many places. They were usually the only people with any education, and consequently managed to find posts in the new administration and become indispensable. Their families were linked by stronger ties than the rest and were to be found in all sections of peasant society, where they opposed the application of legal measures, which sometimes degenerated into private arrangements. The Party had to organize several inspections to make sure that the real benefits of the land reform had gone to the poor and middle peasants and agricultural labourers, and to ascertain that 'class struggle' had not been sacrificed to the love of compromise to which the Chinese are especially prone.

The available figures for the amount of land that changed hands through confiscation and redistribution are all uncertain; the total was probably between 60,000 and 100,000 hectares, if certain Russian sources have been interpreted correctly. It goes without saying that this provided the opportunity for murders and acts of violence to be committed against the landlords and rich peasants; several tens of thousands of them died.[1]

For both ideological and practical reasons, the Chinese Soviet Government endeavoured carefully to create and develop a movement in favour of peasant cooperatives; the experience they gained was later to prove useful. But cooperative organizations made their appearance mainly in the few and rudimentary industrial undertakings in the red territories. Supplies of basic necessities – salt, matches, fabrics and medicines – were to become more and more difficult to obtain after 1931, as the nationalists accompanied their offensives by a strict economic blockade. Mao Tse-tung's appeals for the building of an economic front (essential if the war were to be continued), for the union of workers and peasants, and for maintaining the morale of the population, were to become more and more urgent in tone. One of the chief causes of the elimination of the communist bases in Central China was in fact the poverty of the region itself,

[1] A nationalist author gives a total of 622,000 victims of the communists: Li Tien-ming, *The Chinese Communists and the Peasants* (Hong Kong, 1958).

for it limited the Red Army's development in terms of numbers and equipment.

The labour codes of 1931 and 1933

The First Soviet Congress adopted a labour code, dated 1 December 1931. This extremely modern code in seventy-five articles, presented at length by Hsiang Ying, had little chance of being applied to the red zones, which were almost totally lacking in industry. A few workshops and agricultural wage-earners benefited from it. As early as the following year, it was considered inadequate and a committee was appointed to draw up a new code; it finished its work on 28 April. The new text (15 chapters and 121 articles) was submitted to several organizations for criticism and came into force on 15 October 1933, to be applied to all artisans and employers. Later on, further legal points and, in particular, rules controlling work contracts were added to the 1933 code, sometimes taking the form of corrections. The labour legislation in its final form fulfilled doctrinal requirements, and perhaps answered above all a need for propaganda in the white zones, where the trade unions were gradually slipping entirely from communist influence. The main points in the 1931 and 1933 codes were as follows:

It is forbidden to hire workers through private firms; this must be done through the trade unions or 'Labour Bureaux' organized by the Labour Commissariat.

Contracts of employment are compulsory, whether individual or collective.

The working day is to consist of eight hours for adults, six for adolescents between 16 and 18, and four for children under 14.

Every worker must have forty-two consecutive hours off per week.

An annual holiday of two, in some cases of four, weeks, must be granted.

A list of 'legal holidays', including the anniversary of the Paris Commune (18 March).

Fixing of a minimum wage by the Labour Commissariat, to be doubled for legal holidays and overtime.

Regulations to cover female labour.

Work inspections to be carried out.

The role of the trade unions.

Insurance against illness, unemployment and death, pensions, etc.[1]

[1] The texts of the 1931 and 1933 codes, and others dealing with work contracts, are to be found in Ch'en Ch'eng, *Reactionary Documents of the Red Bandits*, vol. V.

The labour code of the red zones was well ahead of the true situation of a country suffering from a considerable overemployment, and was inspired by concepts of ideology and propaganda; nevertheless, it was a thoroughly praiseworthy effort towards bettering the miserable conditions of the Chinese workers. From this point of view, it stood for an ideal, and was consequently a factor of progress.

The Second All-China Soviet Congress

The Second Soviet Congress, attended by 200 delegates, lasted for eleven days, and met at Juichin on 22 January 1934, a few months before the evacuation of Kiangsi and the beginning of the Long March. Economic questions took up more time than anything else, and formed the subject of Mao Tse-tung's report.[1] Times were growing hard. The Sino-Japanese incidents of 1931 and 1932 had more or less died down, the Fukien revolt had misfired, and the government was in a position to intensify its military pressure and its economic blockade from all sides round the red zones. In spite of Mao Tse-tung's official optimism, the gravity of the problems and the leaders' anxiety as to the loyalty of popular support can still be felt: 'I earnestly suggest to this congress that we pay close attention to the well-being of the masses, from the problems of land and labour to those of fuel, rice, cooking oil and salt.'[2]

The different reports written at the Second Soviet Congress furnish interesting information – both of a statistical nature and with regard to the quality of life – in relation to the red bases. The press was developing steadily; the central district alone boasted thirty-four papers, including the official organ *Red China* whose print run rose from 3000 to 40,000, *The Struggle* published by the Central Committee with a print of 27,000, *Red Star* with a print of 17,300, *Youth's Truth* with a print of 28,000, etc. Revolutionary forms of art were beginning to find an outlet, and propaganda theatre troupes were increasing. The doctrinal attitude to culture was stated thus: 'The general line on culture in the Chinese soviets consists in educating the broad masses in the spirit of Communism, subordinating instruction to revolutionary warfare and the class struggle, and linking work and instruction.'

[1] See Mao Tse-tung, 'Our Economic Policy' and 'Be Concerned with the Well-being of the Masses, Pay Attention to Methods of Work', *Selected Works*, vol. I. Both documents contain interesting details on living conditions in the soviet areas at the time.
[2] 'Be Concerned with the Well-being of the Masses, Pay Attention to Methods of Work', *Selected Works*, vol. I, p. 149.

The principles and methods developed and perfected several years later, during the Sino-Japanese war, were gradually emerging.

The Second Congress made no important changes in the team of government and administrative leaders. The Soviet Central Executive Committee had 175 members and thirty-six members in reserve, instead of sixty-three members, the Council of People's Commissars had eleven members instead of nine, and was presided over by Chang Wen-t'ien, under Mao Tse-tung's guidance; Mao retained his main functions, in spite of the Central Committee's retreat to the red zone, and the growing influence of the 'Twenty-eight Bolsheviks'. The grave setbacks of the past year were, however, going to give rise to a major crisis in the leadership of the movement. This was to weaken Mao Tse-tung's authority considerably, but it was not the first crisis of the Kiangsi period. The Fut'ien Incident in 1930, and the Huangp'o Incident of the following year, all but destroyed the Party's unity.

The Fut'ien Incident (December 1930)

In the last weeks of 1930 Mao Tse-tung and the Front Committee had large numbers of their opponents arrested, accusing them, without evidence, of belonging to a nationalist secret organization known as the 'A.B. League' (the Anti-Bolshevist League), or at least suspected of 'liquidationist' manœuvres. According to the most reliable sources on the subject, 4400 important members of the Kiangsi provincial Action Committee were also imprisoned, among them Li Po-fang, Tuan Liang-pi and Chin Wan-pang. On 8 December Liu Ti, the political commissar of a battalion of the Twentieth Army, rebelled at Tungku, the provincial soviet capital, set the prisoners free and arrested the army's commander, along with about 100 of Mao Tse-tung's supporters. Shortly afterwards, Li Po-fang went off to Yungyang in the 'hsien' of Kian, where he tried to create a rebel provincial soviet, which lasted for two months. At the same time, the rebels attempted to turn the most influential military leaders – Chu Teh, P'eng Teh-huai and Huang Kung-lüeh – against the authority of Mao Tse-tung and the Front Committee. They failed and the repression that followed resulted in the deaths of several thousand people.

The exact origins of this attempt at a real *coup d'état* are still not yet altogether clear today. That it was an accident appears obvious in so far as it happened after the arrests ordered by the Front Committee, but opposition to Mao Tse-tung certainly existed. Most of the rebels belonged to the action committees created just before the July offensive, and gave their allegiance to the Central Committee; their sympathies probably lay with Li Li-san. Their views on the agrarian question also differed from those of the Front Committee. The events should perhaps be interpreted merely as a reaction on a local and provincial scale on the part of men exasperated by Mao Tse-tung's methods of purging. From the beginning, he seems to have been careful not to allow any opposition to form within the Party itself. As inevitably happens in all movements based on an ideology, the opponents were to fall, labelled as heretics and traitors. Authentic communists of long standing, who had sacrificed everything for their cause, were executed at different times under various accusations – reformists, supporters of Wang Ching-wei who was at the time opposed to Chiang Kai-shek once more, 'liquidationists', members of the A.B. League, etc. Although frequent, these Party purges were carried out quietly, with the help of the isolated geographical position of the red zones. Their cruelty and the personal ends they served must not be ignored. A closer study of them will drastically diminish the stature of Mao Tse-tung in the eyes of history.

The Huangp'o purge

Less than a year after the Fut'ien Incident, a large-scale purge was carried out in the red base on the borders of Hupei-Honan-Anhwei (Oyüwan). The pretext for this was the discovery of a plot, whose perpetrator was said to be the commander of the First Army, General Hsü Chi-shen, a former Whampoa (Huangp'u) cadet who at one point deserted the Communist Party for the Third Party. With Chou En-lai's support, he was received back into the Party but was later accused of preparing an uprising fixed for 15 September 1931, in the small town of Mapu. He was arrested and imprisoned at Huangp'o, in north Hupei, and then executed together with 170 members of the First Army's political department. Some authors state that the purge included two divisional commanders, one divisional political commissar, eight regimental commanders, 700 Party members and about 1500 rich peasants.[1]

[1] See the studies by Wu Hsiang-hsiang and the analysis by Hsiao Tso-liang. In *I and the Red Army* (in Chinese) Kung Ch'u gives a few examples of purges in the 34th Division, which he then commanded. Kung Ch'u left the Communist Party in 1935, when he was Chief of General Staff in the south Kiangsi guerrilla zone.

Difficulties also arose at about the same time in the Hupei-Hunan base (the western border of the two provinces, or Hsiangohsi); the famous trade unionist, Teng Chung-hsia, was accused of opportunism and defeatism. While these upheavals were going on within the red zone, the Party was facing serious difficulties in the white zones; government repression, affecting the moderate factions, and the Central Committee above all, was to intensify what was already a tragic situation.

18 The Communist Party in the White Zones

While the Chinese communist movement was going through a period of rebirth, development and change in the Central China bases, it was coming up against insuperable difficulties in the white zones, controlled by the central government or the provincial cliques. These difficulties were to end in the elimination of large groups, whether they were leaders acting clandestinely or members of the opposition. At the same time, the Party was losing almost all its influence over the trade unions. The Japanese policy of aggression and disguised annexation was, however, to enable the communist propaganda to outdo the nationalism of the central government, which, through lack of military and economic preparations, combined with the indifference shown by the foreign powers, was forced to temporize, thereby losing prestige. These events, which were often unconnected, are discussed in this chapter.

The opposition of Ho Meng-hsiung's group and its disappearance

A former comrade of Li Ta-chao and an important trade union leader in North China (and later in Shanghai) and a member of the Kiangsu Provincial Committee, Ho Meng-hsiung was a militant communist of long standing, with great practical experience. His personal reputation, at least in Kiangsu and Shanghai, was such that he could oppose Li Li-san; his opposition was particularly lively in September 1930, after the failure of the offensive against the towns in Central China. The criticisms levelled by Ho Meng-hsiung and his group had much in common with those formulated at the Third and Fourth Plenums of the Central Committee. His was a moderate, prudent line; after accurate evaluation of the movement's weaknesses, he considered that it should be consolidated and, where possible, enlarged systematically through the trade unions in the towns and the Red Army in the rural districts. This shrewdness, which appeared when the question of a successor to Li Li-san was in the air, was not unmarked by personal ambition. Ho Meng-hsiung was not to realize his ambition, however. He was first of all violently attacked by the Party leadership, pronounced guilty of 'rightism', 'opportunism' and 'liquidationism', and accused of wanting to separate the Central Committee from the Comintern. The relevance of some of his criticisms was acknowledged when the Third and Fourth Plenums of the Central Committee were held, possibly with the support of the 'Twenty-eight Bolsheviks', who were also opponents of Li Li-san; Mao Tse-tung, with whom he shared his realism to a certain extent, was later to defend his memory.[1]

The veteran Ho Meng-hsiung was shortly to die a tragic death. In December 1930 he had endeavoured to bring about the creation of an Extraordinary Committee to take over the provisional direction of the Party's affairs, as had already been the case on 7 August 1927 in equally difficult circumstances. This suggestion was bound not to suit the 'Twenty-eight Bolsheviks', who had just got rid of Li Li-san. A few weeks later, on 17 January, Ho Meng-hsiung reshuffled the Kiangsu Provincial Committee, a measure which could be taken as open rebellion in the face of the Central Committee. The next day Ho Meng-hsiung and twenty-two other communists were arrested in Shanghai by the British police, who may have been informed of their whereabouts by Wang Ming's group, the 'Twenty-eight Bolsheviks'. All the members of Ho Meng-hsiung's group were handed over to the Chinese authorities and shot at Lunghua near Shanghai airport on 7 February. Many years later, the great poet Ai Ch'ing was to write a symbolic, poignant poem on Lunghua, where so many martyrs to his cause had ended their lives:

> It is spring.
> At Lunghua the peach-trees are in flower.
> They flower through these nights,
> These nights flecked with blood,

[1] Ho Meng-hsiung's point of view is summarized in a letter he wrote to the Central Committee on 8 September 1930. Hsiao Tso-liang has analysed it in *Power Relations Within the Chinese Communist Movement 1930-1934*.

These starless nights,
These windy nights,
These nights filled with widows' sobs.
But this old earth!
It seems a wild beast, athirst and ravenous
Which laps the blood of the young,
The blood of the unyielding young.
After the long winter days,
After the ice and snow,
After the endless, exhausting wait,
These traces of blood, these flecks of blood,
In a legendary night,
In a black Eastern night,
Burst into bud
And adorn all the south of the River with their spring.
You ask: 'Where has the spring come from?'
And I reply: 'From the graves outside the town.'[1]

Other valuable cadres died alongside Ho Meng-hsiung before the springtime of communism: Lin Yü-nan, an experienced trade unionist, and Li Chiu-shih, one of the leaders of Communist Youth. Opposition from moderate elements was to fade out completely with the fate of Lo Chang-lung, another trade union leader who denounced Li Li-san and Wang Ming far more violently than had Ho Meng-hsiung, and was expelled from the Party in January 1931. After a vain attempt at gathering together others with similar sympathies round a common programme, Lo went over to the counter-revolutionary cause.

The Ku Shun-chang affair: Hsiang Chung-fa's arrest and execution

In the winter of 1930-1, the Hankow police arrested the leader of a troupe of jugglers in the street. This strange disguise concealed Ku Shun-chang, head of the communist Secret Service. Ku agreed to work for the government, and his collaboration rapidly endangered the entire structure of the Communist Party in Central and East China.[2] Little by little, all the secret organizations of the Party and those of the

[1] Translated from the French version in *La Poésie chinoise* (Paris, Seghers).

[2] A former Kinhan railwayman, Ku was already in evidence in Shanghai early in 1927. He had a price of 1000 dollars on his head. He was a member of the municipality of Shanghai created by the communists after the city's third insurrection, and a member of the Central Committee at the Sixth Congress.

International were uncovered: pro-communist trade unions, various centres of communication, the editors of *Red Flag*, and the headquarters of the Provincial Committee, the Kiangsu Provincial Committee, and even the Central Committee.

At roughly the same time, the Comintern was clumsy enough to extend communist propaganda activities to the foreign troops stationed at Shanghai, irritating the authorities of the Concessions, which as a rule provided shelter for the agents, and particularly for those of the Chinese Communist Party.[1] As a result, Hsiang Chung-fa, the Party's Secretary-General and a former Hankow boatman, was arrested on 22 June 1931 in the French Concession above a jeweller's shop in the Avenue Joffre. He was executed almost immediately and his death was to enable Ch'en Shao-yü (alias Wang Ming) to take over his post officially; he remained in office until the middle of 1932, possibly even until March 1933. The chief posts in the Central Committee were held by Chang Wen-t'ien (Propaganda), Chou En-lai (Military Affairs) and Shen Tse-min. Ch'in Pang-hsien was in charge of Communist Youth, and Meng Ch'ing-shu (Ch'en Shao-yü's wife) dealt with questions relating to women. According to other reports, the committee had nineteen ordinary members and twelve deputy members. Five regional committees were set up to cover the whole of China – Manchuria, North China, the Yangtze valley, South China and Kiangnan, the latter divided into four subcommittees, one of which was responsible for the city of Shanghai, split into four districts.

For some time longer the Party tried to adapt itself to the new circumstances, scattering its leading organizations and increasing local activities. But arrests and desertions were to make the situation increasingly difficult. The Central Committee could hold out no longer and its members finally took refuge in the Kiangsi red base at the beginning of 1933. Some authors suggest that this retreat was hoped for and even to a certain extent precipitated by Mao Tse-tung, who 'chose to absorb potential rivals into the soviet structure rather than destroy them'.[2] If this is really so, it proved a false calculation. The 'Twenty-eight Bolsheviks' made their presence felt in the management of the war in a way which drew frequent, sometimes exaggerated reproaches from Mao Tse-tung. Their influence carried more weight than that of the President of the Chinese Soviet Republic in questions of the movement's general policy. Mao Tse-tung, indirectly attacked by the Central Committee's

[1] See Robert Magnenoz, *De Confucius à Lénine*, and U. T. Hsü, *The Invisible Conflict*.
[2] B. I. Schwartz, *Chinese Communism and the Rise of Mao*, p. 178.

charges against the 'opportunist' and 'defeatist' line of Lo Ming (Secretary of the Fukien Party Committee *ad interim*), and replaced by Chou En-lai as Political Commissar of the Red Army, seems to have been left to one side because of his attitude in the question of help for the rebels in Fukien.[1] He did not manage to recover the Party leadership until January 1935, at the Tsunyi Conference at the beginning of the Long March, as will later be seen; even then, his difficulties were far from over.

The Communist Party and the Mukden and Shanghai 'Incidents'

On 18 September 1931 the Japanese Army in Manchuria expelled Marshal Chang Hsüeh-liang's troops, forcing them to retreat south of the Great Wall, and took over the control of the region, except for Jehol. The communists stood to gain from this for two reasons – first of all, an event like this was likely to draw large sections of the government troops away from the red zones, and secondly, it enabled them to take full advantage of a particularly widespread and violent outbreak of nationalist feelings, as the anti-foreign incidents had done in 1925. The Central Committee took up an international rather than a national standpoint and immediately declared its hostility towards Japan: 'The Chinese Communist Party considers the Japanese attack in Manchuria as an imperialist attack and the prelude to the next large-scale imperialist attack on the U.S.S.R.'[2]

Thanks to further serious action on the part of the Japanese, who attacked certain parts of Shanghai from 28 January 1932 onwards, the communists were able to shift the emphasis of their propaganda and use a more national approach. The Nineteenth Army, led by General Ts'ai T'ing-k'ai, engaged the Japanese in hard fighting; this unexpected Chinese resistance excited public opinion enormously. The communists encouraged anti-Japanese demonstrations wherever they could, trying at the same time to direct them towards condemnation of governmental 'weakness'. They endeavoured to take over the leadership of the various Associations for National Salvation formed at the time, from within; their activities were directed mainly towards students, workers and tradesmen.

The Communist Party never hesitated to make a gesture, however unwarranted, which might attract publicity, and the government of the

[1] See Kung Ch'u, *I and the Red Army*, p. 395.

[2] Resolution of September 1931, quoted by R. Magnenoz in *De Confucius à Lénine*, p. 23.

Chinese Soviet Republic made an official declaration of war on Japan on 15 April 1932. Later on, faithful to its policy of making the fullest possible use of all circumstances, it gave the title of Anti-Japanese Army Vanguard to Fang Chih-min's troops, which were sent to north-west Kiangsi to create a diversion just before the bases in Central China were abandoned (see Chapter 19).

For a time the situation in China was so confused that it looked as though the communists would be able to achieve rapid and powerful expansion. The central government had long been exposed to the opposition of a Cantonese faction centred round Wang Ching-wei, Sun Fo and Eugène Ch'en. At the end of 1931 this faction was strong enough to call for the retirement of Chiang Kai-shek, who gave up the leadership of the government on 15 December. His successors' lack of unity and ability restored him to power six weeks later, as he himself had no doubt foreseen would happen.[1] This brief interlude was not followed up and the Communist Party was not in a position to make use of it. The situation was different when the Fukien revolt broke out in November 1933.

The Fukien revolt and the Chinese Communist Party

The Fukien rebellion gathered together men who were dissatisfied with the temporizing policy adopted by the central government with regard to Japan. In November 1933 Generals Ts'ai T'ing-k'ai, Li Chi-shen, Ch'en Ming-shu and Chiang Kuang-nai met at Foochow in Fukien, where they called an Extraordinary People's Assembly and formed an embryo government, in the shape of an Executive Committee. Ch'en Ming-shu presided over the committee, which grouped several members of the Kuomintang left wing, in particular Eugène Ch'en, Foreign Affairs Commissar. The new government repudiated the Kuomintang, announcing that it intended to draw nearer to the communists and Soviet Russia. The Nineteenth Army took the name of People's Revolutionary Army. Nanking replied immediately with a forceful retaliation. Three groups, under orders from General Chiang Kai-shek himself, converged on Fukien from the north-east, the north and the west, while the navy landed large numbers of men on the coasts, especially in the Amoy area.

[1] Chiang Kai-shek, temporarily reconciled with Wang Ching-wei, returned to Nanking on 25 January, a few days before the Shanghai Incident. He did not officially take up his posts again, particularly that of Chairman of the National Military Council, until 6 March.

In February the rebellion was virtually over; the Nineteenth Army was dissolved and reorganized to become the Seventh Route Army.

The Fukien Incident was to provoke a brief crisis within the leadership of the Chinese Communist Party, for two opposing currents of opinion arose as to the question of help for the rebels. The younger members of the Central Committee, among whom were Ch'in Pang-hsien and Chang Wen-t'ien, strongly supported by Chou En-lai, were in favour of putting the new situation to immediate use by sending the First and Third Army Groups of the Red Army to help the Nineteenth Army. If successful, this move would have resulted in large numbers of government troops being held in Fukien. It would also have put the ports of Foochow and Amoy at the communists' disposal, enabling them to receive Soviet military supplies by sea. Mao Tse-tung is reported to have represented another current more prudent than the first. Sceptical as to the movement's 'revolutionary' character and the Nineteenth Army's determination, he wanted the army to come to the Kiangsi base, where it could no doubt be absorbed into the Red Army sooner or later. Eventually, two leading Party members – P'an Han-nien and Chang Yün-i – were sent to Foochow on a liaison mission, while the First and Third Army Groups made a vague move in the direction of Fukien, but Nineteenth Army troops in the neighbourhood of Yenp'ing and Chienou were scattered before they could make contact with the red troops, who then returned to Kiangsi. Mao Tse-tung was blamed for his opposition which brought about the failure of the Central Committee's plans, while helping towards the suppression of Ts'ai T'ing-k'ai, and allowing further nationalist units to be concentrated against the Kiangsi base; according to the account given by one former communist leader, at least, he was excluded from Juichin from August to October 1934.[1]

In his works, Mao Tse-tung expresses regret at the Party's error in denying support to Ts'ai T'ing-K'ai, though he does not dwell on the matter. The Party's official historians, for their part, observe great discretion in their description of the episode, though they are no doubt familiar with the details. It is hardly surprising that the President of the Chinese Soviet Government showed equal prudence, taking the same precautions for the Red Army – his army – in the Fukien affair as he had in Li Li-san's offensives of the summer of 1930. In fact, considering the extent of the resources of men and material which the central government, free of pressure from the Japanese for the moment, was to put into

[1] Kung Ch'u, *I and the Red Army*, p. 395. See also John E. Rue, *Mao Tse-tung in Opposition (1927-1935)*.

action during the fifth campaign, it seems unlikely that the communists could have maintained their bases in Central China for much longer, even with the help of Ts'ai T'ing-k'ai.[1]

The Communist Party and the trade unions in the white zones

The break-up of the collaboration between the Communist Party and the Kuomintang in 1927 was to result in the almost total disappearance of communist influence among the working class and the trade unions. Moreover, the Nanking government did its best to uncover and disband all workers' organizations with communist leanings, replacing them by newly formed trade unions, which either had no political tendencies or else were pro-Kuomintang. Nearly 40,000 trade union members were liquidated in 1927; if the report submitted by Teng Chung-hsia to the Pan-Pacific Trade Union Conference the following year is to be believed, the exact figure was 37,985, of whom 25,000 died fighting and 13,000 were executed. This loss was to enable the government to form committees in charge of reorganization under the jurisdiction of the Ministry of Social Affairs. The government soon passed elaborate legislation on the labour question: a trade union law passed in October 1929 and amended in December 1931 and July 1933, together with various regulations concerning individual unions (seamen, railwaymen, post-office workers). Social Affairs Bureaux dealt with industrial problems in the towns, based, so the communists said, on secret societies; on the whole, they proved to be just and energetic.

A few clandestine or semi-clandestine red unions managed to continue their existence alongside the non-communist unions until 1932. Their membership was not high: 49,826 members for the whole white zone in August 1930, which was not very different from the membership in the red zone at the same time – 64,704, according to Teng Chung-hsia. From 1932 onwards, and up till the Sino-Japanese war, the red trade unions disappeared almost entirely; their eclipse can be explained by the economic crisis, competition from approved unions, and the transfer of the Central Committee to Kiangsi. The only way left open to communists and their sympathizers was that of trying to infiltrate enemy organizations. They were rarely successful, or else once established, were rendered ineffective.

[1] Ts'ai T'ing-k'ai died in Peking in August 1968. The author had previously had the chance to speak to this distinguished revolutionary soldier there; his role had been reduced to that of being present at official occasions.

The Party and the literary and university circles in the white zones

The Party maintained a relatively firm foothold in university and literary circles with the help of the anti-Japanese agitation. It is hard to be accurate in the case of university circles because nationalistic feelings, which were used to the full by the communists, obscure the issue, and teachers with communist leanings had to observe the utmost discretion. In the literary world, the League of Leftist Writers, founded on 2 March 1930 in Shanghai, included authors in favour of social realism and interested in social policy as well as ideology. As the manifesto of the League put it: 'Our art is opposed to traditional tendencies, whether feudal, capitalist or even bourgeois, for the bourgeoisie has lost its social role; we are going to undertake the creation of a proletarian art.'

Kuo Mo-jo, Lu Hsün and Mao Tun, none of whom belonged to the Party, were the most influential figures in the League, but its fifty-odd members included a fair number of communists. The best known were Chiang Kuang-tz'u, founder of the review *The Sun*, whose chief characteristic was its violent tone, Ch'eng Fang-wu, one of those in charge of the Creation Society, Chao P'ing-fu (alias Jou Shih), a playwright and story-teller, executed in 1931, Hsia Yen, who created the communist theatre, Ch'ien Hsing-ts'un (alias A Ying), poet and playwright, P'an Tzu-mien, a journalist, and above all the famous authoress Ting Ling, editor of the review *The Great Bear*, who remained an influential figure until, accused of being a 'rightist', she was eliminated in 1957.

Like the trade union members, the writers suspected of communism had to contend with severe government measures. Censorship became increasingly strict and its legal prohibitions more numerous. Several authors were imprisoned and some were shot. From 1932 onwards the 'leftist writers' remained silent or disappeared, to come to life again on the eve of the Sino-Japanese war. They remained divided, however, on questions which reflected different lines within the Party itself; the supporters of a 'literature of national defence' represented by Chou Yang were opposed to the partisans of a 'literature of the masses for revolutionary war' upheld by Lu Hsün.

These old controversies were recalled officially during the Cultural Revolution in 1966; the writers of the 1930s all vanished.[1]

[1] Chou Yang and Hsia Yen were violently attacked, Jou Shih was criticized indirectly through the adaptation of his novel *February*, as was Mao Tun for the film *The Lin Family Shop*, taken from one of his works.

19 The Period of the Defence of Kiangsi[1]

The nationalists had to mount five campaigns to overcome the communist bases. They took place between October 1930 and October 1934, involving progressively larger numbers on both sides, and using different methods. The communists' initial successes were partly due to the superior morale of the red troops but still more to the fact that their tactics were particularly well adapted to the physical and human situation. The national government was never free to use the majority of its troops against the communists, except in 1934. It was constantly obliged to limit their numbers and quality, owing to provincial rebellions and threats from the Japanese. It is also true to say that those in command found themselves at a loss when faced with the particular style of operations, and their political aspects. The government did, however, get the better of its enemies once it took sufficient trouble, for guerrilla warfare is after all a minor form of operations, rarely, if ever, able to win decisive victories.

The first campaign

The first campaign began in October 1930, once the Kwangsi rebellion was over, and after the temporary loss of Ch'angsha in July of the same year had convinced the central government that it should act without delay. A group of seven or eight divisions was formed (about 100,000

[1] See Maps 12 (p. 230), 13 (p. 231), 14 (p. 233) and 15 (p. 236).

men) commanded in name by Lu Ti-p'ing, the governor of Kiangsi. In fact he stayed in Nanch'ang, controlling the operation from there, while Chang Hui-tsan, the commander of the 18th Division, commanded in the field. Decisive battles were fought from 27 December 1930 to 1 January 1931, in the triangle lying between Kian, Chienning and Ningtu. In the last days of December the nationalist troops, advancing southwards within the communists' territory, reached a line stretching roughly from Kian through Tungku and Kuangch'ang to Chienning, arranged as follows:

Chienning: Liu Ho-ting's division (56th Division)
Kuangch'ang: Hsü K'e-hsiang's and Mao Ping-wen's Divisions (24th and 8th Divisions)
Yüant'ou: T'an Tao-yüan's division (50th Division)
Tungku and Lungkang: Chang Hui-tsan's division (18th Division)
Fut'ien: Kung Ping-fan's division (28th Division = 5th New Division)
Kian: Li Lin's division (77th Division).

General Chang Hui-tsan intended to push straight on, attacking first Ningtu and then Juichin.

The communist troops, commanded by Chu Teh (40,000 regulars), held the Huangp'i and Hsiaopu region, north of Ningtu. They were much more concentrated than their adversaries. When the enemy threatened to encircle them, they turned their attention on Lungkang and Chang Hui-tsan's division, which was being attacked in the rear by red troops from Hsingkuo. Lungkang was occupied after six hours' fighting on 27 December; the nationalist 18th Division was destroyed, losing 9000 men. Its leader, Chang Hui-tsan, was tortured and beheaded, and his head was thrown into a river flowing towards the enemy.[1] The 50th Division, under T'an Tao-yuan, retreated eastwards towards Tungshao. It was also attacked by the largest body of the red troops, losing half of its men near Tungshao. Once their front line was broken, the rest of the government troops, who were extremely mediocre in quality, retreated northwards. The communists, well informed by the guerrilla groups covering their movements, by concentrating large numbers on certain well-defined points against an enemy who was spread over too large an area and who lacked skill in manoeuvring, won an important victory soon to be followed by others.

[1] Cf. Kung Ch'u, *I and the Red Army.*

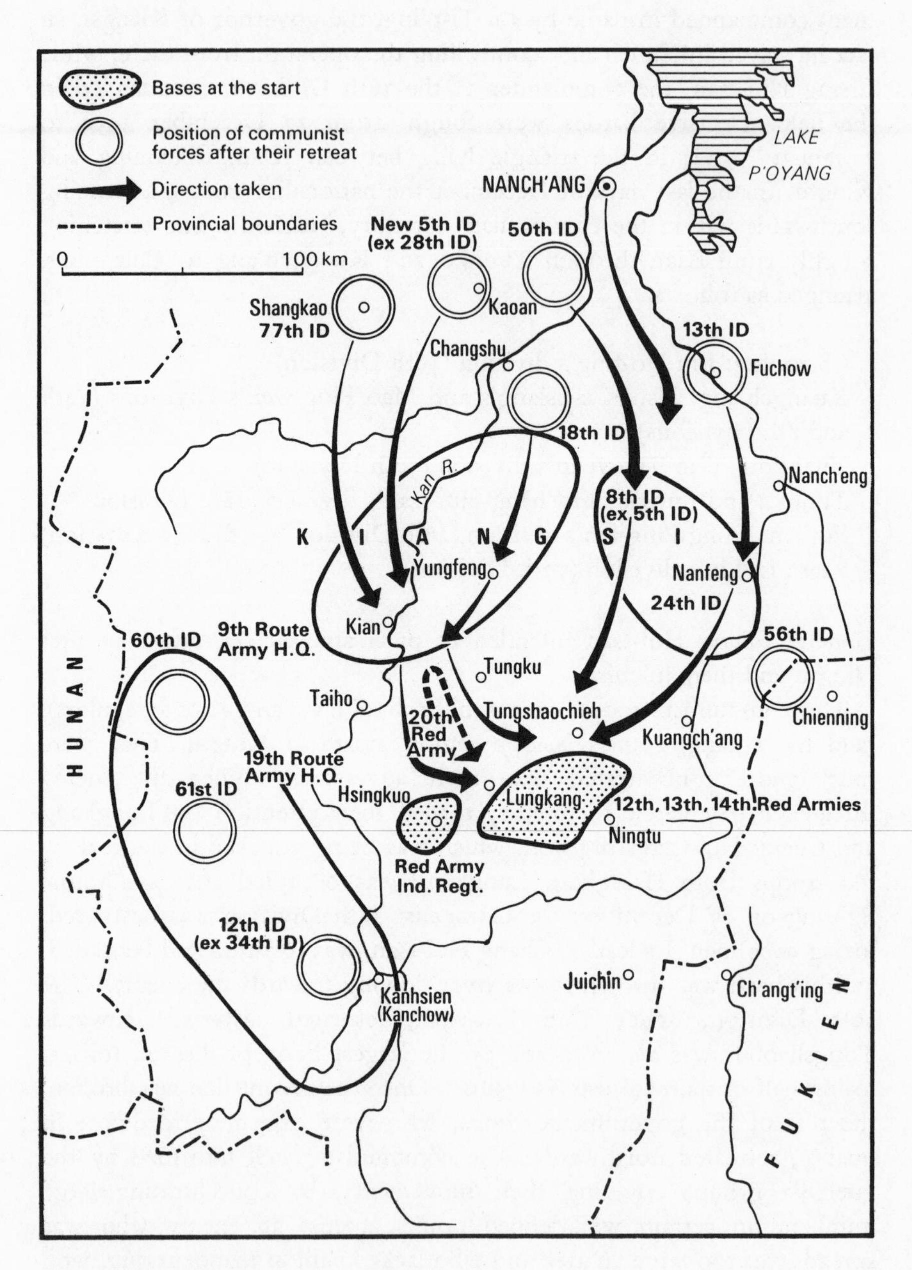

Map 12. The first Kiangsi campaign.

The second campaign

The second campaign was conducted the following May in almost exactly identical circumstances in the same region. The government troops, commanded by General Ho Ying-ch'in, consisted of four armies and two divisions operating separately, making a total of twelve divisions,

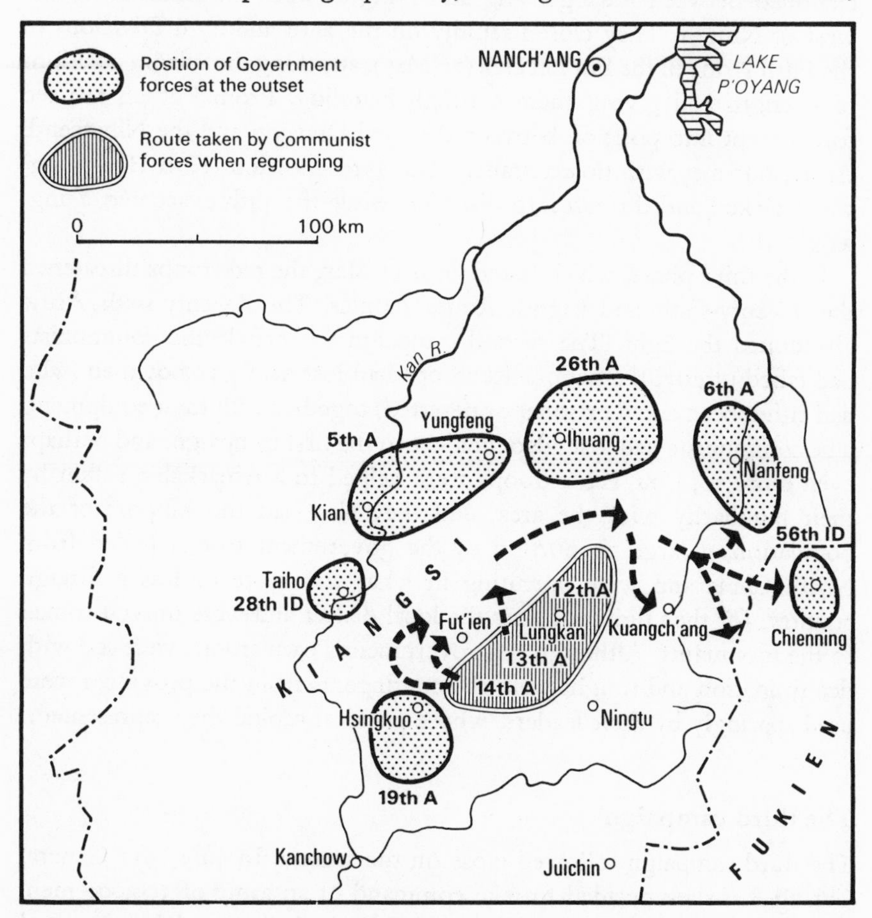

Map 13. The second Kiangsi campaign

with 150,000 men (Mao Tse-tung gives 200,000). Wang Chin-yu's Fifth Route Army (the 43rd, 47th, 54th and 77th Divisions) and the 28th Division commanded by Kung Ping-fan were gathered in the southern area round Kian and Yungfeng. Sun Lien-chung, with the Twenty-sixth Route Army (25th and 27th Divisions) was in the Ihuang region. Chu Shao-liang with the Sixth Route Army (5th, 8th and 24th Divisions) was stationed further east, round Nanfeng. Ts'ai T'ing-k'ai with the Nineteenth Route Army (60th and 61st Divisions and part of the 12th Division) had probably been pushed towards Hsingkuo. Liu Ho-ting with the 56th Division was in the Chienning area, in Fukien.

The communist regular troops, the First and Third Army Groups, stationed between Kuangch'ang and Ningtu, were concentrated to the west of Ningtu. They closed rapidly on the 28th and 47th Divisions of the Fifth Army in the Fut'ien area (16 May), attacking them from positions of strength and giving them a rough handling. From Fut'ien the red forces crept into position between the 43rd Division and the Nineteenth Army, but met with no resistance. The 43rd Division (Kuo Hua-tsung) was attacked and thrown into disorder, while the 54th evacuated Yungfeng.

In the third phase, which lasted until 31 May, the red troops threatened the Twenty-sixth and Eighth Route Armies. The Twenty-sixth Army abandoned the fight. The second campaign to encircle the communists had failed utterly; the nationalist troops had lost nearly 20,000 men (who had either been taken prisoner or deserted) together with their equipment. The communists had lost 4000 men. As in the first campaign, and perhaps even more so, Chu Teh's troops were helped to a remarkable extent by their familiarity with the area, and they also had the support of the population; a large proportion of the government troops hailed from North China and were operating in what was more or less a foreign country, for they did not know the local dialect and were unaccustomed to the mountains. Although the government's own troops were led with determination and fought well, the contingents from the provinces were used sparingly by their leaders, whose political capital they represented.

The third campaign

The third campaign followed close on the second. In July 1931 General Chiang Kai-shek decided to take command of an army of 300,000 men, basing his headquarters at Nanch'ang, where he had several Japanese and German advisers (General Wetzel). The government troops were divided into three large groups: an Eastern group, commanded by General Chu Shao-liang, with its headquarters at Nanfeng, a Central group, commanded by General Ho Ying-ch'in, with its headquarters at Nanch'ang, and a Western group, commanded by General Ch'en Ming-shu, whose headquarters were at Kian. Their plan was to make a rapid advance straight into the heart of the red base, driving Chu Teh's troops back westwards

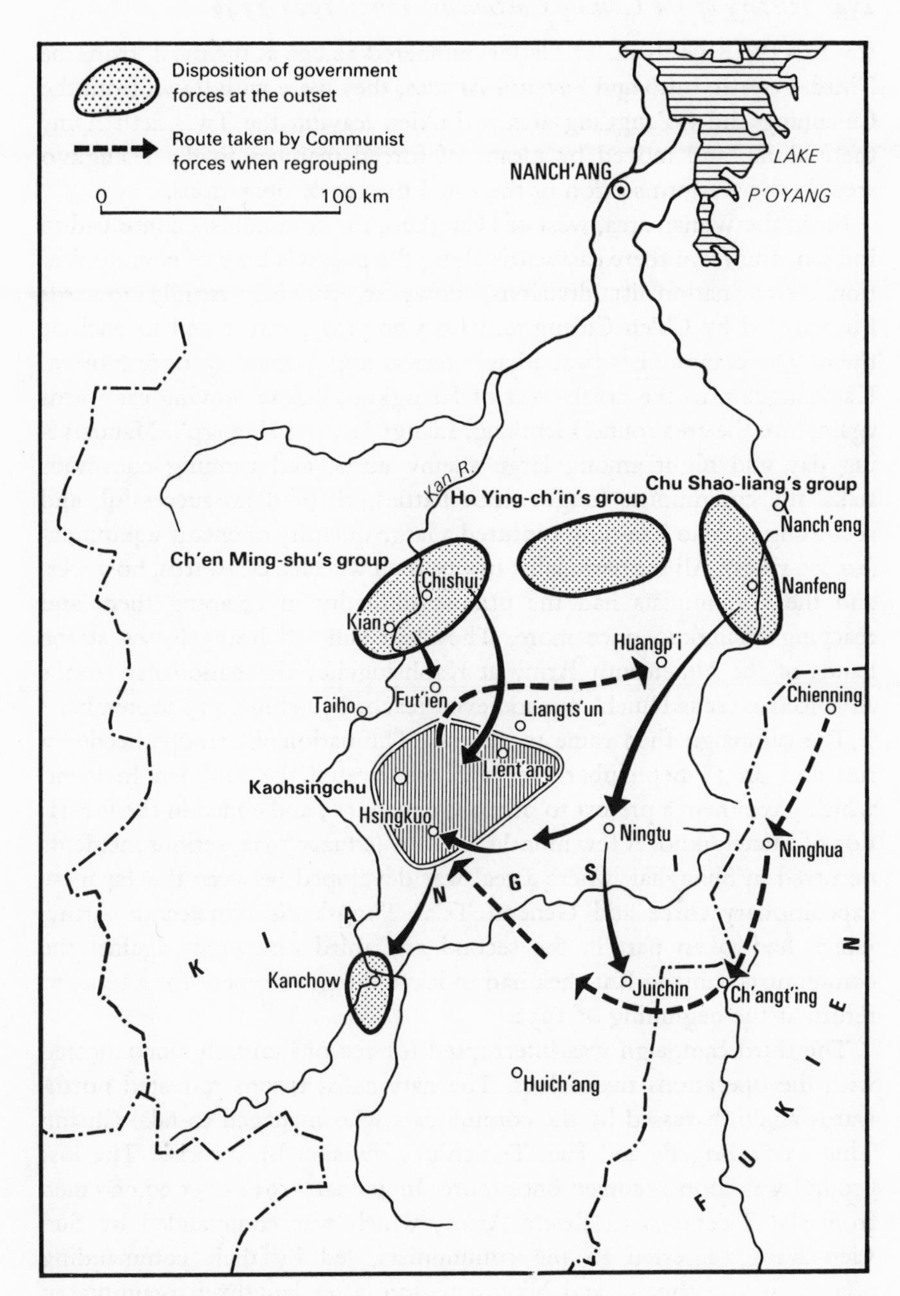

Map 14. The third Kiangsi campaign

towards the River Kan. The latter numbered 30,000 at the most, from the Third, Fourth, Fifth and Seventh Armies; they were withdrawn from the Chienning and Ch'angt'ing area in Fukien leaving the Twentieth Army there alone, and moved by means of forced marches to the Hsingkuo area, in the western section of the usual theatre of operations.

From the Wanan area, west of Hsingkuo, the communists continued to Fut'ien, and from there eastwards along the enemy's lines of communication. Two nationalist divisions, however, moving rapidly towards Fut'ien (led by Ch'en Ch'eng and Lo Cho-ying), threatened to encircle them. The communists beat a hasty retreat and formed up once more at Kaohsingchu, to the north-west of Hsingkuo, before moving eastwards again, into the area round Lient'ang, Liangts'un and Huangp'i. Manœuvring day and night among large enemy units, and running enormous risks, the communists fought three battles, all of them successful, and according to Mao Tse-tung captured a large quantity of enemy equipment (10,000 rifles). All the nationalist troops then wheeled eastwards, however, and the communists had the utmost difficulty in escaping them and reaching Hsingkuo once more. They had suffered heavy losses at the hands of the Nineteenth Army at Kaohsingchu; the nationalist troops advanced as far as Huich'ang, and even reached Juichin on 13 September.[1]

The campaign then came to an end. The nationalist troops needed a rest and on 18 September the Japanese created the Mukden Incident, which gave them a pretext to occupy Manchuria, and ended in the formation of Manchukuo. A few months later, in January 1932, serious incidents occurred in Shanghai, where a real war developed between the Japanese expeditionary force and General Ts'ai T'ing-k'ai's Nineteenth Army, which had taken part in the second and third campaigns against the communists. Chiang Kai-shek had to leave the government for a time, to return at the beginning of 1932.

The third campaign was interrupted for reasons entirely unconnected with the operations themselves. The nationalist troops retreated northwards again, harassed by the communists who managed to take Chiang Ting-wen's brigade and Han Teh-ch'in's division by surprise. The lost ground was soon occupied once more. In January 1932 over 20,000 men from the Twenty-sixth Route Army, which was commanded by Sun Lien-chung, deserted to the communists, led by their commanding officers, in the Ihuang and Ningtu region, after lengthy bargaining, of which countless examples are to be found in the history of China.[2] The

[1] See Hollington Tong, *Chiang Kai-shek* (T'aipei, 1953).

[2] Kung Ch'u took part in the changeover operations. See *I and the Red Army*.

communist victories were indisputable, although less positive than the earlier ones. Two more campaigns were to take place, both larger than the three others; considerable resources were brought into play during the final campaign, which, combined with a strict economic blockade, finally overcame the tenacity of the communists.

The fourth campaign

On 1 May 1932 an agreement put an end to the Sino-Japanese hostilities in Shanghai. The next month Chiang Kai-shek began a fourth campaign against the soviet zones, whose troops had been reorganized and had grown in number during the breathing space allowed to them. This time the central government was to direct its attacks against all the red bases; the effort was to last for nearly a year, from June 1932 until March 1933. The Generalissimo, whose headquarters were based on Hankow and Nanch'ang, launched his first attack against the bases in the Honan-Hupei-Anhwei border area held by Chang Kuo-t'ao and the Fourth Army Group, which had become Hsü Hsiang-ch'ien's Fourth Front Army round Hsinchi and Chinchiachai. The Honan-Hupei-Anhwei border area, attacked by General Wei Li-huang and more easily accessible from several directions than that of Kiangsi, had to be abandoned by the communists. They retreated westwards and settled on the borders of Szechuan and Shensi, in the area round T'ungchiang, Nanchiang and Pachung, where they were to be found at the start of the Long March. A few light units managed to remain in place by scattering. Later on they became Hsü Hai-tung's Twenty-fifth Army, and went to north Shensi where they joined the local Twenty-sixth and Twenty-seventh Armies.

Ho Lung's Second Army Group, based in the Lake Hung area on the Hunan and Hupei border, was attacked by General Hsü Yuan-ch'üan and driven westwards to the Hupei-Hunan-Szechuan frontier area. On the Kiangsi-Hunan border, the Sixteenth Army also retreated to the limits of Hunan and Kiangsi. It joined forces with the Eighth Army, and later formed the Sixth Army Group, commanded by Hsiao K'e, with Jen Pi-shih as its political commissar. Then, in November 1934, the Sixth Army Group went to Kweichow, to the 'hsien' of Yen Ho, where it joined Ho Lung's units; his Second Army Group had become the Second Front Army. In this way, the nationalist troops managed to drive the communist forces away from the great centre of Hankow, and prevent them developing bases in the rich, thickly populated areas of the middle Yangtze valley.

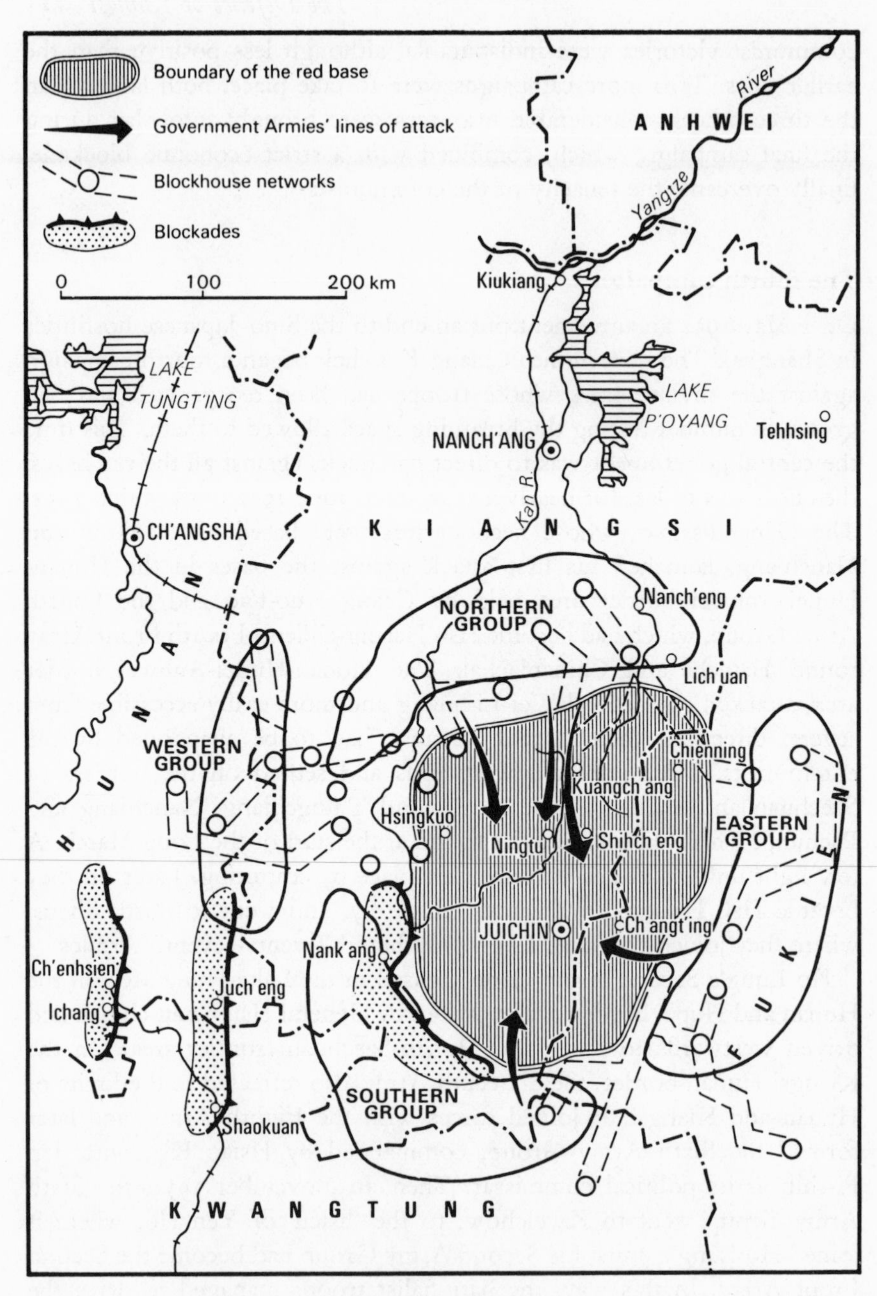

Map 15. The fourth and fifth Kiangsi campaigns

On the other hand, the operations in Kiangsi were no more successful than those of the three earlier campaigns. The Government acted slowly, as its aim was to bring the red zones under proper administrative control once more. The most important operations took place in February 1933. General Ch'en Ch'eng[1] led three groups towards Kuangch'ang, from the Loan, Ihuang and Nanch'eng area. The red troops, operating against the enemy's right wing (General Li Ming-chen), in the Huangp'i area, destroyed two of his divisions (52nd and 59th). Chu Teh then moved in on the rear of the other two groups and threw another division into disorder at Tsaotaikang (the 37th or the 11th Division). Over 20,000 nationalist soldiers were taken prisoner. Chiang Kai-shek had to send the two best central divisions (87th and 88th) rapidly to protect the Nanch'ang area. On 5 April 1933 he arrived in the Kiangsi capital himself, determined to finish with the communists once and for all.

The fifth campaign

The fifth campaign was carefully prepared in every field and large resources were devoted to it. It was no longer limited to military operations, but included elaborate political and economic activities. At the famous Kuling lectures, Chiang Kai-shek declared that the suppression of the communists was 70 per cent a political task, and 30 per cent a military one. He looked for inspiration and examples to Chinese tradition, and especially to the last great conservatives of the nineteenth century – Tseng Kuo-fan, Tso Tsung-t'ang and Li Hung-chang – a fact whose significance extended far beyond the limits of the Kiangsi setting.[2] Confucianism, restored to its former position of honour, was to provide the moral and national basis for anti-bolshevik action. In the context of society, the role of the gentry, who were the examples and guides for the rural population, itself organized by families, was enlarged and rendered more powerful.

In practice, a militia numbering 500 armed and trained volunteers was created in each district in the region. Groups of five districts were organized to draw up plans for self-defence. In the villages, the inhabitants were all responsible for one another according to the old 'pao-chia' system, resurrected for the purpose: ten families made up a 'chia', and a

[1] General Ch'en Ch'eng afterwards held several important posts: Chief of General Staff, Minister of War, Chairman of the Council.

[2] On the role played by tradition in modern times, see Mary C. Wright's outstanding work, *The Last Stand of Chinese Conservatism: the T'ung-chih Restoration 1862-1874* (Stanford, Calif., Stanford University Press, 1957), especially the last chapter.

hundred formed a 'pao'. The organization of the population into militia and 'pao-chia', whose activities were naturally linked, was an attempt to counteract the communists' organization of the population.

The nationalist army, and particularly the troops levied and controlled by the provincial authorities, showed serious weaknesses in loyalty and discipline. To correct these, Chiang Kai-shek created a special control organization, known as the 'Pieh tung tui', a sort of half-overt, half-secret police, whose function was to supply information and organize anti-communist action, and to combat abuses in the administration of the army; it numbered 24,000 men.

A strict blockade of the communist zones was put into operation. This was achieved in the field by networks of blockhouses stretching across the countryside, preventing all movement of traffic and enabling troops and militia to be permanently stationed. Their density was such that near the front lines, the blockhouses were only about 2 to 5 kilometres apart.

Finally, large resources of men and equipment were brought into play: sixty-two regular divisions and about twenty independent brigades; they represented a total of about 800,000 men, counting the supporting units. The air force consisted of about 100 scouting planes and bombers. Radical changes were made in the organization and tactics of the units. As a rule, the ternary system was adopted for the organization of the division. Movement of units was to take the form of short, methodical advances, backed up by heavy fire and careful reconnaissance by the air force. A 'blockhouse doctrine' was evolved, and was discussed plentifully in both camps.

The government strategic dispositions consisted of four large groups:

1 The Northern group, commanded by General Ku Chu-t'ung, with over thirty-eight divisions, stationed in the area south of Nan-ch'ang.
2 The Western group, commanded by General Ho Chien, with seven divisions and three brigades, stationed in the Kiangsi-Hunan border area.
3 The Southern group, commanded by General Ch'en Chi-t'ang, with eleven divisions and one brigade, stationed in the Kwangtung-Kiangsi border area.
4 The Eastern group, commanded by General Ts'ai T'ing-k'ai, with six divisions and one brigade, stationed in the Fukien-Kiangsi border area.

1 Yüan Shih-k'ai, first President of the Republic from 1911 to 1916.

2 Chang Tso-lin, governor of Manchuria, died 1928.

3 Sun Yat-sen, 1921.

4 Mao Tse-tung, 1920.

5 The house in Shaoshan, Hunan province, where Mao Tse-tung was born in 1893.

6 The site of the First Party Congress, Shanghai, July 1921.

Hsin Hua News Agency.

7 Li Ta-chao, joint founder of the Chinese Communist Party, died 1927.

8 Ch'ü Ch'iu-pai, 1920.

9 Mao Tse-tung (third from left) with other leaders of the Autumn Harvest Uprising, 1927.

10 The Ching Kang Shan, occupied by the communists, 1927-1929.

11 Mao Tse-tung's lodgings in Tatsing in the Ching Kang Shan.

12 Chiachin Mountain, on the route of the Long March, 1934-1935.

Hsin Hua News Agency.

Hsin Hua News Agency.

13 The site of the Tsunyi Conference, Kweichow province, January 1935.

14 Yenan, occupied by the communists from 1937 to 1947.

Hsin Hua News Agency.

15 Mao Tse-tung with the peasants of Yenan during the Yenan period.

16 Mao Tse-tung with his teacher Hsü T'e-li, 1938.

17 The authoress Ting Ling, member of the League of Leftist Writers, 1938.

Associated Press.

18 The Peace Preservation Corps being drilled by Japanese officers, Peking, 1945.

19 A unit of the Eighth Route Army heading for the P'inghsing kuan front, 1937.

Hsin Hua News Agency.

Associated Press.

20 Wu P'ei-fu, governor of Hupei, 1937.

Associated Press.

21 The Japanese advance in North China, 1937.

22 Young communist army volunteers in North China, 1937.

Associated Press.

Associated Press.

23 Left to right: Yen Hsi-shan, Feng Yü-hsiang (the 'Christian General'), Chiang Kai-shek, Li Tsung-jen, 1937.

24 Japanese troops advancing on Hankow, 1938. *Associated Press.*

25 Peasant guerrillas in North-West China, 1938. *Associated Press.*

Associated Press.

26 Chu Teh addressing his troops, 1942.

27 Chiang Kai-shek with Mme Chiang Kai-shek and General Stilwell, 1942.

Associated Press.

28 Chinese soldiers marching along the Great Wall, 1943.

Associated Press.

29 Chinese soldiers advancing to the Upper Yangtze front, 1943.

Associated Press.

30 General Wedemeyer (left) greeted by Patrick Hurley on his arrival in Chungking, 26 November 1944.

Associated Press.

Associated Press.

31 General Okamura, Commander-in-Chief of the Japanese forces in China, signs the surrender document, Nanking, 9 September 1945. Facing him is the Chinese mission headed by General Ho Ying-ch'in.

32 General George Marshall with Ho Ying-ch'in, Shanghai, 1945.

Associated Press.

33 Mao Tse-tung and Patrick Hurley arriving in Chungking from Yenan, 24 September 1945.

Associated Press.

34 Chang Ch'ün signing the cease-fire agreement, watched by Chou En-lai and General Marshall, Chungking, 10 January 1946.

Associated Press.

35 Nationalist troops attacking communist positions near Hsuchow, 1948.

Associated Press.

36 The citizens of Peiping welcoming the communist forces entering the city, 1949.

Associated Press.

Associated Press.

37 Mao Tse-tung reviews his troops entering Peiping, 1949.

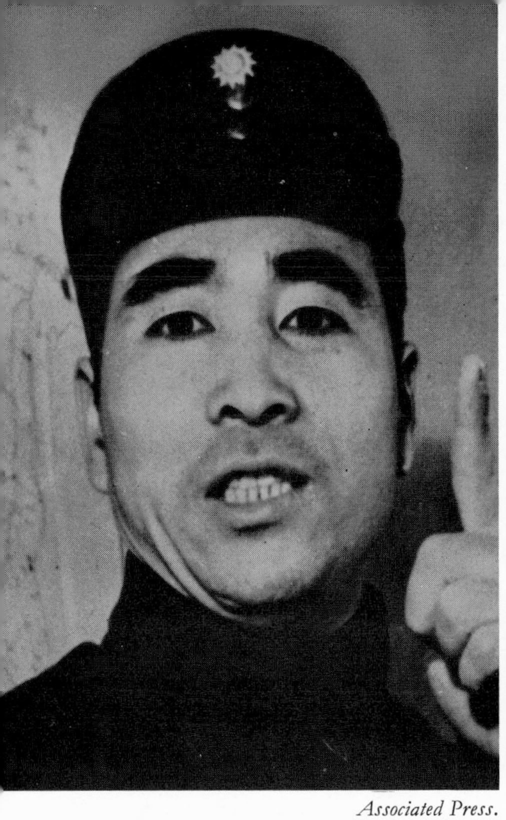

Associated Press.

38 Lin Piao, 1948.

Associated Press.

39 Liu Shao-ch'i, 1949.

40 Nieh Jung-chen, 1949.

Associated Press.

41 Yeh Chien-ying, 1949.

Associated Press.

Associated Press.

42 The communist invasion of Hainan Island, April 1950.

43 Mao Tse-tung proclaims the People's Republic of China, Peking, 1 October 1949.

The government plan consisted mainly in moving the Northern and Eastern groups forward to occupy the communist territory and crush the forces there, leaving the Western and Southern groups to complete the blockade during this vast operation.

The fifth campaign was to last for a year, from October 1933 to October 1934. Initially, the communists tried vainly to win back Lich'uan, a centre that controlled the lines of communication between north-east Kiangsi and Fukien. They failed, and from then on the Red Army dropped its normal tactics of manœuvres on interior lines, consisting of rapid regrouping of its forces, followed by short, sudden massed attacks on the weakest or most adventurous elements of the enemy disposition.

After the failure of the Fukien rebellion (December 1933 to January 1934), the communist territory shrank continuously. The turning point in the campaign came at Kuangch'ang, a hard battle which the communists lost (10-12 April 1934). Distant diversions were unsuccessful or useless. The diversion attempted by Fang Chih-min (Tenth Army Group) in the direction of south Anhwei (the Tehhsing area) was a total failure; Fang Chih-min himself was taken prisoner and executed in January 1935. Another diversion led by Hsiao K'e in the direction of Kweichow had no effect on the government forces. The Red Army, lacking in supplies, with progressively less support from a dwindling population whose sufferings were becoming unbearable, and no space in which to manœuvre, was in danger of complete annihilation. Serious disagreements arose between the majority faction in the Central Committee and certain leaders of the Chinese Soviet Government – chiefly Mao Tse-tung – as to the conduct of the operations.

Early in October 1934 the government forces reached a line running roughly through Shihch'eng, Ningtu and Hsingkuo; the evacuation of the Kiangsi base, which had been contemplated ever since the battle of Kuangch'ang and had been in preparation since August, was put into action. The red forces were organized in two large groups:

1. A Field Army (First, Third and Fifth Army Groups, and the Sixth and Nineteenth Armies) consisting of 90,000 fighting members and 30,000 non-fighting elements (cadres, civilians and families).
2. The Central Military Zone Reserve Army (24th and 37th Divisions, several independent regiments and other small elements), commanded by Hsiang Ying, with Ch'en Yi as his political commissar.

The latter was to cover the retreat of the Field Army and remain in Kiangsi to try to carry on guerrilla warfare.

Towards 10 October the Field Army gathered in the area round Yütu in south-west Kiangsi and began to move on 14 October. On 19 October without much difficulty its vanguard broke through the first line of the nationalist blockade in the Kiangsi, Hunan and Kwangtung border area. The Long March had begun.

20 The Results of the Kiangsi Period
Mao Tse-tung and his Comrades

Mao Tse-tung's assumption of the leadership of the Party and the army is without doubt the most important result of the Kiangsi period, even though the take-over was not officially sanctioned (after a few final, useless shows of resistance) until the Tsunyi Meeting in January 1935 at the beginning of the Long March. The moment has come to give a summary of the early years of the future leader of the Chinese revolution.

No fully complete biography of Mao Tse-tung has yet been written. He himself gave a long account of his life to the American journalist Edgar Snow in 1936, reported in *Red Star Over China*; a few limited works exist on episodes of his childhood, and Li Jui has written of his early revolutionary activities, but the rest is deliberately veiled in legend and mystery. Nothing has yet been revealed as to Mao's activities within the Kuomintang, and his minor role in the Party's central organizations, at least until 1928, is also left conveniently in obscurity. The legend sheds light on several important events which have been seized on by popular and official artists. Mao Tse-tung's true personality will not be fully known until the opening of the secret records or further political upheavals reveal it in its entirety.[1]

Mao Tse-tung comes of peasant stock and until the age of 16 he lived the life of a peasant. He was born on 26 December 1893 in the village of Shaoshan, set in a delightful landscape of rice fields and wooded hills, in

[1] The most complete biography is Stuart Schram, *Mao Tse-tung*. See also Stuart Schram, *The Political Thought of Mao Tse-tung*.

the district of Hsiangt'an, in the heart of Hunan, whose inhabitants have the reputation of being rough and proud. His father, Mao Jen-sheng, a former soldier who became a poor peasant, then a middle peasant, and eventually a rich peasant, also did a little business. Between the ages of 8 and 13 Mao went to the village private school, where he learned his characters by reciting the classics like all the children of his generation; like them, he also read stories from the old popular novels: *Record of a Journey to the West* or *Monkey*, *The Water Margin* or *All Men Are Brothers*, and *The Romance of the Three Kingdoms*, the last two of which influenced him especially. From the age of 13 Mao helped his father in the fields and in his rice and pig business. Nothing worthy of note happened to him; his father's strictness and swift anger, the conscientious kindness of his mother, Wen Ch'i-mei, the companionship of his two brothers, Mao Tse-min and Mao Tse-tan, and his sister, Mao Tse-hung, combined to create a family atmosphere, typical both of China and elsewhere. There he acquired a deep understanding of the peasant mentality, and a thorough knowledge of land problems. He also witnessed social disturbances which were inevitable in years of famine.

In 1909 Mao Tse-tung was given permission to leave his village to continue his studies; he started at the Tungshan Primary School in Hsianghsiang, his mother's birthplace. This was his first contact with the modern world, as Western science formed part of the curriculum, along with the classics. It was also his first contact with national problems, which he had merely glimpsed until then, through books he borrowed. He read writings by the great reformers, K'ang Yu-wei and Liang Ch'i-ch'ao, for his tastes inclined him towards geography, history and the lives of famous men rather than the exact sciences, to which he never referred in his works, in spite of contemporary trends.

In 1911 Mao Tse-tung went to Ch'angsha and enrolled at the Hunan Middle School, where his true initiation to politics began. The provincial capital had a strong patriotic and revolutionary tradition. Mao barely had time to read a few reformist papers (*Min-li pao*), and to hear of the T'ung-meng hui founded by Sun Yat-sen, and of the sacrifice of the seventy-two comrades of his fellow Hunanese, Huang Hsing, when the 1911 Revolution broke out. The army took up the rebel cause, and Mao Tse-tung enlisted in a unit of regulars, serving for six months without distinguishing himself in any way. Then, at 18, he was released from the army, and hesitated between several institutions – the Police School, the Commercial School, the Law School and the Middle School. After a few disappointing experiences, Mao Tse-tung momentarily gave up the idea of receiving a formal education, and embarked on a programme of reading of his own personal choice at the Ch'angsha library. Finally, he entered the Hunan Teachers' Training School in 1913, staying there for five years.

The determined, ardent side of Mao Tse-tung's personality began to develop at this time, as did his taste for reflection and criticism. He also began to take part in politics. In 1917 he helped to organize the 'Hsin-min hsüeh-hui', the New People's Study Society. It had a membership of about sixty, few of whom were to follow their organizer's astounding destiny through to the end. Many joined the Kuomintang, some died, like Ts'ai Ho-shen and Ho Shu-heng; only Li Wei-han (alias Lo Mai), later head of the 'united front' department, was to reach fame with Mao Tse-tung.

However, although Mao was beginning to turn from reformism towards social revolution, becoming more interested in the contributors to *New Youth*, especially Hu Shih and Ch'en Tu-hsiu, than in K'ang Yu-wei and Liang Ch'i-ch'ao, his political ideas were still far from being coherent or clear cut.

> At this time my mind was a curious mixture of ideas of liberalism, democratic reformism and Utopian socialism. I had somewhat vague passions about 'nineteenth-century democracy', Utopianism and old-fashioned liberalism, and I was definitely anti-militarist and anti-imperialist.[1]

One of his teachers, Yang Ch'ang-chi, who taught him moral philosophy, had a profound influence on him. Although Yang Ch'ang-chi, a liberal educated in England and Japan, a lover of virtue who was steeped in the classics, encouraged Mao Tse-tung to take up social action, he was not one to guide him towards Marxism. Later on, in 1921, Mao married his daughter, Yang K'ai-hui, ignoring the wife chosen for him in the village by his parents when he was 14. His second wife was to meet a tragic end – the governor of Hunan, Ho Chien, had her beheaded at Ch'angsha in 1930.

'Knowledge without action is not true knowledge', as Mao Tse-tung was to say later on, and it is true to say that at Ch'angsha his personality developed at the same time as his intellect. Unlike traditional Chinese students, he liked physical exercise, swimming and walking.[2] Both in what

[1] Edgar Snow, *Red Star Over China*, p. 148.

[2] 'A Study of Physical Culture' dates from this period. Extracts are to be found in S. Schram, *The Political Thought of Mao Tse-tung*, and in his complete translation of Mao Ze-dong, *Une Étude de l'éducation physique* (Paris, Mouton, 1963).

he said and in what he did he showed that he possessed an unusually powerful will and ambition. He was ardent and unyielding in argument, totally lacking in the frivolity of others of his own age, and deeply concerned by the transformations taking place in the world around him.

In the spring of 1918 Mao Tse-tung left the Hunan Teachers' Training School and in September he went to Peking with about twenty other young men from Hunan who were getting ready to go to France. Life was not easy for him in the material sense. His future father-in-law helped him to find his way into the Peking University Library, where he was given a humble post. This minor event was to have far-reaching consequences, for it enabled Mao to meet Li Ta-chao, the librarian, and to take part in the work of a small Marxist study group which met in the little room where he worked. He may possibly have come into contact with Ch'en Kung-po, T'an P'ing-shan, Chang Kuo-t'ao and Ch'en Tu-hsiu in this way.

Mao Tse-tung was also in more or less close contact with various groups meeting for the study of journalism and philosophy, who were interested in mass education, and especially with the group run by the future trade unionist, Teng Chung-hsia. He seems to have been briefly attracted by anarchism, but the lack of consistency shown by these little groups discouraged him from becoming permanently involved with any of them.

At the beginning of 1919 Mao Tse-tung went from Peking to Shanghai, where several of his friends were embarking for France. In March he returned to Hunan. He taught in an elementary school, and at the same time began to re-establish the New People's Study Society; then, spurred by the May 4th Movement, he gave himself up entirely to political and social activities. These had as their background and support the boycott on Japanese goods, the creation of a United Students' Association of Hunan and of the Hunan United Association of all Circles, which embraced the Groups for National Salvation. He then founded a review, which was issued for the first time on 14 July 1919. Mao Tse-tung wrote the most important articles for this review, the *Hsiang River Review* (*Hsiang-chiang p'ing-lun*), a weekly paper with an issue of several thousand, based more or less on Li Ta-chao's review, the *Weekly Critic*. The *Hsiang River Review* was one of a profuse number of papers appearing at that time, particularly in the universities, and it did not last long. Mao also organized an Association for Book Learning, which was as short lived as the review.

Early in 1920 Mao Tse-tung made another brief visit to Peking, as the delegate of the New People's Study Society, followed by a journey to

Shanghai in April, when he met Ch'en Tu-hsiu once more. It was at this point in his life that he became an avowed Marxist. On his return to Ch'angsha, he took an active part in local political agitation, began to approach the workers and organized a Marxist study society like those already existing in several towns.

On 1 July 1921 Mao Tse-tung was present at the First Party Congress, but his role was negligible (see Chapter 6). In October he went back to Ch'angsha and organized the provincial branch of the Party there, becoming its secretary. He was also secretary of the Hunan trade union associations, which he helped to found. He missed the Second Party Congress, but was present at the Third when he was elected a member of the Central Committee, and put in charge of the United Front. This was to bring him into close contact with the Kuomintang. After the First Kuomintang Party Congress, which elected him a deputy member of the Central Committee, he went to Shanghai, where he took part in trade union activities and worked in local Kuomintang organizations. He appears to have been in particularly close collaboration with Hu Han-min and Wang Ching-wei. At the Second Kuomintang Party Congress in 1926 he was once more elected a deputy member of the Central Committee and, as temporary head of the Propaganda section, Mao Tse-tung ran the Party's official organ, the *Political Weekly* (*Cheng-chih chou-pao*). Soon after, he was put in charge of the training of peasant movement cadres, also for the Kuomintang (see Chapter 10, p. 112).

Meanwhile, Mao Tse-tung had transferred his attention from workers' agitation to peasant agitation, and on his return to Hunan in the spring of 1925, he began to organize Peasant Associations there. He wrote a great deal at this period of his life. His works are said to be lost today, and the first important text in existence, 'Analysis of the Classes in Chinese Society' (3 March 1926), tries to establish a demarcation line between the revolution and its enemies, and to stress the importance of the peasantry as an ally of the proletariat.[1]

A year later, in March 1927, Mao Tse-tung wrote the *Report on an Investigation of the Peasant Movement in Hunan*, which gained him recognition for his interest and competence in peasant politics, marking his true entry into history and contemporary Marxist literature. His radical views were, however, in opposition to the policy of collaboration with

[1] See the *Selected Works* for the official version, which is different from the original version translated by S. Schram, *The Political Thought of Mao Tse-tung*. The text is said to have been written at the Peasant Movement Training Institute in Canton, already mentioned above.

the Kuomintang left wing and Ch'en Tu-hsiu refused to allow them publication. Similar reservations were made at the Fifth Congress of the Chinese Communist Party, though at least Mao had the satisfaction of seeing the creation of an All-China Peasants' Union, of which he later became Chairman. A few months later, the break between the Kuomintang and the Communist Party, Ch'en Tu-hsiu's elimination at the Conference of Kiukiang on 7 August 1927, and the decision to extend the revolution to the country districts were to lay a new way open to him. He entered on it without hesitation, as has already been described, with the Autumn Harvest Uprising, the Ching Kang Shan episode, and the creation of the Kiangsi base; from then on, his own personal history becomes identified with that of the Party and its leadership.

Chu Teh

To find a career similar to that of Chu Teh, it would no doubt be necessary to turn to some of the extraordinary military adventurers of the eighteenth century or of the period of the French Revolution and Empire. Chu Teh is older than Mao Tse-tung; he was born in 1886, in north-east Szechuan, in the district of Yilung. He became an orphan early in life, and was brought up by an uncle, a peasant of considerable means, who intended his nephew to take the official examinations. He sent him to a secondary school in the district of Shunch'ing, after which he went to the Physical Training Institute at Ch'engtu, the provincial capital, and then, in 1909, to the Yunnan Provincial Military Academy. His military career was a rapid one; he commanded a battalion on the Tongking frontier, became colonel in 1916 and then general in 1919. At that time he was an example of the type of 'militarist' so often condemned by the revolutionaries, unpredictable, self-seeking and fond of luxury. In 1922, when he was head of the Yunnan provincial police force, Chu Teh had to leave because of local disturbances; he fled to Szechuan, and from there went to Central China where he came came into contact with the Kuomintang, became a member, and decided to go to Germany to complete his military education. He went there in 1922, and in Berlin Chou En-lai won him over to the newly created Chinese Communist Party. He stayed in Germany until the end of 1925, when he returned to Szechuan; during the Northern Expedition he won over a fellow-officer from Yunnan, Chu P'ei-teh, in command of the Third Army. At the time of the Nanch'ang Uprising he was head of the provincial Public Security Bureau, and commander of a local training unit.

The meeting between Mao Tse-tung the peasant and Chu Teh the professional soldier was no doubt one of the main causes of the communists' victories, yet the credit has gone almost entirely to Mao Tse-tung alone. Chu Teh's modesty has furnished outsiders with little to enable them to judge of his personality and his professional merits. His writings are few in number, appeared late and deal with tactics rather than great strategic concepts. Whatever the circumstances may be, he was brilliant in action during the Kiangsi period and the Red Army owed its organization and methods of combat mainly to him. When this period came to an end, Mao and Chu seemed to be in perfect agreement; a few dissimilarities in their approach did arise during the Long March, but no satisfactory explanation for this has yet been found.

Other prominent communists

All those of any importance in the Chinese Communist Party today gathered round Mao Tse-tung and Chu Teh during the Kiangsi period. They included survivors from the years from 1921 to 1927, nationalist officers who had changed sides and other Hunanese whom Mao Tse-tung had brought with him. Almost all of these came from the urban bourgeoisie or the great landowning families, and few were of humble origins; most of them came from provinces already swept by the nationalist revolution – central provinces like Hunan, Hupei and Kiangsi, and southern provinces like Kwangtung and Fukien. As they had joined the revolution as young men, few of them had had the time to undergo full professional training or acquire proper experience of a profession. They were above all 'cadres', in the Party, the administration or the army (usually in all three at once); differences in origins or vocation were effaced by the activities in which they shared. The most senior among them – Tung Pi-wu, Chou En-lai and Liu Shao-ch'i – already had a revolutionary past comparable to that of Mao Tse-tung. They sometimes showed independence of thought, at least until Mao Tse-tung's position was fully established.

Chou En-lai

Chou En-lai, who is five years younger than Mao Tse-tung, was born into a great country-dwelling family of civil servants from Huaian in Kiangsu. He was brought up in North China and, as a student, went to Japan, France, Germany, and even Russia; his origins and his experience of different foreign countries combined to give him great subtlety and flexibility of intellect. The ease with which he handles human relations is largely responsible for his popularity in the West, sometimes misleading those dealing with him, as it hides revolutionary orthodoxy and a strong will. After the Li Li-san affair, when he tried to remain on good terms with both sides, he drew nearer to Mao Tse-tung, though apparently without any particular personal attachment for him.

Liu Shao-ch'i

Liu Shao-ch'i, like Mao Tse-tung a Hunanese and a former pupil of the Hunan Teachers' Training School, was born in Ninghsiang in 1898, into a family of rich peasants. In 1921 he went to Russia, where he was trained for trade union activities. Until 1949 he devoted his time to the labour question in all its different aspects. He acted as agitator, organizer and trade union delegate, usually working in secret; in 1931 he became Chairman of the red zone trade unions.

His activities were completely different from those of Mao Tse-tung, as were his temperament and behaviour. A self-effacing man, his speech and his style totally lacked Mao's personal magnetism. On the other hand, all those in contact with him were impressed by his common sense and attention to detail. Up till 1934 Liu Shao-ch'i wrote nothing of importance. His writings after 1939 revealed his strictness and doctrinal orthodoxy, just as the Cultural Revolution was later to reveal his firmness and fidelity to the traditional concept of the Party and classic Marxism-Leninism.[1]

Tung Pi-wu

Tung Pi-wu, a landowner's son from Huangan in Hupei, six years older than Mao Tse-tung, joined first of all in the activities of the T'ung-men Hui organized by Sun Yat-sen. In 1911, as a young man, he was Financial Commissar for his native province. He then spent some time in Japan, before belonging to the little Hupei socialist study group, and, as a result, taking part in the First Party Congress. He worked in close cooperation with the Kuomintang, and consequently after the break in 1927 he had to flee to Japan, and then to Russia. On his return to Kiangsi in 1931 he was appointed Chairman of the Supreme Court and Director of the Party School. His loyalty won him the highest of posts later on in the government: the administration of justice, the training of cadres and even that of Vice-President of the Republic, which he still holds today, perhaps in virtue of his age.[2]

[1] On Liu Shao-ch'i's writings, see Chapter 27. For a short biography of him, see Howard L. Boorman, 'Liu Shao-ch'i, a political profile', *The China Quarterly*, No. 10, 1962.

[2] Since the removal from office of Liu Shao-ch'i, Tung Pi-wu has in fact been fulfilling the duties of President of the Republic.

The outstanding communist military leaders received their training in the Kiangsi Red Army. P'eng Teh-huai, Ch'en Yi, Lin Piao, Liu Po-ch'eng, Ho Lung, Nieh Jung-chen, Yeh Chien-ying and Hsiao K'e distinguished themselves early and, because of the Sino-Japanese war, soon became known outside China as well. The style of operations, the way in which the bases were separated from each other, and the close links between political, administrative and military affairs, proved to be a severe test of talent, character and loyalty. The constant variety of problems and situations called for ceaseless intellectual flexibility. This schooling was to bear fruit throughout the Party's history, and these guerrilla leaders ended their military careers commanding armies, army groups and zones of operations, and handling several hundred thousand men on battlefields stretching over several provinces.

The Kiangsi period was to produce or establish, alongside the military leaders, men whose interests lay in the problems of government, administration and economy; they were to assume greater importance with the development of the New China. Ch'en Yün, born in Shanghai in 1901, one of the rare Chinese communists who came of humble origins, acted as a trade union agitator in the great strikes of 1925 and 1927 and, with Liu Shao-ch'i, was in charge of the trade unions in the bases forming the Chinese Soviet Republic until it came to an end. Li Fu-ch'un, another Hunanese, a returned student from France, was Secretary of the Kiangsi Provincial Committee, before becoming known as an economist, like his rival Ch'en Yün. Li Wei-han (Lo Mai), yet another Hunanese, held important posts in the Party structure in Kiangsi and was for a long time the tactician of the United Front. Teng Tzu-hui, from Fukien, was Financial Commissar, after commanding an army. Teng Hsiao-p'ing, from Szechuan, who was also educated in France, was put in charge of Propaganda and the press, as well as being editor of the paper *Red Star*. Lo Jui-ch'ing, also from Szechuan, was Political Commissar of several units before becoming a specialist in questions of Information, Public Security and National Defence. Lu Ting-i, the son of a rich landowner from Wuhsi, in Kiangsu, was head of the Propaganda section of Communist Youth in Kiangsi, before becoming the official Party spokesman. Li Hsien-nien, a native of Hupei, who came of a poor family, gained his first experience in the Hupei-Honan-Anhwei border base; he returned to the same area as Commander-in-Chief during the Sino-Japanese war. He is now Minister of Finance and a possible successor to Chou En-lai.[1]

[1] Ch'en Yün, Li Wei-han, Teng Tzu-hui and, above all, Lo Jui-ch'ing, Lu Ting-i and Teng Hsiao-p'ing, were removed from political life by the Cultural Revolution of 1966.

A few other important men, now dead, should be added to this list, which is all too short: Hsiang Ying, Wang Jo-fei, Lin Po-ch'ü (alias Lin Tsu-han), along with a few deserters. Only a few recent or current leading figures in the Party did not belong to the Kiangsi period – they include Po I-po, Ch'en Po-ta, K'ang Sheng, P'eng Chen, and a few other, lesser known communists.

The Kiangsi period did more than merely train cadres of great value both to the Party and the army. The Chinese communists had a territorial base and its population to organize and administer, which gave them practical experience and a clear insight into the problems involved in the expansion of the movement. After the Li Li-san adventure, fewer and fewer attempts were made to apply policies inspired by Moscow and formulated in secret meetings of the Central Committee in Shanghai. The Party's planning now began to recognize the limitations imposed by time and place. The whole Party hierarchy was concerned with practical considerations, particularly Mao Tse-tung and Chu Teh, whose only hope was to make their troops last as long as possible against the Kuomintang, and to safeguard their development against the Central Committee, which was more interested in the cities and the proletariat.

A certain measure of unity in doctrine, and certain habits, seem to have evolved during this difficult period. This may be the origin of the realism and solidarity among military commanders often noticeable during the Yenan period and the last civil war.

The Kiangsi period also gave the Communist Party a political and moral renown which was not due solely to propaganda and to a skilful use of attendant circumstances. Now that it had become a peasant movement, the communist movement was to a greater extent part of Chinese traditional history, and aroused more sympathy and understanding than a city-born workers' movement of foreign inspiration. This aspect obviously opened far wider prospects in terms of numbers and geographical extent. This peasant colouring also won interest and approval for the Party from many foreign observers who were quick to forget its orthodoxy. Aided by the role imposed upon them by the war against Japan, the Chinese communists soon became simply patriotic agrarian reformers in the eyes of foreign public opinion.

Ready, as ever, to put the Kuomintang, its enemy, into an awkward position and ward off its attacks, the Chinese Communist Party encouraged the war against Japan as much as possible; this effort to outdo the Kuomintang was made easier by the Japanese themselves, as they increased their military provocations. By creating the legend of the communists' intense patriotism, the Kiangsi period was behind the movement which attracted many students to Yenan rather than Chungking during the Sino-Japanese war.

However, in spite of these moral advantages, and the formation of a framework of cadres, chosen and hardened by seven or eight years' testing, the Chinese Communist Party was seriously weaker than before. In 1927 it had lost the support of the cities; it had just lost all support in the country districts. About 10 million peasants became subject to the government's authority once more, and the example of their sufferings and their final abandonment could hardly do much for red propaganda among the peasants in other provinces. The Party membership fell drastically, from 300,000 at the end of 1933 to less than 40,000 in 1937, and it was probably even lower between these two dates. The majority were naturally peasants turned professional soldiers. This military proletariat was to form the backbone of the Party for a further ten years. The Kiangsi period ended in disaster for the Chinese Communist Party, a disaster as complete as that of 1927; its survival and eventual resurrection were entirely due to an extraordinary combination of favourable circumstances.

21 The Long March (October 1934-October 1935)

The Long March appears in the history of modern China as an awe-inspiring, epic undertaking, as is only right; thousands of stories and popular pictorial reproductions exist centred round the different episodes. It inspired Mao Tse-tung himself:

> The Red Army fears not the trials of a distant march;
> To them a thousand mountains, ten thousand rivers are nothing;
> To them the Five Ridges ripple like little waves,
> And the mountain peaks of Wumeng roll by like mud balls.
> Warm are the cloud-topped cliffs washed by the River of Golden Sand,
> Cold are the iron chains that span the Tatu River.
> The myriad snows of Minshan only make them happier,
> And when the Army has crossed, each face is smiling.[1]

In fact, movements covering a similar distance – 12,000 kilometres – and lasting as long (one year) were relatively frequent in the past and even up till modern times. Less than 100 years earlier, the T'ai p'ing adventure led Shih Ta-k'ai, one of the generals of the Heavenly King, as far as Szechuan, along the route which the Chinese Communists were to follow. In 1927 and 1928, during the Northern Expedition, several armies crossed the continent, or almost crossed it. Some nationalist armies sent in pursuit of the communists, such as the Second Route Army under General Hsüeh

[1] Mao Tse-tung, *Nineteen Poems*, with notes by Chou Chen-fu and an appreciation by Tsang Keh-chia.

Yüeh, covered the same distance as their enemies. In 1949 Lin Piao and his Fourth Field Army moved from Manchuria to the Yangtze, and from there to the Canton area in South China, in less than a year. Credit must be given to the leaders of the Long March, particularly Mao Tse-tung and Chu Teh, for surviving, rather than for undertaking the march – for survival was due to their military and political skill, and also to the courage and discipline of the army, under constant threat of disintegration. Their exploit was obviously made easier by the lack of cohesion of the Nanking government, whose authority was particularly weak in the western provinces.

From Kiangsi to the Yangtze: the Tsunyi Conference

The Long March was carried out by three separate groups, completely different as far as their composition, leadership, place of departure, route and timing of their movements were concerned – Chu Teh's group came from Kiangsi, Ho Lung's from the Hunan-Kweichow-Hupei-Szechuan border region, and Chang Kuo-t'ao's group was stationed at first in north-east Szechuan (see Maps 16, p. 254, and 17, p. 256).

The First Front Army, commanded by Chu Teh, had P'eng Teh-huai as its second in command; Yeh Chien-ying was Chief of General Staff, and Liu Po-ch'eng head of the Operations Bureau. It included the First, Third, Fifth, Eighth and Nineteenth Army Groups and a training division. These names must not create a false impression and mask the smallness of their numbers and their mediocre weapons and equipment; the five army groups formed a total of 90,000 men, 30,000 of whom were recruits, all virtually unarmed. Nearly 30,000 civilians marched alongside the army, including workers belonging to a small arsenal and a printing press, whose materials were carried by the men themselves.

Chu Teh left the area south of Kanchow on or about 16 October 1934, his troops divided into several columns, and kept to the mountains separating Hunan from Kwangtung and Kwangsi. He broke through four light defence lines, all more or less well manned by the enemy – one along the River Kan, another in the region of Jenhua in Kwangtung, a third parallel to the Canton-Hankow road (13 November), and the fourth south of Ch'üanchow, north-east of Kueilin – and reached the province of Kweichow in December (the Lip'ing district). The numbers of his troops appear to have fallen considerably, perhaps by half, as a result of fighting and desertion on the part of soldiers afraid to leave their native regions. Equipment was mainly abandoned to increase mobility. Large

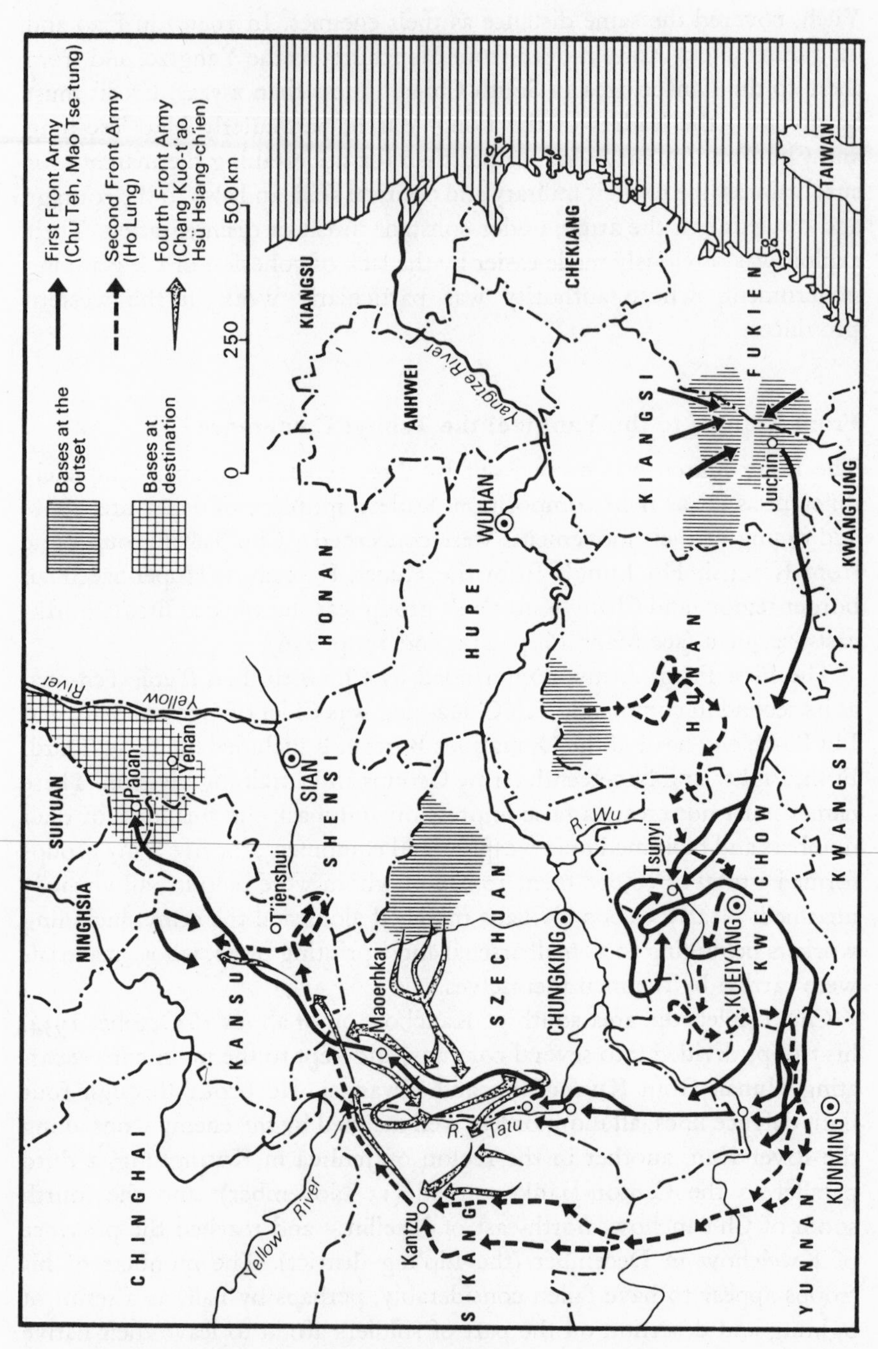

Map 16. Routes taken on the Long March

government units were gathered round Kueiyang, the capital of Kweichow, commanded by General Wang Chia-lieh, who was in charge of the province; Chu Teh gave up his plan to continue westwards, and set off in a north-westerly direction towards Chenyuan and Tsunyi. He intended to cross the Yangtze not far from Chungking and join up with Chang Kuo-t'ao's group, which was already in Szechuan. A difficult engagement led by Liu Po-ch'eng on 4 January 1935 enabled Chu Teh to cross the River Wu and avoid most of the nationalist troops pursuing him. On 6 January the communists entered Tsunyi, where they were to stay until 18 January. A conference held at this halt (in fact an enlarged meeting of the Political Bureau) was to make Mao Tse-tung temporary Chairman of the Central Committee – in other words, leader of the Communist Party.[1]

Nothing is known for certain about the conditions surrounding this conference. Scraps of information to be found in the official history mention a violent discussion between the former leaders, particularly Po Ku (Ch'in Pang-hsien), and their supporters, who were held responsible for the 'third leftist deviation', and the 'Maoist' Kiangsi faction. Nor does any information exist as to the composition of the new Central Committee, and no mention is made of consultation by telegram with the leaders of the other groups – Chang Kuo-t'ao and Ho Lung. Nothing suggests that Moscow could be approached or even informed. Much later, in 1945, Mao Tse-tung wrote no more than this:

> The Tsunyi Meeting was entirely correct in concentrating all its effort on rectifying the military and organizational errors, which at that time were of decisive significance. The meeting inaugurated a new central leadership, headed by Comrade Mao Tse-tung – a historical change of paramount importance in the Chinese Communist Party.[2]

The Tsunyi Conference was in fact indispensable, not to condemn past 'military errors' or to decide on a new strategy, for no possible alternatives existed, but to deduce the effect on the Party leadership of the abandonment of Kiangsi. Mao Tse-tung, as President of a Soviet Republic that no longer existed, was in a false and potentially dangerous position. Having lost the support of the governmental and administrative structure of the Central China bases, reduced once more to the status of a member of a Political Bureau in which his friends were probably in the minority,

[1] See Jerome Ch'en, 'Resolutions of the Tsunyi Conference', *The China Quarterly*, No. 40 (October-December 1969).

[2] 'Resolution on Certain Questions in the History of our Party', *Selected Works*, vol. III, p. 193.

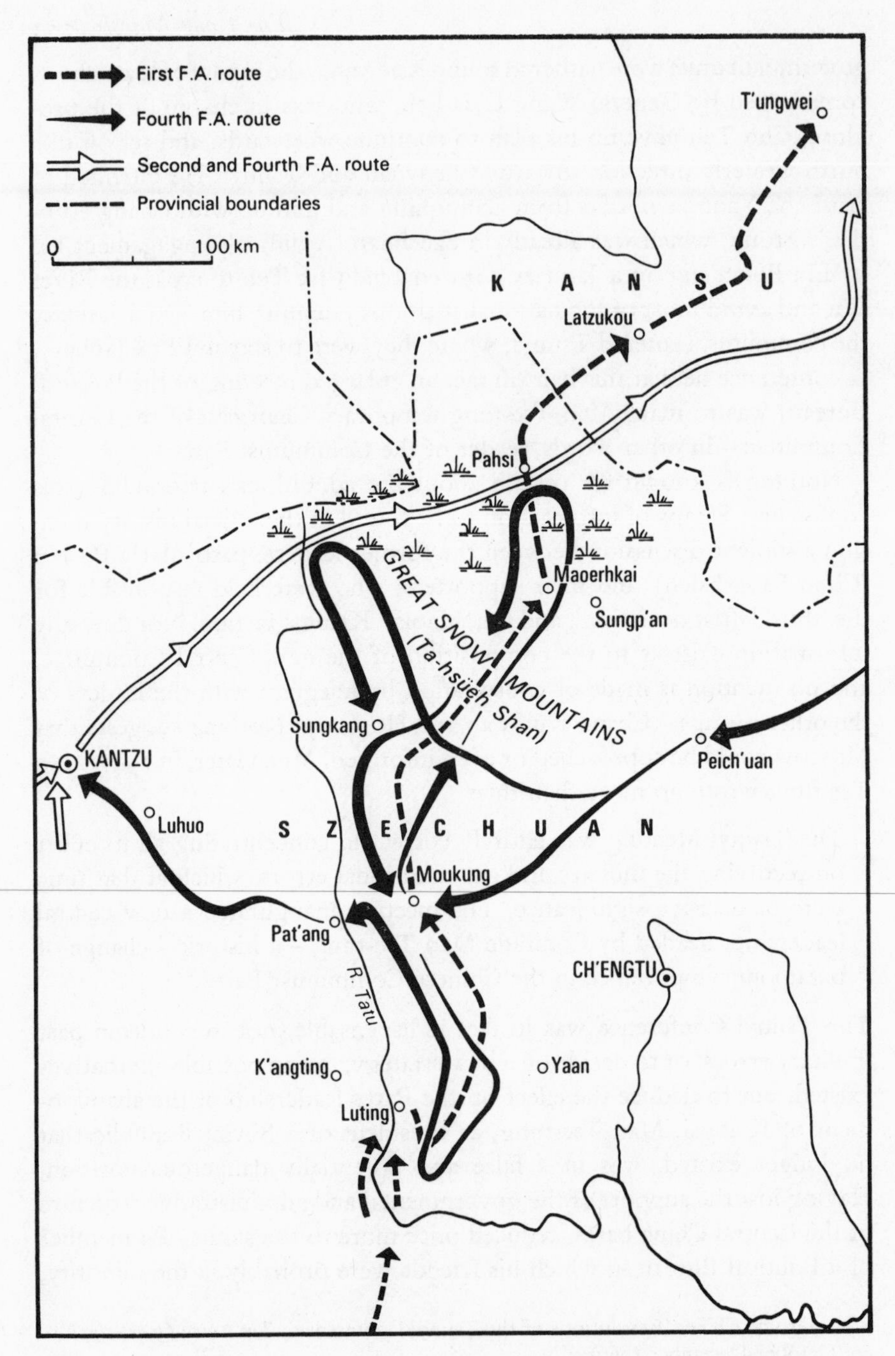

Map 17. The Long March: the crossing of Szechuan, Kansu and Shensi

he was bound to have to give way to the authority of the 'Young Bolsheviks' and the Secretary-General.

In fact, everything suggests that Mao Tse-tung rapidly made use of the considerable credit he still had in the Party and the army to forestall these unpleasant possibilities. The criticism of past operations was a pretext to eliminate rivals conveniently accused of 'leftist deviationism', just as Ch'ü Ch'iu-pai and Li Li-san had been in their turn. Mao Tse-tung does not appear to have succeeded completely. Ch'in Pang-hsien in particular still held posts of responsibility in the movement, which he maintained at least until the Party settled once more in Shensi, and until Mao Tse-tung consolidated his position of authority. During the Sino-Japanese war, he was editor of the communist press agency (Hsin-hua agency) and of the Party's paper *Emancipation*, and member of several missions of liaison with the central government, before being killed in a plane crash, along with Yeh T'ing and Wang Jo-fei, on 8 April 1946.

The Red Army's ultimate destination also gave rise to disagreements at Tsunyi. Some, among them Mao Tse-tung, were in favour of north Shensi, where a small base had already been formed, while the rest suggested Sinkiang, or Chinese Turkestan, which was nearer the Russian frontier, and aroused the interest, not wholly altruistic, of the Russians. It is conceivable that these considerations guided Mao Tse-tung in his preference, particularly as his credit in Moscow stood less high than that of his rivals. In any case, the choice of Sinkiang was not a good one, because only a small proportion of its inhabitants were Chinese, and because of the predominant influence of Islam. No solution was found to this question, which arose again, with further variations, at Maoerhkai.

The crossing of the Yangtze and the Tatu

It turned out to be impossible to cross the Yangtze in the Chungking area, as the Szechuanese generals put up a determined opposition. The First Front Army, which had reached Chishanting, had to decide to return south-eastwards. After sending a small force westwards as far as Pichieh as though to move straight on to the upper Yangtze valley, it turned in a south-easterly direction once more. It passed between Tsunyi and Kueiyang, turning east and then south round Kueiyang to avoid entering the town, and at last was able to march westwards again. The whole of this complicated route was punctuated by several battles against sections of four enemy divisions. For several weeks, the communist troops took a route corresponding roughly to a line from Kueihua to Chengfeng, along mountain paths parallel to the main road from Kueiyang to Kunming.

Chu Teh then decided to cross the Yangtze in the Yunnan-Szechuan border area, in the reaches where the river is still known as the Gold Sand River (Chinshachiang). With this end in view, a group commanded by Lin Piao made a feint attack on Kunming, causing considerable disturbance. While this was under way, the rest of the army, divided into two main columns, marched towards the river's great southern loop. The right column, heading for Süanwei and Tungchwan, crossed near Luki, south of Ch'iaochia, and the left column crossed about 100 kilometres further south, at the Luch'e and Hungmen ferries; Lin Piao crossed further upstream, east of Lungkai. The crossing of the Yangtze, which is about 300 metres wide at this point, lasted for about ten days, ending in the middle of May, with no events worthy of note. Leaving the Yangtze valley, the First Front Army moved northwards, through Hueili, where it stopped for five days, and through the territory of the Lolos. It had to win over this belligerent minority race, traditionally hostile to the Han. Liu Po-ch'eng's diplomacy, backed up by the communists' experience in dealing with the common people, avoided all dangerous complications.

In the last weeks of May, Lin Piao's group reached the south bank of the River Tatu, a tributary of the Min, itself a tributary of the Yangtze. His advance troops (the 1st Regiment of the 1st Division), coming from Mienning, took the little town of Anshunch'ang, defended by two Szechuanese companies (22 May). Liu Po-ch'eng (more fortunate than the T'ai p'ing leader Shih Ta-k'ai) and the 1st Division, of which he was in command, with Nieh Jung-chen as his political commissar, set foot on the north bank of the river. But the means of crossing the river, amounting to a few boats only, were not enough to carry all the First Front Army over the Tatu, which was 300 metres wide, with an extremely strong current at that particular time of year. The army followed the south bank for nearly 150 kilometres upstream, in an attempt to reach Luting. The landscapes surrounding them were impressive – high mountains, covered in snow in spite of the season, and furrowed by swift mountain torrents. More impressive still was the bridge itself, made up of thirteen iron chains stretching above the boiling waters. The Fourth Army arrived at the west end of the bridge on the morning of 26 May, after a series of forced marches which had brought them from Anshunch'ang. Two lines from an old poem were inscribed on the tablet at the entry to the bridge:

Lofty mountains surround the bridge of Luting,
Their peaks rise a thousand li among the clouds.

The walled town of Luting rose out of the mountainside at the other end of the bridge and, if the communists are to be believed, its centre and surroundings were held by two Szechuanese regiments. At 4 p.m. twenty-two volunteers from the 2nd Company launched an attack on the bridge, and two hours later both the bridge and the town were in the hands of the 4th Regiment. Admittedly, the operation was made considerably easier by the 1st Division's progress along the north bank, and also, probably, by the poor quality of the provincial troops resisting them. The assailants lost no more than seventeen men, but the magnificence of the setting, the ghost of Shih Ta-k'ai, and the enemy's numbers, if not his quality, could not fail to fire the imagination; the crossing of the Tatu has earned a place among the most glorious of the Red Army's exploits.[1]

The meeting of the First and Fourth Front Armies at Maoerhkai

Once Luting was taken, west Szechuan was open to the First Front Army, which arrived a few weeks later in the Moukung area, west of the important centre of Yaan, after passing through Tiench'üan. There it met the Fourth Front Army, commanded by Chang Kuo-t'ao and Hsü Hsiang-ch'ien. Leaving the Shensi-Szechuan border region where it had settled in 1933, the Fourth Front Army had begun its journey westwards again in March 1935. In June after crossing the Chialing and the Min, it halted in the region of Moukung, Lianghok'ou, Lifan and Maohsien. Much less sorely tried than the First Front Army, it numbered at least 50,000 men, all properly armed and equipped. The two armies made preliminary contact on 16 June; a little later a military ceremony took place in the village of Eulhokuo to celebrate their meeting. Leaving Moukung, the two armies, following parallel routes, moved northwards across the Mengpi range and reached Maoerhkai on 10 July.

A meeting of the Political Bureau was held at Maoerhkai.[2] Mao Tse-tung and Chang Kuo-t'ao came into serious disagreement over the direction to be taken by their armies. The latter, who was afraid that they would be unable to break through the government defences in the Shensi and Kansu areas, proposed settling in west Szechuan and in Sikang, in the Tatsienlu area. He came round to Mao Tse-tung's view, however,

[1] Hang Teh-chih, and an officer of the 4th Regiment, Yang Ch'eng-wu, who was Chief of General Staff *ad interim* from 1966 to 1968, have left two accounts of the operations.

[2] The first meeting, during which Mao Tse-tung and Chang Kuo-t'ao had already disagreed, is said to have taken place at Moukung.

which was still in favour of north Shensi, and the two armies marched on again, in two columns.

The western column consisted of the Fourth Front Army under Chang Kuo-t'ao and Hsü Hsiang-ch'ien and – for reasons unknown – part of the First Front Army (the Fifth and Ninth Armies). The eastern column, which included Mao Tse-tung, was commanded by Lin Piao and P'eng Teh-huai, and moved along a line stretching westwards of Sungp'an and Latzukou. After a few days Chang Kuo-t'ao changed his mind once more, on the pretext that the difficulties ahead of them were insuperable, and decided to move westwards once again, taking with him Chu Teh, against his will according to the official historians. This new mystery in the extremely eventful life of the Chinese Red Army's Commander-in-Chief has yet to be explained. It is implied that Chu Teh gave way under threat of violence, and it may be that he was unwilling to risk a confrontation between the men from the First Front Army who had followed him and the vastly superior troops commanded by Chang Kuo-t'ao. At the same time, it inevitably comes to mind that Chu Teh, a native of Szechuan with personal links with the province's military circles, would be likely to do better work for the revolution in Szechuan than in Shensi. This hypothesis would find further support if it were true that Moscow, when asked to solve the problem of the final destination, advised the formation of two bases, one with Chang Kuo-t'ao, and the other with Mao Tse-tung.[1] The split must have gone a long way, for Chang Kuo-t'ao is now accused of having created another Central Committee.

While this was taking place, in July and August 1935, the First Front Army was still a long way from its destination, and severe trials lay ahead. Before reaching Maoerhkai, it had to cross the Ta-hsüeh Shan, the Great Snow Mountains, over 4000 metres high, often cutting a path through rocks, and abandoning men and animals as it went. After Maoerhkai, it was confronted by the swamps south of Latzukou on the Shensi border. Narrow passages had to be found through the tall swamp grasses. The soldiers, lacking all provisions, had to eat wild plants, suffering twenty days of appalling hardship, which reduced the First Front Army, already two armies short of its full complement, to under 7000 men. Even so, it managed to reach Minhsien in south Kansu and from there, taking a circuitous route to avoid central Shensi, where large government forces were stationed, it moved towards T'ungwei, and then towards Kuyuan and Huanhsien. It entered north Shensi in the district of Paoan, where it

[1] Declaration made by Chang Kuo-t'ao to R. North. Cf. *Kuomintang and Chinese Communist Elites.*

joined troops commanded by Liu Chih-tan and Kao Kang, who had come to meet the First Front Army, on October 1935. For a few months, Paoan was to become the capital of the Chinese Communist Party and the headquarters of the First Front Army.

The Second and Fourth Front Armies reach north Shensi

Ho Lung's group, the Second Front Army, leaving the region of Sangchih and Shanyang, on the borders of three provinces – Kweichow, Hunan and Szechuan – started on its way in November 1935. After crossing Kweichow from east to west, and north Yunnan, the Second Front Army crossed the Yangtze near Lichiang, much further west than the position chosen by the First Front Army the year before. From there, it moved up the upper Yangtze valley as far as Atuntzu on the threshold of Tibet, then split into two columns to go on towards Kantzu. Near Kantzu it met the Fourth Front Army, commanded by Chang Kuo-t'ao, with which it had made contact near Lit'ang. The choice of such a circuitous route can be explained by anxiety to avoid interception by government or provincial troops, who were on the alert, and to escape being harassed by air attacks. In fact, it seems that the Second Front Army had to fight few battles.

Meanwhile, Chang Kuo-t'ao's troops – the Fourth Front Army – had not managed to spread out satisfactorily in Szechuan from their base in the Moukung and Maoerhkai area (to which they had returned at one point) and they had been forced to stay on the borders of Sikang, in a poor, difficult area, which was partly hostile to them. This unfortunate situation, and the fact that Mao Tse-tung seemed to have settled in complete security in north Shensi, appears to have decided Chang Kuo-t'ao (encouraged by Chu Teh and Jen Pi-shih, as the communist historians say) to join the new red base in his turn, after sending some of his troops on a remarkable expedition towards Sinkiang.

Leaving Pat'ang, the Second and Fourth Front Armies went directly north-eastwards. They left Maoerkhai to the east, avoided the Latzukou swamps by taking a northerly route, sent their right wing (Second Front Army) towards central Shensi, and crossed Kansu. On 6 October 1936 the two armies made contact at Huining with units sent from the First Front Army to meet them; soon all the communist troops were gathered in North Shensi, and the Long March was over.

The political consequences of the Long March

The Long March was a political event with far-reaching results, not merely an outstanding military achievement. First of all, it ensured the survival of the communist movement as a whole. The armies did not march alone; they were accompanied by all the Party's superstructure – the Political Bureau, the Central Committee with its attendant services – in short, all the military and political leaders of that time. Had the army been destroyed, the Party would have been annihilated, if not for good, at least for many years. The proletariat was small, and had lost its most dynamic members during the upheavals of 1927; consequently it was not in a position to serve as a basis for a new revolutionary formation. The peasantry was still unable to organize itself without the military and intellectual framework provided by the rebel officers from Nanch'ang and the students from the cities. Public opinion was becoming increasingly concerned with resistance to Japan and, as the Sian Incident was soon to show, it turned towards Chiang Kai-shek.

The communist movement on the march was also in a sense the 'République Voyageuse' described by Taine in connection with the 'Dix Mille'. The Political Bureau dealt with doctrinal questions as well as problems arising from the circumstances, as at Tsunyi and Maoerhkai. On a lower level, the lower ranks of the Party and particularly the army Political Department held meetings as often as possible at which ideology was inseparable from the current situation. It was the difficulties that arose from day to day that tried and proved the strongest characters; today's leaders are still the leading cadres of the Long March.

For the minor cadres, the Long March was also a test – physically, intellectually and morally. After seven years' ceaseless fighting and activity among the population, it perfected the qualities that were soon to be used in the eminently suitable context of a war on a national scale. It was with the Kiangsi period and the Long March that the tradition originated of the communist cadre who was at the same time doctrinaire and tough, determined and devoted to his cause, with a political training in the communist sense of the term, convinced of his duty to serve the people. The cadres trained after the victory of 1949 were not to match their elders. In 'On Tactics Against Japanese Imperialism' Mao Tse-tung exaggerated the importance of the Long March, turning it into an event on an international scale:

> The Long March is the first of its kind in the annals of history, . . . a manifesto, a propaganda force, a seeding-machine. Since Pan Ku divided the heavens from the earth and the Three Sovereigns and Five Emperors reigned, has history ever witnessed a long march such as ours? . . . It has announced to some two hundred million people in eleven provinces that the road of the Red Army is their only road to liberation. . . . In

> the eleven provinces it has sown many seeds which will sprout, leaf, blossom and bear fruit, and will yield a harvest for the future.[1]

There is no doubt that for the communist movement, the Long March was not only an achievement that won considerable prestige, but also a political success, which was to do much to facilitate the formation of a new united front. The Party spread propaganda directly among a population, which up till then had been in ignorance of its aims, and generally of its existence as well. The political commissars seized every opportunity of holding meetings to explain the communists' political and, above all, social programmes, and encourage the population to share out the land, emancipate the women, etc. The Party also came in contact with different races, which had to be won over, giving birth to their policy towards the national minority races, to be developed fully after 1949.

The propaganda spread by the Long March obviously achieved its most useful effects in the government zones, and first and foremost in the cities. The Red Army was in flight, but it regularly managed to escape an enemy whose material means were infinitely superior. Inspired by admiration, sympathy or romantic revolutionary leanings aroused by the Long March, many students endeavoured to go to Yenan as soon as the relaxing of the government's blockade and the Sino-Japanese war allowed them to. As it gradually extended from one end of China to the other, the Long March shifted the civil war from a provincial to a national level. This in itself stressed the obvious incongruity of waging a civil war at a time when the Japanese aggressions were increasing in their intensity. The military commanders in the North-West realized this, and pursued their anti-communist campaign with less and less conviction, until they eventually rebelled against the principle itself at the time of the Sian Incident in December 1936.

Lastly, in a different field, the Long March helped the Chinese Communist Party to achieve a greater independence of Moscow. Everything tended in the same direction – Mao Tse-tung's appointment as Chairman of the Party, happening as it did in unusual conditions, practical difficulties in maintaining contact, the Comintern's tendency to keep in the background to help the creation of popular fronts, under cover of patriotism or anti-fascism. In fact, after the Tsunyi Conference, the Russians seem to have had less and less influence in the Chinese Communist Party's internal affairs. In the light of more recent history, this was perhaps one of the major consequences of the Long March.

[1] Mao Tse-tung, *Selected Works*, vol. I, p. 160.

Part 4

The Yenan Period and the Sino-Japanese War (October 1935-August 1945)

In a struggle that is national in character the class struggle takes the form of national struggle.

Mao Tse-tung, 'The Question of Independence and Initiative within the United Front'

I told them they ought not to regret it. If the Imperial [Japanese] Army had not occupied half of China, the Chinese people would not have become united in their struggle and the People's Republic of China would not have been born.

Mao Tse-tung, in an address to a delegation from the Japanese Socialist Party, July 1964

22 The Party's Re-establishment in North Shensi and the Formation of an Anti-Japanese United Front

North Shensi

The new communist base was in one of the poorest regions of China, except for the deserts of Turkestan and the Tibetan mountains. North of it lay the Great Wall, bounding the southern edge of the Ordos plateau; to the east lay the Yellow River, flowing southwards after its Great North Bend. The area was roughly square in shape, each side measuring about 400 kilometres, and covered twenty or so districts, of which the most important were Paoan, Anting, Suiteh, Chingpien and Yenan, which was occupied a little later than the rest. The countryside was one of hills and bare loess plateaux, interspersed with precipitous cliffs, the average altitude being about 1000 metres above sea level. Frequent droughts cancelled out the natural fertility of the soil, which yielded crops of wheat, oats and cotton. Its mineral resources – salt, coal and oil – were little exploited, if at all. The area had no modern roads; a rough track that could take lorries led from Sian to Yülin, passing through Yenan.

The population had fallen to less than a million as a result of the Dungan Moslems' revolt in the second half of the last century. But this frontier region, where nearly all the towns still had their walls and fortifications, had harboured many imperial garrisons in the past and was one of the high places of Chinese military history, immortalized in countless stories of misery and splendour. Li Hua, as early as the eighth century, wrote:

Again, since the Ch'in and the Han dynasties, countless troubles have occurred within the boundaries of the empire, desolating the Middle Kingdom. No age has been free from these. . . .

Alas! methinks I see them now, the bitter wind enveloping them in dust, the Tartar warriors in ambuscade. Our general makes light of the foe. He would give battle upon the very threshold of his camp. Banners wave over the plain; the river closes-in the battle array. All is order, though hearts may beat. Discipline is everything: life is of no account. . . .

Faintly and more faintly beats the drum. Strength exhausted, arrows spent, bow-strings snapped, swords shattered, the two armies fall upon one another in the supreme struggle for life or death. To yield is to become the barbarian's slave: to fight is to mingle our bones with the desert sand.[1]

Mao Tse-tung, faithful as ever to the Chinese historical and literary tradition, could not resist recalling past battles, while thinking of those in store for him.

The communist movement was not unknown in north Shensi. As early as 1929 Liu Chih-tan, a native of Suiteh and a former Peking University student, had tried to spread communism among the peasants. He was soon joined by Kao Kang, another native of Shensi, born in 1902 into a family of poor peasants in Hengshan and liquidated mercilessly by Mao Tse-tung in 1953, in spite of his glorious career as a revolutionary.[2]

In 1931 or thereabouts a communist organization took shape north of the River Wei, in the 'hsien' of Sanyüan, Yaohsien, Ichün and Chengning. A little later, in about 1934, it spread northwards to include the region of Yench'uan, Yench'ang, Paoan, Anting and Chingpien, near the Kansu and Ninghsia borders. The communists from Central China settled in this same zone, transferring their capital to Yenan in December 1936.

The new regime gave itself a fairly modest name at first: The North-west Bureau of the Central Soviet Government, a title that made concessions to present realities, while allowing for basic principles and for the future. Four administrative districts were created: (1) the North Shensi Revolutionary Base, (2) the Shensi-Kansu Revolutionary Base, (3) the Kuanchung Special Zone, near the Great Wall, (4) the Shenfu Special Zone.

[1] Herbert A. Giles, *Gems of Chinese Literature* (New York, Paragon Books, 1965), pp. 145-7.

[2] For details of the communists' first attempts at settling in Shensi, see Meng Po-chien, *Hui Shiang jen-1ao* (*Return to Humanity*) (in Chinese), and an article by Mark Seldon, 'The guerrilla movement in north-west China: the origins of the Shensi-Kansu-Ninghsia Border Region (part I)', *The China Quarterly*, No. 28 (1966).

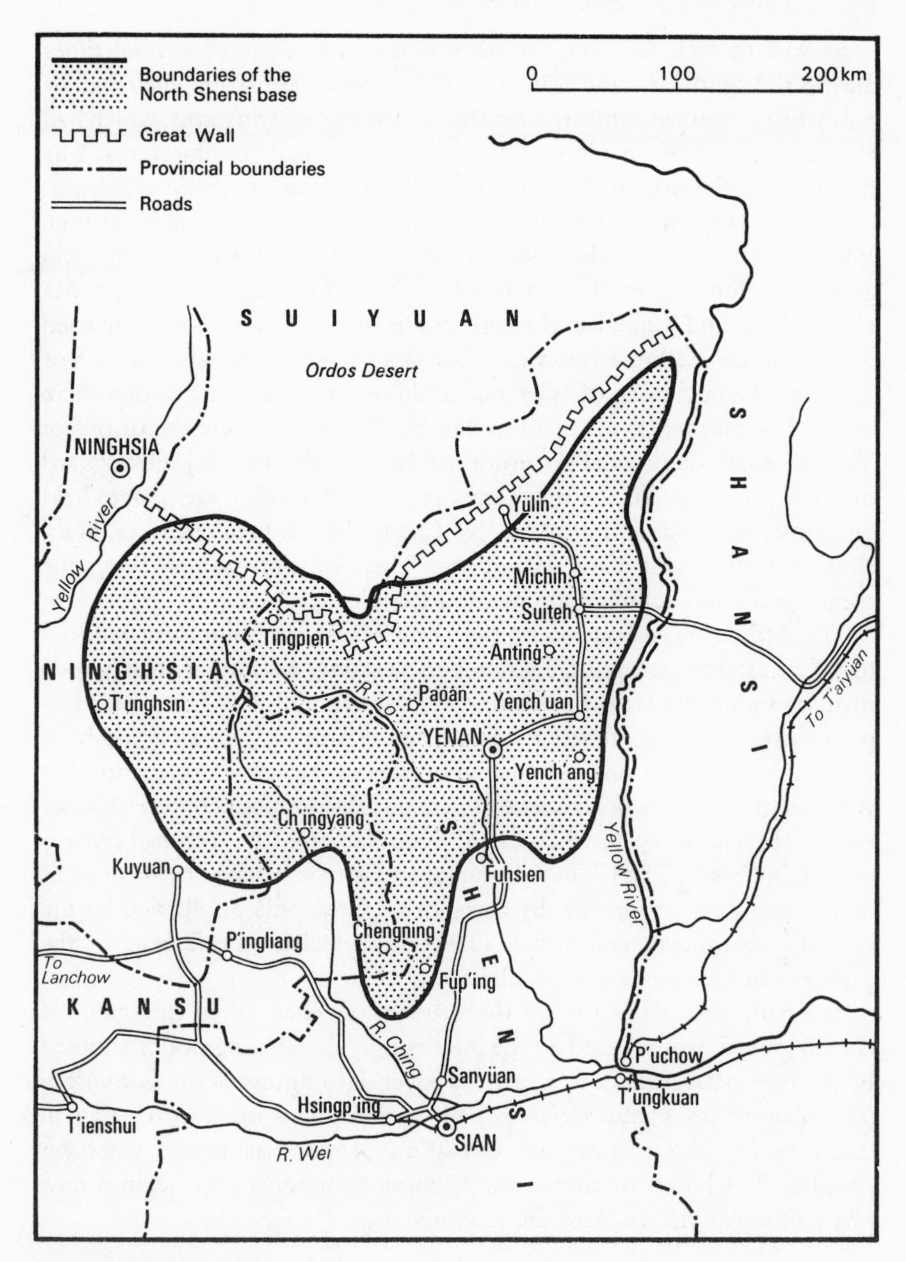

Map 18. North Shensi

As will be seen later on, the organization was changed several times during the Sino-Japanese war. The red troops were to be encircled by powerful government and provincial armies in this outlying area, which had few links with the outside world even under normal circumstances. The province of Suiyuan to the north was held by an energetic governor, Fu Tso-yi, who was later obliged by adverse circumstances to change sides. To the west were the troops commanded by the formidable Moslem generals belonging to the Ma family, who held Ninghsia through Ma Hung-k'uei, and Chinghai through Ma Pu-fang. Chang Kuo-t'ao tried to settle in the Yellow River valley downstream of Lanchow at the end of 1936 and the beginning of 1937, but could not maintain his position there and had to make a rapid return to Shensi. To the east were the troops of Yen Hsi-shan, the 'model governor' of Shensi, who kept a jealous guard over his province. To the south the Sian and Wei valley areas were held by numerous units commanded by Chang Hsüeh-liang (former Manchurian armies) and Yang Hu-ch'eng. Their mission was to bring the communists into submission once and for all.

The Red Army, exhausted by the Long March, its equipment reduced to a few infantry weapons, its numbers certainly no higher than 50,000 men (counting the local troops of Liu Chih-tan and Kao Kang), made a poor showing at first. It was a miracle that it survived, for it would have been at the mercy of one determined operation. No clear explanation has yet been given for the inactivity of the nationalist armies between October 1935 and October 1936, when Chang Kuo-t'ao and Chu Teh had not yet arrived in Shensi. The Chinese Communist Party was saved by the lack of unity among its opponents, by the short-sighted policy followed by the central government, and above all by the ceaseless interference of the Japanese in Chinese domestic affairs.

The truly oriental factors of the situation were set in an international climate, which was affected by the increasingly threatening policy adopted by the European Axis Powers. At the Seventh Congress of the Comintern (July-August 1935) the Kremlin had carried out a masterly change in direction by encouraging the formation of popular fronts wherever possible. It advised or forced the Chinese communists to begin a new phase of collaboration with the Kuomintang.

Japanese intervention in China after the Mukden Incident

The Mukden Incident on 18 September 1931, leading to the loss of Manchuria for China, showed to what extent the Nine Power Treaty signed in Washington on 6 February 1922 had ceased to be effective, and above all it marked the beginning of a phase of determined expansion as far as Japanese foreign policy was concerned.[1] During 1932 the League of Nations had made as though to intervene, the Lytton Report, published on 2 October 1932, was submitted to the General Assembly, and on 27 March 1933 Japan left the League, thereby creating a dangerous precedent. In January 1934 Tokyo put ex-Emperor P'u Yi, regent since 9 March 1932, and now Emperor K'ang Teh, on the throne of Manchuria. The annexation of Manchuria naturally aroused violent reactions in China, causing a boycott on Japanese goods in several large towns, and finally resulted in open war in Shanghai lasting five weeks, beginning on 26 January 1932 (the first incident occurred on 19 January) and ending, theoretically, at the armistice on 5 May 1932 (see Chapter 18).

From then on Japanese aggressions increased both in number and frequency. On 27 February 1933 the province of Jehol, beyond the Great Wall but traditionally Chinese, was invaded, and its capital was occupied on 3 March; Jehol was eventually annexed to Manchukuo. On 31 May of the same year the Japanese forced the Chinese to evacuate their troops from east Hopei, by means of the T'angku Military Agreement; its twenty-two districts became the East Hopei Autonomous Anti-Communist Zone in November 1935, with T'ungchow as its capital. A carefully chosen collaborator, Yin Ju-keng, was placed in charge of the zone, through which enormous quantities of Japanese goods were smuggled. The Chinese customs suffered considerable losses, but, worse still, the existence of the East Hopei zone furnished the Japanese with a permanent pretext for interventions within the Great Wall.

1934 passed with no major incidents, in spite of the stir caused by the Amau Declaration, by which the Japanese government affirmed that it was entitled to special rights and interests in China (17 April). But in May and June 1935, following incidents in Jehol and Chahar, the Japanese instigated the formation of an Autonomous Government of Inner Mongolia. This was organized by a Mongol, Prince Teh Wang, and a Chinese, Li Shou-hsin (5 June 1935).

At about the same time the Japanese demanded that the former Manchurian troops, commanded by Chang Hsüeh-liang, should be withdrawn from Hopei and Chahar, and that the Kuomintang offices in the

[1] During the night of 18 September, the Japanese, using an incident at Mukden (sabotage of railway lines) as a pretext, took over the control of the surrounding area and then of the north-eastern provinces, and drove out Marshal Chang Hsüeh-liang and his armies into China.

two provinces should be closed. Mysterious negotiations began, ending in a secret agreement, the Ho-Umezu Agreement signed on 7 July by Ho Ying-ch'in, the Nanking Minister of War, and General Umezu, the commander of the Japanese forces in North China. The Chinese government was forced to give way. The Japanese planned to separate the Five Northern Chinese Provinces (Hopei, Shantung, Shansi, Chahar and Suiyuan) from the rest of China, as the first phase of an even larger project drawn up in the Tanaka Memoir, whose authenticity was to remain doubtful but whose contents nevertheless were borne out by events of the succeeding years. To satisfy Japanese ambitions and at the same time preserve Chinese national integrity, a Hopei-Chahar Political Council was set up in Peking, and inaugurated on 16 December 1935; its Chairman, General Sung Che-yuan, tried to avoid the insistent pressure from the Japanese as far as possible. His troops (the Twenty-ninth Army) were attacked on 1 July 1937 at Lukouch'iao, and were the first to take part in the war.

In 1936 Japan embarked on a policy of large-scale expansion. The Hirota cabinet, which had come to power after the abortive military *putsch* in February 1936, gave its sanction to the ambitions of the Japanese army and navy, as defined in a document which appeared in the following August. The main aim was to enlarge the continental base of Manchukuo, a buffer against the Soviet Union, by adding North China to it and making it independent, and to keep the Western powers out of South-East Asia and the South Seas. This policy led to the signature of the Anti-Comintern Pact (November 1936) in the field of foreign affairs, whereas economic measures were adopted within Japan itself to build up the nation's defences.

The Tokyo government still nourished the hope of coming to a general arrangement with the Nanking government leading to cooperation against communism throughout the world, and opposing the privileged position of Westerners in Asia. In June 1937 the Hirota cabinet was replaced by the cabinet of Prince Konoe, while Hirota remained Minister of Foreign Affairs. The new cabinet was considered more moderate than the preceding one, but Japanese policy had reached a point where the slightest incident, if exploited in the right way, could lead to war; this was to happen in the following month.

Chinese nationalistic reactions

Public opinion, at least in the towns, shocked by the loss of Manchuria in 1931, excited by the resistance put up by the Nineteenth and Fifth

Armies in Shanghai in 1932, and worried as to the future of the northern provinces, particularly of the historic town of Peking, began to react more and more violently to Japanese encroachments. It was less and less able to understand the procrastinations of the central government, itself justifiably conscious of its own military weakness. The Generalissimo's political enemies made full use of the profitable theme of armed opposition to the Japanese. With the ostensible aim of resisting the aggressor, Ts'ai T'ing-k'ai and his Nineteenth Army, covered with glory by their defence of Shanghai in 1932, staged a rebellion in Fukien and attempted to set up a government to rival that in Nanking. The whole affair was over in a few months – it lasted from November 1933 to January 1934 – but it caused a considerable stir, owing to the personality of Ts'ai T'ing-k'ai (see Chapter 18).

At the end of 1935 the creation of the East Hopei Autonomous Anti-Communist Zone gave rise to a series of demonstrations later known as the December 9th Movement. On that day over 10,000 students demonstrated in Peking against Japan; to a certain extent the movement resembled the May 4th 1919 Movement. This time, however, the Communist Party was in existence, and the avowed hostility of the Japanese proved an advantage; the ending of the civil war figured among the slogans. Further demonstrations took place in Peking at the Bridge of Heaven on 16 December, when the creation of the Hopei-Chahar Political Council was announced. The movement spread to students in other towns – Hangchow (11 December), Shanghai, Wuhan, Ch'angsha and Wuchow (20 December) – and it also embraced part of the general population of the towns. In some places in North China, particularly along the main railway lines, the students tried to arouse the peasants to join in the agitation. Associations for National Salvation were formed almost everywhere; in May 1936 they set up a national federation in Shanghai, which the communists tried to take under their control.

The ostensible aim of resistance to Japan was used once more by the generals of Kwangtung and Kwangsi – Ch'en Chi-t'ang, Li Tsung-jen and Pai Ch'ung-hsi – who stirred up a rebellion from June to September 1935. This ended in typically Chinese fashion, by a distribution of titles and posts for the rebels.

The development of the anti-Japanese movement not only endangered the central government's stability; it also affected its entire policy towards Japan. The Japanese army in Manchuria (Kwangtung Army) immediately made use of the patriotic reactions of the various sections of Chinese opinion, treating them as proof of the duplicity and impotence of the

Nanking government, and as justifying further interventions. They led the Tokyo government to ratify local initiatives whether it wanted to or not. Thus, an already dangerous situation worsened, helped by the efforts of the leading Japanese officers and the Chinese communists, the former acting in the name of the defence of East Asia against communism, and the latter in the name of national salvation, for which they assumed the total responsibility.

The Chinese Communist Party versus Japan

For a long time, the Chinese communists adopted an extremist position on the question of resistance to Japan. Their wisdom and foresight, the special enmity shown them by the Japanese, and lastly events themselves, could not fail to provide them with excellent propaganda, helping them to win back a nationwide audience which they had almost entirely lost.

As early as February 1932, with a gesture as spectacular as it was gratuitous, the Chinese Communist Party declared war on Japan. The declaration was obviously not followed by any action. Later on, with the same keen sense of the impact of propaganda, it gave the title of Anti-Japanese Army Vanguard to Fang Chih-min's troops, sent to create a diversion towards Kiangsi on the eve of the Long March (see Chapter 19, p. 228). At one of the most serious moments of its history, 1 August 1935, when it was on the move in the Maoerhkai area and shaken by disputes within its ranks, the Central Committee published an 'Appeal to all our Compatriots for Resistance to Japan and for the Country's Salvation'. This extremely violent document enumerated the ceaseless Japanese aggressions, and denounced indiscriminately Chiang Kai-shek, Wang Ching-wei and even Chang Hsüeh-liang, the future ally of the Sian Incident, describing them as 'human dregs lacking all shame', and 'men with human faces and the hearts of beasts'.

This outburst did not prevent the Chinese Communist Party from proposing the formation of a United Popular Pan-Chinese Government for National Defence, to include the Chinese Soviet Government and the Anti-Japanese Authorities in Manchuria. They declared themselves ready to begin talks with all other Chinese parties and political groups. Lastly, they proposed a common programme in ten points, in which practical measures and basic principles were mingled, often in unexpected ways:

1 Armed resistance to Japanese expansion and the recovery of lost territory.

2 Struggle against famine, floods and drought.
3 Confiscation of the property of collaborators with the Japanese.
4 Confiscation of Japanese property.
5 Reorganization of the economy and finances.
6 Improvement of the living conditions of workers, peasants, soldiers and intellectuals.
7 Democratic freedom, release of political prisoners.
8 Compulsory education and security of employment.
9 Equal rights for the different nationalities.
10 Establishment of contact with the masses in countries hostile to Japanese policy.[1]

In the circumstances, the appeal and the programme could not be given wide circulation and had no practical effects. Another anti-Japanese declaration made by the Central Committee of the Party on 13 November, shortly after it had settled in north Shensi, provoked no further echoes.

The scope of the December 9th Movement, which it was anxious to use as widely and as rapidly as possible, led the Political Bureau to hold a meeting at Wayaopao on 25 December 1935 to adopt tactics based on a National United Front, which, in spite of the memories of 1927, included the bourgeoisie. Although no written record of the meeting exists, two contemporary documents indicate how far the Party had swung, notwithstanding persistent opposition from the 'leftist sectarians' whose mistrust of the bourgeoisie remained as strong as ever. The first of these is the article by Wang Ming for the *Communist International* (special issue of January 1936). Although probably written before the Wayaopao meeting, the article lists all the modifications in policy which the Party should be prepared to make, to bring about 'the broadest anti-Japanese popular front'. Recognition of the property of small landlords who do not work their own land, but have acquired it through their own work, encouragement for privately owned commercial and industrial capital, acknowledgement of the civil rights for all those opposing the Japanese, no matter what their class allegiance may be, more careful handling of foreign representatives – diplomats, businessmen, missionaries, etc. – except, of course, the Japanese – all foreshadow the policy of the Yenan period.

The second document, dated 27 December 1935, entitled 'On Tactics Against Japanese Imperialism', was to be of vital importance in the Party's history, providing clear, decisive instructions. Once more,

[1] For details on this subject, see the special issue of the *Communist International* of January 1936.

Mao Tse-tung endeavoured to analyse the feelings of the different classes towards 'imperialism', and to prove through history that the petty bourgeoisie and even part of the national bourgeoisie – the section that was not inextricably tied up with foreign capital – were hostile to Japan, whose intention was to make China into a colony for herself alone. The situation in 1935 seemed to him to be entirely different from that of 1927. As he said: 'China was then still a semi-colony, but now she is on the way to becoming a colony'; he gives Ts'ai T'ing-k'ai, Feng Yü-hsiang and several bourgeois militarists as examples. Mao Tse-tung also lays down the 'basic tactical task' of the Party: 'none other than to form a broad revolutionary national united front'. He advocates the 'united front' tactics as opposed to 'closed door tactics', which correspond to an 'infantile disorder'. He rejects the arguments used by the advocates of 'closed-doorism'; for them the revolutionary forces must remain 'pure' and the road of the revolution must be straight, absolutely straight: 'Like every other activity in the world, revolution always follows a tortuous road and never a straight one.'

It seems to him that everything should fade into the background in the face of the prodigious task awaiting the Party:

> In order to attack the forces of the counter-revolution, what the revolutionaries need today is to organize millions upon millions of the masses and move a mighty revolutionary army into action. . . . Therefore, united front tactics are the only Marxist-Leninist tactics. The tactics of closed-doorism are, on the contrary, the tactics of regal isolation. Closed-doorism just 'drives the fish away into deep waters and the sparrows into the thickets', and it will drive the millions upon millions of the masses, this mighty army, over to the enemy's side, which will certainly win his acclaim. . . . We definitely want no closed-doorism; what we want is the revolutionary national united front, which will spell death to the Japanese imperialists and the traitors and collaborators.

Working from this theory, Mao Tse-tung considers that the 'workers' and peasants' republic' should be changed into a 'people's republic', representing the whole nation. The 'people's republic' will respect property, and regulate the relations between capital and labour, at least during the period of the 'bourgeois democratic revolution'. Although the 'socialist revolution' is inevitable, it will not come about 'for some time to come', and not before the political and economic conditions necessary for its accomplishment have been fulfilled. Much of this great document foreshadows the style of 'On New Democracy', although the latter was not written until five years later. Finally, the enlarging of the struggle to take in the 'national front' must also be extended to the 'international front':

> All just wars support each other . . . our war against Japan needs the support of the people of the whole world, and above all, the support of the people of the Soviet Union. . . .

The Chinese were to meet with a fair degree of disappointment as to this last point.

It would seem that the communists first began to take steps towards constituting a National Anti-Japanese Front in the summer or autumn of 1935, by sounding public opinion. Tseng Yang-fu in Hong Kong and Ch'en Li-fu and his brother Ch'en Kuo-fu in Shanghai were approached by Chou En-lai, who was shortly to become a sort of communist ambassador to the Kuomintang. On 25 January 1936 the Red Army sent a circular letter to the officers and men of the Manchurian armies, which had retreated to the provinces of Shensi and Kansu, in the hope of achieving joint action against Japan. This gesture was not aimed solely at demoralizing the troops, and fell on particularly fertile ground.

In March, Liu Chih-tan undertook a deliberately spectacular action, crossing the Yellow River to march against the Japanese in Manchuria. He was no luckier than Fang Chih-min had been a year earlier in the same circumstances. North of Chihsien, Liu Chih-tan's 'anti-Japanese detachment' was intercepted by the provincial troops of Yen Hsi-shan; its leader was killed, and the troops were dispersed. In memory of Liu Chih-tan the Party changed the name of the town of Paoan to Chihtan, one of the rare examples of this kind in the history of the movement and indeed of modern China as well.[1]

In order to avoid a politically awkward position, while appealing to those most sensitive to the concept of national self-respect, the Communists' Revolutionary Military Committee sent a message on 5 May to the Military Affairs Committee, proposing that the civil war should be brought to an end, and negotiations opened straight away. The message contained none of the usual linguistic excesses and showed the courtesy

[1] The real purpose of Liu's expedition may have been to establish a base in Shansi. In July 1962 a novel about Liu Chih-tan appeared in the *Workers' Daily*. Mao Tse-tung, suspecting that it would rehabilitate the memory of Kao Kang, who committed suicide during the 1954 trial, suspended its publication. 'South are the Ching Kang Shan, north are the Yung Ning Shan', wrote the author. Yung Ning Shan was Kao Kang's base.

habitual between soldiers. A little later the two parties established direct, though secret contacts in Shanghai, where Chou En-lai and P'an Hannien, another born diplomat, are said to have met General Chang Ch'ün, a representative of the Generalissimo. The subjects forming the basis of the agreement reached the following year – respect for the Three People's Principles, obedience of the communist troops, abolition of the soviet administration, etc. – were discussed. On 25 August 1936 the Central Committee of the Communist Party in turn sent an open letter to the Kuomintang Central Executive Committee. Although the letter contained criticism of the opposing party, the communists offered to collaborate in setting up a 'democratic government', and even recalled their former collaboration. They then became increasingly urgent in their efforts. On 17 September the Central Committee passed a new, important resolution, entitled 'Resolution on the New Situation of the Anti-Japanese Resistance and National Salvation Movement, and on the Democratic Republic'. The Democratic Republic was in fact the People's Republic, the change of name being a formal concession to the Kuomintang, with the intention of counteracting the latter's monopoly of politics by merging the party with a group of much more 'progressive' forces. A month later, using an intervention by combined Mongolian and Japanese troops in the east of Suiyuan as a pretext, the communists pressed the central government to renounce its policy of passivity. The successful recapture of Pailingmiao by provincial troops appeared to justify their exhortations to bold action.

The Sian Incident and the communists

The central government's military operations against the communists came virtually to a standstill after November 1935. Only one minor attack had taken place, in October and November 1936. General Hu Tsung-nan in command of the First Army sent three divisions northwards beyond Huanhsien in east Kansu. His advance came to an abrupt end on 21 November at Mengch'engpao and Shanch'engpao, while the communists claimed that victory was theirs.

In December, the Generalissimo, rid of the Kwangsi rebellion and less hard pressed by the Japanese, decided to settle with the Red Army once and for all. With this end in view, he made plans to fly to Sian, where Chang Hsüeh-liang was becoming increasingly sensitive to the slogans proclaiming the United Front, and had already shown signs of independence. He was said to have regular contacts with Chou En-lai, and his blockade of the red zone was half-hearted. During his visit to Sian the central government leader intended to put the finishing touches to the coming military campaign which he hoped would be a decisive one, and to check up on the loyalty of Chang Hsüeh-liang, possibly thinking of replacing him by Chiang Ting-wen. The Generalissimo arrived in Sian on 7 December and stayed in the small neighbouring town of Lint'ung, where he began his discussions and inspections. In the night of 11-12 December Chang Hsüeh-liang and Yang Hu-ch'eng, Commissar for the Pacification of Shensi and commander of the Seventeenth Route Army, arrested Chiang Kai-shek, who injured his spine trying to escape.

On the same day Chang Hsüeh-liang drew up a circular telegram addressed to the nation, proposing an eight-point programme:

1 Reorganization of the government on a broader basis.
2 End to civil war.
3 Release of those condemned for political and patriotic activities and held in Shanghai (leaders of the Association for National Salvation).
4 Release of all political prisoners.
5 Freedom of action for patriotic movements.
6 Freedom to hold meetings and form associations.
7 Execution of Sun Yat-sen's political will.
8 Convocation of a meeting for National Salvation.

Contrary to his hopes, Chang Hsüeh-liang's proposals were not approved by the central government or by Chinese public opinion. In the face of such hostility, and under threat of military action from Honan where large government forces were stationed, the 'Young Marshal' let his prisoner free. Chiang Kai-shek and Madame Chiang, who had come to join him on 22 December, left for Nanking once more on Christmas Day, accompanied by Chang Hsüeh-liang, soon to be a prisoner himself.[1]

Chiang Kai-shek's detention seems to have caught the communists unprepared; they may even have been in total disagreement with Moscow for several days as to the meaning of the incident and the political use to be made of it. The Chinese communists may have thought that the elimination of their longstanding enemy would make possible the formation of the broad national defence government, which they had been urging since the middle of 1935. But the central government's authority

[1] Chang Hsüeh-liang remained the personal prisoner of Chiang Kai-shek until 1962. He is still in Taiwan today, and is probably not allowed to leave. The Generalissimo's rancour against Yang Hu-ch'eng was such that he had him executed in his prison in Chungking, at the same time as the communists entered the town.

was still precarious in many provinces; had its leader's disappearance resulted in a split within its ranks, where several opposing tendencies already existed, a period of political and military anarchy might have ensued. A further possibility was that members of the Kuomintang right wing, such as General Ho Ying-ch'in, who were relatively well disposed towards Japan, might seize power and, in their hatred of the communists, draw nearer to Tokyo, as Wang Ching-wei was to do four years later in the middle of the war. Wang Ching-wei, who was in Europe when the Sian Incident occurred, hurried back to Nanking by air, after having an interview with Hitler.

The Chinese communists' first intention appears to have been to execute the Generalissimo, after a trial by the people, which had for a long time been promised to the militants by the Party's propaganda. The Comintern's decision was different, however. It realized immediately that Chiang Kai-shek and the Kuomintang were the only forces capable of rallying China as a whole to resist Japan, and that should Chiang disappear, serious repercussions might follow in the international field, and Japanese designs on the Chinese continent might even be speeded up.

On 14 December the Russian press made its position clear. Without demur, *Pravda* attributed the responsibility for the plot to Japanese anxiety to thwart the Generalissimo's work of unification. *Izvestia* accused Chang Hsüeh-liang of being in the pay of Japanese imperialism, which alone stood to gain from the incident. Consequently, Chou En-lai, who had been fetched from Yenan by plane on Chang Hsüeh-liang's orders on 13 December, had to adopt a position in favour of the release of his Party's mortal enemy. Chou En-lai, Yeh Chien-ying and Ch'in Pang-hsien (alias Po Ku), President of the Soviet Government in the North-West, took an active though indirect part in the talks which followed between Chiang Kai-shek, Chang Hsüeh-liang and Yang Hu-ch'eng; Wang Ping-nan, later one of Chou En-lai's chief collaborators, was then private secretary to Yang Hu-ch'eng. The communists have revealed nothing about the details of their intervention, though the line they took is clear, as Mao Tse-tung reported on it in 'A Statement on Chiang Kai-shek's Statement':

> Chiang should remember that he owes his safe departure from Sian to the mediation of the Communist Party, as well as to the efforts of Generals Chang and Yang, the leaders in the Sian Incident. Throughout the incident the Communist Party stood for a peaceful settlement and made every effort to that end, acting solely in the interests of national survival.

The leader of the Chinese government has written an account of his captivity, and has always denied having pledged himself in any way either to the Japanese or to the communists. The communists had to admit that no document had been written or signed, but they maintained that Chiang Kai-shek was nevertheless under a moral obligation to reply to the demands of Chang Hsüeh-liang.[1] Whatever the case may be, his release was followed by a long period of secret or half-secret bargaining with the communists, while several measures were taken to ease the general situation and help pave the way for an eventual agreement.

On 10 February 1937 the Central Committee of the Communist Party presented the Central Executive Committee of the Kuomintang with a five-point programme:

1 End civil war and concentrate national troops to resist aggression from abroad.
2 Freedom of expression, and freedom to hold meetings; release of all political prisoners.
3 Call a national congress of representatives from all sections of society to ensure national salvation.
4 Take immediate measures for national defence.
5 Improve the people's standard of living.

In exchange the Communist Party made the following promises:

1 To end armed anti-government action.
2 To abolish its own government, turning it into a 'special administration'.
3 To put democratic principles into effect in its zone, and especially to hold elections.
4 To end confiscations of land.
5 To place its army under the orders of the government and its Military Affairs Committee.

The Kuomintang Central Executive Committee (the Fifth Committee, Third Plenary Session) answered these demands with a resolution published on 21 February. It asked the communists for:

1 Total integration of the Red Army into the national army.
2 Integration of red zone administration within the framework of the normal administration.

[1] Mao Tse-tung, 'A Statement on Chiang Kai-shek's Statement', *Selected Works*, vol. I, p. 255. See also 'Urgent Tasks Following the Establishment of Kuomintang-Communist Cooperation', *Selected Works*, vol. II, p. 35.

3 Suspension of communist propaganda as the communist doctrine was incompatible with the Three People's Principles and with Chinese traditions.
4 Renunciation of the class struggle.

This series of proposals from both camps could not be accepted by either side, but hostilities came to an end, the blockade of the soviet zone became less strict, and visits were exchanged. Chou En-lai, who apparently made several journeys into the government zone, is said to have been even to Nanking and Kuling, the Generalissimo's summer residence. General Ku Chu-t'ung began discussions with the communists on the integration of the red troops, and a Kuomintang mission went to Yenan in June. As is only to be expected, modern Chinese authors, both communist and nationalist, observe the utmost discretion as to this period in their history which they shared in common. The Lukouch'iao Incident of 7 July allayed mistrust on both sides and hastened the conclusion of a formal agreement.

On 15 July 1937 the Communist Party handed a manifesto to the Kuomintang, which the Kuomintang published on 22 September and partly endorsed in a declaration made the following day. Meanwhile, the Sino-Japanese war was in full development and an event took place on the political level which is important for the understanding of the Chinese communists' attitude – a pact of non-aggression, which had been under discussion between Moscow and Nanking since 1936, was signed in Nanking on 21 August.[1]

The declaration of 22 September, which was theoretically to rule relations between the central government and the Communist Party throughout the Sino-Japanese war, defined the aims of the common struggle and stated the principles underlying the new agreement. There were three aims, which can be summarized as follows:

1 Launch the war of resistance, take back lost territory, struggle for independence, liberty and national emancipation.
2 Establish a democratic regime.
3 Improve the living standards of the people.

In exchange the Communist Party pledged itself to carry out four obligations:

[1] According to Feng Yü-hsiang, a meeting between Chiang Kai-shek, Chang Ch'ün and Shao Li-tzu on one side, and Chou En-lai, Po Ku and Lin Tsu-han on the other, took place at Lushan on 19 July 1937; Chiang Kai-shek is said to have acknowledged the existence of the frontier district: Shansi, Kansu and Ninghsia (Shenkanning).

1 Apply the Three People's Principles of Sun Yat-sen.
2 Not to overthrow the Kuomintang by force, and not to confiscate landlords' lands.
3 To reorganize the government of the red zone to become the Democratic Government of the frontier regions.
4 To change the name of the Red Army to National Revolutionary Army and submit it to the control of the Military Affairs Commission of the national government.[1]

The government's declaration on 23 September echoed the communist ones. It took official note of each of these pledges and remarked, with feigned candour, that 'national consciousness had prevailed over all other considerations'. The communist declaration and programme of 15 August, sometimes called the Loch'uan Declaration, is even more worthy of note than the 22 September manifesto, only the forms of which were respected, and that briefly, for the earlier declaration's ten points foreshadowed the communists' intentions as to their activities during the war that had just begun. Its impassioned, intransigent style reveals real determination and the wish to claim all patriotic initiatives for the Party. Mao Tse-tung later included its relatively long text in a speech to the Central Committee, 'For the Mobilization of all the Nation's Forces for Victory in the War of Resistance'.[2] A short summary follows.

1 Overthrow Japanese imperialism, fight to the finish, opposing all compromise, until the aggressors are forced to withdraw.
2 Mobilize the whole nation; adopt an active strategy, arm the people, develop guerrilla troops, unite the people and the army in a single whole, reform political work in the army, adopt general military service to replace the army of volunteers.
3 Mobilize the people of the whole country, except for traitors and collaborators. Allow all political parties free activity. Mobilize the national minority races, in the name of the right of all peoples to self-determination.
4 Reform the government, call a genuinely representative national assembly, elect a government of national defence to include revolutionaries, and practise 'democratic centralism'. Eliminate all forms of corruption.
5 Conclude pacts with all countries opposed to Japan and support the

[1] See Wang Shih *et al.*, *History of the Chinese Communist Party* (*source material*) (Shanghai, 1958: in Chinese).
[2] See Mao Tse-tung, *Selected Works*, vol. II.

international peace front, in opposition to Japanese, German and Italian aggression.

6 Adopt wartime financial and economic policies, tax the rich, combat speculation.

7 Improve the people's living conditions, particularly those of families of soldiers, simplify and readjust the taxation system.

8 Introduce a new education system, aimed at resisting Japan and saving the nation.

9 Consolidate the rear, by liquidating traitors and pro-Japanese elements.

10 Build up a National Anti-Japanese United Front, based on cooperation between the Kuomintang and the Communist Party.

The deplorable policy of the Japanese, by providing the context for the birth and development of a climate of national unity in China, was to save the Communist Party, enable it to achieve a military strength far surpassing any previous degree and almost unseat the nationalist regime. The Chinese communists realized immediately that three great possibilities lay open to them. They realized that a foreign war would first of all provide the means of forcing the Kuomintang to give up its monopoly of political power. On 3 May 1937, in an address to a national Party conference, Mao Tse-tung foretold the Kuomintang's future.[1] A new phase in the Chinese revolution had begun with the December 9th 1935 Movement and with the formation of an Anti-Japanese National Front. The communists' task was now to continue the struggle both within and without and 'win democracy'; 'Armed resistance requires the mobilization of the people, but there is no way of mobilizing them without democracy and freedom.'

As he put it, China had to carry out democratic reforms in two ways:

> First, in the matter of the political system, the reactionary Kuomintang dictatorship of one party and one class must be changed into a democratic government based on the cooperation of all parties and all classes. . . . The second matter concerns freedom of speech, assembly and association for the people. Without such freedom, it will be impossible to carry out the democratic reconstruction of the political system, mobilize the people for the war of resistance and victoriously defend the motherland and recover the lost territories.

The progress achieved in this way would also contribute to the advance

[1] Mao Tse-tung, 'The Tasks of the Chinese Communist Party in the Period of Resistance to Japan', *Selected Works*, vol. I, p. 263.

of communism, which was not to be abandoned: 'Communists will never abandon their ideal of socialism and communism, which they will attain by going through the stage of the bourgeois-democratic revolution.'

The Party's ideological level must constantly be raised: 'To overcome the undesirable tendencies we have described, it is absolutely necessary to raise the Marxist-Leninist theoretical level of the whole Party, for Marxism-Leninism alone is the compass which can guide the Chinese revolution to victory.'

In spite of these democratic aspirations, the Party did not abandon its claims to a privileged position: 'The preservation of the Communist Party's leadership over the Special Region and in the Red Army, and the preservation of the Communist Party's independence and freedom of criticism in its relations with the Kuomintang – these are the limits beyond which it is impossible to go.'

A few months later, after hostilities began, Mao Tse-tung, in a violent declaration, stated the need to 'arouse the masses of the people':[1]

> We are not satisfied with the War of Resistance in its present state because, though national in character, it is still confined to the government and the armed forces. . . .
>
> The masses of workers, peasants, soldiers, and urban petty bourgeoisie and a large number of other patriots have not yet been aroused, called into action, organized or armed.
>
> The only way to save it [the situation] is to put Dr Sun Yat-sen's Testament into practice, to 'arouse the masses of the people'.

The government turned a deaf ear to these injunctions, but the vast theatres of operations and the peculiar form of war engaged by the Japanese along the chief lines of communication, leaving huge spaces between them untouched, were to enable the communists to carry out the 'people's war' directly and on their own account. Thanks to this 'people's war', their power soon spread over vast areas where the government's administrative control was extremely uncertain.

[1] Mao Tse-tung, 'Urgent Tasks Following the Establishment of Kuomintang-Communist Cooperation', *Selected Works*, vol. II, p. 35.

23 General Outline of the Sino-Japanese War[1] from 7 July 1937 to 14 August 1945

The military operations of the communist troops between 1937 and 1945 fit naturally into the whole context of war in the Chinese continent at that time. Generally speaking, the development of hostilities between the Chinese and the Japanese can be divided into two main phases. From July 1937 to October 1938 the Japanese Imperial Army directed its attacks along the main railway lines and occupied the Five Northern Chinese Provinces (Hopei, Chahar, Suiyuan, Shansi and Shantung), the territories alongside the lower and middle Yangtze valleys as far as the Ich'ang Gorges near the Szechuan border, and the Canton area in South China. Little change took place in the front lines between October 1938 and the spring of 1944. The Japanese concentrated their efforts on huge consolidation and cleaning-up operations, particularly in North China, and not until March 1944, when the United States air force and navy were presenting a serious threat to their communications by sea, did they begin a new series of campaigns. Their aim was then to take the last stretches of railway lines in South China (Canton-Hankow, Hengyang-Kueilin) and Central China (Chengchow-Hankow, Chengchow-Loyang) to ensure a direct overland route from the Indo-Chinese peninsula as far as the Straits of Korea. They also intended to destroy the United States air force bases, which by then were beginning to threaten Japan itself.

Aerial warfare played an important part throughout the war. The Japanese had no difficulty in eliminating the Chinese air force; they then

[1] See Maps 19 (p. 289), 20 (p. 293) and 21 (p. 297).

did their best to destroy the population's morale by huge, merciless bombing raids, carried out at no risk to themselves over the most heavily populated areas of China. From 1941 onwards the American volunteers commanded by Colonel (afterwards General) Chennault, and later the United States air force, attacked the enemy's communications, defending the towns and helping to restore the population's confidence, which was beginning to ebb after the long years of hardship.

The Lukouch'iao Incident

During the night of 7-8 July 1937 the Japanese garrison at Fengtai, a little railway junction a few kilometres south of Peking, was carrying out manœuvres near the small walled town of Wanp'ing at the end of the famous Marco Polo Bridge. When one of their soldiers was reported missing – he was found shortly afterwards – the Japanese accused the Chinese garrison at Wanp'ing of taking him prisoner and demanded to search the town. The Chinese garrison commander refused, whereupon fighting broke out in the night, with, however, few casualties. During the next few days Japanese and Chinese troops moved into position facing each other between Peking and the Yungting River; Wanp'ing and the Marco Polo Bridge remained in Chinese hands. Negotiations were begun at a local level between the Japanese and General Sung Che-yuan, Chairman of the Hopei-Chahar Political Council and commander of the Chinese Twenty-ninth Army. A Japanese military clique in Tokyo, and possibly the Japanese army in Manchuria, whose Chief of Staff was General Tojo, later sentenced to death in 1945, insisted on making use of the incident, though it has not yet been proved that it was premeditated. General Sugiyama, the Minister of War, made strong representations to Prince Konoe's cabinet. On 11 July, under pretext of ensuring the safety of the many Japanese residents in North China, several large units began to move from Korea, Japan and Manchuria towards the Peking-Tientsin area (the 5th and 20th Divisions and two or three brigades), while three reserve divisions were mobilized in Japan. Within a month, the Japanese troops in North China, commanded by General Kawabe, increased from 7000 to 160,000 men.

The Nanking government took an extremely firm line. On 17 July, at Kuling (Kiangsi), General Chiang Kai-shek stated that he intended to use force to resist all Japanese attempts to sever North China from the rest of the country. Nanking also insisted on shifting the settlement of the July 7th incident from the local to the more responsible government level. Central government and provincial troops (four divisions) were sent north of the Yellow River, contrary to the stipulations of the Ho-Umezu Agreement, as the Japanese claimed.

More and more incidents took place around Peking from 25 July onwards. On 26 July the Japanese speeded up events and called on the Chinese to withdraw to the west bank of the Yungting. When, on 28 July, their ultimatum had been ignored, the Japanese destroyed an entire column of Chinese troops marching from Nanyüan airport to Peking, and bombed the barracks round the former capital.[1] On the night of 28-9 July General Sung Che-yuan quietly evacuated Peking, while nearly 300 Japanese civilians were massacred at T'ungchow. Hard fighting broke out round Tientsin; the war which had begun was to last eight years.

The War of Movement (July 1937-October 1938)

Three principal groups of Japanese troops operated in North China; their line of advance followed, broadly speaking, the three main railway lines: 1, Pingsui (Peking-Suiyuan railway); 2, Kinhan (Peking-Hankow railway); 3, Tsinpu (Tientsin-P'uk'ow railway – P'uk'ow is opposite Nanking on the north bank of the Yangtze).

The Japanese force on the Pingsui line tried first of all to take the famous Nank'ou Pass, 50 kilometres or so north of Peking, the traditional gateway to Mongolia. General T'ang En-po's government troops put up strong resistance but were outflanked to the south and threatened from the rear by Japanese units from the Dolonor region on the Manchurian border. The latter troops moved straight into the region of Kalgan and Huailai, inadequately defended by General Kao Kuei-tzu and General Liu Ju-ming. The Nank'ou Pass had to be abandoned towards 15 August and Kalgan fell on 27 August. The Japanese Pingsui Army continued westwards, beating back the troops commanded by Fu Tso-yi, the governor of Suiyuan, and took the twin towns of Kueihua and Suiyuan on 14 October. By 16 October the Japanese had reached Paotou on the Great North Bend of the Yellow River, on the edge of the Gobi desert; this was roughly the most westerly point of their advance during the whole of the war. From the Pingsui line and also from the Kinhan line (the Chengtingfu area), the Japanese then occupied the province of Shansi, defended in vain by Yen Hsi-shan.

[1] The column was part of the 132nd Division; its commander was killed, along with Feng Yü-hsiang's nephew.

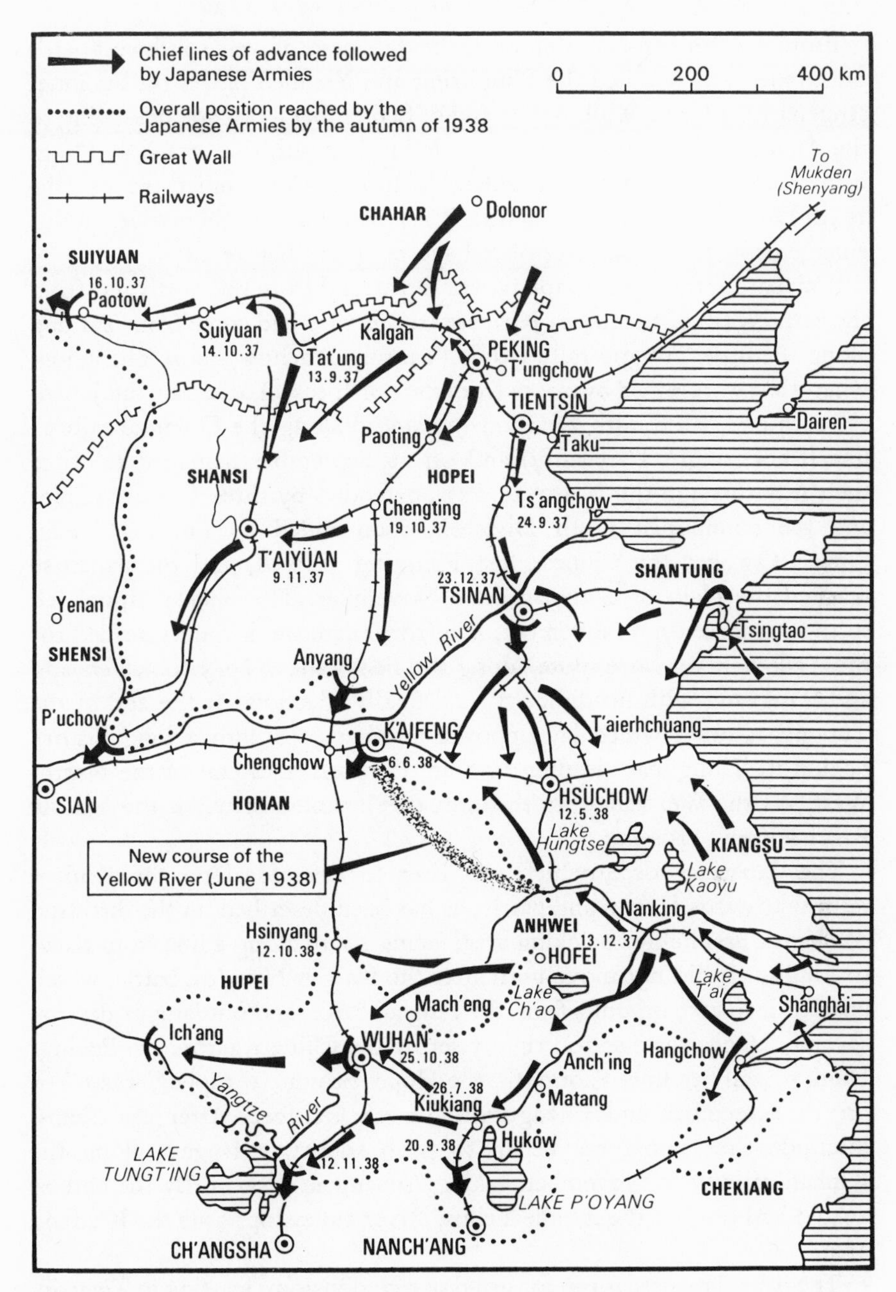

Map 19. Sino-Japanese operations from July 1937 to October 1938

From the Kalgan-Nank'ou area, the Japanese moved southwestwards once more and attacked the P'inghsing and Yenmen passes on the inner stretch of the Great Wall. At the end of September a brigade belonging to the Japanese 5th Division was the victim of a surprise attack at P'inghsingkuan, and suffered considerable losses. Communist troops (the 115th Division commanded by Lin Piao) distinguished themselves in this engagement, but it was an isolated success (see Chapter 24).

T'aiyüanfu, the Shansi capital, was threatened from the north and from the east. North of the town, Japanese troops who had come from Tat'ung along the little Tungpu railway line (Tat'ung-P'uchow) took Yüanp'ing, where they were joined by troops from the north-east. To the east, the Japanese 20th and, later, 14th Divisions advanced along the Chengtai railway line (Chengtingfu-T'aiyüanfu) and on 26 September managed to force their way through the Niangtzu Pass, defended by three Chinese armies and the communist 129th Division, commanded by Liu Po-Ch'eng. On 30 October the Chinese lost P'ingting as well, and the Japanese reached the plain of T'aiyüan on 2 November. The Shansi capital fell to the Japanese on 9 November, and from there the invaders headed for the Yellow River once more, along the Fen Valley. They took Fenyang and P'ingyang with no difficulty, and finally P'uchow, at the end of the Tungpu railway, which lay opposite another pass with a long history behind it: T'ungkuan, leading to Sian, the former capital of the North-West, via the Wei valley. In this area the Japanese halted at the Yellow River without crossing it.

The Japanese force, which was later to operate along the Kinhan railway towards Honan and partly, as has been described, in the direction of Shansi, first held the Peking area, facing south along a line from Kuan to Liuliho. It did not move until after the Kalgan-Nank'ou battle, which enabled it to take on units from the Pingsui force, and outflank or destroy several defence systems too rigidly set by the Chinese across the Peking-Hankow railway line. Paotingfu, the Hopei provincial capital, was taken on 24 September and Chengtingfu on 10 October. After the Shansi interlude the same force began to push southwards again along the Kinhan railway in November, taking Anyang in Honan. By the end of 1937 it had reached the middle Yellow River valley, opposite the K'aifeng area.

The third Japanese force consisted of two divisions; starting in Tientsin, it followed the Tsinpu railway line. After breaking through Chinese defence lines in the Mach'ang area (10 September), it took Ts'angchow (24 September), entered Shantung to take Tehchow on 3 October for the first time, then evacuated the town, entering it again and completely destroying a heroic Chinese regiment (the 485th Infantry Regiment). The governor, Han Fu-chü, tried in vain to keep his province, by temporizing and negotiating with the Japanese; they entered Tsinan and Tsingtao on the same day – 13 December.

By the end of 1937 the Japanese had reached their main objectives in North China. They did their best to find Chinese collaborators, and after fruitless overtures to General Wu P'ei-fu, now an old man, they managed to form a Provisional Peking Government headed by Wang K'e-min, a politician with a long career behind him and a former member of the Hopei-Chahar Political Council. An Autonomous Government of Mongolia, independent of Peking, was set up by the Japanese army in Kalgan.

While all this was going on, Shanghai had been the scene of operations on an even larger scale, in terms of the number and quality of the Chinese troops involved, from 13 August 1937 onwards. A few days earlier, on 9 August, Second Lieutenant Oyama and his driver Saito, a seaman, were killed by a Chinese sentry near the Hungjao (Hungch'iao) aerodrome; this incident, probably less of a coincidence than that of 7 July, was used by the Japanese as a pretext for armed intervention. Marines were put ashore in Shanghai itself, and in the evening of 22 August large numbers of troops were landed from Wusung, at the confluence of the Yangtze and the Whampoo (Huangp'u), up to a point east of Liuho, 30 kilometres or so upstream; the 3rd, 11th and 13th Divisions, part of the 1st and the 8th, and later the 6th and 16th Divisions, were sent into action, in that order. A front line was gradually formed, parallel at first to the south bank of the Yangtze.

The Chinese retaliated rapidly. Memories of the battle of Shanghai in 1932 were still fresh and the government did not want to be accused once more of weakness and lack of patriotism. The large-scale hostilities in Central China furthermore disrupted the plans of the Japanese headquarters, which was more concerned with North China, and made a greater impact on the Western Powers, particularly Great Britain, whose interests in the Yangtze valley were considerable.

Chinese regular troops were moved into the demilitarized zone laid down by the 1932 agreement. Three groups were formed, commanded by Generals Chu Shao-liang, Lo Cho-ying and Hsüeh Yüeh, with General Ku Chu-t'ung at their head, to resist the various Japanese forces. They soon amounted to over 300,000 men. The Japanese numbers rose to nearly 200,000 when parts of the 102nd, 106th, 107th, 114th and 116th

Divisions (a brigade from each division), and the Formosa Brigade, joined in the fighting. The Commander-in-Chief, General Iwane Matsui, also had the support of the guns of the Third Fleet and, most important of all, an efficient air force, which disposed of the 200 planes belonging to the heterogeneous and improperly used Chinese air force in the space of a few weeks.

Between 13 August and 9 November there was bitter fighting on a stationary front amidst the canals and ricefields. The Chinese troops fought with the utmost determination, but their most highly trained units were either destroyed or thrown into disorder. The front, which had originally stretched from the north-west to the south-east, gradually shifted until it followed a line from Liuho, at the western tip of the International Concession, to Hungjao, reached in mid-October. Once the front had become stationary, the Japanese command tried to initiate decisive action, landing troops in the bay of Hangchow (Chap'u area) on 5 November. Two divisions (the 6th and the 18th) were put ashore and threatened to encircle the Chinese armies on the Shanghai front. The Chinese began to retreat on 7 November and turned out to be incapable of taking up position once more, as had been planned, and as should have been easily possible, given the lie of the land, particularly in the Wuhsi area, between Lake T'ai and the Yangtze. The Japanese troops then advanced unimpeded on the unprotected capital. They entered Nanking on 13 December, massacring the civilian population with no justification whatsoever; several tens of thousands were killed. Outrage at this was such that it reached Japan and General Matsui was recalled.

When attempts to negotiate a peace through the mediation of the German Ambassador, Doctor Trautman, failed, the Konoe Cabinet announced (16 January) that the war would continue until the enemy was eliminated completely, and military operations began once more. In 1938 the Japanese-occupied zones in North and Central China met in the Hsüchow area, while two great towns, Hankow in the Yangtze valley and Canton in South China, fell to the enemy.

Three sets of operations took place during this phase of the war. From the Nanking area, the Japanese moved up the Tsinpu railway towards Hsüchow, to join troops on their way from Tsinan to Hsüchow with the aim of surrounding and destroying twenty Chinese divisions belonging to seven armies, commanded by Li Tsung-jen, in a great and possibly final battle. Twelve Japanese divisions were used for this great plan – to the north the 5th, 10th, 103rd, 105th and 110th Divisions, all part of the Japanese army in North China (headquarters in Peking) commanded by

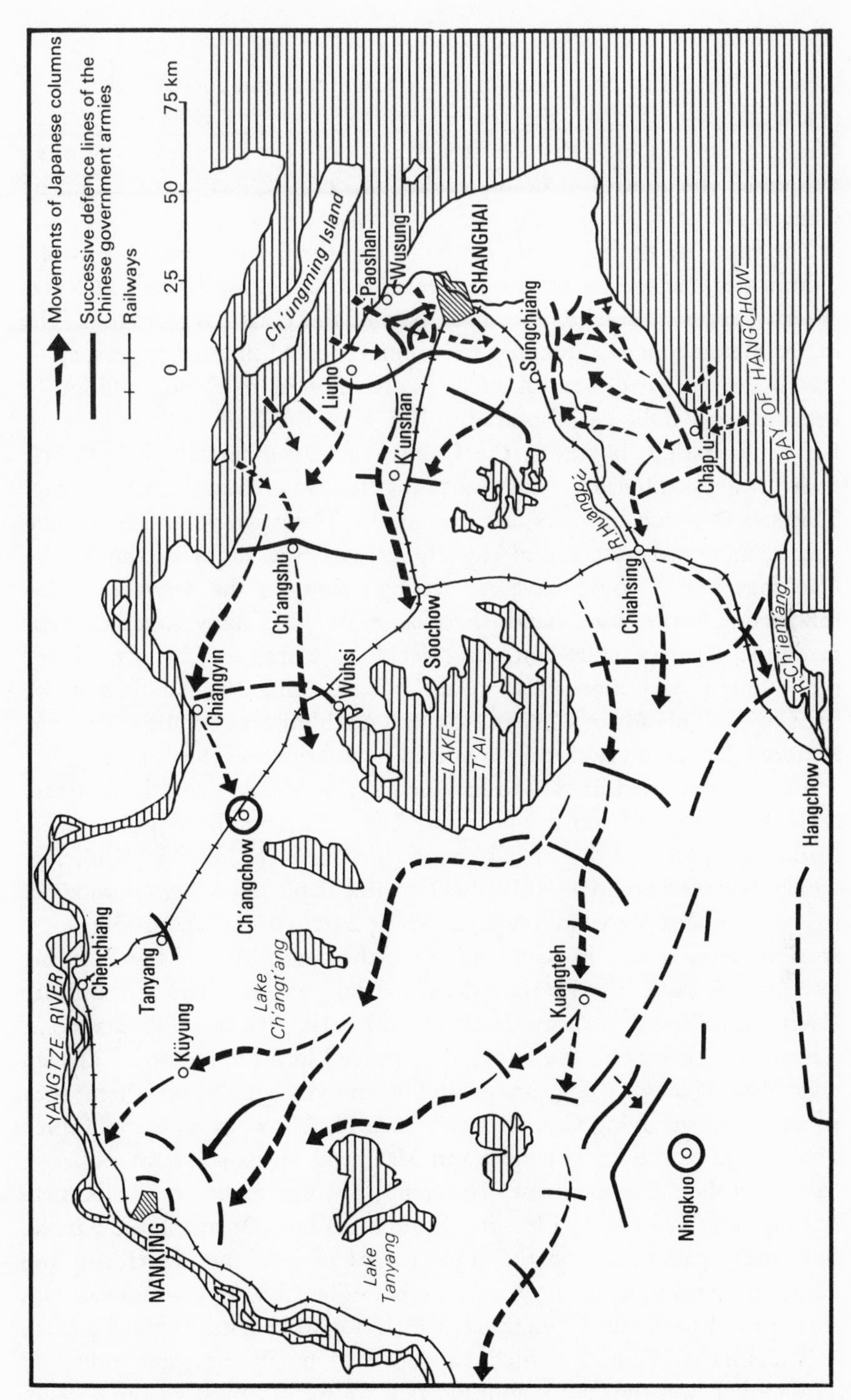

Map 20. The Shanghai front and the retreat to Nanking (August-December 1937)

General Terauchi, and to the south the 3rd, 101st and 106th Divisions in north and east Kiangsu, the 102nd, 107th and 111th Divisions north of Nanking, and the 9th Division in west Anhwei; the latter group of units was under the control of headquarters in Central China, commanded by General Hata.

The Japanese encirclement plan failed and the Chinese armies from the Tsinpu area managed to retreat, protected by the Yellow River, which was diverted from its course, becoming part of the Huai River system. The incredible destruction involved was unprecedented in military history. A few dikes breached near K'aifeng were enough to flood millions of hectares; and millions of peasants died after the loss of their harvest. Before retreating, however, the Chinese managed to halt the 5th and 10th Japanese Divisions north-east of Hsüchow, near T'aierhchuang. This success, won by units commanded by T'ang En-po and Sun Lien-chung, increased morale and slightly lessened the shock of the loss of Nanking, but it could have no lasting effect on the operations that followed. On the other hand, the change in the Yellow River's course made the Japanese chief command decide to march on Hankow, where the Chinese government had taken refuge, using the Yangtze valley as its route. This advance began from the Anch'ing area on about 12 June. A dozen Japanese divisions, supported by a large fleet, took part.

The Chinese tried in vain to bar the river at Matang, and downstream at Hukow, roughly on a level with Lake P'oyang. Both points were inadequately defended and fell on 26 June and 26 July. At Kiukiang, which they reached on 23 July, the Japanese deployed a large number of troops to attack the Hankow area. The 9th, 101st and 106th Divisions, working from a base in Kiukiang along the south bank of the Yangtze, advanced towards the Hankow-Yochow railway line. The 3rd and 6th Divisions followed the north bank, and the 10th, 13th and 16th Divisions, which had come from the Hofei area, moved into the region of Loshan and Shangch'eng, using an encircling movement. From there they pursued the surviving Chinese units from Hsüchow, crossed the Tapieh Shan range, and took Huangan and Mach'eng on its southern slopes in early October. To the west, Hsinyang, a large town on the Kinhan railway, was taken on 12 October. From the Tapieh Shan and the Kinhan line, the Japanese fell on the three towns of Hankow, Wuch'ang and Hengyang and took them on 25 October. The Chinese government was forced to flee towards Chungking, which was to become its third capital.

The loss of Canton, which happened at much the same time, on 21 October, was the end of an important source of supplies from abroad.

Two Japanese divisions and a brigade gathered in Taiwan, commanded by General Furusho, landed in Bias Bay, east of Hong Kong, on 12 October. They advanced on Canton, via Tanshui, Huiyang, Polo and Shihlung, without meeting any serious resistance. The great port of Amoy, further east, had been taken on 10 May.

The years of stagnation

After the fall of Hankow and Canton, the Japanese made no more big advances until 1944. The military history of the next five years is more or less spread over all the occupied regions; operations were generally on a smaller scale and their aims were often political and economic as much as military.

The chief events of 1939 were the conquest of Hainan (10 February) and the battle of Nanch'ang (March-April) when the capital of Kiangsi fell to the Japanese. Large-scale operations were carried out in west Honan at about the same time. The most important military event of the year was the first battle of Ch'angsha (Hunan) in September and October. The Japanese troops numbered nearly 100,000 men; they seized a large part of this rich province's harvest. On 24 November the large town of Nanning, between Canton and the frontier of Tongking, was taken after a landing west of Pakhoi.

1940 and 1941 were calm years. The Chinese lost Ich'ang on the Yangtze valley (12 June 1940) and took back Nanning (25 October 1940). In March 1941 things became lively in the western sector of Nanch'ang, in the region of Anyi and Kaoan. Chengchow, in Honan, was temporarily lost in October. The second battle of Ch'angsha broke out after the autumn harvest in September and October. On the eve of Pearl Harbour (7 December 1941) the total of Japanese troops in China was relatively small, considering the size of the theatre of operations. According to later official Japanese sources, the Expeditionary Force in China, commanded by General Nishio, consisted of twenty-one infantry divisions, twenty mixed brigades, one general reserve division, one cavalry group and sixteen air squadrons. The total number, including elements that did not belong to divisions, amounted to roughly 800,000 men. Japanese troops in Manchuria on the Russian frontier, on the other hand, amounted to thirteen divisions, twenty-four mixed brigades and fifty-six squadrons.

The entry of the United States into the war against Japan and Germany was to shift the Sino-Japanese war on to a different plane. It provided justification for the Chungking government's resistance, since it justified real hopes of eventual victory, but on the other hand, the expansion of the war in South-East Asia, particularly Burma, was to close the last routes carrying supplies to China from the outside world. The Soviet Union, the United States and Great Britain were also too much engrossed by their own war efforts to come to the aid of their new ally immediately.

The Chinese government therefore kept up the war, in spite of strong currents of defeatism in public opinion, of which Wang Ching-wei's defection is an illustration; at the same time, its army's deplorable condition, logistic difficulties and the certainty that the West would take the leading part in Japan's defeat, encouraged it to keep its own efforts to a minimum and husband its resources for the confrontation with the communists which was now inevitable. The stagnation lasted for several more years and the Chinese theatre of operations shrank still further.

One battle alone was fought in 1942 – the third battle of Ch'angsha. Four Japanese divisions beat back eleven Chinese armies and seized Ch'angsha, which they again evacuated soon after (4 January 1942). Even fewer major events took place in 1943; in June the Japanese launched a small attack on Ich'ang in west Hupei, and in December they captured Ch'angteh, west of Lake Tungt'ing in Hunan, only to abandon it. The presence of a small American air force in China, composed of volunteers commanded by Colonel Claire Chennault, and of the Fourteenth U.S. Air Force equipped with B25 bombers, was beginning to worry the Japanese supreme command. Its fears increased when it became obvious that plans were going ahead for an Allied offensive in Burma, and above all when its losses at sea grew heavier. From then on it concentrated on keeping up land transport from Indo-China to Korea, and eliminating the American air bases in Central and South China (Operation Ichigo).

In May and June 1944 the Japanese Twenty-second Army, under orders from the North China headquarters, and the Thirty-fourth Army, under orders from the Sixth Regional Army at Hankow, took the whole of the Kinhan railway line, by occupying the section between Chengchow and Hsinyang. The Twelfth Army also entered Loyang, along the great transversal Lunghai line (from Kansu to Haichow on the north-east coast of Kiangsu); about thirty Chinese divisions, commanded by Generals Chiang Ting-wen and T'ang En-po, were thrown into total disorder. The Japanese action was helped at a political level by the unpopularity of the nationalist troops who, underfed and undisciplined, laid waste countryside already hit by severe famine.

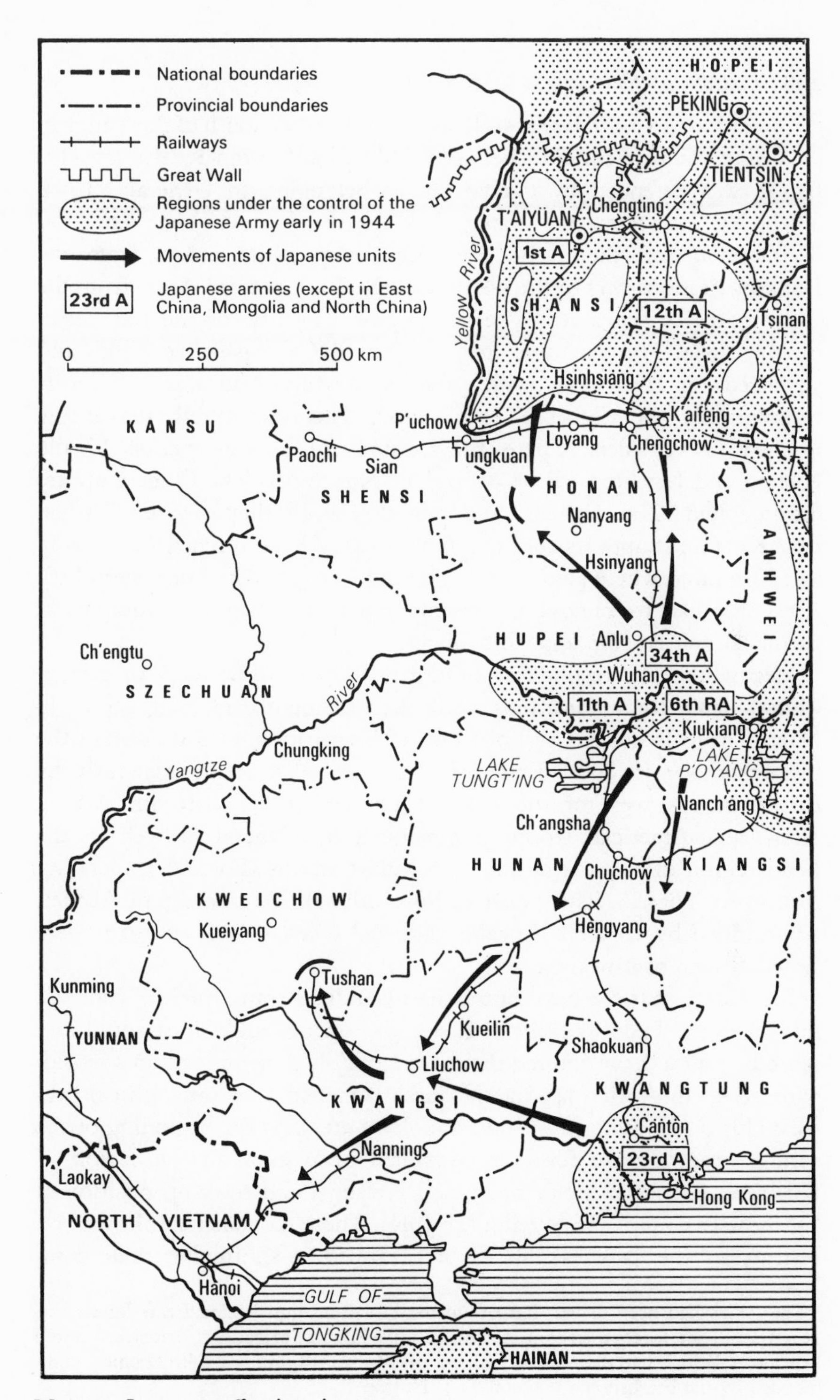

Map 21. Japanese offensives in 1944

Operations on a still larger scale were to take place south of the Yangtze, on a line roughly running between Ch'angsha-Kueilin-Kueiyang. This region was defended by twelve armies belonging to Generals Hsüeh Yüeh, Yu Han-mou and Chang Fa-k'uei; the Japanese sent ten good divisions against them, the Eleventh Army under orders from the Hankow headquarters to the north, and the Twenty-third Army from the Canton area to the south. The last large-scale battle of the war began in May 1944. The Japanese first recaptured Ch'angsha (20 June) and advanced on Hengyang, which fell on 8 August in spite of heroic resistance by the Chinese Tenth Army. The next month the enemy reached Ch'üanhsien, where they rested for several weeks. Finally Kueilin and Liuchow fell on 10 and 11 November. The Chinese armies disintegrated. The Japanese did not stop until they reached Tushan near Kueilin; it appears that they could easily have reached Chungking and Kunming, where panic was beginning to reign. The Fourteenth U.S. Air Force had to remove or destroy much of its ground equipment, particularly at Kueilin and Chihchiang.

Meanwhile, the reconquest of north Burma, which was to restore China's land communications with the outside world, had begun in March 1944.[1] It was led by Lord Louis Mountbatten, in command of the theatre of war in South-East Asia, and carried out simultaneously by British troops west of the River Chindwin (the Fourteenth Army), Sino-Anglo-American troops commanded by General Stilwell in the Ledo region in the north, and by Chinese troops (Force Y) operating from west Yunnan. The Japanese Fifteenth and Twenty-eighth Armies, commanded by General Kawabe who had taken Peking in 1937, were slowly driven southwards.

In January 1945 the New Burma Road (India, Assam, Burma, Yunnan), known as the Ledo or Stilwell Road, was opened and China could in a sense be said to have entered the theatre of Allied operations on a world-wide scale. In April 1945 the Japanese launched a last attack in north-west Hupei (the Siangyang and Laohok'ou area). At the beginning of the summer the Chinese forces reassembled once more in the region of Kueiyang (Group Alpha), re-entered Kwangsi and took up position at Liuchow (27 June) and Kueilin (27 July). These movements followed on retreats by the Japanese, which were aimed at shortening their com-

[1] The Allies had been driven out of Burma in a campaign lasting from January to May 1942. Their forces then consisted of: 5 Indian infantry brigades, 1 British armoured brigade, 1 British battalion and 9 Chinese divisions (5th, 6th and 66th Armies) commanded by the Englishman General T. J. Hutton.

munications lines, now difficult to maintain, and above all at getting back troops to defend their own country. They were also the first move in an attack intended to open a Chinese port, either Fort Bayard or Canton, on the Pacific coast (Plan Beta). The second half of 1945 seemed to be the beginning of the reconquest of the Chinese continent.

The Hiroshima bomb on 6 August and Japan's capitulation a week later brought the hostilities to a sudden end, but in less than a year the Chinese armies were thrown into a new and decisive civil war.

The conduct of the war on the Chinese side

Responsibility for the leadership of the war, in the widest sense of the term, lay above all with General Chiang Kai-shek, then at the zenith of his power and popularity. He did his best to delay hostilities, aware of his lack of preparation, but once they seemed to him to be inevitable, his actions appear to have been guided by the light of certain principles, as well as by reference to the actual circumstances. From the point of view of the world outside China, his main concerns were to prevent the war from becoming limited to North China, which was too vulnerable, too particularist, and too far removed from the currents of foreign interest, and to gain time and ground by waiting for a second world war to break out, which was easy enough to foresee given the international situation in 1937. Within the country, he had to make use of the circumstances to advance the work of political unification, eliminate or integrate the great provincial warlords, keep a constant watch on the communists, and remain the undisputed leader of his own party.

These principles transcended personal interests and corresponded to real needs which many Western observers, ill informed about the state of China, and particularly about Chinese political forces and customs, did not fully realize. They fell victim to their own democratic ideals – or, more accurately, irritated by the prevailing incompetence, apathy, and administrative and political corruption, they tended to forget that one person alone, Chiang Kai-shek, was able to embody the idea of resistance, and objectively, if not deliberately, they became the allies of the communists, his worst enemies. They revealed themselves poorer judges than Moscow at the time of the Sian Incident, which was not yet far away. The most severe criticisms that can be levelled at Chiang Kai-shek have nothing to do with his lack of liberalism (except for a few rare exceptions, the country adapted itself to this), but concern his narrow views, his obstinate adherence to old governmental practices, his lack of trust and his habit of rating the loyalty of his collaborators far above their talents or their honesty.

Since it affected every province, the war could have brought about a total national and social upheaval, and radical transformations in social structure and mentality. Changes of this kind could have created a new China for the people, a China full of enthusiasm, well organized and revolutionary in the best sense of the word – the only China capable of successfully opposing the communists when the time came. The Generalissimo had outlived his time and probably could no longer fully perceive the possibilities the circumstances offered; from the start, he also lacked an instrument of sufficient strength and purity to fulfil the task. The Kuomintang was an old, worn and tame party, embodied by a leader who was skilful but lacked real political genius. Worse still, this same leader wrote 'The Kuomintang is therefore the state's blood stream [artery] and the San Min Chu I [Three People's Principles] Youth Corps provides the new corpuscles in that blood stream',[1] but either could not or pretended not to see that his party was dying of sclerosis or leukemia; the war was to reveal this.

When the Sino-Japanese war broke out on 7 July 1937, China was still in the phase of political tutelage established by Sun Yat-sen. The provisory constitution of 1 June 1931 was still in force; the Kuomintang, and particularly its Central Executive Committee, was in charge of the government. In fact, the Central Political Council, whose members were appointed by the Party, formulated the policy which the government – chiefly the President and the ministers belonging to the Executive Yüan – was responsible for putting into action. On 29 January 1939 the Central Political Council made way for the Supreme Council for National Defence presided over by Chiang Kai-shek. The government and the Military Affairs Commission both came under its control. A Minister of War, attached to the Executive Yüan, was responsible for mobilization and materials, while the Military Affairs Commission consisted of: the General Staff, whose head was for a long time General Ho Ying-ch'in with two assistants (Generals Pai Ch'ung-hsi and Ch'eng Ch'ien), the Military Training Department, the Political Instruction Department, and the Arms and Services Departments. The Military Affairs Commission directed and prepared operations through these different bodies. Another organization frequently intervened in this field, however, sometimes without informing the regular hierarchy – Generalissimo Chiang Kai-shek's headquarters, where Chiang's chief collaborator was General Lin Wei.

[1] Cf. *China's Destiny*

For the purpose of military operations, China was divided into War Areas, which varied in number and outline as time went on. When they were created in the early months of 1938, they were as follows:

First War Area, Honan (Kinhan railway line); Commander, General Ch'eng Ch'ien: 25 infantry divisions, 2 infantry brigades, 2 cavalry divisions.

Second War Area, Shansi, Chahar, Suiyuan; Commander, General Yen Hsi-shan: 27 infantry divisions, 3 infantry brigades, 3 cavalry divisions.

Third War Area, south Kiangsu, Chekiang, south Anhwei; Commander, General Ku Chu-t'ung; 24 infantry divisions and 6 infantry brigades.

Fourth War Area, Kwangtung and Kwangsi; Commander, General Ho Ying-ch'in: 9 infantry divisions and 2 infantry brigades.

Fifth War Area, north Kiangsu, north Anhwei, south Shantung; Commander, General Li Tsung-jen: 27 infantry divisions and 3 infantry brigades.

Sixth and Seventh War Areas (created later on).

Eighth War Area, Kansu, Ninghsia, Chinghai; Commander, General Chiang Kai-shek: 3 divisions and 4 brigades of infantry, 5 divisions and 4 brigades of cavalry.

Wuhan Defence Area; Commander, General Ch'en Ch'eng: 14 infantry divisions and 1 infantry brigade.

Sian Headquarters; Commander, General Chiang Ting-wen: 14 infantry divisions, 4 infantry brigades and 3 cavalry divisions.

Defence of Fukien; Commander, General Ch'en Yi: 2 divisions and 4 brigades of infantry.

Troops under direct control of the Military Affairs Commission: 17 infantry divisions.

Units in formation: 40 divisions and 7 brigades of infantry.

Counting several special units not included above, Chinese troops at that time totalled 210 infantry divisions, 35 infantry brigades, 11 cavalry divisions, 6 cavalry brigades, 18 artillery regiments and 8 artillery groups on general reserve.[1]

In theory, the commander of a War Area had all the troops of his area at his disposal, but their availability was not often forthcoming in practice. The Chinese army in 1937 in many ways still reflected the lack of political unity in the country as a whole. The central troops, mainly

[1] General Ho Ying-ch'in, *Eight Years of War of Resistance* (in Chinese).

commanded by officers from the Whampoa (Huangp'u) Military Academy, were unquestionably loyal to the Generalissimo, though less so to his Chief of Staff, Ho Ying-ch'in. Provincial troops were still the most numerous; their obedience varied in degree from one province to another, with their needs in the way of supplies, and in different circumstances. It is easy to imagine how this state of affairs affected military operations. If other problems are added to these – difficulties resulting from distance, lack of transport, differences in dialects and even in eating habits, it will be realized that the Sino-Japanese war was in some ways like a series of regional wars in progress simultaneously.

Within the War Areas the large Chinese units were organized into army groups, armies, divisions and, initially at least, brigades. The threefold system was gradually brought into use within the armies, divisions and regiments. The composition of army groups was generally ruled by political considerations. These definitive Western terms hid infinite variety in numbers, materials and services. The units trained by the German military mission, and later those trained by the U.S. military mission, were the only ones to conform to Western standards in these respects. Generally speaking, the numbers of each unit were lower than they should have been. Divisions that ought to have had 9529 men rarely had more than 5000 or 6000. For what were nearly always political reasons, the total number of units maintained was absurdly high. Whereas the Japanese were content with about 25 divisions and the same number of independent brigades, in 1941 the Chinese had 246 divisions and 44 brigades taking part in operations, and 66 divisions and 3 brigades behind the front lines, amounting to a total of nearly 350 divisions.

At the start of the war China had an army totalling 1,788,000 men. Nearly 14 million men were mobilized as time went on, over a third of whom deserted or perished before joining their unit at the front. Recruiting was left in the hands of the local gentry, which meant that all the relatively well-off families escaped conscription. Consequently the poorest and physically weakest sections of the population found themselves herded into primitive depots, and then had to cover several hundred or thousand kilometres on foot to join their units. Out of 1,670,000 men conscripted in 1943, 750,000 never reached their destination. The U.S. advisers, and Generals Stilwell and Wedemeyer in particular, commented more harshly than did any other observers on this situation. A brief quotation from General Wedemeyer's writings sums up the appalling negligence on the part of the authorities and the Chinese administration, even after the creation of a Ministry of Recruitment in November 1944:

'Conscription comes to the Chinese peasant like famine or flood, only more regularly – every year twice – and claims more victims. Famine, flood, and drought compare with conscription like chicken pox with the plague.'[1]

More Chinese died of privation or illness during the war than in action. Official figures for military losses give 3,211,419 as the total, of which 1,761,335 were wounded, 1,319,958 killed and 130,116 reported missing. These figures fail to take into account the millions of unfortunate people who died, victims of an inhuman society and a thoroughly deplorable system. As the philosopher Meng-tzu said in his time, 'Is there any difference between killing a man with the sword or by bad administration?'

Keeping the troops alive was a major military problem. The country's poverty, transport difficulties, the extremely mediocre services in charge of supplies and upkeep, and the corruption, meant that most units were underfed and therefore given to marauding, while the soldiers' morale and physical fitness were reduced to zero. For sheer inefficiency, the Quartermaster-General's department was outdone only by the Health Service, of which the most that can be said for it is that it was non-existent in the modern sense of the term. In 1937 China had fewer than 10,000 doctors with Western-style training for 500 million inhabitants; the Army Health Service reflected this situation. It never had more than 2000 doctors worthy of the name in spite of the creation of the Military Medical School in Ch'angsha. The few large hospitals behind the lines could alone offer the wounded some hope of survival, but dysentery and malaria claimed many more victims than did the fighting.

From the first months of the war the Chinese army suffered a severe shortage of material and ammunition. Before 1937 Chinese arsenals produced approximately enough weapons for the infantry, using German and Czech models. To provide equipment for the artillery and other forces the government or the provinces called on several different countries, thus maintaining a measure of autonomy in politics and trade, to the detriment of uniformity in types of material used.

The fighting at Shanghai and the hasty retreat that followed had put the best equipped sections of the army to a severe test, while the biggest arsenals – Nanking, Hankow and T'aiyüan – were quickly lost. The Russians, the French and the English then handed over some equipment. From 1941 the U.S.A. took over and granted limited money, but not until 1943, when an air lift was organized over the Himalayas, and 1945, when the Burma Road was reopened, could a steady stream of supplies be

[1] C. F. Romanus and R. Sunderland, *Time Runs Out in CBI* (Washington, D.C., U.S. Dept of the Army, Office of the Chief of Military History, 1959).

established and maintained. Until then, the Chinese army could be described as a vast infantry totally lacking in support, except from its own mortars.

The strategy and tactics used by the Chinese troops obviously suffered badly from all these insufficiencies. The army lacked modern materials, it was badly trained and badly led, and had virtually no support from a population with no sense of public spirit; it usually sought refuge in a hasty retreat or passive defence, which could not last long in the face of an enemy as determined and as skilful in manœuvre as the Japanese. It was admitted that a Japanese division could easily outdo a Chinese army group with three times as many men.

On several occasions the Chinese showed great fortitude, however, and in various battles – Shanghai, T'aierhchuang and Ch'angsha – whole units were sacrificed. Later on the Chinese units in Burma, properly equipped and fed by supply corps under U.S. control, led by good generals with Western training and working with the Allies in a morally and professionally healthy climate, proved themselves equal to their Japanese enemies.

Following the communists' example, the government endeavoured to create a few guerrilla units behind the Japanese lines, with 2000 to 3000 men, according to common reckonings. The men belonging to the political structure of these units were not sufficiently experienced to organize the population thoroughly. Because of this, and because of their origins, these units tended to work in too orderly a fashion, and in large groups. They also suffered from the weaknesses inherent in the central administration. In its efforts to check communist expansion even more than Japanese expansion, Chungking probably did not wish to give too much encouragement to an experiment that helped local individualism. Wherever the regular army could not give support, the government guerrilla forces had to give way to their communist rivals. The U.S. advisers saw guerrilla action as a way to carry out sabotage and set up information networks. They found it hard to shift the action to a political level.[1]

Foreign advisers and foreign aid

In 1928 a group of German officers took over the training of part of the Chinese army. Colonel Bauer, General von Seeckt, Lieutenant-General Wetzell and, lastly, General von Falkenhausen from 1934 onwards,

[1] See Milton E. Miles, *A Different Kind of War: the little-known story of the combined guerrilla forces created in China by the U.S. navy and the Chinese during World War II* (New York, Doubleday, 1967).

managed to bring about a remarkable improvement in about thirty divisions. When the Germans were recalled at the request of the Japanese in 1938, they were replaced by a small group of French officers with General Berger of the air force, and a much larger group of Russians with General Cherbachev (about 300 officers and technicians of various kinds). In 1941 the U.S.A. extended the Lend-Lease Act (11 March) to China, in its anxiety to keep China in the war, and soon afterwards, in July, a military instructors' mission was organized. Led by General Magruder, it began work in September.

Foreign aid was to prove even more necessary for the air force. In 1937, the Chinese air force had about 200 fighting planes – Curtiss and Fiat fighters, Northrop and Caproni bombers, etc. It had an assembly plant at Nanch'ang, run by Italians. Its pilots were trained at Hangchow by Americans and at Loyang by Italians. Even so, a few weeks' fighting in the Yangtze valley was to eliminate the air force almost entirely. Pilots from the Soviet Union, using Russian planes (E15 and E16), and international volunteers helped the Chinese air force without causing much anxiety to the Japanese. The situation changed in October 1941 when Colonel Claire Chennault of the American Reserve created a group of volunteers, the Flying Tigers, consisting of about 100 pilots using P40s. In 1942 the Japanese air force almost stopped its daytime raids; at least 300 Japanese planes were shot down in the first six months of 1942.

When, after 7 December 1941, the United States entered the war, the question of American participation in operations in China was again brought to the fore. China had to be kept in the war at all costs, in spite of the Japanese blockade; as many Japanese units as possible had to be kept on Chinese soil, and as soon as the situation elsewhere would allow, East China was to be reconquered and used as a base for strong air attacks on Japan itself. Military relations between the new allies were difficult and complicated. China's isolated position, the greater importance of the battlefields in Europe, the mistrust displayed by the Generalissimo who was more worried by the danger represented by the communists than by the Japanese – 'the Japanese are a disease of the skin, the communists are a disease of the heart', as was to be said later on – and the feeling that the Chinese had lost interest, all slowed down U.S. aid and created serious friction. General Stilwell's memoirs bear witness to the disillusion and bitterness of the U.S. advisers. Their opinions were divided as to the line they should adopt. General Chennault, now at the head of the Fourteenth Air Force, thought that the Japanese could be paralysed simply by stepping up air attacks. General Stilwell, on the other hand, wanted to base all action on the Chinese army, but its grave inadequacies and his anxiety to remedy them led him to intervene in the country's internal politics. He thought that above all the number of Chinese units should be cut down drastically, that they should be better equipped, and their capacity for fighting increased.[1] He also considered it profitable to use communist troops, helping them by handing over weapons and ammunition. This last suggestion, and also his wish to gain supreme control of the whole Chinese military organization, finally led the Generalissimo to ask for his recall to the United States (October 1944).

The opening of the Burma Road, largely due to General Stilwell's tenacity, and the satisfactory development of the war in the West, both enabled the United States to make a considerable effort to help China. In 1944 and 1945, the Chinese were given supplies to equip thirty-nine modern divisions; the equipment belonging to the whole of the Japanese army in China, forced to capitulate on the spot, was soon to be added to this. By the end of the war, the central government's army was infinitely better equipped than it had been in 1937. These materials were to be used against the communist rebellion. In spite of its quantity, equipment alone could not make up for weaknesses in leadership and organization, which were so serious that in two or three years the communists managed either to destroy or obtain the surrender of all the enemy's armed forces. It is true to say that political and economic factors played as large a part in their final victory as purely military factors.

[1] General Wedemeyer, who succeeded General Stilwell, had greater consideration for Chinese self-respect than his predecessor; he also thought that the number of Chinese divisions should be reduced, from over 300 to 81 (36 using U.S. equipment and 45 using existing equipment).

24 The Chinese Communist Party's Territorial and Military Expansion during the Sino-Japanese war (July 1937-August 1945)

The Sino-Japanese war was to enable the Chinese Communist Party to accomplish a complete political and military resurrection. Thanks to the war, it was able to add to its numbers by attracting young patriots, who were trained to become enthusiastic cadres; it also increased its regular and auxiliary armed forces, and considerably enlarged the territories under its control. Anti-Japanese military action naturally provided the pretext and the means for expansion; 'anti-Japanese guerrilla zones' were formed, which turned into 'liberated areas', whose organization closely resembled that of the earlier bases created in Central China between 1927 and 1934. In fact, the development of the liberated areas was more harmful to the government administration than to the Japanese army and the new pro-Japanese administrations.

The reorganization of the Red Army to form the Eighth Route Army

Within the terms of the agreement of 15 July 1937 the Red Army disappeared, to be reorganized as the Eighth Route Army with three divisions of two brigades each, which in turn were each divided into two regiments, making a total of twelve regiments and 45,000 men. The order of battle of the Eighth Route Army, later to become the Eighteenth Army Group, was as follows:

Eighth Route Army: Commander, General Chu Teh. Deputy Commander, General P'eng Teh-huai. Chief of Staff, General Yeh Chien-ying. Political Commissar, Jen Pi-shih.

115th Division: Commander, General Lin Piao. Deputy Commander, General Nieh Jung-chen. Political Commissar, General Nieh Jung-chen. *Note:* the 115th Division was formed of elements from the former First Front Army.

120th Division: Commander, General Ho Lung. Deputy Commander, General Hsiao K'e. Chief of Staff, General Chou Shih-ti, later Li Ta. Political Commissar, General Kuan Hsiang-ying. *Note:* the 120th Division was based on the former Second Front Army.

129th Division: Commander, General Liu Po-ch'eng. Deputy Commander, General Hsü Hsiang-ch'ien. Political Commissar, Teng Hsiao-p'ing. *Note:* the 129th Division corresponds to Chang Kuo-t'ao's former Fourth Front Army.

As well as these troops, which the central government recognized as regulars forming part of the national military organization, from 1937 onwards between 30,000 and 50,000 men were stationed behind the lines in various services, depots and training centres, although theoretically one of the four regiments in each division was a training unit. When in the field the Eighth Route Army came under the Second War Area, commanded by the governor of Shansi General Yen Hsi-shan; in September and October parts of it took part in engagements in the north and east of the province, where they acquitted themselves with credit.

On 23 September the 115th Division under Lin Piao (the 344th Brigade commanded by Ch'en Keng) took part in operations carried out by the Sixth Army Group in the area round Lingch'iu north of P'inghsingkuan which was under attack from the Japanese 5th Division (Itagaki) from the Peking-Kalgan region. While the Sixth Army Group (Fifteenth and Thirty-third Armies) covered the approaches to the pass, the 115th Division came up on the rear of a Japanese column on the move, taking it by surprise and inflicting considerable losses. The division captured 1000 weapons and about 100 vehicles belonging to the Japanese 21st Brigade (25 September). Communist propaganda made extensive use of this victory, though the part played by the government units was not mentioned.[1] A few weeks later the 129th Division commanded by Liu Po-ch'eng distinguished itself in similar though less spectacular circumstances, in the Niangtzukuan region in east Shansi. The 769th Regiment of the 192nd Division, working with the government Third Army, carried out a successful raid in Japanese territory at Yangmingpao and

[1] See the article by Li Tien-yu in the Peking paper on 15 August 1965, and also Sydney Liu's article in the *China Mainland Review* of December 1966.

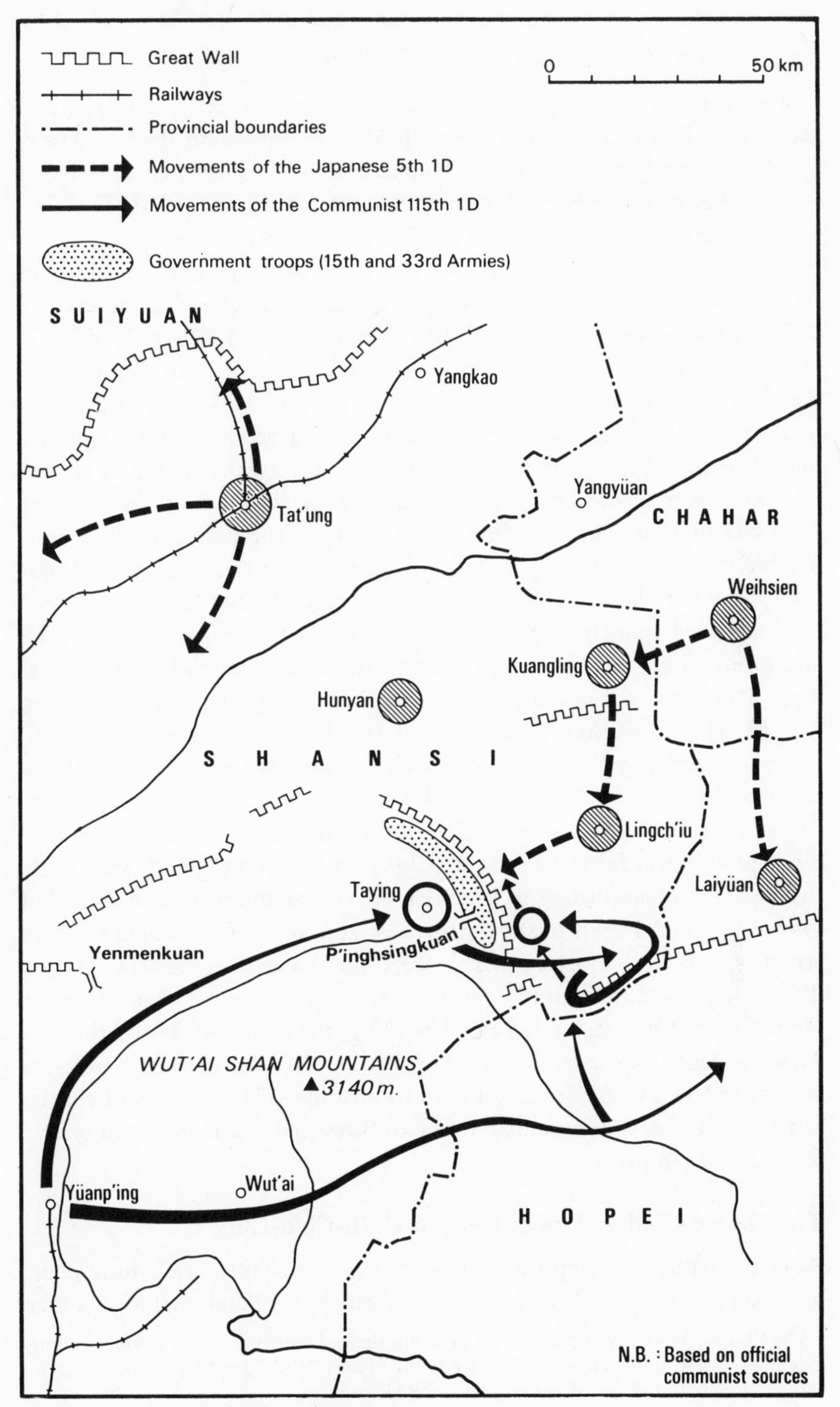
Great Wall
Railways
Provincial boundaries
Movements of the Japanese 5th 1D
Movements of the Communist 115th 1D
Government troops (15th and 33rd Armies)
0
50 km
SUIYUAN
Yangkao
Yangyüan
Tat'ung
CHAHAR
Weihsien
Kuangling
Hunyan
SHANSI
Lingch'iu
Laiyüan
Taying
P'inghsingkuan
Yenmenkuan
WUT'AI SHAN MOUNTAINS
3140 m.
Yüanp'ing
Wut'ai
HOPEI
N.B.: Based on official communist sources

Map 22. The battle of P'inghsingkuan

destroyed about twenty grounded planes. A few days later, the 771st and the 772nd Regiments, working with the Twenty-sixth Route Army, fought an engagement with the Japanese 20th Division in the Hsiyang and Changlots'un region. At about the same time the 120th Division under orders from the government Thirty-fourth Army near the Yenmen Pass in north Shansi destroyed a column of 500 Japanese vehicles and reoccupied the pass, which the Japanese then bypassed (16 October).

When the national and provincial armies retreated to the south and west of the province after the evacuation of T'aiyüan, the Eighth Route Army was free to act independently once more. Instead of taking up a position on the front alongside the government units, it stayed behind the Japanese lines, for lack of adequate numbers of troops forced the enemy to restrict its occupation to the chief towns and lines of communication. A large zone was allotted to each of the three divisions of the Eighth Route Army, in which the army began the political, administrative and military organization of the population, while at the same time gathering together isolated or abandoned elements belonging to the national and provincial armies and even willing elements belonging to the former administrative structure. The three communist divisions gradually spread beyond Shansi, towards Hopei, Chahar, Shantung and Honan, using methods similar to those used during the Kiangsi period. As time went on, about fifteen different bases with shifting boundaries grew up, first of all in North China, then in Central China, when the Fourth Army was created once more, and even as far away as South China, in Kwangtung and Hainan. By the end of 1944, according to Chou En-lai, the communists had control of twelve regional administrative structures and 591 district administrative structures (hsien), most of which were not located in the chief town. Three different administrative systems sometimes coexisted in the same district's territory, answering to Chungking, the communists and the pro-Japanese regimes; the wretched lot of the population under three different administrative authorities is not hard to imagine. The history and characteristics of the new communist 'bases' or 'liberated areas' are given below, for each one in turn.

The Shansi-Chahar-Hopei base, or Chin-Ch'a-Chi[1]

After the battle of P'inghsingkuan in north-east Shansi, Nieh Jung-chen, who had formerly studied chemistry in France and Belgium and was then

[1] The Chinese have kept up the habit of using the old names for the provinces alongside the modern ones. Here, 'Chin' stands for Shansi, 'Ch'a' for Chahar and 'Chi' for Hopei. 'Lu' is found for Shantung, 'Yü' for Honan, etc.

Deputy Commander of the 115th Division, received orders to take up a position in the Wut'ai Shan range, in an area enclosed on four sides by the Kinhan, Chengtai, Tungpu and Pingsui railway lines. For this he was allotted one independent regiment, a few cavalry squadrons and two incomplete companies, making a total of 2000 men, which was an extremely modest beginning. On 7 November the Shansi-Chahar-Hopei Command was created, a title revealing ambitious intentions. It gradually spread almost entirely over a territory of 800,000 square kilometres, with a population of 25 million, administered by 108 'hsien'. Three subdivisions were formed – Peiyueh,[1] Central Hopei (Chichung) and Hopei-Jehol-Liaoning (Chi-Jih-Liao).

Politically speaking, Chin-Ch'a-Chi came into being on 10 January 1938 at the Congress of Regional Representatives held at Foup'ing in north-west Hopei. The congress created a Provisional Administrative Committee led by Nieh Jung-chen. It was the only administrative authority of its kind to receive recognition from the central government, apart from the Border Region in north Shensi. In the spring of 1938 Lü Cheng-ts'ao, a former officer in the Manchurian army won over to the communists, brought two battalions from Shansi to central Hopei and on 1 April created a local executive organization, which subsequently was to change its name several times. A little later, in June, communist groups commanded by Li Yün-ch'ang infiltrated into seven districts in east Hopei and stirred up risings against the pro-Japanese administrative authorities.

The arrival of part of Ho Lung's 120th Division in central Hopei in February 1939 maintained and increased the communist hold there, which was under threat from Lu Chung-lin, one of Feng Yü-hsiang's former officers, and the new provincial governor. Hsiao K'e placed units to the west of Peking; in the spring of 1939 they moved on to Jehol and even to parts of Liaoning. By the end of 1939 the communists were spread over five provinces.

The new administrative systems had great difficulty in gaining a foothold and their power was precarious right to the end. As the region was important both strategically and politically, the Japanese felt obliged to purge it from time to time. 'Cleaning up campaigns' often laid bare the communist administrative structure and acted as a deterrent to the inhabitants, who as far as possible avoided taking part in elections, with the risks they involved, and provided few office-bearers. Sometimes the Japanese played into communist hands for their reprisals were so savage

[1] This area is called after one of China's five sacred mountains, the Northern Peak, in the mountains in north-west Hopei.

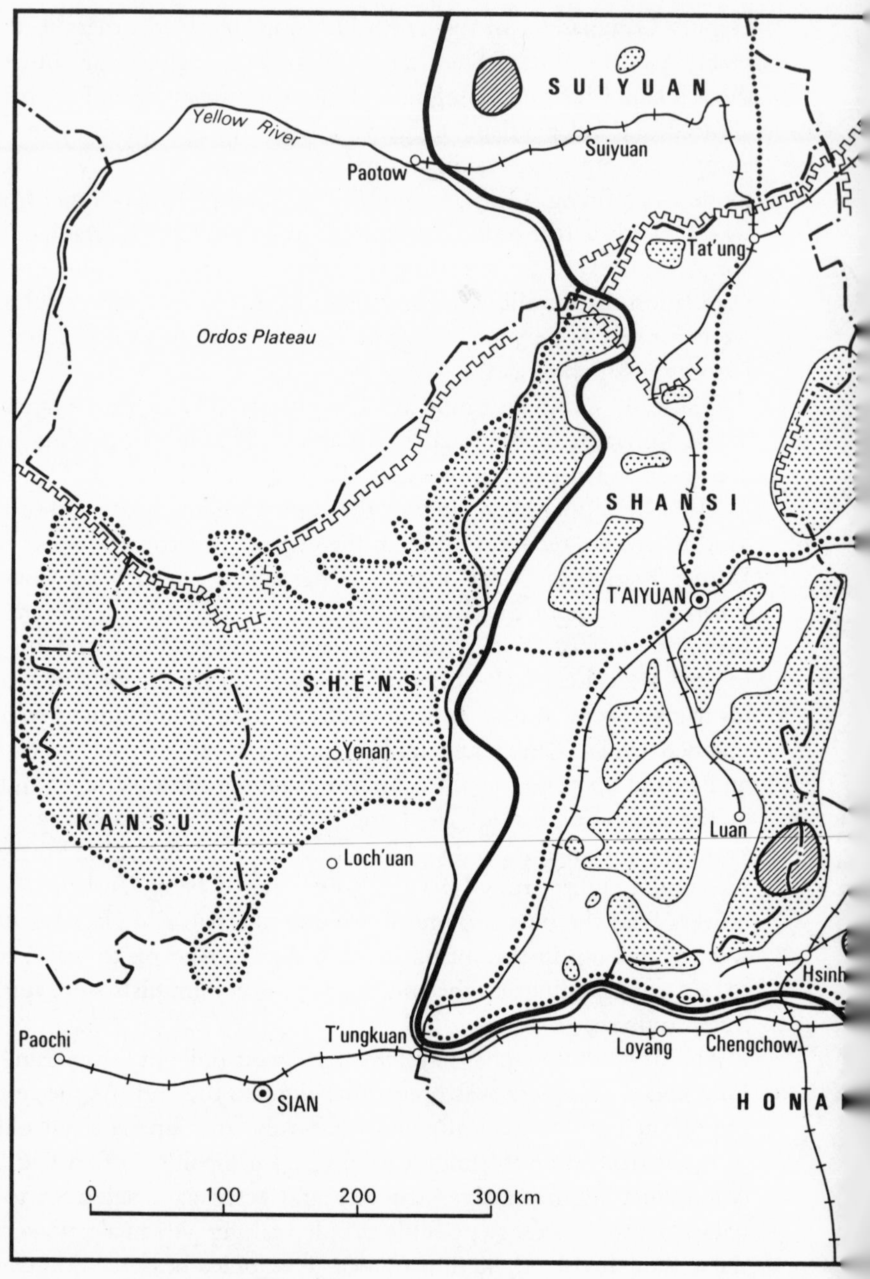

Map 23. The communist bases during the Sino-Japanese war: North China

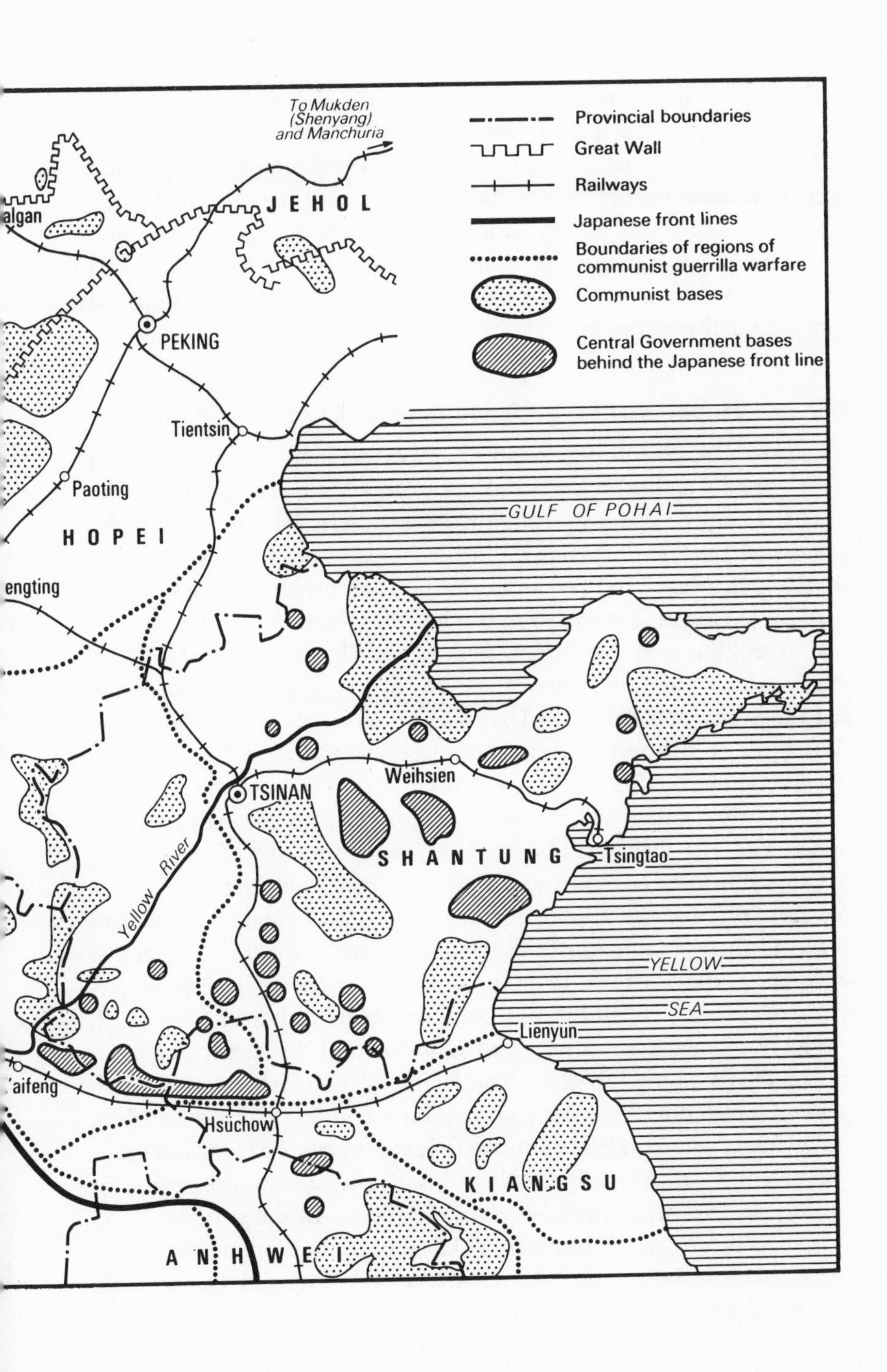

To Mukden (Shenyang) and Manchuria
Provincial boundaries
Great Wall
Railways
Japanese front lines
Boundaries of regions of communist guerrilla warfare
Communist bases
Central Government bases behind the Japanese front line
algan
JEHOL
PEKING
Tientsin
Paoting
HOPEI
engting
GULF OF POHAI
Weihsien
TSINAN
Yellow River
SHANTUNG
Tsingtao
YELLOW
SEA
Lienyün
'aifeng
Hsüchow
KIANGSU
ANHWEI

that numerous ruined peasants went over to the communists. Guerrilla warfare was to take on a special form in central Hopei, owing to the lack of hills and scarcity of watercourses. In some areas the Japanese and their Chinese auxiliaries formed whole networks of earth banks and ditches. The peasants' reply was to dig hundreds of kilometres of underground passages and galleries in the light soil, where they hid with their harvests and sometimes their animals as well. These strange conditions soon lent a relentless quality to the war.

The Shansi-Hopei-Shantung-Honan base, or Chin-Chi-Lu-Yü

The Shansi-Hopei-Shantung-Honan base was gradually formed between the Tungpu railway line in Shansi to the west, and the Tsinpu line to the east. The Lunghai line was roughly its southern boundary, and the Chengtai and Tehshih (Tehchow-Shihchiachuang) lines bounded it to the north. For purposes of military operations, it was divided into two parts: Shansi-Hopei-Honan, covering 219,000 square kilometres with a population of 7 million and 59 'hsien'; and Hopei-Shantung-Honan, which covered 315,000 square kilometres and 18 'hsien'. The base was created by Liu Po-ch'eng and the 129th Division, or, to be even more exact, the 386th Brigade, which retreated to south-east Shansi, to the T'aihang and T'aiyüeh mountains, after the Japanese reached the centre of the province. One of its earliest organizers was Po I-po, formerly one of the provincial governor Yen Hsi-shan's auxiliaries, later to become one of the leading figures in the field of economy and finance of the Peking regime.

In February 1938 the Eighth Route Army sent a mounted regiment from the T'aihang mountains to the plains of south Hopei and the north bank of the Yellow River. In May, when the battle of Hsüchow was fought, Hsü Hsiang-ch'ien brought reinforcements to join it – the 769th and 771st Regiments from the 129th Division and the 668th Regiment from Lin Piao's 115th Division. The laying of political foundations in Hopei was directed by Teng Hsiao-p'ing, then Political Commissar of the 129th Division, commanded by another fellow countryman from Szechuan, Liu Po-ch'eng.[1] Contact was established with the communist groups in Shantung, and a Tsinpu Detachment was formed. In the autumn Hsiao Hua, later to be one of the international figures in the Communist Youth movement before becoming head of the army's Political Department, arrived to organize west Shantung.

[1] Teng Hsiao-p'ing was one of the victims of the Cultural Revolution, and Liu Po-ch'eng also seems to have suffered from it.

The central government, whose regular troops still held part of the neighbouring province of Honan, were worried by the communist expansion and retaliated sharply. Lu Chung-lin, the official governor of Hopei province and commander of the Hopei-Chahar Military Area wanted to dissolve the Executive Bureau in south Hopei. At the same time government troops from the Chungt'iao Shan on the borders of Honan and Shansi tried to gain a foothold in the T'aihang mountains. Although personal contacts were established between Lu Chung-lin and P'eng Teh-huai, armed clashes increased in number and the situation was further confused by the ambiguous attitude of certain generals from Chungking who were plotting with the Japanese. Shih Yu-san, the most notorious of these generals, was shot by order of the government. The communists finally eliminated their rivals from the whole of Hopei, in both a military and political sense; Lu Chung-lin was forced to return to Chungking (March 1940).

The communists' progress resulted in the establishment of new administrative systems and authorities which owed allegiance to them. In south Shansi this was accomplished by the end of 1938. During the summer of 1939 local assemblies were elected in south Hopei. In August 1940 an executive organization shared by the subdivisions of south Hopei, the T'aihang mountains and the T'aiyüeh mountains was inaugurated. Then in 1941 a provisional assembly for the four provinces was elected. The communists held seventy-two seats, representing a third of the total, in accordance with the rule which they had laid down for themselves; several men known to be members of the Kuomintang or non-party patriots were brought to the fore. A nationalist revolutionary, a returned student from France later to be governor of Hupei, was elected chairman of the assembly; Po I-po and Jung Wu-shen (later deputy Minister of Finance to Po I-po) were vice-chairmen.

On the eve of the Japanese capitulation, the Shansi-Hopei-Shantung-Honan base included four regional executive bureaux and 198 administrative bodies at the 'hsien' level. But only fourteen chief towns were held among the 'hsien', and out of 25 million inhabitants, 5 million only were fully under control. The Japanese could not allow communist power to take root in south or north Hopei. They sent frequent expeditions there, which the communist militia, estimated at 400,000, could not prevent. The Eighth Route Army managed to maintain a hold in only the most outlying and unapproachable zones. Its battles became mingled with history and legend, for the same area had already seen countless peasant risings and secret societies and countless battles against the barbarian invaders, and it was no mere coincidence that it had formed the backcloth for the fabled heroes of Liang Shan Po in their revolt against the injustice of the central authorities.

The Shansi-Suiyuan base, or Chin-Sui

After the fighting at Yenmenkuan in north Shansi in October 1937, Ho Lung's 12th Division slipped away to the north-east and the Shansi-Suiyuan base gradually grew up round it. Eventually its boundaries were the Tungpu railway to the east, the vertical stretch of the Yellow River to the west, the Mongolian desert to the north, and to the south a line running through Chiehsiu, Chungyang and Chüntu, roughly in the middle of Shansi province. Two subdivisions were created, one in north-west Shansi, with Hsinghsien as its capital, and one in the Tach'ing mountains in Suiyuan. It covered a total area of 330,000 square kilometres sparsely populated by 3 million inhabitants, with an extremely poor economy.

The communists' progress appears to have been slow. In August 1938 Ho Lung went to help Lü Cheng-ts'ao in Hopei, leaving only the 358th Brigade and a few miscellaneous units behind him in north-west Shansi. In Suiyuan the situation was even more difficult. The population was quicker to support its governor, Fu Tso-yi, with his Thirty-fifth Army within easy reach of the province; the Mongolian elements under Prince Teh gave their wholehearted support to the Japanese.

From February 1940 the communists tried to gain a better hold by setting up administrative structures elected on the 'three-thirds' system, and tightening their organization of the population. The Japanese replied by a 'nibbling' policy of patient psychological action carried out by groups of civilians working in the name of peace and the revival of the economy, who developed the New People's Association founded in Peking by the collaborating government. The communists themselves admitted that the campaign achieved good results. They took up the challenge in their turn in 1942. A 'maintenance' policy was launched to oppose the 'nibbling' policy – land rent was reduced, the militias were developed and the economy was encouraged. In October 1942 a North-West Shansi Provisional Assembly met; from then on, the region may be said to be almost entirely under the control of Yenan. Its geographic situation was such that it never assumed as much importance as the other bases, and none of the leading figures made a name for himself there.[1]

[1] In its first issue in 1954, the Chinese review *Modern Historical Material* (*Chin-tai shih tzu-liao*), published in Peking, printed part of the reports and statistics presented to the North-West Shansi Assembly held in October 1942.

The Shantung base

At the end of 1937, before the Japanese advance had reached the province, thirty communists from Shantung, scantily armed, organized the first anti-Japanese detachment in the T'aian area, south of Tsinan. They were joined by students who had escaped from Peking and Tientsin; by March 1938 the detachment boasted 500 men and, in a brave show of optimism, took the title of Fourth Group (chih-tuei) of the First Column (tsung-tuei) of the Shantung Anti-Japanese Defence Troops. It then split into two groups, North and South, and carried out a few raids to obtain supplies in various districts in central Shantung – Laiwu, Poshan, Szushui, etc. In May 1938 fugitives from the battle of Hsüchow swelled its numbers and it became the 4th Brigade of the Shantung Column of the Eighth Route Army.

On 24 December 1937 a small group of seventeen people was formed in the extreme east of the province (in the area known as Kiaotsi). Two months later it had over 1000 members and was capable of attacking several districts on the north coast, such as Moup'ing and Huanghsien. By the autumn of 1938 the armed communists in Shantung were said to amount to 30,000; they were formed into the Shantung Column of the Eighth Route Army, divided into nine groups (chih-tuei).

The communists were not alone, however. In the west of the province, Fan Chu-hsien, a local rebel who appears to have been a provincial army officer, was active over about twenty districts. At the end of 1938 the Kuomintang provincial governor, Admiral Shen Hung-lieh, took charge of the defence of Shantung and the Hopei border region (Chi-Lu lien-fang) once more, trying to gather all members of resistance movements together and hindering communist expansion considerably. At this point, outside elements intervened – first of all part of the 115th Division (March 1939) and later General Hsü Hsiang-ch'ien, assisted by Lo Jung-huan. Hsü was a former pupil of the Whampoa (Huangp'u) Military Academy, an excellent general later to be Chief of Staff of the People's Liberation Army; Lo was in charge of the political department, and took over the leadership of the communist troops in Shantung.

From 1939 to 1941 the Shantung Column's situation was extremely difficult. The Japanese, traditionally interested in the province, placed three good brigades there and had the help of over 100,000 Chinese auxiliaries;[1] there was a similar number of government troops. Armed

[1] Communist sources give the following figures for the auxiliaries: 1940, 80,000 men; 1941, 122,000; 1942, 155,000; 1945, 180,000. They hold that this regular rate of growth was the result of desertions from the government troops, whose numbers fell just as regularly in that area: 1940, 166,000; 1941, 110,000; 1942, 80,000; 1943, 30,000.

clashes were frequent. In order to retain a foothold in Shantung, the Party had to send a number of energetic cadres there in 1941; for the next two years they conducted an intense campaign to reduce land rent and give the population some military organization. By the middle of 1943 half the population – 15 million inhabitants out of 29 million – was more or less under communist control and the militia numbered nearly 500,000, if Peking authors are to be believed.

The Shantung base was to remain much the same from then on until the end of the war of resistance. Its boundaries were not entirely the traditional provincial boundaries, particularly to the west and the south, where its frontiers were the Tsinpu and Lunghai railway lines. On the other hand, it included several districts in east Hopei. The interior was divided into five subregions or 'ch'ü': 1 Lu chung ch'ü (central Shantung), 2 Lu nan ch'ü (south Shantung), 3 Po Hai ch'ü (Gulf of Po Hai region), 4 Kiao tung ch'ü (the eastern region of the peninsula), 5 Pin Hai ch'ü (coastal region west of Tsingtao). With its jagged relief, its unique geographical position and its large population, Shantung was destined to become an extremely important part of the communist military disposition. It formed a bastion, threatening both North and Central China, and was to facilitate the reconquest of Manchuria, which was in a sense a colony peopled by inhabitants of Shantung. The government tried in vain to take it in 1947; the loss of Tsinan in 1948 marked the beginning of the communists' decisive victories.

The New Fourth Army and the Central China bases

From 1938 onwards the Communist Party extended its bases as far as the lower Yangtze valley. This movement was the work of troops left behind in 1934 on the borders of Kiangsi-Fukien-Anhwei during the Long March. They numbered about 20,000 men at the time, many of whom were ill or wounded. An old militant trade unionist from Hupei, Hsiang Ying, a former vice-president of the Chinese Soviet Republic, was their commander, and Marshal Ch'en Yi, later Minister of Foreign Affairs, was his political commissar. This lost army managed to maintain some measure of unity in spirit, in spite of the fact that it was scattered, and in spite of government action. Several thousand men also managed to survive in the north Hupei, Anhwei and Honan border regions, in Chang Kuo-t'ao's former base. When the Sino-Japanese war broke out, these men reappeared, after being more or less forgotten. The Communist Party obtained permission for them to leave their mountain hide-outs and join in military operations. They took the title of the New Fourth Army, and their numbers were officially fixed at 10,000 men divided into four detachments (chih-tuei), each of which was equivalent to a regiment with reinforcements. Yeh T'ing, a professional soldier with a distinguished record in the Northern Expedition who had taken part in the Nanch'ang Uprising, was appointed commander of the new army, although he no longer belonged to the Party. Hsiang Ying became deputy commander and Ch'en Yi political commissar.[1]

The New Fourth Army, attached to the Third War Area commanded by General Ku Chu-t'ung, fought its first engagement in May 1938 in south Anhwei near Wuhu and Nanking. One of its detachments joined in engagements in north Anhwei among the lakes between Anch'ing and Hofei. As it was part of a closely knit government formation, the New Fourth Army could not gain a firm and lasting foothold in the region, but its numbers increased, swelled by refugees from the Nanking and Shanghai area. This development, which occurred in a zone of great political and economic importance, and the deterioration of relations between the national and the communist troops north of the Yangtze, were at the root of a serious crisis which all but put an end to the principle of collaboration between the central government and the Communist Party. The result on a local scale was the elimination of the New Fourth Army troops operating south of the Yangtze in January 1941 (see Chapter 26).

Although it was officially dissolved by the government in 1941, the New Fourth Army continued to exist and expand north of the Yangtze. The communists made it a point of honour to reorganize it on a regular pattern. It consisted of seven divisions north of the river and a column to the south; each division was instructed to create its own territorial base and, naturally enough, to refuse to enter into cooperation, whether military or political, with the government troops. The order of battle of the New Fourth Army was as follows:

Commander: Ch'en Yi
Assistant Commander: Chang Yün-i
Chief of Staff: Lai Ch'uan-chu

[1] According to Yeh T'ing himself, in his statements published by I. Epstein in *The People's War*, in 1937 the New Fourth Army was made up as follows: 2000 men under Chang Ting-ch'eng from west Fukien, 1500 men under Ch'en Yi from south Kiangsi, 1200 men under Fu Ch'iu-t'ao from east Hunan (Ho Lung's former base), 2000 men under Liao Ying from the borders of Chekiang and Fukien. The old bases north of the Yangtze were reported to have furnished between 4300 and 5000 men under Kao Chung-ting.

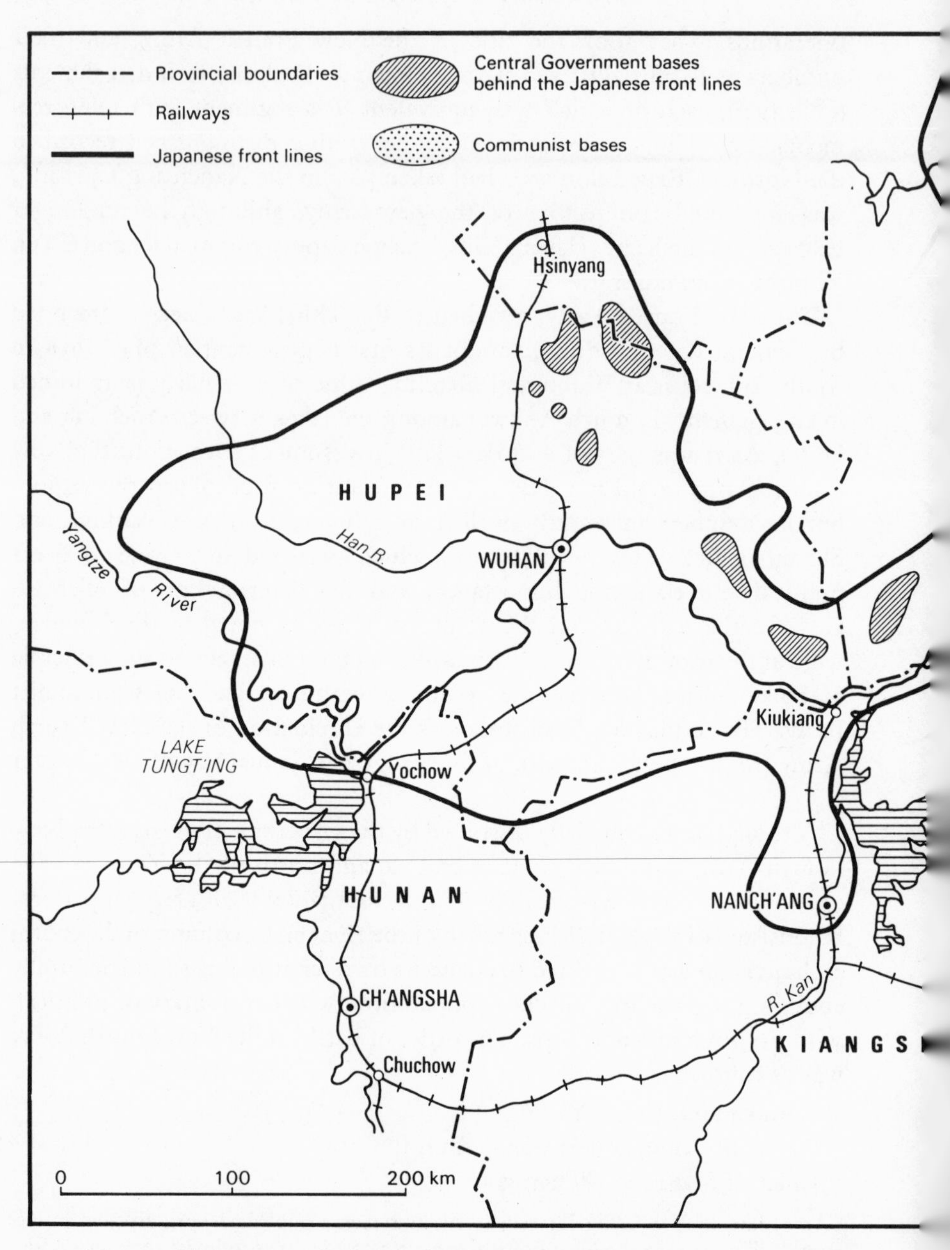

Map 24. The communist bases during the Sino-Japanese war: Central China

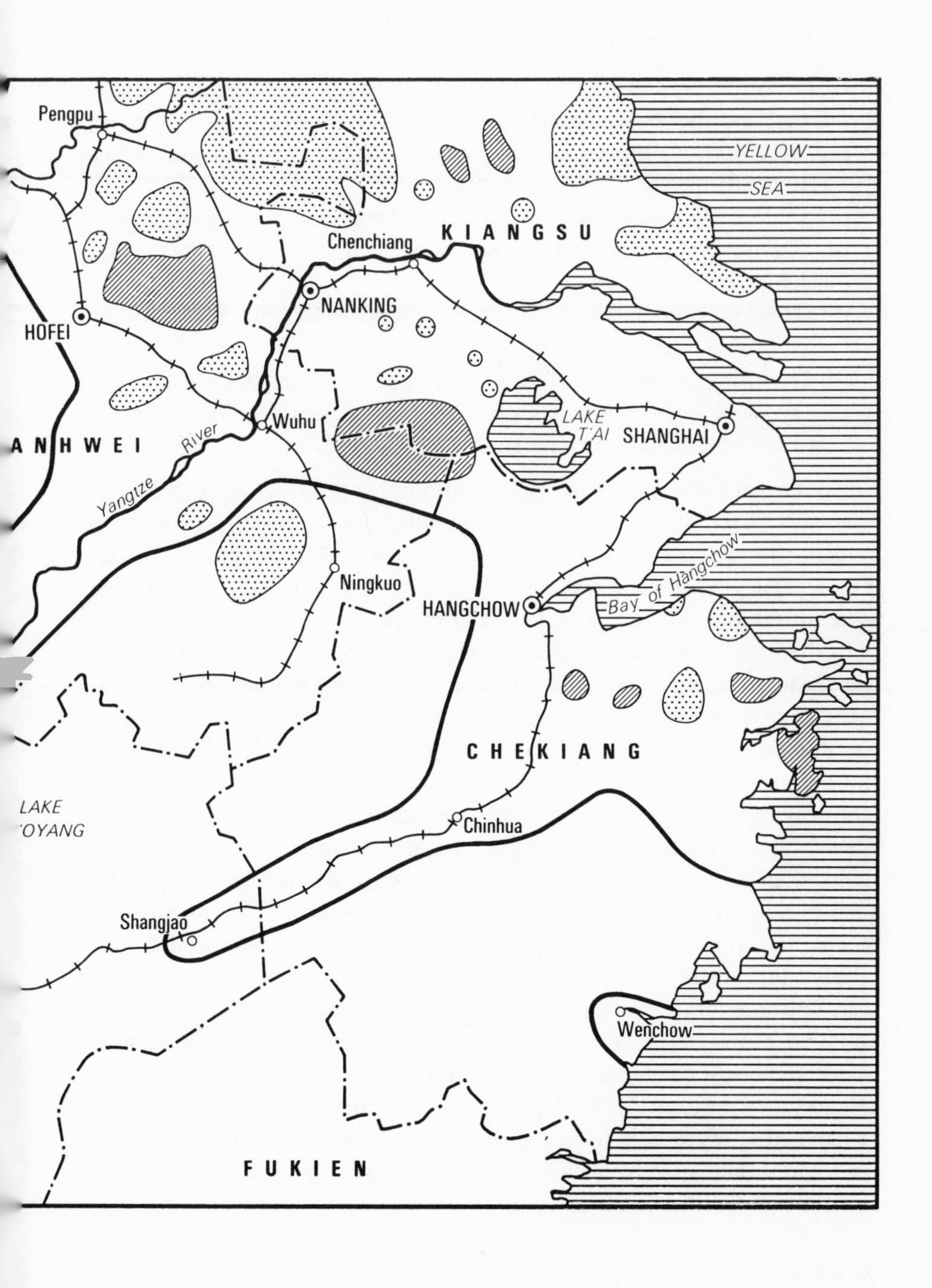

Pengpu
YELLOW
SEA
KIANGSU
Chenchiang
NANKING
HOFEI
LAKE
T'AI
SHANGHAI
Wuhu
ANHWEI
River
Yangtze
Ningkuo
HANGCHOW
Bay of Hangchow
CHEKIANG
LAKE
OYANG
Chinhua
Shangjao
Wenchow
FUKIEN

1st Division: Commander Su Yü; Central Kiangsu between the Grand Canal and the sea (Suchung)
2nd Division: Commander Lo Ping-hui; south of the Huai river (Huainan)
3rd Division: Commander Huang K'o-ch'eng; north Kiangsu (Supei)
4th Division: Commander P'eng Hsueh-feng; north of the Huai (Huaipei)
5th Division: Commander Li Hsien-nien; Hupei-Honan-Anhwei border area (O-Yü-Wan)
6th Division: Commander T'an Chen-lin; south Kiangsu (Sunan)
7th Division: Commander T'an Hsi-lin; central Anhwei (Wanchung)
East Chekiang Column: Commander Ho Ko-shih

Ch'en Yi had some important figures among his political assistants – Liu Shao-ch'i, later President of the Republic, Jao Shu-shih, a returned student from France who was one of the chief conspirators in 1953, Chang Yün-i, later governor of Kwangsi, and Teng Tzu-hui, later in charge of agricultural questions on the Central Committee.

In the overlapping zones of activity of the different armies involved – the Japanese and the governments of collaboration, the national government, the communists, not to mention the private armies – it is not easy to follow the fluctuations of the red influence in the area, which was twice the size of France and had a population of 60 million. Top cadres from Yenan were sent there, and the communists claimed to have carried off great political successes. In fact, the regular government armies maintained their hold on huge enclaves scarcely ever penetrated by the Japanese, such as the region between the Tapieh Shan and the new course of the Yellow River (the Huai valley); they had no difficulty in driving the communists out of the Central Plain in 1946, at the beginning of the last civil war. The communist troops then amounted to 60,000 men, commanded by Li Hsien-nien. On the other hand, the communists were firmly implanted in east and north Kiangsu, between the Tsinpu railway line and the sea (the Grand Canal region). As the Japanese were indifferent and Shantung near at hand, they were able to organize the population thoroughly, in their own time. The government found it extremely difficult to extend its authority there once more in 1946.

The South China bases

In places where it had been in existence for some time, the Chinese communist movement had left behind a clandestine structure, which enabled it to reconstitute its organization with the help of a longstanding revolutionary tradition. This was true of the East River districts, where P'eng P'ai had created the first Chinese Soviets, near Canton and Hong Kong. The communists did not reappear there until after the Japanese landings at Bias Bay in October 1938. They began their activities first of all in the Hueiyang area, where some 100 militants formed a group entitled the Independent Detachment of the 3rd Guerrilla Zone of Kwangtung, obtaining tacit recognition from the local authorities. After an incident at

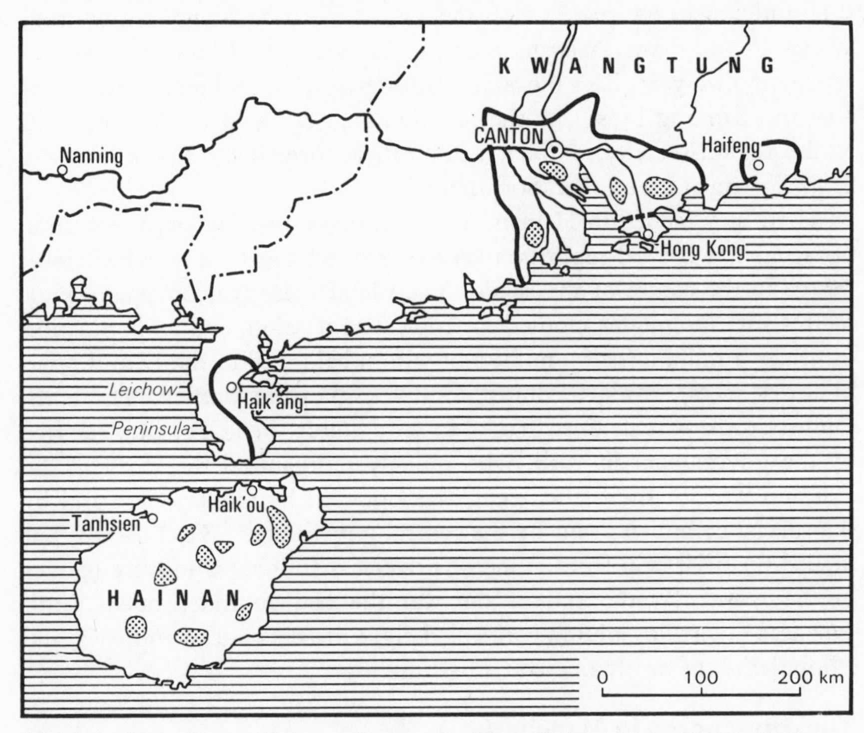

Map 25. The communist bases during the Sino-Japanese war: South China

P'ingshan, however, the new detachment was dissolved and almost entirely disarmed. Part of it then joined communists engaged in activities in the district of Tungwan, commanded by Wang Tso-yao, forming the East River Column in 1941.

The fall of Hong Kong to the Japanese in December 1941 brought more cadres to the communists; their development was helped by the relative passivity of the Japanese army, which did no more than to cover the Canton-Hong Kong railway line, as it did not consider Kwangtung important from a political point of view. One fairly large attack was launched against the communist guerrilla forces in the area, in the spring of 1944, by the Japanese 57th Division and four divisions under Wang Ching-wei, and groups responsible for propaganda and psychological action. The results appear to have been mediocre and the Party continued its work without much difficulty.

By 1944 1 million of the local inhabitants were under communist organization, and the East River Column numbered nearly 10,000 men, commanded by Tseng Sheng, a returned student from Australia who had been militant in the trade union movement in Hong Kong and Canton; Wang Tso-yao was assistant commander, and Lin P'ing the political assistant. Two years later the cadres belonging to the column were evacuated to Shantung by sea by the Kuomintang. Some of them came back to the region secretly in 1947, while others formed the Column of the Two Kwangs in the Liberation Army.

When they landed in Hainan on 10 February 1939 the Japanese came up against two local regiments (Peace Preservation Corps), which took refuge in the centre of the island. The island's size (34,000 square kilometres), its mountains clothed in tropical vegetation, and its population of nearly 3 million (half a million of whom belonged to the Li and Miao minority races), made it almost ideal for guerrilla warfare. The communists took part in this, thanks to an agitator, Feng Pai-chü, set free by the government in 1937, who quickly reorganized the Party in the east and west of the island. Feng was opposed by the Japanese and by the special commissar sent by the central government, Wu Tao-nan, but he had financial help from numerous overseas Chinese who were natives of the island. By the end of the war the Hainan Independent Anti-Japanese Guerrilla Column controlled eight districts out of eighteen, and a population of nearly one and a half million.

The communists in Manchuria

Manchuria had been firmly held since 1931 by Japanese armies and the Manchukuo troops; the chances of establishing durable bases there were slender. However, resistance movements had grown up at an early date. Several generals led them for a few years – Ma Chan-shan (the Hero of the River Nonni), Su Ping-wen and Li Tu, who was to take command of all the Manchurian Volunteers in the name of Nanking after 1937, were the best known of them. Ruined peasants, demobilized soldiers, secret society members, and traditional style bandits gradually organized 'armies' whose high-sounding names caused great confusion. These all developed further after the events of 1937. A dozen or so armies existed, one of them an army of Koreans commanded by Kim Il sung, now Marshal. Out of a possible total of 150,000 men, it seems that the communists were not strongly represented. They did not move far out of south and west Liaoning and, under the title of the People's Revolutionary Army, they more or less formed part of the anti-Japanese armies commanded by Li Tu. In spite of the assertions of official historians, the communists did not gain a firm foothold in Manchuria until after the Japanese capitulated.

The military organization of the population

Whereas the central government, mainly supported by its regular army, was playing for time, abandoning vast areas and large sections of the population if necessary, the Communist Party was trying to spread its influence wherever possible, and to gain control of and organize as many people as it could. It was helped in this by a natural tendency towards 'working with the masses', by experience gained in Kiangsi and in the Central China bases, and by the form taken by military operations, owing to the geographical characteristics of the country and the low numbers of the Japanese troops. Even before the opening of hostilities, the Chinese communists were not afraid to state that their main aim was to win over the people. In June 1937 General Chu Teh, in his speech of welcome to a central government military mission, proclaimed like a challenge: 'After the war begins [however], all our troops will go to the front. We will root ourselves in the people as we have always done and mobilize, train, arm and educate them. We will survive and fight. . . . *We* are not afraid of the Chinese people.'[1]

This theme reappeared frequently and forcefully throughout the war. Mao Tse-tung declared on 25 October 1937: 'The principle of unity between the army and the people, which means maintaining a discipline that forbids the slightest violation of the people's interests, conducting propaganda among the masses, organizing and arming them. . . .'[2] The expressions 'mobilization of the army and the people', 'war of the masses', and 'total revolutionary and national war' appear constantly, even in official texts. The Communist Party was to organize the people for its own ends in the name of this mobilization.

As we have seen, the process of organization was at first the work of three large army units – the 115th, 120th and 129th Divisions, which were allotted north-east Shansi, north-west Shansi and south-east Shansi as their

[1] Agnes Smedley, *The Great Road: The Life and Times of Chu Teh*, p. 355.

[2] Mao Tse-tung, *Selected Works*, vol. II, p. 53.

original bases. Within each of these regions, the large units broke down their subordinate units as far as local security would permit. Gaps in the administrative framework were filled and potential opponents eliminated. The new watchwords were spread by meetings and the press, patriotic mass organizations multiplied, 'elections' were held at progressively higher levels, and the administrative structures of a new regime emerged; when the army had completed its task of political organization, the Party took over.[1]

In principle, the communist military organization in North China closely resembled that in Central China several years earlier. The circumstances were different, however – constant pressure from the enemy, the isolated position of the bases, which were hemmed in by different enemy defence networks, rapid increase in numbers, due to political reasons, out of all proportion to the army's resources in the way of arms and ammunition, assimilation of heterogeneous elements which had to be treated with care at least for a time, etc. The organization was therefore less systematic and uniform than before. The use of Chinese terms, which were either inaccurate or untranslatable, or else had a purely local, sometimes temporary value, renders attempts at evaluation and analysis even more difficult. Two large categories of troops existed in any case:

(*a*) Regular troops, used constantly in any region whatsoever.
(*b*) Local troops, which fought in their own native area only, as need arose.

The Eighth Route Army and the New Fourth Army were theoretically formed of regular troops, but their lower echelons, such as divisions and brigades, had little meaning in terms of organization. Division and brigade had become collective expressions to denote all the regular troops in one area; the division was also a unit of reckoning used in dealings with the government when the size of authorized and subsidized communist forces had to be calculated. On the other hand, in view of the fact that all military operations conducted by the regular troops were virtually guerrilla operations, as far as their theoretical or their real structure was concerned they should be considered as independent guerrilla units. Contemporary texts give the ideal composition of companies, battalions, regiments and divisions; a brief summary follows:[2]

Independent Company: Company commander and assistant, company headquarters, political commissar, mobile propaganda unit, three

[1] See next chapter, 'The administration of the liberated areas'.
[2] See Gene Z. Hanrahan, *Chinese Communist Guerrilla Tactics.*

platoons each with three sections (6-12 to a section). Total numbers: 115-128 men (cadres and fighting men).

Independent Battalion: Battalion commander and assistant, political commissar, battalion headquarters, machine gun platoon, reconnaissance platoon, between two and four companies. Total numbers: 343-488 men.

Independent Regiment (*Detachment = Chih-tui*)*:* Regimental commander and chief of staff, political commissar, headquarters, supply group, medical and first aid group, three battalions. Total numbers: between 1262 and 1589 men.

Independent Division (*Column = Tsung-tui*)*:* Divisional commander, staff, services, etc., political commissar and political bureau, company of engineers, company of machine-gunners or artillerymen, three regiments. Total numbers not given (probably minimum 5000 men).

An effort was made to create one regiment for each subregion of two to six 'hsien'. No accurate figures are given for supplies of arms, which were doubtless low (between two and five rifles to each combat group; the rest consisted of a motley collection of rifles or non-firearms). Local troops consisted mainly of militia or 'min-ping' and various other less important auxiliary forces.

The militia, sometimes called 'self-defence corps' (tzu-wei-tui), was the descendant of the red guards of the Kiangsi days. It took in all able-bodied volunteers between 18 and 45 years of age. It was made up of groups (from five to twelve men each), sections with two or three groups, companies of two or more sections, and battalions of at least two companies. The village naturally provided the foundations for the organization. The cadres were theoretically elected and confirmed in office by the military authorities, and maintained their civilian occupations. The militia's chief function was to help the regular troops and the guerrilla units by taking over the responsibility for all duties in the way of transport and supplies, evacuation, security, etc. The whole population could be called upon to help with these tasks, under the militiamen's leadership. As in Kiangsi, the best and youngest members of the militia were grouped in model units, which acted as instantly available reserve units for the regular troops. As arms were so short, the model units were generally the only ones required to take part in fighting.

The auxiliary forces were varied – groups of adolescents, who kept a watch on all strangers in the village or obtained information on the enemy or 'traitors', women who looked after clothing, tended the sick and the wounded and were sometimes willing to fight alongside the men. The weapons were always rudimentary – bad, locally made shotguns, primitive grenades, big traditional sabres, pikes, sickles, etc.; no uniforms were worn.

It is hard to trace the figures for the communist regular and militia troops with any degree of certainty between 1937 and August 1945. Yenan tended to magnify the numbers of its regulars to obtain Chungking's recognition of more divisions and, more important, to obtain more arms. The Yenan authorities consequently claimed the right to have twelve, and later forty-eight, regular divisions. Furthermore, as the differences in fighting methods had virtually disappeared, classification of troops as belonging to the regulars or the militia became purely arbitrary. The wearing of a uniform of some sort, which was often left off, could no longer serve as a criterion. It is even harder to estimate the figures of the militia, as their numbers and true situation varied from day to day with the political and military fluctuations in the so-called 'liberated areas'. The statistics for the intervening years are so uncertain that only those for the years marking the beginning and the end of hostilities will be given.

Communist sources:

1937: 92,000 regular troops, 80,000 belonging to the Eighth Route Army and 12,000 to the New Fourth Army.

1945: 910,000 regulars and 2,200,000 militia (figures quoted in April at the Seventh Party Congress).

Government sources:

1937: 54,000 regular troops belonging to the Eighth Route Army and 10,000 to the New Fourth Army.

1945 (September): 320,000 regulars armed with 160,000 rifles, plus 600 mortars or various pieces of ordnance.

The Party's military successes, like its political successes, were due to the fine quality of its cadres. Its strict discipline ruthlessly eliminated all those whose personality or devotion were found wanting. It also imposed a unified attitude on moral and doctrinal issues, which was essential for leaders called upon to act alone and deal with military, political and administrative problems, all equally important and closely linked up with each other. The Party was also on the watch for any tendency that might remove the army from its control. The change of enemy, the collaboration with the government, the assimilation of young patriots with no political convictions, the switching of loyalties on the part of former central government or provincial cadres, all created new conditions which could affect the former military structure. Mao Tse-tung grew apprehensive in the early months of the war:

> A struggle has been started against the tendency towards new warlordism in the Eighth Route Army. This tendency is manifest in certain individuals who, since the redesignation of the Red Army, have become unwilling to submit strictly to Communist Party leadership, have developed individualistic heroism, take pride in being given appointments by the Kuomintang (i.e. in becoming officials), and so forth.... Both the system of political commissars, which was abolished because of Kuomintang intervention, and the system of political departments, which were renamed 'political training offices' for the same reason, have now been restored.[1]

Mao Tse-tung often referred to this point. The army cannot be other than an army led by the proletariat, with the support of the masses: 'Therefore, the Red Army must oppose the purely military point of view and the roving-rebel ideology, according to which the military does not obey the political, or even commands the political.'[2]

As may be expected, the Party gave its cadres a closely supervised and systematic training, organizing schools and institutes. The first of these was the Anti-Japanese University (K'ang-jih Ta-hsüeh), shortened to K'ang Ta. It eventually had fifteen annexes and trained 10,000 cadres a year. Teaching consisted of politics and warfare, with special emphasis on guerrilla warfare as expounded by Mao Tse-tung or by Russian writers translated by P'eng Teh-huai. Middle cadres were trained in a staff school (K'ang-jih ts'an-mou hsüeh-yuan). The Anti-Japanese War Institute (K'ang-jih chan-cheng Yen-chiu hui) was a sort of staff college, and it was there that Mao Tse-tung expounded his theories of 'protracted war' in May 1938.

On the whole, the amalgamation of the former members of the Kiangsi base, young patriotic elements from the occupied cities, and others from the provinces, went through satisfactorily. Few cadres defected to join the pro-Japanese collaborators or the central government. The regional leaders were almost entirely unchanged; a great sense of solidarity had grown up among them, and their long acquaintance with their particular zones and their problems, and with the men fighting alongside them, prepared them for the final confrontation with the Kuomintang. Considering the country's normal standards and customs, the troops were excellent.

[1] Mao Tse-tung, *Selected Works*, vol. II, p. 66.
[2] Ibid., vol. III, p. 205.

American observers, following events as closely as they could without taking part in them, reported on this.

> The consensus of opinion of United States observers is that the Chinese communist regular army is a young, well-fed, well-clothed, battle-hardened volunteer force in excellent physical condition, with a high level of general intelligence, and very high morale. Training of these troops may be rated as fair for their present capabilities even though it is woefully inadequate judged by American standards. Military intelligence, for their purposes, is good. The most serious lack of the Communist forces is in equipment.[1]

The worth of the communist soldiers was beyond question. This was to a large extent due to the fact that the soldier now occupied an honoured position in society. He was no longer the parasite he had been under the Manchu, nor the mercenary serving the warlords, nor the conscript handed over to the national army by the head of the village. He now not only defended his country, but also safeguarded the people against the return of feudalism; he was the soldier of the revolution, sometimes even taking part in production, and his family was given help and respect. In short, he was accepted by a world that until then had cast him out. The qualities of the race itself supplied the rest, justifying Mao Tse-tung's sally: 'Chiang Kai-shek's soldiers are good, only they need a little political education.' The Communist Party's new units were guided by the Kiangsi tradition; the 'Three Rules and the Eight Points' became their charter.

Military operations by communist troops were extremely fragmented, partly because their political aims led them to spread over as large an area as possible in order to establish contact with the population, and partly because their arms and equipment were infinitely inferior to those of the Japanese. Their guerrilla warfare was even further removed from regular war than were the Kiangsi campaigns; they worked in small units, never larger than a regiment. Mao Tse-tung dealt at length with this type of warfare, trying to rehabilitate it and increase its importance by giving it strategic significance:

> For all these reasons, China's guerrilla warfare against Japan has broken out of the bounds of tactics to knock at the gates of strategy, and it demands examination from the viewpoint of strategy. The point that merits our particular attention is that such extensive as well as protracted guerrilla warfare is quite new in the entire history of war.[2]

[1] Herbert Feis, *The China Tangle*.

[2] Mao Tse-tung, 'Problems of Strategy in Guerrilla War Against Japan', *Selected Works*, vol. II, p. 80.

Even so, in Mao Tse-tung's opinion, guerrilla activities are the first stage only, and must lead to the formation of base areas, and from there, to 'mobile war', conducted by regular troops: 'Since the war is protracted and ruthless, it is possible for the guerrilla units to undergo the necessary steeling and gradually to transform themselves into regular forces, so that their mode of operations is gradually regularized and guerrilla warfare develops into mobile warfare.'[1]

The operations conducted by the Eighth Route Army and the New Fourth Army did not have the chance to move on to this stage or even to the stage Mao Tse-tung called 'guerrilla warfare at a higher level', or, using a rather strange term, 'a regular war in Chinese style'. Not until the last revolutionary civil war did this transformation take place, when it unfolded exactly as intended.

Mao Tse-tung was not the only military writer of his period; several other military leaders also wrote on guerrilla warfare, though from a more practical aspect. Their writings are important, for they were used not only by the Chinese communist troops, but also by other Eastern revolutionary movements:[2] Chu Teh, *On Guerrilla Warfare*; P'eng Teh-huai, *Our Strategy and Tactics*; Liu Po-ch'eng, *How We Beat Back the Enemy's Southward Drive along the Ch'engt'ai Railroad*; Lo Jui-ch'ing, *Political Work in Military Units*; Lin Piao, *Experiences and Lessons*; Hsiao K'e, *On Plain Guerrilla Warfare*. Other less known names are also to be found: Ming Fan, *A Textbook on Guerrilla Warfare*; Ts'ai Ch'ien, *Japanese Army Methods Against Guerrillas*; anon., *Tactical Problems in Guerrilla Warfare*.

Twenty years later, Marshal Lin Piao, when Minister of National Defence, referred once more to the military problems of the Sino-Japanese war in a document of the utmost importance, in both a contemporary and a historical context: 'Long Live the Victorious People's War' (3 September 1965), while Marshal Ho Lung also dealt with the same period in 'The Democratic Tradition in the Chinese People's Liberation Army' (1 August 1965).

Seen from the communist angle, the Sino-Japanese war offered all the usual forms of guerrilla warfare, right through to the end: harassing of communication lines and small outposts, surprise attacks on isolated units, establishment of information and sabotage networks, planting primitive mines, etc. Even action on a general scale, like the so-called 'hundred regiments' attack in the summer of 1940 on enemy communications, was

[1] Mao Tse-tung, *Selected Works*, vol. II, p. 107.

[2] These texts have been translated into English by Gene Hanrahan in his work entitled *Chinese Communist Guerrilla Tactics*.

equally fragmented and it is hard to find any real battles that can be quoted by name after 1937. Comparing their own bravery with the apathy of the government troops, which was no fiction, the communists claimed that they held the strongest enemy contingents in check, amounting at times to 56 per cent of the Japanese units and 55 per cent of the Chinese troops belonging to the governments collaborating with the Japanese. They reckoned losses inflicted on the enemy at 500,000.

The facts do not support this view. The Japanese later gave their losses in actions against guerrillas of all allegiances as 50,000 men at the most. This figure seems low for a war lasting eight years, conducted over an area of vast size. An examination of the Japanese order of battle shows that in November 1944, for example, eight Japanese divisions out of twenty-five, and ten independent brigades out of twenty-two, were in North China, where the communists were not alone. It should be stressed here that the Japanese main striking force gathered in Central China took relatively little interest in the countryside behind the lines. This was not so in North China, where the Japanese intended to stay once the war was over, either in person or by proxy, to exploit its economic resources – cotton, iron and coal – and so consolidated their occupation there as far as possible.

The Chinese communist army was powerless in the face of the Japanese army, which maintained complete freedom of action at a strategic level; it was bolder in its dealings with units belonging to the governments collaborating with the enemy. The loyalty of these troops was uncertain and their fighting spirit weak, so that they were quick to come to an agreement with the communists and avoid fighting them, in response to the slogan 'Chinese do not fight Chinese'. The communists obtained most of their arms from them, and it was they who supplied most of the victims for the impressive casualty lists. Figures for enemy losses for the whole of the war were 960,000 killed and wounded, 280,000 prisoners and 100,000 deserters. The number of Japanese taken prisoner never amounted to more than a few hundred (among whom were a tiny minority of revolutionaries), a fair indication of communists' limited efficacy in the military field.

The army's political work

The Party intended the communist army to be a political as well as a military organization, its political role being the more important of the two:

> Another highly significant and distinctive feature of the Eighth Route Army is its political work, which is guided by three basic principles. First, the principle of unity between officers and men. . . . Second, the principle of unity between the army and the people. . . . Third, the principle of disintegrating the enemy troops and giving lenient treatment to the prisoners of war.[1]

It is true to say that the communist armies, recruited by normal methods, kept in hand both by the officers and their political commissars, drawing inspiration from the twin ideals of the defence of the fatherland and the service of the people, were to prove themselves beyond reproach in their morals and discipline. Here they showed real merit only by comparison with the inadequacies of the government army. Their true importance and originality lie in their role in the expansion of the Party.

> It is most essential to maintain absolutely independent Communist Party leadership in what was originally the Red Army and in all the guerrilla units, and communists must not show any vacillations on this matter of principle.[2]

When written, this text referred to the possibility of the subordination of the communist military forces to the central government. The anxiety expressed remained nonetheless one of the Party's chief preoccupations everywhere, whatever the circumstances, throughout the war. Consequently the army was empowered to introduce the new administrative systems in the liberated areas, followed up by the Party itself, as has already been described. The instrument in this was naturally the army's Political Department, organized in much the same way as it had been in the Kiangsi days.

The Political Department of the Military Committee occupied the highest rank of all. It directed each region's political department, which in turn controlled the political departments of the large units stationed in the area. The two levels given overleaf are the most interesting of all, that of the division and the company, as they were the lowest, and closest to the population.[3]

These five basic divisions were the same at the brigade and regimental levels, the political departments being directed by chairmen and vice-chairmen, which makes it seem likely that a committee existed with

[1] Mao Tse-tung, *Selected Works*, vol. II, p. 53.
[2] Mao Tse-tung, 'Resolution of 5 September 1937', *Selected Works*, vol. II, p. 73.
[3] Lo Jui-ch'ing, *Political Work in Anti-Japanese Forces* (1939), quoted in Gene Z. Hanrahan, *Chinese Communist Guerrilla Tactics*.

members drawn both from the local territorial administrative body and from among the local Party members. At the battalion level political work was in the hands of a Political Instructor or a Political Commissar. They were above all responsible for the execution of decisions on political orientation taken theoretically at the divisional level or above. The exclusion of military responsibilities from their functions seems to be even clearer than it had been in the Kiangsi days, though the commissars had to have undergone suitable military training. Theoretically, political commissars were forbidden to 'keep a watch' on military cadres. In communist China, as in Russia, the war helped to make the commanding officers more emancipated than the political leaders.

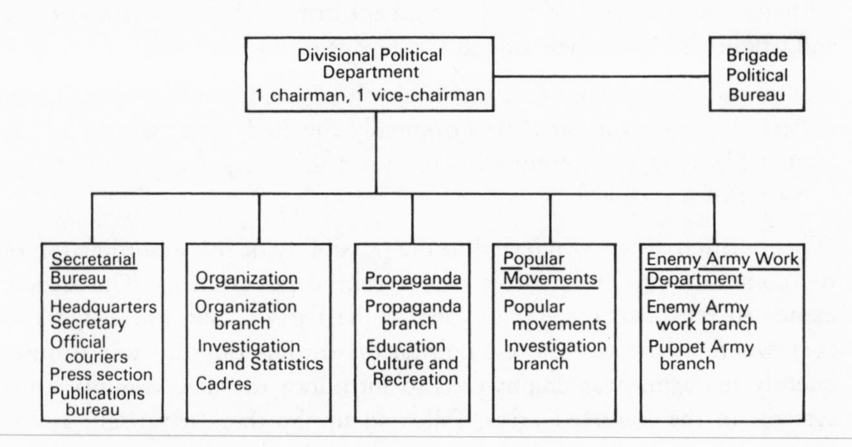

The precision and flexibility of the system was naturally illustrated best of all at the lowest level – that of the company. Five men or groups of men gave their backing to the political commissar's work. Each section had a 'political combatant', a model soldier, picked for qualities as a soldier as well as for his devotion to the Party and his understanding of it. Though he had no real authority, he was invested with his duties at a little introduction ceremony. He led political debates in his section, dealt with propaganda among the local inhabitants, and tried to win over the enemy during military engagements. He was obedient to the regular hierarchy, though he had no special duties, and furnished a concrete example for all to follow – a perfect communist soldier. A small committee ran a sort of soldiers' club in the widest sense of the word, including cultural, educational, sporting, economic and even medical activities. Small groups of qualified and responsible men were in charge of the activities. A correspondence group dealt with the correspondence of the illiterate, and the censorship. A so-called 'people's movement' group was in charge of cooperation with the local inhabitants and particularly propaganda. This group was responsible for good relations between the army and the population, and also for its conversion, or for maintaining it at a satisfactory political atmosphere. Lastly a propaganda group was formed to work among the enemy, responsible for writing slogans, tracts and posters, etc. It aimed its activities mainly at the troops of collaborating regimes, and sometimes at government and provincial troops. This homely propaganda conducted by ordinary people among other ordinary people who were their fellow-countrymen, in the language of their region or even of their profession, could not fail to succeed among the Chinese. It met with no success among the Japanese, however, for the language barrier, the different temperaments and cultures, and the opposition of two peoples separated by their national interests, all doomed it to failure.

In short, the communist army that developed between 1937 and 1945, for whom the battle front was nowhere and everywhere at the same time, was better prepared for a civil war than for war with a foreign enemy, which it had not the material resources to carry on effectively. It managed to turn the population away from the government, organizing it from the roots by means of a widespread, yet flexible system: regular units, guerrilla troops, militia and self-defence corps, gaining the firmest possible support in all fields. It perfected extremely mobile tactics, enabling it to carry out the rapid concentration or dispersion of its troops to compensate for its technical inferiority. Quite apart from ideology, it gave a new soul and a new faith to the troops, and trained cadres of primitive mentality and ability, who were nonetheless energetic, completely unselfish and devoted to their cause.

The government troops were committed to defend several vital communication lines leading to well-defined and important targets (the Yangtze valley, the Kweichow railway), and maintained rigid dispositions, while their growing apathy took further hold on them. Regular warfare did nothing to encourage them to look to the population for support. In spite of a surge of real patriotism, the army had not become the expression of all the nation's purest and most enthusiastic feelings. The communists' superiority arose from their concept of the army's role in society. Their superiority was such that it even took them by surprise. They were expecting the civil war to last ten years; two were enough to bring about the government's military downfall.

25 The Chinese Communist Party and the Administration of the Liberated Areas

The Institutions

The agreement announced at Yenan and in Nanking on 22 and 23 September 1937 planned the dissolution of the North Shensi Soviet Government and the transformation of the communist-controlled territory round Yenan into a 'special border region', an expression usually used in its abbreviated form, 'Pien ch'ü', by Chinese and foreigners alike. The same anxiety to maintain the appearance of national unity and keep up the fiction of an anti-Japanese front was to be found in the structure and the running of the new 'liberated areas', which gradually developed behind the Japanese lines. The 'Pien ch'ü' served on the whole as a model which the liberated areas – a total of nineteen by the end – followed. Owing to variations in the military situation and different political conditions, the political structures were not always identical from one area to another at the same time. This absence of uniformity and logic had numerous precedents, as each region reacted to outside events in its own way, and according to the personalities of its leaders. An omnipresent and highly centralized Communist Party maintained the unity by extending its leadership to every field by means of the new administrative structures.

Although each liberated area was autonomous and no government existed at the head of them all, Yenan's role was that of a real capital. It was the chief town in the Border Region, the area to which all the later ones turned for inspiration. The Central Committee of the Party met and had its offices there; it was the headquarters of all the regular and irregular armed forces and of the political and military training centre for cadres who almost all spent some time there; the Party's supreme heads, Mao Tse-tung and Chu Teh, who had become glorious symbols of the Party and its destiny, were also to be found there. By comparison with the pro-Japanese regimes in Nanking and Peking, and the Chungking regime, and with the help of propaganda from the international communist movement, Yenan was beginning to appear as the capital of a new 'democratic' state. The little square town, surrounded by its old walls, overlooked from afar by its slender pagoda, was a former military stronghold against the barbarians from the steppes, and has often been described by Western journalists and visitors. It was flanked by a meagre river, the Yen Shui, and encircled by bare hills of easily workable yellow earth; it was soon to have a population of 40,000, almost all of whom lived in caves, which sheltered them from Japanese air attacks and from the particularly hard winters.

The 'Pien ch'ü' territory, also known as 'Shen-Kan-Ning' (Shensi-Kansu-Ninghsia), had shifting borders and varying subdivisions. In 1941, for instance, it contained 5 'subregions' (fen ch'ü), 29 districts (hsien), 270 subdistricts (ch'ü) and 1549 'administrative villages' (hsiang). The population amounted to one and half million. The general administrative organization followed the same pattern as that of the Kiangsi period, except for the names. At the head of it was a Border Region Assembly, which elected a permanent administrative body of thirteen people who formed a sort of local government. Lin Po-ch'ü (alias Lin Tsu-han), although a native of Hunan, was its chairman; Chang Kuo-t'ao was vice-chairman until he deserted the Party and fled in 1938. The assemblies and the committees attached to them do not appear to have existed at the level of the five subregions, one of which had only a theoretical existence anyway, as its districts were directly controlled by Yenan. The 'fen ch'ü' was more of a relay post for instructions from the central administrative authority. On the other hand, assemblies met at the levels of the 'hsien', the 'ch'ü' and the 'hsiang', and executive bodies were formed alongside them. According to the electoral law, everyone from the age of 20 upwards had a vote. Unlike the system of the Kiangsi days, all professions and social categories had equal representation. At the lowest level, that of the village (hsiang), one delegate represented 30 inhabitants, in the district (hsien) the proportion was one to 700, so that the assembly had on the average less than 100 members, while the 300 or so delegates at the 'Pien ch'ü' assembly each represented 5000 people.

Theoretically, elections were held every year, but this was not the case in practice. The communist authors themselves report that the first elections at the 'hsiang', 'ch'ü' and 'hsien' levels were held in November 1937, although the order had been given in September. The Border Region Assembly did not meet for the first time until January 1939. In February 1941 general elections had to be held at all levels in accordance with the rule of 'three-thirds', which had been neglected, and in the following November the second regional assembly was able to hold its first session; the second was not held until 1944. The tradition of convening the National Assembly several years late, still apparent today, is of long standing.

The regular administrative structure, like the Party itself, had the support of a large number and variety of mass organizations, whose apparent *raison d'être* was the war effort. They included the Association for National Salvation, the Vanguard of Anti-Japanese Youth, etc. Women, adolescents, children, tradesmen, students and patriots of every kind took part in these movements, which were somewhat at a loss when faced with the Japanese, but had the incalculable advantage of awakening the population to politics and winning it over to the regime. The Anti-Japanese United Front was used to attract the masses at first. The Party made no secret of this and Mao Tse-tung discussed it at length in 'Current Problems of Tactics in the Anti-Japanese United Front' (11 March 1940). The chief aims were to develop the progressive forces (proletariat, peasantry, urban petty bourgeoisie), to win over the intermediary forces of the middle bourgeoisie and the 'regional power groups', and to isolate the reactionary 'die-hards'.

To start with at least, great care was taken when setting up administrative structures like those in the Border Region behind the Japanese lines. They were described as representing the Anti-Japanese National United Front political power, but it was a power already hostile to reactionaries, who, under cover of equality in electoral procedures, took over the right of being the sole representative of the great majority of the people. Mao Tse-tung is enlightening on this point:

> It is the political power of all who support both resistance and democracy, i.e. the joint democratic dictatorship of several revolutionary classes over traitors and reactionaries. . . . Places in the organs of political power should be allocated as follows: one third to the communists, representing the proletariat and the poor peasantry; one third to the left progressives, representing the petty bourgeoisie; and the remaining one third to the middle and other elements, representing the middle bourgeoisie and the enlightened gentry. Traitors and anti-communist elements are the only people disqualified from participation in these organs of political power.[1]

[1] Mao Tse-tung, 'Current Problems of Tactics in the Anti-Japanese United Front', *Selected Works*, vol. II, p. 427.

These last words excluded in advance all possibilities of opposition to the Party or of real democracy. Appearances were kept up for a long time, however, to help propaganda in the white zones and for the benefit of foreign opinion. The army appointed officials, or confirmed those already in office, until elections could be held; the central government was asked to sanction the new administrative structures. The Party was careful to leave leading posts as far as possible to accommodating allies.

Economic policy and agrarian measures

To maintain the united front and save the mediocre, fragile economy from total ruin, the communists observed a fairly liberal economic policy in the areas under their control. This was particularly obvious in their agrarian measures. As early as the summer of 1937 confiscation and redistribution of land stopped, except in the case of absent pro-Japanese collaborators. All efforts were directed towards measures to reduce land rent. The Central Committee's decision of 28 January 1942 was a reminder and a summary of what was to be the Party's agrarian policy for nearly ten years, between 1937 and 1947. It defined the principles involved and stated how they were to be applied:

Principles:

The Party recognizes that the peasants constitute the basic strength in the anti-Japanese war and the battle of production. They must be helped and their living conditions improved.

Most landlords are anti-Japanese and some are even in favour of democratic reform. They must be allowed to keep their political rights and their interests must be protected.

The capitalist mode of production is a relatively progressive mode of production in present-day China. The rich peasants are the capitalists of the rural areas and are an indispensable force; their work must be encouraged.

Legislation must provide for the reduction of land rent and stipulate that rent be paid. The landlord must keep his right to dispose of his land in accordance with existing legal provisions.

The Peasant Association for National Salvation must help the government and not go against its decisions.

Rules for Application:

As far as possible, land rent should be reduced by 25 per cent of the pre-war rate.

Rents are to be collected after the harvest; payment may be postponed or reduced in times of natural or man-made disaster.

Rent in arrears for many years is to be exempted from payment.

The land tax is to be paid by the owner of the land.

Local customs or existing contracts must be respected concerning the tenant's rights when the land changes hands.

The rate of interest is fixed at 1·5 per cent per month; total interest may not exceed the capital.

Land belonging to absent landowners or to those forced to become traitors will be temporarily managed by the government, if there is no one to look after it.

Land belonging to a religious group will not be confiscated.

The resolution of 28 January 1942 was certainly not fully applied everywhere. In many places, the administrative authorities were inexperienced, or their position was precarious, particularly near zones held by the Japanese army, and the influence of the landowners was still considerable. At the same time, in other places, old cadres were probably inclined to fall back on the old radical practices of Kiangsi, which had now become leftist deviations. It should also be borne in mind that communication difficulties created by the Japanese networks weakened the orders from Yenan, with the result that local leaders gained a fair degree of freedom.

The Party leaders were torn between two somewhat contradictory desires – heightening revolutionary awareness in the rural areas and increasing production. Reductions in land rent ought not to arise solely from administrative decisions or friendly arrangements on a local scale, but from real class struggle. 'To bestow rent reduction as a favour instead of arousing the masses to achieve it by their own action is wrong, and the results will not be solid. Peasant organizations should be formed or reconstituted in the struggle for rent reduction.'[1]

Collective work was encouraged for the same reasons – mutual aid groups, cooperatives, etc. But Mao Tse-tung's numerous and urgent appeals seem to indicate that agricultural production won the day over ideological targets. The mobilization of every source of manpower, and the encouraging of the civilian and military cadres to take part in individual production, became a general custom; Mao Tse-tung and Chu Teh themselves were not exempted from it. The well-known image of the two great

[1] Mao Tse-tung, 'Spread the Campaigns to Reduce Rent, Increase Production and "Support the Government and Cherish the People" in the Base Areas', *Selected Works*, vol. III, p. 131. See also 'Get Organized', ibid., p. 153.

communist leaders tending their turnips and cabbages may have recalled the old imperial ploughing ceremonies, but none would have dared overlook its value as an example. If the official history is to be believed, the agrarian measures and the periodic mass movements to encourage production together raised the area under cultivation in the 'Pien ch'ü' alone from 8,431,006 to 15,205,553 'mou', roughly equivalent to 56,000 and 100,000 hectares respectively, between 1936 and 1945.

Trade policy was equally liberal. The economies of the liberated areas, almost totally lacking in industry, could not get by without a system of exchanges with the outside world, either with government zones, or with occupied zones. These trade exchanges were vital for the population and for the army. Commercial taxes were reduced or even abolished, and the risks run by merchants operating through the government blockade, which was strict at times, were compensated. The number of shops in Yenan rose from 123 to 473 between 1937 and 1943; trade cooperatives also appeared. The Yenan regime made a great effort to help production by artisans – cotton fabrics, paper, matches, salt, etc. 'Induscos', or industrial cooperatives on the same lines as similar institutions in government zones, were created, under the leadership of Rewi Alley, originally financed by the administrative authority and managed by staff from it; they were scattered to avoid bombing raids and draw closer to the sources of raw materials used. In 1945, 882 Induscos with 265,000 members were working in the 'Pien ch'ü' alone. The army was encouraged to produce its own food as far as possible, as well as its consumer goods; it seems to have managed to do so, more or less.

Even so the economy of the red zones remained primitive and precarious, split into regional divisions, each of which minted its own money, but on the whole this state of chaos was prevalent before the war, and could even be described as the normal state of affairs for most regions of modern China. The relatively healthy situation in the Border Region, out of reach of Japanese destruction and requisitions, was not shared by the much larger, more thickly populated liberated areas which went through years of horrifying misery, particularly between 1941 and 1943.

Education and information

As in Kiangsi, the communists, in their eagerness to take control of the youth and obtain cadres, gave their full attention to education. Mao Tse-tung's old teacher, Hsü T'e-li, was put in charge of it – he was already over 80 and had been to France as a student after the First World War. The task was made easier for him by the arrival of a number of teachers and students in the red zone. Higher education was given at five universities, schools or institutes all in existence by 1941.

1 The Anti-Japanese Military and Political University (shortened to K'ang Ta), already mentioned in connection with army cadres. It was founded in Wayaopao in June 1936, and transferred to Yenan at the beginning of 1937; its courses lasted between six and eight months. Lin Piao was the dean, and the deputy dean was Lo Jui-ch'ing, a dour native of Szechuan who became Chief of General Staff in 1959, and who was more interested in political activities than in military affairs. The University turned out cadres for the administrative authorities and the army; the second generation of communist leaders all went there. After 1945 K'ang Ta became the Political and Military Institute of the People's Liberation Army.[1]
2 The North Shensi School produced cadres who specialized in technology.
3 The Lu Hsün Academy of Literature and Arts. As well as writers and artists, the Academy turned out propagandists for the troupes of travelling players and other artists and its importance in the political field outweighed its cultural importance.
4 The Health School.
5 The Marx-Lenin Institute.

Other institutions were founded later on, as the need for them arose: the Political and Military Institute, the Institute of Administration, the Natural Science Institute, the Institute of Nationalities (an early version of the present institute in Peking), the University for Girls, and the Mao Tse-tung School for young cadres. The last two institutions combined with the North Shensi School in 1941 to become the University of Yenan. A Japanese Workers' and Peasants' School was created to train Japanese prisoners and deserters for propaganda work among their compatriots.

Above all, elementary and secondary education progressed in the 'Pien ch'ü'. It was still inadequate, however, for official sources give 1341 schools and 43,625 pupils for a million and a half inhabitants in 1940.[2] Classes for adults were organized during the winter. The army did much to eliminate illiteracy, both among the population and within its own ranks.

[1] Life in the Anti-Japanese University has been described in detail by a former pupil who has now left the Party, Ma Fu-yao, in *I and the Communist Party* (Hong Kong, 1953), which has not been translated.

[2] According to Edgar Snow, who visited the area roughly at this time, the number of primary schools rose from 120 to 773, not counting a further 77 model primary schools and 16 middle schools, between 1937 and 1939. Cf. *The Battle for Asia.*

As was to be expected, the communist interest in propaganda led to the creation of a press to back up the other activities, which was circulated as far and as widely as possible, in spite of material difficulties and the difficult and somewhat unappetizing contents. The chief communist paper at the time was the *New China Daily* (*Hsin-hua jih-pao*), which became the *Liberation Daily* (*Chieh-fang jih-pao*) after 16 May 1941. Other, more specialized publications existed alongside these two – *The Communist*, founded in 1939 to be the Party's organ, *Liberation* (*Chieh-fang*), *The Eighth Route Army Political and Military* Review (*Pa lu-chün chün cheng tsa-chih*), *Unity* (*T'uan-chieh*), *Chinese Culture* (*Chung-kuo wen-hua*), *The Cry of the Fatherland* (*Tsu-kuo hu-sheng*), *The Chinese Worker* (*Chung-kuo kung-jen*), *Chinese Youth* (*Chung-kuo ch'ing-nien*), *The Chinese Woman* (*Chung-kuo fu-nü*).[1] Two publications were allowed to circulate in government territory (at least in a few large towns) – the *New China Daily* and a periodical, *The Masses* (*Ch'ün-chung*). The communist press, after an almost total disappearance lasting several years, helped the Party to renew contact with large areas of the country. It also was used to keep cadres and other officials informed of the leaders' chief lines and decisions; this was probably its most important role.

After the press and meetings, the theatre was the other main vehicle for communist propaganda. In an illiterate country where radio sets were rare and the cinema barely existed, the theatre had the great merit of being universally understood and having its place in customs common to everyone, even to the humblest of villages. The Party made wide use of the theatre, either putting on the classical plays best suited to the circumstances, or producing new modern ones, though no real masterpieces appeared.[2] Mao Tse-tung's two declarations on the problems arising from Literature and Art (2 and 23 May 1942) gave renewed impetus to cultural activities, including the theatre, encouraging those responsible to direct their efforts still further towards the service of the masses and of propaganda (see Chapter 27). The nation's resistance to the Japanese could be said to have been conducted in the name of a cultural heritage adapted by the communists. This argument could not fail to arouse a population that had always considered cultural expansion as the highest form of nationalism.

[1] There was even a newspaper in the Latin alphabet: *Shin Dzung Hwa Bao*. Cf. James Bertram, *North China Front* (London, Macmillan, 1939).

[2] Robert Payne describes Mao Tse-tung's astonishing reactions to a classical opera in a passage valuable both as a historical and a psychological document. Cf. *Mao tse-Tung, Ruler of Red China*.

26 Relations between the Central Government and the Chinese Communist Party during the Sino-Japanese war Early American Arbitration

The united front policy, prepared in 1936, confirmed in 1937 and put into practice by the declarations of 22 and 23 September that year, was to be maintained, theoretically at least, throughout the whole of the war of resistance against Japan. But although the worst – renewal of widespread civil war – was avoided, there was constant friction and armed engagements were frequent; some of them involved large numbers of men and heavy losses on either side. As tension alternately rose and fell, it rapidly became obvious that the Communist Party's territorial expansion and military development would sooner or later make open conflict inevitable. From 1944 onwards, American official representatives, fully conscious of the danger, did their best to prevent it and managed to delay it until the spring of 1946.

Several variable factors influenced the behaviour of the two opponents between 1937 and 1945 – the changing military situation within China itself, possibilities of a peaceful compromise, the international situation in Europe and particularly in the Pacific, after the summer of 1941, and, naturally, the expansion of the communists' military forces in North and Central China. These factors, and other less important ones, sometimes working together and sometimes in opposite directions, were to shape the evolution of events, which can be divided into four main periods:

1 Satisfactory collaboration in 1937 and 1938.
2 From the spring of 1939 to the spring of 1941: a crisis, which steadily

worsened, culminating in the New Fourth Army incident in January 1941.

3 An easing of tension from the summer of 1941 until the autumn of 1944.

4 Renewed tension beginning with the autumn of 1944.

The government's relations with the Communist Party were composed of a mixture of anxiety, mistrust (which was largely justified), more or less unavoidable blunders and, lastly, powerlessness. The government watched its rival's steady military and territorial expansion far outreach the three divisions of the Eighth Army and the eighteen districts in the 'Pien ch'ü' laid down by the agreement of September 1937. Overflowing first Shensi and then Shansi, the Eighth Route Army bases spread to the plains of Hopei, then beyond them to the Shantung mountains, and the Huai and Yangtze valleys, until they reached those of the New Fourth Army; the latter were dangerously near Nanking and Shanghai, while the northern bases were within striking distance of Peking, Tientsin and Tsingtao. The population under communist control was to increase almost a hundredfold in eight years.

However, except for beginning a new civil war in presence of the enemy, or reversing the political situation, as Wang Ching-wei tried to do by entering into an agreement with Japan against the communists, the Kuomintang could do little to prevent its rival's development. It denounced the disobedience of the communists in the name of national unity, of the authority of the state, and of the non-partisan allegiance of the army, but in vain. To this, the insolent communist reply was that their disobedience was admirable, in that it preserved whole regions from Japanese occupation, and from administration by their Chinese collaborators. They in turn denounced the partisan spirit rife in the government and the army, both controlled by the most reactionary section of the Kuomintang. The communists also said that the government did not dare mobilize the population as a whole, 'arouse the masses', as Sun Yat-sen had wished them to. They added that Chungking refused to modify and enlarge existing political structures and draw up a 'common programme' which would have enabled them to put up a better resistance to the Japanese and improve general living conditions.

In the face of these challenges, the government could do no more than take limited measures, which engendered unpopularity, if not hatred, and harmed its position abroad: economic blockade of the communist regions, reduction of freedom for the press, cutting off of financial help for the troops of the Eighth Route Army and the New Fourth Army. In so doing, it seemed to be opposing part of the nation's war effort, and intent on continuing the dictatorship in its own name, a principle condemned by all the allied nations. The communists maintained a firm line over their rights, but manœuvred with great flexibility, so that they managed to avoid a true break in relations, at the same time taking full advantage of local situations and basing their propaganda on patriotism and democracy, the two most telling themes of the moment.

They tried to prove that the true spirit of resistance was now to be found in Yenan alone, and pretended that the united front was about to collapse under the influence of an 'ultra-reactionary and capitulationist clique' of pro-Japanese persuasion. Extremely violent writings were produced throughout the whole of the war, though only a few titles can be mentioned here. In 1937 'In the Country as a Whole, Oppose National Capitulationism' attacked the big landowners and the big bourgeoisie supposed to embody defeatism. 'Oppose Capitulationist Activity', written in 1939 (30 June), accused Chiang Kai-shek of hiding behind 'Wang Ching-weis, both overt and covert'. In January 1940 'Overcome the Danger of Capitulation and Strive for a Turn for the Better' made further attacks on the capitulationist spirit in the landowners and the big bourgeoisie, who in this opposed the determination expressed by the proletariat and the peasantry. 'Expose the Plot for a Far Eastern Munich' (25 May 1941) directed identical reproaches at the Japanese, the Americans and Chiang Kai-shek, who were supposed to be preparing a peaceful compromise to bring about the downfall of communism and the Soviet Union; Russia's agreement with Germany in the pact between the Soviet Union and Germany had nevertheless received abundant approval.[1] By skilful calculation, defeatism, lack of patriotism and anti-communism were assimilated together to share in the same disgrace.

Although the Communist Party would never have tolerated any hostile propaganda at Yenan, it set itself up as the nation's defender of all civic and political rights, continuing the work of Sun Yat-sen and supporting a democratic and centralized republic.[2] This won it the support of a large proportion of liberals educated in the West or with leanings in that direction, as yet not fully aware of communist methods and ultimate

[1] 'Interview with a *New China Daily* correspondent on the New International Situation' (1 September 1939).

[2] See 'Interview with the British Journalist James Bertram' (25 October 1937), 'On New Democracy' (January 1940) and, naturally, 'On Coalition Government' (24 April 1945).

aims, but who had met with intolerance from the Kuomintang. As they despaired of gaining the support of popular opinion, these liberals eventually threw in their lot with the communists, either rallying to them directly, or joining small parties forming the convenient, safe and purely fictitious united democratic front.

Relations between the government and the communists in 1937 and 1938

From the beginning of the war until the end of the period of large-scale operations – that is, until the fall of Hankow and Canton in October 1938 – everything behind the relations between the government and the Communist Party pointed towards collaboration. Neither party could take upon itself the responsibility of a break while the Japanese columns were advancing on the Yellow River and the Yangtze valley. The government probably took some time to realize how much the communists would gain from their expansion behind Japanese lines. Three influential rivals had a stake in North China – the hitherto autonomous provincial governors, the Japanese and their collaborators' regimes, and the Communist Party. The central government represented a fourth; it seemed reasonable to hope that the first three would neutralize each other, leaving a situation which the government could put to good use when the time came. In any case, its position was strongest in Central China.

At an international level, the Soviet Union had to be treated with tact, for Nanking had signed a pact of non-aggression with Moscow on 21 August 1937; Stalin had hinted to the Chinese Chargé d'Affaires in November 1937 during the Brussels Nine Power Conference that the Soviet Union might supply military aid against Japan.[1] The Changkufeng incident in July 1938 and the Nomohan incident lasting from May to August 1939 had been small-scale wars and showed that relations between Japan and the Soviet Union had deteriorated. Finally, a point to remember, Russian advisers and materials had been sent to lend support to Chinese efforts in the earliest months of the war.

The halting of the civil war and the renewal of collaboration with the Kuomintang were important as far as the communists were concerned. Their next task was to renew contact with public opinion as a whole, and to continue the Party's seizure of the available, or partially available, territory in North and Central China, in the name of common resistance to the enemy. The leaders in Yenan were perfectly aware that the supporters

[1] See Chiang Kai-shek, *Soviet Russia in China.*

of an honourable peace with Japan still carried weight in the government; the negotiations following on the fall of Nanking had achieved nothing, but should negotiations follow the fall of Hankow, they might be more successful, at considerable cost to the communists.

Both sides were therefore prudent and tolerant; efforts were made to continue the fiction created by the September agreement and the government even promised to make a new study of the basic proposals. The communists were invited to take part in the People's Political Council convened in July 1938 instead of the National Assembly, which could not now meet in the circumstances. At the first sitting, on 6 July, the Council adopted a Programme of National Resistance and Restoration, the terms of which were often recalled later on by the two parties who had accepted them.[1] Meanwhile, Chou En-lai was invited to attend the Kuomintang National Executive Congress, as in the good old days in Canton (March-April 1938). He was even appointed Deputy Minister of Political Training in the army, maintaining the post until 1940, though its attributions were entirely honorific.

In 1937 the government rashly gave its authorization for the New Fourth Army's operations in the Yangtze valley; in January 1938 it sanctioned the creation of the Shansi-Hopei-Chahar administrative structure. The communists had permanent representatives at Hankow and later at Chungking, led by Chou En-lai and Tung Pi-wu, with the help of distinguished collaborators – Wang Ping-nan, Kung P'eng (Madame Ch'iao Kuan-hua), etc. Communist liaison offices (local delegations from the Eighth Route Army) were set up in several large towns, where they organized or at least facilitated the emigration of volunteers to Yenan. The communist press reappeared in the government zone; the *Hsin-hua jih-pao* was directed by talented journalists, nearly all of whom had had a sound foreign training, such as two present deputy Ministers of Foreign Affairs, Chang Han-fu and his brother-in-law Ch'iao Kuan-hua.

Just before the fall of Hankow, a first, minor incident occurred there; the government dissolved a mass organization suspected of having strong communist sympathies. In the following month the Kuomintang rebuffed communist overtures towards forming a new inner block like the one that had existed from 1923 to 1927. If the Generalissimo himself is to be believed, it was no less than a proposal to institute simultaneous member-

[1] The Political Council had 200 members chosen by the government from lists compiled for it, and included delegates from 'small parties' and some independent members. It was a purely consultative assembly, but it furnished the communists with a useful platform for their propaganda.

ship of both parties once more.[1] The possibility of success was so remote that the communist move seems to have had no other aim than that of propaganda. Even so, it shows how anxious the Party (which had just held the Sixth Plenum of its Central Committee) was to maintain the united front.

First signs of tension (1939-1940)

The relative stability of the Chinese front lines, the communist military expansion behind them, and the evolution of the climate in international affairs in the summer of 1939, began to have an adverse effect on relations between Chungking and Yenan. The government was beginning to have a clearer idea of communist progress in the field, while the halt in the Japanese advance enabled it to devote more attention to the subject. Its former good relations with the Soviet Union also began to deteriorate. Russian supplies of war materials diminished and were soon to stop altogether, while it became apparent that the Americans could possibly replace the Russians in 1940. The pact of non-aggression signed by Germany and the Soviet Union on 23 August 1940, which was highly praised by the Chinese communists in their indignation against the 'intrigues' and 'duplicity' of the 'international reactionary bourgeoisie', brought Chungking closer to its Western allies.[2]

The communists had by then consolidated their position in North China and had little to fear from armed intervention from the Kuomintang. The Russians were now less committed to help China and already engaged in preparations for the *rapprochement* with Japan which was to result in the Russo-Japanese pact of neutrality signed on 13 April; this gave them more liberty to reduce their war effort and concentrate on their own political aims.

From December 1938 onwards armed engagements between communist troops and non-communist troops more or less in the service of the government became more and more frequent. They also increased in scope and spread gradually eastwards and southwards from Shansi. The methods of the communists were always identical: local troubles were used

[1] Chiang Kai-shek, *Soviet Russia in China*.

[2] For Chinese communist reactions to the signature of the pact between Germany and Russia, see Mao Tse-tung, 'Interview with a *New China Daily* Correspondent on the New International Situation' (1 September 1939), and 'The Identity of Interests between the Soviet Union and all Mankind' (28 September 1939), in *Selected Works*. The tone is insulting both for French and British statesmen. On the other hand, the Communist Party remained silent when the neutrality pact between Russia and Japan was signed.

or instigated, small autonomous bands either of patriots or traditional-style bandits were liquidated or else won over, government elements accused of collaboration with the Japanese or banditry were encircled and disarmed, and new people's administrative structures were set up. These engagements sometimes involved several thousand men, and fighting often lasted for several days: losses were heavy, and were often accompanied by brutality and traditional forms of torture, of which burying alive seems to have been one of the most often used. A few foreign witnesses have left horrifying descriptions of what they saw. The list of incidents, starting with the disarming of the nationalist 7th Regiment at Poyeh, south of Paotingfu in Hopei in December 1938, up till the final elimination of the Kuomintang from the same province in February 1940, is both long and confused.[1]

On 10 June 1939 the Generalissimo presented a warning to Chou En-lai, the communist representative at Chungking, and addressed another to Yeh Chien-ying, Chief of Staff of the Eighth Route Army in Yenan; counter-measures were already under way, however. On 12 June the New Fourth Army's office and rear depots at P'ingchiang in Hunan were disbanded and a number of communists arrested and some executed. The incident was exploited to the full at Yenan; Mao Tse-tung made a speech on the necessity for unity, condemning the Kuomintang Central Committee's recent decisions with regard to other parties.[2] The government had also ordered a purge in the administrative structures and the army, where elements sympathizing with the communists and opponents of various tendencies had made their appearance. A special security organization, the 'Pao-mi ch'u', was created for the purpose. The communists naturally replied by reinforcing their clandestine organization. At the same time, the communists' liaison offices were prevented from working normally. Lastly, the government seized the five districts of Shen-Kan-Ning (Ch'unhua, Hsünyi, Chengning, Ninghsien and Chenyuan) and set a closer watch on the Border Region. The object was to prevent small communist detachments from infiltrating the government zone where they could freely carry on their propaganda, to keep up the economic pressure, and possibly to force the communists to immobilize some of their regular troops by keeping them in position opposite nationalist troops under General Hu Tsung-nan, and consequently far away from zones where they could continue their expansion. The Americans found this waste of good

[1] See Lin Yü-t'ang, *The Vigil of a Nation*, and the official report (in Chinese) on the eight years' war of resistance by General Ho Ying-ch'in.
[2] Mao Tse-tung, 'The Reactionaries Must be Punished' (1 August 1939).

troops on either side excruciatingly irritating. The result was that in 1944, when the Chinese had nothing to send into action against the Japanese advancing on their air bases in the south-west except mediocre units whose morale had collapsed, 150,000 fully equipped nationalist troops and 50,000 communists stayed in Shensi with arms at the ready. Urgent representations were needed before some of the former were transferred by plane.

In spite of all this, the nationalist blockade, and the concentration camps at Lanchow and Sian in the North, and at Kanchow and Shangjao in the South, could not prevent individuals or small groups of volunteers from reaching Yenan; this weeding-out process was perhaps preferred by the Kuomintang in the long run.

A few attempts at modifying the 1937 agreement were made through the communists' representation in Chungking. In July 1940 (apparently on 11 July) the government put forward the following proposals:

1 The Eighteenth Army Group (in fact the Eighth Route Army) should be increased to three armies, each with two divisions, with a further three, and later five, independent regiments. The New Fourth Army should be split into two divisions.
2 The communist troops in Hopei, Chahar and Shantung should move north of the Yellow River, and the New Fourth Army should do likewise. They were to acknowledge the authority of General Yen Hsi-shan, commander of the Second War Area, and Chu Teh was to become his deputy commander.

These suggestions were handed on to Yenan on 16 July; they were not followed up, but formed some sort of basis for later discussions, and some of them were agreed upon, theoretically at least.

The New Fourth Army incident in south Anhwei (January 1941)

The most serious military engagement between the government and the communists occurred at the beginning of 1941: units belonging to the New Fourth Army, then in south Anhwei near the south bank of the Yangtze, were attacked and disarmed. As is to be expected, versions of the incident and of preceding events vary considerably, depending on the source.

The government held that the incident arose from the failure of the communists to act upon their word. Instead of giving orders for the New Fourth Army to cross the Yangtze and then the Yellow River once more, as they had agreed to do in July, the communists wanted to consolidate their occupation of part of Kiangsu north of the Yangtze, and attacked several important centres held by nationalist troops, particularly Jukao and T'aihsing on the Grand Canal. The nationalist provincial governor Han Teh-ch'in had to retreat eastwards to Tungt'ai, where he found it impossible to maintain his position. In view of the development of the situation, the government Chief of Staff, General Ho Ying-ch'in, ordered the New Fourth Army to cross the Yangtze (19 October). The Generalissimo renewed this order on 9 December, at Yenan, to General Yeh T'ing; it was stated that all communist troops were to have crossed the Yangtze by 31 December 1940, and the new course of the Yellow River by 31 January 1941. According to the official version, elements of the New Fourth Army in the area of Sanch'i, south of Wuhu, made a sudden attack on the government's 40th Division, which was on the move in the same area. General Ku Chu-t'ung, Commander of the Third War Area, retaliated vigorously by encircling and attacking the communist troops (6-11 January). Ten thousand men were disarmed, and the New Fourth Army's commander, General Yeh T'ing, was taken prisoner and was tried shortly afterwards. The deputy commander, Hsiang Ying, an old militant trade unionist, was killed. A government order was passed, disbanding the New Fourth Army on 17 January.

The communists claimed that the north Kiangsu government troops and the governor, Han Teh-ch'in, had opened hostilities in the region as a whole, in order to dislodge the New Fourth Army. Aided by units from south of the Yangtze, commanded by Ch'en Yi, the New Fourth Army fought off the government attacks. Meanwhile, the staff from the Army's headquarters, together with nearly 9000 men, had gathered near Chinghsien and Maolin and were preparing to cross the Yangtze as planned. At that point they were attacked by troops ten times superior to them in number, and lost 1000 men.[1]

It is easy to understand why the government, worried to see its troops in north Kiangsu shrinking under the repeated attacks from New Fourth Army units, which had already crossed the Yangtze with Ch'en Yi, seized on the pretext offered by the communists' delays to destroy all that was still left south of the river. Its own superiority and the fact that the Japanese were not active in this region should have made it an easy task. Seen in this light, the New Fourth Army incident had only local significance, as a gesture of reprisal and a measure intended to ease the position of the government troops in north Kiangsu, where they were hard pressed by the communists and the Japanese.

The communists, without any doubt, justified Chungking's brutal

[1] Two declarations made by the Party in January 1941, to be found in the *Selected Works* of Mao Tse-tung, supply further details on the facts themselves.

retaliation by their actions and their cynicism; they admitted as much in a directive published by the Central Committee on 4 May 1940, addressed to Hsiang Ying as Secretary of the Communist Party Bureau in the South-East – Hsiang Ying was reproached for his moderation and given a new line to follow:

> The Central Committee has pointed out this policy of expansion to you time and again. To expand means to reach out into all enemy-occupied areas and not to be bound by the Kuomintang's restrictions but to go beyond the limits allowed by the Kuomintang, not to expect official appointments from them or depend on the higher-ups for financial support, but instead to expand the armed forces freely and independently, set up base areas unhesitatingly, independently arouse the masses in those areas to action and build up united front organs of political power under the leadership of the Communist Party. In Kiangsu province, for example, despite the verbal attacks and the restrictions and oppression by anti-communist elements such as Ku Chu-tung, Leng Hsin and Han Teh-chin, we should gain control of as many districts as possible, from Nanking in the west to the sea coast in the east, and from Hangchow in the south to Hsuchow in the north, and do so as fast as possible and yet steadily and systematically.[1]

The Communist Party still made a violent denunciation of the disarming of the New Fourth Army, describing it as the first phase in a plot perpetrated by the 'pro-Japanese clique', which intended to repeat the same operation on the Eighth Route Army, conclude a peace treaty with Japan, and then lead China into the tripartite pact. It also made a point of honour, as has already been described, of re-forming the New Fourth Army and keeping the same name, in defiance of the decisions of the Military Affairs Commission. The Party was not indifferent, however, to the halt inflicted by the government and showed genuine anxiety at the determined speech given by the Generalissimo at the People's Political Council session on 6 March 1941. In plain, magnanimous terms, Chiang Kai-shek stressed the basic need to maintain the state's political and military authority in the face of the enemy, and gave a lofty denunciation of the presumptuous nature of some of the communists' demands. Although the government's cause was unassailable as far as principles were concerned, events showed it to be less secure in practice; the fact that some criticisms were justified made it all too easy to excuse Yenan's indiscipline and duplicity.

The serious nature of the crisis itself, and Germany's invasion of Russia

[1] Mao Tse-tung, *Selected Works*, vol. II, p. 431.

which threatened the existence of the Soviet Union and the future of communism in the world as a whole, prevented the worst from happening. Regular contacts were maintained at Yenan, where there was a permanent representative of the Military Affairs Committee and at Sian, where Lin Piao was sent in October with a conciliatory message from Mao Tse-tung to Chiang Kai-shek, whose pupil Lin Piao had been at the Whampoa (Huangp'u) Military Academy, and lastly at Chungking.

On 28 March 1942, Chou En-lai and Lin Piao presented a number of demands in their Party's name:

1 Legal status for the Chinese Communist Party over the whole national territory, where it was tolerated only to a limited extent.
2 Reorganization of the administrative structures in the liberated areas; their existence to be given official recognition.
3 Increase in the numbers allotted to the Eighth Route Army, which would then be enlarged from three to twelve divisions, organized in four armies.
4 Authorization for the communist units south of the Yellow River, i.e. the re-formed New Fourth Army, to remain there until the end of the war.

The demands were not accepted. They were taken up once more the following year. Lin Piao went to Chungking to discuss them in November 1943. In May 1944 the dialogue was enlarged. General Chang Chih-chung and Mr Wang Shih-chieh on the government side met Mr Lin Tsu-han from the communist side, in Sian, for discussions lasting from 4 to 11 May at which a list of twenty points, including military, administrative and political questions, was examined. On 27 May the negotiators went to Chungking, where conversations continued from June to September. Two reports were subsequently produced, one by the government and one by the communists, and presented to the People's Political Council at its meeting on 15 September 1944.[1]

The government proposals (memorandum of 5 June 1944) were an attempt to place the communist administrative structure and army directly under government control once more, while the Eighth Route Army was enlarged to ten divisions, the 'Pien ch'ü' boundaries were revised, and the liberated areas placed under the authority of the provincial governors. Questions pertaining to politics and organization were shelved until they could be discussed by a national assembly, to be elected at the end of the war. In the meantime, the Programme of Armed Resistance and National

[1] The English text is to be found in the *China Handbook* (1937-1945), pp. 81-90.

Reconstruction remained the charter of the government and the political parties. The lifting of the military and commercial blockade of the communist regions depended on whether or not the government's proposals were accepted. On the same day, the communist delegate to the Political Council put forward a demand in ten points; their tenor shows how much more exacting Yenan's requirements had become, now that the development of the war in Europe and the Pacific was becoming more satisfactory:

1 Civil and political liberty for all citizens throughout the whole Chinese territory. Creation of elected local administrative bodies. Liberation of political prisoners.
2 Organization of the communist troops in sixteen armies, or forty-seven divisions with 10,000 men in each; five armies and sixteen divisions to be created straight away. The *status quo* to be observed regarding the stationing of troops. Communist troops to be supplied with arms, materials and food by the government.
3 Lifting of the economic blockade on the 'Pien ch'ü'.
4 Legal acknowledgement of the administrative structures in the liberated areas, etc.

As these proposals emphasized the need to introduce democracy into the administrative structure and to enlarge individual rights, they aroused the sympathy of foreign representatives and observers, who as a rule knew more about the lack of truly democratic institutions in the government zone than in the communist zone.

The Americans reacted most violently of all, for they were particularly involved in the Chinese war and therefore more sensitive to the action of a press showing no indulgence for their ally. In the autumn of 1944 the communists carried off a great success with the arrival of official U.S. representatives to take part in discussions; their relations with the central government moved virtually on to the international scene and a new phase opened which was to win considerable advantage for Yenan.

In June 1944 Henry A. Wallace, Vice-President of the United States, visited China; he made known to Generalissimo Chiang Kai-shek Washington's eagerness to see his difficulties with the communists settled, and spoke of the possibility of American mediation to settle them. Although he was reticent at first, Chiang Kai-shek agreed to consider the possibility and authorized a small American military mission to be sent to Yenan.[1]

[1] This mission was originally composed of Colonel David D. Barrett, two young diplomats, John Service and Raymond P. Ludden. Later on, Colonel Barrett, a sound expert on Chinese affairs, was replaced by Colonel Yeaton, an expert on Soviet Union and communist problems. See Col. Barrett's outstanding book, *Dixie Mission*.

Worried by the Japanese attacks in the summer and autumn of 1944, the Americans intervened earlier than expected, in both political and military fields. General Patrick J. Hurley was sent to Chungking as ambassador and plans for military cooperation with the communist troops were drawn up. When General Wedemeyer replaced General Stilwell as the Generalissimo's Chief of Staff, the plans came to a halt before being put into operation. Their substance shows how important they were in the eyes of the American command, however:

> *The first plan* was to supply munitions to the Chinese communists, as their activities were seriously hampered by difficulties in obtaining supplies. This plan was rejected by the Generalissimo on 27 November 1944.
>
> *The second plan* proposed to organize three communist infantry regiments (5000 men), to be armed, equipped and advised by the Americans, and send them to operate in government-held territory. Like the first plan, it was laid before the Generalissimo; he rejected it on 2 December.
>
> *The third plan* suggested sending American airborne units, amounting to 4000 or 5000 well-trained technicians, into communist-held territory to carry out raids, in collaboration with guerrilla units, to demolish and sabotage Japanese communications, and to set up an intelligence network. This plan – known as the McClure plan – was abandoned by the Americans themselves.[1]

General Hurley's political mission had an unfortunate beginning. His fiery personality and lack of diplomatic experience made him ill prepared for dealings with Asian interlocutors, and, after a long conversation with Mr Molotov, his opinion of the true nature of Chinese communism was candid in the extreme:

> At the time I came here Chiang Kai-shek believed that the Communist Party in China was an instrument of the Soviet government in Russia. He is now convinced that the Russian government does not recognize the Chinese Communist Party as communist at all and that (1) Russia is not supporting the Communist Party in China, (2) Russia does not want dissension or civil war in China, and (3) Russia desires more harmonious relations with China.[2]

[1] The above is a summary of passages from C. F. Romanus and R. Sunderland, *Time Runs Out in CBI* (Washington, D.C., U.S. Department of the Army, Office of the Chief of Military History, 1959), pp. 72 ff. The O.S.S. (Colonel Bird) also entered upon negotiations with the Chinese communists, an initiative which naturally provoked violent reactions. Cf. *Time Runs Out in CBI*, p. 252.

[2] See U.S. Department of State, *U.S. Relations with China: The China White Paper*, p. 73.

On 7 November 1944 General Hurley went to Yenan and, after discussions with Mao Tse-tung, endorsed a project in five points which virtually put relations between Chungking and Yenan on an equal footing:

1 Both Parties undertake to work for the unity of the armed forces, the defeat of Japan and national reconstruction.
2 The National Government is to be reorganized as the National Coalition Government, the Military Affairs Committee is to be reorganized and the communists are to be represented on it.
3 The National Coalition Government is to adhere to Sun Yat-sen's principles and to democratic and liberal principles.
4 All military forces to submit to the new National Coalition Government. Foreign aid to be divided equally among the armies.
5 The Kuomintang, the Communist Party and all anti-Japanese political parties to be given legal recognition.

The question of coalition government arose yet again; this time it seemed to be viewed with favour by the Americans. The Chinese communists quickly added several concrete, specific demands: dissolution of the Kuomintang special service, lifting of the blockade of the 'Pien ch'ü', recognition for the administrative structures in the liberated areas. The Chinese government did not appreciate the new American ambassador's contribution and T. V. Soong's exclamation to him has become famous: 'The communists have sold you a bill of goods!' On 22 November it replied to Yenan by a note in three points amounting quite simply to a rejection of the proposal to form a coalition government:

1 The Chinese Communist Party will be given legal recognition when the communist military forces have been integrated in the national army.
2 The Chinese Communist Party will give its full support to the National Government's conduct of the war, and to the work of reconstruction to follow. The government will control the communist troops through the Military Affairs Committee, to which communist officers may belong.
3 The National Government will continue to develop democratic forces. In accordance with the programme of armed resistance and national reconstruction, civil rights will be granted within the limits imposed by security and the continuation of the war.

Chou En-lai returned to Yenan with the government proposals; as was only to be expected, they were turned down, and direct contact between the government and the communists virtually came to an end. It was to begin again in January 1945, thanks to the indefatigable efforts of the United States.

The new conversations, with Mr T. V. Soong, Dr Wang Shih-chieh and General Chang Chih-chung as the government spokesmen, were centred, naturally, round the unification of military forces and the use of the entire force against Japan. The communists would agree solely on condition that the arrangement allowed for the reorganization of all government troops and the transformation of the Kuomintang government into a fully representative coalition government. This brought political questions to the fore once again, and the discussions raised the possibility of a Political Consultative Conference, which would be responsible for preparing the way for a constitutional government, and, more specifically, for drawing up a common programme for both parties (3 February).

But on 1 March 1945 the Generalissimo summed up his government's position and announced:

1 The calling of a National Assembly for 12 November 1945, the eightieth anniversary of Sun Yat-sen's birthday, to inaugurate a constitutional government.
2 The granting of legal status to all parties, after the inauguration of the constitutional government; the communists would be granted legal status as soon as they allowed their administrative structures and armies to be integrated in the corresponding government structures.

Taking the declaration as a pretext, the Communist Party broke off negotiations. It had nothing to gain from the convocation of a national assembly, in which Kuomintang influence would predominate; its aim was to obtain the convocation of a Political Consultative Conference, whose composition and attributions were to be decided beforehand by the two chief parties. The communist position was clarified a few weeks later when the Seventh Party Congress met at Yenan from 23 April to 11 June. Mao Tse-tung marked the occasion by publishing 'On Coalition Government', a document of supreme importance, which retraced the history of the relations between the Kuomintang and the Communist Party from the beginning, and noted the current trends. The substance of the document was briefly that a coalition government should be created in China as quickly as possible, as the approaching victory would be a victory not only over fascism, but over reactionaries all over the world. As the Russian people had played the chief part in the war, the worldwide situation in 1945 would be totally different from that of 1918. The struggle would henceforth oppose 'democratic forces' and the rest. The Chinese people, from then on, had two great advantages to help them in their struggle against the reactionaries and the Japanese: a higher degree of political awareness and powerful support from the liberated areas.

A long and interesting description of the 'tortuous history' of Chinese resistance to Japan is used by Mao Tse-tung as an illustration of the two different policies and lines of action existing in China. The first is that of the Kuomintang, for a long time indifferent to the Chinese people, who were eventually victims of oppression from both the government and the enemy; the second is the policy of the Chinese Communist Party, endeavouring to gather the Chinese people together once more to conduct a people's war, which was to be both national and all-embracing as well. The development of these two themes, often put forward since 1937, gives rise to a violent indictment of the Kuomintang's defeatism and its dictatorship, and provides a setting for a telling comparison between the situation in the government regions and that in the nineteen liberated areas. As the fact that the two lines coexist is likely to lead to civil war after the anti-Japanese war, a truly democratic coalition government is essential. Should this government become a reality, the Communist Party sets forward proposals for a common programme, consisting of general principles and specific measures.

The principles were composed chiefly of a refusal to accept a 'feudal' or 'bourgeois' dictatorship, and a proposal for all who shared in the united front to form an alliance under the auspices of 'New Democracy'. The latter point is followed by an interesting description of new democratic structures in every field; it is interesting to note that Mao Tse-tung considered that New Democracy would be applied for 'several decades'. A question arises here as to whether the Chinese Communist Party leader's views were closer at this point to the real situation in China than they were after 1949.

The specific demands to be brought gradually into effect were numerous and varied:

(*a*) Creation of a democratic coalition government and a unified supreme command.
(*b*) Legal recognition for all democratic parties.
(*c*) Strengthening and expanding of liberated areas.
(*d*) Abolition of measures limiting basic freedom.
(*e*) Strict control of 'bureaucrat-capital'.
(*f*) Reduction of land rent.
(*g*) Political and military reorganization of the army, etc.

These measures could be effected only after the establishment of a provisional coalition government, created with the agreement of all groups, parties and leading figures, and later a regular government born of a national assembly.

The second part of this vitally important text states the communist position in a large number of fields – the army, agriculture, industry, cultural affairs, foreign policy, national minority races, etc.; relations between the Party and the Kuomintang are treated from a distance. Many of the ideas already to be found in 'On New Democracy' occur here as well, but the writing is more violent in tone and invective is more frequent – hypocrite, traitor and criminal being commonplace insults.

The subject matter and style of this document indicate the extent of the Communist Party's astonishing development between 1937 and 1945; its ending is virtually a call to arms, or at least a call to be on the alert, and a distribution of missions to be accomplished in the fight. The carrying out of the democratic movement is the chief task in government zones, while in regions under enemy occupation internal resistance must be developed, taking recent events in France as an example; in liberated areas, more and more troops must be mobilized, organized and trained, and the cooperation between the army and the population must be improved still further.

The Party itself must get ready for the new tasks awaiting it, remaining lucid and constantly practising criticism, for 'running water is never stale', and 'political dust and germs' must be prevented from contaminating 'the minds of our comrades and the body of our Party'. Once more Mao Tse-tung stresses the value of experience gained in the Chinese revolution, taking the Party's history as an example; he looks beyond the victory over the Japanese towards the building of a New China.

The negotiations between the government and the communists were broken off after 9 March; they did not reopen until the following July. The Japanese capitulation on 14 August changed the state of affairs completely and made the need for an immediate solution appear all the more urgent. On 28 August Mao Tse-tung arrived in Chungking, fetched from Yenan by the U.S. ambassador himself. He was to stay there until 11 October; although his presence there took on briefly the value of a symbol of peace and unity, the illusion was short lived.

27 Life within the Communist Party and its Doctrinal Evolution during the Yenan Period The Seventh Party Congress

During the Yenan period the Chinese Communist Party expanded over huge areas of North and Central China; the Party itself went through a period of rebirth with regard to numbers and doctrine. The development of numbers is impressive: from 40,000 in 1937, the membership jumped to 800,000 in 1940, and 1,211,128 in April 1945, when the Seventh Congress was held. Members from the central provinces – Hunan, Hupei and Kiangsi – were in the minority compared with the influx of new members from North China, at least as far as the basic structure and the lower ranking cadres were concerned; this situation did not make itself felt in the higher levels of the Party until much later on. In any case, peasants from Hunan have the same fundamental characteristics as peasants from Shansi – endurance, patience, willingness, intelligence and manual dexterity; both showed the same devotion to the hierarchy. As in the Kiangsi period, the basic structure was composed essentially of peasants, along with the soldiers, who were, however, recruited from among the peasants. Again, as in the Kiangsi period, the proletariat was scarcely represented at all; even artisans were few in number. On the other hand, intellectuals in the widest sense of the term were more numerous. They were above all, if not exclusively, young men from universities and middle schools fleeing the Japanese occupation, and inspired by patriotic feelings rather than real revolutionary aspirations. The most enthusiastic among them were interested in the methods of action peculiar to the communist forces – guerrilla warfare and the work carried out among the local inhabitants.

The communists' reputation for uprightness and efficiency, as opposed to the government's negligence, attracted many of them. Lastly, it was often easier to reach communist territory than government territory, which was further away; this was particularly true for North China.

The newly arrived intellectuals had to be re-educated in politics, whether they wanted it or not. Most of them underwent this trial willingly and became new cadres, who were badly needed, as the movement was expanding rapidly. The satisfaction they found in their new responsibilities could not fail to appeal to people of their age. They were military as well as political cadres. The peculiar characteristics of guerrilla warfare, and its relatively independent aspect, helped develop their love of responsibility and an ability to take decisions. The Party became more and more imbued with a military sense of organization and discipline. This approach was extended to the state administrative bodies, and the structure and working of the People's Communes, where it lasted at least until the troubles arising from the Cultural Revolution.

The political leaders were also given important military commands, as had been the case during the Kiangsi period and as was now even more frequent than before. In the liberated areas, they represented all forms of authority, including the Party, as they were usually regional secretaries. The consequences of this can never be overrated. It is one of several factors which have combined to make the present leaders acutely aware of the importance of military affairs while preventing the creation of an entirely rival military power. This synthesis of political and military responsibilities is more obvious in Mao Tse-tung's writings than anywhere else; at that time much of his work was devoted to military questions, considered from every angle: 'Problems of Strategy in Guerrilla War against Japan' (May 1938), 'On Protracted War' (May 1938), 'Problems of War and Strategy' (6 November 1938). These titles are typical examples; indeed almost all of his articles revealed the extent of his preoccupation with military affairs.

'On New Democracy'

From 1940 onwards, the political doctrine was put forward in texts arousing wide interest; 'On New Democracy', published in January 1940 in the first issue of the review *Chinese Culture* (*Chung-kuo wen-hua*), is without any doubt the most important of them all, in so far as it is an attempt to adapt Marxism-Leninism to concrete Chinese conditions. In 1940 Mao Tse-tung held that the Chinese revolution would be carried out in two phases – the New Democracy, followed by socialism. The New Democracy was, and would for a long time continue to be, the most appropriate regime for China. It bore no resemblance to the regimes in Western republics controlled by the bourgeoisie, nor to those in the proletarian soviet republics. The new democratic republic was to be a union of the four anti-imperialist and anti-feudal classes – the proletariat, the peasantry, the petty bourgeoisie and the national bourgeoisie; the proletariat was to take over the leadership of the alliance. These were the characteristics linking the old style bourgeois new democratic revolution to the world-wide socialist revolution.

The economy of a new democratic republic had to be new democratic as well. The state had therefore to take control of the large industrial and commercial enterprises, but would not confiscate the rest, which were not powerful enough to enslave the people, as the backwardness of the Chinese economy justified the maintenance of some forms of capitalism. In the same way, large country estates would be confiscated and the land shared out according to Sun Yat-sen's formula: 'land to the tiller'. Rich peasants would remain, however, for the theory mentioned above was equally applicable to them, and in any case they played a useful part in production. Equal distribution of land, Mao Tse-tung adds, though without undue emphasis, should enable the first steps to be made towards co-operative organizations. Lastly, the new culture, 'the ideological reflection of the new politics and the new economy', must serve both politics and the economy. Semi-feudal culture (that is, traditional culture) and imperialist culture, 'devoted brothers', as Mao Tse-tung puts it, are engaged in a 'life-and-death struggle' with the new culture, and must be eliminated. A national, scientific, new democratic 'culture of the broad masses' will emerge in their place, until a real socialist culture can make its appearance.

The New Democracy, with its liberal and nationalist tone, was to facilitate the conversion of many young intellectuals to communism. It also helped maintain a stable social climate in the rural districts of the liberated areas, and had a reassuring and calming influence on many liberal members of the bourgeoisie, landowners, industrialists and tradesmen. The Party reaped the benefits of its new democratic propaganda between 1945 and 1949, in spite of the fact that its attitude had hardened in the meantime.

The Rectification Movement

The Rectification or Cheng-feng[1] Movement, which began to develop in the Communist Party in 1941 and was active particularly in 1942, arose

[1] The literal meaning of the two characters composing this expression is 'readjustment in style'.

to meet real needs – to maintain the orthodoxy of the older members, give ideological training to new members, and to keep up the cohesion and discipline of the communist movement in general. The aim, as Mao Tse-tung was to say several times, was to 'clarify ideas and unite comrades'.

The old cadres, who had had time to undergo a solid training in Marxism during the long years of the period of collaboration with the Kuomintang, and then in Kiangsi, were often troubled by the moderate policy adopted by the Party in the style of the 22 September declaration. The allegiance to the central government, changes of titles, the renunciation of the soviets, the abandoning of the land policy, and even details in the uniform (the replacement of the red star by the Kuomintang emblem of the white sun, for instance) could not fail to provoke confusion and heart-searching. The swing from the five Kiangsi campaigns and the Long March to the United Front must have seemed abrupt to many militants.

The new arrivals from the white zones lacked Marxist foundations, and, owing to their social origins, they brought liberal and bourgeois ideas which were dangerous, or at least out of place, and their nationalist feelings tended to dim all other political concepts. Some went as far as to propose to reorganize the regime in the bases along parliamentary lines, as in capitalist countries, and others even made up the quarrel with the landowners, blurring 'the difference in principle between the Kuomintang and the Communist Party'.[1]

'On New Democracy' probably helped towards a synthesis of some points of view, but on the whole it was a text destined for the public rather than Party members. A series of fundamental texts appeared exclusively for them. Mao Tse-tung wrote the most important ones himself: 'Reform our Study' (May 1941), 'Rectify the Party's Style of Work' (1 February 1942), 'Oppose Stereotyped Party Writing' (8 February 1942).

Other authors were regarded as authorities on more limited subjects. It was at this time that Liu Shao-ch'i wrote: 'How to be a Good Communist' (1939),[2] 'On the Intra-Party Struggle' (1941), and 'Liquidation of Menchevik Ideas in the Party' (1943). It need hardly be said that some earlier writings also provide insight into the Cheng-feng Movement, such as 'On Practice' and 'On Contradiction', which completes it, both by Mao Tse-tung.

The texts referring to the movement do not show great originality. They give a classic picture of a 'good' communist, along with the analysis and

[1] See Mao Tse-tung, 'On Policy' (25 December 1940) and 'The Situation and Tasks in the Anti-Japanese War after the Fall of Shanghai and Taiyuan' (12 November 1937).
[2] This text must not be confused with an article by Ch'en Yün, written at the same time: 'How to be a Member of the Communist Party'.

justification of the methods used inside the Party. The good communist was not simply a member of the Party; he had to be an active member, and a propagandist, using his judgement to try and spread the doctrine, particularly among intellectuals and workers. He had to be honest, disciplined, ready to make the supreme sacrifice, an example for all, constantly striving to improve his Marxist learning, his general knowledge and his military knowledge, and to 'learn from the masses'. Ch'en Yün was to declare that the ultimate aim of this training was not solely to make the individual fight for communism, but to give him a revolutionary conception of life which would lead him to struggle ceaselessly for the Party. To achieve this, he added, members first had to understand the proletariat's role in society. Generally speaking, knowledge and understanding of ideology would prevent Party members from going astray among the inevitably winding paths of the revolution.

The methods used within the Party were intended to maintain all its doctrinal purity, efficiency and impetus. 'Inner struggle' had a special place in this respect. It was meant to bring ideas and not individuals into play, remaining free from all personal considerations and after-thoughts and following clearly defined lines. It could be described as the exercising of democracy, though it was a narrow form of democracy, reserved to communists alone, and contained within strict limits imposed by the instructions and interpretations of official Party organizations.

The inner struggle, whose chief instruments were study (hsüeh-hsi), criticism and self-criticism, was intended to enable the Party to avoid three main errors, defined in the texts, before it was too late:

1. 'Subjectivism' cut the militant off from doctrine and reality, and occurred in two forms – dogmatism and empiricism.[1]
2. 'Sectarianism' was a particularly grave fault, as it brought with it disunity arising from contradictions which were inevitable among Party members of different origins and in different situations; in its clearest forms, it appeared as 'particularism' and 'authoritarianism'.
3. 'Formalism' was related to 'dogmatism', and was shown by empty words which engendered irresponsibility and false authority, and meant nothing, like 'shooting [an arrow] without a target'; the arrow was obviously Marxism-Leninism, and the neglected target was the Chinese revolution.

These doctrinal declarations naturally masked more specific preoccupations, such as consolidating the authority of the leaders, discrediting or

[1] In June 1943 the Central Committee published a decision on this deviation.

eliminating rival factions, and preventing the formation of opposing tendencies. Some rival trends of thought had survived the Tsunyi meeting and the resettling of the Party in north Shensi. The first of them was that of Chang Kuo-t'ao, though it had been seriously weakened by the failure of the Szechuanese venture headed by Chang. In April 1937 diverging opinions became clearly apparent at an enlarged meeting of the Political Bureau. At the time Chang Kuo-t'ao was still influential enough to be given the post of Vice-Chairman of the North-Western Bureau of the Central Soviet Government, or, in other words, the north Shensi area. More disagreements arose at the Loch'uan meeting, in August 1937. Chang Kuo-t'ao, who up till then had been violently anti-Kuomintang, is supposed to have changed his mind and stressed the need for loyal collaboration with the other party. He was then reported to have been placed under a close watch. Finally, in April 1938, he made use of a visit from a government mission to the communist zone to escape, whereupon he went to Wuhan and broke off his allegiance to the Communist Party, which expelled him immediately. His former supporters or subordinates still in Yenan were either purged or won over to orthodoxy. Chang Kuo-t'ao has now taken refuge in Hong Kong; the passing of time and his ardent loyalties reduce the value of his testimony.

Ch'en Shao-yü, alias Wang Ming, another of Mao Tse-tung's rivals, came back from Moscow at the beginning of 1938, powerfully supported by the Comintern, whose representative he was. He was at first the Chinese Communist Party's delegate to the central government, but he returned to Yenan after the fall of Wuhan, where he and his assistants, Chou En-lai and Ch'in Pang-hsien, had been in residence. When he denounced formalism of foreign origin at the Sixth Plenum of the Central Committee in October 1938, stressing yet again the impossibility of separating internationalism from national forms of revolution, Mao Tse-tung was no doubt using this as a disguised attack on Ch'en Shao-yü, whose return had probably made him uneasy.

Ch'en Shao-yü is also indirectly under fire when Mao Tse-tung attacks subjectivism, under its two forms of 'dogmatism' and 'empiricism', and 'envoys' who 'are always right, they are the Number One'. He probably had Ch'en Shao-yü in mind when he quoted the classical couplet:

> The reed growing on the wall – top-heavy, thin-stemmed and shallow of root;
> The bamboo shoot in the hills – sharp-tongued, thick-stemmed and hollow inside.

For a time, Ch'en Shao-yü embodied 'rightist opportunist' trends, which no doubt tallied with Moscow's wishes. His importance soon waned, however. 'On New Democracy' and the Rectification Movement of 1942 gave final confirmation of Mao-Tse tung's role as virtually the sole theorist of the revolutionary movement; Mao himself bore witness of the evolution when he declared in 1944 that the 'old factions' had disappeared from the Party, leaving only 'remnants of dogmatist and empiricist ideology' and, temporarily, a ' "mountain-stronghold" mentality'.[1]

The Rectification Movement was also a purge. The Party had to get rid of numbers of uncertain elements, petty bourgeois or rich peasants, who had come over to communism more or less sincerely, through the united front. As they were opportunists, the Party had nothing to fear in the way of active opposition, but by using their local influence, or by remaining passive, they could effectively counteract the leaders' actions. The Chinese habits of inaccuracy, *laissez-aller* and compromise were more accentuated among them than among the old, convinced, militant Party members, and could alter the image the Party wanted to give.

In practice, the Movement began in 1942 and lasted throughout 1943. Cadres at all levels took part in it. Meetings took on the form of autobiographical accounts, and studies of texts, after which each person present had to compare his own behaviour with the theory studied and find material for criticism and self-criticism. The conduct of the other members of the study group was also examined, making no allowances, using the classic method of 'unity, critic, unity', in order to 'cure the sickness to save the patient'. Many cadres were expelled from the Party, in the first place those who did not seem determined to struggle actively against the Kuomintang for national reasons; some cases show that Mao Tse-tung was not prepared to suffer any attacks on his authority, or even on his pride.

The communists have never given any figures enabling the extent of the purge to be reckoned. If the normal rate of 5 to 10 per cent of 'bad elements' is observed, between 40,000 and 80,000 people must have been involved. This estimate seems to tally with the fall in Party membership, which was 800,000 in 1940 and 736,151 in 1942, whereas no figure was published for 1943. Former communists testify to widely generalized expulsions and numerous executions. The inquiries, confessions and denunciations accompanying the Party purge gave rise to a widespread hunt for 'traitors', 'collaborators', 'Kuomintang special agents', etc. Countless excesses, none of them peculiar to China, were committed under cover of patriotism.

[1] See 'Our Study and the Current Situation' (12 April 1944), *Selected Works* vol. III.

The Rectification Movement was an event of great ideological impact, compared by some communist authors with the May 4th Movement, and an event of great political impact as well, for it left Mao Tse-tung in complete control of the Party. It was used as a precedent and a model for other movements with the same name, with the same aim of consolidating unity under the leadership of the Party and Mao Tse-tung. This was particularly true of the Rectification Movement of 1957, which followed the failure of the 'Hundred Flowers' experiment.

Problems of literature and art

Mao Tse-tung made two declarations on literature and art, in the same spirit as the Rectification Movement, which still constitute the basis of the Party line in both fields today. They were dated 2 and 23 May 1942.

After the May 4th 1919 Movement, the fighter representing the new culture had taken his place alongside the political fighter. He attacked both the so-called feudal, or traditional culture, and the so-called imperialist or Western culture. Literature and art had to be included in the general mechanism of the revolution. In practice, writers and artists had to take up the same political position as the proletariat, that is, the Communist Party. They had to fight the 'enemies of the people', both help and criticize the allies of the united front, and serve the masses, while drawing on them for inspiration and contributing to their progress. Writers and artists had therefore to undergo a difficult ideological transformation; they had to express themselves in such a way as to be understood by the masses and by the militant communists who were slightly more advanced, collaborate with the propagandists, and encourage petty bourgeois writers and artists to take part with them in a 'cultural front', itself part of the united front.

Mao Tse-tung deals with all the problems – the respective values of political and artistic criticism, the theme of human love, literature used to denounce, to exalt or to satirize. In the last analysis it is clear that he is chiefly concerned with the ideological alignment of writers and artists; he concludes with an image borrowed from Lu Hsün, saying that they must humble themselves before the masses, as the ox bows to the child who leads it. This bending of literature and art to serve Party ideology and bureaucracy deeply shocked some writers, and they showed great courage in their reaction to it. The case of Wang Shih-wei, author of *The Wild Lily*, followed a little later by that of Hu Feng and his magazine *Hope*, the disgrace of the novelist Hsiao Chün and of the great poet Ai

Ch'ing, and the disillusion of the novelist Ting Ling, all foreshadowed the difficulties that the upper ranks of the Party were to experience after 1949 in their dealings with the intellectuals.[1]

The Seventh Congress

The Seventh Congress of the Chinese Communist Party, attended by 544 regular members and 208 deputy members at Yenan from 23 April to 11 June 1945, when victory was only a few weeks away, gave a striking picture of the Party's progress and its strength. The outside world had to be shown that the communists were capable of taking their part in the leadership of the state; from within, the Party had to be drawn together round its leaders to prepare it for further battles. 'The fate of 480 million Chinese depends on our Congress', said Mao Tse-tung at the start; with some measure of self-satisfaction, he reckoned the total communist forces as follows: a Party with a membership of 1,210,000; a population of 95,500,000; a regular army of 910,000 men; a militia of 2,200,000 men; the support of the masses throughout the country; the support of the peoples throughout the whole world, and particularly of the Soviet Union.

The great text set before the congress was 'On Coalition Government', whose name alone was a programme.[2] Its style was harsh, almost insulting towards the government, with whom the communists had virtually broken off relations at that point; it left little doubt as to the reality and ruthlessness of Yenan's demands, and it is vital for the understanding of the complicated events of the following year.

Chu Teh dealt with the military situation; his report was little more than a development of ideas stated by Mao Tse-tung, and an appeal for the reorganization of the Chinese armies on the same basis as the people's troops of the Eighth Route Army.

The Seventh Congress gave new statutes to the Party. This decision was justified in the light of the considerable changes that had come about since the Sixth Congress was held, seventeen years earlier; Liu Shao-ch'i stated the reasons when he gave the introductory report. It contained some interesting points. He laid strong emphasis on the value of practical experience in the Chinese revolution; it is hard not to interpret this as a mark of independence combined with homage to Mao Tse-tung's leadership. The characteristic features of Chinese society were mentioned, to

[1] See Merle Goldman, 'Writer's criticism of the Party in 1942', *The China Quarterly* (January-March 1964).
[2] See the analysis of this document in the preceding chapter.

stress the need for a new democratic revolution to precede the socialist revolution. All 'anti-feudal' and 'anti-imperialist' bourgeois elements should take part. The central government and the Kuomintang were isolated still further. As for the Party itself, the struggle against leftist and rightist opponents was to be intensified; the adoption of a document of the utmost interest on past events, 'Resolution on Certain Questions in the History of our Party',[1] by the Seventh Plenary Session of the Sixth Congress, on 20 April, three days before the opening of the Seventh Congress, paved the way for this harsher attitude to some extent. Mao Tse-tung's work was magnified or placed to the fore throughout this article, which was a review of nearly thirty years of revolutionary activities.

The Seventh Congress elected Mao Tse-tung chairman of the Central Committee, renewing the legitimacy of a title which none could now contest. The decision taken at Tsunyi was ten years old, and had been the outcome of exceptional circumstances. From now on, Mao Tse-tung was to be the sole leader of the Party, in every respect; the leaders in Moscow do not seem to have had any say in the new election. The accounts given by Peking's historians of this congress state the unification of the Party round Mao Tse-tung, and his correct interpretation of Party leadership, as its main theme; the Seventh Congress was in fact the first congress of the present Communist Party.

China victorious

To all appearances, China and the Chinese government emerged from the war in a far better position than they had occupied before it. Thanks to the efforts of President Roosevelt, China had risen to become one of the five world powers; it was to take back all the territories lost to Japan since 1895, particularly Taiwan and Manchuria. A century of humiliation was wiped out with the abolition of the Unequal Treaties. For the first time, an independent China was to take its place in world politics; Chiang Kai-shek's name aroused the same interest as that of Roosevelt, Churchill, de Gaulle or Stalin. The reality behind this façade, embellished still further by the Allies' war propaganda, was totally different and China was already no longer able to make use of its new rise to the international scene.

The war had aged and exhausted the central government and its administrative structures. The country's economy and finances were verging on chaos. What was worst, the Communist Party, the regime's implacable

[1] See Mao Tse-tung, *Selected Works*, vol. III.

enemy, was publicly making insolent claims to a share in government, under threat of civil war. The Kuomintang, in the hands of a man whose temperament, education and origins inclined towards uncompromising conservatism, had completely lost its revolutionary spirit, and indeed all urge for renewal. The different currents of opinion splitting it – Whampoa (Huangp'u), the C.C. (Organization) clique, and the Political Sciences group, to mention only the most important of them – represented as many groups spurred on by personal interests, with no national programme. The Generalissimo played them off against each other as earlier on he had dealt with the rival semi-independent provincial governors. All appointments were made on the criterion of loyalty, which explains the numerous government posts held by members of his family: Madame Chiang Kai-shek, her brother Sung Tzu-wen (T. V. Soong), their brother-in-law Dr K'ung Hsiang-hsi (H. H. Kung) all succeeded one another in the chief government posts. Their personal wealth and at times their behaviour shocked public opinion and damaged the Generalissimo's reputation for austerity and integrity.

The necessities of war, the fear of spectacular desertions like that of Wang Ching-wei, and the anxiety to parry Yenan's intrigues, all made Chiang Kai-shek more suspicious than ever. He could not be over-watchful, surrounded as he was by his mortal enemies, the communists, liberals who were unconsciously his enemies, the advocates of agreement with Japan, who were few but influential, and provincial leaders, particularly those from Szechuan and Yunnan. In 1937 the Generalissimo's credit throughout the country was such that he could have launched the revolution once more in the name of war, giving national and social targets to the Kuomintang, and infused new life into the Party and senior army officers by gathering about him energetic men of integrity inspired by the true tradition of Sun Yat-sen. It would have been a difficult, even dangerous undertaking. Had it been attempted at the beginning, it could have succeeded, giving real vigour to the conduct of the war, thwarting the communists' progress, and avoiding the economic disintegration which, bringing other catastrophes with it, was to prove the death blow.

In the summer of 1939 the Chinese currency began to collapse rapidly. The cost of the war, the loss of much of the state revenue to the enemy, a poor taxation policy and difficulties over foreign exchange provoked galloping inflation. Between June 1937 and June 1939, the price index in Chungking rose from 101 to 216. By December 1939 it was 325, and in December 1940, 1121.[1] In spite of U.S. financial aid amounting to

[1] Cf. Yuan-li Wu, *An Economic Survey of Communist China* (New York, Twayne, 1955).

$1,515,700 over the whole of the war,[1] the Chinese dollar had fallen to 2020 for one U.S. dollar at the beginning of 1946.

The gradual fall of the currency, and all sorts of economic disturbances arising from the invasion affected the material conditions and the morale of the middle classes, and above all the civil servants. The result was a huge increase in dishonest practices, which had been all too common before the war, and particularly in administrative corruption of all kinds. The unfortunate result was loss of popular support inside the country and discredit abroad; the civil war, when it came, only made things worse. Chang Hsi-jo's sally, made at Kunming on 13 January 1946, 'The Kuomintang claims to be a revolutionary political party, but for a long time it has simply been a cause for revolt', soon came true.

At the close of the war the Communist Party's image was that of a young, new and dynamic party, considered, rightly or wrongly, as possessing everything its rival lacked; the quality of its members and the appropriateness of its social programme were certainly superior to that of its enemy. This superiority and the immense lassitude of the population, partly explain the swiftness of its victory.

[1] Cf. U.Department of State, *U.S. Relations with China: The China White Paper*, p. 817.

Part 5

The Winning of Power and the Accession of People's China (15 August 1945–1 October 1949)

The seizure of power by armed force, the settlement of the issue by war, is the central task and the highest form of revolution.

Mao Tse-tung

28 Negotiations or Civil War

'But never in my experience with human beings have I encountered anything like the suspicion on both sides, especially among the communists.'

Dr Leighton Stuart

From the point of view of relations between the central government and the Chinese Communist Party, the short period of four years from the capitulation of the Japanese on 14 August 1945 to the accession of the People's Republic of China on 1 October 1949 is without any doubt one of the most complicated stages of all. Phases of negotiations alternated with phases of open warfare, and covert warfare sometimes went on at the same time as high-level discussions.

The policy of the United States complicated the situation still further. It took on several forms – military intervention, economic support and good offices, which were sometimes accepted, sometimes rejected, by one side or the other. It was uncertain and sometimes contradictory, and was given wide coverage by the United States press, which dwelt on the sensational aspects. The Soviet policy, which was one of the utmost reserve, provides a striking contrast.

The period can be divided into two chief phases. The first was dominated by negotiations, and continued until the Chinese communist delegation left Nanking, on 5 March 1947. Although military engagements were frequent, they were on a local, limited scale. The second phase, lasting from the spring of 1947 until the end of 1949, or, in other words, until the communist occupation of the whole of China except for Hainan and Tibet was complete, was one of uninterrupted military operations on a larger scale than ever before, spreading to all the theatres of war. Yet contact was maintained secretly and brief official negotiations took place even at the beginning of 1949.

The period of negotiations

The central government and the Chinese Communist Party had scarcely had time to make contact once more after the crisis of the spring of 1945 before the Japanese capitulated on 14 August, an event which was itself preceded by the Soviet Union's entry into the war against Japan on 8 August, in accordance with the agreement signed at Yalta on 11 February 1945. This sudden change in the military situation caught everyone by surprise, particularly the government, which had intended to move its armies nearer the main centres in Central and North China, using the opportunity supplied by the offensives planned for the autumn of 1945. A race immediately began to disarm the Japanese armies and to occupy the regions under their control. A great deal was at stake, especially for the communists, whose fighting materials amounted to a fifth of those of their adversary, and whose territories did not form a continuous area, as they were thoroughly penetrated by the invaders. The Japanese military equipment soon to become available amounted to that used by 1,313,420 men, as well as enormous reserve stocks.

As for the territories to be reoccupied, the communists were naturally most interested in North China and Manchuria, which the Russians had just entered. Had the communists occupied the large towns in these areas – Peking, Tientsin, Tsingtao, T'aiyüan and Kalgan, to speak of North China alone – this would have given them a valuable card to play off against the government, and caused considerable stir in the world as a whole (see Map 26, p. 377).

As soon as the Soviet Union entered the war, three days after Hiroshima, and without waiting for the official announcement of the Japanese capitulation, which seemed inevitable, Mao Tse-tung quickly made use of the results of the American atom bomb. On 9 August he launched a 'nationwide counter-offensive' against the invaders, 'in close and effective coordination with the operations of the Soviet Union and the other allied countries'.[1] The aim of the operation was clearly stated to those carrying it out – they were to annihilate the enemy, 'capture their arms and *matériel*, vigorously expand the Liberated Areas' and arouse and organize the millions of people living in the occupied regions, the ultimate aim being to 'avert the danger of civil war and make efforts to bring about the

[1] The 9 August declaration, 'The Last Round with the Japanese Invaders', *Selected Works,* vol. III, does not refer to the American victory over Japan or to the effects of the atom bombing. The United States are not even mentioned by name and the entry of the Soviet Union into the war is made responsible for the Japanese capitulation.

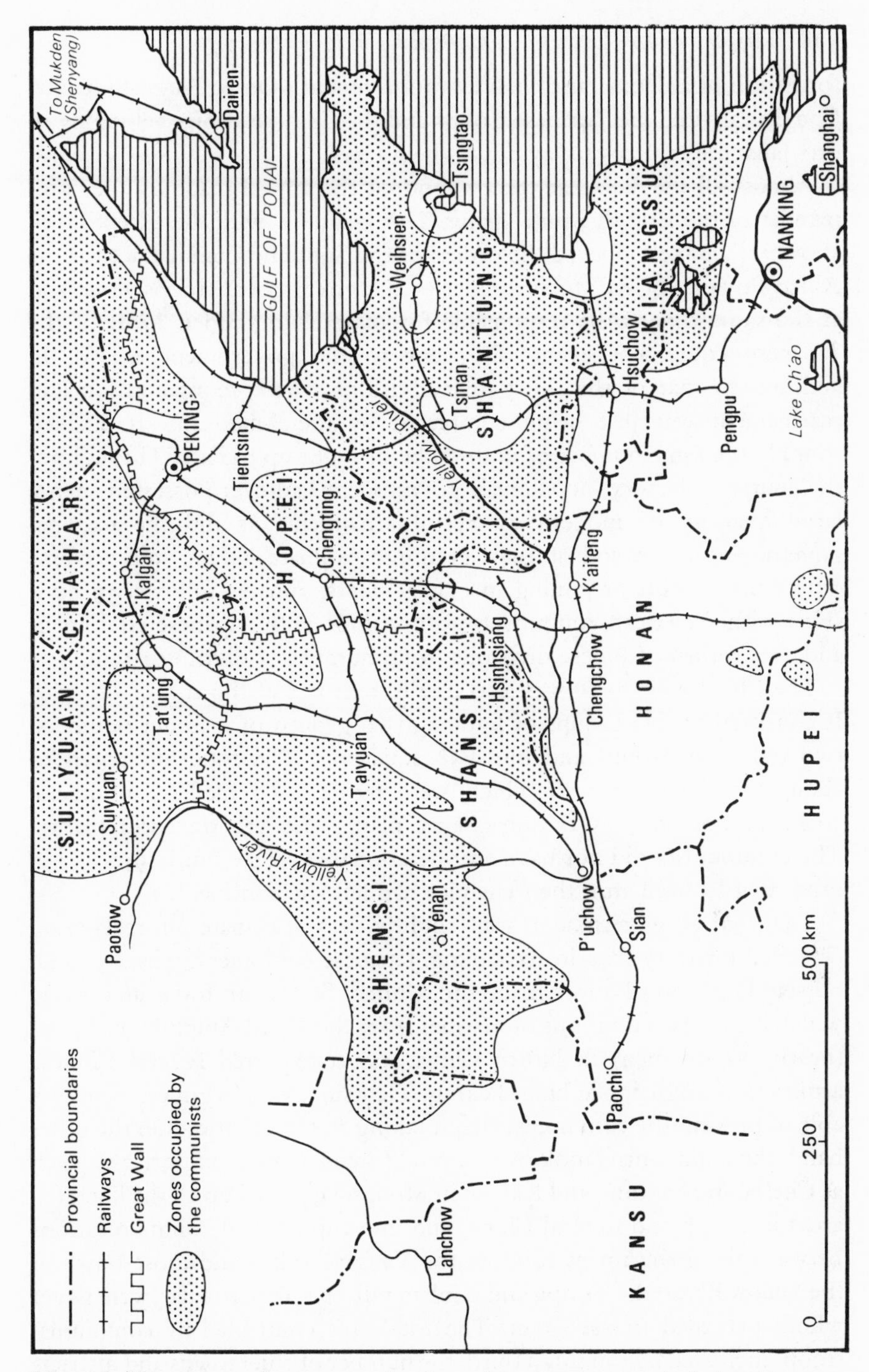

Map 26. The communist zones at the time of the Japanese capitulation (August 1945)

formation of a democratic coalition government'. On 10 August General Chu Teh invited the Japanese troops and the Chinese armies belonging to pro-Japanese regimes to lay down their arms.

Almost all the Japanese troops ignored the appeal made by the commander of the Eighth Route Army. The Japanese, with the exception of about 30,000 men, obeyed the orders of the Supreme Commander for the Allied Powers (SCAP) to surrender to the government troops alone and at the same time to be responsible for maintaining order. Most of the Japanese equipment eventually went to the government troops, in addition to that of the thirty-nine divisions whose reorganization and rearmament was just being completed by the Americans. It enabled roughly the same number of units to be brought up to date. Throughout the course of history, no Chinese government had ever possessed such a large quantity of modern, powerful armaments as did the national government at the end of 1945. A rough estimate, taking into account only units capable of joining in engagements, runs as follows: 39 divisions with American equipment, 40 divisions with Japanese equipment and 120 ordinary Chinese divisions (total number of divisions: 199).

The Chinese air force was also totally renewed at the end of the war. It consisted of five groups of fighters, two groups of medium bombers, two transport groups and one P38 squadron. The total amounted to about 500 planes, 200 of which were fighters, 60 medium bombers, 30 heavy bombers, 15 reconnaissance planes and 120 transport planes. The communists did not have an operational air force until 1950, or, in other words, until after their enemies had left the continent.

The central government was slightly less fortunate in reclaiming occupied territory than in reclaiming Japanese equipment. Thanks to an outstanding contribution from the United States air force and navy, which landed two divisions of marines from the Third Amphibious Corps (nearly 50,000 men) in North China and transported several Chinese armies to Shanghai, Nanking, Peking, Tientsin, etc., the government was able to prevent the communists from taking the large cities. On the other hand, the communists took over several towns of lesser importance, such as Chefoo in Shantung and Kalgan in Mongolia, joined up all the liberated areas in North and Central China, and interrupted land communications between the government zones in the Yangtze valley and those north of the Yellow River; the Tsinpu and Kinhan railways, in particular, were never wholly returned to use again. The total area controlled by communist troops increased by roughly a third; the number of chief towns and districts occupied rose from 70 to 200.

The race for armaments and territory abandoned by the Japanese army soon resulted in brisk engagements between national and communist troops. In south-east Shansi, five divisions from the Nineteenth Army commanded by General Shih Tse-po were destroyed on about 15 October, in the area near Hsiangyüan and T'unliu.[1] Fighting also broke out near Kalgan on about 10 September. The largest engagement took place in Honan. Two nationalist armies, the New Eighth Army commanded by General Kao Shu-shun and the Fortieth Army under Ma Fa-wu, and part of the Thirtieth Army, were trying to reopen the Kinhan railway line near Hant'an in north Honan, when they were either wiped out by Liu Po-ch'eng, or else went over to the enemy, as did Kao Shu-shun and the two divisions he commanded. This was a bitter blow to the nationalists' pride, for three out of the six divisions were at least partially equipped by the United States. The incident occurred on 31 October, a few weeks after the communiqué published on the 'Double Tenth', which had given rise to hope of an agreement between Chungking and Yenan.

Manchuria presented the largest problem of all, and the situation there was further complicated by the presence of the Soviet Army. It had disarmed the Japanese army there, meting out rough treatment, and had sent the men to Siberia, where they were to stay for several years. It also dismantled and removed all the industrial equipment, which the Pauley mission reckoned would cost 2000 million U.S. dollars to replace, and was worth 858 million dollars as it stood; this implied that the Russians intended to impose their economic cooperation on the future occupants of this region, which was vitally important to the economy of Siberia.

The Sino-Soviet agreement of 14 August 1945, which in a sense sanctioned the proposals put forward at Yalta on 11 February of the same year, gave explicit acknowledgement, by means of a series of notes exchanged alongside the agreement, of the Nanking government's sovereignty over Manchuria. But it was difficult for the Russians to refuse legally to allow Chinese troops to enter Manchuria; they could only create delay, using all kinds of pretexts, or complicate matters by ensuring that local conditions were unfavourable. This is precisely what happened. The Russians, basing their arguments on the 14 August treaty, which made Dairen a commercial port, and using the pretext that the state of war with Japan had not come to an end, refused to allow American ships

[1] The communists claimed to have destroyed thirteen divisions, but the composition of the Nineteenth Army stated that it contained the 46th and 49th provincial divisions, the 66th and 68th Divisions, and the 37th Temporary Division.

carrying Chinese troops to enter the harbour (6 October). Admiral Barbey, in command of the U.S. Seventh Fleet, found the ports of Hulutao and Yingk'ou already in the hands of troops 'of unknown origin and obedience', to use the expression of the Russian admiral who reported the situation to him.

As soon as the Japanese capitulation came about, the communists quickly moved troops towards Manchuria via Chahar and Jehol, and sent others from Shantung across the stretch of sea between Shantung and the Kwantung peninsula. Nearly 100,000 men were on the move towards the north-east provinces, and among them were leading figures who were natives of Manchuria – Lü Cheng-ts'ao, Wan I and Chang Hsüeh-shih, the son of Chang Tso-lin and brother of Chang Hsüeh-liang. Lin Piao soon took the command of these various elements, who were joined by soldiers from the former Manchukuo army, anti-Japanese volunteers and some Koreans. They were later reorganized into eight columns (ts'ung-tui) each with several divisions, seven cavalry divisions, one artillery division and three independent divisions, equipped with Japanese armaments captured by the Russians. This equipment was handed over to the Chinese communists in open violation of the 14 August treaty; it amounted to that of 594,000 Japanese and 75,000 Manchukuo soldiers.[1] Its completion and upkeep was ensured by the Mishan arsenal and a few secondary arsenals.

The Russians had intended to leave Manchuria gradually in October and November, leaving the way open to the Chinese communists. At the request of the central government, which had not finished its plans for the complete reoccupation of the area, they agreed to delay their departure until the following April. The Americans for their part, anxious to avoid being drawn into fighting between the nationalist and communist troops, limited the landing of nationalist soldiers to the North China ports. As they were convinced that the Chinese government was not capable, in terms of logistics, of taking Central and North China and Manchuria simultaneously, they strongly advised it, though in vain, to reconquer the two great railway lines of Tsinpu and Kinhan before pushing on beyond the Great Wall. Eventually, the nationalists did not move into Chinchow, on the threshold of North China, until 26 November. They did not reach Mukden before 26 January 1946. This town had been occupied by Russians and communists for five months, and the

[1] According to the *China Handbook*, it consisted of 300,000 rifles, 4836 machine guns, 1226 pieces of artillery, 2300 motor vehicles and 369 tanks, without counting equipment in the depots.

communists had had time to do some thorough groundwork in the rural districts in the area. They held on to Ch'angch'un, the capital of Manchuria, for a short time and managed to stay on permanently in Harbin, in the north of the region. Manchuria was to be the graveyard of the best of the nationalist troops; countless political mistakes were made there, which Chiang Kai-shek was to acknowledge years later.

The continuing of negotiations

Although the reverse was to be feared, the state of severe tension resulting from the sudden ending of the war did not stop Kuomintang and communist efforts to negotiate a solution to their differences. At the end of June 1945 the central government appointed a committee with seven members, drawn from the Kuomintang, from the Democratic League and from non-party men, to renew contact with the communists. The committee went to Yenan on 1 July and returned on 5 July, bringing new proposals from the communists:

1 The government should abandon its intention to convene a national assembly on 12 November, as planned.
2 A political conference consisting of three communist members, three Kuomintang members, three members from the Democratic League, and three members from independent parties, should be called.

The Japanese capitulation, the Sino-Soviet Treaty, and the hostility of the Great Powers towards possible war, all made Mao Tse-tung decide, after some hesitation, to accept the Generalissimo's invitation to go to Chungking. He arrived there on 28 August, two days after the Central Committee of the Party had published a declaration giving the general conditions necessary for negotiations, and stating openly that negotiations would not prevent the movement from continuing its territorial expansion.[1] The communists' main concern was to play for time, in order to enable them to set up a solid political, administrative and military structure wherever possible, particularly in North China and Manchuria.

The Sino-Soviet Treaty of Friendship and Alliance, signed on 14 August, put the Chinese Communist Party in a delicate position. It had been concluded with Chiang Kai-shek's government, and appeared to imply a disavowal of communist use of force in advance. It also seemed

[1] See Mao Tse-tung, *Selected Works*, vol. IV, p. 47.

to put Russian national interests before those of communism in general, for certain points recalled irresistibly some of the Unequal Treaties and showed total disregard of traditional Chinese claims to Outer Mongolia.

In the general state of well-being that followed the victory it was hard for either side to refuse discussions, thus shouldering the moral responsibility for civil war straight after war with the foreigner. The U.S. ambassador left discreetly on a mission to Washington (22 September), while difficult negotiations went on between Mao Tse-tung (assisted by Chou En-lai and Wang Jo-fei) and Chang Ch'ün and Shao Li-tzu representing the Kuomintang. Both sides were probably quick to realize the limits within which agreement was possible, for, if the Generalissimo is to be believed, only five sessions were held in six weeks. Even so, on the national day (10 October), a joint communiqué was drawn up, though it was not published until the next day. Its terms, written in the most neutral style possible, showed a disquieting lack of precision. Generally speaking, both parties agreed to accept certain principles, though they withheld all details on how they were to be put into effect. The three main headings of the agreement were democratization, local administration and nationalization of troops.

Democratization. The period of political tutelage was to end. The evolution towards constitutional government was to be prepared by the calling of a national assembly, and before that, by calling a 'Political Consultative Conference' attended by delegates from all parties, and also by non-party delegates.

Local administration. Administrative autonomy was to be greatly encouraged. The government refused, however, to recognize the administrative structures of the liberated areas, which had now no reason to continue. Several suggestions put forward by the communists concerning the organization of administrative bodies and nominations to administrative posts were set aside, the *status quo* was maintained and the whole question reserved for consideration by the Political Consultative Conference.

Nationalization of troops. Reorganization was to take place in stages. The communists agreed to accept a system which would assign them definite zones in which to station their troops, which they reduced from between eighty and a hundred divisions to twenty or twenty-four for the whole of China. They would withdraw their troops from South and Central China, except for north Kiangsu, north Anhwei and north Honan. A committee of three, representing the Military Affairs Commission, the Ministry of War and the Eighteenth Army Group, was to make a general study of military affairs.

The vague, fragile agreement signed on 10 October was rendered invalid less than two weeks later, as a result of military difficulties. The communists were becoming increasingly alarmed by movements of government troops in or towards North China, and especially along the Kinhan railway. They felt that the safety of their own areas was threatened. Fighting grew more frequent, particularly along lines of communications; the worst incident was the one in north Honan, already mentioned. Contact between the two parties was maintained, but the delegates' discussions were fruitless. On 30 November the government put forward a proposal in six points, five of which dealt with the military situation, while the sixth urged that the Political Consultative Conference be called straight away. It was to meet on 20 November and consist of thirty-seven members – eight from the Kuomintang, seven from the communists, thirteen from various different parties, and nine non-party members. The communists used the worsening military situation as a pretext to refuse to attend. The atmosphere was one of pessimism.

The United States, in justifiable alarm, returned to the scene once more with a new, important move. On 27 November 1945 President Truman announced that he was going to send a personal representative to China – General George Marshall, who was still surrounded by the prestige earned as Chief of General Staff of the U.S. forces. The day before, the U.S. ambassador Patrick Hurley, irritated by the criticisms levelled against him in certain political circles at home, had handed in his resignation, which was accepted. The communists made a gesture straight away. On 1 December they went back to their former decision and agreed to attend the Political Consultative Conference. Wang Ping-nan, Chou En-lai's usual collaborator, was sent to Chungking to give this information to the Americans, and to find out what their intentions were.

General Marshall, who arrived in Chungking at Christmas in 1945, intended to base his action on the declaration made by the President of the United States on 15 December.[1] According to this, the Americans wanted a 'strong, united and democratic' China, in the interests of the world, of peace and of the United Nations. They hoped that the Chinese would resolve their differences themselves by means of peaceful negotiations, and should they be successful, they promised to give substantial help towards the restoration and development of their agricultural and industrial economy. As the United States saw it, two things were needed to achieve this:

[1] For the complete text see U.S. Department of State, *U.S. Relations with China: The China White Paper*, annex 62, p. 607.

1 The signature of a cease-fire agreement between government and communist troops.
2 The convocation of a national political conference, which would restore unity and put an end to government by one party alone.

For several months all U.S. efforts towards arbitration and reconciliation worked in these two directions. At first, these efforts seemed about to succeed, for on 10 January 1946 a cease-fire agreement was signed and on the same day the Political Consultative Conference, for which the communists had so long been asking, opened at last in Chungking.

The cease-fire agreement, prepared by a committee of three – General Marshall, General Chang Ch'ün and Chou En-lai, contained three main clauses:

1 All hostilities to come to an end on 13 January 1946.
2 All movements of troops to cease, except for those of government troops south of the Yangtze, and those necessary for the reoccupation of Manchuria.
3 A tripartite – United States, central government and communist – General Executive Headquarters to be created in Peking, to organize military inspection teams responsible for enforcing the cease-fire and dealing with any incidents that might arise; Mr Walter Robertson was to represent the United States, General Cheng Kai-min the government, and General Yeh Chien-ying the communists at the General Executive Headquarters in Peking.

The Political Consultative Conference, which met in Chungking from 10 to 31 January, had communist members, as agreed – Chou En-lai, Teng Ying-ch'ao (Madame Chou En-lai), Tung Pi-wu, Wang Jo-fei, Yeh Chien-ying, Wu Yü-chang and Lu Ting-i. After three weeks' work, five proposals were put forward, resembling moral obligations rather than precise formal agreements.

1 *Reorganization of the government.* Until the National Assembly could be called, the Council of State (which was in fact the government council) was to be reorganized, so that it had forty members, half of whom belonged to the Kuomintang.
2 *National reconstruction.* National reconstruction was to be based on the doctrine of the 'Three People's Principles' of Dr Sun Yat-sen.

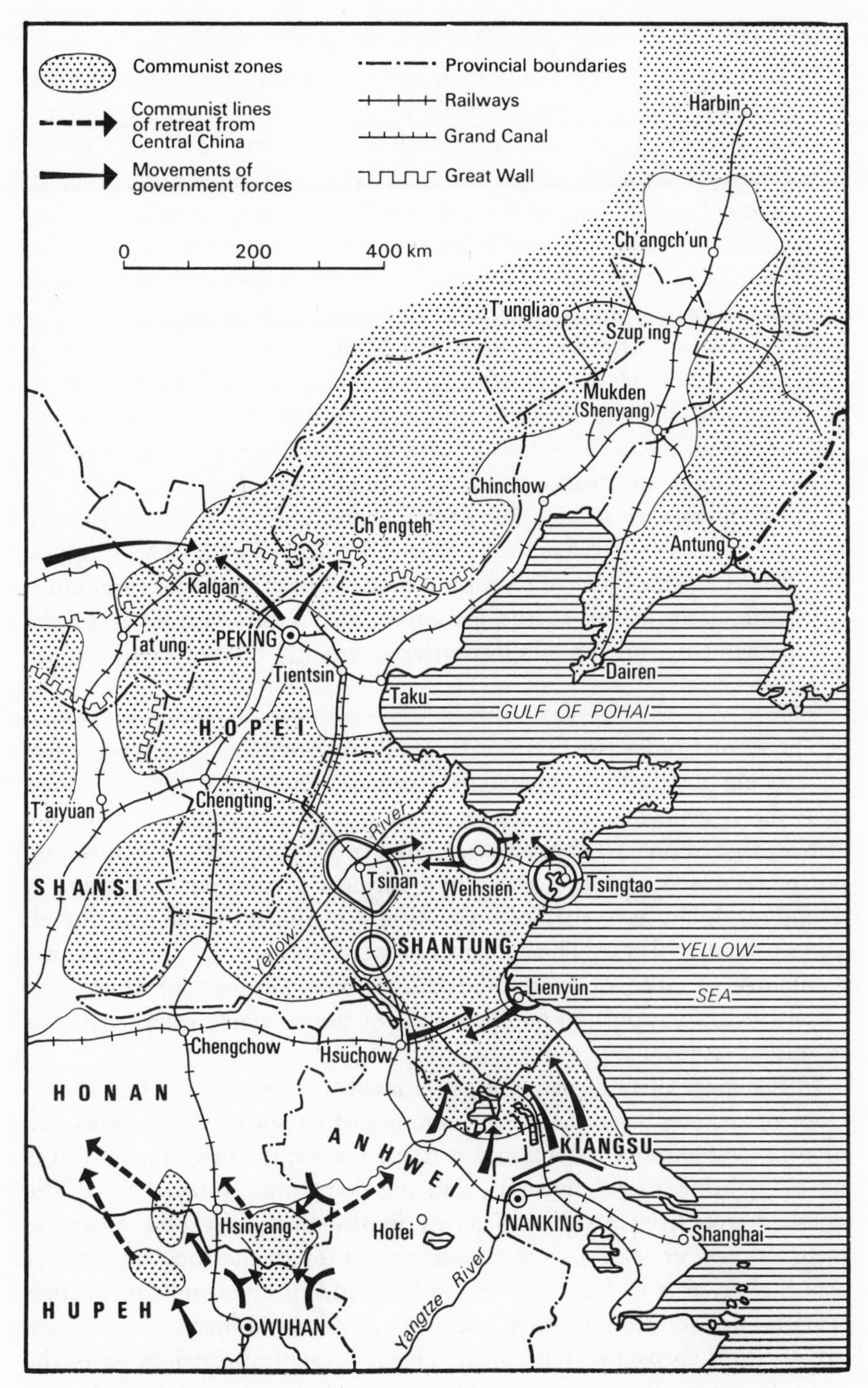

Map 27. The Third Revolutionary Civil War: operations during 1946

Civil rights, political and administrative questions, military affairs, relations with foreign countries, economic and financial questions, cultural affairs, etc., were each dealt with at some length.

3 *Reorganization of the army.* The army was to be dissociated from all political parties. The Military Affairs Commission was to be replaced by a Ministry of National Defence, under the control of the Executive Yüan. The communist and government troops were to be reorganized on the basis of ninety, and later of fifty or sixty divisions.

4 *The National Assembly.* A National Assembly was to meet on 5 May 1946. It was to consist of 2050 members, 1350 of whom were to represent different regions or professions, and 700 of whom were to be delegates from political parties. It was to be responsible for adopting a constitution, with a 75 per cent majority.

5 *The Constitution of 1936.* The 1936 constitution was to be revised by a committee of twenty-five, helped by ten experts. The proposal lists the principles which should guide the work of the committee, particularly as far as the executive body's responsibilities to the parliament, and the administrative autonomy of the provinces, are concerned.

The resolutions passed by the Political Consultative Conference upset all existing institutions. In practice, though, they were less important than the agreement on the reorganization and new deployment of the armies, signed on 25 February 1946. Had this document – which should not be confused with the cease-fire agreement – been put into effect, it would no doubt have enabled a coalition government to be constituted, and avoided civil war. The agreement of 25 February was the work of a committee of three – General Marshall, General Chang Chih-chung and Chou En-lai; it stipulated numbers and the zones where each party was to station its troops.

In the space of one year, the government troops were to be reduced from 394 to 90 divisions, and the communist troops to 18 divisions. Six months later another reduction was to take place; the government forces were to shrink to 50 divisions, and the communist forces to 10. The numbers were fixed at 14,000 men to a division, making a total of 840,000 men, 140,000 or whom were communists, though the total was 15 per cent higher, as it included men from independent units and the different services. In addition to this, each province could maintain a 'peace preservation corps' of 15,000 men. The geographical distribution of the sixty divisions, divided into twenty armies of three divisions each, was eventually as follows:

	Gov. div.	*Comm. div.*
North-East (Manchuria)	14	1
North-West	9	0
North	11	7
Central China	10	8
South	6	0
	—	—
Total	50	10

It was understood that the Executive Headquarters in Peking was to be responsible for the application of these new military arrangements.

A few months were going to be enough to reduce these carefully drawn up agreements to nothing and bring back a state of civil war; the chief cause of this unfortunate development was the two parties' irrepressible mistrust of each other. The Kuomintang, the party in power, hesitated to sacrifice either itself or the individual interests of its members, who were to be found throughout the administrative structure and in much of the army. Its leaders knew that the country was ill prepared for life under a constitutional government and a parliament, and that, if they gave way, the Communist Party alone stood to gain, for it was the only other organized party. The communists practised a far stricter political tutelage in their zones than did the Kuomintang in theirs, and the government knew that this would continue whatever happened. For their part, the communists would possibly have foregone the safeguard furnished by their armies and administrative structures under a completely liberal regime, which would have allowed them to develop at will their political activities and the organization of the Party throughout China. This was clearly not to be the case. As long as the memory of April 1927 remained fresh in people's minds, they could not hand themselves over to the enemy on trust and allow military integration priority over total political integration. On 13 August 1945 Mao Tse-tung attacked the Generalissimo in a withering speech, recalling Ch'en Tu-hsiu and the mistakes he made: 'This time we must be on our guard. Our policy is absolutely different from Chen Tu-hsiu's; no trickery can fool us. We must be clear-headed and have a correct policy; we must not make mistakes.'[1]

As the U.S. ambassador, Leighton Stuart, pointed out, the two men

[1] Mao Tse-tung, 'The Situation and Our Policy after the Victory in the War of Resistance against Japan', *Selected Works*, vol. IV, p. 11.

were personal enemies of twenty-five years' standing, a fact which was probably more significant in China than elsewhere.

It need hardly be added that neither party valued the concepts of parliamentary democracy highly enough to feel morally bound by engagements entered into because they served immediate interests, and enabled each side to avoid shouldering the responsibility for a civil war which both wanted more than anything else. As no pressure from outside was strong enough to restrain them, for the Russians and the Americans were both unwilling to become involved in an internal Chinese conflict and consequently in further international complications, the situation was to worsen rapidly.

New struggles arose over Manchuria. The cease-fire agreement of 10 January allowed the government to move troops south of the Yangtze and in Manchuria. In virtue of this clause, the government considered it unnecessary to allow tripartite teams from the Executive Headquarters in Peking to enter Manchuria, as their intervention was likely to hinder the government's advance. After lengthy discussions, they agreed to do so on 27 March, but until then the two enemies had been alone, face to face, and numerous incidents had occurred.

With this knowledge that it was acting within its rights, the government rapidly advanced its divisions along the main channels of communication, concentrating its efforts towards Ch'angch'un, the former capital of Manchukuo. It had 137,000 choice troops to hand; the communists had to avoid large-scale engagements. Instead, in obedience to instructions given by Mao Tse-tung to the Party Committee for the North-East,[1] which turned out to be remarkably prophetic, they spread out as much as possible throughout the countryside and small towns. Their regular and their local troops were rapidly organized and, if some Kuomintang historians are to be believed, two Mongolian divisions from Outer Mongolia were brought in to help Lin Piao for a time.[2]

The communists, who had occupied Ch'angch'un on 11 April, straight after the departure of the Russians (15 April), tried to hold on to the city or at least gain time by various moves to delay the enemy. The government refused to be taken in by their manœuvres, and, brushing American objections aside, they pushed on towards Szup'ing, an important

[1] See Mao Tse-tung, 'Build Stable Base Areas in the Northeast', *Selected Works,* vol. IV, p. 81.

[2] Ku Kuan-chiao, *The Chinese Communists over the last Thirty Years* (Hong Kong, 1955: in Chinese).

railway junction; violent fighting broke out there on 19 May. Eventually nationalist troops commanded by General Tu Yü-ming entered Ch'angch'un on 23 May, and moved on eastwards and northwards towards Kirin and Harbin. General Marshall managed to negotiate a fortnight's truce, starting on 7 June, in an attempt to find a solution to the question of Manchuria, which the government looked on as its own private affair. At one stage he went so far as to propose that the area be divided between the communists, who were to keep the north of the province of Kirin and Heilungkiang, and the government, who were to keep the rest. This bargaining was rejected by Chou En-lai. An agreement – 'Instructions for the Ceasing of Hostilities in Manchuria' – was eventually drawn up on 26 June; it lasted for only a few weeks.

Once the Manchurian question was half settled, negotiations were reopened for the enforcing of the military agreement of 25 February. The government demanded the control of several towns, roads and railways, among them the railway from Tsingtao to Tsinan (Kiaotsi); it also wanted the communists to leave several provinces where they were not in fact within their rights – Jehol, Chahar and Kiangsu. The communists for their part demanded that the numbers laid down for nationalist and communist troops stationed in Manchuria be revised; they claimed the right to five divisions instead of one. They were shortly to reorganize all their armies. In July 1946 the Eighth Route Army, the New Fourth Army and the 'Democratic Forces in Manchuria' all took on the collective title of People's Liberation Army.

Roughly at the same time (June 1946) the government also carried out a so-called military reform, said to fall within the realm of the tripartite agreement. The Military Affairs Commission was dissolved and replaced by the Ministry of National Defence, while the armies were renamed 'reorganized divisions', and what had been divisions became 'reorganized brigades' – changes that did little more than add to the confusion.

General Marshall tried to end the deadlock by putting forward a draft proposal entitled 'Preliminary Agreement to Govern the Amendment and Execution of the Army Reorganization Plan of 25 February 1946', but the truce of 30 June expired before he could get it accepted. Although both parties officially declared on 1 July that they would not resort to the use of force to settle their differences, the situation deteriorated rapidly.

The government took the initiative in operations everywhere, initially meeting with great success (see Map 27, p. 385). In north Kiangsu, General T'ang En-po, in command of about fifteen good divisions, attacked Ch'en Yi and Hsü Yü from 13 July onwards, driving them back towards Shantung. Hard fighting continued throughout the summer; the government won back the towns along the Grand Canal, and to the east of it, among them Huaian (17 September) and Huaiyin. By the autumn the eastern section of the Lunghai line was completely free of communist troops. The Kiaotsi railway line in east Shantung was also occupied once more, but the government Third Army, commanded by Chao Hsi-t'ien, was destroyed at Tingt'ao, in the Hotseh area (3-8 September) in the south-west of the province. In Jehol, government troops took Ch'engteh, the provincial capital, on 28 August. Kalgan, the capital of Chahar, and the largest communist town beyond the Great Wall, was occupied by Fu Tso-yi on 11 October. The government's most important victory was perhaps the elimination of the communist troops under Li Hsien-nien who held Central China, on the northern slopes of the Tapieh Shan. Five nationalist armies drove the remains of them into west Honan and south Shansi. A serious threat on the middle reaches of the Yangtze was averted for the moment, at least.

The communists carried off a few local victories, maintaining their position in their traditional mountain bases, but they were in real difficulties. Mao Tse-tung admitted as much and tried to restore confidence to the cadres. He declared that some towns and territories should be abandoned, guerrilla methods should be adopted once more, and that the communists should unite themselves as widely as possible with all sections of the rural and urban populations, in order to isolate the Kuomintang.[1] Everything seemed to indicate that a long civil war had begun; the result appeared doubtful, to say the least, to all those who realized how weak the national army was, taken as a whole.

General Marshall, helped by the new United States Ambassador to China, Dr Leighton Stuart, a former teacher and missionary who had grown up in China, continued his now hopeless efforts towards mediation in a climate that was growing increasingly difficult. The Kuomintang right wing challenged him, reproaching him with giving the communists time to get organized and expand. Even the Generalissimo himself became less and less receptive to Marshall's suggestions.

The communists for their part launched open attacks on the United States accusing it of fostering civil war through its military aid to the national government. One of their chief grievances was that on 20 February 1946 the Americans created a mission of military advisers to

[1] See Mao Tse-tung, 'Smash Chiang Kai-shek's Offensive by a War of Self-Defence', *Selected Works*, vol. IV.

the Chinese government.[1] They reproached them for continuing to supply equipment for the thirty-nine national divisions covered by the programme of 1944, and for handing over 800 million dollars' worth of 'surplus' military supplies from the zone of operations in the Pacific to the Chinese government. Incidents intended to mislead international opinion or American opinion were put to full use, or instigated if necessary. On 28 July 1946 a small American military convoy was attacked at Anping, in Hopei, losing twenty men; a little later, a Chinese student was supposedly raped by an American soldier, with the result that anti-American demonstrations were staged in Peking. The fact that several American journalists sympathized with the Chinese communists – Edgar Snow, Israel Epstein and Anna Louise Strong were the best known of them – helped further the aims and manœuvrings of Yenan. Mao Tse-tung, in an interview with Anna Louise Strong at this time, said: 'If the American people stay the hand of the American reactionaries who are helping Chiang Kai-shek fight the civil war, there is hope for peace.'[2]

During this same interview, which in places took on the tone of an incitement to turn the American people against its government, Mao Tse-tung, in his attacks on the American 'reactionaries' and the atom bomb, described them as 'paper tigers', an expression borrowed from popular imagery with a considerable future ahead of it. When, in 1958, Peking tried to shift the policy of the worldwide communist movement towards a harder line, it was taken up and widely used; it had already acquired its full meaning at the time of the interview in 1946.[3]

> The atom bomb is a paper tiger which the U.S. reactionaries use to scare people. It looks terrible, but in fact it isn't. Of course the atom bomb is a weapon of mass slaughter, but the outcome of a war is decided by the people, not by one or two new types of weapon.

America's willingness to help, and the sincerity of General Marshall and Dr Leighton Stuart, both of whom wanted above all to promote peace and serve the Chinese people by attributing their fair share of the responsibilities to the communists, were utilized by the latter for their

[1] See Mao Tse-tung, 'Talk with the American correspondent Anna Louise Strong', *Selected Works*, vol. IV, p. 97.

[2] Ibid., p. 100.

[3] The Chinese review, *Knowledge of the World* (*Shih-chieh Chih-shih*) made a collection in 1958 of all the passages in articles and speeches by Mao Tse-tung on the theme 'imperialism and all reactionaries are paper tigers', which was published under the same title in several foreign languages.

own ends, with total shamelessness and dishonesty. The communists did their best to stir up the most primitive forms of nationalism and pacificism, directed against the United States, in a population exhausted by a century of national humiliations and forty years of foreign or civil war.

The American attempts at mediation and the political changes within the country could no longer disguise the real military situation; General Marshall eventually acknowledged its gravity and withdrew definitively on 6 January 1947. In the meantime, the most eminent United States representatives tried to prevent civil war by every means at their disposal, short of direct intervention. On 10 August General Marshall and Dr Leighton Stuart appealed to Chinese public opinion, though it was limited and in any case powerless. Their appeal was based on the themes of the seriousness of the economic situation, the expansion of the civil war and the inability of the government and the communists to find solutions to these questions.

On the same day, President Truman sent a message to the Generalissimo expressing great anxiety and regret at the fact that General Marshall's mission had not been successful. The U.S. president, using a frank, vigorous tone rarely to be found in documents of this kind, denounced the harmful action of Kuomintang and Communist Party extremists, and the assassination of public figures with liberal views, and threatened China with complete economic abandonment:

> The firm desire of the people of the United States and of the American government is still to help China achieve lasting peace and a stable economy under a truly democratic government. There is an increasing awareness, however, that the hopes of the people of China are being thwarted by militarists and a small group of political reactionaries who are obstructing the advancement of the general good of the nation by failing to understand the liberal trend of the times. The people of the United States view with violent repugnance this state of affairs.
>
> It cannot be expected that American opinion will continue in its generous attitude towards your nation unless convincing proof is shortly forthcoming that genuine progress is being made towards a peaceful settlement of China's internal problems.[1]

This showed, in the clearest possible terms, that for the Americans at least the Kuomintang's share in the responsibility was even greater than that of the communists.

[1] *U.S. Relations with China: The China White Paper*, p. 652.

Chiang Kai-shek did not agree; on 28 August he gave an energetic reply, shifting the responsibility on to the enemy's side and pointing out their totalitarian ambitions. He listed the violations committed by the communists and promised to carry on efforts towards peace, for which he considered U.S. support indispensable. A few weeks earlier, on 13 August, in a long speech to the nation in memory of the Japanese surrender, the Generalissimo had stated the government's democratization policy and denounced the communist rebellion once more. American efforts towards mediation still went on. On the basis of proposals put forward by Dr Stuart on 1 August an attempt was made to set up a 'Committee of Five' to be put in charge of reorganizing the State Council. The Committee was to consist of one American (Dr. Stuart), two members of the Kuomintang (General Wang Ta-chen and Mr Chang Li-sheng) and two communists (Chou En-lai and Tung Pi-wu). The reorganization of the State Council was still dependent on the development of the military situation, and particularly on the execution of five conditions, which the Generalissimo had laid down at the beginning of August, and which were to precede any agreement:

1 Withdrawal of the communist troops from Kiangsu to north of the Lunghai railway line.
2 Evacuation by the communists of the railway line from Tsinan to Tsingtao in Shantung.
3 Evacuation by the communists of the capital of Jehol.
4 Regrouping of the communists in Manchuria in the provinces of Heilungkiang, Nenkiang and Hsingan.
5 Abandoning by the communists of all points occupied by their troops after 7 June 1946.

Some of these conditions were shortly to be obtained by government military action.

The conditions the communists laid down for their participation in the Committee of Five were equally unacceptable to the government; they were accompanied by a demand that the Military Committee of Three (General Marshall, General Chang Ch'ün and Chou En-lai) should meet to end the now increasing hostilities. A deadlock had been reached once more. General Marshall, thoroughly disheartened and deeply hurt by the personal attacks levelled at him by the communist press, informed the Generalissimo that he intended to return to the United States, giving up all further efforts towards mediation. On 5 October he asked Washington to recall him, suspending his request for a time when the central government granted a ten-day truce to enable him to look into proposals, which were immediately rejected by the communists.

The national government, urged on by its victories, and particularly by the taking of Kalgan, was increasingly unwilling to make concessions. On 11 October it decided to call a meeting of the National Assembly for 12 November. On 16 October it put to the communists the proposals that were delaying General Marshall's departure. On 24 October the communists rejected all eight points. The small parties and several independent figures of some note tried to bring about a reconciliation on 25, 29 and 30 October, but met with failure. Briefly, the differences of opinion arose over the ceasing of hostilities, the meeting of the National Assembly, and the reorganization of the government. The communists gave a cease-fire and the reorganization of the government as the conditions for their attending the assembly, whereas the government wanted to reverse the order of operations. After three days' delay, filled by last moment attempts at arbitration and government proposals, the National Assembly eventually met on 15 November. The Communist Party and the Democratic League did not attend, although their seats were kept for them. On 19 November Chou En-lai left Nanking, leaving part of his delegation behind him, however, headed by Wang Ping-nan.

On 16 November the communist representatives in Nanking made a long declaration, stating their Party's point of view. They denounced the one-sided initiative taken by the government in calling the National Assembly, and declared once more that three points ought to have been fulfilled:

1 The proposals put forward by the January Political Consultative Conference ought to have been carried out.
2 The government ought to have been reorganized.
3 The Assembly ought to have been called by the new government.

Lastly, the responsibility for the break in relations was naturally attributed to the central government, which had just 'slammed the door on negotiations'. On 4 December the Communist Party adopted a still harder line and virtually brought all conversations to an end when it stated the conditions necessary for them to begin again, conditions that were totally unacceptable to the government:

1 The dissolution of the National Assembly.
2 Return of all troops to the positions occupied on 13 January 1946, the day the first cease-fire was put into application.

Until the last moment the U.S. mediators retained their illusions to some extent, owing to the comparatively liberal proposal for the new constitution (adopted on 25 December 1946 and promulgated on 1 January 1947), and also possibly relying on the influence of some neutral elements. They may also have attached more importance than was deserved to the government's military victories. The illusion seems to have been particularly long lived as far as the influence of the neutral personalities was concerned, as is borne out by a passage from the American *China White Paper*:

> In furtherance of the idea of endeavouring to build up a liberal group in China to a position of influence, General Marshall took every opportunity in conversations with minority and non-party Chinese to emphasize the necessity of the unification of the minority parties and the organization of a liberal group which could serve as a balance between the two major parties.

This same illusion occurs once or twice more in the melancholy official communiqué, which followed the departure of General Marshall, on 7 January 1947: 'The salvation of the situation would be the assumption of leadership by the liberals in the government and in the minority parties and successful action on their part under the leadership of the Generalissimo would lead to unity through good government.'

General Marshall left China a justifiably embittered man, though his appointment to the post of Secretary of State helped to alleviate his sorrow. Soon after, the withdrawal of the U.S. members of the Military Committee of Three and the Executive Headquarters in Peking (29 January 1947) confirmed the U.S. abandonment of efforts towards mediation, at least as General Marshall had conceived them.

Contact between the national government and the Communist Party was maintained for a few weeks longer through the mediation of Dr Stuart. On 16 January 1947 the government proposed to send a mission to Yenan, led by General Chang Chih-chung, a man of integrity, liked by the communists, to bring all matters in abeyance under discussion once more, including a cease-fire. The Communist Party rejected the suggestion and stood by its declaration made on 4 December. Its increasingly hard attitude was underlined by a speech given by Chou En-lai on the Yenan radio on 10 January, and by a declaration by the official Yenan spokesman, Lu Ting-i, made at the same time. The communists appear to have wanted to shift the whole Chinese question on to an international level. On 1 February the Central Committee of the Communist Party repudiated all agreements made with the government after 10 January 1946, the date of the first cease-fire agreement. Once the way had been opened, Mr Molotov proposed, on 10 March 1947, to insert the Chinese civil war question on the agenda before the Foreign Ministers' Conference. The United States refused.

On 10 March contacts between the government and the Chinese Communist Party officially came to an end, with the departure of Wang Ping-nan from Nanking (5 March) and the withdrawal of the American liaison detachment in Yenan. A few days later, on 19 March, Yenan fell to government troops. The period of large-scale military operations had begun.

29 The Period of Large-scale Military Operations (April 1947-December 1949)

The period of large-scale military operations, ending in the military and economic collapse of the government, forced to fall back on Taiwan, was made up of three different stages. In the spring and summer of 1947 the government troops maintained the upper hand more or less everywhere. The communists, with far fewer regular troops and less equipment and transport facilities, did not generally try to hold towns and communications channels against them, or to maintain an unbroken front. Instead, they maintained or, where necessary, won back the control of the rural areas. Their mobility, their discipline when in combat, the high quality of their commanding officers and above all, their superior morale, began to achieve results and to wear down the national troops.

Between the summer of 1947 and that of 1948 the communists gradually gained control; they won a foothold once more in Central China between the Yellow River and the Yangtze and managed to break the chief nationalist lines of communication in North China and Manchuria. The government hung on to several large towns and their surrounding areas: Peking, Tientsin, Mukden and Ch'angch'un.

The third phase began in the autumn of 1948. In all the theatres of war – Manchuria, North China and Central China – powerful communist attacks shattered the nationalist dispositions, which were completely lacking in flexibility. The communists had won superiority in numbers and equipment. In the spring of 1949 they crossed the Yangtze. In the autumn the communist advance reached Canton and Szechuan. By the end of the year the entire Chinese continent, except for Yunnan, Hsinkiang and Tibet,

The communists did not try to put up serious resistance. Small engagements occurred in the Wayaopao region round about 13 March, and Yenan was taken without a fight on 19 March. The Party leadership retreated to Suiteh, and later to north-east Shansi, near Shihchiachuang, where it was to stay until virtually the end of the civil war.

The return of communist troops to Central China

In the summer of 1947 the communists made an extremely daring move in Central China. It was not a real offensive, but a vast infiltration operation, which was not in itself dangerous, but it still paralysed government action by keeping most of its strategic reserve south of the Great Wall. Three main groups took part in this audacious undertaking. One group, under Liu Po-ch'eng, consisting of seven 'columns' (armies) amounting to between 50,000 and 60,000 men, moved in from south Hopei, crossed the Lunghai railway line east of K'aifeng and marched towards the Tapieh Shan mountains (30 June to 27 July). Another group under Ch'en Keng, of two 'columns' and the Thirty-eighth Army, amounting to about 20,000 men, coming from south Shansi, crossed the Yellow River east of Loyang and took up position along the Kinhan railway line, and also to the west of the line (August). The third group, under Ch'en Yi, consisting of eight 'columns' from Shantung, crossed the Tsinpu railway line north of Hsüchow and took up a position in east Honan, south of the K'aifeng area, thus isolating the towns on the Lunghai railway (August). Hsü Yü meanwhile took charge of the defence of the Shantung peninsula. These three relatively small groups – about 150,000 men in all – spread out over the area enclosed by the main railway lines of Tsinpu, Lunghai and Kinhan, threatening all three of them. They also set about organizing the population in the area, which the communists had already occupied, at least partially, during the Japanese war. Their sudden appearance there naturally caused a great stir in the capital.

The Wedemeyer mission

At roughly the same time an event occurred which seemed briefly to herald a decisive change in U.S. policy in China, and to involve the possibility of the Chinese question becoming an international issue: General Wedemeyer was sent to Nanking on a mission of information. The arrival of a general well known for his anti-communist feelings aroused the Kuomintang to further hopes of large-scale U.S. military aid, or even of direct military intervention. The communists were correspondingly alarmed and denounced American plans for 'aggression' with unprecedented violence. In fact, according to General Wedemeyer himself, the aim was to calm criticisms formulated by a group of Republican senators rather than to make a change of policy and oppose the extension of communism to the whole of China at any cost. General Wedemeyer's report could add nothing new to what was already known. The faults of the system were ruthlessly enumerated once again, and communist methods and designs were condemned. It appears that the situation could still have been stabilized by the application of far-reaching reforms, with the help of U.S. aid in the spirit of the United Nations Charter. The worsening situation in Manchuria, combined with the region's geographical position at the crossroads of conflicting international interests, seemed to indicate that it would be preferable to set up an international tutelage to be supervised by the five Great Powers. General Wedemeyer was hardly more optimistic than the United States ambassador, though he differed from him on two points – the inappropriateness of setting up a coalition government, and a greater faith in the Generalissimo's goodwill.[1] The Wedemeyer mission did damage in that the negative results were the only ones made known. It discredited the central government still further, while the seriousness of the diagnosis and the cost of the remedies proposed made the abandonment of the patient still more inevitable.

The taking of Loyang and the reoccupation of Yenan by the communists (April 1948)[2]

By the spring of 1948 it was becoming obvious that the communists had won the strategic initiative. Their regular troops were divided into ten army groups, fifty or so 'columns' (armies) and 156 brigades, which were really small divisions similar to the central government divisions before the reorganization of the army. Their numbers amounted to 1,320,000, all of whom could be used in the front line, as the communist military organization made the local militia responsible for the security of the rear; the militia amounted to 2,490,000 men. The central government constantly replenished its troops so that their numbers were kept up, but the good units trained and equipped by the United States were beginning to tire. The breaking up of the theatres of war into twenty 'pacification zones' suggested that territorial safety had gained in importance over the attacks in the grand style which had marked the beginning.

[1] See the text of the report in 'Wedemeyer Report', appendix VI, or in *U.S. Relations with China: The China White Paper*, annex 135.

[2] See Map 29, p. 402.

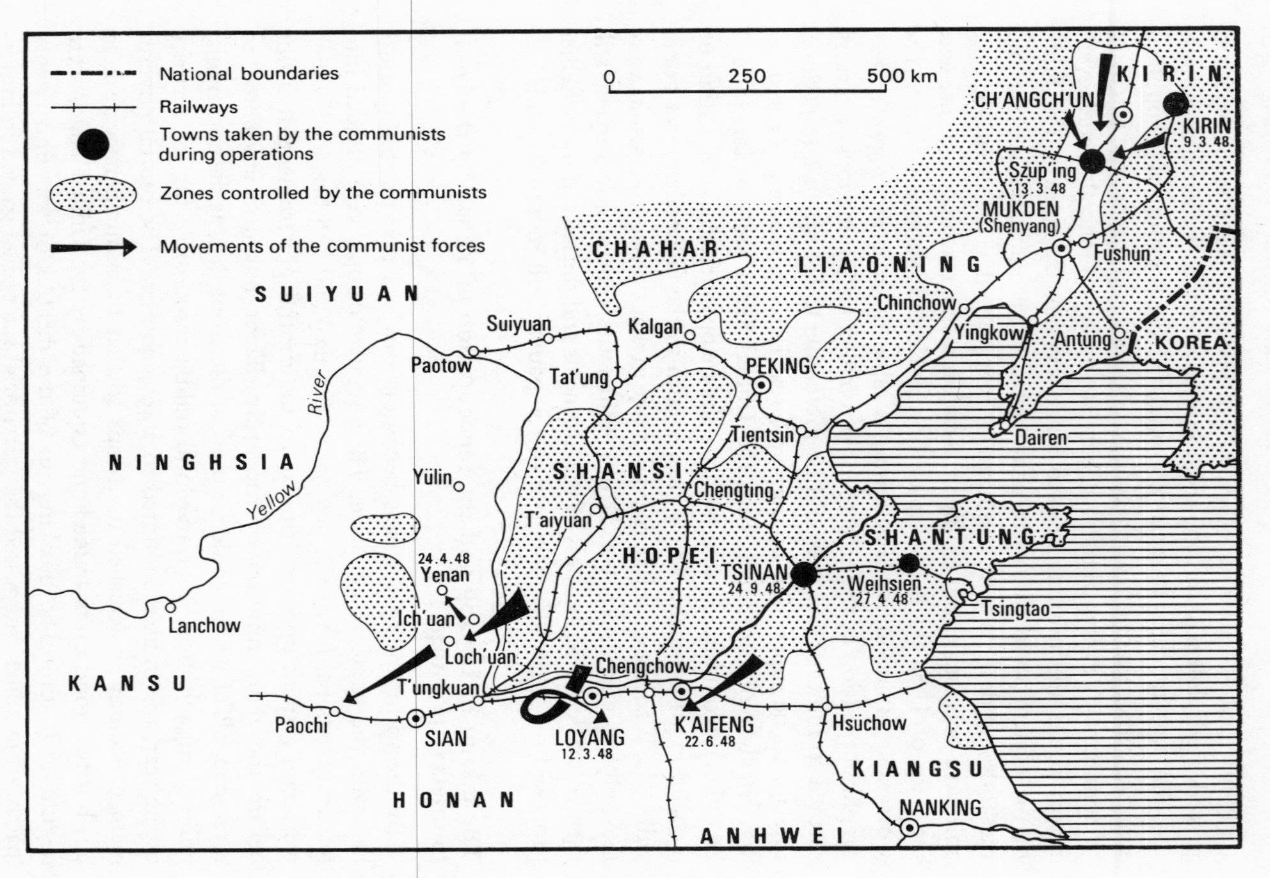
National boundaries
Railways
Towns taken by the communists during operations
Zones controlled by the communists
Movements of the communist forces
0
250
500 km
KIRIN
KIRIN 9.3.48
CH'ANGCH'UN
Szup'ing 13.3.48
MUKDEN (Shenyang)
Fushun
KOREA
Antung
Dairen
Yingkow
Chinchow
LIAONING
CHAHAR
PEKING
Tientsin
Kalgan
Tat'ung
Suiyuan
Paotow
SUIYUAN
SHANSI
T'aiyuan
Chengting
HOPEI
TSINAN 24.9.48
Weihsien 27.4.48
SHANTUNG
Tsingtao
Hsüchow
KIANGSU
NANKING
ANHWEI
K'AIFENG 22.6.48
Chengchow
LOYANG 12.3.48
HONAN
Loch'uan
24.4.48 Yenan
Ich'uan
Yülin
T'ungkuan
SIAN
Paochi
Yellow River
NINGHSIA
Lanchow
KANSU

Map 29. The battles of the spring and summer of 1948

On 12 March 1948 General Ch'en Keng took the important town of Loyang which to a certain extent controlled liaisons between Shansi and Honan. The communists lost the town on 18 March, but won it back for good on 7 April. A few weeks later P'eng Teh-huai and his First Field Army, based on the Anyi area in Shansi, took Ich'uan and Loch'uan in Shensi. The government troops quickly evacuated Yenan (24 April), at considerable sacrifice to their pride, though it enabled them to reopen the road from Sian to Lanchow, which had been cut at Paochi by P'eng Teh-huai on his way south-westwards; he managed to stay there until 28 April. The national Eighty-second Army inflicted a serious defeat on the 2nd, 4th and 6th communist columns in the same region. On the other hand, a national division was surprised and destroyed in Shensi, in the Ich'uan and Huangling region; its leader, General Liu Kan, committed suicide, as several other Kuomintang generals were soon to do. The Shensi front moved back roughly to the Wei valley.

The battles of K'aifeng and Tsinan

The battle of K'aifeng involved more troops on either side than any other engagement so far. The communist troops, commanded by Ch'en Yi, consisted of eighteen 'columns', or nearly 200,000 men. The government troops assembled against them consisted of three army groups, commanded by General Chiu Ching-chuan (Second Army Group), General Huang Po-tao (Seventh Army Group) and General Wu Shao-hien (Eighth Army Group). The nationalist numbers were roughly the same as those of the communists, in spite of the fact that 23,000 men had been flown to Sian.

Ch'en Yi took K'aifeng on 22 June and withdrew from it again on 25 June. The battle, fought over the whole of north Honan, remained indecisive to the end, but it proved that the communists were capable of handling large-scale operations and bringing several hundreds of thousands of men into action. From then on military operations became more powerful and more frequent than ever before. The communists were henceforth strong enough and well enough prepared in the technological field to dare to attack the enemy's large formations and cities.

Three months after the battle of K'aifeng the government suffered a grave defeat in the fall of Tsinan, the capital of Shantung, defended half-heartedly by the governor, Wang Yao-wu, and lost through the treachery of the 84th Division and its commander Wu Hua-wen, who had already changed sides several times in the past. Tsinan fell on 24 September; its loss, following that of Weihsien on 27 April, left the whole of the province of Shantung in the hands of the communists. This had a considerable effect on morale. From a purely military point of view, it meant that the communists gained 100,000 men and their equipment. Operations were shifted to the Hsüchow area once more. The road to Nanking had soon to be defended. However, events in Manchuria were already taking a dramatic turn.

The battle of Manchuria[1]

In Manchuria the 'United Democratic Army of the North-east', which had developed considerably since 1945, had become the Fourth Field Army, commanded by Lin Piao. It was better equipped than the others, and had plenty of good recruits on hand from a population which was both robust and well prepared psychologically by years of foreign occupation; but it had the best government troops as its opponents. The government troops had changed their position little since their spectacular advances of the spring of 1946. Although they controlled nearly half the population, amounting to a total of 40 million inhabitants, they held only a fifth or a sixth of the territory, as well as the large towns in the centre and the south, and the main railway lines, as was their usual practice.

At the beginning of 1947, in the midst of the bitter Manchurian winter, Lin Piao launched the first of a series of minor attacks round Ch'angch'un and Kirin, with the two aims of preventing the government troops from extending their occupation and of hindering or interrupting their internal liaisons. The attacks took place on 6 January, 15 February, 10 March and 10 May; the last attack forced the nationalist command to evacuate Kirin (17 May) and T'unghua (25 May) for a time, and to withdraw from the Liaotung peninsula in the south. The nationalist command had to concentrate its troops round the large towns, a purely defensive attitude which lessened the troops' will to fight still further, when their morale was already beginning to suffer. The situation was further complicated by an unsatisfactory sharing out of responsibility between the Generalissimo's delegate, then General Hsiung Shih-hui, and General Tu Yü-ming, in command of the whole theatre of war in Manchuria. General Ch'en Ch'eng was appointed Commander-in-Chief in the autumn of 1947, but this did not improve matters and he was replaced by General Wei Li-huang shortly afterwards.

The communists carried out two fairly successful operations at the end of 1947. They aimed at isolating Ch'angch'un by cutting communications

[1] See Map 30, p. 405.

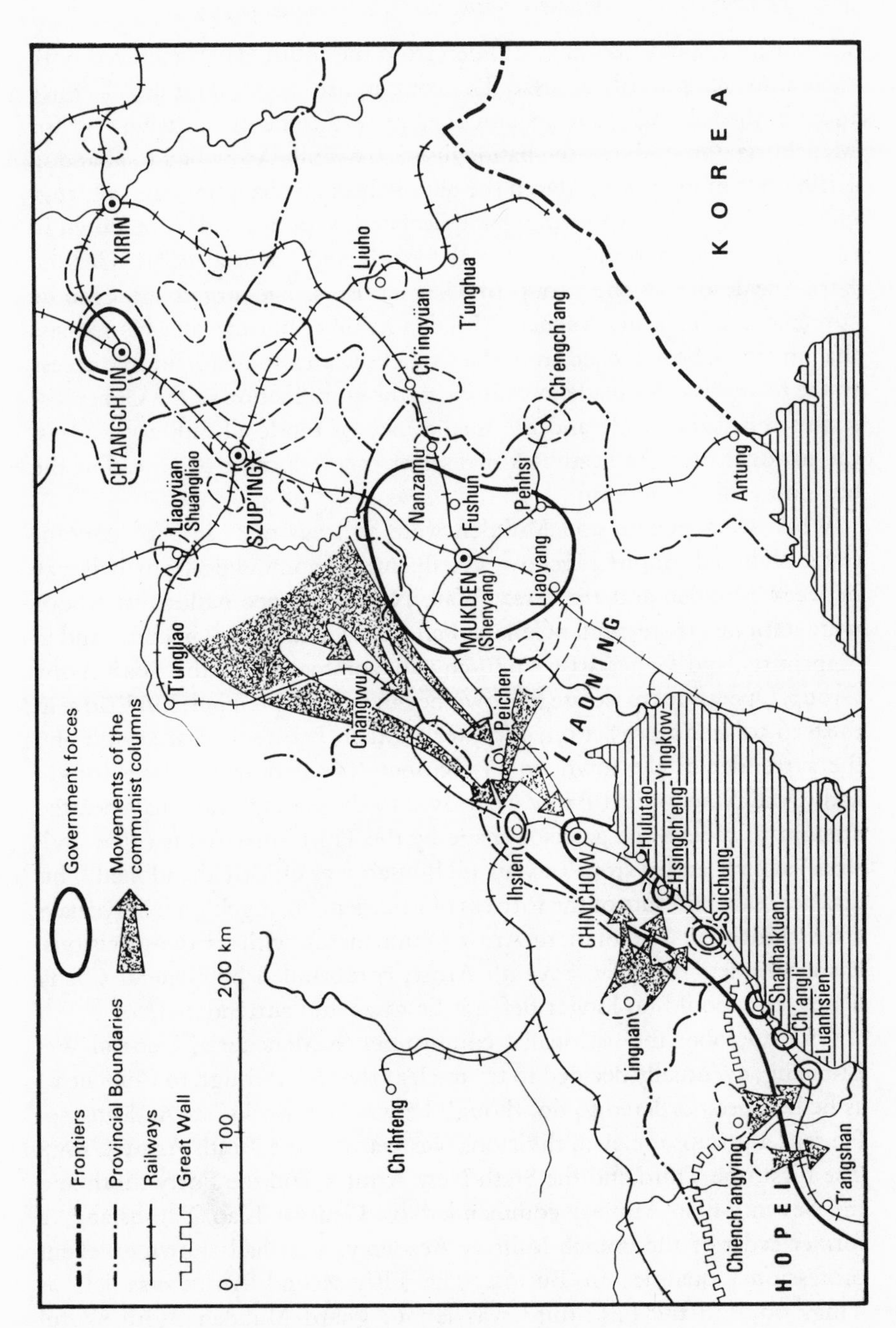

Map 30. The battles of Manchuria (autumn 1948)

with Mukden, and isolating Mukden from the south. They achieved both their aims, temporarily at least. The communists began their attacks once more in the following spring, and 1948 proved to be the decisive year for Manchuria. On 9 March the nationalist Sixty-ninth Army had to abandon Kirin once more. On 13 March the nationalists lost Szup'ing, and Ch'angch'un and Mukden were completely isolated; supplies had to be flown in to both towns, involving a colossal logistic and financial effort. General Barr, the leader of the group of U.S. advisers, had urged the Chinese supreme command to evacuate Mukden in time, but in vain; his request that an attack be launched from the Chinchow area to maintain free access to the town was also made in vain. With the combination of the Generalissimo's misplaced pride and the inefficiency of the local military leaders, the nationalists were heading for disaster; matters came to a head at the beginning of the autumn.

While Ch'angch'un and Mukden were still cut off, Lin Piao concentrated all his efforts on Chinchow, a vital centre of communications, half way between Mukden and the Great Wall. Nearly 100,000 nationalist troops were stationed there, under General Fan Han-chieh, second in command in Manchuria, and General Lu Chün-ch'üan, commander of the Sixth Army Group. Operations to isolate the town began on 12 September; Lin Piao sent thirteen columns into action, one after another, before the last assault and the surrender of the town on 15 October. The nationalist forces fought badly, the Ninety-third Army went over to the enemy, and a half-hearted attempt to relieve the garrison made by the Thirty-first Army (nine divisions), which landed from Taiwan at Hulutao, was quickly abandoned. This disaster sealed the fate of the fortress of Mukden. Ch'angch'un fell five days after Chinchow. The Sixtieth Army (Yunnanese), with its two divisions, changed sides; the New Seventh Army, commanded by General Cheng T'ung-kuo, could no longer defend the town and surrendered.

On 9 October the nationalist commander in Manchuria, General Wei Li-huang, eventually decided to try to clear the way through to Chinchow, as he had been ordered to do, though he was two weeks late in doing so. He sent a group of eleven divisions westwards – the Ninth Army Group (the First, the Third and the Sixth New Armies, and the Forty-ninth and the Seventy-first Armies) commanded by General Liao Yao-hsiang, a former cadet of the French Military Academy, who had shown excellent professional qualities in Burma. The Fifty-second Army was left at Yingk'ou, and the Fifty-third was left to guard Mukden. With skilful manœuvring by Lin Piao, who once more had ample means at his disposal after the fall of Chinchow, the Ninth Army Group was encircled, partially destroyed and eventually forced to surrender between 27 and 30 October. On 2 November the fortress of Mukden surrendered, with the Fifty-third Army and part of the 207th Youth Division. The Fifty-second Army alone managed to re-embark at Yingk'ou.[1] Manchuria had cost the government over thirty good divisions, half of which had American equipment. A large proportion of the men and all the equipment went over to the communists, who now were superior in numbers and armaments. All the communists' troops in Manchuria were free to undertake the conquest of North China, which was about to begin.

The fall of Peking and Tientsin

North China was in fact reduced to the Peking-Tientsin-Kalgan-Taku area, where the government troops were divided into five groups commanded by General Fu Tso-yi, formerly under the orders of Yen Hsi-shan and respected for his simplicity, his uprightness and his talents as an administrator and a military leader. The five groups consisted of over 500,000 men. The communists brought in the Fourth Field Army (probably a dozen or so columns), and two army groups from the North China forces commanded by Nieh Jung-chen; the numbers were roughly equal.

General Fu Tso-yi, well aware of the inferiority of his troops in terms of morale at least, aware too that the end of the regime was inevitable, and impressed by the resounding victories the communists were winning in Central China at the same time, was inclined to open negotiations; he can be partly excused by his anxiety to save the ancient city of Peking and its art treasures. In November Lin Piao finished deploying his troops along an approximate line running from Shanhaikuan to Jehol; Jehol, or, as it is also known, Ch'engteh, was occupied on 9 November. To the south, Nieh Jung-chen threatened the Peking-Kalgan railway from positions in north Shansi and north-west Hopei, where Paoting had been abandoned by the nationalists on 23 October. The communists planned to exert pressure on Fu Tso-yi at either end of his disposition, isolating him in the Peking region, where they tried to get him to stay as long as possible. Mao Tse-tung himself drew up the main instructions for these operations, as he had done for the battles in Manchuria.[2]

[1] General Wei Li-huang escaped from Mukden by air. Later on, in 1955, he joined the communists on the mainland. When he died in 1959, his new friends organized grandiose funeral celebrations, no doubt to express their gratitude.

[2] Cf. Mao Tse-tung, 'The Concept of Operations for the Peiping-Tientsin Campaign' and 'The Concept of Operations for the Liaoshi-Shenyang Campaign', *Selected Works*, vol. IV, pp. 289 and 261.

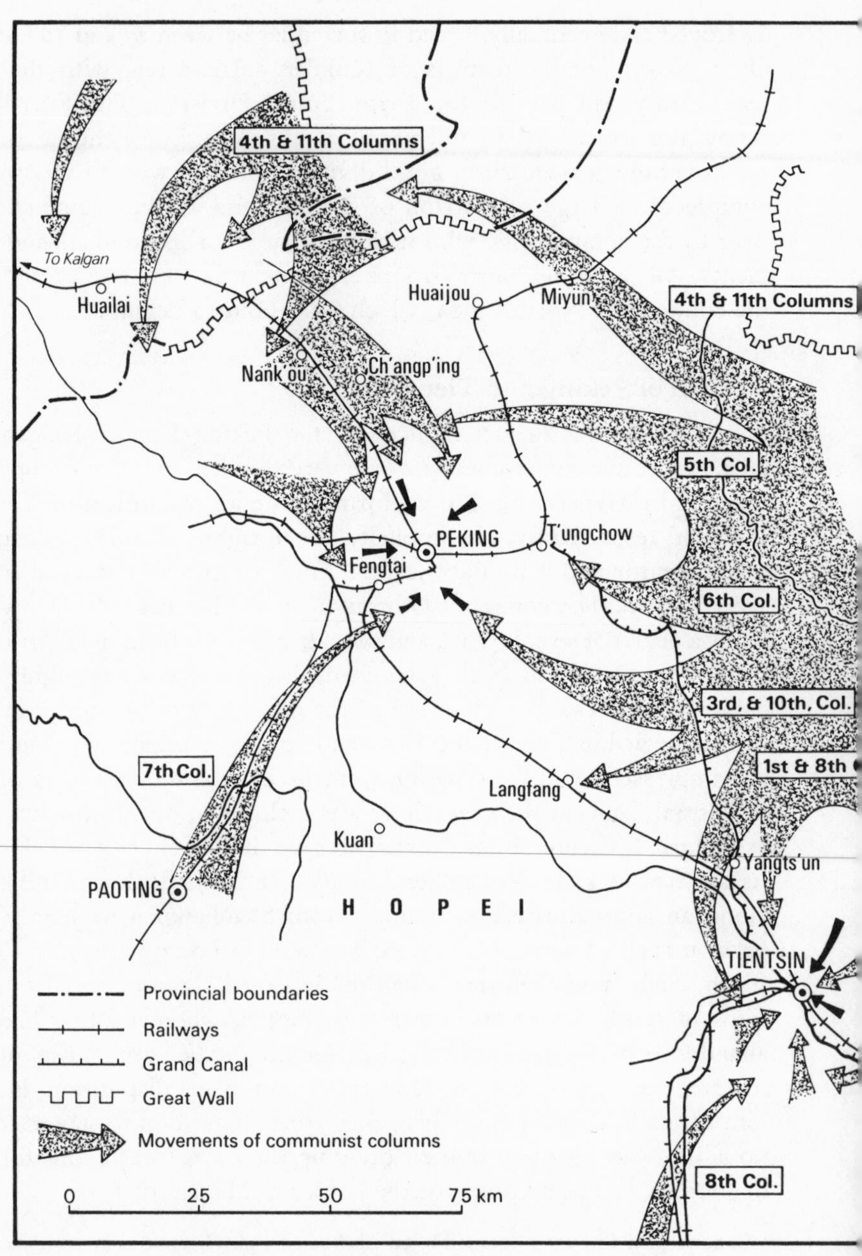

Map 31. The Peking-Tientsin campaign

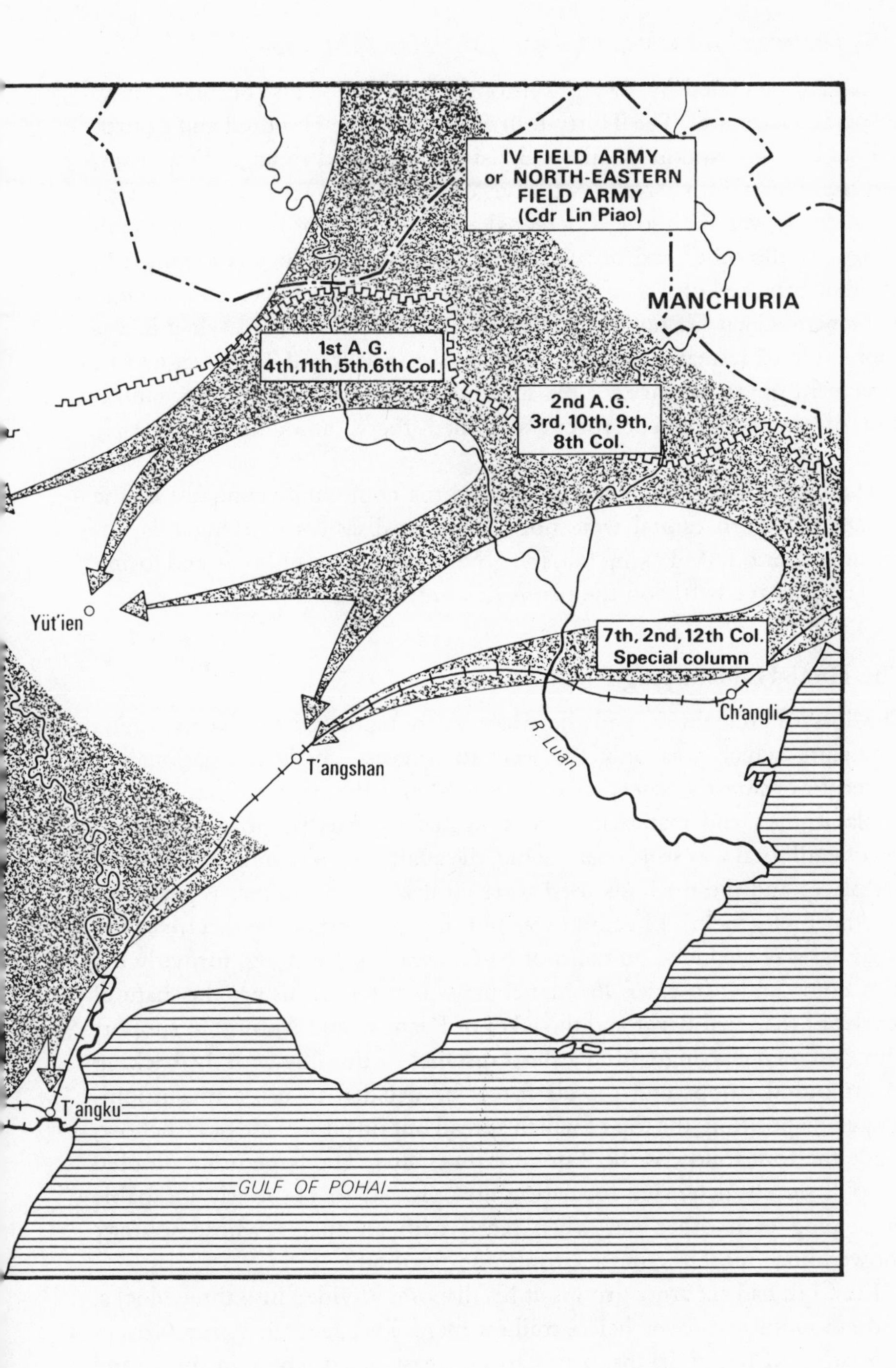
IV FIELD ARMY
or NORTH-EASTERN
FIELD ARMY
(Cdr Lin Piao)
MANCHURIA
1st A.G.
4th,11th,5th,6th Col.
2nd A.G.
3rd, 10th, 9th,
8th Col.
Yüt'ien
7th, 2nd, 12th Col.
Special column
Ch'angli
R. Luan
T'angshan
T'angku
GULF OF POHAI

Kalgan, defended by seven divisions of the nationalist Second Army, fell on 24 December. The Thirty-fourth and the One Hundred and Fourth Armies had to abandon Huailai and Hsinpaoan round about 22 December, and the Thirty-fifth Army (two divisions) was thrown into disorder or captured. It was Fu Tso-yi's personal army and one of the best in North China. At the other end of the theatre of war, Tientsin was hemmed in and then attacked on 15 January; its garrison of 150,000 men commanded by General Chen Chang-chieh had to surrender. Eventually, when it was impossible to retreat either eastwards or westwards, Fu Tso-yi signed an agreement on 23 January for the surrender of Peking and the reorganization of the government forces stationed there, amounting to nearly 200,000 men.

The loss of half a million soldiers and the communist conquest of the former Northern capital were not the worst disasters marking this unfortunate period. As Peking fell, the government was fighting – and losing – a last decisive battle on the plains of Central China.

The Huai-Hai campaign[1]

The loss of Manchuria and the probable outcome of the North China campaign, which was only too easy to forecast, made the nationalists hasten to ensure the safety of their capital and the Shanghai region. All available men and materials were collected for this purpose. Although the overall total was still considerable, the affair was mishandled. The men, the places and the methods used were all disastrous choices. A loyal but incompetent general, Liu Chih, was put in command of the theatre of the Huai; he was seconded on the spot by General Tu Yü-ming, formerly the first commander-in-chief in Manchuria. Instead of using the natural barrier of the Huai River and the lakes of Kiangsu and Anhwei to support him, and manœuvring within a short distance of this line with the backing of armoured troops and the air force, he decided to use a mushroom-shaped disposition, the top of which spread out on either side of Hsüchow, while the foot followed the Tsinpu railway line. The large units adopted a rigid, purely defensive formation and proved to be utterly incapable of helping each other out when faced with an enemy whose strategy showed once more the most astonishing flexibility.

Liu Chih had six army groups at his disposal, divided into three blocks, and amounting to over half a million men. The Seventh Army Group, consisting of ten divisions, was stationed east of Hsüchow in the Grand

[1] See Map 32, pp. 412-13.

Canal area, with its headquarters at Hsinanchen; it was commanded by General Huang Po-tao. West of Hsüchow lay the Second Army Group under General Chiu Ching-chuan, and the Thirteenth Army Group under Li Mi. The Sixth Army Group under Li Yen-nien and the Sixteenth Army Group under Sun Yüan-liang were in position around Hsüchow. Several units were kept in reserve between Hsüchow and Pengpu: the Twelfth Army Group commanded by General Huang Wei, and the Eighth Army under Liu Ju-ming.

On the communist side, Chu Teh had assembled all the troops of the Third Field Army, commanded by Ch'en Yi (at least six columns, or armies) and most of the Second Field Army under Liu Po-ch'eng. From 16 November 1948 onwards the combined Second and Third Field Armies were led by a 'Front Committee', which took over the command of operations, consisting of Liu Po-ch'eng, Ch'en Yi, Teng Hsiao-p'ing, Su Yü and T'an Chen-lin. The two communist field armies probably did not outnumber the government troops, but the latter were made up largely of recent levies who were poorly trained and even lacking in the will to fight.

The assailants began by attacking the Seventh Army Group, which tried to retreat to Hsüchow, since no help was forthcoming. It was eventually brought to a halt in the Nienchuang region, and destroyed between 6 and 22 November. Huang Po-tao was killed; two of his generals had turned traitor on him, making defeat all the more inevitable, and took with them to the other side three divisions holding part of the area north-east of Hsüchow (8 November). Others were soon to follow their example. A few days later the Twelfth Army Group, on its way up the Tsinpu to Hsüchow, was intercepted in the Suhsien area. One of its divisions (the 110th Division of the Eighty-fifth Army) rebelled on 27 November; between then and 15 December the Twelfth Army Group was destroyed and its commander taken prisoner. The Sixth Army Group alone managed to retreat southwards.

The worst was to happen a few days later. The Second, Thirteenth and Sixteenth Army Groups, General Tu Yü-ming and all the services entrenched in the fortified town of Hsüchow retreated, first towards Suhsien and the Twelfth Army Group, and then south-westwards. On 4 December this mass of over 200,000 people was encircled near Yungch'eng in Honan. Cut off from their supplies, at the mercy of a severe winter, and encumbered with families and baggage, the armies eventually surrendered in the open country on 10 January 1949. The government made a few ineffectual gestures of help, sending troops in their direction, but the latter had to

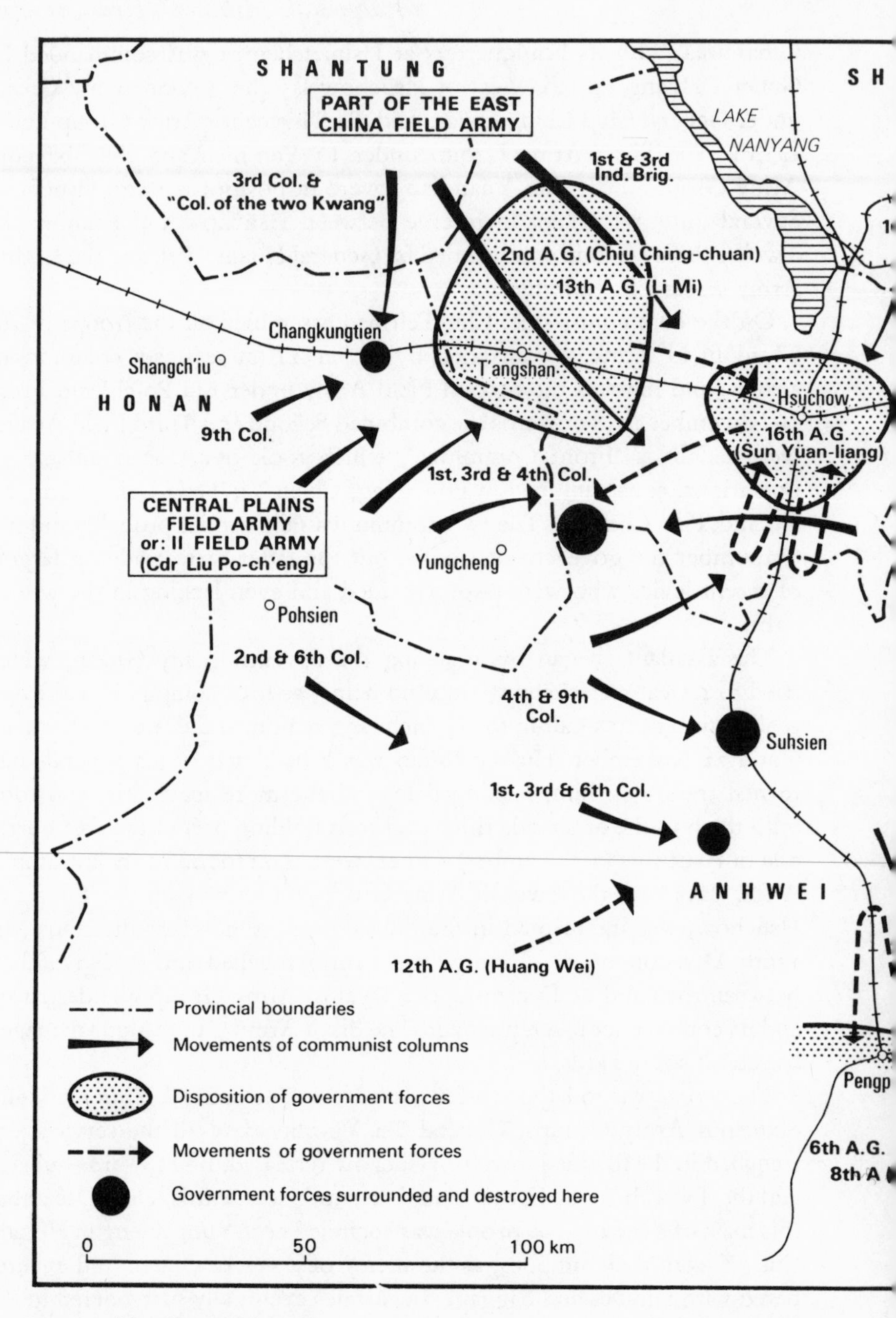

Map 32. The Huai-Hai battle.

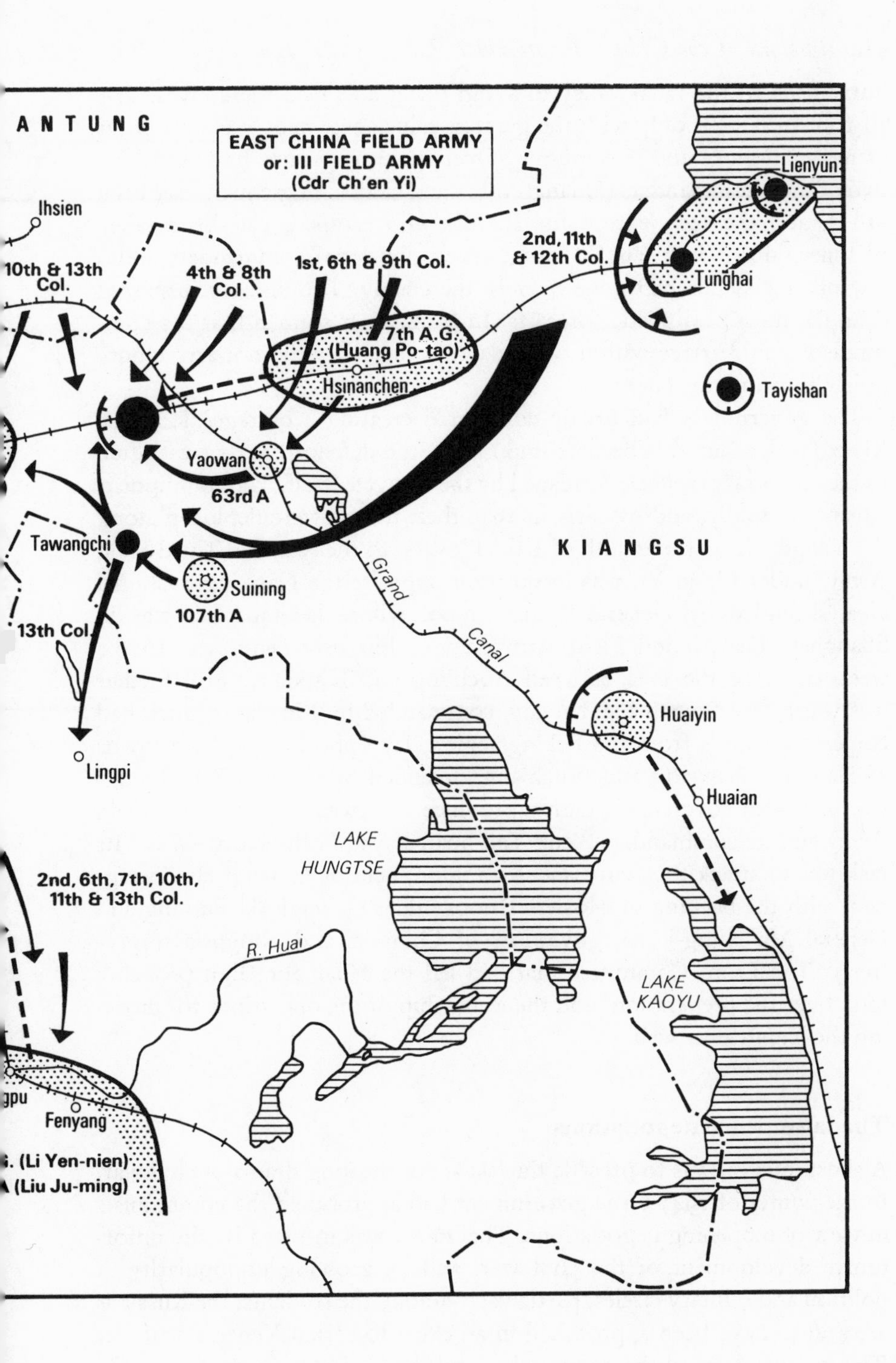
ANTUNG
EAST CHINA FIELD ARMY
or: III FIELD ARMY
(Cdr Ch'en Yi)
Ihsien
10th & 13th Col.
4th & 8th Col.
1st, 6th & 9th Col.
2nd, 11th & 12th Col.
Lienyün
Tunghai
7th A.G. (Huang Po-tao)
Hsinanchen
Tayishan
Yaowan
63rd A
Tawangchi
Suining
107th A
KIANGSU
Grand Canal
13th Col.
Huaiyin
Lingpi
Huaian
LAKE HUNGTSE
2nd, 6th, 7th, 10th, 11th & 13th Col.
R. Huai
LAKE KAOYU
Fenyang
(Li Yen-nien)
(Liu Ju-ming)

hurry back to the Huai valley to avoid being encircled themselves. The air force was used only with the greatest reluctance, mainly for purposes of reconnaissance and parachuting. Over six army groups had been lost, two of their commanders (Huang Po-tao and Chiu Ching-chuan) had been killed, and the rest, except for Li Mi, who escaped, had been taken prisoner, along with Tu Yü-ming; seven divisional commanders and a few other generals had gone over to the enemy. The disaster surpassed even the most pessimistic forecasts. In Nanking it seemed that the communists would arrive within a few days; in fact, they did not arrive until nearly four months later.

The government had briefly considered creating a barrage along the River Huai; when this became impossible, the defence lines were shifted to the temporary obstacle furnished by the Yangtze itself. The communists advanced rapidly, and by early in 1949 their troops were deployed along the Yangtze from the mouth of Lake P'oyang to the sea. The Third Field Army, under Ch'en Yi, was in position opposite the Nanking-Shanghai area, defended by General T'ang En-po, whose headquarters was in Shanghai. The Second Field Army, under Liu Po-ch'eng, was to the west, covering the area between Anch'ing and Kiukiang. Still further westwards, the Fourth Field Army, commanded by Lin Piao, which had come southwards from the Peking region, lay opposite the three towns of Hankow, Hanyang and Wuch'ang, defended by General Pai Ch'ung-hsi, who also covered his native province of Kwangsi. The First Field Army and its commander, P'eng Teh-huai, stayed in the North-West. Its task was to attack the Sian-Lanchow region, held by General Hu Tsung-nan, with the backing of Moslem troops under General Ma Pu-fang and General Ma Hung-k'uei, governors of Chinghai and Ninghsia respectively. The Front Committee that had led the Huai campaign probably took over the preparations and the leadership of the operations for crossing the Yangtze as well.

The false peace negotiations

A short interval was to precede the last act of the long drama of civil war. In the winter of 1947-8 the government had approached the communists in view of reopening negotiations. This move was inspired by the unfortunate development of the civil war, and its growing unpopularity in political and military circles, particularly among the students; the Russians are said to have been approached in an effort to soften Yenan's attitude. The intransigence of the communists and the obstinacy of the Generalissimo condemned these attempts to failure; a certain degree of balance had come about in the military field and it looked as though the war could go on for several more years with no means of forecasting what its final outcome might be.

Owing to these prospects, the Generalissimo's authority was challenged, at first with great caution, then more and more openly. Reformist and even pacifist tendencies began to make themselves felt within the Kuomintang itself. These had a chance to come out into the open in April 1948 when the new National Assembly designated the new President and Vice-President of the Republic, in accordance with the constitution promulgated on 1 January of the same year. Chiang Kai-shek was elected President, but he had to give up his intention of having his own candidate, Sun Fo, the son of Sun Yat-sen, elected to the Vice-Presidency. General Li Tsung-jen, Sun Fo's most serious rival, beat him by a small margin; opposition to the right wing of the Kuomintang and to the Generalissimo's personal policy began to take shape round him. The Generalissimo's failure was the harder to bear since his relations with Li Tsung-jen, the Kwangsi leader who had resorted to armed opposition after 1927, had always been tinged with a deep mistrust.

The military collapse of the autumn of 1948, and the abandoning of China by the United States, led the Generalissimo to retire, or, to put it more accurately, to pretend to retire, at the beginning of 1949, leaving his Vice-President to carry out the extremely difficult and humiliating negotiations with the communists. As the former balance in the military situation had been destroyed, General Li Tsung-jen had little hope of success, particularly as Chiang Kai-shek maintained a clandestine control over part of the army and the government, where his supporters still held the most important posts. Interventions or strong pressure from outside could alone give the Vice-President time to consolidate his power and succeed in his tasks. On 1 January 1949 President Chiang Kai-shek addressed a new year message to the nation referring to the conditions for peace laid down by the communists:

> If the communists sincerely wish for peace and give proof of their wish, the government will be only too happy to open discussions with them on ways to end the war. If a negotiated peace left national independence and sovereignty intact . . . but worked towards the well-being of the people. If the constitution is not violated, if the constitutional principles are preserved, and democratic forms of government are maintained, if the national character of the armed forces is safeguarded, etc., . . . I would be satisfied.

While waiting for the communists to reply, the government made a last diplomatic move, on 8 January, asking the Americans, the British, the French and the Russians to act as intermediaries. This dangerous effort to save the regime, while running the risk of provoking an international crisis, was rejected by all the powers concerned.

On 14 January 1949 the communist radio made known the eight conditions for the opening of peace negotiations. They were preceded by an insulting indictment in which Chiang Kai-shek was labelled as 'China's number one war criminal', 'chieftain of the Kuomintang bandit gang', 'bogus president of the Republic', and accused of having 'sold out the national interest wholesale to the U.S. government'. It was in fact a proposal for a formal surrender with which not only the Nanking government, but also all the Kuomintang military groups and regional authorities could comply separately. As it was, most of the territory in the West and South-West was occupied after local decisions to surrender. The eight conditions were as follows:

1 Punish the war criminals.
2 Abolish the bogus constitution.
3 Abolish the bogus 'constituted authority'.
4 Reorganize all reactionary troops on democratic principles.
5 Confiscate bureaucrat-capital.
6 Reform the land system.
7 Abrogate treasonable treaties.
8 Convene a political consultative conference without the participation of reactionary elements, and form a democratic coalition government to take over all the powers of the reactionary Nanking government and of its subordinate governments at all levels.[1]

The communist declaration ended with a sentence intended to be awe-inspiring, whose author was not afraid of using a multitude of adverbs: 'Any reactionaries who dare to resist must be resolutely, thoroughly, wholly and completely annihilated.' As for the 'war criminals', a list of forty-three names had already been published on 25 December, headed by Chiang Kai-shek; generals and ministers followed in order of importance.

On 21 January the Generalissimo announced he was going to retire. He delegated his powers to Vice-President Li Tsung-jen, as stipulated by Article 49 of the constitution, and returned publicly to his native village. Shortly afterwards, the government was transferred to Canton, enabling

[1] Mao Tse-tung, 'Statement on the Present Situation', *Selected Works*, vol. IV, p. 318.

Mao Tse-tung to give full play tc his irony as he wrote of the emptiness surrounding Nanking, the 'Stone City', quoting a poem written under the Yuan dynasty:

From the ramparts of the Stone City
One sees the sky brooding low over the land of Wu and Chu,
With nothing between to meet the eye.
Pointing to strategic points famous in the Six Dynasties,
Only the green hills stand out like walls.
Where army flags blotted the sun
And masts of war vessels touched the clouds
Snow-white skeletons lie scattered.
North and south of the River
How many warriors died![1]

The departure of the Generalissimo enabled contacts to begin once more between the government and the Chinese Communist Party. On 14 February an unofficial mission left Shanghai for Peking and Shihchiachuang, where the Party leaders still were. It was led by Dr Yen Hui-ch'ing (W. W. Yen), a former diplomat who had been Foreign Minister and even Prime Minister in his time, and it included Shao Li-tzu, an early member of the communist movement who quickly abandoned it, two lawyers, Tsang Chih-ch'ao and Chiang Yung, and Chiang Kai-shek's personal envoy, Huang Chi-lu, the former Rector of Szechuan University. The mission returned on 27 February in fairly optimistic mood.

On 3 March a Committee for Peace with ten members was created in Nanking. Its chairman was Dr Sun Fo, head of the Executive Yüan, or, in other words, President of the State Council since 31 December 1948; he had to relinquish the post to General Ho Ying-ch'in on 12 March 1949. This ten man committee led the talks on the government side and on 24 and 26 March the government and the communists each named their delegation. General Chang Chih-chung represented Nanking, assisted by five members and fourteen advisers, while Chou En-lai, Lin Piao, Lin Po-ch'ü, Li Wei-han and General Yeh Chien-ying, Army Chief of Staff, represented the communists. Conversations began on 2 April in Peking where the Central Committee had finally been transferred. The communists, certain of their moral and military superiority, took up a hard line. The provisional president, Li Tsung-jen, had no leading cards left to play; Chiang Kai-shek played his own game from Fenghua, as did the

[1] Cf. Mao Tse-tung, 'Why do the Badly Split Reactionaries Still Idly Clamour for "Total Peace"?', *Selected Works*, vol. IV, p. 343.

government from its retreat in Canton and the leaders of the Western provinces. He tried to gain the support of the United States, hoping for a declaration linking their own security to the observance of the limit set by the Yangtze, but in vain.

It seems that Li Tsung-jen received help from an unexpected quarter during these decisive days, though it turned out to be useless. It appears that the Russians, possibly uncertain of U.S. reactions to the sudden collapse of Nanking, urged the Chinese communists to adopt a moderate line, and advised them in particular not to cross the Yangtze too soon. This intervention tallied with precedents for which the Yugoslav leaders blamed Stalin, and recent allusions in the Chinese press seem to bear them out.[1] However this may be, Russian intervention was fruitless, if indeed it happened.

The communists produced their final proposals on 15 April, ready to come to a compromise over the question of war criminals. They laid down an official ultimatum, to expire on 20 April. Their requirements were roughly the same as the Eight Points of 14 January, which had already been more or less accepted by the government, but they added demands amounting to nothing less than a surrender, such as:

1 Freedom to cross the Yangtze for the communist armies.
2 Reorganization of the national armies to bring them under communist control.
3 The government gradually to hand over its administrative powers, in preparation for the formation of a coalition government.[2]

The communist ultimatum, with its preamble forcing the government to shoulder the moral responsibility for the war, was totally unacceptable even to a regime reduced to its last stand; Nanking rejected it on 19 April, trying vainly to put forward counter-proposals in its turn. By this time, the communist armies were more or less fully deployed along the north bank of the Yangtze. They began to cross the river in the night of 20-21 April. The general orders issued to the troops to begin the movement contained an appeal to President Li Tsung-jen and to local governments and military groups, inviting them to sign the proposals of 15 April. Two days later, a proclamation by the People's Army ordered everyone to remain at his post, forbidding sabotage, strikes, disorder of any kind, and arrests; the traditional protection extended to foreigners, including their possessions, was not forgotten.

[1] Cf. in particular Milovan Djilas, *Conversations with Stalin,* trans. M. B. Petrovich (Harmondsworth, Penguin, 1969).

[2] The complete, definitive version of the communist proposals is to be found in Mao Tse-tung, *Selected Works*, vol. IV, p. 391.

The final operations[1]

The communists forced their way across the Yangtze with ease, in spite of the immense obstacle presented by a river several kilometres wide. The nationalist troops strung out along the south bank were mediocre; morale was low, their attitude was one of defeatism and desertions were frequent. The Third Field Army, commanded by Ch'en Yi, who was assisted by Hsü Yü and T'an Chen-lin, crossed on either side of Nanking. To the east operations were made easier by the instant surrender of the fortress at Chiangyin.[2] A handful of ships belonging to the Yangtze fleet put up a show of resistance. Nanking was abandoned by the nationalists during the night of 22-23 April and occupied on the morning of 24 April. A peace preservation committee handled the changeover and looting was reduced to a minimum. The communist infantry entered a silent, anxious town, ashamed of having been the capital of the Kuomintang for twenty-two years.

The Third Field Army pushed on from Nanking straight to Hangchow, the capital of Chekiang, which was taken on 3 May. Shanghai was then cut off; General T'ang En-po began to re-embark his troops, already partly stationed in the Choushan archipelago and Taiwan. Shanghai was occupied on 27 May without much fighting.

To the west of Wuhu, which fell on 22 April, the Second Field Army under Liu Po-ch'eng crossed the Yangtze with no difficulty, for the south bank there was even less well defended than on the Nanking-Shanghai front. The army marched on south-westwards and entered Nanch'ang on 22 May, where Liu was no doubt proud to remember the events of 1 August 1927. The vanguard of the Second Field Army, moving on up the Kan valley, reached Kanchow in south Kiangsi; this was the nearest point to Canton reached by the communists in the present phase of operations.

The government troops collapsed just as rapidly in Central China. On 15 May General Pai Ch'ung-hsi and his forces abandoned the triple town of Wuhan, which was occupied by Lin Piao and the Fourth Field Army over the next two days. The communists marched southwards, taking Chuchow on 2 July. Ch'angsha, the capital of Hunan, was about to be surrounded. The Kuomintang was once more betrayed by those to whom

[1] See Maps 33 (p. 420) and 34 (p. 422).

[2] It seems that the commander of the fortress, Tai Lung-chiang, and the commander of the fleet had been approached by the communists long before; the former was won over with no difficulty.

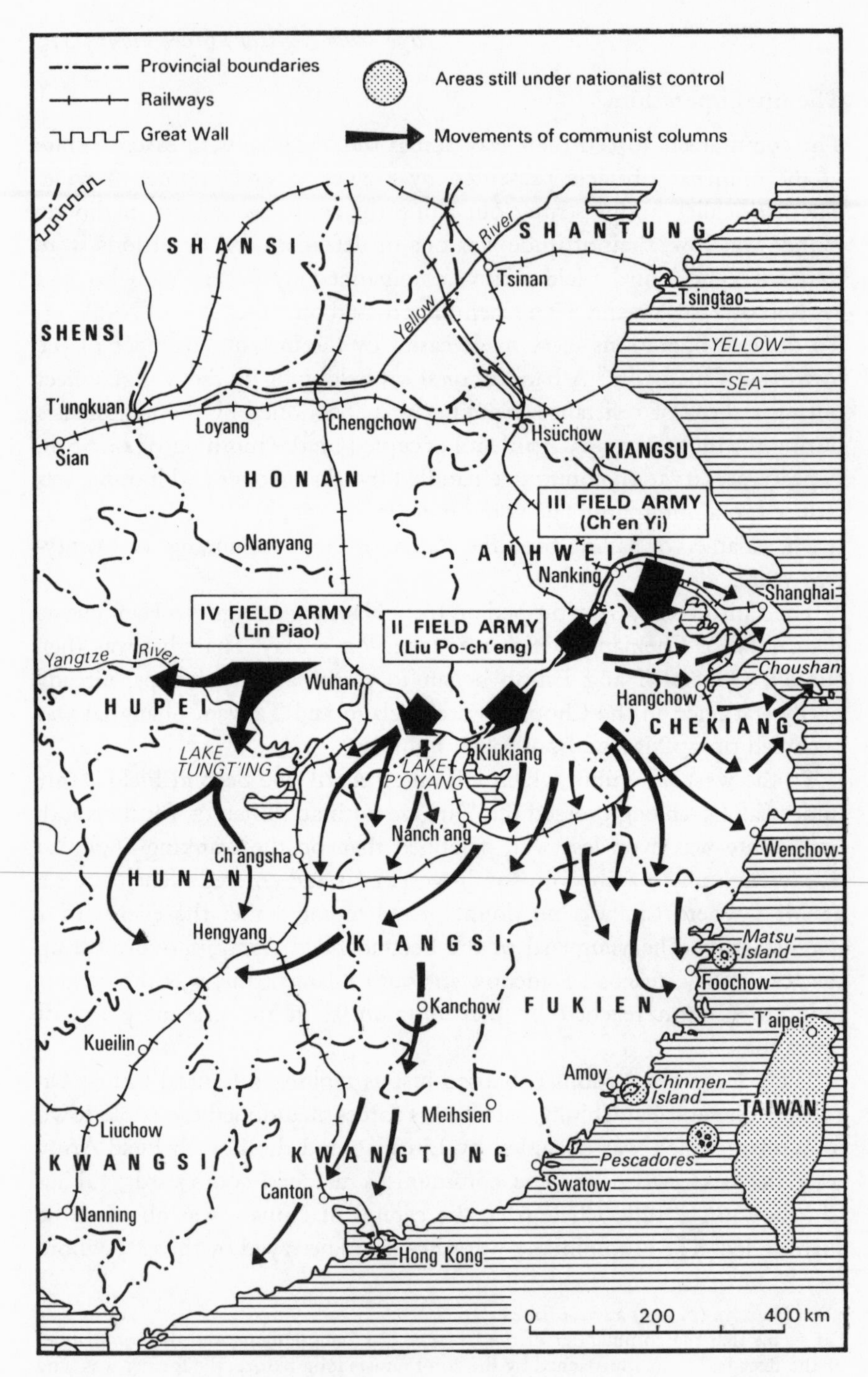

Map 33. The battle of the Yangtze and the conquest of South China

it had been most generous. On 1 August Ch'en Ming-jen, governor of Hunan and commander of the First Army Group, and General Ch'eng Ch'ien, commander of the Headquarters for the Pacification of the Region and Li Tsung-jen's rival for the Vice-Presidency of the Republic, both went over to the communists. General Huang Chieh, appointed governor of Hunan after his predecessor's desertion, managed to delay Lin Piao's advance southwards for a short time, with attacks eastwards towards Yungfeng, Anjen and Hsiangt'an in mid-August, but nothing could save the government, which was heading for disaster in both political and military fields.

In September the Second and Fourth Field Armies moved forward once more. Liu Po-ch'eng started from the Kanchow region, sending two columns towards east and north Kwangtung. The first overran the east of the province, taking Meihsien and Hsingning. The communists found themselves once again in what had been the scene of their earliest soviets, founded by P'eng P'ai along the East River. The other column, commanded by Ch'en Keng, made for Ch'üchiang and the Canton-Hankow railway, via Nanhsiung. It followed the railway line southwards towards Canton, still theoretically the capital of the government. On 15 October the government announced that it was leaving for Chungking, a useless piece of deception which managed to maintain the fiction of its existence on the continent for a few weeks longer. Vice-President Li Tsung-jen alone briefly nourished the illusion that the resistance could be made to last longer in the rich, thickly populated Szechuan Basin. He ordered the troops of Hu Tsung-nan to retreat into the mountains surrounding the area to the north, while Sung Hsi-lien and his troops were to retreat into the mountains forming the southern and eastern borders; Huang Chieh and his forces were to be sent in the direction of Kweichow. He lacked the means, the time and the money needed to carry out his plan.

The communist armies began their advance towards the south-western provinces and Szechuan in early October. Liu Po-ch'eng and the Second Field Army were mainly responsible for it, but the Fourth Field Army carried out the first phase of the operations and performed a sort of '*chassé-croisé*' with the Second Field Army, taking over or accepting responsibility for troops from Kwangtung. Eventually part of the First Field Army moved down from the north-western provinces and hastened the decision by threatening Szechuan from the north. On 8 October the Fourth Field Army entered Hengyang; Lingling, on the road to Kueilin, fell on 28 October. Lin Piao advanced towards the south-west while the Second Field Army began to move towards Kueiyang, the capital of

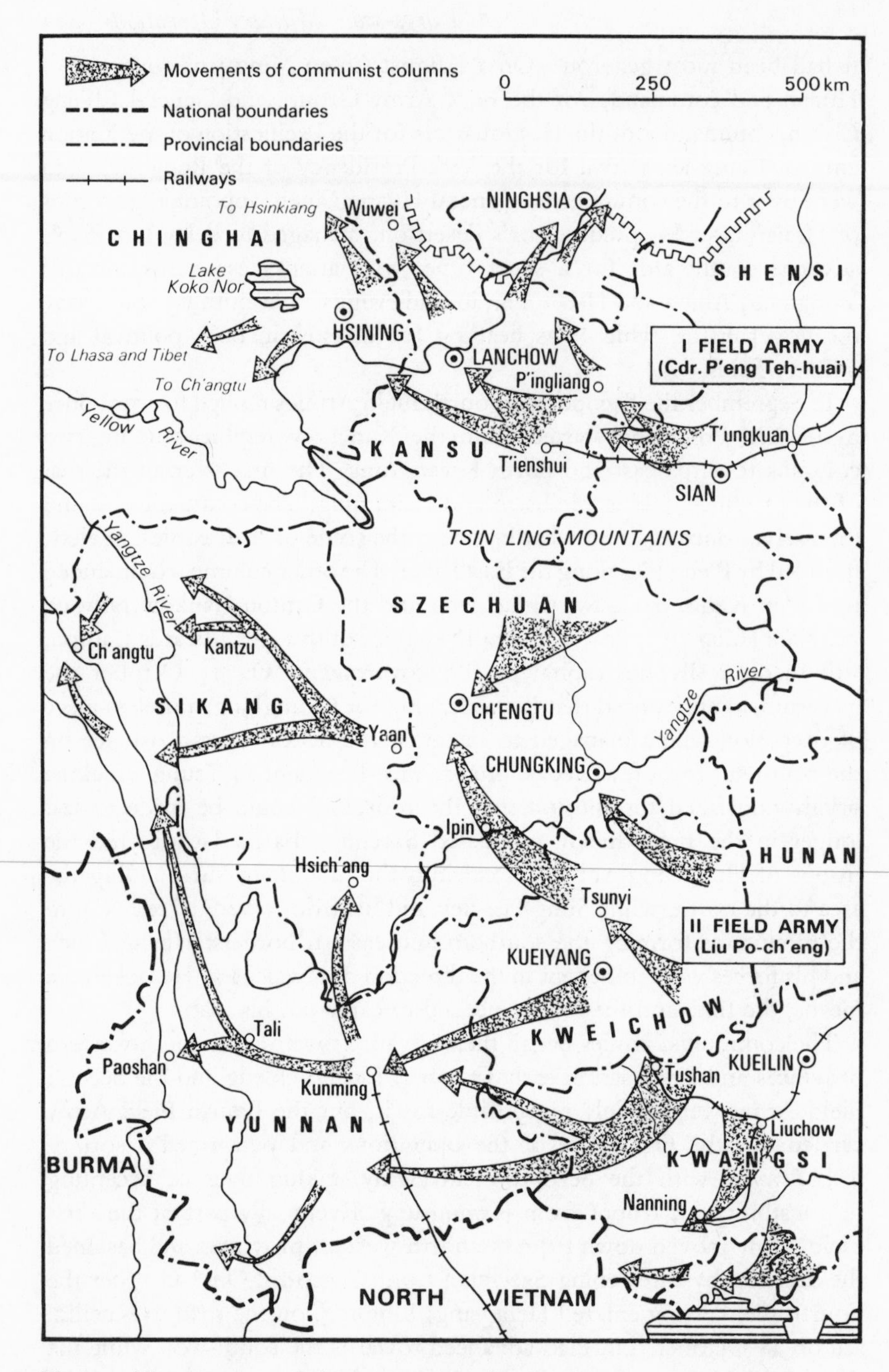

Map 34. The conquest of the western provinces.

Kweichow. Kueiyang was taken on 15 November without a blow being struck and the government had the officer in charge of its defence shot. Kueiyang being an important junction of roads to Kunming and Chungking, the communists then threatened both Yunnan and Szechuan. Sung Hsi-lien put up a brief and vain resistance, which came to an end once his Second Army, the last sound unit in the area, had been destroyed. On 22 November Liu Po-ch'eng reached Tsunyi and a week later, on 30 November, his troops entered Chungking. The whole course of the Yangtze downstream of the town was in communist hands; they had occupied the region round Enshih, on the borders of Szechuan and Hupei, on 6 November.

Lin Piao, in Kwangsi, took Kueilin on 22 November and Nanning on 6 December. The remains of Pai Ch'ung-hsi's troops hastily retreated to the peninsula of Leichow and Hainan island, where Pai Ch'ung-hsi set up his headquarters for a time. Another nationalist group, commanded by General Huang Chieh, reached the North Vietnam border, where French troops disarmed it.

General Lu Han, governor of Yunnan, handed his province over to the communists on 10 December. Confusion reigned for a short time as central government troops, commanded by General Li Mi, stationed at Kunming, took control of the town from 19 to 22 December. Eventually, communist troops from Kweichow came to relieve Lu Han. General Li Mi retreated towards the border of the Shan States in Burma, where his presence was a source of international tension for several years.[1]

The conquest of the North-West

The First Field Army, commanded by P'eng Teh-huai, was responsible for operations in the North-West. They began in May; Sian fell almost immediately (20 May). The government troops commanded by General Hu Tsung-nan retreated southwards to the passes in the Tsin Ling mountains covering the way into Szechuan. The North-Western command was then in the hands of the Moslem general, Ma Pu-fang, governor of Chinghai. In June he brought P'eng Teh-huai to a halt west of Sian, taking back Hsienyang and part of the Wei valley, and cutting off Sian for a time; communist losses were heavy, amounting to 50,000 men

[1] General Li Mi commanded the Thirteenth Army Group at the battle of Huai-Hai, and managed to flee in disguise. His troops entrenched in the Shan States received regular supplies from the nationalist government in Taiwan. Eventually, most of them were evacuated by international agreement.

according to some reckonings. The situation was righted by the arrival of reinforcements sent by Nieh Jung-chen and Hsü Hsiang-ch'ien. P'ingliang, between Sian and Lanchow, was taken in July; bitter fighting took place in August at Kuyuan, near Lanchow. Lanchow itself, the capital of Kansu, was taken on 26 August; Hsining fell on 2 September. The long reign of the Moslem generals of the region was soon to come to an end. Communist troops moved down the Yellow River from the Lanchow area, and advanced on the province of Ninghsia; its governor Ma Hung-k'uei abandoned its defence and the capital, Ninghsia, was taken on 28 September. A few days earlier the nationalist troops in Suiyuan, commanded by the provincial governor, General Tung Ch'i-wu, had agreed to undergo 'peaceful reorganization', as the current expression had it, and the whole of the Yellow River then flowed through communist territory.

The great frontier region of Hsinkiang had still to be overcome. Its conquest was achieved without difficulty, on the same pattern as most of the western provinces. On 26 September its governor, Burhan, and the commander of the nationalist troops, T'ao Chih-yüeh, went over to the communists. The nationalist troops in Hsinkiang retained their organization and their leaders for a long time; though officially transformed into pioneer units, they remained security troops in what was colonial territory.

The troops of General Hu Tsung-nan, one of the communists' most constant enemies, still had to be overcome, and with them the provincial troops from Szechuan and Sikang, commanded by Marshal Teng Hsi-hou and Marshal Liu Wen-hui. Political intrigue and military action combined once more to the advantage of the communists. Szechuan had been constantly torn by internal rivalries, between Ch'engtu and Chungking, or between the provincial clans and the central authority. The collapse of the Kuomintang brought these to life again. General Chang Ch'ün, a native of Szechuan who had for years been loyal to the Generalissimo and had just given up his post of Chairman of the State Council (Executive Yüan), was sent to Chungking first of all; Chiang Kai-shek himself went there for a short time (24 August). When Liu Po-ch'eng arrived at Chungking in November, Hu Tsung-nan retreated to Ch'engtu, where Teng Hsi-hou, who had for several months been in contact with the communists, was becoming uncertain in his loyalties. P'eng Teh-huai and Hsü Hsiang-ch'ien followed close on the heels of Hu Tsung-nan; Liu Wen-hui handed over his province of Sikang to the communists, and Teng Hsi-hou followed suit. On 27 December Hu Tsung-nan had to abandon Ch'engtu. He made a vain attempt to prolong government resistance in the region of Hsich'ang and Hueili, where the communists had fought several engagements and even tried to gain a permanent foothold during the Long March. This reversal of the situation lasted only a few months. In March 1950 the troops of Liu Po-ch'eng entered the Hsich'ang and Hueili region, marking the end of all nationalist resistance on the continent. All that remained was to bring Tibet under control, including it once more in a united China, but avoiding local revolts and complications of an international kind, particularly as far as India was concerned. The Chinese communists managed to achieve this by an astonishing combination of military pressure and political concessions.

On 7 October 1950 the Second Field Army advanced westwards and on 9 October seized Ch'angtu (Chamdo) on the border of Sikang and Tibet. The army scattered and destroyed a small Tibetan army, which lost 6000 men. Negotiations were opened in Delhi, and then in Peking, between the government of the People's Republic of China and the local Tibetan government. An agreement was drawn up on 23 May 1951, abolishing the independence of Tibet in foreign affairs, and maintaining some local political and social institutions for the time being. In the autumn, Chinese troops entered Lhasa; the 'peaceful liberation' of Tibet was completed.[1]

The islands off the coast and the defence of Taiwan

While the First, Second and Fourth Field Armies continued operations in the west and the south, the Third Field Army, commanded by Ch'en Yi, was deployed along the coast of Chekiang and Fukien opposite Taiwan, with a view to planning amphibious operations against the government's last refuge. Wenchow and Foochow were taken with ease in July and August 1949; Amoy was taken in October of the same year. To block the ports now in communist hands, and to provide cover at a distance for Taiwan and the Pescadores, the nationalists maintained their position in three groups of islands lying off the mainland coast. The Choushan islands off the Ningpo region were densely occupied. A garrison of over 100,000 men held the region under constant threat of sudden landings, and the islands provided shelter for the nationalist warships, which were cruising off shore and paralysing the port of Shanghai. The appearance of a communist air force and the need to reinforce the defence of Taiwan led the nationalist government to abandon the archipelago in May 1950. The Tach'en islands further south, off Wenchow, were kept

[1] The Chinese gradually moved into the province, which tried to revolt in March 1959; the Dalai Lama then fled to India.

until January 1955, when they were evacuated under United States protection. The Quemoy (Chinmen) and Matsu islands off Amoy are still in nationalist hands today; although their legal status is clear, the United States still defend them as an advance post of Taiwan.

When they left the Choushan islands, the nationalists also lost Hainan (April 1950). The island was difficult to supply and defend and, as the United States did not at that point guarantee the safety of Taiwan, its abandonment was justified in military terms. On the other hand, it came after the loss of the three coastal provinces from which come most of the overseas Chinese; the abandonment of Hainan amounted to a further loss of prestige and influence abroad for the central government.

The H.M.S. Amethyst Incident

On the night of 20-21 April, in apparent disregard of the communists' ultimatum to the government, the British gunboat H.M.S. *Amethyst*, under Commander Kerans, sailed up the Yangtze from Shanghai to Nanking. The official reason for her presence in such a dangerous spot was to ensure the safety of British residents in the capital, and possibly also to keep a watch on the military developments which had been announced. The communists naturally saw it as the familiar and hated image of a century-old foreign occupation, a true manifestation of Western 'imperialism'. The *Amethyst* was shelled by the artillery of the Third Field Army; several of her crew were killed or wounded before she went aground on a sand-bank. The British naval command in Shanghai sent a cruiser, H.M.S. *London*, and a destroyer, H.M.S. *Consort*, to help out, but both ships had to turn back rapidly. The British losses were forty-four killed and eighty wounded; the Chinese losses amounted to 252 killed and wounded

An awkward debate opened in the House of Commons. True to the imperial tradition, Winston Churchill demanded that two aircraft-carriers should be sent in; Mr Attlee spoke of the treaties. Mao Tse-tung used the incident as an excellent opportunity to appear as the real defender of his nation's rights and sovereignty after its long humiliation; his words no doubt found an echo in every Chinese heart.

The Chinese Communist Party leader published a truly statesmanlike declaration on 25 April. Firm but not injurious, it left the way open for future diplomatic recognition on a basis of total equality. Within less than a year, London broke off relations with the nationalists and sent a Chargé d'Affaires to Peking. The *Amethyst* Incident was the close of an era, which ended as it had begun, with the thunder of guns from the British navy; the definitive break with an outmoded epoch had a touch of grandeur about it. The communists seemed to sense this; perhaps they were secretly grateful to the British for providing the opportunity for such a brilliant and resounding reversal.[1]

[1] The British also earned a last share of glory, for on 30 July Commander Kerans managed to refloat his ship with great skill, and escaped screened by a Chinese trading vessel.

30 The Chinese Communist Party during the Third Revolutionary Civil War: Administration of Liberated Areas

Life of the Party and Doctrinal Evolution

From 1945 to 1949, during the period referred to in communist terminology as the Third Revolutionary Civil War, the Party naturally concentrated its chief efforts on developing its military power. This development was impossible without widespread support from the population, which was particularly necessary at the first stage of operations – guerrilla warfare; all great political or administrative decisions were taken with a view to maintaining or acquiring this support. The Communist Party's approach to the matter was one of great flexibility and realism. A fundamental distinction was made between 'formerly' and 'recently' liberated areas. In the latter, won after the Japanese capitulation, reforms, especially land reforms, were moderate and gradual.

The communists were also concerned with destroying the morale of the enemy, particularly that of his armed forces, and of the urban bourgeoisie, still the chief if not sole support both of the Kuomintang's economy and of its political and administrative structure. For this, the communists used every appropriate theme, especially those of nationalism, democracy and peace. Skilful propaganda, at once insidious and violent, was aimed at isolating the government by inciting all possible opponents and forms of opposition against it, rallying the moderate and indecisive elements by a process combining intimidation and persuasion, and exploiting mercilessly all the mistakes and deficiencies of which the regime was guilty. Frequent declamations by the Central Committee, the Revolutionary Military Committee, or by Mao Tse-tung himself, were among the most effective psychological weapons used; the government was at a total loss for adequate methods to oppose them.

The administration

One of the first results of the retreat of the Japanese was to achieve some measure of territorial continuity among the eighteen 'liberated areas'.[1] After various administrative adjustments carried out in 1946 six large regions were created or maintained: Shansi-Hopei-Shantung-Honan (Chin-Chi-Lu-Yü), Shansi-Chahar-Hopei (Chin-Ch'a-Chi), Shansi-Suiyuan (Chin-sui), East China (the former bases of Shantung, Kiangsu and Anhwei), North-East China (Manchuria), the Central Plain (Hupei-Honan).

In May 1948 the first three bases were combined into one single North China base. By then, the communist territory was roughly as follows: North China (44 million inhabitants), East China (43 million inhabitants), North-West China (7 million inhabitants), North-East China (about 10 million inhabitants), the Central Plain (here the population varied constantly, owing to the fluidity of military operations).

The administrative structure remained as it had been during the anti-Japanese war of resistance. From the village (hsiang) up to the regional people's governments, by way of the subdistricts (ch'ü) and districts (hsien), elected assemblies in their turn still elected 'executive committees', which amounted in fact to different administrative levels. After the civil war, the rule of 'three-thirds' was no longer respected as far as the Kuomintang was concerned; well-known local figures, with a reputation for being progressive in spite of their social origins, retained administrative functions, which were decorative but a mere pretence. These were the people to whom Mao Tse-tung gave the unexpected name of 'enlightened gentry': 'We should not abandon the enlightened gentry who cooperated with us in the past and continue to cooperate with us at present, who approve of the struggle against the United States and Chiang Kai-shek and who approve of land reform.'[2]

The avowed aims of this policy of tolerance were to isolate Chiang Kai-shek, and win over the intellectuals from the gentry and from families of rich peasants.

[1] The nineteenth, in South China, disappeared when communist troops were evacuated to North China on board nationalist ships.

[2] See 'On the Question of the National Bourgeoisie and the Enlightened Gentry' (1 March 1948), *Selected Works*, vol. IV, p. 207.

Agrarian measures

The Party's line on land questions between 1945 and 1949 was a slow, consistent movement towards the confiscation of lands belonging to landlords and some rich peasants. The poorest peasants in the 'formerly' liberated areas had to be granted more than a mere reduction in land rent. But at the same time landlords and rich peasants living in areas under government control or areas where the Party's military situation was precarious should not be worried in advance. These two concerns gave rise to extremely varied, flexible measures. Mao Tse-tung played a leading part in drawing them up. A directive dated 7 November 1945 gave instructions for the reduction of rent in liberated areas, by means of a vast movement 'so as to arouse the revolutionary fervour of the great majority of the peasant masses'. A reminder was given that land was not, however, to be confiscated. The main stress was laid on the importance of agricultural production, the most important task of the moment.[1]

The first major change in this situation was brought about by the directive of 4 May 1946. The official policy was then to confiscate public lands and lands belonging to landowners, at least in the 'formerly' liberated areas. The reform was applied with moderation. Wherever possible, the landlords were left alive, and the rich peasants were not unduly harassed. The principle of land rent was still applied in the 'recently' liberated areas. Official commentaries and journalists' reports concur, stating that the decree of 4 May was a reply to pressing demands from the peasants who in some places had shared out the land of their own accord. In February 1947, while expressing satisfaction at the application of the directive of 4 May in two-thirds of the liberated areas, Mao Tse-tung found it necessary to speak up forcefully in support of the middle peasants, and even the rich peasants and some landlords:

> . . . we must unite firmly with the middle peasants; and it is absolutely impermissible to encroach on the interests of the middle peasants. . . . Moreover, during and after the land reform, appropriate consideration in accordance with the will of the masses should be given to ordinary rich peasants and middle and small landlords, and it should be given in accordance with the 'May 4th Directive'.[2]

[1] This directive, to be found in the *Selected Works*, vol. IV, p. 71, was written by Mao Tse-tung in the name of the Central Committee.

[2] 'Greet the New High Tide of the Chinese Revolution', *Selected Works*, vol. IV, p. 119.

In 1947 a tendency arose towards a harder line, particularly in respect of landlords. In September a 'National Land Conference' was held at Hsipaip'o in the 'hsien' of P'ingshan in Hopei; the result of its work was the law of 10 October 1947. The principle of confiscating public lands and lands belonging to landlords was given a more formal definition. Confiscations were to be enlarged, and would include livestock and implements as well as the land. Surplus lands of rich peasants would also be seized. A year later land had been distributed to 100 million peasants; Sun Yat-sen's phrase 'land to the tiller' had become a reality in communist areas.

The 1947 reform gave rise to excesses, which Mao Tse-tung condemned wholeheartedly, recalling once more the importance of the middle peasants who were in the majority in the 'formerly' liberated areas, defending the rich peasants, particularly those whose riches were newly acquired, and even protecting those landlords who were not tyrants or counter-revolutionaries. As he put it, 'Our task is to . . . wipe out the landlords as a class, not as individuals'. The interests of the revolution also required that 'criminal' landlords and rich peasants be sentenced and executed. When so doing, the masses should use correct procedure and avoid brutality. Mao Tse-tung the Head of State was a long way from the author of controversial writings who in 1927 considered that 'excesses' were an important part of the revolution.[1]

In February 1948 new rulings appeared stating how the land law of 10 October 1947 was to be enforced. Important distinctions were made between the regions; formerly liberated areas, semi-recently liberated areas and recently liberated areas were to receive different treatments. In the formerly liberated areas redistribution of land was to cease, and the position of the poor peasants within the rural organizations was to be strengthened, as they helped to heighten the revolutionary spirit. Nevertheless, middle peasants were to be shown consideration, as they were in the majority, and active. In semi-recently liberated areas – that is, liberated between September 1945 and August 1947 – the decree of 4 May 1946 no longer applied, and the law of 1947 replaced it. Lastly, in regions liberated after August 1947, the earlier laws were not yet to be applied; the influence of the landlords and rich peasants was to be weakened in preparation for the confiscation of land. The tactics to be used were described with unusually cynical precision:

[1] Cf. Mao Tse-tung, 'On Some Important Problems of the Party's Present Policy' (18 January 1948), *Selected Works*, vol. IV, p. 181. If Liu Shao-ch'i is to be believed in his self-criticism of 1966, he was chiefly responsible for this hard line, which he described as a 'leftist' mistake, admitting that it resulted in many people being killed.

> Therefore, we should not try to enforce the Land Law all at once, but should do it in two stages. The first stage is to neutralize the rich peasants and strike blows exclusively at the landlords. This stage should be further subdivided into several steps, namely, propaganda, preliminary organization, distribution of the movable property of the big landlords, distribution of the land of the big and middle landlords with some consideration being given to the small landlords, and finally the distribution of the land of the landlord class. During this stage poor peasant leagues should be organized as the backbone of leadership, and peasant associations may also be organized with the poor peasants as the main body. The second stage is to distribute the land rented out by the rich peasants, their surplus land and part of their other property, and to distribute that portion of the land of the landlords which was not thoroughly distributed in the first stage. The first stage should take about two years and the second a year.[1]

This programme gives a good summary of the whole policy; its aims were clear, its methods realistic, and it was based on practical experience. In another, slightly later text, Mao Tse-tung gives further advice: 'Do not start the work in all places at the same time, but choose strong cadres to carry it out first in certain places to gain experience, then spread the experience step by step and expand the work in waves. This applies to a whole strategic area as well as to a single county.'[2]

This remark could be applied to China as a whole. The experience gained through the reforms of 1946, 1947 and 1948 was used as the basis for the great Land Law passed on 30 June 1950, which launched a series of far-reaching transformations in the structure of rural life – Mutual Aid Teams, Elementary (and later Advanced) Agricultural Producers' Cooperatives and People's Communes.

Meanwhile, the measures taken during the Third Revolutionary Civil War appear to have yielded the results expected of them. As far as the communists were concerned, no outstanding social or economic difficulties arose. A harsh, new 'Rectification Movement', which will be mentioned later, no doubt helped maintain revolutionary order in the countryside.

The Communist Party's policy concerning industrial economy and trade was much more conservative than their land policy; the reasons for

[1] Mao Tse-tung, 'Different Tactics for Carrying out the Land Law in Different Areas' (3 February 1948), *Selected Works*, vol. IV, p. 194.

[2] Mao Tse-tung, 'Essential Points in Land Reform in the New Liberated Areas' (15 February 1948), *Selected Works*, vol. IV, p. 202.

this difference in attitude are fairly obvious. In the red zones it was important not to disorganize the existing, mediocre production; the Party lacked the urban experience to take it over. In the white zones the so-called 'national' bourgeoisie had to be reassured, alienated from the regime and prepared for future collaboration. Party committees and cadres received instruction to protect industrialists and tradesmen; the protection was extended to cover industry created by landlords. Mistakes already made in this field were to be rectified. Generally speaking, capital was respected as much as labour, and a short term policy aiming only at the workers' well-being was set aside. One of the most revealing instances of the communists' careful, yet perplexed approach to the towns is to be found in a telegram from Mao Tse-tung to the commander of the Loyang front, after the taking of the town, one of the few large towns in communist territory. He uses unusual expressions and pressing entreaties to moderation:

> Be very prudent in the liquidation of the organs of the Kuomintang rule, arrest only the chief reactionaries and do not involve too many persons . . . do not designate as bureaucrat-capital and do not confiscate all the industrial and commercial enterprises run by Kuomintang members. . . . On entering the city, do not lightly advance slogans of raising wages and reducing working hours. In war time it is good enough if production can continue and existing working hours and original wage levels can be maintained.[1]

The economy of the communist zones, based mainly on agriculture and handicrafts, was infinitely less fragile than that of the Kuomintang zones. Their only difficulties were monetary, and even these were limited by the use of different coinage in each liberated area, and by a system of tax paid in grain, which helped reduce the use of paper money considerably. The practice of holding meetings at which all tax-payers had to make a public declaration of their income, the collective compulsion typical of the regime, and the climate of honesty and revolutionary solidarity, all gave immense help to the governors and reduced their difficulties to a minimum. The communist zones did not escape inflation, but it did not assume the same proportions as in government zones. After the communist victories, local and regional banks gradually disappeared and the problems that arose were on a national scale. The scattered nature of their economy helped the communists as much as the scattering of their military forces.

[1] Cf. Mao Tse-tung, *Selected Works*, vol. IV, pp. 247, 248.

Anti-American nationalism

Nationalism and land reform were the two great weapons used by the communist movement during the Third Revolutionary Civil War. Nationalist feeling had lessened in the countryside with the departure of the Japanese, but it was still powerful in the large towns, traditionally more aware of the presence of foreigners, even when they were allies. In propaganda from Yenan, and particularly in declarations made by Mao Tse-tung, the United States immediately replaced Japan, just as the name of Chiang Kai-shek replaced that of Wang Ching-wei; this substitution gave new impetus to nationalist feelings already excited by war, and, oddly enough, by the American victory over Japan.

With the failure of the Marshall mission and the beginning of the cold war in the West, the tone became one of unprecedented violence. The communists shamelessly falsified obvious historical facts, attributing the defeat of Japan to the Soviet Union's entry into the war, for instance, and tirelessly slandering the United States, accused of wanting to enslave or colonize China. Appearances were in their favour; it was easy for them to show up disinterested gestures, such as economic and military aid, handing over surplus materials, and completely unexceptional treaties like the Sino-American Treaty of Commerce and Navigation, signed on 2 November 1946, from the angle best suited to their own purposes. Minor incidents were violently exploited and many more created. General Marshall and Dr Leighton Stuart were constantly insulted in spite of their openly liberal views and their severity towards the Kuomintang. In 'Farewell, Leighton Stuart' and 'Why it is Necessary to Discuss the White Paper' (18 and 28 August 1949), Mao Tse-tung does little more than summarize four years of outrages in an ironical style inspired by the circumstances:

> When the People's Liberation Army crossed the Yangtze River, the U.S. colonial government at Nanking fled helter-skelter. Yet His Excellency Ambassador Stuart sat tight, watching wide-eyed, hoping to set up shop under a new signboard and to reap some profit. . . . In short, he was left out in the cold, 'standing all alone, body and shadow comforting each other'. There was nothing left for him to do, and he had to take to the road, his briefcase under his arm. . . . Leighton Stuart has departed and the White Paper has arrived. Very good. Very good. Both events are worth celebrating.[1]

1 Mao Tse-tung, *Selected Works*, vol. IV, pp. 438, 439.

The United States had to be kept out of Chinese affairs, and the ground prepared for the policy of friendship with the U.S.S.R., later described by the expression 'leaning to one side';[1] but, above all, the movement needed support from nationalist and anti-Western feelings.

The anti-American propaganda was fairly successful in the government zone. Xenophobe students, tradesmen worried by the worsening economic situation, extremists from the Kuomintang itself, either threw in their lot with it openly, or approved in secret. The climate it engendered helped discourage the Americans, making them reject the idea of direct intervention, which was the only way of halting the communists at the Yangtze, and decide to open frank negotiations with the Vice-President, Li Tsung-jen. The theme of democracy was put to a wide use alongside that of nationalism, bringing with it the theme of a coalition government, and consequently of peace. The 'fascist' dictatorship of Chiang Kai-shek was not opposed by the dictatorship of the proletariat, but by a genuine liberalism, which purported to defend the 'small parties' who had joined up to become the 'Democratic League'. When the Kuomintang dissolved the League on 27 October 1947, this act was described as a counter-revolutionary crime.

At the same time, the communists bandied insults at a few 'small parties' whose views brought them closer to the Kuomintang than their own party – the 'Young China Party', founded in France and led by Tseng Ch'i, and the 'Socialist-Democrat Party' of Carsun Chang (Chang Chün-mai), a lawyer educated in America. Even Mao Tse-tung himself often referred to them as 'parasites', 'political mercenaries' and 'feudal residues'. The excesses and clumsy moves committed by the Kuomintang drove other groups over to the communist side, where they met with the utmost scorn; Mao Tse-tung ironically called them 'confused, short-sighted, individualistic democrats', who were 'much too engrossed in their books'.

The communists had the satisfaction of winning over rebel elements of the Kuomintang, under the title of Kuomintang Revolutionary Committee. The most outstanding of these were Li Chi-shen, who defeated the Canton Commune, Ts'ai T'ing-k'ai, who rebelled in Fukien, and Madame Sun Yat-sen.

The communists wanted to stand for the 'common front' of all revolutionary classes – national bourgeoisie, petty bourgeoisie, workers and peasants, or, in other words, almost the whole of society united against

[1] It appears for the first time in Mao Tse-tung, 'On the People's Democratic Dictatorship' (30 June 1949), *Selected Works,* vol. IV, p. 415.

the traditional evils of imperialism, feudalism, militarism, bureaucrat-capitalism, etc., rather than for a 'common front' of political parties.

The Kuomintang, unable to become a strong revolutionary party once more, or to move towards a new democracy, eventually lost all its support and prestige. The population's lassitude and its wish for peace at any price made its downfall complete. The communist victory was due to the fact that their enemies were worn out and unable to react rather than to any massive popular movement.

The development of the Party from 1945 to 1949: the chief documents of the period

The extension of zones under communist control naturally increased the Party membership. Between 1945 and 1947, it rose from 1,200,000 to 2,700,000. The Party was now gaining a hold on areas where it had no tradition behind it. Many people deserted the government administrative organizations and the army to join its ranks. In the countryside many hitherto uncertain elements also joined it hurriedly. The land reform measures gave rise to various 'conservative' and 'leftist' deviations. In 1947 another 'rectification movement' was launched. It involved the examination of each individual's standpoint as far as social origins, ideological training and working style were concerned. The usual practices were brought into play, particularly mutual and self-criticism sessions. It eventually spread to the army as well, which was in great need of being taken in hand once more, owing to the large numbers of enemy soldiers absorbed. The spirit of the 1947 Rectification Movement was similar to that of the 1942 Rectification Movement, and was in a sense a continuation of it; it was designed to maintain discipline within the Party, and its doctrinal purity, as understood by the theorists behind the movement.

The leaders also turned their attention to methods of work. Committee secretaries were to lead their committee like a squad, but they also had to organize discussion of problems, exchange information, consult the lower ranks, be able to handle every question with skill, be firm and accurate, organize meetings, be modest, and be able to tell the difference between friends and enemies, success and failure.[1]

Mao Tse-tung's thought and his intentions had also to be taken into account. As victory seemed to be drawing nearer, he began to move

[1] Cf. Mao Tse-tung, 'Methods of Work of Party Committees', *Selected Works*, vol. IV, p. 377.

away from the New Democracy and the conciliatory spirit it implied. The title alone of 'On the People's Democratic Dictatorship' revealed a hardening attitude which the facts themselves were beginning to bear out.[1] This important text states the leaders' official views on the introduction and development of communism in China, drawing up several principles at the same time and putting forward several views of the future. China belonged entirely 'to the side of the anti-imperialist front headed by the Soviet Union'. Individual or national neutrality is an untenable 'illusion'. No possibility of compromise with the reactionaries exists, any more than between Wu Sung, the hero of the popular novel *The Water Margin*, and the tiger attacking him. Wu Sung had to kill the tiger or be devoured by it; the communists must destroy the reactionaries or be destroyed. In an astonishingly pertinent passage, Mao Tse-tung exclaims:

> 'You are too irritating.' We are talking about how to deal with domestic and foreign reactionaries, the imperialists and their running dogs, not about how to deal with anyone else. With regard to such reactionaries, the question of irritating them or not does not arise. Irritated or not irritated, they will remain the same because they are reactionaries.

This tough attitude does not exclude diplomatic and trade relations:

> 'We want to do business.' Quite right, business will be done. . . . When we have beaten the internal and external reactionaries by uniting all domestic and international forces, we shall be able to do business and establish diplomatic relations with all foreign countries on the basis of equality, mutual benefit and mutual respect for territorial integrity and sovereignty.

These remarks naturally lead to the definition of the 'democratic dictatorship', which is 'democracy for the people and dictatorship over the reactionaries'. The 'democratic dictatorship' will be maintained as long as classes, the reactionaries within the state, and the imperialists continue to exist.

Distant prospects such as these do not prevent Mao Tse-tung from being aware of the great difficulties in the tasks immediately to hand; his anxiety is apparent when he says: 'The serious task of economic construction lies before us. We shall soon put aside some of the things we know well and be compelled to do things we don't know well. This means difficulties. The imperialists reckon that we will not be able to manage

[1] Cf. Mao Tse-tung, 'On the People's Democratic Dictatorship', *Selected Works*, vol. IV, p. 411.

our economy; they are standing by and looking on, awaiting our failure.'

Mao Tse-tung turns to the example of the Soviet Union once again: 'The Communist Party of the Soviet Union is our best teacher and we must learn from it.'

Another contemporary text, equally important from the point of view of the history and the hopes of the communists, if not from that of the doctrine itself, is to be found in the resolution passed by the Seventh Central Committee at its second plenary session at Shihchiachuang, from 5 to 13 March 1949. The attention of the Party as a whole was drawn to the difficulties to be expected with the return to the towns – difficulties concerning the Party itself, administrative questions, and the question of cooperation with the useful bourgeoisie. Using a grave tone, the resolution gives several wise exhortations:

1 Party members must learn to administer the cities, for 'the period . . . of the city leading the village has now begun'. They must be ready to struggle overtly or covertly against the dangerous remains of the bourgeoisie and imperialism.
2 Leaders in the towns must learn to restore their production and to get to know techniques of production.
3 Private industrial capitalism must continue to develop within the framework fixed by the State.

These efforts will be crowned with success: 'The day is not far off when China will attain prosperity. There is absolutely no ground for pessimism about China's economic resurgence. . . . Not only can the Chinese people live without begging alms from the imperialists, they will live a better life than that in the imperialist countries.'

The resolution of 5 March 1949 ended with this promise, which history was to leave unconfirmed.

The rise to power of People's China

Preparations were going ahead for the creation of a real government. A Political Consultative Conference was convened to ensure the transition from the former institutions (nationalist government or Revolutionary Military Committee). The former government had itself intended to use this method to effect the changeover from the Kuomintang regime of tutelage to the constitutional regime; the Consultative Conference met from 10 to 31 January 1946. The convening of a Consultative Conference was also one of the conditions for armistice laid down by the communists on 15 April 1949. The New Political Consultative Conference met in Peking from 21 to 30 September 1949. The Communist Party decided how it was to be composed, acting with great skill and refraining from forming a majority, at least as far as representation of political parties was concerned. The conference was made up of 662 delegates, 585 of whom were regular members, and the other 77 deputy members, divided as follows:

	Regular members	*Deputy members*
Political parties	142	23
Regional representatives	102	14
Army delegates	60	11
Miscellaneous (professions, cultural associations, overseas Chinese, minority races)	206	29
Guests	75	—

The Political Consultative Conference had a double task:

1 To adopt the organic law of the People's Government.
2 To vote a 'common political programme', to be a sort of charter for the new regime.

This was carried out on 29 September.

On 1 October 1949 Mao Tse-tung, Chairman of the Central Committee of the Communist Party, proclaimed the People's Republic of China from the top of the crimson Gate of Heavenly Peace at the entrance to the old Imperial Palace. The Party that he had re-created twice over had triumphed, after twenty-eight years of bitter struggle. Political and territorial unity, lost since 1911, had been achieved once more, or would be achieved, with the exception of Taiwan. The building of the New China, 'new democratic' and then 'socialist', was to begin.

Conclusion

The causes of the communist victory

To analyse the causes of the communists' triumph in China naturally calls for a previous study of all the main political, economic, social, cultural, military and international factors at work, both in the country's situation and in its evolution over the last fifty years. Various authors have made either individual or collective attempts to clarify this complicated question; the study of it is by no means finished.[1] A few facts stand out clearly against a still confused background, and are sufficiently important in themselves to suggest that all that remains to be discovered will apparently be of secondary importance.

The chief fact lies outside the Communist Party's activities; it is the development, from the Mukden Incident of 18 September 1931 onwards, of an international state of affairs which became increasingly favourable to the communists' designs, until the end of the Sino-Japanese war on 15 August 1945. In this respect, by shirking their obligations, the League of Nations and the Powers who signed the Treaty of Washington in 1922, thereby guaranteeing the integrity of Chinese territory, can be said to have been instrumental in the birth of the New China. The Sino-Japanese war of 1937 to 1945, as has already been said, brought about the resurrection of the Communist Party, after the Long March had maintained a flicker of life. At the same time, the war achieved the economic and moral downfall

[1] See Lucien Bianco's excellent book, *Les Origines de la Révolution chinoise 1915-1949*, and also A. Doak Barnett, *China on the Eve of Communist Takeover,* for a work of a different kind.

of the Kuomintang, a party lacking the preparation and organization needed to sustain seven hard years of warfare.

The Nanking government of 1937 obviously suffered from serious failings inherent in the slow transformation of an old society, which was gradually, almost regretfully, casting off its old traditions in order to evolve towards Western customs, though these were not as yet fully understood. It was a precarious government, potentially an easy prey for a military coalition liable to plunge China again into the anarchy that had reigned between 1916 and 1928, or allow the communist spark to set the prairie alight once more; even so, it still carried on with the great national tasks ahead of it, in spite of rivalries within and pressures from outside. Political unity was growing stronger, as the Sian Incident on 12 December 1936 had proved, an economic structure was beginning to take shape, particularly in the field of transport, the currency was stable and the army partly modernized. The government's early achievements encouraged the Japanese to speed up the rhythm of their attacks; owing to its national character and irresponsible pressure from the communists, it could not play for time and had to come to terms with the enemies within the country.

When times became hard, after the valiant Battle of Shanghai was over, the central government turned out to be incapable of leading the war by making the necessary intellectual adjustment, and adapting the means at its disposal to the only possible form of warfare, by shifting the 'resistance' to a national scale and allowing it authentically popular expression. This lack of flexibility can be ascribed to several reasons – the influence of Western-type strategy with regular armies only, the failure of both the new and old bourgeoisie to fulfil their military and civic duties, loyalty to traditional political concepts, which left the people to shift for itself as far as possible, and the fear that the creation of semi-independent theatres of operations would destroy national unity.

In this state of affairs, ill suited to its rivals, the Communist Party was to benefit from its own particular characteristics and its past activities. All things considered, these characteristics, combined with its sound experience in land and military policy, were to result in victory in a war which can be described as 'revolutionary' in comparison with the war in the style of the 'ancien régime' carried on by the Kuomintang.[1]

Centralization. The Chinese Communist Party, highly centralized organically, politically and ideologically, could found and direct isolated bases

[1] The comparison with the context of the French Revolution can obviously be carried no further than this.

behind Japanese lines without the slightest risk of their rebelling or going over to the enemy. As a result, the war against the invader and the simultaneous struggle against the Kuomintang were conducted with incomparable firmness and flexibility. At the same time, the Generalissimo, although he had a reputation as a dictator, had to deal craftily or come to terms with the different factions within his party, the provincial leaders, still all-powerful in places, and his foreign advisers. The transfer of his capital from the zone where it had direct influence, in the middle and lower Yangtze valley, towards outlying, almost autonomous provinces (Szechuan, Yunnan, Kwangsi, Hsinkiang, Kansu and Chinghai), was an immense, and often overlooked, handicap.

Organization. The Communist Party, with its simple, precise principles of organization, quickly set up the structure it needed to approach the masses, win them over, train them and control them. With its solid foundations in the population, which, unlike the Kuomintang, it wanted to arouse politically and supply with cadres, the Party's mass organizations were powerful weapons which its enemies, reduced to exhortation and external constraint, lacked entirely.

Ideology. The ideology was a unique and convenient source of reference, and a touchstone for cadres and party members, collected into concise slogans for use by the masses; its own strictness ensured strict uniformity of behaviour. The Three People's Principles, when set beside it, appeared as vague as in the past; its ageing conservative ideas had by this time lost their attraction and their social content.

Cadres. The new cadres who had joined a movement that had for a long time been outlawed did so through patriotism or on a revolutionary impulse, or through a combination of both reasons. Their selflessness and energy usually made them superior to the Kuomintang cadres, who often joined their party under a moral or administrative obligation. It might be said that the Chinese bourgeoisie had paradoxically given the most ardent of its members to the Communist Party, instead of upholding the regime that embodied its duties, its interests and its traditions.

The Party's missionary role. The Chinese communist movement set out to be more than a patriotic movement, in which it was on an equal footing with the Kuomintang; it also claimed to educate, whether by eliminating outdated customs or introducing newer ideas of 'justice' and above all, of 'equality'. Its 'liberating' action (in both the national and social applications of the word) was carried out in the name of the people and consequently individuals were sometimes held cheap. The system it encountered was not a liberal democracy – even the very notion of this was virtually lacking in the countryside – but a social and family system often creating practices generating as much restraint as those that the Party eventually imposed. Inertia and fear on the part of the population, and fanaticism and undue haste on the part of the cadres, were to constitute the real obstacles to the propagation of communism.

The Communist Party was superior to the Kuomintang as far as centralization, organization, propaganda and cadres were concerned; in the two most important fields, land policy and the army, it was also superior, through both its principles and its application of them. From 1937 onwards particularly, intelligent and moderate land measures, aimed at lightening the burden on the peasants and encouraging small-scale production, helped the Communist Party to implant its authority in the first place, ensured its authority and provided an excuse for its despotism. At the same time, the central government had great difficulty in lowering land rent and even had to resort to heavier taxation of agriculture to compensate for a loss of resources in the industrial areas. As in the Kiangsi period, once the Chinese peasants had been 'aroused', if they lived in villages relatively far away from zones controlled by the Japanese, their collaborators or the central government, they upheld the Party through gratitude and above all because their fate was bound up with that of the 'revolution'. The youngest among them defended their newly acquired land and rights by serving willingly in the Red Army.

The communists gave outstanding proof of their superiority in the military field above all, as regards the fighting qualities of the individual soldier, the flexibility of the organization, the tactical use of units and the conduct of operations in general. Several chapters have touched on the first three points, and it may be said that by the end of the Kiangsi period, the Chinese communists had achieved everything they hoped for, given the circumstances and the means at their disposal (see Chapter 15). During the Sino-Japanese war, their target of political expansion became more important than the purely military target. Furthermore, they were completely outclassed by the Japanese in terms of arms, strategic mobility and manœuvring. The communist command could not show its usual ability; instead, it wisely adapted itself to existing possibilities and covered up its weakness with unexpected formulae and theories. 'Regular warfare of the Chinese type' is 'only guerrilla warfare raised to a higher level', in the words of Mao Tse-tung, for whom guerrilla warfare sometimes took on the role of primary strategic importance, while operations of a regular type were 'supplementary'.

This was not so during the Third Revolutionary Civil War. The leaders of the Red Army – an anonymous term which could mean Mao Tse-tung, and the Chu Teh and Yeh Chien-ying partnership, either separately or all together – the Military Committee,[1] began by gradually building itself up on new lines, helped by political truces and contributions of Japanese military equipment recuperated in Manchuria, thanks to the Soviet Union. It then progressed gradually from the conduct of small guerrilla units to the conduct of large units – armies, army groups and field armies with several million men with all the logistic organization entailed, even in the case of a sober, rustic army with the solid support of a thoroughly mobilized countryside behind it. The operations carried out in 1948 were masterpieces in terms of the adaptation of the means to the objectives, the choice of objectives, the rapidity of movement and the excellent coordination of the different elements of the armies in action. It is no exaggeration to describe them as operations of the Napoleonic type, in their style as well as in the unrefined means used, and the almost total absence of modern transport. In this sense, the battles of Chinchow, Mukden and Huai-Hai were perhaps the last great battles of the classical age before those of the nuclear epoch.[2] All things considered, in spite of initial inequalities in numbers, resources and territory, the communists triumphed easily because they managed to synthesize the political, military and psychological factors in their favour and apply them accurately and intelligently. The Sino-Japanese war was responsible for creating the conditions needed.

The Party and its future in 1949

In 1949 the situation of the Chinese Communist Party was reversed. Its task from then on was to restore and build up instead of destroying, and to govern instead of conquering. Its coming to power was only the first step in the amazing political, economic, social and cultural revolution it intended to carry through: the first and easiest, as Mao Tse-tung said. It does not fall within the scope of this book to pass judgement on the work accomplished up to the date of writing, or even to analyse the characteristics that make the Chinese Communist Party totally different from its Western equivalents. It is only possible to say how far thirty years of past struggle had prepared it for its new mission.

[1] It has already been pointed out that Mao Tse-tung took the credit for some directives during operations, particularly during the Manchurian and the Peking-Tientsin campaigns.

[2] Operations in Korea and Vietnam did not take on the same geographical development or flexibility of movement; equipment and armaments were far more important than in China.

On the whole, the Party appeared to be strong, dynamic, homogeneous and united behind the outstanding leader who had forged it. The population, humiliated and wearied by endless civil or foreign wars, both feared and accepted it. It had already gained valuable experience of administration in large areas. Its victory owed virtually nothing to outside forces. The Party was deeply nationalistic, born as it was of the anti-foreign movements of the 1920s; it had grown up during the war of resistance against Japan, and was in tune with a tradition of Chinese grandeur and superiority which the century of Unequal Treaties (1842-1943) had been unable to break. The leaders, brought up under the empire and witnesses of the 'national shame', were doubly sensitive to this point. The intellectuals, the masses and even the enemies of communism were quick to realize that the rise of an energetic regime, intransigent in its dealings with foreigners, represented above all a revenge on the West and the promise of a rise to the status of a modern power.

The Party's composition, its spirit and its preoccupations, all reflected its own experience. Some Chinese intellectuals, all convinced communists, had made use of a difficult agrarian situation – a normal phenomenon – and an international state of affairs which was both exceptional and extremely promising for them, to rise to power through military action. Three factors in this short cut to power were going to help the new regime and yet weigh heavily on it at the same time.

The exclusively intellectual origins of the leaders seemed to guarantee that ideological unity would be easy to maintain. The leaders closely resembled each other – they came from the same petty bourgeois social background, they had received the same education, and had shared the same personal experiences, with only a few shades of difference. They all believed in Marxism-Leninism, completed by Stalinism. After 1931, no outstanding deviation or rival doctrine emerged; no rival socialist, labour or workers' party managed to form and gain a hold, even in non-communist zones. The differences of opinion and the frictions that arose at Yenan and after were centred on the appropriateness of certain actions or on personal ambition. Until the Cultural Revolution, at least, the inner strife reflected conflicting methods or recipes for development, rather than real doctrinal conflicts.

The peasantry, both pretext and instrument for the revolutionary movement, was at the centre of the regime. Its huge masses and problems provide ample justification for this. The countless experiments in land policy carried out in Kiangsi between 1927 and 1934, and in the liberated areas between 1937 and 1949, have presumably earned for the leaders an ability to make sound judgements and choices in practical measures; it is to be hoped that, as far as structure, rulings and working rhythms are concerned, they will be able to provide solutions that are both revolutionary and profitable to the economy as a whole.

Lastly the army: the Chinese communist movement has never ceased to be a military movement. The Party and the army hierarchies were almost identical, for the same men figured in both; they helped build each other up throughout. The militarization of the Party spirit, a result of the path it took to power, is to be found in the methods of leadership, the vocabulary and the army's place and role in the nation. After a brief interlude from 1955 to 1959, the old tradition of the people's revolutionary army was born again, an army ever-present spiritually and sometimes physically among the masses, helping with their ideological training; during the Cultural Revolution it maintained a remote though real control over the large administrative organizations and industrial undertakings, and may perhaps have saved the country from total anarchy.

These rapidly summarized characteristics are not uniquely happy in their effects. The party office-bearers, trained in the countryside for rural and military jobs which were often scattered geographically, were not adequately prepared for the work of building up a modern economy on a national scale. Few of them were economists, scientists or technicians. The slogan 'Politics in command' resulted from ignorance and a habit of thought rather than from a careful choice. Planners from the Soviet Union were called in at first, although from 1958 onwards a 'Chinese way' policy was adopted with no prior investigation, founded on blind faith in the docility and devotion of the masses. There is reason to believe that the presence of a powerful proletarian nucleus in the Party (it still represents 14 per cent only), and adherence to the higher requests of experts in urban administration or industrial and commercial undertakings, would have been useful in limiting over hasty and irrational decisions on planning and organization of production.

In the name of the military effort, and as a counterpart to the land measures they had wanted for so long, the Chinese Communist Party could ask what it wanted of the peasants. This habit was continued and carried too far, beginning with the People's Communes, and explains the mistakes made when collectivization was put through too hastily in 1956-7, and particularly those of the People's Communes in 1958. Generally speaking, the Party was too quick to wield the scalpel when dealing with social structures; operations that were undergone without a murmur at first eventually became insupportable and provoked post-operational reactions within the structure of the Party itself. The 'militarist' spirit, in spite of its great tradition of devotion and loyalty to the Party, furnished an example of methods which were too rigid and rough, and too political in comparison with the complexity and the technical aspects of the problems involved. The attitude of independence towards the outside world and particularly the Soviet Union during the rise of the Party, given various ideological pretexts, was to become systematic hostility towards all great powers and powerful neighbours. It was to create further complications in China's adjustment to the rest of the world, even though she was free of the complexes born of the Unequal Treaties.

Mao Tse-tung's overriding personality, which had conferred unity and strong leadership on the Party, on the revolutionary movement, and on the whole of China after 1949, was eventually to become a source of embarrassment both inside the country and outside it. After introducing the People's Communes, the Great Leap Forward, the Socialist Education Movement of 1962, and the Cultural Revolution in the years that followed, he gradually encountered so much resistance within the Party that he had to outmanœuvre his enemies by stirring the masses into movement and overthrowing established structures. In the ideological field, the growing pretensions of the Maoist theses to inspire every revolution, whether in an underdeveloped or a highly industrialized country, and the resulting revolutionary extremism, have hardened Chinese foreign policy to a harmful degree; when seen alongside the Chinese advance in the field of nuclear weapons, they create a new danger for world peace.

All this was hard to foresee in 1949. Haloed with the glow of victory, presenting a startling contrast to the central government and its grave failings, and surrounded by a world still convalescing after the Second World War, New China seemed bound for an era of peace, progress and prestige. This mood of optimism lasted for ten years before signs of disorder appeared, first in the realm of the economy and then in politics. As they still continue, the causes may be surmised. Is the work to be done out of proportion to the means available? Is the trouble due to factors inherent in a Chinese society which is still largely traditional? Is the population growing uncontrollably? Was the technological level too low at the start? All these questions are based on elements which are hard to grasp and deserve far-reaching and difficult analyses. One more reason ought probably to be added – the characteristics of a whole party whose aim has for too long been the winning of power by war, and the illusions of a leader whose revolutionary vision has prevailed over the realities of the nation before him.

Bibliography

Western works

This bibliography deals mainly with the history of the Chinese Communist Party during the period from 1921 to 1949. General works, works on the history or other aspects of the People's Republic of China, and works on present-day events in China are not included. The following general bibliographies may be found useful:

HUCKER, CHARLES O., *China: A Critical Bibliography*. Tucson, University of Arizona Press, 1962.

YUAN TUNG-LI, *China in Western Literature*. New Haven, Conn., Yale University Far Eastern Publications, 1958.

Bibliography of Asian Studies, an annual publication of the *Journal of Asian Studies*. Ann Arbor, Mich., The Association for Asian Studies Inc.

Revue bibliographique de Sinologie. Paris, École Pratique des Hautes Études. Annual publication.

Index Sinicus: A Catalogue of Articles Relating to China in Periodicals and Other Collective Publications, 1920-1955. Cambridge, Heffer, 1964.

BERTON, PETER, and WU, EUGENE, *Contemporary China, a Research Guide*. Stanford, Calif., Hoover Institution, 1967.

As a rule, articles in newspapers or periodicals have not been listed, as they are too numerous and scattered.[1] The most reliable of them usually appear in a few specialized periodicals:

[1] Some of them have nevertheless been quoted in footnotes to the text.

The China Quarterly. London, Congress for Cultural Freedom. Quarterly.

The Journal of Asian Studies. Ann Arbor, Mich., The Association for Asian Studies Inc. Quarterly.

Asian Survey. Berkeley, Calif., University of California, Institute of International Studies. Monthly.

Problems of Communism. Washington D.C., U.S. Information Agency. Bimonthly.

Works on the Chinese Communist Party usually fall into one of three categories:

1 Eye-witness accounts, generally written by journalists or diplomats. Although these may be extremely valuable, they sometimes suffer from a lack of adequate perspective, or from the fact that they reflect contemporary preoccupations, or the sympathies or antipathies of their authors.
2 Studies and research based on documents. These are usually the work of able academics who frequently have plentiful material available, and they help to throw light on historical events. American authors have made a particularly large contribution in this field.
3 Biographies. They fall into one of the two above-mentioned categories, or more rarely into both. Some, such as those by Edgar Snow in *Red Star Over China* or by Howard Boorman in *Men and Politics in Modern China*[1] are of outstanding interest.

The books are listed with no attempt to distinguish between them or comment on them, as the reader should have no difficulty in judging them for himself.

Apart from a few exceptions, texts published by the Foreign Languages Publishing House in Peking have not been listed. Relatively few appeared during the years before 1 October 1949. Some – particularly those by Mao Tse-tung – have been included in later editions of selected works.

BAND, CLAIRE, and BAND, WILLIAM, *Two Years with the Chinese Communists*. New Haven, Conn., Yale University Press, 1948.

BARNETT, A. DOAK, *China on the Eve of Communist Takeover*. New York, Praeger, 1963.

BARRETT, DAVID D., *Dixie Mission: The United States Army Observer Group in Yenan, 1944*. Berkeley, University of California Press, 1970.

[1] See also H. Boorman and Richard Howard, *A Biographical Dictionary of Republican China*.

BELDEN, JACK, *China Shakes the World.* New York, Harper, 1949.

BERTRAM, JAMES M., *First Act in China.* New York, Viking, 1938.

BIANCO, LUCIEN, *Les Origines de la Révolution chinoise 1915-1949.* Paris, Gallimard, 1967.

BOORMAN, HOWARD L. (ed.), *Men and Politics in Modern China: Preliminary 50 Biographies.* New York, Columbia University, 1960.

BOORMAN, HOWARD, and HOWARD, RICHARD C., *A Biographical Dictionary of Republican China,* Vols I-V. New York and London, Columbia University Press, 1967, 1968.

BRANDT, CONRAD, *Stalin's Failure in China (1924-1927).* Cambridge, Mass., Harvard University Press, 1958.

BRANDT, CONRAD, SCHWARTZ, BENJAMIN, and FAIRBANK, JOHN K., *A Documentary History of Chinese Communism.* Cambridge, Mass., Harvard University Press, 1958.

BRIEUX, JEAN JACQUES, *La Chine du nationalisme au communisme.* Paris, Le Seuil, 1951.

BROUÉ, PIERRE, *La Question chinoise dans l'Internationale communiste (1926-1927).* Paris, Études et documentation internationales, 1965.

CARLSON, EVANS FORDYCE, *Twin Stars of China.* New York, Dodd Mead, 1941.

CARRÈRE D'ENCAUSSE, H., and SCHRAM, STUART, *Le Marxisme et l'Asie, 1853-1964.* Paris, A. Colin, 1965.

CHANG, CARSUN, *The Third Force in China.* New York, Bookman Associates, 1952.

CHAO KUO-CHÜN, *Draft Survey of Materials Relating to Communism in China, 1927-1934.* Stanford, Calif., Hoover Institution, 1948.

CHAO KUO-CHÜN, *Agrarian Policy of the Chinese Communist Party, 1921-1959.* London, Asia Publishing House, 1960.

CHASSIN, L. M., *La Conquête de la Chine par Mao Tse-tung (1945-1949).* Paris, Payot, 1952.

CHASSIN, L. M., *L'Ascension de Mao Tse-tung (1921-1945).* Paris, Payot, 1953.

CHEN CH'ANG-FENG, *On the Long March with Chairman Mao.* Peking, Foreign Languages Press, 1959.

CH'EN, JEROME, *Mao and the Chinese Revolution.* London, Oxford University Press, 1965.

CH'EN, JEROME (ed.) *Mao Tse-tung papers: Anthology and Bibliography.* London, Oxford University Press, 1970.

CH'EN KUNG-PO, *The Communist Movement in China,* ed. C. Martin Wilbur. New York, East Asian Institute of Columbia University, 1960.

CH'EN PO-TA, *Notes on Ten Years of Civil War, 1927-1936*. Peking, Foreign Languages Press, 1954.

CHESNEAUX, JEAN, *Sun Yat-sen*. Paris, Club Français du Livre, 1959.

CHESNEAUX, JEAN, *Le Mouvement Ouvrier chinois 1919-1927*. Paris, Mouton, 1962.

CHIANG KAI-SHEK, *China's Destiny*, trans. Wang Chung-hui. New York, Macmillan, 1947 (official translation).

CHIANG KAI-SHEK, *China's Destiny* and *Chinese Economic Theory*, trans. Philip Jaffe. New York, Roy, 1947 (unofficial translation).

CHIANG KAI-SHEK, *Soviet Russia in China: A Summing-up at Seventy*. New York, Farrar, Straus and Cudahy, 1958. 2nd ed. pub. by Farrar, Straus and Giroux, 1965.

CHOW TS'E-TSUNG, *The May Fourth Movement: Intellectual Revolution in Modern China*. Cambridge, Mass., Harvard University Press, 1960.

CHU HAO-JAN, 'Mao's Wife Chiang Ch'ing'. *China Quarterly*, No. 31, July-September 1967.

COHEN, ARTHUR A., *The Communism of Mao Tse-tung*. Chicago, University of Chicago Press, 1964.

COLLOTI PISCHEL, ENRICA, *Le Origine ideologiche della rivoluzione cinese*. Turin, Giulio Einaudi, 1958.

COMPTON, BOYD (trans.), *Mao's China: Party Reform Documents, 1942-1944*. Seattle, University of Washington Press, 1952.

DANIELS, ROBERT V. (ed.), *A Documentary History of Communism (from Lenin to Mao)*. New York, Random House, 1960.

DUBARBIER, GEORGES, *La Chine du XXe siècle: des Mandchous à Mao*. Paris, Payot, 1965.

ELEGANT, ROBERT S., *China's Red Masters*. London, Bodley Head, 1952.

EPSTEIN, ISRAEL, *The People's War*. London, Gollancz, 1939.

EPSTEIN, ISRAEL, *The Unfinished Revolution in China*. Boston, Mass., Little, Brown, 1947.

EUDIN, XENIA J., and NORTH, ROBERT C., *Soviet Russia and the East, 1920-1927*. Stanford, Calif., Stanford University Press, 1957.

FAIRBANK, JOHN K., and LIU KWANG-CHING, *Modern China: A Bibliographical Guide to Chinese Works, 1898-1937*. Cambridge, Mass., Harvard University Press, 1950.

FEIS, HERBERT, *The China Tangle: the American effort in China from Pearl Harbour to the Marshall Mission*. Princeton, N.J., Princeton University Press, 1953.

FEUERWERKER, A., and CHENG, S., *Chinese Communist Studies of Modern Chinese History*. Cambridge, Mass., Harvard University Press, 1961.

FITZGERALD, CHARLES PATRICK, *Revolution in China*. New York, Praeger, 1952.

Foreign Languages Press, *China's Revolutionary Wars: Stories of the Long March*. Peking, Foreign Languages Press, 1958.

FORMAN, HARRISON, *Report from Red China*. New York, Holt, 1945.

Fundamental Laws of the Chinese Soviet Republic (with an introduction by Bela Kun). New York, International Publishers, 1934.

GARVEY, J. E., *Marxist-Leninist China: Military and Social Doctrine*. New York, Exposition Press, 1960.

GASSTER, MICHAEL, *Chinese Intellectuals and the Revolution of 1911*. Seattle, University of Washington Press, 1969.

GELDER, STUART (ed.), *The Chinese Communists*. London, Gollancz, 1946.

GRIFFITH, SAMUEL B. (trans.), *Mao Tse-tung on Guerrilla Warfare*. New York, Praeger, 1961.

GRIFFITH, SAMUEL B., *The Chinese People's Liberation Army*. London, Weidenfeld & Nicolson, 1968.

GUILLERMAZ, JACQUES, *La Chine Populaire*. Paris, Presses Universitaires de France, 1959. 5th ed. 1971.

HANRAHAN, GENE Z., *Chinese Communist Guerrilla Tactics*. New York, Columbia University Press, 1952.

HINTON, WILLIAM, *Fanshen: A Documentary of Revolution in a Chinese Village*. New York and London, Monthly Review Press, 1967.

HO KAN-CHIH, *A History of the Modern Chinese Revolution*. Peking, Foreign Languages Press, 1959.

HSIA, C. T., *A History of Modern Chinese Fiction, 1917-1957*. New Haven, Conn., Yale University Press, 1961.

HSIA, TSI-AN, *The Gate of Darkness*. Seattle and London, Washington University Press, 1968.

HSIAO SAN (EMI SIAO), *Mao Tse-tung: His Childhood and Youth* (trans. from Chinese). Bombay, People's Publishing House, 1953.

HSIAO TSO-LIANG, *Power Relations Within the Chinese Communist Movement 1930-1934*. Seattle, University of Washington Press, 1961.

HSIAO TSO-LIANG, 'Chinese Communism and the Canton Soviet of 1927'. *China Quarterly*, April-June 1967.

HSIAO TSO-LIANG, *The Land Revolution in China, 1930-1934*. Seattle and London, Washington University Press, 1969.

HSIAO YÜ ('SIAO-YU'), *Mao Tse-tung and I were Beggars*. Syracuse, N.Y., Syracuse University Press, 1959.

HSU KAI-YU, *Chou En-lai*. Paris, Mercure de France, 1968.

HSU, U. T., *The Invisible Conflict*. Hong Kong, 1958.

HSÜEH CHÜN-TU, *The Chinese Communist Movement, 1921-1937*. Stanford, Calif., The Hoover Institution, 1960.

HU CHIAO-MU, *Thirty Years of the Communist Party of China*. Peking, Foreign Languages Press, 1952.

HUANG SUNG-K'ANG, *Lu Hsün and the New Culture Movement of Modern China*. Amsterdam, Djambatan, 1957.

HUANG SUNG-K'ANG, *Li Ta-chao and the Impact of Marxism on Modern Chinese Thinking*. Paris and The Hague, Mouton, 1965.

ISAACS, HAROLD ROBERT, *The Tragedy of the Chinese Revolution*. London, Secker & Warburg, 1938. Rev. ed., Stanford, Calif., Stanford University Press, 1951.

JOHNSON, CHALMERS, *Peasant Nationalism and Communist Power: the Emergence of Revolutionary China 1937-1945*. Stanford, Calif., Stanford University Press, 1962.

KLEIN, DONALD W., and CLARK, ANN B., *A Biographic Dictionary of Chinese Communism 1921-1965*. 2 vols. Harvard East Asian Series, 57. Cambridge, Mass., Harvard University Press, 1971.

KUO and WARREN, *Analytical History of the Chinese Communist Party*. 3 vols. T'aipei, Institute of International Relations, 1970.

LANG, OLGA, *Pa Chin and His Writings: Chinese Youth between the Two Revolutions*. Cambridge, Mass., Harvard University Press, 1967.

LENG SHAO-CHUAN and PALMER, NORMAN, *Sun Yat-sen and Communism*. London, Thames, 1961.

LENG SHAO-CHUAN, 'Pre-1949 Development of the Communist System of Justice'. *China Quarterly*, April-June 1967.

LEVENSON, JOSEPH R., *Liang Ch'i-ch'ao and the Mind of Modern China*. Cambridge, Mass., Harvard University Press, 1953.

LÉVY, ROGER, *Mao Tsö-tong*. Paris, Seghers, 1965.

LEWIS, JOHN WILSON, *Leadership in Modern China*. New York, Cornell University Press, 1963.

LI CHIEN-NUNG, *The Political History of China, 1840-1928*, trans. Teng Ssu-yü and Jeremy Ingalls. Princeton, N.J., Van Nostrand, 1956.

LI TIEN-MIN, *Chou En-lai*. T'aipei, Institute of International Relations, 1970.

LIAO KAI-LUNG, *From Yenan to Peking*. Peking, Foreign Languages Press, 1954.

LIN YÜ-TANG, *The Vigil of a Nation*. New York, John Day, 1944.

LINDBECK, JOHN M., 'Research Materials on Communist China; U.S. Government Sources'. *Journal of Asian Studies*, XVIII (1958-9).

LIU, F. F., *A Military History of Modern China, 1924-1949*. Princeton, N.J., Princeton University Press, 1956.

LYNN (JERMYU CHI HUNG LYNN), *Political Parties in China*. Peking, Henri Vetch, 1930.

MAGNENOZ, ROBERT, *De Confucius à Lénine*. Saigon, France-Asie, 1951.

MAGNENOZ, ROBERT, *L'Expérience communiste en Chine*. Paris, Les Îles d'or, 1954.

MAO TSE-TUNG, *Nineteen Poems*. Peking, Foreign Languages Press, 1958.

MAO TSE-TUNG, *Selected Works*, Vols I-IV. Peking, Foreign Languages Press, 1960-1965.

MAO TSE-TUNG, *Selected Writings from the Works of Mao Tse-tung*. Peking, Foreign Languages Press, 1967.

MACGREGOR-HASTIE, ROY, *The Red Barbarians: The Life and Times of Mao Tse-tung*. Philadelphia, Chilton, 1961; London, T. V. Boardman, 1962.

MCLANE, CHARLES B., *Soviet Policy and the Chinese Communists, 1931-1946*. New York, Columbia University Press, 1958.

MEISNER, MAURICE, *Li Ta-chao and the Origins of Chinese Marxism*. Cambridge, Mass., Harvard University Press, 1967.

MIF, P., *Heroic China: Fifteen Years of the Communist Party in China*. New York, Workers' Library Publishers, 1937.

NEUBERG, A., *L'Insurrection armée*. Paris, L'Imprimerie Centrale, 1931. See chapters on the Shanghai insurrections and the Canton Commune.

NORTH, ROBERT C., *Kuomintang and Chinese Communist Elites*. Stanford, Calif., Stanford University Press, 1952.

NORTH, ROBERT C., *Moscow and Chinese Communists*. Stanford, Calif., Stanford University Press, 1953.

NORTH, ROBERT C., *M. N. Roy's Mission to China, the Communist-Kuomintang Split of 1927*. Berkeley, University of California Press, 1963.

PALOCZI-HORVATH, G., *Mao Tse-tung, Emperor of the Blue Ants*. London, Secker & Warburg, 1962.

PAYNE, ROBERT, *Journey to Red China*. London, Heinemann, 1947.

PAYNE, ROBERT, *Mao Tse-tung, Ruler of Red China*. London, Secker & Warburg, 1950.

PAYNE, ROBERT, *Portrait of a Revolutionary Mao Tse-tung*. New York, Abelard-Schuman, 1961.

PECK, GRAHAM, *Two Kinds of Time*. Boston, Houghton Mifflin, 1950.

PÉLISSIER, ROGER, *La Chine entre en scene*. Paris, Julliard, 1963.

PÉLISSIER, ROGER, *De la Révolution chinoise*. Paris, Julliard, 1967.

RHOADS, EDWARD J. M., and others, *The Chinese Red Army 1927-1963 (An Annotated Bibliography)*. Cambridge, Mass., Harvard University Press, 1965.

ROMANUS, C. F., and SUNDERLAND, R., *Stilwell's Mission to China*. Washington, D.C., U.S. Department of the Army, Office of the Chief of Military History, 1953 (United States Army in World War II: China-Burma-India theater).

ROY, M. N., *My Experiences in China*. Calcutta, Renaissance Publishers, 1938.

ROY, M. N., *Revolution and Counter-revolution in China*. Calcutta, Renaissance Publishers, 1946.

RUE, JOHN E., *Mao Tse-tung in Opposition, 1927-1935*. Stanford, Calif., Stanford University Press, 1966.

SCALAPINO, R. A., and YU, GEORGE T., *The Chinese Anarchist Movement*. Berkeley, Institute of International Studies, University of California, 1961.

SCHRAM, STUART R., 'The Military Deviation of Mao Tse-tung'. *Problems of Communism*, January-February 1964. Washington, D.C., U.S. Information Agency.

SCHRAM, STUART R., *Mao Tse-tung*. Harmondsworth, Penguin, 1966. Rev. ed. 1967.

SCHRAM, STUART R., *The Political Thought of Mao Tse-tung*. New York, Praeger, 1963; Harmondsworth, Penguin, 1969.

SCHWARTZ, BENJAMIN I., *Chinese Communism and the Rise of Mao*. Cambridge, Mass., Harvard University Press, 1951. New ed., New York, Harper & Row, 1967.

SHIRATO, ICHIRO, *Japanese Sources on the History of the Chinese Communist Movement*, ed. Martin Wilbur. New York, Columbia University Press, 1953.

SMEDLEY, AGNES, *Chinese Destinies: Sketches of Present-day China*. London, Hurst & Blackett, 1934.

SMEDLEY, AGNES, *China's Red Army Marches*. London, Lawrence & Wishart, 1935.

SMEDLEY, AGNES, *Battle Hymn of China*. New York, Knopf, 1943.

SMEDLEY, AGNES, *The Great Road: The Life and Times of Chu Teh*. New York, Monthly Review Press, 1956.

SNOW, EDGAR, *The Battle for Asia*. New York, Random House, 1941.

SNOW, EDGAR, *Random Notes on Red China (1936-1945)*. Cambridge, Mass., Harvard University Press, 1957.

SNOW, EDGAR, *Red Star Over China*. New York, Random House, 1938. Revised and enlarged edition, London, Gollancz, 1968.

STEIN, GUNTHER, *The Challenge of Red China*. New York, Whittlesey House, 1945.

STEINER, H. ARTHUR, 'The Curriculum in Chinese Socialist Education: An Official Bibliography of "Maoism"'. *Pacific Affairs*, Vol. 31, No. 3, September 1958.

STILWELL, JOSEPH W., *The Stilwell Papers*. New York, Sloane, 1948.

STRONG, ANNA LOUISE, *China's Millions, the Revolutionary Struggles from 1927-1935*. London, Gollancz, 1936.

STRONG, ANNA LOUISE, *J'ai vu la Chine nouvelle*. Paris, Hier et aujourd'hui, 1949.

STRONG, ANNA LOUISE, *The Chinese Conquer China*. New York, Doubleday, 1949.

STUART, JOHN LEIGHTON, *Fifty Years in China*. New York, Random House, 1954.

T'ANG LEANG-LI, *China in Revolt*. London, Noel Douglas, 1927.

T'ANG LEANG-LI, *Inner History of the Chinese Revolution*. London, Routledge, 1930.

T'ANG LEANG-LI, *Suppressing Communist Banditry in China*. Shanghai, China United Press, 1934.

THORTON, RICHARD C., *The Comintern and the Chinese Communists, 1928-1931*. Seattle and London, Washington University Press, 1969.

TROTSKY, LEON, *L'Internationale communiste après Lénine*. 2 vols. Paris, Presses Universitaires de France, 1969.

TUCHMAN, BARBARA W., *Sand Against the Wind: Stilwell and the American Experience in China*. London, Macmillan, 1971.

Union Research Institute, *Who's Who in Communist China*. Hong Kong, 1970.

U.S. Department of State, *United States Relations with China, with special reference to the period 1944-1949*, based on the files of the Department of State. Washington, Government Printing Office, 1949. Publication No. 3573, Far Eastern Series 30. Re-issued as *The China White Paper*. Stanford, Calif., Stanford University Press, 1967.

United States General Staff, Intelligence Division, *The Chinese Communist Movement*.

VAN SLYKE, LYMAN P., *Enemies and Friends: The United Front in Chinese Communist History*. Stanford University Press, 1968.

WALES, NYM, *Inside Red China*. New York, Doubleday, Doran, 1939.

WALES, NYM, *My Yenan Notebooks*.

WALES, NYM, *The Chinese Labor Movement*. New York, John Day, 1945.

WALES, NYM, *Red Dust*. Stanford, Calif., Stanford University Press, 1952.

WANG, ANNA, *J'ai combattu pour Mao*. Paris, Gallimard, 1967 (orig. pub. Hamburg, 1964).

WANG SHIH, etc., *A Brief History of the Chinese Communist Party*. Shanghai, The Shanghai Publishing House, 1958. English translation, Washington, 1961.

WEDEMEYER, ALBERT, 'Wedemeyer Report'. In *The China White Paper*. Stanford, Calif., Stanford University Press, 1967.

WHITE, THEODORE H., and JACOBY, ANNALEE, *Thunder out of China*. New York, William Sloane Associates, 1946.

WHITING, ALLEN SUESS, *Soviet Policies in China, 1917-1924*. New York, Columbia University Press, 1954.

WILBUR, C. M., *Chinese Sources on the History of the Chinese Communist Movement: an annotated bibliography of materials in the East Asiatic Library of Columbia University*. New York, Columbia University Press, 1950.

WILBUR, C. M., and HOW, JULIE LIEN-YING, (eds), *Documents on Communism, Nationalism and Soviet Advisers in China, 1918-1927*. New York, Columbia University Press, 1956.

WINT, GUY, *Dragon and Sickle*, New York. Praeger, 1959.

WITKE, ROXANE, 'Mao Tse-tung, Women and Suicide in the May Fourth Era'. *The China Quarterly*, No. 31, July-September 1961.

WOO, T. C., *The Kuomintang and the Future of the Chinese Revolution*. London, Allen & Unwin, 1928.

YAKHONTOFF, VICTOR A., *The Chinese Soviets*. New York, Coward-McCann, 1934.

Works in Chinese

For research into, or for a detailed study of the history of the Chinese Communist Party, specialized bibliographies are essential:

HSÜEH, CHÜN-TU, *A Bibliography of Source Materials on Chinese Communism 1931-1937*. Stanford, Calif., The Hoover Institute, 1960.

FEUERWERKER, A. and CHENG, S., *Chinese Communist Studies of Modern Chinese History*. Cambridge, Mass., Harvard University Press, 1961.

RHOADS, EDWARD J. M., and others, *The Chinese Red Army 1927-1963 (An Annotated Bibliography)*. Cambridge, Mass., Harvard University Press, 1965.

FAIRBANK, J. K., and LIU KWANG-CHING, *China: A Bibliographical Guide to Chinese Works, 1898-1937*. Cambridge, Mass., Harvard University Press, 1950.

It is also essential to refer to the chief official texts (works of Mao Tse-tung and the most important leaders), to editorials of newspapers and periodicals (particularly periodicals for political cadres) as these amount to instructions, and naturally to the chief historical periodicals published in Peking – *Li-shih yen-chiu* (*Historical Research*), *Chin-tai shih tzu-liao* (*Modern Historical Material*) – or in Taiwan – *Chung-kuo Hsien-tai shih tsung k'an* (*Contemporary China Historical Review*), etc.

As for collections and important documents, it is difficult if not impossible to discover their whereabouts or get access to them, as the Peking authorities treat foreigners or even Chinese engaged in research with the utmost reserve. The Taiwan authorities, although more liberal in their attitude, are extremely careful in their choice of documents made available to the public.

For this reason, it is usually necessary to fall back on works in general circulation, often those intended for teaching purposes, or on apologetics taking the form of stories or memoirs written by revolutionary cadres. These stories and memoirs are often of interest but as they are scattered throughout the national and provincial press, it is extremely difficult to list them in a general work such as this.

Many works have been systematically destroyed either by the Kuomintang before 1949, or by the Peking government after that date. The new regime has taken great care to eliminate not only works by its enemies, but also those of communists with a reputation for being 'deviationists' or 'counter-revolutionaries'.

The Cultural Revolution of 1966 provoked two opposing tendencies. On one hand, it resulted in the destruction of the remaining personal or family archives, works dating from before or after the beginning of the present regime, leaving only the works of Mao Tse-tung, or paraphrases of them, untouched; the damage, from the point of view of Chinese history taken as a whole, will certainly prove incalculable.

On the other hand, through the Red Guards, it produced an outburst of aggressive and generally unjust writings aimed at many leading personalities. 'Revelations' often throw light on the biography of one of the leaders, or on the facts underlying an affair or an event. It is clearly impossible to use them as a basis for a new interpretation of the history of the Party, particularly before 1949. It is impossible, however, to neglect them altogether; each case must be considered separately, stripped of the obvious exaggerations and falsehoods.

The following, limited list comprises works in Chinese which are useful towards an understanding of the way in which the Chinese communist movement developed, and towards a knowledge of some aspects of it. It can, obviously, serve only as an indication.

Academy of Science, *Chin-tai shih tzu-liao* (*Modern Historical Material*). Peking. This periodical has ceased publication.

CHANG CH'I-YÜN, *Tang-shih kai-yao* (*A Summary of the History of the Kuomintang Party*). 2 vols. T'aipei, 1950.

CHANG CHING-LU, *Chung-kuo hsien-tai ch'u-pan-shih liao* (*Material for a History of Modern Chinese Publishing*). 4 vols. Peking, 1955.

CHANG CHÜN-YING, *Ko-ming yü fan-ko-ming ti chüeh-chan* (*Decisive Battles between Revolutionaries and Counter-revolutionaries*). Peking, 1961.

CHANG CHÜN-YING, *Ti-san-t'zu kuo-nei ko-ming chan-cheng* (*The Third Revolutionary Civil War*). Peking, 1964.

CHANG HSIAO-KAN, *Chung-kuo chin-tai cheng-chih shih* (*A Political History of Contemporary China*). Hong Kong.

CHANG HUI, PAO TS'UN, etc., *Shang-hai chin-pai-nien ko-ming shih-hua* (*Essay on the Revolutionary History of Shanghai during the Last Hundred Years*). Shanghai, 1962.

CHANG TA-CHÜN, *Chung-kung-jen ming-tien* (*Who's Who in Communist China*). Hong Kong, 1965.

CH'EN CH'ENG, *Ch'ih-fei fan-tung wen-chien hui-pien* (*Reactionary Documents of the Red Bandits*). 6 vols. T'aipei, 1960.

Cheng-feng wei-hui (*Documents on the Cheng-feng movement of 1942*). New ed., Shanghai, 1950.

CH'EN PO-TA, *Kuan-yü shih-nien nei-chan* (*Ten Years of Civil War*). 1944.

CH'EN PO-TA, *Chung-kuo ssu ta-chia-tsu* (*The Four Great Families of China*). 1946.

CH'EN PO-TA, *Jen-min kung-ti Chiang Kai-shek* (*An Enemy of the People: Chiang Kai-shek*). Peking, 1954.

CH'EN YÜN, *Tsen-yang tso i-ko kung-ch'an-tang tang-yuan* (*How to be a Communist*). New ed., Canton, 1950.

CHIN I-KUNG, *Chung-kuo t'u-kai yü Chung-kuo t'u-ti wen-t'i* (*The Communist Land Reform and the Land Question in China*). Hong Kong, 1950.

CHU TAO-NAN, *Tsai ta ko-ming ti hung-liu chung* (*In the Upsurge of the Revolution*). Shanghai.

CHU TAO-NAN, *Hui-i Kwangchow ch'ii* (*Memories of the Canton Rising*). Shanghai, 1958.

Chung-kuo chin-tai ssu-hsiang-chia yen-chiu-lun wen-hsüan (*Selected Studies on Contemporary Chinese Thinkers*). Peking, 1957.

Chung-kuo hsien-tai jen-wu lun-tsung (*A Discussion on a Few Figures of Modern Chinese History*). Peking, 1965.

Chung-kuo hsien-tai-shih-liao tsung-shu (*A Collection of Materials on Contemporary Chinese History*). T'aipei.

'Chung-kuo jen-min chieh-fang-chün san-shih-nien', Cheng wen-pien-chi wei-yuan-hui (Editorial Committee of 'Thirty Years of the P.L.A.'), *Hsin-huo liao-yuan* (*A Single Spark Can Start a Prairie Fire*). Peking. Note: the collection is to consist of about ten volumes, of which No. 7 appeared in 1963.

CHUNG-KUO LU-CHÜN TSUNG-SZU-LING-PU, *Shou chiang pao-kao-shu* (*Report on the Japanese Capitulation*). Nanking, 1946.

CHUNG YÜ-FEI, *Liao-Sheng chan-i* (*The Mukden and Liaoning Campaign*). Peking, 1964.

Erh-wan-wu-chien li ch'ang-chen (*The Long March*). Peking.

FANG CHIH-MIN, *K'o-ai ti Chung-kuo* (*Beloved China*). Peking, 1957.

HO CH'ANG-KUNG, *Ch'in-kung-chien-hsüeh sheng-huo hui-i* (*Memories of my Life as a Student Worker*). Peking, 1958.

HO YING-CH'IN, *Pa-nien K'ang-chan chih ching kuo* (*Eight Years of War of Resistance*). Nanking, 1946.

HO YING-CH'IN, *Ho Shang-chiang K'ang-chan ch'i chien chün-shih pao-kao* (*General Ho's Report on the Operations of the Anti-Japanese War*). 2 vols. T'aipei, 1962.

HSIAO PAI-FAN, *Chung-kuo chin-pai-nien ko-ming shih* (*Revolutionary History of the Last Hundred Years*).

HSIAO YING, *Wo shih Mao Tse-tung ti nü mi shu* (*I am Mao Tse-tung's Secretary*). Macao.

HSÜEH YÜEH, *Chiao-fei chi-shih* (*Notes on the Campaigns for Exterminating the Communist Bandits*). T'aipei, 1962.

HU CH'IAO-MU, *Chung-kuo kung-ch'an-tang ti san-shih-nien* (*Thirty Years of the Chinese Communist Party*). Peking, 1951. This work has been translated.

HU HUA, *Chung-kuo hsin-min-chu-i ko-ming shih, ch'u kao* (*A History of the Chinese Neo-Democratic Revolution*). Peking, 1952.

HUA KANG, *Chung-kuo min-tsu yün-tung shih* (*A History of the Chinese National Liberation Movement*). Peking, 1950.

HUANG HO, *Chung-kuo kung-ch'an-tang san-shih-nien chien-shih* (*A Summary of Thirty Years' History of the Chinese Communist Party*). Peking, 1957.

HUANG YEN-PEI, etc., *Yenan kuei-lai* (*Return from Yenan*). Chungking, 1945.

Hui-i Chingkangshan chü ti tou-cheng (*Memories of the Struggle in the Chingkangshan*). 1955.

HUNG HUAN-CH'UN, *Wu-ssu chih-ch'i ti Chung-kuo ko-ming yün-tung* (*The Chinese Revolutionary Movement at the Time of the Fourth of May*). Peking, 1956.

KAN YU-LAN, *Mao Tse-tung chi chi chi-t'uan* (*Mao Tse-tung and his Band*). Hong Kong, 1954.

K'ang-chan pa-nien lai ti pa-lu-chün yü hsin-ssu-chün (*The Eighth Route Army and the New Fourth Army during Eight Years of War of Resistance*). Yenan, 1946.

K'ang-Jih chan-cheng shih-ch'i chieh-fang-ch'ü kai-k'uang (*The General Situation in the Liberated Areas during the War of Resistance Against Japan*). Peking, 1953.

K'ang-Jih chan-cheng shih-ch'i ti Chung-kuo jen-min chieh-fang-chün (*The People's Liberation Army during the War of Resistance Against Japan*). Peking, 1953.

KAO SHU-KANG, *Chung-kung shou-kung-yeh kai-lun* (*On Chinese Handicrafts – a Résumé*). 1946.

KO KUNG-CHEN, *Chung-kuo pao-hsüeh shih* (*A History of Chinese Journalism*). Hong Kong.

KU KUAN-CHIAO, *San-shih-nien lai-ti Chung-kung* (*The Communists Over Thirty Years*). Hong Kong.

KUNG CH'U, *Wo yü hung-chün* (*I and the Red Army*). Hong Kong, 1954.

KUO-FANG-PU, SHIH-CHENG-CHÜ, *Chiao fei ch'an-shih* (*A History of Operations against the Bandits*). 6 vols. T'aipei, 1967.

KUO-FANG YEN-CHIU-YUAN, *Kang-Jih chan-shih* (National Defence Institute, *A History of the War of Resistance Against Japan*). T'aipei, 1966.

KUO, WARREN, TING, etc., *Chung-kung jen-ming-lu* (*A Biography of the Chinese Communists*). T'aipei, 1967.

LI ANG, *Hung se wu-t'ai* (*The Red Scene*). Chungking, 1942.

LI CH'ANG, *'I-erh-chiu' hui-i lu* (*Memories of the December 9th Movement*). Peking, 1961.

LI CHIH-MING, *Ch'ang-cheng shih-tsao* (*Poems on the Long March*).

LI HO-LIN, *Chin erh-shih nien Chung-kuo wen-i ssŭ-ch'ao lun* (*Literary and Artistic Currents of the Last Twenty Years*). Shanghai, 1948.

LI JUI, *Mao Tse-tung t'ung-chih ti chu-ch'i ko-ming huo-tung* (*Early Revolutionary Activities of Comrade Mao Tse-tung*). Peking,1957.

LI WEI, *Ching kang shan* (*The Ching kang shan*). Shanghai, 1956.

LIANG SHEN-CHÜN, *Chiang Li tou-cheng nei-mu* (*The Hidden Struggle between Chiang Kai-shek and Li Tsung-jen*). Hong Kong, 1954.

LIAO KAI-LUNG, *Chung-kuo jen-min chieh-fang chan-cheng chien-shih* (*A Brief History of the People's War in China*). 1952.

LIU LI-K'AI, WANG CHEN, etc., *Chung-kuo kung-jen yün-tung* (*1919 chih 1927 nien ti*) (*The Chinese Workers' Movement between 1919 and 1927*). Peking, 1953.

LIU SHAO-CH'I, *Lun tang-nei tou-cheng* (*The Struggle Within the Party*). 1941.

LIU SHAO-CH'I, *Lun kung-ch'an-tang-yüan ti hsiu-yang* (*On the Training of Members of the Communist Party*). 1939.

LO CHIA-LUN, *Kuo-min ko-ming-hua* (*Pictures of the Chinese National Revolution*). T'aipei, 1958.

LU CHIANG, *Ching kang shan ti ying-hsiung* (*The 'Heroes' of the Ching Kang Shan*). Hong Kong, 1953.

MAO TSE-TUNG, *Hsüan-chi* (*Selected Works*). 4 vols.

MAO TSE-TUNG, *Mao Tse-tung shih-tzu shih-chiu-shou* (*Nineteen Poems*). 1958.

MENG PO-CHIEN, *Hui hsiang jen-tao* (*Return to Humanity*). Hong Kong, 1954.

MIU CH'U-HUANG, *Chung-kuo kung-ch'an-tang chien-yao li-shih* (*A Brief History of the Chinese Communist Party*). Peking, 1957.

P'AN TZU-NIEN, *Hsin-hua-jih-pao ti hui-i* (*Memories of the 'New China' Newspaper*). Chungking.

Shang jao chi-chung-ying (*The Shang jao Concentration Camp*). Shanghai.

SHIH CH'ENG, *Lun chung-kung ti chün-shih fa-chan* (*The Military Development of the Chinese Communists*). Hong Kong.

SZU MA-LU, *Tou-ch'eng shih-pa nien* (*Eighteen Years of Combat*). Hong Kong, 1952.

TENG CHUNG-HSIA, *Chung-kuo chih-kung yun-tung chien-shih* (*A Brief History of the Chinese Workers' Movement*). Re-edition, Shanghai, 1949.

Ti-i-tz'u kuo-nei ko-ming chan-cheng & shih-ch'i ti nung-min yün-tung (*Peasant Movements during the Period of the First Civil War*). Peking, 1953.

Ti erh-tzu kuo-nei ko-ming chan-cheng shih-ch'i shih-shih lun tsung (*Historical Events of the Period of the Second Revolutionary War*). Peking, 1956.

TI SAN YEH-CHÜN CHENG CHIH-PU, *Huai-Hai ta-chan* (Political Department of the Third Field Army, *The Great Huai-Hai Battle*).

TING WANG, *Chiang ch'ing chien-chuan* (*A Short Biography of Chiang Ch'ing*). Hong Kong, 1967.

TSO SHUN-SHENG, *Chin san-shih-nien chien-wen tsa-chi* (*Memories of the Last Thirty Years*). Kowloon, 1952.

Tsui-chin san-shih-nien Chung-kuo chün-shih shih (*A Military History of the Last Thirty Years*). 2 vols. T'aipei, 1962.

TSUNG-CHENG-CHIH-PU HSÜAN-CH'UAN-PU, *Chün min kuan-hsi* (Department of Politics and Propaganda, *Relations Between the Army and the Population*). Shanghai, 1949.

TSUNG-CHENG-CHIH-PU HSÜAN-CH'UAN PU, *Pu-tui ti pao-chih t'ung hsin kung-tso* (Propaganda Service of the Army Political Department, *The Work of War Correspondents*). Shanghai, 1949.

WANG CHIEN-MIN, *Chung-kuo kung-chan-tang shih kao* (*A History of the Chinese Communist Party*). 3 vols. T'aipei, 1965.

WANG SHIH, etc., *Chung-kuo kung-ch'an-tang li-shih chien pien* (*A brief History of the Chinese Communist Party*). Shanghai, Shanghai jen-min ch'u-pan-she, 1958.

WANG YA-KANG, *Chung-kuo kung-ch'an-tang chien shih* (*A Brief History of the Chinese Communist Party*). Hong Kong, 1950.

WANG YA-KANG, *Kung-ch'an-tang yü nung-min wen-t'i* (*The Communist Party and the Peasant Question*). Hong Kong, 1956.

WANG YAO, *Chung-kuo hsin-wen-hsüeh shih kao* (*A History of the New Chinese Literature*). Shanghai, 1953.

YANG SHANG-KUN, *Hung-se Kan-Yeh pien* (*The Kiangsi-Kwangtung Red Frontier Region*). Peking, 1959.

YANG TZU-LIEH, *Chang kuo-t'ao fu-jen hui-i-lu* (*The memoirs of Madame Chang kuo-t'ao*). Hong Kong, Tzu-lien ch'u-pan-shih, 1970.

YEH TIEH-SHENG, *Chingkangshan ti hung-ch'i* (*The Red Flag of the Chingkangshan*). Peking, 1954.

YEN CHUNG-P'ING, *Chung-kuo chin-tai ching-chi shih t'ung-chi tzu-liao hsüan-chi* (*Selected Statistics on the Economical History of Contemporary China*). Peking, 1955.

YÜ YEN-KUANG, *Ti-i-tz'u kuo-nei ko-ming chang-chen shih-ch'i ti Kwangtung nung-min yun-tung* (*Peasant Movements in Kwangtung during the First Civil War Period*).

Note: *Historical Studies Review* (*Li shih yen-chiu*), September 1958.

Index